Business Systems

DOEACC "O" LEVEL

Business Systems

M2–R3

(also Covers Syllabus for A2–R3 for DOEACC 'A' Level)

STRICTLY AS PER NEW DOEACC SYLLABUS

Ramesh Bangia

B.Sc. Dip. Comp. Sc.(IIT D)

Formerly: Incharge Computer Centre,
Hindustan Copper Limited, New Delhi
Ex. Managing Editor: Software Today

FIREWALL MEDIA

(An Imprint of Laxmi Publications Pvt. Ltd.)

BANGALORE • CHENNAI • COCHIN • GUWAHATI • HYDERABAD
JALANDHAR • KOLKATA • LUCKNOW • MUMBAI • RANCHI
NEW DELHI

Published by :
LAXMI PUBLICATIONS (P) LTD
113, Golden House, Daryaganj,
New Delhi-110002

Phone : 011-43 53 25 00
Fax : 011-43 53 25 28

www.laxmipublications.com
info@laxmipublications.com

Price : **Rs. 250.00** *Only.*

New Edition

OFFICES

India

© **Bangalore**	080-26 61 15 61
© **Chennai**	044-24 34 47 26
© **Cochin**	0484-239 70 04
© **Guwahati**	0361-254 36 69, 251 38 81
© **Hyderabad**	040-24 65 23 33
© **Jalandhar**	0181-222 12 72
© **Kolkata**	033-22 27 37 73, 22 27 52 47
© **Lucknow**	0522-220 95 78
© **Mumbai**	022-24 91 54 15, 24 92 78 69
© **Ranchi**	0651-230 77 64

USA

Boston
11, Leavitt Street, Hingham,
MA 02043, USA

FBU-2712-250-BUSINESS SYSTEMS M2-R3
Typeset at : Goswami Printers, Delhi.

C—14571/07/07
Printed at : Sanjeev Offset Printers, Delhi.

Preface

There had been a long struggle between Training Institutes and Government Organizations, since these organizations would not recognize the degree/diploma given by them. Students passing out from these institutions were not given jobs based upon the said diplomas/degrees. Ultimately, the Government formed a society under the Department of Electronics, called DOEACC, who conducts tests and gives grades to the students irrespective of the institutes where they have studied. It is also possible to give the test without having any proper institutional studies. This is more or less on the terms of SET and GRE conducted by USA. The only difference is that this is not online. There are fixed dates for the exams.

The course for this has been designed for students to appear in the exams at various levels. These levels are O-level, A-level, B-level, C-level. The most popular among these is the O-level, since it is the entry level. Once you have cleared the O-level, you are eligible for a government job. Each course has been divided into various modules. Various books are available for various modules. This book is also made for you to prepare for the O-level course.

This book has been written totally in accordance with the syllabus provided. Each chapter has been embedded with the screen shots for you to know what to expect on the screen, while running the application. Each chapter contains examples which can be attempted to supplement the reading. At the end of the chapter, there is a thorough revision of the text read. Not to mention of the questions provided in the beginning, both in the form of objective and subjective. The book also contains Sample papers which are based on the samples provided by DOEACC society. These would help you in preparing for the exams.

I am thankful to Firewall Media (An imprint of Laxmi Publications Pvt. Ltd.) for giving me an opportunity to write this book. They have provided the complete assistance in bringing out the book in the present form. Without their help it would not have been possible to complete the book and present it in the shape and form.

Lastly, I would like to thank my wife, Sadhna, and sons Mayank and Samarth for their support. Without their help I would not have been able to complete this book in time.

I would welcome the suggestions given.

Ramesh Bangia

SYLLABUS

M2-R3: Business Systems

The objectives of this module are to give the students an in depth knowledge about the development of applications of business processing. The students will be able to understand how the business activities are conducted and very specifically, how the concerned data is managed. They will know about business environmment, it's requirements and how they are fulfilled.

The students will learn the following:-

- Database and its efficient handling.
- Principles and Techniques of Programming.
- Visual FoxPro as a Database Management package.
- Storing and retrieving the data, in situation specific manner.
- Develop various business applications.

Outline of Course

S.No.	*Topic*	*Minimum Hours*
1.	Introduction to Business Data Processing	06
2.	Concept of Files	02
3.	Principles and Techniques of Programming	06
4.	Visual FoxPro	38
5.	Business Applications	08

Theory	=	60
Practicals/tutorials	=	60
Total	=	120

Detailed Syllabus

1. Introduction to Business Data Processing **6 Hrs.**

Overview of Business Systems: Management functions, Levels of management, Information requirements for planning, Co-ordination and control for various levels in Business, Industry and Government.

Profile of data in Business systems: Large volumes of data and data handling implicit, Identification of relevant data. Classification of data elements by function and by source, Primary and Secondary. Historical data for reference and analysis. Need for ensuring accurate, reliable and timely processing of data. Basic tasks in

Business data processing, data origination, capture, sorting, merging, calculating, summarizing, managing output-results, storing and retrieving transmission, both interim and final, Examples of business data processing and applications, Payroll, Financial, Accounting, Inventory, etc.

Computer System as a potential tool to meet business data processing needs, facilities available in computerized systems for Data capture; online and offline; validation; storage; processing and output; Transmission.

2. Concept of Files **2 Hrs.**

Master and transaction files, File organization; sequential, relative and indexed, Modes of processing; batch, online, real-time.

3. Principles and Techniques of Programming **6 Hrs.**

Introduction to programming; Program definition, Life cycle, characteristics of a good program, data handling(flow charts, pseudocods).

Report production and file updation; simple report generation, overview of control break procedure for report production.

Operation on files; Input, Output and I/O; processing a file, multiple handling file updation; sequential file updation, random file update.

Programming paradigms: Unstructured programming, structured programming, procedural programming, modular programming.

Program design; Top down and bottom up design, program documentation.

4. Visual FoxPro **38 Hrs.**

Introduction to Visual FoxPro: The menu system, File Types, The toolbars, Visual Design and Wizards, The Command window and the View window, Other features of the Visual FoxPro Interface. **2 Hrs.**

Tables in Visual FoxPro: Creating a new Table, Table Wizard, Using Table Designer, Using Tables, Opening a table, Working on a table, Modifying a table. Managing data: Switching from Browse to Edit display, Entering and Editing Data, Appending data, Editing data, Moving through a Table, GoTo Record command, Find and Replace, Deleting a Record, Altering the display of the Browse Window. **2 Hrs.**

Using Queries: Creating a Query, Query Wizard, Query Designer, Running the Query, Using the Query, The Cross Tab Wizard, Modifying the Query, The Query Designer. **4 Hrs.**

Using Forms: AutoForms, The Form Wizard, Choosing fields, Choosing a style, Choosing a Sort Order, Generating the Form, Using Forms, Running a Form, Using the Form's Control Panel. **2 Hrs.**

Using the Report Wizard: Auto Reports, Using the Report Wizard, Using the Group/ Total Report Wizard, Printing Reports, Filtering records for the printed report, Mailing

Labels and Mail Merge, Working with Mail Labels, The Label Wizard, Using Mail Merge Wizard. **4 Hrs.**

Working from the Command Window: Using the Command Window, Creating a new table, Modifying the structure of the table, Displaying and editing the data, Deleting and recalling the records, Using commands; RUN, SET DEFAULT, DISPLAY, LIST, ?, Using logical expressions, Logical functions, Relational operators, Logical operators, IIF() function, Sorting a table, creating Indexes, Setting the index order, Re-indexing, Filtering data, Use of Macro (&) command, Data functions, Use of multiple tables. **4 Hrs.**

Working with relational Databases in Visual FoxPro: Concept of relational databases, Entering and Viewing data using the Form Wizard, Query Wizard to work with Relational databases, Using one-to-many Report Wizard, Using the View Window, Queries versus Views, The Query designer, Working with multiple tables, Directing output, Using SQL, Viewing SQL code, maximizing the Table View, Running the Query, One-to-many and Many-to-one Queries, Filtered Joins, A grouped Query, The SQL SELECT command, Other SQL commands, Using Visual FoxPro databases. **8 Hrs.**

Visual FoxPro Utilities: Importing and Exporting data using Import Wizard, Editing text, Edit menu, Format menu, Spelling tool, Object Linking and Embedding, Programming and developing applications using Visual FoxPro; An overview of programming, Creating files, Running the program, Input/output, Variables, Simple output using '?', Command, Getting Input from the User, @...SAY...GET command, Picture clauses, Control Flow, Looping, Selection, EXIT and LOOP, Procedures and Parameters, scope of Variables and Passing Parameters, User-Defined Functions, Using the Menu Designer, Using the Project Manager, Techniques of writing efficient FoxPro programming codes. **12 Hrs.**

5. **Business Applications** **8 Hrs.**

Design, analysis and development of: Computerized Financial Accounting, Computerized Inventory Control, Computerized Payroll, Computerized Invoicing application.

Contents

1 Introduction to Business Data Processing

OVERVIEW OF BUSINESS SYSTEMS

Long before the modern way of doing business, the stone age people are known to have done business on barter system. They used to exchange food stock with animals and precious items. No monetary system was developed in those times. Even now when the monetary system is thoughly developed the method remains the same. Only thing is that the money is now involved. You will spend some money to create something which you will sell to other person for money and then you will buy more from that money. The buying and selling more or less remains the same. Since in the modern age the businesses have expanded beyond the boundaries of cities and even countries, the methods of transaction have become more meaningful. To a large extent computer plays an important part. To manage a business, organizations need resources like manpower, materials, etc., but as the size of an organization increases, it is faced with the task of managing large volume of relevant data and information. This is where computers come in, to streamlining the various aspects.

SYSTEM DEFINITION

To run any business you need to develop a system to run it. You must be very clear in your mind, from where the raw material is going to come, how the object is to manufactured, and then how it is to be sold. For all these you need to have manpower and to manage them, you need to have managers. On the top of the managers you have the people who are directly responsible for the profit and loss of the unit. In fact all of them starting from a small peon to the managing director of the company, everybody is concerned about the welfare of the company. So for all purposes it is the system which must be foolproof to make it happen.

A business sytem can however be broadly described as consisting of the following:

Purchasing	Resarch
Manufacturing	Sales/Marketing Research
Billing	Shipping
Accounting	Personnel

All these departments are there to coordinate with each other. If there is no manufacturing then what will the sales department sell. If you are not selling then there is no shipping, etc. Once you start going into details of each, then you will see that how dependent these departments are. Since it is the management to see that all these departments work in tandem, the function of management becomes more crucial. So let us study what the management functions are.

MANAGEMENT FUNCTIONS

Broadly the management functions can be described as below:

1. Controlling the working of the whole comapny.

2. Directing others to do the work as their calibre.
3. Integrating the working to do the work accordingly.
4. Organizing the resources to run the company.
5. Planning to get the maximum output by making the minimum efforts.
6. Controlling the staff.

Let us go into details of these.

Controlling

It includes the various aspects which can enhance production. It can include laying down of the standards for performance for each worker and machine. The perfomance can be measured on weekly basis and appreciated accordingly. It the variance is high, then try to find out the reasons for it. If the machine has become rusty, take measures to have it either replaced or upgraded.

Directing

Management job is more like a director of the film. He does not do anything himself but directs others to do it. The main idea is to supervise the whole procedure. If there is problem or something is not understood, guide the same to the worker. So it is very important that the management should be very thorough in the job. How else can they guide, if they do not know themselves. One of the most important part of the management is to communicate to all the departments and wherever need motivate them to show better results. In most of the cases the decision making part is kept to the management.

Integrating

As mentioned above the management's responsibility is to integrate the workers to take the best out of them.

Organizing

Establishment of authority-responsibility relationships. It includes identification and grouping of activities, definition and delegation of responsibility, authority.

Planning

Definitly the most important part of the management. It has to foresee the outlook of the company. So for this the management has to have a mission to succeed. For this they have to set up the objectives to achieve it. Based on the objectives, policies are drawn and implemented. Each policy has its own program and budget. Then once the budgets are decided the procedures and schedules are laid down and stictly followed.

Staffing

Workers make the company and not the vice versa. If you have dedicated workers, your company is bound to do well. For them to be good, you need to have a good selection method. Once selected there should be a constant communication with the staff/worker. To include them in the decision making and participation you need to have counselling. Other major factors concerning the staff are: Training, Compensation and Dismissal.

There are various levels of mangement, read on.

LEVELS OF MANAGEMENT

In most of companies you have 3 levels of management. These levels are:

Top Level

Middle Level

Lower Level

Each level of management has different set of responsibilities. They can be divided as follows:

(i) **Top level** managers must have a general understanding of the organization's activities. Since they are charged with weighing risks and making major policy decisions on such matters as new product development, new plant authorizations and so on, they need the type of information that will support these long-range strategic plans and decisions.

(ii) **Middle level** managers are responsible for making the tactical decisions that will allocate the resources and establish the control needed to implement the top level plans.

(iii) **Low level** managers make the day-to-day operational decisions to schedule and control specific tasks. The actual results of an operation may be checked daily against planned expectations and corrective actions may be taken, if needed.

WHAT IS INFORMATION?

The term information in general is considered to be designate data arranged in ordered and useful form. Thus, information will usually be thought of as relevant knowledge, produced as the output of processing operations. Information is needed in virtually every field of human action. At a personal level, if you always had high-quality information you could take better advantage of your future career opportunities and you would be better equipped to make other personal decisions. But besides being essential to individuals, information is also needed by managers in organizations.

Managers at all levels must perform such basic management takes or functions as planning, staffing and controlling. A common need basic to all managers is an understanding of the purpose of the organization, i.e., its policies, its programmers, its plans and its goal. Managers at the lower operating levels need information to help them make day-to-day operating decisions. At the top levels, however, information is needed to support long range planning and policy decisions.

INFORMATION REQUIRED FOR MANAGEMENT PLANNING

Planning is most important of all the managerial functions. For this you need to have maximum information support for decision making. Normally planning is done at three levels in organizations:

1. Long-term planning
2. Medium-term planning
3. Short-term planning

Let us look into them in details.

Long Term Planning

The various type of information which is needed for long term planning is:

1. Definition of long term planning mission which you want to achieve.

2. Setting up of different goals and objectives for achieving the mission
3. Setting up policies and guidelines for the same
4. Utilizing the organizational capabilities and performance
5. Having full knowledge of the competitive market
6. Prospects of the industry as a whole.
7. Opportunities, strategies and resource projections in connection with the product.

Medium Term Planning

The various type of information which is needed for medium term planning is:

1. Planning for resources acquisition and their utilization.
2. Preparation and monitoring of budgets for achieving the optimum results.
3. Always be on the lookout for new products, new facilities required, source of funds, post data and long term plans.

Short Term Planning

The various type of information which is needed for short term planning is:

1. Day-to-day planning for efficient utilization of available resources and facilities.
2. Budgets and schedules, resources availability, customer orders.
3. Inventory status.

Besides these there are other factors which also add to the information requirements of the organization. These are:

Information for Planning, Coordination and Control

This can be discussed under the various factors, among them are: Scope, Competitive Edge, Specifications of Targets and Assignment of Resources.

Scope: It covers the various aspects of the product as far as the market is concerned. Whether the product stands a chance in the market, what is the competition, which part of the country it is going to sell more and if there is any chance of seasonal marketing. All these aspects have to be looked into.

Competitive Edge: To sell a product you must know, what others are doing. How much discount are they offering and how? These days the trend is offer various discount schemes with the products like if you buy 3, you will get the 4th free. These type of marketing strategy of the competitors should be known beforehand to overcome the competition.

Specifications of Targets: As mentioned earlier, there should be a clear concept of the target audience. You must know where your product is going to sell. Like for example these days Reliance is selling their mobile connection to one and all. They know that mobile is needed by everyone in the rural sector.

Assignment of Resources: These are definitely for the top level management. They should know in advance when the resources are needed and when not. I remember the Hamdard people would pick up money from the market every year in the months of March to May for a period of 6 months. Since those were the months when they would manufacture Rooh Afzha to the maximum and then by the month of September they would stop production and return the amount collected from selling of the product. This is called the rotation of funds.

Information for Long Term Planning

This can be discussed under the following terms: Analyzing the Environment, Identifying the Company's Strengths and Weaknesses, Identifying Opportunities and Risks and Defining Product/Market Scope.

Analying the Environment: You must be able to identify the environment conditions which are going to affect your product and the whole marketing strategy as a whole. The management should be aware of the new trends arising in the market. One must be flexible to adopt to those changes.

Identifying the Company's Strengths and Weaknesses: With the reference to the trends and developments of the new product, one must be able to access the strengths and weaknesses of the company. The advance knowledge of this can be very useful and changes if needed can be done without effecting the flow of production.

Identifying Opportunities and Risks: Studying the products in details is very important. Everybody cannot do everything. If Tata's have done well in cars, that does not mean that everyone can get into car business and make profit. Look at Standard Motors and Premier Automobiles. So the mangement must look into the risks before venturing into the new product.

Defining Product/Market Source: This involves explicit definition of the future scope of the company's activities. The main idea is to concentrate on a very limited number of carefully defined product/market segments.

Tactical Information

Middle level manages are responsible for making tactical decisions that will allocate the resources and establish the controls needed to implement the top level plans. To do so, the middle level will need the type of information which we call as tactical information.

Short Term Planning

This information states objectives and sets standards of performance in terms of financial results on quarterly or half-yearly basis. The basic requirement is to decentralize the reponsibility, and achieve the result in shorter periods.

Day to Day Activity Information

This planning is done at the lowerst level of management. This includes taking care of Stock in Hand, Pending Orders, Bills Payable, Production Control. One must have enough stock in hand to cater to an unexpected huge demand. One must see that the pending orders do not pile up beyond the expected stage. Bills payble should be streamlined so that you have the credibility of the market. Good paymaster always stands to get good credits. One must plan the production in such a way that if tomorrow the product moves slowly, there is not piling of the stocks.

BUSINESS DATA PROCESSING APPLICATIONS

Raw data is what makes the information. This data has to be drawn from various sources. This data when put into meaningful form is called Information. This process can be done in a very convinient way by using the computers and it is called in the computer terminilogy as Data Processing. Today the processing of data has been one of the important tasks in any organization, whether commercial, scientific, governmental social, etc. The input data used to produce information originates form the internal and external sources. These sources include such categories as customers, suppliers, competitors, business publication, industry associations and government agencies.

BUSINESS ORGANISATION

In each and every business, there exists a system. This system controls the whole flow of data and supplies relevant info to the concerned decision makers. Information systems, serve all the functions or department of a business, linking them in such a way that they effectively work towards the organizational purpose.

Modern organizations have to maintain large volumes of data about various entities of interest — products, processes, people, customers, competitors, equipment, facilities, suppliers, etc. Therefore efficient data management/information systems are essential for managing organizations effectively. Data is the basic building block of organizational information system.

LARGE VOLUMES OF DATA AND DATA HANDLING

When the computers where introduced in India, they were introduced mainly for the jobs which had large volume of data and it was not possible to handle it manually. Take the case of Telephone billing, Electricity billing, Share Applications processing, etc. All needed to handle large volume of data and give the results in time. For example, in the case of telephone billing all the data had to be processed within one month to send out the bills for payment.

Similary as per the Stock Exchange regulations the share applications, irrespective of the numbers, had to be processed and the refunds sent out within two months of the closing of the issue. All these needed were good handling of the data. But, you could not rule out the human errors. In most of the fields which had numeric in it could be checked by validation and totals. The alphanumeric fields like addresses, etc., had to be maually checked. There are no shortcuts and these resulted in wrong addresses and wrong delivery of the refund orders.

In most of the cases the problem has now been solved by entering the data from its source. This is called the online data entry, about which you will read later. Another thing which has really helped is the concept of networking which allows the data to be sent across the various computers. So instead of processing the data at one place and on one computer, now you can do that at various computers and merge the information on one computer.

IDENTIFICATION OF RELEVANT DATA

If you are making a report, then the manager in most of the cases, would not be interested in the full report, but he would rather look at the last page where the summary of the whole report appears. I am not saying that you do not print the whole report. It is here you have to make the demarkation. The whole report goes to the department and the summary goes to the manager. So the information should not be given in quantity but in quality wherever possible.

There are two types of data that must be input when processing transactions:

Variable Data

These are data items that change for each transaction handled or decision made. For example, the identify of a specific item withdrawn from inventory various from order to order. Therefore, it must be entered.

Identification Data

This is the element of data that uniquely identifies the item being procesed. This item is sometimes called the key too. For example, in all inventory transactions, the transaction is done with the help of a unique number given to each item.

CLASSIFICATION OF DATA ELEMENTS

Data elements can be classified into two main categories, one which are function based and the other which is source based. They are:

By Function

Transaction	Reference	Planning
Control	Security	Validation

By Source

Raw or Input	Stored	Derived

DATA ELEMENTS BY FUNCTIONS

We take up the above mentioned elements one by one.

Transactional Data Elements

Most of the transactions give rise to the data. If it is an inventory transaction then you would need data like Product description, Quantity sold, Gross sale value, etc. Similarly, if the payment has been made to the vendor, then the transaction will be an accounts transaction data.

Reference Data Elements

Some data in a business are generated for the purpose of reference. In a sales transaction, when the sale is made, an invoice or a cash memo is prepared and the transaction data are recorded in the relevant document. However, in the course of a business, it is often necessary to trace and refer to that transaction. So a reference number is given to the invoice number, sales order number, invoice or cash memo.

Planning Data Elements

Some data are not generated due to a transaction but are created on the basis of the policy decision. These can also be on the basis of some budget transactions, etc.

Control-Related Data Elements

Some data elements are generated for control purposes by the management. These can of the nature of the upper credit limit of an account, etc.

Security-Related Data Elements

Security concerns everyone. To guard against unauthorized access to data, users are often assigned codes. The data related to these is security related data.

Validation Data Elements

Some data are used to ensure completeness and accuracy of processing. While processing a batch of invoices, the total value of all invoices can be provided as validation data. The computer, while processing the invoices, will calculate this total and match with the one that is provided.

DATA ELEMENTS BY SOURCE

We take up the above mentioned elements one by one.

Raw or Input Data

New variable data entering the system for the first time is called the raw or input data. This can include the data pertaining to a new product, a new employee, etc. Sometimes raw data may be in coded forms, e.g., instead of department name, a code can be assigned to the value.

Stored Data

A lot of data are stored in the system in computer files which may be required for processing purposes at various points in time, e.g., Employee data, Product data, Sales data, Budget data, Cost data, etc.

Derived Data

Derived data are the result of processing or manipulation of raw or stored data.

PRIMARY AND SECONDARY DATA ELEMENTS

When several depatments use the same file, a record may have more than one record key. For example, an inventory file might be used by both an inventory manager who refers to inventory file records by item number, therefore uses stock numbers as records keys, also by an accountant who refers to inventory records by vendor code. The record key that is unique to each record is called the primary record key or just the primary key. For inventory records, for example, this wold be the inventory item number field. The data fields in the computer record that are given lower priority are called secondary record keys. For inventory records, a secondary record key would be the vendor code.

Secondary record keys are not necessarily unique. They enable multiple uses to access information from the same file or, alternately, enable the same user to access a computer file in more than one way. Secondary record keys, therefore, lessen the number of computer files a company must maintain to perform its business operations.

HISTORICAL DATA FOR REFERENCE AND ANALYSIS

The form of data that gives an idea of the history of an organization or the formation of a document comes under this heading. Historical data are stored on archive files. These files record data in a serial manner which means that you can retrieve data fields one after the other in a serial manner. Magnetic tapes and magnetic cartridges are normally used for storing this type of data. For example, the storage of old songs on compact audio disk is very similar to the historical data recorded on CD's.

Need for Ensuring Accurate, Reliable and Timely Processing of Data

Once, data is inputted and processed, they form an information. The business information so achieved should have the following characteristics.

Accuracy: It is a ratio of correct information to the total amount of information produced over a period. Sometimes even 80 to 90% accuracy is enough but in some cases, 100% accuracy has to be ensured specially in the cases, where it is easier to do so. For example, bank transactions, where the data is all numeric.

Brevity: When important information is accompanied with relatively useless data, then assimilation of the important information may become very difficult and thus may escape from the attention of the users.

Completeness: Information should be complete so that a manager can take decisions confidently. Information received in bits and pieces may have to be connected together to make out the meaning.

Timeliness: The value of information also depends on when it is made available to the decision maker and how quickly system responds to the user request for information. The response time should be short enough that the information does loose its freshness and value.

Decision Making: Information is of some value when it can be used for taking the right kind of decision.This information will be very useful for him as he can take decision to sell his shares to reduce loss.

Receiver Relevant: Information is of value to a receiver only when he can make use of it. It will be useful only when it pertains to the field in which the user operates.

All these qualities of information are major concerns of the information system manager. Not only the information must be readily available but it not stored properly, intact in a classified and indexed manner, its retrieval time will be high even for a computer.

BASIC TASKS IN BUSINESS DATA PROCESSING

Following are the basic functions carried out in any data processing:

Data Organization

The first function involved in the processing of data is the origination of the data to be processed. Unless the data is organized, you cannot do any processing. While organizing you have to make sure that the documents are complete and checked for validity.

Data Input

Data must be recorded or captured in some form or other before they can be processed. For this you can use any of the off-line or on-line machines. While inputting the data, you must make sure that the data is validated and removed from possible errors.

Data Processing

Once the data is available for processing, then you have to see how it can be best processed. It is always easier to work on sequential records. So sort the data in a particular format and then start the processing. This is called **Sorting**.

It is not that your data would be there in a particular file, it could be in more than one file. To process the whole data, you need to merge various files. This merging can be done on the same key field on which you have sorted the data. This is called **Merging**.

Then comes the main part, i.e., calculation. Before doing the actual calculations you must know what formulas you have to use and on which fields. This is called **Calculating**.

Finally, you have to summarize the results in the form of maybe graphs, etc. This is called **Summarizing**.

Managing Output Results

Once data have been captured and processed there are two things which can be done, outputting or storing. The final output can either be stored or printed. Transferring data from one location or operation to another, for use or further processing, is data **transmission**, a process that continues until information in a usable form reaches the final user. Sometimes, of course, it is necessary to copy or duplicate output documents. Finally, the results of the processing of data must be retained for further use of reference. This function is called **storage**.

TYPICAL BUSINESS PROCESSING APPLICATION

There are 5 main steps any business application would take place. A typical business data processing system consists of the five parts as shown below.

Inputs: For producing outputs, the system will require data about various activities that are taking place both within as well as outside the organization.

Processing Logic: Step-by-step logic of generating outputs, starting with inputs and using stored data. This becomes the basis for writing computer programs.

Procedures: Procedures are designed to link and tie-up the above mentioned four components of business system together. Procedures laydown the methods, schedules and responsibilities for various activities necessary to operate the business system successfully.

Outputs: The very purpose of designing a business system is to produce outputs which should help managers in taking various decisions.

Stored Data: For producing useful outputs, a business system needs to store a lot of data about entities of concern to the system. The stored data may relate to the past as well as current status of business.

Let us now look at various of business applications.

THE PAYROLL SYSTEM

Payroll is probably the most important application of any company. Why not, it is going to effect all the employees of the company. Well, after all everyone works for earnings and most of those who work in companies look forward to the pay day. This is the day for which they have already made up the plans. It is true that most of the salaried people distribute 80% of their salary within a week of getting it. All this is mostly planned during rest of the 3 weeks. It is also true that most of the salaried people are short of money in the last of the month, irrespective of their immaculate planning.

Most of the companies prepare payroll whether there are 4 employees or 400 or even 4000. Only thing is that for preparing a payroll of 4000 employees you would need the help of computer. It is not humanly possible. Since payroll is a time bound system, you have to prepare a time bound schedule for it too. Have you ever imagined what will happen if the salary is not distributed in time? Well, nothing less than chaos can happen. So for the preparation of payroll, the most important is timing and strictly adhering to it.

Well, the officer or the worker takes away the salary slip and salary on the 1st or 7th of the month. For he is not concerned for what goes on in the payroll section during the whole of the month. Obviously, the staff here does not sit idle for the whole month. Their main work is coordination with the various departments, getting all the information from them and putting it to the meaningful form and sending it for computerization. Following could be the rough schedule for the events to be happening at the payroll section.

Date	*Activity*
5	Receive all corrections to the payroll
7	Send corrections of payroll to computer centre
11	Receive all PF, FPF, and loan registers
12	Receive and send muster roll to various department for filling up the next month data

14	File all FP, LIC, etc., to the respective departments
18	Send all corrections of the muster roll to computer centre
23	Send attendance register for preparing payslips
26	Receive the payslips from the computer centre
29	Distribution of salary to various collection centres for making paypackets

This could again vary from company to company, specially if you have the salary distribution on 7th.

The above dates are subject to the fact that all corrections received from the various collection centres are fed into the computer and a parallel salary run is done to make all the possible corrections. This helps in making the master data up to date and all the monthly reports like PF ledger, Loan registers, etc., are printed only after the corrections have been made.

FINANCIAL ACCOUNTING SYSTEM

Another important area of computerization is the Accounting System. Usually this is the second application to be computerized in any organization, the first being the Payroll System. A well maintained accounting setup with capabilities of the quick production of reports and summaries is an asset to any business activity in that the management is aware of the latest up to date financial standing of the business thereby facilitating right decision making. In a non computerized accounting system the books of accounts are normally completed only by two to three months after closing of the period and knowledge of what happened before two or three months is only of historical importance.

An accounting system is ideally suited for computerization, since the system involves mass processing of data which otherwise take many man hours to complete. Accuracy is of paramount important as regards accounting data is concerned which is often lost in a manual system. Also the type of accounting data are of simple numerical in nature involving large volumes and laborious calculations.

In olden days, in a manual system, closing of accounts of production of periodical reports were done rather infrequently after days of poring over the books of accounts and painstakingly arriving at the required totals during which time all routine accounting activities were to be suspended. Today, with the advent of computers, it has become possible to prepare profit and loss figures monthly or if necessary even on a daily basis.

Unfortunately to the technical uninitiated, the accounting system will remains a mystery and except for students with a commerce background, computer professionals are generally unaware of the nuances of the system. This is primarily because the terminologies used and the concept of accounts are rather strange to students of other faculties.

To understand a computerized accounting system it is therefore imperative that one should have a clear background to this field of study as otherwise when talking to the accounting personnel, he would be faced with terminologies like debits and credits which would be rather incoherent to a software personnel.

Let us now try to understand the accounting system using our household as a typical example. You must have heard many a times "to put your house in order" usage when things go wrong. Is it not?

While a household is strictly not a business organization, we need to make "both ends meet" in a household. What does this means? You should be able to live off well without much difficulties with your income from all sources. In other words, you should control your expenditure so that it never exceeds your income and even if at some stage it exceeds due to unavoidable reasons, you should be able to mobilize enough funds to offset such expenses. This is exactly what is required in a business organization too, except that in a business, success is measured in terms of profits you make. Even in a household, if you can make a saving, well and good. Is it not so.

How do we achieve this objective? First and foremost is that we should account very pisa that is being spent and earned under different heads of accounts. We will now see what are the different heads of accounts possible in a household to maintain a typical accounting system.

1. Land and Buildings.
2. Machineries – for e.g. Mixer Grinder, Refrigerator etc.
3. Furniture – e.g. Cots, Chairs, table etc.
4. Tools – e.g. Stove, Utensils, Hammer, Screw driver etc.
5. Stocks – Many items Like Rice, Sugar, Bulbs, etc kept in stock.
6. Cash – Amount of cash kept in a Cash box for day to day minor expenditure.
7. Bank – Amount kept in a Bank account for expenditure of a larger nature.
8. Debtors – There may be persons who owe money to you for various reasons. For example, you have given a loan to Mr. X.
9. Creditors – You may perhaps owe money to M/s ABC traders for purchases made.
10. Loans taken – From may be the Bank for construction of the house.
11. Salaries and allowances – Paid to domestic systems.
12. Telephone charges
13. Electricity charges
14. Cost of stationery
15. Travelling expenses
16. Cost of Provisions
17. Cost of Milk
18. Cost of Vegetables
19. School Fees
20. Entertainment Expenses
21. Salary received from employer
22. Proceeds of Coconut Sales
23. Interest received on deposits from the bank
24. Proceeds of sale – other agricultural products
25. M/s. ABC Coconut traders – They buy Coconut from you regularly
26. M/s. XYZ Agricultural traders – They buy other agricultural products from you
27. Varkey's supermarket – From whom you regularly buy your domestic requirements.
28. Pramod Kumar – The milk man who supplies milk regularly
29. Moosa Koya – Supplier of Vegetables
30. Bank of India – A loan has been taken from this bank for an emergency

The above accounts heads are by no means all that there is to it. There could be many more account heads. But for understanding an accounts system, the above heads would suffice.

On analysis, you can find heads 1 though 8 are of a peculiar nature. They are all some from of an ASSET as far as a household is concerned. You could sell them and get money according to the worth of the assets. Cash is hard cash, you can use them, money in the bank can be encashed, money from debtors can be realized and so on. If you decide to migrate to America, you can convert these heads into solid cash. Do you get the concept of an ASSET?

ASSETS are of two kinds, Fixed Assets and Current Assets. Items 1 through 4 are fixed assets, while items 5 through 8 are examples of current assets. Fixed assets are those which cannot be very easily sold while it is easy liquidity as far as current assets are concerned, i.e. easy it convert to into cash. Items 9 and 10 are LIABILITIES to the household. If you are going away for good, Creditors should be paid off, loan taken should be repaid. Thus these items are a burden to you. Isn't it?

In an actual business environment, there will be appearing a major account head under the caption "LIABILITIES", titled Capital Account. This represents the initial investment or money received from shareholders to start the organization or for further expansion of business. Until the organization is wound up or liquidated, these funds received remain as a liability in the books of accounts.

Items 11 to 24 represents heads coming under the Profit and Loss accounts (generally known as P & L account heads). These are further divided into INCOME heads (items 21 to 24) and EXPENDITURE heads (item 11 to 20). Expenditure could also be subdivided into direct and indirect expenditure heads. We have considered here only direct expenditures and indirect expenditure will be discussed later.

Finally items 25 and 26 are the debtors to the household while items 27 to 30 are the creditors. Debtors are those who owe you money for whatever reasons it may be like in this case, they owe you money for purchases made from you. Creditors are those to whom you owe money in the course of business transactions with them. Here we owe them money for purchases made form them. In the case of item 30, you owe Bank of India money to be repaid against a loan taken from them.

INVENTORY CONTROL SYSTEM

This system controls the contents and changes made in the inventory of various items in the organization. By achieving the overall objectives of inventory mangement, which are maximizing sales, meeting target service-level objectives and achieving profitablity objectives, requires much more than merely buying correctly or buying efficiently.

An important aspect of improving profitability is to make the right merchandising decisions, ones that determine what level of profitability is achievable. Without going deep into the details of the various aspects of the system (you need the full book for this), I am giving

Input Data

Vendor invoices	Data in the form of various invoices for the items sold.
Memos of Goods	Movement of goods from one stock depot to another.
Received	Items received from the production.
Returned	Items returned back after sold.
Transferred	Goods transferred from various stock depots.
Requests for stock	Requisition of stocks.

Output Reports

Listings of all inventory Items	Once in a while the whole list of the stock items is printed. It is useful specially when you have to pledge the stock with the bank and take loan on that basis.
Stock on Order	This report is very important since on the basis of this you have to prepare yourself for placing the order for raw material, etc.
Specially Ordered Goods	There are times when you have to prepare special items for this you have to have the list of that items ready with you.
Critical Stock Items	There are some items which are considered as critical. These items are made only when the demand comes.
Cost data of the outputs	Cost wise analysis of all the goods available in the stock.

Considering the amount of money that can be tied-up in inventory, management must have reliable information.

BUSINESS DATA PROCESSING APPLICATIONS

Computer based data processing systems can be used in practically all areas of business to improve efficiency and increase productivity.

Major Applications

Listed below are some of the major data processing applications in a typical manufacturing organization:

- Marketing and sales management
- Market research
    - Order processing
    - Sales Analysis
- Production management
    - Production planning and scheduling
    - Progress monitoring and control
    - Maintenance planning and control
- Materials management
    - Materials requirement planning
    - Purchasing
    - Stores and inventory control
- Human resources management
    - Manpower planning
    - Recruitment and selection
    - Training and development
- Accounting and financial management
    - Payroll

- Budgeting and budgetary control
- Financial

FACILITIES AVAILABLE IN COMPUTERIZED SYSTEM

So far we have learned about the various aspects of business systems as per the company's viewpoint. Let us now learn how the computer system is used to enhance the working of these bussiness systems. Data processing covers all the various methods that can be used to manipulate facts. The processing methods used may be manual, mechanical or electronic (as with the electronic computer). The technology of computers is electronic and this lends them two significant capabilities – SPEED and ACCURACY. In view of the fact that the functions of computer are broader than just computing, the computer is sometimes more descriptively called Electronic Data Processoring (EDP).The central processor of any computer system processes the information in the form of program fed into the computer by means of the peripheral units. Peripheral units are the devices attached to the main computer. It is through these devices, that the programs coded on cards, paper-tapes, magnetic tapes, etc., are entered into the computer system whereas some peripheral units produce the output depending upon the information processed.

Computer System

We all know about the vast opportunities which computer gives us for processing. Here I highlight 6 of them:

Speed: Computers speed up data processing by many orders of magnitude as compared to the manual system.

Data Volume: Vast amount of data can be stored and processed very quickly.

Repetitiveness: The more repetitive the task, the more profitable it is to automate it.

Complexity: Problems with several interacting variables can be solved quickly and accurately.

Accurate Output: As high accuracy can be obtained as needed; also accuracy is not affected by boredom and fatigue and is not subjective.

Declining Costs: There has been a steady decline in the cost of per unit of data processed.

DEVICES AVAILABLE IN COMPUTERIZED SYSTEM

To enter the data into the computer, you can either the off-line method or the on-line method. First I will talk about On line methods. These include Keyboard, Light Pen, Touch screen, Microphone and Speech Recognizer, Mouse, Scanners, MICR, OCR, OMR, Bar Code Readers, POS Terminals, Smart Cards.

Keyboards

One look at it and you would be reminded of the old typewriter keypad. Well yes, the placing of alpha keys is exactly the same. This is called the QWERTY type of keyboard. This has been done specially keeping in mind the migration of people from typewriter to keyboard.

It is the most important part of the computer. I am yet to see a computer without it. It is there in each computer. There are some software available in the market which teach you how to master the keyboard, but the old asdf method of typing would be sufficient. If one does not have speed for typing, it is ok but, the placement of keys is very important before you sit down on computer.

Let us see how the various keys are placed on the keyboard.

Keyboard Keys

Most keyboard layouts are still a variation of the key layout of a typewriter, at least for the alphabetic, numerical and special character keys. Keyboards are available for various other languages than English too, but, for our purposes we would stick to the English one. There are mostly **101 keys** on the keyboard. The important keys are as follows:

Alpha Keys

Alphabet keys are marked from A to Z. As in typewriter, you can use SHIFT to make them capital, i.e., ABCDE, etc. So if you press a b c d e .... etc., with SHIFT key already pressed, you will get A B C D E .... etc. Similar results can be obtained by putting CAPS LOCK key ON. For typing capital A, you press SHIFT key and then while keeping SHIFT key pressed, press the "a" key. Otherwise for typing a, you don't need to press the SHIFT key, just press the a key.

Numeric Keys

The numeric keys (with the characters 0 to 9) are located on the computer's keyboard at two places. You can see them in the top row above the alpha keys (as in typewriter). A second set of these keys is provided on the right-hand side of the keyboard. The numeric keys in the top row can be used straightaway to type in numeric characters. By simultaneously holding down the Shift key (as in the typewriter), you can also type in special upper characters like ! % $ *, etc. However, to type numeric characters by using the keys on the right side, you will need to press the Num Lock key ON.

Function Keys

These keys are marked F1 to F12. These keys are used for specific purposes as defined in the computer (a computer program is a set of instructions given to a computer to perform a specific task) which you may be using. For example, in BASIC programming (BASIC is a computer language used for writing programs) F3 will load the program, F1 will list the program after loading and F2 will run the program.

Arrow Keys

On 101 keys keyboard these are placed at two places. The first is called the cursor pad which works independently. The other is the numeric-cum-cursor pad. It is similar to the one on the 84 key keyboard. When the Num Lock key is not in the ON position, pressing the key of the numeric keypad moves the cursor in the direction shown on each key. Otherwise, this portion is used to enter numbers.

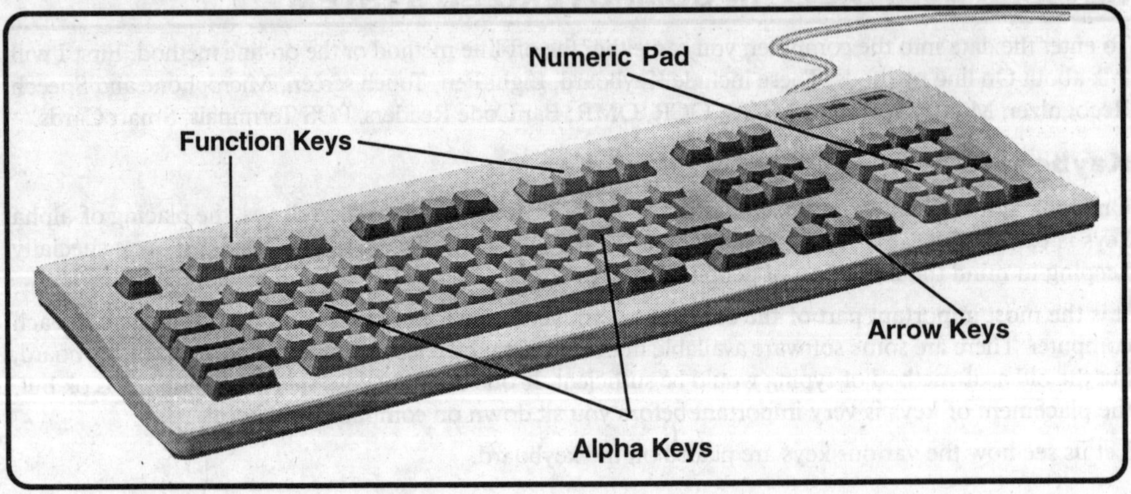

Special Keys including Spacebar

There are several other keys which serve some definite purposes. Some of these keys are available on the typewriter too. The special keys are:

Key	Description
Shift Key	It is used for typing capital letters and special characters. In combination with both Control and Alternate keys, it is sometimes used to execute a particular command too.
Control Key	On its own, this key does not have any purpose. However, combined with different keys, it performs some useful operations. For example, in WordStar software, Control if pressed alongwith B, will make the character Bold.
Backspace	It allows the cursor to go back by one character. Some types of computer programs allow the backspace to delete the last character. A cursor is usually a blinking line (_), on the screen, which shows where he character you type on your keyboard will appear.
Spacebar	As in the typewriter, the Spacebar is used to leave space between words.
Enter Key	It informs the computer that the line of the matter, you are typing, has come to an end. After that you begin typing from a new line. It is also used, while programming, to tell the computer to execute certain commands which you give. Thus, while writing a computer program, you can also use this key to indicate the end of a given command.
Del Key	If, by mistake, you have typed in something which you did not want to, you can erase the wrong character by pressing the DEL (short for Delete) key.

The Numeric Pad

As mentioned earlier the numeric pad is used for entering the numeric data, from 0 to 9. But, there are other keys too, which are shown here.

Key	Description
NUM LOCK	As mentioned you need to put this ON for typing the numeric data. When you put on the computer system, this key is put on.
Arithmetic operators	The number pad includes keys for the four standard arithmetic operators, / (divide), * (multiply), - (subtract) and + (add).
Numbers/cursor keys	When the Num Lock key is off, the various keys here act differently. They act as they are mentioned on the keys. For example, there is Home on the 7 key, there is Up Arrow at the 8 key. So while the Num Lock key is off, you can use the numeric pad for other purposes.
INSERT/DELETE	These two keys are the zero and period of the number pad when it is in number mode; in cursor control mode, they duplicate the actions of the INSERT key and the DELETE keys.
ENTER	This is a second ENTER key that remains an ENTER KEY regardless of the number pad's mode.

Special-Purpose Keys

These keys are used for some special purposes. Each key has a special purpose attached to it and can be used for it:

Esc	The Escape key is typically enabled as an exit key by most software applications. It is used to cancel out of a command or to exit an application. It is also used in combination with other keys to create special key values and to indicate other actions. For example, in Windows the ESC key can be used to close a context menu.
Print Screen/SysRq	The PRINT SCREEN mode of this key got its name back in the MS-DOS days, when pressing it sent the image of the display to the printer. On a Window system, the image of monitor's display is sent to the Windows Clipboard.
Pause/Break	In its default mode (PAUSE), this key will, it enabled by software, pause the display or the action of an application program. If used in combination with the CTRL key, the alternate mode of this key interrupts or halts some software programs, primarily MS-DOS commands and applications. Using the CTRL and BREAK keys together is the same using the CTRL and C keys to break an action.

Light Pens

A light pen is a small pen-shaped wand, which contains light sensors. The light pen is used to choose objects or commands on the screen either by pressing it against the surface of the screen or by pressing a small switch on its side. This sends a signal to the computer, which then works out the light pen's exact location on the screen. The advantage of a light pen is that pen is that unlike a touch screen it doesn't need a special screen on screen coating. Used like an ordinary writing pen, this electronic pen is used to enter data by writing on the screen. The data you write is displayed on the monitor.

Touch Screens

Similar in use to the light pen is the touch-screen, which enables users to input instructions by merely touching on-screen prompts. The edges of the monitor of a touch-screen emit horizontal and vertical beams of light that criss-cross the screen. When a finger touches the screen, the interrupted light beams can pinpoint the location selected on the screen.

Such screens are especially helpful when people are unfamiliar with computers. Information systems in shopping malls, airports, and amusement parks are now being developed using touch-sensitive screens as the only input hardware.

Voice Input/Microphone

Speaking to a computer, known as voice input or speech recognition, is another form of source input. Voice recognizers accept the spoken word through a microphone and convert it into binary code (0s and 1s) that can be understood by the computer. Most voice recognizer systems are speaker dependent - that is, they must be separately trained for each individual users.

Therefore, a database of words must be created for each person using the system. To create this database, each person using the system must repeat - a minimum of 20 times - each word to be interpreted by the system. This training is necessary because we seldom say a word the same way each time.

Voice Recognizers

Voice recognizers are used in some graphic workstations as input devices to accept voice commands. The voice-system input can be used to initiate graphics operations or to enter data. These systems operate by matching an input against a predefined dictionary of words and phrases.

Mouse

These days even the mouse has become very important part of computer. It has become integral part of computer since Windows has become the operating system for computers. It is in fact a pointing device. With this you can point at any place on the monitor and start the typing or clicking from that point. All Windows-based programs use mouse, making working with computers easier as you are not required to type commands.

Types of Mouse

There are three basic types of Mouse

1. Mechanical Mouse
2. Optomechanical Mouse
3. Optical Mouse

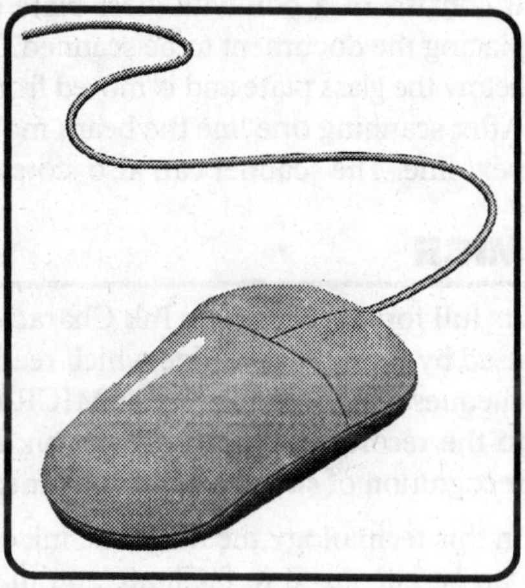

Mechanical Mouse

A mechanical mouse has a rubber or metal ball on its underside that can roll in all directions. Mechanical sensors within the mouse detect the direction of the rolling ball and make a movement of the screen pointer accordingly.

Optomechanical Mouse

Optomechanical mouse is also similar to a mechanical mouse except that it uses optical sensors to detect the movement of the ball on the Mouse Pad.

Optical Mouse

Optical mouse uses a laser beam to detect the movement of mouse on specially designed Mouse Pad. We must move the mouse along a special mat with a grid so that optical mechanism has a frame of reference. This type of mouse has no mechanical moving parts. Optical mouse respond more quickly and precisely than any other mouse. These are expensive than the other two.

Scanners

Whereas a keyboard, mouse or trackball requires manual input of data, scanners allow input of printed data. A scanner reads text, photographs and graphics from paper which are then converted into bit patterns for processing, storage or output. Scanner is a device that examines a spatial pattern one part after another and generate analog or digital signals corresponding to the pattern. Scanners are often used in mark sensing, pattern recognition or character recognition.

Practically scanner uses light for examining the spatial patterns. In a scanner, as the image is scanned, it is converted into light and dark picture elements, or pixels, similar to newspaper photo. Colour scanners can assign a specific colour to a pixel. The pixel are then stored as bit patterns. This technique makes the images usable by word processing, desktop publishing, and graphic packages.

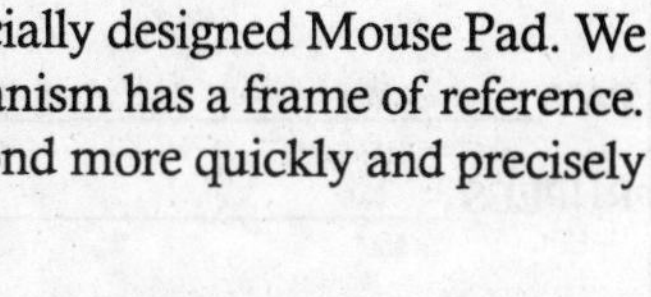

There are two types of scanners, Hand-held scanner and Flat-bed scanner

Hand-Held Scanner

These devices read data on price tags, shipping labels, inventory part number, book ISBNs, and the like. Hand-held scanner, sometimes called wand scanners, use either contact or laser technology. It has a set of light emitting diodes. It is placed over the material to be scanned and slowly dragged from the top to the bottom. The light emitted by the diodes are not reflected by black lines and are reflected by whole areas. The material is converted and stored in a bitmap. Typical applications are to store images and reproduce them in publications.

Flat-bed Scanner

It consists of a box with glass plate on top, which is used for placing the document to be scanned. The light beam is situated below the glass plate and is moved from left to right horizontally. After scanning one line the beam moves up little and scans the next line. The scanner can also store colour images.

MICR

Its full form is Magnetic Ink Character Reader. This process is used by a special machine which reads coded numbers you see on your bank cheques. These days most cheques issued and used bear MICR numbers to speed up clearing of cheques. It is a technology related to the recording of information on document by means of magnetized ink characters and automatic recognition of such characters by means of machines.

In this technology the magnetic ink contains particle of magnetizable material (viz., iron oxide), which can be energized to facilitate automatic reading of printed characters. Magnetic ink document reader helps in translating the information read into a coded format usually for direct insertion into an input area of a computer's core storage in an order according to the digits recorded in a specified field, i.e., account number, etc.

PAY ______________________________ OR BEARER

RUPEES ______________________________

______________________________ **Rs.**

A/c. NO.			TR NO.		INTLS	

Bank of Punjab Ltd.

10166-67, Gurdwara Road,

Karol Bagh,

New Delhi - 110 005

DHS - KRB

222287″ 110237003: 10

Optical Character Recognition (OCR)

A special kind of devices called scanners use the principle of OCR to input the printed matter on the paper or any other object. This matter can be in the coded form (bar codes) or simple text/ graphics (pictures). Bar Code Readers and Scanners come into this category of devices. OCR is a technique which permits the direct reading of printed character. Optical character recognition readers or scanners typically examine each character as if it were made up of a collection of minute spots.

Once the whole character has been scanned, the pattern detected is matched against a set of patterns stored in the computer. Whichever pattern it matches, or nearly matches is considered to be the character read. Patterns which can not be identified are rejected.

Optical Mark Recognition(OMR)

It is an automatic optical sensing of marks recorded on a data medium. In this method special preprinted forms are designed with boxes which can be marked with a dark pencil or ink. These documents are applicable in areas where responses are one out of a small number of alternatives and the volume of data to be processed is large. Thus they are used for

1. Objective type answer papers in examinations (e.g., in UPSC) in which large number of candidates appear.
2. Market surveys, population surveys etc., where responses can be restricted to one or more out of a few possibilities.
3. Order forms containing a small choice of items.

These preprinted documents filled by user are passed under a light source and presence of mark is detected by measuring very accurately the infra-red light levels. A mark reader may be able to detect coloured marks. It can also be designed to be insensitive to certain colours. Now these particular colours could be safely used in the pre-printing of the documents without the risk of their being read as marks intended for recognition.

Bar Code Readers

These represent alphanumeric data by varying the width and combination of adjacent vertical lines. These zebra strips can be sensed and read by a bar code reader, a photoelectric device that reads the code by means of reflected light. When a bar code is scanned, the light source is reflected off the spaces between the marked bars. This returned light is then converted into bit patterns. A decoder in the scanning system translates the bit patterns into meaningful letters and numbers.

The bar code merely identifies the product to the store's computer; the code does not contain the price, which may vary. The price is stored in a file that can be accessed by the computer. This is because of the reason that it is easier to change the price once in the computer than to have to restamp the price on each book. The computer automatically tells the point-of-sale terminal what the price is; a printer prints the item description and price on a paper tape for the customer.

POS Terminals

Called the Point of Sale Terminals, they are used in departmental stores. Usually an optical bar code reader is provided with a point of sale terminal. Bar codes are marked on most packets of commodities to be sold by merchants to identify them. The point of sale terminal is connectd to a computer for processing sales. The sold packets are passed though a scanning window. The optical bar reader reads the bar code of the item to identify it. The computer stores its price and othe details. The computer prints name of the item, rate, price and other details on the receipt and issues the receipt to the customer.

Smart Cards

They are alternatives to magnetic cards. A smart card contains a built in processor chip instead of magnetic tape. In case of smart cards there are less chances of fraud. How much cash a customer has to his credit is stored in the chip before it is issued to him. When the customer uses the card to make purchases, the required amount is deducted from the balance by a special electronic machine used by merchants.

Off-Line Mode

In this case the computer is free as long as the entry is being done. This is so because there are special machines which do this and are not connected to the computer. Data which is put either on floppy disk, magnetic tape or on any other such media is then brought to the computer for processing.

Key-T-Tape

A Key-to-tape device, also known as magnetic tape encoder, is designed to record keyed data directly onto magnetic tape. A tape unit in this case is attached to the keyboard where the actual data entry is done and the data is recorded into the tape attached to it. Once done this tape can be carried over to the computer and data copied onto the computer for processing.

Key-To-Floppy

These data entry machines are used to store data directly on flexible disks, called diskettes or floppies. Here the process is almost similar to the above. Instead of using the magnetic tape you are using the floppy disk here.

Key-To-Disk

Used as data recording stations in systems where data from different points has to be recorded for processing at one point. As above here the data is directly entered into the disks of smaller sizes.

Data Validation

In computer accuracy is the key. While there are lots of mistakes in electricity billing, people blame computer for it. In fact, computer has to just feed in the data which has been recorded by the meter reader who has gone from home to home noting the readings. If he makes mistakes then it is not the computer fault.

Well the computer can have its own checks. For example, it can check that the reading is not less than the previous reading. Nobody can use the electricity in negative. I remember we used to compare the monthly reading with the average of last six month readings. If high variance was found, it was rechecked. Similar other checks can be performed, for example:

Checking Totals

It is easier to compare a total of 10 entries then checking all the 10 entries. A manual total is generated while manually recording the data on the sheets. This total is also keyed in. This total is generated from the various entries of the computer. The two totals are then matched. If not found okay, then this particular batch is printed out for rechecking.

Built-In Checks

While writing the programs for checking the data, you can provide checks like the one I mentioned above about the average of 6 months. Similar controls can be developed. I remember that in the case of Telephone billing we use to provide a check digit which was nothing but the total of all digits of telephone number and then the remainder after dividing by 9.

Storage and Retrieval

Once the valid data has been entered in the system, it is essential that this data is stored securely for future use. Major types of external storage devices used in computerized systems are: Magnetic tapes or cartridge, Hard disks, Floppy disks and Compact disk (CD). The last one is more commonly used now because of its ease to handle and capacity to hold good amount of data (about 640MB)

Outputting Methods

There are two basic categories of computer-produced output: Output for immediate use by people, and Output that is stored in computer-usable for later use by the computer. Output can be in either hardcopy or softcopy form. Let us first study the hardcopy devices.

Hardcopy Output Devices

The commonly used hardcopy output devices are:

Printers: These are the most popular commonly used output devices. Capable of printing characters, symbol and sometimes graphics on paper. Printers are categorized according to whether the image produced is formed by physical contact (impact printers) or not (non-impact printers) of the print mechanism with the paper.

Plotters: A plotter is a specialized output device designed to produce high-quality graphics in a variety of colors. There are two basic types of plotters: those that use pens and those that do not. Drum plotters and flatbed plotters both uses pens.

Microfilm and Microfiche: In this technique the output from the computer is recorded on a microfilm as microscopic film images. The information recorded on the microfilm can be read with the help of a microfilm reader. A microfiche (pronounced as fish, French word, which means card) is a 4 x 6 inch film sheet. It can store up to 270 pages of information. It is easier to read a microfiche as compared to a microfilm.

Softcopy Output Devices

Cathode Ray Tube (CRT): Probably, the most popular softcopy output device. Used with terminals connected to large computer systems and as a monitor for microcomputer system. The CRT's screen display is made up of small picture elements, called pixels for short. The smaller the pixels, the better the image clarity or resolution.

Voice Output Systems: Relatively new and can be used in some situations where traditional display screen softcopy output is inappropriate. Two different approaches to voice output have evolved, speech coding and speech synthesis. Used in applications such as automobiles, toys and games.

Transmission

The most exciting developments in data processing today is data communication. Communications, the transfer of information is the basis of office automation. Data communication takes on several forms. These are given below:

1. Data can be transferred between two geographically distant personal computers by using modems, the dial-up telephone system and a communication program in each computer.
2. Data can be transferred between two side-by-side computers by hooking up a cable from one computer's serial port to the other computer's serial port.
3. PC can act like a remote to a mini or mainframe computer.
4. PC can be part of a local area network, in which software and hardware resources can be shared among many users.

Let us Revise

1. Computers are very effectively used in running business.
2. To run any business you need to develop a system to run it.
3. Controlling includes the various aspects which can enhance production.
4. Directing means getting the job done by directing the workers.
5. Integrating means getting the best out of workers.
6. Organizing means identification and grouping of activities, definition and delegation of responsibility, authority.
7. Planning means to foresee the outlook of the company.
8. Information on the Web is made available in the form of Hypertext.
9. Top level managers must have a general understanding of the organization's activities.
10. Middle level managers are responsible for making the tactical decisions.
11. Low level managers make the day-to-day operational decisions.
12. Information is needed in virtually every field of human action.
13. Scope covers the various aspects of the product as far as the market is concerned.
14. Competitive Edge is to sell a product, you must know what others are doing.
15. You must know where your product is going to sell.
16. Top level management should know in advance when the resources are needed and when not.
17. Short term planning includes taking care of Stock in Hand, Pending Orders, Bills Payable, Production Control.
18. The system controls the whole flow of data and supplies relevant info to the concerned decision makers.
19. Most of the transactions give rise to the data.
20. New variable data entering the system for the first time is called the raw or input data.
21. Derived data are the result of processing or manipulation of raw or stored data.
22. Secondary record keys are not necessarily unique.
23. The first function involved in the processing of data is the origination of the data to be processed.
24. Data must be recorded or captured in some form or other before they can be processed.
25. Usually Financial Accounting System is the second application to be computerized in any organization, the first being the Payroll System.
26. Inventory Conrol System controls the contents and changes made in the inventory of various items in the organization.
27. Computers speed up data processing by many orders of magnitude as compared to the manual system.
28. Keyboard is an important part for entering the data into the computer.
29. A light pen is a small pen-shaped wand, which contains light sensors.
30. Mouse is in fact a pointing device.
31. A scanner reads text, photographs and graphics from paper which are then converted into bit patterns for processing, storage or output.
32. Point of Sale Terminals, are used in departmental stores.
33. In off-line method, you can put data using keys to floppy, tape or even disc.
34. Data validation can be done performing various checks.
35. For outputting you can use printers, plotters or even microfilms.
36. Softcopy output can be taken on terminals and voice output systems.
37. Using Data communication you can transmit data from one place to another.

Multiple Choice Questions

1. In Stone age, business was done using :
   (a) Computers (b) Pebbles
   (c) Money
2. Policy decisions are made by which level of mangement:
   (a) Top level
   (b) Middle level
   (c) Lower level
3. Source data elements are Raw, Stored and :
   (a) Developed (b) Designed
   (c) Derived
4. Merging is done on key:
   (a) Field (b) Lock
   (c) Master
5. In Payroll system, most important print out is :
   (a) Earnings (b) Payslips
   (c) Deductions
6. Numeric keys are there on the keyboard at top line and .
   (a) Numeric keypad
   (b) Above arrow keys
   (c) Above function keys
7. Mouse are of 3 types: Mechanical, Optomechanical and :
   (a) Elliptical (b) Optical
   (c) Spherical
8. MICR is mostly used in :
   (a) Schools (b) Banks
   (c) Railways
9. Point of Sales Terminals are used mostly in:
   (a) Banks (b) Schools
   (c) Department Stores
10. Printers can be used for outputting the results, which copy it is called:
    (a) Soft (b) Medium
    (c) Hard

True/False Questions

1. Computers are very effectively used in running business.
2. Controlling includes the various aspects which can enhance production.
3. Directing means getting the job done by directing the management.
4. Organizing means identification and grouping of activities, definition and delegation of responsibility, authority.
5. Planning means to foresee the outlook of the company.
6. Top level managers must have a general understanding of the organization's activities.
7. Lower level managers are responsible for making the tactical decisions.
8. Information is needed in virtually every field of human action.
9. Scope covers the various aspects of the product as far as the market is concerned.
10. You need not know where your product is going to sell.
11. Top level management should know in advance when the resources are needed and when not.
12. The system controls the whole flow of data and supplies relevant info to the concerned decision makers.
13. Most of the transactions give rise to the data.
14. Derived data is not the result of processing or manipulation of raw or stored data.
15. Secondary record keys are not necessarily unique.
16. Data must be recorded or captured in some form or other before they can be processed.

17. Usually Financial Accounting System is the second application to be computerized in any organization, the first being the Payroll System.
18. Computers speed up data processing by many orders of magnitude as compared to the manual system.
19. Keyboard is an important part for getting the data out of computer.
20. Mouse is in fact a pointing device.
21. A scanner reads text, photographs and graphics from paper which are then converted into bit patterns for processing, storage or output.
22. In off-line method, you can put data using keys to floppy, tape or even disc.
23. Data validation can be done performing various checks.
24. Softcopy output can be taken on terminals and voice output systems.
25. Using Data communication you can transmit data from one place to another.

Matching Columns

Match the text in Column A with the text in Column B.

Column A	Column B
1. Keyboard	a. Magnetic Ink Character Reader
2. Light Pen	b. Device to read bar codes
3. Printer	c. Optical Character Recognition
4. Touch Screen	d. Used in department stores
5. Voice Input	e. Optical Mark Recognition
6. Mouse	f. Magnetic cards
7. Scanner	g. Performing checks on input data
8. MICR	h. Information on the screen by touch
9. OCR	i. Plotting the output
10. OMR	j. Output device to get hard copy
11. Bar Code Reader	k. Media to key in the data
12. Point of Sale Terminals	l. Device to scan text and image
13. Smart Cards	m. A pointing device
14. Data Validation	n. Device like pen to put data into computer
15. Plotters	o. Recording data by speaking

Fill in the Blanks with Appropriate Words

a. Processed b. Pointing c. Transactions d. Keyboard
e. Validation f. System g. Manupulation h. Middle
i. Light pen j. Terminals

1. _________ is an input device.
2. ______ level managers are responsible for making the tactical decisions.

3. Derived data are the result of processing or __________ of raw or stored data.
4. To run any business you need to develop a __________ to run it.
5. Data must be recorded or captured in some form or other before they can be __________.
6. Mouse is in fact a __________ device.
7. Most of the __________ give rise to the data.
8. Data __________ can be done performing various checks.
9. Softcopy output can be taken on __________ and voice output systems.
10. A __________ is a small pen-shaped wand, which contains light sensors.

Descriptive Type Questions

1. How would you define the system?
2. What are the various management functions?
3. What all the different levels of management?
4. What is information?
5. What information is required by management?
6. How would you handle large volume of data?
7. How would you identify the relevant data?
8. Which are the data elements by functions?
9. Which are the data elements by source?
10. Which are primary and secondary data elements?
11. Which are the basic tasks in Data Processing?
12. What are the facilities available in computerized system?
13. Write short notes on the following:

Keyboard	Light Pen
Touch Screens	Voice Input
Voice Recognizers	Mouse
Hand held scanner	Flat bed scanner
MICR	OCR
OMR	Bar Code Readers
POS Terminals	Smart Cards
Data Validation	Transmission
Controlling	Directing
Organizing	Planning
Staffing	Raw Data
Variable Data	Identification Data
Stored Data	Derived Data
Data Organization	Data Input
Data Processing	
Long Term Planning	
Medium Term Planning	
Short Term Planning	
Tactical Planning	
Transactional Data Elements	
Reference Data Elements	
Planning Data Elements	
Control Related Data Elements	
Hardcopy Output Devices	
Softcopy Output Devices	

Answers to Objective Type Questions

Multiple Choice Questions

1. b	2. a	3. c	4. a
5. b	6. a	7. b	8. b
9. c	10. c		

True/False Questions

1. T	2. T	3. F	4. T
5. T	6. T	7. F	8. T
9. T	10. F	11. T	12. T
13. T	14. F	15. T	16. T
17. T	18. T	19. F	20. T
21. T	22. T	23. T	24. T
25. T			

Matching Columns

1. k	2. n	3. j	4. h
5. o	6. m	7. l	8. a
9. c	10. e	11. b	12. d
13. f	14. g	15. i	

Fill in the Blanks with Appropriate Words

1. d	2. h	3. g	4. f
5. a	6. b	7. c	8. e
9. j	10. i		

Recommended Readings

1. Fundamentals of Computer Programming and Information Technology *by J.B. Dixit*.
2. Comprehensive Computer and Languages *by Ashok Arora & Shefali Bansal.*
3. 1000 IT Quizzes *by Dheeraj Mehrotra*.
4. Pictorial Computer Dictionary *by Dheeraj Mehrotra*.

—Published by Firewall Media (An Imprint of Laxmi Publications Pvt. Ltd.)

2 Concept of Files

INTRODUCTION

So far we have learned about the various aspects of data and its entry into the computer. Now we would learn how this data is stored in the computer in terms of files and how these files are arranged and worked on. Since as far as computer is concerned, all data goes into files. For working with it you have to work with a file and extract data from it. When large volume of data has to be processed again and again, it is stored as a file on a secondary device like hard disk for future processing. Different applications require a variety of record types and file structure of the files. There are various kinds of the file structures. The simplest kind of file is the one in which all the records are in sequence (sequential files). Another kind of file organization is the index sequential organization. The files can also be stored on direct access storage. There is yet another type of file organization called direct or random file organization.

CONCEPT OF FILES

As mentioned most of the data that is stored in computer is in the form of a file. So there are various types of files. Some of them are listed here:

1. Data file
2. Program file
3. Object code file
4. Executable file
5. Text file (unformatted file)
6. Formatted file

Let us look into them one by one.

Data File

As the name sounds it is used to store data records. Here the data is stored in random and may not have any sequence or even groupings. However, each data has a Header and Trailer record, which take care of the data headings and summary. Depending upon the nature of data, data files can be categorized as: Master file, Transaction file, Work file, Audit file or Backup file.

Data in files can be organized in different ways. These data records can be organized in any one of the following ways Serial, Sequential, Indexed Sequential or Directly Acesible/Random.

Program File

These files are used to store programs in different languages provided by different software vendors. These files have different extensions depending on the language used to write a program. For example, a program file of C will have the extension .C while that of C++ will have the extension of .CPP.

Object Code File

Programs are written in source language the language which you and I would understand. Then these programs are compiled into object language which the computer understands. These files contain the machine codes and are created with an extension .OBJ.

Executable File

Mostly few .OBJ files are linked together to form a single executable file which is used to run an application. These files have an extension of .EXE and are used for running the programs.

Unformatted Text Files

These files are simple files containing simple text and can be created using any text editor or line editor. These are used as feedback to the various programs which accept only unformatted text files.

Formatted Text File

These are text files with formatting done on them using some software or the other. These files are output of some software applications. Such as .DOC files are outputs of word processor Microsoft Word.

CLASSIFICATION OF DATA FILES

There are two main categories of data files used in any information system:

1. Master file
2. Transaction file

There are others too but are of less important.

1. Work file
2. Security (or Backup) file
3. Audit file

Let us now concentrate on the first two type of data files.

Master File

A master file contains the master records, which contain data that are relatively permanent. For example, the name, address, roll number, sex, and date of birth of a student would appear on his master record. Similarly, name, address, and credit information would appear on the master record of a customer master file.

Most of these attributes of the master file do not change but there is always a provision to change them. Mostly you would be performing the following operations on the master file:

Addition of data/records

Deletion of data/records

Amending of data/values

These ammendments can be done on periodic basis.

Transaction File

A tansaction file contains the records that are used to update the records of the master file. For example, a transaction file may contain the roll number of the student whose home address has recently changed. This file will be used to update the record of the student whose roll number in the master file matches with the transaction file record.

FILE ORGANIZATIONS

File organization refers to the relationship of the key of the record to the physical location of that record in the computer file. The two main objectives of computer – based file organization are: ease of file creation and maintenance and providing an efficient means of storing and retrieving information.

The four file organization methods that are commonly used in business data processing applications are:

1. Sequential
2. Serial
3. Direct or Random
4. Indexed Sequential

Let us learn more about them.

Sequential File Organization

Here the records are arranged in the ascending or descending order or chronological order of a key field. To access these records, the computer must read the file in sequence from the beginning to the record which needs to read. The retrieval search ends only when the desired key matches with the key field or the currently read record. Sequentially organized files are normally created and maintained on storage media such as magnetic tape, cartridge tape, magnetic disks, etc.

Let us look into various advantages and disadvantages of using this method.

Advantages

1. Easy to organize, maintain and understand.
2. There is no overhead in address generation locating a particular record requiring only the specification of the key field.
3. Relatively inexpensive I/O media and devices can be used.
4. It is the most economical and efficient file organization where the activity ratio (the ratio of the total number of records in transaction file and the total number of records in master file) is very high. That is why this file organization is most suitable for transaction files.

Disadvantages

1. It proves to be very inefficient and uneconomical for applications in which the activity ratio is very low.
2. Since an entire sequential file may need to be read to retrieve and update few records, accumulation of transactions into batches is required.
3. Transactions must be stored and placed in sequence prior to processing.
4. Timeliness of data in the file deteriorates while batches are being accumulated.
5. Data redundancy is typically high since the same data may be stored in several files, sequenced on different keys.
6. Random enquiries are virtually impossible to handle.

Serial File Organization

Here the records are stored without any consideration of their order or sequence. Records have to be accessed in the serial way only. Each record is written after the last record in the current file. The order of records in the serial file is according to the time when the data was generated.

Relative or Random File Organization

A direct file (also referred to as a relative or random organization) consists of records organized in such a way that it is possible for the computer to directly locate the desired record without having to search through any other records first. A record is stored by its key field. For mapping the key fields to the locations, an arithmetic procedure called hashing algorithm is frequently used. This address generating function is selected in such a manner that the generated addresses should be distributed uniformly over the entire range of the file area and a unique address must be generated for each record key.

Let us look at various advantages and disadvantages of this system of file organization.

Advantages

1. The access to and retrieval of a record is quick and direct (within a fraction of a second).
2. Transactions used not be sorted and placed in sequence prior to processing.
3. Accumulation of transactions into batches is not required before processing them. They may be processed as and when generated.
4. It can also provide up-to-the minute information in response to enquiries from simultaneously usable online stations.
5. If required, it is also possible to process direct file records sequentially in a record key sequence.
6. A direct file organization is most suitable for interactive online applications.

Disadvantages

1. These files must be stored on a direct access storage device. Hence, relatively expensive hardware and software resources are required.
2. File updation (addition and deletion of records) is more difficult is compared to sequential files.
3. Address generation overhead is involved for accessing each record due to hashing function.
4. May be less efficient in the use the storage space then sequentially organized file.
5. Special security measures are necessary for online direct files that are accessible from several stations.
6. System design around it is complex and costly.

Indexed Sequential File Organization

An indexed file is one that has an index for looking up locations of records on a disk. This index enables the user to access a disk file randomly. The index or reference table is created on the disk at the same time that the data are recorded on the disk. This index stores each record's key field and the corresponding disk address of that record. The index on a disk is similar to a book's index, which has unique subjects (keys) and their corresponding page numbers (addresses). There would be two ways to find a topic in the book. You can read the book sequentially, from the beginning until that topic is found, but this would be very time-consuming and inefficient. The best method wold be to look up the topic in the index, find the page number, and go directly to that page. This is precisely how records can be accessed on a disk file.

Let us look at various advantages and disadvantages of using this system.

Advantages

1. Allows the efficient and economical use of sequential processing techniques when the activity ration is high.
2. Allows direct access processing of records in a relatively efficient way when the activity ratio is low.

Disadvantages

1. These files must be stored on a direct access storage device. Hence, relatively expensive hardware and software resources are required.
2. Less efficient in the use of storage space than some other alternatives.

FILE OPERATIONS AND DATA PROCESSING

In order to manipulate data in files, various operations are performed on files. Firstly, the file needs to be created and operations like adding a record, deleting a record and modifying existing records have to be performed on files.

By now we have seen how computer systems process data with speed, accuracy and efficiency. However, is efficiency depends primarily on the way the system is utilised. Human interaction with computers is very slow as compared to the CPU speed. Even at the highest typing speed, the CPU has to wait a lot for data input thus wasting its time which could be better utilised for processing. Secondly, all the I/O devices are basically mechanical devices – comparatively slow speeds of data transfer thus again curtailing the throughout of CPUs. To overcome both these restraints, many innovations, both in hardware and software, have been made. We now processed to discuss them in detail.

MODES OF DATA PROCESSING

It is not that every organization would follow the same method of data processing. There are several ways and each organization has its own preference. The various systems are:

Batch Processing

On line Processing

Real time Processing

Let us look into them in details.

Batch Processing

Well as the name goes here the processing is done in small batches. They are easier to handle. Remember I had given an example of making small batches of electricity reading records and generating their totals manually then comparing those totals with the computer generated ones. That in fact is an example of batch processing.

Here each user prepares his program off-line and submits it to the computer centre. A computer user collects the programs which have been stored on tapes and stocks one program or job on top of another. When a batch of programs have been collected, the operator loads this batch of programs into the computer at one time where they are executed one after another. Finally, the operator retrieves the printed outputs of all these jobs and returns them to the concerned users.

Various advantages and disadvantages of using this system are:

Advantages

1. This method of batch processing reduces the idle time of a computer system because transition form one job to another does not require operator intervention.
2. It is the most appropriate method of processing for many types of applications such as payroll or preparation of customer statements where it is not necessary to update information on daily basis.

Disadvantages

1. Reduces timeliness in some cases.
2. It makes each job wait in line at each step and often increases its turnaround time.
3. It is difficult to provide the desired priority scheduling.

On-line Processing

Here the processing is done on-line and the data is immediately transferred from nodes to the main computer simultaneously. The data may be keyed in by the user of a typewriter like terminal, or they may be produced by a variety of other data collection and transaction recording devices. The CPU can make programmed input control checks during this process. Using these input data, appropriate records may be quickly updated. The access to and retrieval of, any record is quick and direct.

This type of processing also provides a satisfaction to the users that they are able to command the machine. However, this type of processing can not be used in all circumstances as otherwise the processing time will increase.

Real Time Processing

The world of communications is really playing an important role in processing. There are applications which need immediate processing, for example, the money transfer of banks. Here the response time has to be negligible. In these cases a Real time system is used. Real time processing provides immediate (not periodic, as in batch processing) transaction input capability from all input originating stations.

The essential requirements of a real time processing system include: direct connection (on line) between input/output devices and the central processor and fairly fast response time, allowing two-way communication. The characteristic of real time data processing that truly distinguishes it from the more common batch and on-line processing systems is the immediacy of its response on receipt of a message.

Real time system finds extensive application in airlines booking, banking system, air and ground traffic control, automatic radar connected defence and space programs.

DATA PROCESSING TERMS

There are various terms which are used in data processing, some of them are listed here.

Bit	The term bit is short for binary digit. It can assume either of the two states, representing numeric value 0 or 1.
Byte	In a computer system, basic unit of information is called a byte. A byte of information is generally stored by using 8 bits in a specified combination.
Field or Item	A field or item of data is one or more bytes that contain data about attributes ofan entity.
Record	A record is a collection of field relating to a specific entity.

File — A file is a collection of related records. The concept of a computer file is very similar to the manual file in a filing cabinet.

Database — A database consists of all the files of an organization, structured and integrated to facilitate updation of files and retrieval of information from them.

Format of a record — It can be either of Fixed length record or Variable length record format

Fixed Length — This record format contains the records of the same length (fixed format). So the information does not expand with time or use. For this type of format, record is designed by specifying a fixed number of storage positions.

Variable Length — This record format may contain the records of different lengths. So the information may vary with time and use. It is a record in which the data is allowed to occupy only the spaces which it needs.

Record Layout — Arrangement of data fields in a record, which normally contains two types of data fields: Key field and Non-key field. Key field is a field which contains a unique identifier for the entity about which data is being stored in the record. Non-key field store values of attributes of the entity identified by the key field value.

Data Codes — Data about entities can be recorded in two formats: Clear form and Coded form. Using clear or natural format, attributes of the entity are described or narrated using normal language.

Alphabetic Codes — Alphabetic codes contains alphabetic characters. These codes are easily rememberable and their meanings often seems obvious. For example, M is used for male and F for female.

Numeric Code — Numeric code contains digits and are widely used primarily for their convenience of showing the classification of hierarchy or related data items.

Alphanumeric Code — Alphanumeric code contains both numeric and alphabetic characters. Alphanumeric codes allow a large number of codes using fewer positions.

FILE PROCESSING ACTIVITIES

Four major file processing activities are:

1. File updation
2. File referencing
3. File maintenance
4. File enquiry

File Updation

The active lifetime of a file is usually short. Very soon the information stored on a file becomes old and it becomes necessary to modify the file with current information. This process of modifying an old file with current information is known as file updation.

The process of file updation may include:

1. Insertion of new records.
2. Modification of data in existing records.
3. Deletion of obsolete records.

4. Copying of those records which are neither obsolete nor require modification.

For example, Master file contains the information: subscriber number, name, address, age, sex.

File Referencing

When access is made to a particular to ascertain what is contained therein, e.g., reference is made to a Process file during an invoicing sum.

File Maintenance

File maintenance is the process of reorganizing the file structure or changing the physical layout of a reference or a master file.

File Enquiring

File enquiring is the examination of both reference and master files to obtain information contained therein

Let us Revise

1. Data is stored in the computer in terms of files.
2. The files can also be stored on direct access storage.
3. Data files are used to store data records.
4. Program files are used to store programs in different languages provided by different software vendors.
5. Object code files contain the machine codes and are created with an extension .OBJ.
6. Executable files have an extension of .EXE and are used for running the programs.
7. Unformatted text files are simple files containing simple text and can be created using any text editor or line editor.
8. Formatted text files are text files with formatting done on them using some software or the other.
9. A master file contains the master records, which contain data that are relatively permanent.
10. A tansaction file contains the records that are used to update the records of the master file.
11. File organization refers to the relationship of the key of the record to the physical location of that record in the computer file.
12. Sequential file organization has the records are arranged in the ascending or descending order or chronological order of a key field.
13. Serial file has the records are stored without any consideration of their order or sequence.
14. Random file consists of records organized in such a way that it is possible for the computer to directly locate the desired record without having to search through any other records first.
15. An indexed file is one that has an index for looking up locations of records on a disk.
16. Batch processing is done in small batches.
17. On line processing is done on-line machines and the data is immediately transferred from nodes to the main computer simultaneously.
18. Real time processing provides immediate (not periodic, as in batch processing) transaction input capability from all input originating stations.
19. The term bit is short for binary digit. It can assume either of the two states, representing numeric value 0 or 1.
20. In a computer system, basic unit of information is called a byte. A byte of information is generally stored by using 8 bits in a specified combination.
21. A field or item of data is one or more bytes that contain data about attributes ofan entity.

22. A record is a collection of field relating to a specific entity.
23. A file is a collection of related records. The concept of a computer file is very similar to the manual file in a filing cabinet.
24. A database consists of all the files of an organization, structured and integrated to facilitate updation of files and retrieval of information from them.
25. Record length can be either of Fixed length record or Variable length record format
26. Fixed length record format contains the records of the same length (fixed format). So the information does not expand with time or use. For this type of format, record is designed by specifying a fixed number of storage positions.
27. Variable Length record format may contain the records of different lengths. So the information may vary with time and use. It is a record in which the data is allowed to occupy only the spaces which it needs.
28. Record Layout of data fields in a record, which normally contains two types of data fields: Key field and Non-key field. Key field is a field which contains a unique identifier for the entity about which data is being stored in the record. Non-key field store values of attributes of the entity identified by the key field value.
29. Data about entities can be recorded in two formats: Clear form and Coded form. Using clear or natural format, attributes of the entity are described or narrated using normal language.
30. Alphabetic codes contains alphabetic characters. These codes are easily rememberable and their meanings often seems obvious. For example, M is used for male and F for female.
31. Numeric code contains digits and are widely used primarily for their convenience of showing the classification of hierarchy or related data items.
32. Alphanumeric code contains both numeric and alphabetic characters. Alphanumeric codes allow a large number of codes using fewer positions.
33. This process of modifying an old file with current information is known as file updation.
34. File maintenance is the process of reorganizing the file structure or changing the physical layout of a reference or a master file.

Multiple Choice Questions

1. In computer data is stored in terms of :
   (a) files (b) records
   (c) marbles
2. Object files have an extension of :
   (a) .doc (b) .exe
   (c) .obj
3. Executable files have an extension of :
   (a) .doc (b) .exe
   (c) .obj
4. Sequential file orgranization has records in :
   (a) serial (b) sequence
   (c) random
5. In batch processing, processing is done in terms of :
   (a) batches (b) groups
   (c) items
6. A bit can have two values 0 and .
   (a) 3 (b) 1
   (c) 4
7. A byte of information is stored using how many bits:
   (a) 8 (b) 7
   (c) 6

8. Data about entities can be recorded in two formats: Clear form and :
   (a) Non-clear form (b) Coded form
   (c) Alpha form
9. Alphanumeric code contains characters both numeric and :
   (a) alphabetic (b) special
   (c) physcial
10. Record Layout of data fields in a record, normally contains two types of data fields: Key field and :
   (a) Alpha field (b) Non-key field
   (c) Numeric field

True/False Questions

1. The files can also be stored on direct access storage.
2. Data files are used to store data records.
3. Object code files contain the machine codes and are created with an extension .EXE.
4. Executable files have an extension of .OBJ and are used for running the programs.
5. A master file contains the master records, which contain data that are relatively temporary.
6. A tansaction file contains the records that are used to update the records of the master file.
7. Sequential file organization has the records are arranged in the ascending or descending order or chronological order of a key field.
8. Serial file has the records are stored without any consideration of their order or sequence.
9. An indexed file is one that has an index for looking up locations of records on a disk.
10. Batch processing is done in small patches.
11. The term bit is short for binary digit. It can assume either of the two states, representing numeric value 2 or 1.
12. A field or item of data is one or more bytes that contain data about attributes of an entity.
13. A record is a collection of fields relating to a specific entity.
14. A database consists of all the files of an organization, structured and integrated to facilitate updation of files and retrieval of information from them.
15. Record length can be either of Fixed length record or Variable length record format
16. Variable Length record format may contain the records of different lengths.
17. Record Layout of data fields in a record, which normally contains two types of data fields: Key field and Non-key field.
18. Data about entities can be recorded in two formats: Clear form and Coded form.
19. Alphabetic codes contains numeric characters.
20. Alphanumeric code contains both numeric and alphabetic characters.
21. The process of modifying an old file with current information is known as file updation.
22. File maintenance is the process of reorganizing the file structure or changing the physical layout of a reference or a master file.

Matching Columns

Match the text in Column A with the text in Column B.

Column A	Column B
1. Bit	a. Records of different length

2.	Byte	b.	Containing only alphabets
3.	Field	c.	Collection of all files relating to an application
4.	Record	d.	Containing both alphabets and numerics
5.	File	e.	Modification of an existing file
6.	Database	f.	Containing only numerics
7.	Record length	g.	Basic unit of information
8.	Variable length	h.	Collction of related records
9.	Alphabetic code	i.	Fixed or variable
10.	Numeric code	j.	Binary digit
11.	Alphanumeric code	k.	Collection of field relating to an entity
12.	File updation	l.	Data about attributes of an entities

Fill in the Blanks with Appropriate Words

a.	Permanent	b.	exe	c.	Transaction	d.	programs
e.	files	f.	Serial	g.	indexed	h.	obj

1. Data is stored in terms of ________.
2. Program files are used to store ______.
3. Object code file has an extension of____.
4. Executable files have an extension of ____.
5. A master file contains records which are of ________ nature.
6. ________ file contains data which is used to update the master file.
7. ________ file has the records are stored without any consideration of their order or sequence.
8. An ________ file is one that has an index for looking up locations of records on a disk.

Descriptive Type Questions

1. Describe the various types of files.
2. How would you classify the different data files?
3. What is difference between formatted and non-formatted text files?
4. What is a Master file?
5. What is a Transaction file?
6. Describe the various type of file orgranizations?
7. What is Data Processing?
8. What are the different advantages and disadvantages of Data Processing
9. What are the different mode of data processing?
10. Write short notes on the following:

File updation	File Referencing
File maintaining	File Enquiring
Bit	Byte
Field or Item	Record
File	Database
Format of a record	Fixed Length
Variable Length	Record Layout
Data Codes	Alphabetic Codes
Numeric Code	Alphanumeric Code

Answers to Objective Type Questions

Multiple Choice Questions

1. a	2. c	3. b	4. a
5. a	6. b	7. a	8. b
9. a	10. b		

True/False Questions

1. T	2. T	3. F	4. F
5. F	6. T	7. T	8. T
9. T	10. F	11. F	12. T
13. T	14. T	15. T	16. T
17. T	18. T	19. F	20. T
21. T	22. T		

Matching Columns

1. j	2. g	3. l	4. k
5. h	6. c	7. i	8. a
9. b	10. f	11. d	12. e

Fill in the Blanks with Appropriate Words

1. e	2. d	3. h	4. b
5. a	6. c	7. f	8. g

Recommended Readings

1. Fundamentals of Computer Programming and Information Technology *by J.B. Dixit.*
2. Comprehensive Computer and Languages *by Ashok Arora & Shefali Bansal.*
3. 1000 IT Quizzes *by Dheeraj Mehrotra.*
4. Pictorial Computer Dictionary *by Dheeraj Mehrotra.*

—Published by Firewall Media (An Imprint of Laxmi Publications Pvt. Ltd.)

3 Principles and Techniques of Programming

INTRODUCTION TO PROGRAMMING

There are two aspects to computers. One, you use the computer and the other is to make the computer work for you. This first one is very easy. You run the program which has been designed and created for use. But, it is the second which is very important. This covers the programming part. With programming you design the process where you ask the computer to work according to you. Here the privledge of making any error is not there. Because, you are going to be tested by the computer, which is very accurate.

Programming is one of the step in system development cycle and it starts once the detailed design is over and program specification have been obtained. Flow charts are the first tool developed for design. Flow charts are drawn up as a pictorial guide by programmers for planning the procedure for the solution of a program.

PROGRAM DEFINITION

We had learned in our earlier classes that a computer program is a set of instructions to be followed by the computer. These instructions are basically the steps to be followed sequentially in order to achieve the result. Systematic notations for these steps are the computation steps referred to as programming languages. A person engaged in the activity of programming is referred to as programmer.

Steps in Program Development

The following basic steps are involved in writing computer programs:

1. Problem identification
2. Task analysis and data analysis
3. Output identification
4. Designing the solution
5. Data validation
6. Implementation and debugging
7. Final documentation and maintenance

These steps are mostly performed in sequence mentioned, however, in some cases you can do otherwise too.

PROGRAM LIFE CYCLE

No computer program is ever lasting. Each program overgrows itself. A program is actually the result of your own logic and thought process. If you think something today then it is not possible that you will think the same way a month onwards. If so then probably your mind has struck and is not developing. So once you read your own program, there is every likelihood that you will think of some improvements.

The change in program can also occur owing to expansion or changes in the nature of the business, the economic environment, the need to keep up with the new technology or other factors, a program may become inadequate to meet the future needs.

Characteristics of a Good Program

A good program has to have the following characteristics:

Accuracy	The program must do what it is supposed to do and meet the criteria laid down in its specification.
Reliability	The program must ALWAYS do what it is supposed to do and never crash.
Efficiency	The program must use the available store space and resources in such a way that the system's speed is not wasted.
Robustness	The program should cope with invalid data without stopping with no indication as to the cause and without creating errors.
Usability	The program must be easy to use and well documented.
Maintainability	The program must be easy to amend, having good structuring and documentation.
Readability	The code in the program must be well laid out and explained with comments. Since it is that you are one who is going to read the program always, there will be others too.
Portability	It should be seen that the program is easy to transfer to other machines as well.

DATA HANDLING AND DECLARATION

Data handling is basically the level of manging data. This can be divided into the following levels.

1. In the first step it is the operating system which handles the data. It manages the physical storage and retrieval of data on floppy disk, CD or other storage device.
2. It refers to the software that allows for the creation, storage, retrieval and manipulation of files interactively at a terminal or personal computer.
3. It is also the management of all data and information within an organization and includes data administration.
4. Lastly it is a function within an organization that manages data. It analyses, classifes and maintains all the data and data relationships. Data handling or administration coordinates the development of data models and data dictionaries which, combined with transaction volume, are the raw materials for database.

Types of Data

Let us see the type of data which can be used for running the program.

Constants

This is the data which is predetermined before a program is used. Values remain unchanged during the execution of a program.It has a fixed range in computer applications.

Variables

Here the data may change or be assigned different values as the program runs. There are limitations imposed by language on maximum number of characters used to form variable names.

INTRODUCTION TO FLOW CHARTS

Flow chart is the representation of the programming steps. These steps show the various steps in sequence which are needed to run the program. Flowchart uses boxes of different shapes to denote different types of instructions. The actual instructions are written within these boxes using clear and concise statements. These boxes are connected by solid lines having arrow marks to indicate the flow of operations, that is, the exact sequence in which the instructions are to be executed.

Flowchart helps in detecting errors in the programming logic too. Once the flowchart is ready, the programmer can forget about the logic and can concentrate only on coding the operations in each box of the flowchart in terms of the statements of the programming language. This usually ensures an error-free program.

Flow Charts Symbols

Terminal Box — The beginning, end of a point of interruption in a program, is represented by the terminal box.

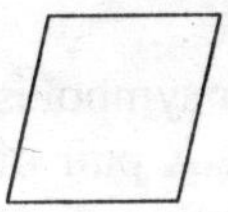

Input/Output Box — Any function of an input/output device (marking information available for processing, recording, processing information, etc.) is represented by input/output box.

Processing Symbol — A group of program instructions that perform a processing function of the program is represented by this symbol.

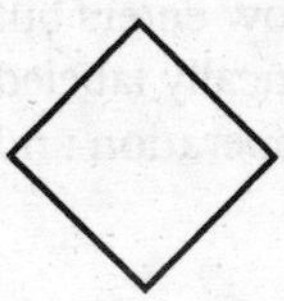

Decision Box — This box is used to document points in the program where a branch to alternate paths is possible based upon variable conditions.

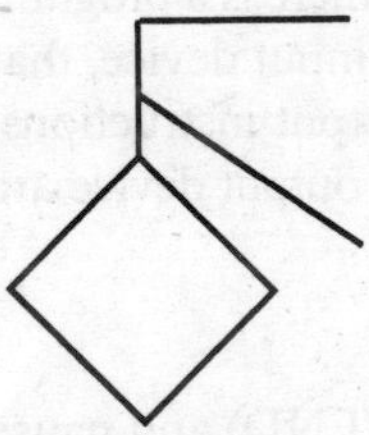

Connector — An entry to, or an exit from another part of the program flow chart is represented by this symbol.

Flow Lines — Flow lines connect symbols to show the sequence of logical setups.

Predefined Box — A group of operations not detailed in the particular set of flow charts are represented by the predefined box.

But, before actually making the flowcharts, let us understand some of the symbols shown here. A brief introduction of them was given able.

Decision

This symbol is used in a flowchart to indicate a point at which a decision has to be made and a branch to one of two or more alternative point is possible. The criterion for making the decision should be indicated clearly within the decision box. Moreover, the condition upon which each of the possible exit paths will be executed, should be identified and all the possible paths should be accounted for. During execution, the appropriate path is followed depending upon the result of the decision.

Processing

It is used in a flowchart to represent arithmetic and data movement instructions. Thus, all arithmetic processes such as adding, subtracting, multiplying and dividing are shown by a processing symbol. The logical process of moving data from one location of the main memory to another is also denoted by this symbol. When more than one arithmetic and data movement instructions are to be executed consecutively, they are normally placed in the same processing box and they are assumed to be executed in the order of their appearance.

Connector

If a flowchart becomes very long, the flow lines start crisscrossing at many places that causes confusion and reduces the clarity of the flowchart. Moreover there are instances when a flowchart becomes too long to fit in a single page and the use of flow lines becomes impossible. Thus, whenever a flowchart becomes so complex that the number and direction of flow lines is confusing or it spreads over more than page, it is useful to utilize the connector symbol as a substitute for flow lines.

This symbol represents an entry from, or an exit to another part of the flowchart. A connector symbol is represented by a circle and a letter or digit is placed within the circle to indicate the link. A pair of identically labeled connector symbols are commonly used to indicate a continued flow when the use of a line is confusing.

So two connectors with identical labels serve the same function as a long flow line. That is, they show an exit to some other chart section or they indicate an entry from another part of the chart. How is it possible to determine if a connector is used as an entry or an exit point? It is very simple: if an arrow enters but does not leave a connector, it is an exit point and program control is transferred to the identically labeled connector that does have a outlet. It may be noted that connectors do not represent any operation and their flowchart is only for the sake of convenience and clarity.

Input/Output

This symbol is used to denote any function of an input/output device in the program. If there is a program instruction to input data form a disk, type, card reader, terminal or any other type of input device, that step will be indicated in the flowchart with an input/output symbol. Similarly, all output instructions, whether it is output on a printer, magnetic, tape, magnetic disk, terminal screen or any output device are indicated in the flowchart with an input/output symbol.

Terminator

This symbol, as the name implies, is used to indicate the starting (BEGIN) stopping (END) and pause (HALT) in the program logic flow. It is the first symbol and also the last symbol in the program logic. In addition, if the program logic calls for a pause in the program, that also is indicated with a terminator symbol. A pause is normally used in the program logic under some error conditions or in case the forms had to be changed in the computer's line printer during the processing of that program.

Flow lines

Flow lines with arrowheads are used to indicate the flow of operation, that is, the exact sequence in which the instructions are to be executed. The normal flow of a flowchart is from top to bottom and left to right. Arrowheads are required only when the normal top to bottom flow is not to be followed. However, as a good practice and in order to avoid confusion, flow lines are usually drawn with an arrowhead at the point of entry to a symbol. Good practice also dictates that flow lines should not cross each other and that such intersections should be avoided whenever possible.

Rules for Drawing Flow Charts

Rule 1	Program flow charts should use conventional symbols.
Rule 2	The logic of a program flow chart should flow from top to bottom and from left to right.
Rule 3	Each symbol should have one entry point and one exit point.
Rule 4	Instructions within symbols should be in language.
Rule 5	Clearly label the exits of a decision symbol.

Advantages of Flowcharts

Following are the various advantages of flowcharts.

Conveys Better Meaning

Since a flowchart is a pictorial representation of a program, it is easier for a programmer to understand and explain the logic of the program to some other programmer.

Effective Joining of a Part of a System

A group of programmers are normally associated with the design of large software system. Each programmer is responsible for designing only a part of the entire system. So initially, if each programmer draws a flowchart for his part of design, the flowcharts of all the programmers can be placed together to visualize the overall system design. Any problem in linking the various parts of the system can be easily detected at this state and the design can be accordingly modified. Flowcharts can thus be used as working models in the design of new programs and software systems.

Efficient Coding

Once a flowchart is ready, programmers find it very easy to write the concerned program because the flowchart acts as a roadmap for them. It guides them in processing from the starting point of the program to the final point ensuring that no steps are omitted. The ultimate result is an error free program developed at a faster rate.

Systematic Debugging

Ever after taking full care in program design, some errors may remain in the program because the designer might have never thought about a particular case. These errors are detected only when we start executing the program on a computer. Such type of program errors are called bugs and the process of removing these errors is known as debugging. A flowchart is very helpful in detecting, locating and removing mistakes (bugs) in a program in a systematic manner.

Systematic Testing

Testing is the process of confirming whether a program will successfully do all the jobs for which it has been designed under the specified constraints. For testing a program, different sets of data are fed as input to that program to test the different paths in the program logic.

Drawbacks of Flow Charts

1. Flow charts are something new and strange to work with for beginners.

2. When modifications are made in the original program, corresponding changes must be made in the flow charts of the program in the documentation.
3. Flow charts may not reveal significant steps to be followed in actual coding.
4. Flow charts are often cumbersome to use and costly to produce.
5. Flow charts do not constitute a programming language, they are person-to-person means of communication, not person-to-computer.
6. Flow charts are difficult to produce at a summary level.

Rules for Writing Flow Charts

1. Keep the flowchart as simple as possible. The crossing of flow lines should be avoided as far as possible.
2. Be consistent in using names and variables in the flowchart.
3. Do not give every detail on the flowchart. A reader who is interested in more details can refer to the program itself.
4. If a new flowcharting page is needed, it is recommended that the flowchart be broken at an input or output point. Moreover, properly labeled connectors should be used to link the portions of the flowchart on different pages.
5. Go from left to right and top to bottom in constructing the flowchart.
6. First formulate the main line of logic, then incorporate the details in the flowchart.
7. Maintain a consistent level of detail for a given flowchart.
8. Words in the flowchart symbols should be common statements and easy to understand.

Types of Flow Charts

The two major varieties of flow charts used presently in practice are:

System flow charts
Program flow charts

System Flow Charts

1. In system flow charts, the unit of data transformation is usually an operation, i..e it usually shows the work done by an entire computer program. For example, Sorting a file of data, Inverting a matrix, Producing a report.
2. System charts stress on what data is used and produced at various points in a sequence of operations.
3. It represents the flow of documents, the operation or activities performed, the persons or work station.
4. It is an important tool of system analysis and plays a key role in the evaluation of existing system, designing and documentation of new systems.
5. System flow charts are usually prepared as an aid to the management and systems analysts.

Program Flow Charts

1. In Program flow charts the unit of data transformation is usually an operation or short sequence of operations that a computer performs.

2. Program flow charts stress on how data is transformed.
3. Such a diagram provides complete and detailed sequence of logical operations, to be performed in the central processing unit of the computer for executing the program.
4. Generally the programmer will use these flow charts to translate the elementary steps of a procedure into a program of coded instructions.

PSEUDOCODES

It is another program analysis tool that is used for planning program logic. "Pseudo" means imitation or false and "Code" refers to the instructions written in a programming language. Pseudocode, therefore, is an imitation of actual computer instructions. These pseudo instructions are phrases written in ordinary natural language (e.g. English, French, German, etc.)

Instead of using symbols to describe the logic steps of a program, as in flowcharting, pseudocode uses a structure that resembles computer instructions. Because it emphasizes the design of the program, pseudocode is also called Program Design Language (PDL).

Pseudocode is made up of the following basic logic structures that have been proved to be sufficient for writing any computer program:

1. Sequence
2. Selection (IF…THEN…ELSE or IF….THEN)
3. Iteration (DO…WHILE or REPEAT ….UNTIL)

Sequence

Sequence logic is used for performing instructions one after another in sequence. Thus for sequence logic, pseudocode instructions are written in the order, or sequence, in which they are to be performed. The logic flow of pseudocode is from the top of the bottom.

Selection

Selection logic, also known as decision logic, is used for making decisions. It is used for selecting the proper path out of the two or more alternative paths in the program logic. Selection logic is depicted as either an IF…THEN…..ELSE or IF…THEN structure. The flowcharts shown in figure illustrate the logic of these structures.

The IF…..THEN….ELSE construct says that if the specified condition is true, then do process 1, else (if the condition is not true) do process 2. Thus, in this case either process 1 or press 2 will be executed depending on whether the specified condition is true or false. However, if we do not want to choose between two processes and we simply want to decide if a process is to be performed or not, then the IF…THEN structure is used.

The IF…THEN structure says that if the condition is true, then do process 1 and if it is not true, then skip over process 1. in both the structures, process 1 and process 2 can actually be one or more processes. They are not limited to a single process. ENDIF is used to indicate the end of the decision structures.

Iteration

Iteration logic is used when one or more instructions may be executed several times depending on some condition. It uses two structures called the DO….WHILE and the REPEAT….UNTIL. Both DO…..WHILE and REPEAT….UNTIL are used for looping.

Differences between Pseudocode and Flowchart

Pseudocode differs from the flowchart in the following ways:

1. Pseudocode is self-explanatory and does not requires a separate documentation. This is so because it is written in plain English language.
2. Pseudocode has a structure similar to that of a programme written in BASIC or PASCAL language. But flowcharts have a tendency to extend flow lines in all directions and thus their paths of instructions do not parallel the final BASIC code.

REPORT GENERATION

Commercial outputs used formatted output. These formatted outputs are known as reports. A formatted report may have the following:

1. Report heading
2. Page heading
3. Page numbering
4. Footers
5. Some remarks
6. Date, month and year of printing

Commercial outputs may also extend over multiple pages. In that case, one will have to keep a provision in his program so that certain details get printed on every page. For example, one may have to print page headings on every page. Report may be of

1. Single page
2. Multiple page

Multiple page reports in general may consist of following parts:

Report Heading

It represents the title of the report and appears, only on the first page of the report.

Report Sub Heading

It is printed as and when required on each page.

Page Heading

It is printed on the top of each page.

Page Footer

It is printed at the bottom of each page. It is generally the total number of records on the page, sum of the numeric data, etc.

Report Detail

This constitutes the main body of report. The output details or the information of the main consequence are listed in this group.

Reports with Control Break

The most important objective of a program is reporting. We need summarized information for decision making. For presenting the summarized information one can use the concept of control break. In control break report, one need to group information based on some common criterion, maybe department, cost centre, etc.

A control break report can have the following:

1. Records of a particular region are grouped together and printed at one page.
2. When the control break occurs, certain procedures are followed. Such as total sales of that region.
3. It may be necessary that performance of each region is printed on each page, i.e., when the control break occurs the report is printed on a fresh page.
4. At the end of the report, it may be necessary to calculate and print the grand totals.

OPERATION ON FILES

There are some basic operations which can be performed on the files. They are:

Writing on the file

Reading the file for updating or outputtting

Deleting the file

Let us see each one of them in details.

Writing to a File

This is the process of making the data permanent on the tape or disk. It can be done with the help of data which has been keyed in either by off-line or by on-line method. Here the data is first stored in the memory and then written on the output medium.

Reading the File for Updating or Outputting

File created in the above step is used here. Once the data from the file comes to the memory, use have the option of making changes or doing calculations based on it or even send the data for printing.

Deleting the File

It is a process in which you delete the file from the storage media making way for some other data to be stored in.

FILE UPDATION

It is a process in which a data file is processed for changes in the records. These changes can be many to one records or one to many records. You may have to skip various records which do not have any changes or you may have to make several changes in the same record. Updation can be done on both sequential and non-sequential, i.e., random access files.

Sequential File Updation

This process is mostly used in the case of files being on the magnetic tapes. Because of the possibility of record insertions and/or deletions, during an update run, the computer processing creates new master file records. In many applications, some master file records are also deleted from the file. So you need to have one file having the master record before updation and the second having master records after affecting the changes in the master file.

Random File Updation

This process is mostly used in the cases where the file is on floppy disk or hard disk where the data is stored in random. Here a record is added, deleted or modified without affecting any other record in the file. Also when the record is to be accessed the same mapping function, key to address transformation, is used to transform the key to obtain its address. Thus while storing or accessing the record the same mapping function is used to find the address of the record.

Multiple Handling of Updation

Here since you are using more than one file, all the files in use must have the same sequence. Either all of them should be in sequence or all of them in random access mode. The records from all the files are called into the memory and converted into a single stream for updating. Once updated the data is transferred back to the files.

PROGRAMMING PARADIGMS

It is not that there are no rules for writing programs, there are a few of them. You must adhere to these rules to write good programs. Some of these are listed below:

Unstructured Progamming

This type of programming is straight forward programming. Here the everything is in a sequential manner. It does not involve any decision making. A general model of these linear programs is:

1. Read a data value.
2. Compute an intermediate result.
3. Use the intermediate result to compute the desired answer.
4. Print the answer.
5. Stop.

Structured Programming

Structured programs are the ones that are divided into functional modules and arranged in an hierarchical order instead of programs written in a sequence. Structured programming refers to the process in which we break the overall job down into separate piece of modules. These modules, in turn, are broken down into smaller pieces which can also be further subdivided. Modules must be chosen in such a way that we can specify how they have to interact. In effect, there is a contact between each pair of modules.

Advantages of Structured Programming

1. Decreases the complexity of the program by breaking it down into smaller logical units.
2. Allows several programmers to perform coding simultaneously.
3. Allows common functions to be written once and then used in all the programs needing it.
4. Decreases debugging time, because modules make it easier to isolate errors.
5. Amendments to single modules do not affect the rest of the program.
6. It saves time to use modular structures rather than using self made structure. If a job can be done well by using what is already available and known to be well tried and tested then trying out something new for sake of it, is a waste of effort.

7. Standard method; so, less time is required in writing programs.
8. It is easier to name modules in such a way that they are easy to find in the documentation and consistent.

Various characteristics of Structured Programs can be listed out as:

1. Two-way decision statements are based on IF...THEN, IF...THEN...ELSE and nested IF statements.
2. A rule of thumb is that the modules should not be more than one half page long. If they are longer than this, they should preferably be split into two or more submodules.
3. The programs are based on top-down modular design. In other words, the problem at hand is analyzed or broken down into major components, each of which is again broken down it necessary. Therefore, the process involves working from the most general down to the most specific. The design of the modules is reflected in hierarchy charts.
4. Loops and not custom designed with the use of the GO TO statement, but are based on the consistent use of WHILE...WEND and FOR...NEXT. In WHILE...WEND, the loop is based on the truth of a condition and in FOR...NEXT, on a counting process and the number of repetitions that can easily be predicted.
5. Each module has one entry point and one exit point. The GOTO statement is never used to jump from one module in the program to another.

Procedural Programming

As the name sounds it is based on certain procedures. A procedure call is used to invoke the procedure. After the execution of statements, flow of control returns to the postion from where call was made. Procedures can be further divided into sub procedures. With the help of sub procedures, programs can be written more structured and error free. For example, if the procedure is correct, every time it is used it produces correct results.

Modular Programming

One of the key concepts in the application of programming discipline is the design of a program as a set of units referred to as blocks or modules. A program module is defined as the part of a program that perform a separate function, e.g., input, input validation, processing of one type of input. A program module may be quite large, so that it may be further divided into logical sub modules. The process of subdivision continues until all modules are of manageable size in terms of complexity of logic and numbers of instructions.

Advantages of Modular Programming

1. Program maintenance becomes easier because the affected modules can be quickly identified and changed.
2. If a programmer leaves the the project midway, it is easier for someone else to take over a set of self contained modules.
3. In a very large project, several programmers may be working on a single program. Using a modular approach, each programmer can be given a specific set of modules to work on. This enables the whole program to be finshed sooner.
4. Some modules will be standard procedures used again and again in different programs or parts of the same program.

5. More experienced programmers can be given a more complex module to write and the junior programmers can work on the simpler modules.
6. Since module is small, it is simpler to understand it as a unit of code. It is therefore easier to test and debug, especially if its purpose is clearly defined and documented.
7. A large project becomes easier to monitor and control.
8. Modules can be tested independently, thereby shortening the time taken to get the whole program working.

SYSTEM DESIGN TECHNIQUES

Following are the main desinging techniques called Top Down and Botton Up.

Top Down Design

Top down design approach is performed in a special way. The main program is written first. It is tested before sub programs are written. To do this, the actual sub programs are replaced with stubs. The stubs simply test to see if the data is passed correctly. After the main program is written and checked each module is written and tested in turn. This should first be done without the main program in order to isolate a stub if an error occurs.

If the module and the main program run properly then the next module is written and checked and so on. To describe the program at its highest level, we use something called the universal program and then by a process of stepwise refinement work out the details of each part of the program.

Advantages of Top Design

1. At each stage, the sub programs are tested by themselves and then the main program is tested. Whenever modules are added, they are tested with the main program so if any error occurs it will probably be in a module only and this will be easy to debut.
2. It is desirable for modules to be kept small in general. As far as possible a module should be less than 100 statement lines long.

Top Down Implementation

1. Start with a very simple and short statement of what the program does. This is the top level in the design.
2. Go to the next level of details for the whole program, try to describe the program as sequence, selection or repetition of main tasks. Each of these tasks should be complete in itself but will be described in greater detail at the next level lf program development. These tasks are called module. A module should have just one entry point and just one exit point.
3. This process is repeated step by step and at each step all the modules at that levels are refined or developed to the next level of details. This is called step-wise-refinement. The step-wise-refinement stops when there are sufficient details for the procedure to be written in a programming language.
4. At the intermediate steps in the refinement, pseudo code or flowcharts are used to represent the procedure.
5. At every state unnecessary details are left out.
6. It is important that at each state the individual modules are checked to make sure that they perform the correct actions on the appropriate data.

Bottom Up Design

A bottom up approach would be to write the most basic subroutines in the hierarchy first and then use them to make more sophisticated subroutines. The pure bottom approach is generally not recommended because it is difficult to anticipate which low level subroutines will be needed for any particular program. It can often be a useful first step to produce a library of basic functions and procedures before embarking on a major project. In the bottom up approach it is usually assumed that the basic routines created will be general enough to be used more than once.

Using the subroutines, to construct a program, save yourself repeating the same lines of code by reusing it. A routine that is used many times has a very difficult status to those higher in the hierarchy. It is more like a basic instruction in the programming language than a large scale program component.

PROGRAM DEVELOPMENT PROCESS

So far I have talked about the various programming concepts. Here I define the various steps that are involved in writing and developing software:

Program Definition

Unless you define it how would you know what is to be done. So this is the first step. Various activities involved in this are:

1. Determine objectives of the current system
2. Study the current system
3. Analyse new objectives
4. Prepare design specifications.
5. Identify user's responsibility of data inputs and outputs to other systems
6. Prepare plan for design and implementation phases
7. Produce a report for the user and systems management.

Program Design

We have recently read about the various types of program designs. Choose one of them to design your program. This should envisioned as a step-by-step procedure. The programmer's problem is then to design a process (or algorithm) which, on being given the correct inputs, produced the required outputs. A program specification also includes a description of the constraints which must apply to the solution. This step consists of preparing documents that will guide the actual coding of the program. This step is considered complete when a clean compile walk-through has been held and the program design has been approved.

Coding

This step is the process of transforming the program logic design documents into a computer language format. This stage translates the program design into computer instructions. When the coded program is ready in a high level language, it is entered in a source file using any editor or word processor.

Debugging

Who does not make error? When you type the program and try to run it, you are bound to get errors. This process of correcting errors is called Debugging. Debugging aids the built in the computer which give diagnostic messages about any error in the program language either during coding or during keypunching. The errors are corrected and the program is debugged again to find out further errors, if any. This process is repeated till the program is error free. Debugging does not point out logical or arithmetic errors. Debugging program is an important part of program preparation and may even take more time than the actual program writing.

Type of Errors

Once a program has been typed in, different types of errors may show up. These include:

Syntax/Semantic Errors

Syntax is a set of rules governing the structure of an relationship between symbols, words and phrases in a language statement. A syntax error occurs when a program cannot understand the command that has been entered. Computer does not have any intelligence. Therefore, it can do what it is made to do provide it known how to do it. For this, a computer has an operating system and the compiler for programming language. These software convert the instructions given to a computer into a machine language equivalent. When we give the same instruction in a high level language, i.e., similar to English, then the computer compiler first translates it into the machine language and then the switches in the microprocessor of the CPU are so set that the computer performs these instructions one by one.

The compiler which translates the high level language instructions will be able to translate into exact machine language instructions, provided it has received the instructions correctly. If not, then the result will be absurd. For example, when we say Mangoes and Man goes, the meaning totally changes in English. Similarly, in computer language also, a little change in the position of comma or semicolon or a gap will make all the differences in the meaning of the entire instruction. This type of error is called **syntax error** and it is very harmful to the working of the computer. The compiler is able to detect such errors and gives the indication about those locations where the instructions are not understandable. A programmer then correct such instructions and then retypes the syntax errors.

Logic Errors

Logic refers to a sequence of operations performed by a software or hardware. Software logic or program logic is the sequence of instructions in a program. Logic errors are the errors that have been entered in the instructions created because of the mistake made by a program. Suppose you wanted the sum of A and B and put the result in the variable C. This is accomplished by typing:

```
C:=A + B
```

But while typing, the programmer has typed the following expression:

```
C:= A - B
```

Such a program will run properly but will give erratic result because the value of C will not be the sum of A and B but it will be the difference of A and B which is quite different. Such errors can only be detected with the help of test data that will give the input values of A and B and the resultant value that should come out of the program as a result of the operation performed on A and B. If the result given by the computer an the result calculated manually with the help of a calculator are the same, then you can say that there is no logical error. Otherwise a logic error may be present in the program.

The logical error given above is very simple. However, all logic errors used not be the result of wrong typing. They could also be the result of wrong definition, as for example. When the sales turnover of a company is checked on the printed price instead of the discounted price. Here if sales are defined as Y and the quantity is defined as X. If we by mistake interpret these two quantities differently, i.e. sales as X instead of Y. Then also the error committed is a logical error. In such a case the result will be logical.

Runtime Error

Runtime errors occur when a program is run on the computer and the results are not achieved due to some misinterpretation of a particular instruction. This could be some thing like dividing a number by zero which results in a very large value of quotient. At the time of executing a program, the runtime error is detected. Because, one of the values for which a program needs to calculate the result may be to divide the quantity by a very small quantity and the resultant value will be so large that it cannot be interpreted by the computer. This will then be shown as a runtime error. For example, the mass of an electron is very small value. If one divides a quantity by the mass of the electron, the result may be so large that it is beyond the capacity of the machine.

To overcome this problem, there is a built-in error detector in the language interpreter or compiler which will give the message and that will reflect the reason for run time error.

Program Testing

It is the job of the program to test, as far as possible, that all parts of the program work correctly. It should be realized that complete testing is not possible except in the case of the most trivial program; one can never be completely certain that all errors have been removed, but sufficient tests can be performed to give a reasonable measure of confidence in the program. The situation is analogous of testing children on multiplication tables; once a child has answered a certain number of multiplication table tests correctly, at some point or other the teacher assume that all other tests will be answered correctly and testing ceases.

Designing a Test Plan

Since we cannot test everything because there may be many number of if then else decision and all the test data may not be able to test all the loops. Each test must be carefully planned to provide more information about the program. A major benefit of preparing a comprehensive test plan with expected results is that it forces the programmer to think carefully about the program and often errors are spotted even before running the test.

Testing requires the following:

1. A thorough knowledge and understanding of what the program is supposed to do.
2. Plan out in advance what ought to be tested.
3. To work out expected results for each of the test cases.
4. Writing out the test plan.

Methods of Testing

The objectives of testing can be stated in two basic questions:

1. Does the logic work properly? This means, answering the following:
   (i) Does the program work as intended?
   (ii) Can it be made to crash?
2. Is the necessary logic present? This means answering the following:
   (i) Are there any functions missing?
   (ii) Does the program or module do everything specified?

There are two different ways of testing. These are:

1. Functional testing

2. Logical or structural testing

Functional Testing

Functional testing is carried out independently of the code used in the program. It involves looking at the program specification and creating a set of test data that covers all types of inputs and getting outputs and program functions. This type of testing is also known as "black box testing".

Logical (structural) Testing

Logical testing (white box testing) is dependent on the code logic and derives from the program structure rather than its function. In other words, we study the program code and try to test each possible path in the program at least once. The problem with logical testing is that it will not detect the missing functions. One method of devising a test plan is to start with a set of functional test cases and then add additional tests to exercise each statement in the program at least once, making sure that each decision is tested for all outcomes.

DOCUMENTATION AND PROGRAM MAINTENANCE

Documentation of a software system involves collecting, organizing, storing and maintaining a complete historical record of programs and other documents used or prepared during different phases of the system development. The documentation of a program is a continuous process. The program specifications, the algorithmic representation and the program itself can all be considered part of the documentation of a program. However, after successfully completing the program, we must ensure that our documentation us complete and it is in a finished, usable form. This includes both technical documentation for the programmers who maybe working with and modifying the completed program and user-level documentation for the users of the program.

One of the mistaken ideas held by too many programmers is that the documentation for a program should be written only after the program is "finished". This is a very dangerous point of view! It will certainly lead to inadequate documentation and might result in an incomplete or incorrect program. Documentation is a continuous process. It starts when we first begin to formulate a clear problem statement and continuous as we device a solution, express the solution algorithmically and code the algorithm as a computer program. The proper point of view is that documentation is an inherent part of a program. It is therefore meaningless to assert that documentation should be written after the program is finished.

Most programs that are written by professional programmers are used in a production environment. This means that once a program is deemed operational it is used on a regular basis, usually by people other than the author(s). For example, programs to process payrolls, maintain inventories, or handles hotel or airline reservations are invariably used by people who did not write them. Moreover, these people are usually not even programmers. In this sort of environment, we can appreciate the need for the following two different kinds of documentation.

User Documentation

It provides the information that one needs in order to use a program. This information includes a number of different items. These items are:

1. A description of the application area of the program or what will this program do?
2. A description of the input data that the program requires.
3. A description of the output produced by the program.

4. A description of the commands needed to start the program.
5. A description of the kinds of interactions that are possible with the program.
6. An explanation of all the messages that the program can produce.
7. A discussion (in nontechnical terms) of the performance capabilities and limitations of the program.

Technical Documentation

This kind of documentation is addressed to programmers who might be faced with the task of modifying the program at some time. Perhaps a mistake will become apparent after the program has been placed into use, or a decision may be made to enhance the program by adding a new feature. In either case, good technical documentation is a necessity.

Uses of Documentation

The uses of documentation are as follows:

1. They facilitate communication about an application between the technical development personnel and the non-technical users.
2. Documents are very helpful in initiating and training not just new employees, but old employees changing jobs or learning to use a computerized version of an old job. Good documentation will provide a self-instructional approach that will allow employees to advance at their own pace.
3. The documents are essential during abnormal maintenance when a new programmer must maintain a system after the original programmer or analyst has left. This is very common and serious problem. There are numerous cases where an application was left undocumented and could not be maintained. When this occurs, the application must be developed all over again.
4. Documents are essential even among technical personnel not only during developing of a system but also during operations and normal maintenance.
5. The provides a package that will contain the information needed to change the system should the environment or management's needs alter.
6. Documentation prevents system dislocation and cost that might otherwise occur if knowledge of the system were centered in a few individuals who resigned, relocated or were subsequently reassigned other duties.

Limitations of Documentation

Documentation has the limitations inherent in human communication. The difference in the backgrounds of the user and the documenter and the nature of the high technology that is being documented. This makes the test of a sound documentation more difficult.

Every thing can not be conveyed through the documentation only. It may be difficult for an analyst to convey one's assumptions and one's view of how the system could and should be improved given changed circumstances (of technology or user), interaction which would be invaluable to maintenance and redevelopment.

EXAMPLES OF FLOWCHARTS

Example1: This is a very simple program to make tea.

The possible steps could be:

BEGIN
Put pot on the stove
Add water
Light stove
Add tea leaves
Add milk
Wait till boil
Pour tea in the cup
END

This can be represented as a flowchart in the following manner. In the above program supposing I add an option to check whether the tea has come to boil or not, then I would have to use a Conditional option, this flowchart is also shown here.

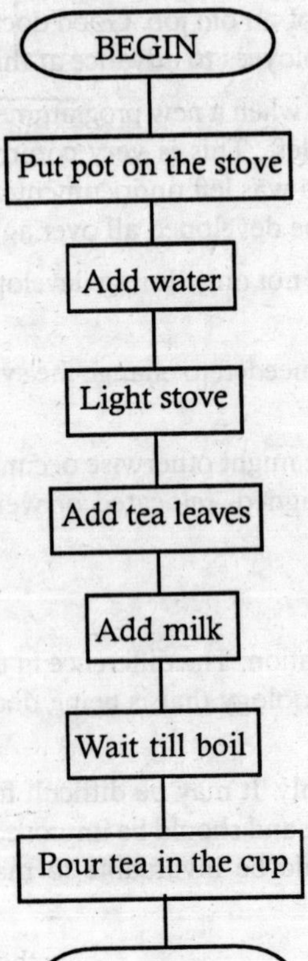

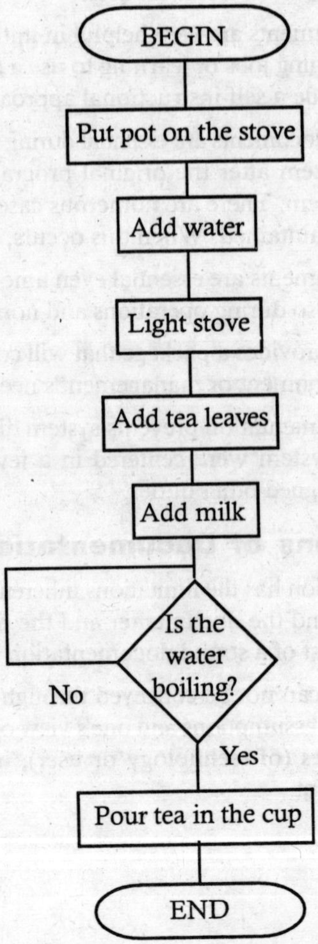

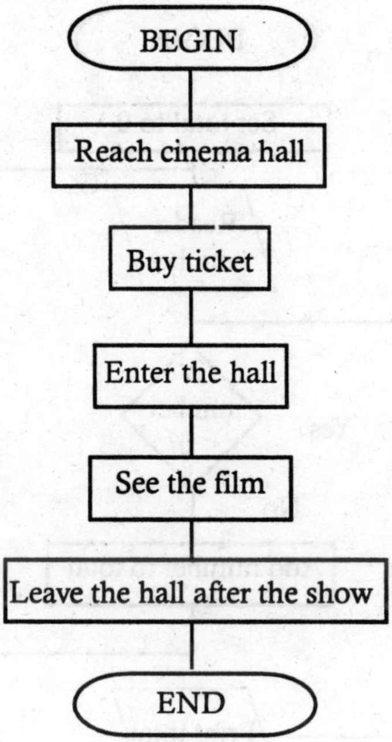

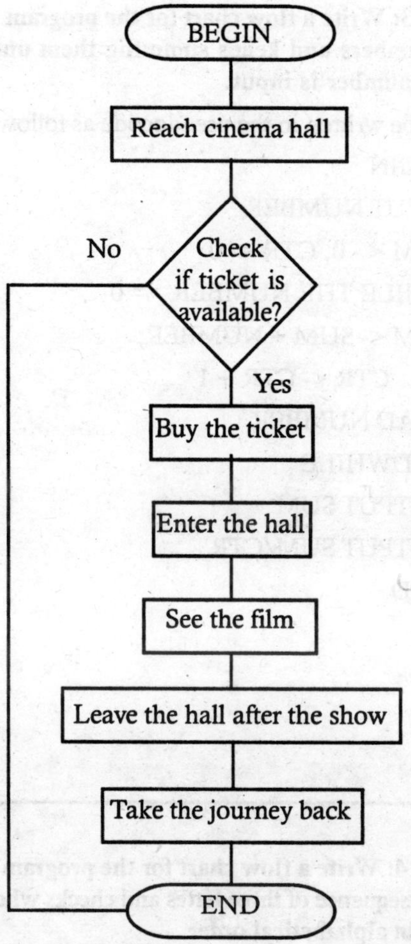

Example 2: Going to cinema hall to see the movie.

This can be done in the following steps.

BEGIN

Reach cinema hall

Buy ticket

Enter the hall

See the film

Leave the hall after the show

END

These steps are shown as a flowchart above. If now there is a chance you do not get the ticket, i.e., there is a housefull, then the flowchart would be different. It is also shown above.

Example 3: Write a flow chart for the program that inputs numbers and keeps summing them until a negative number is input.

This can be written in the pseudocode as following:

```
BEGIN
INPUT NUMBER
SUM < - 0, CTR <- 0
WHILE THE NUMBER >= 0
SUM <- SUM + NUMBER;
     CTR <- CTR + 1
READ NUMBER
ENDWHILE
OUTPUT SUM
OUTPUT SUM/CTR
END
```

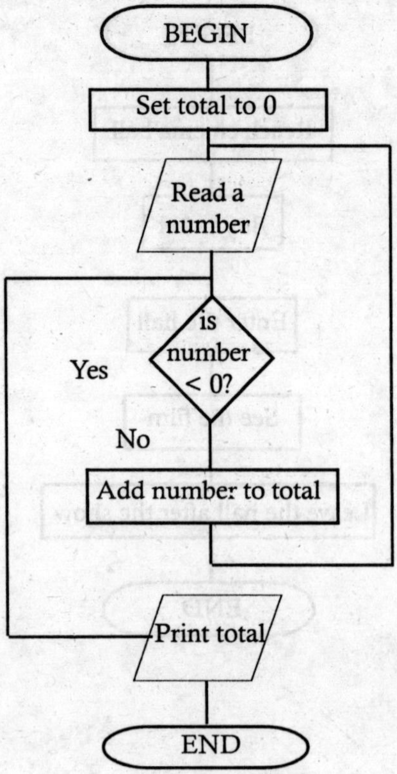

Example 4: Write a flow chart for the program that accepts a sequence of three lettes and checks whether they are in alphabetical order.

This can be written in the pseudocode as following:

```
BEGIN
Input letters
Check if first letter is lesser than the second
The second letter is lesser than the third
Then the letters are in alphabetic order
else
They are not in alphabetic order
END
```

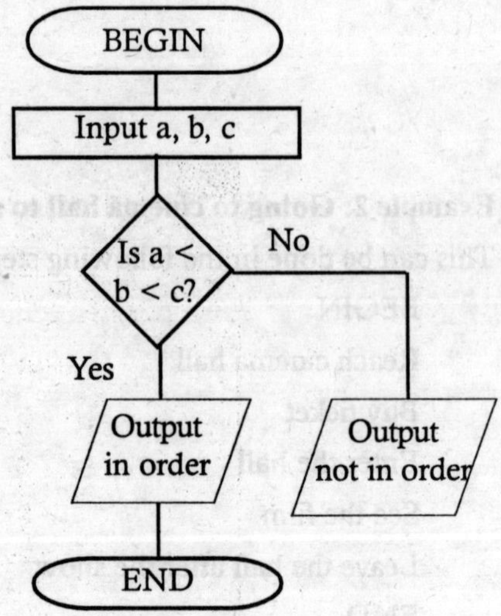

Example 5: Write a flow chart for the program that inputs three numbers and outputs whether they can be the angles of a triangle. If they can, it also outputs what kind of a triangle.

This can be written in the pseudocode as following:

```
BEGIN
    Input the three angles
    If the sum <> 180, output the angles cannot make a triangle : End
    Else
    If all angles are < 90 then output that the triangle is acute endif
    If one angle is 90 then output the triangle is right angles endif
    If one angle > 90 then output the triangle is obtuse endif end
    If any two angles are equal, then output the triangle is isosceles endif
    If all angles are different then output the triangle is scalene endif
    endif
END
```

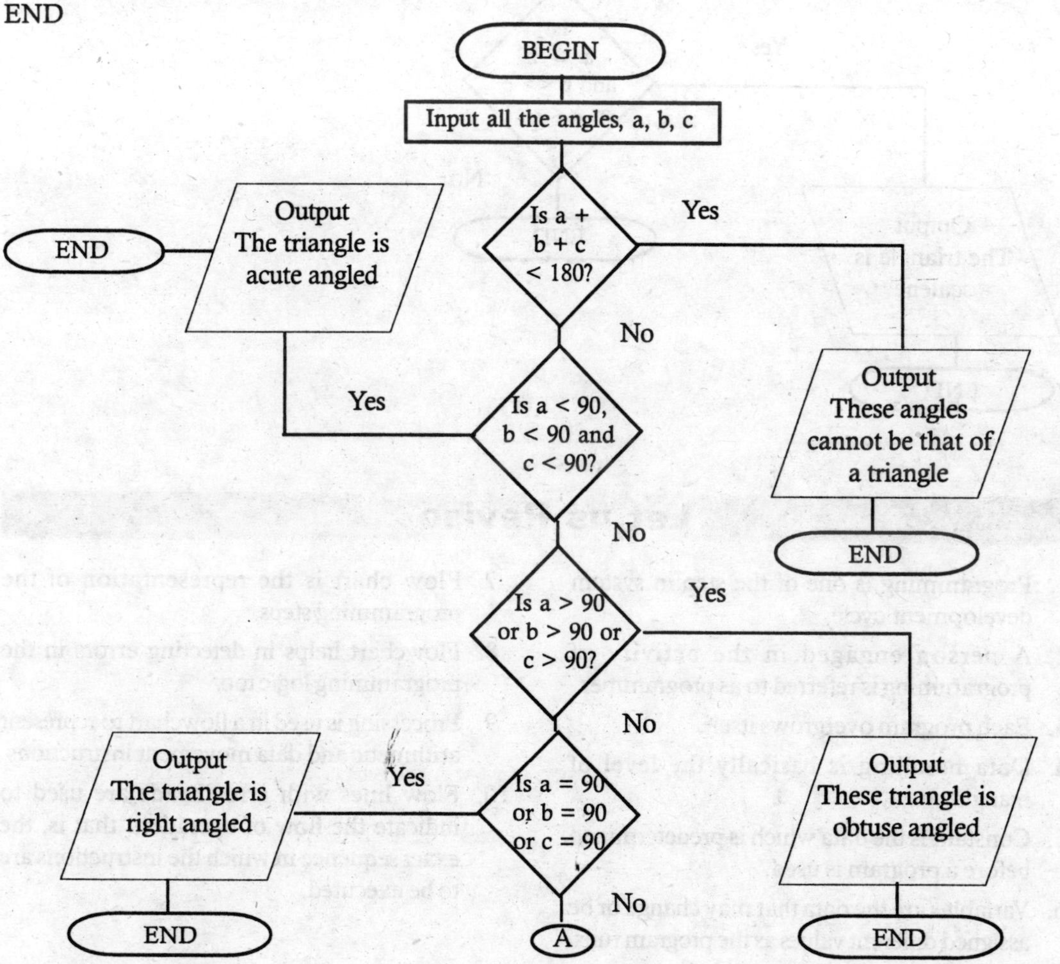

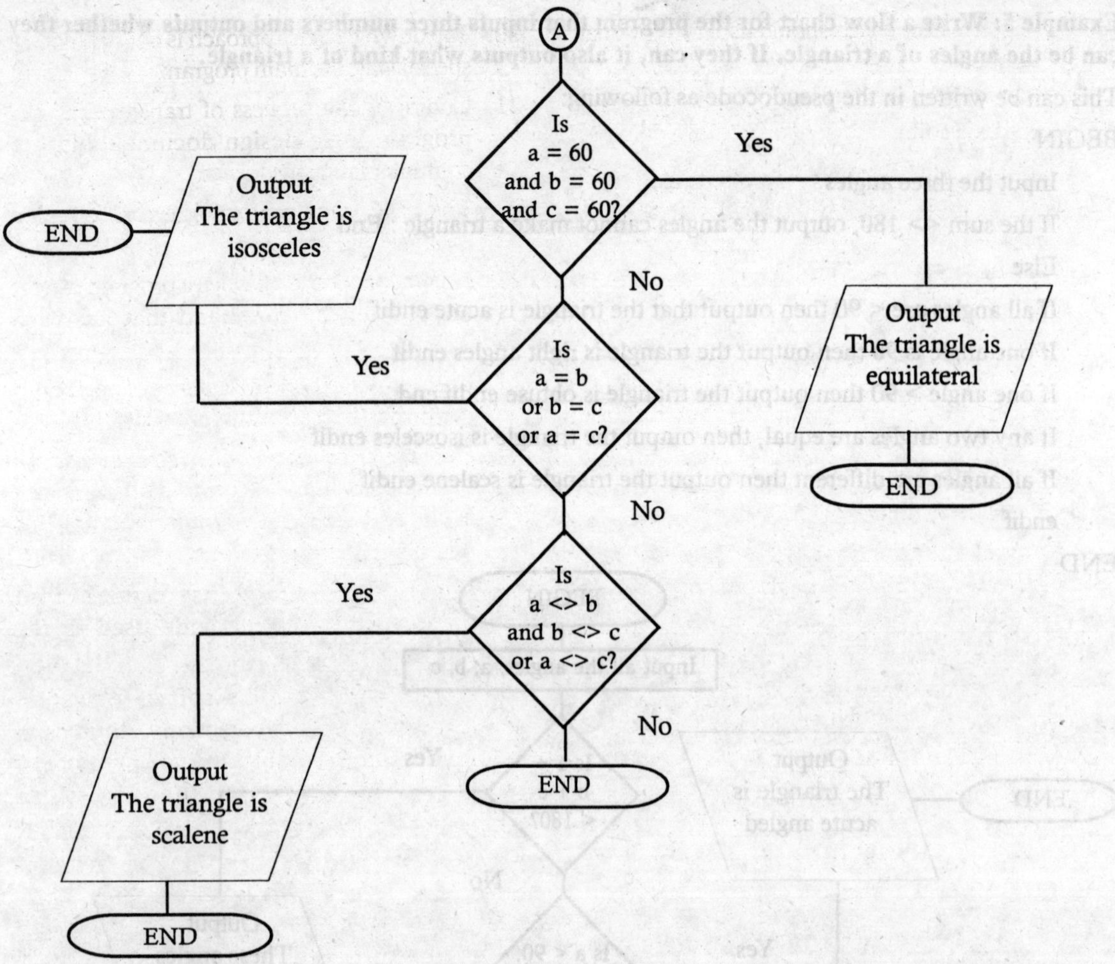

Let us Revise

1. Programming is one of the step in system development cycle.
2. A person engaged in the activity of programming is referred to as programmer.
3. Each program overgrows itself.
4. Data handling is basically the level of manging data.
5. Constant is the data which is predetermined before a program is used.
6. Variables are the data that may change or be assigned different values as the program runs.
7. Flow chart is the representation of the programming steps.
8. Flowchart helps in detecting errors in the programming logic too.
9. Processing is used in a flowchart to represent arithmetic and data movement instructions.
10. Flow lines with arrowheads are used to indicate the flow of operation, that is, the exact sequence in which the instructions are to be executed.

11. Program flow charts should use conventional symbols.
12. Each symbol should have one entry point and one exit point.
13. System charts stress on what data is used and produced at various points in a sequence of operations.
14. Program flow charts stress on how data is transformed.
15. Pseudocode is self-explanatory and does not requires a separate documentation. This is so because it is written in plain English language.
16. File updation is a process in which a data file is processed for changes in the records.
17. Random file updation is mostly used in the cases where the file is on floppy disk or hard disk where the data is stored in random.
18. Structured programs are the ones that are divided into functional modules and arranged in an hierarchical order instead of programs written in a sequence.
19. Procedural programming is based on certain procedures.
20. Top down design approach is performed in a special way, the main program is written first.
21. Coding is the process of transforming the program logic design documents into a computer language format.
22. The process of correcting errors is called Debugging.
23. A syntax error occurs when a program cannot understand the command that has been entered.
24. Logic errors refers to a sequence of operations performed by a software or hardware.
25. Runtime errors occur when a program is run on the computer and the results are not achieved due to some misinterpretation of a particular instruction.
26. Functional testing is carried out independently of the code used in the program.
27. Documentation of a software system involves collecting, organizing, storing and maintaining a complete historical record of programs and other documents used or prepared during different phases of the system development.

Multiple Choice Questions

1. A person engaged in programming is called :
   (a) Operator (b) Programmer
   (c) Analyst
2. Data whose value remains the same thoughout the program is called :
   (a) Variable (b) Constant
   (c) Communicator
3. If a flow chart goes from one page to another, it is connected using :
   (a) Connector (b) Flow lines
   (c) Decision box
4. Different options of a step are shown using :
   (a) Connector (b) Decision box
   (c) Input/output box
5. In top down design, the main program is written:
   (a) Fist (b) Last
6. The process of correcting errors is called:
   (a) programming (b) flow charting
   (c) debugging
7. A syntax error occurs when the system cannot understand a :
   (a) command (b) logic
   (c) flow
8. Pseudocode is written in :
   (a) machine language
   (b) English language
   (c) programming language

True/False Questions

1. Programming is one of the step in system development cycle.
2. A person engaged in the activity of programming is referred to as operator.
3. Data handling is basically the level of manging data.
4. Constant is the data which is predetermined before a program is used.
5. Flow chart is the representation of the programming steps.
6. Flowchart helps in correcting errors in the programming logic too.
7. Flow lines with arrowheads are used to indicate the flow of operation, that is, the exact sequence in which the instructions are to be executed.
8. Program flow charts may not use conventional symbols.
9. System charts stress on what data is used and produced at various points in a sequence of operations.
10. Program flow charts stress on how data is transformed.
11. File updation is a process in which a data file is processed for changes in the records.
12. Random file updation is mostly used in the cases where the file is on floppy disk or hard disk where the data is stored in random.
13. Procedural programming is not based on certain procedures.
14. Top down design approach is performed in a special way, the main program is written first.
15. The process of correcting errors is called Debugging.
16. A syntax error occurs when a program cannot understand the command that has been entered.
17. Runtime errors occur when a program is run on the computer and the results are not achieved due to some misinterpretation of a particular instruction.
18. Functional testing is carried out independently of the code used in the program.

Matching Columns

Match the text in Column A with the text in Column B.

Column A	Column B
1. Flow chart	a. Changing file with corrections
2. Programming	b. Checking program for errors
3. Constant	c. Program divided into modules
4. Variable	d. Error while running the program
5. Flow lines	e. Program following various procedures
6. Pseuecode	f. Error due to wrong command
7. File updation	g. Errors occuring due to error in logic
8. Structured program	h. Program logic design to computer format.
9. Procedural programming	i. Value of which remains constant
10. Logic errors	j. Codes written in English
11. Syntax error	k. Pictorial representation of program

12. Runtime error
13. Debugging
14. Coding

l. In flow chart the connecting lines
m. Writing instructions for computer
n. Value of which changes in the program

Fill in the Blanks with Appropriate Words

a. programming b. movement c. English d. Procedural
e. Constant f. data g. program h. exit
i. Top down j. Debugging

1. Program flow charts stress on how ______ is transformed.
2. Each symbol should have one entry point and one ______ point.
3. The process of correcting errors is called ________.
4. Functional testing is carried out independently of the code used in the ______.
5. ________ design approach is performed in a special way, the main program is written first.
6. Flow chart is the representation of the ________ steps.
7. ________ is the data which is predetermined before a program is used.
8. Processing is used in a flowchart to represent arithmetic and data ________ instructions.
9. ________ programming is based on certain procedures.
10. Pseudocode is written in plain ______ language.

Descriptive Type Questions

1. What is programming?
2. What is data handling?
3. What all the steps in program life cycle?
4. Describe the various flow chart symbols.
6. What are the advantages and disadvantages of flow chart?
7. What are the rules for writing a flow chart?
8. What are Pseudocodes?
9. What is the difference between Pseudocode and flow chart?
10. Which are the various parts of reports?
11. What operations you can perform on the files?
12. Which are the different methods of file updation?
13. What do you understand by top down design?
14. How program testing is done?
15. Describe the various type of errors you get when the program is run?
16. What do you understand by documenation of program?
17. What are the usuage and limitations of program documentation?
18. Write short notes on the following:

Constants	Variables
System Flow Charts	Program Flow Charts
Sequence	Selection
Iteration	Deleting the File
Writing on a file	Reading the file
Bottom down design	Functional Testing
Sequential File Updation	
Random File Updation	
Multiple Handling of Updation	

Reports with Control Break
Unstructured Programming
Procedural Programming
Modular Programming
Logical (structural) Testing
User Documentation
Technical Documentation

Answers to Objective Type Questions

Multiple Choice Questions

1. b	2. b	3. a	4. b
5. a	6. c	7. a	8. b

True/False Questions

1. T	2. F	3. T	4. T
5. T	6. F	7. T	8. F
9. T	10. T	11. T	12. T
13. F	14. T	15. T	16. T
17. T	18. T		

Matching Columns

1. k	2. m	3. i	4. n
5. l	6. j	7. a	8. c
9. e	10. g	11. f	12. d
13. b	14. h		

Fill in the Blanks with Appropriate Words

1. f	2. h	3. j	4. g
5. i	6. a	7. e	8. b
9. d	10. c		

Recommended Readings

1. Fundamentals of Computer Programming and Information Technology *by J.B. Dixit*.
2. Comprehensive Computer and Languages *by Ashok Arora, Shefali Bansal.*
3. Practical Project Management *by Ivan Bayross.*
4. Programming and Problem Solving Through "C" Language *by Harsha Priya, R. Ranjeet.*
5. Learning Computer Programming : It's not about Languages *by Mary Farrell.*

—Published by Firewall Media (An Imprint of Laxmi Publications Pvt. Ltd.)

4 Database Concepts

INTRODUCTION

Each office has to maintain details of its several employees. It may, for example, maintain the files of the followings:

Personal File

Accounts File

Leave Record File

Details of these files can be worked out (it may be different from office to office) as follows:

Personal File

- ☐ Name
- ☐ Address
- ☐ Telephone number
- ☐ Joining Date
- ☐ Designation
- ☐ Qualifications

Accounts File

- ☐ Name
- ☐ Basic Salary
- ☐ HRA
- ☐ DA
- ☐ I Tax
- ☐ PF

Leave Records File

- ☐ Name
- ☐ Casual Leave
- ☐ Privileged Leave
- ☐ Sick Leave
- ☐ Accumulated Leaves

If you notice all these files have one field in common which is **Name** and this is called the **Primary** key and is the link between all the 3 files. A look at the fields of the Personal file will give us an idea about the database to be created for it.

Personal File

Name	Alphanumeric
Address	Alphanumeric
Telephone number	Numeric
Joining Date	Date
Designation	Alphanumeric
Qualifications	Alphanumeric

Once we create all these tables the **office database** will be created. A database therefore comprises of tables. Tables in turn contain records. If we are to decide what tables should be part of the office database, we have to ask ourselves what is the information which needs to be stored in the database. Once we have this information we can decide about the tables.

A Database is a collection of all the required information pertaining to a particular subject. Thus, all the data pertaining to a office is put together in a database.

Two things should be borne in mind while storing data.

- ☐ The data is to be stored in a single database since it pertains to a single subject.
- ☐ The distinction between the various groups should be maintained since different types of details are stored for each group.

To satisfy these conditions, the data for each category is stored in a separate table. All the tables are part of a single database. Thus, in the Office Database we have 3 tables as follows:

Office Database

- ☐ Personal Table
- ☐ Accounts Table
- ☐ Leave Record Table

The point to note here is that data in this database is stored in the form of tables, is also known as relations.

RELATIONAL DATABASE MANAGEMENT SYSTEMS

It would definitely make things easy for the user if software that enables the user to create a database also allows the user to maintain it. Maintaining a database would involve performing the various data manipulation operations on the tables in the database.

These operations are:

- ☐ Adding Records
- ☐ Querying
- ☐ Modifying Records
- ☐ Deleting Records

These operations enable the user to store, retrieve and update data in the database. In addition to this the system should also allow the user to create relationships between the various tables. The system that provides all these facilities is called a **Relational Database Management System** (RDBMS).

Examples of Relational Database Management Systems are:

- ☐ Microsoft Access
- ☐ Oracle
- ☐ Sybase

But, it is Access which is more popular, since it works equally well on both **Personal Computers** (PCs) and on mainframe computers. Whereas Oracle is more popular with bigger computers where you have more than one computer networked together.

Each RDBMS will facilitate the following:

Tables Containing data

Queries Selected information is displayed on the screen

Reports Formatted printed information

Forms Screen created to add, modify and delete records

Let us consider the tasks that have to be performed when we are working with each one of the entities given above.

TABLES

In the case of tables, the tasks involved are as follows:

Creating a table

- ☐ Specifying the field names
- ☐ Specifying the data names
- ☐ Specifying the field sizes
- ☐ Specifying a field in the table that will have unique value

Adding records to the tables

Modifying data in the table

Deleting records from the table

Creating relationships between tables

The RDBMS will provide the facility to perform all these tasks. For example, using an RDBMS we can create the Office database. We can create the 3 tables described in the case of Office database. We can also create the relationships between the tables.

QUERIES

In the case of queries, the tasks involved are as follows:

Creating queries to obtain information

- ☐ Specifying the conditions on the basis of which the data is fetched from one or more tables
- ☐ Specifying the fields on the basis of which the data is to be sorted

Creating queries to update data

- ☐ Specifying the conditions to determine which records are to be updated

Creating queries to delete data

- ☐ Specifying the conditions to determine which records are to be deleted

For example, the RDBMS allows us to create a query to obtain the names and designation of all the employees working in the office. We can also have the records sorted in the ascending order by their names.

A report is data presented in an easy-to-understand, good-to-look-at manner. This data can be taken directly from a single table. Or we can use the relationships between tables to fetch the data from more than one table via a query.

REPORTS

In the case of reports the tasks involved are as follows:

Creating a report

- ☐ Specifying the table or query from which the report is to be created

- ☐ Specifying the fields from the above that are to be included in the report
- ☐ Formatting the data

For example, we can use the query created above. Using the facility provided by the RDBMS, we can highlight the records of employees who have salary over Rs. 10,000. A bold typeface can be used for these records.

FORMS

The easiest way to understand forms is to think of them as paper forms. The only difference being that these forms are available on the computer and not on paper. They are used to data entry or to view the data in the table. They can also be used to print the reports created in the above example.

In the case of forms the tasks involved are as follows:

Creating Forms

- ☐ Specifying the table or query from which the form is to be created
- ☐ Specifying the fields from the above that are to be displayed in the form
- ☐ Formatting the form

For example, using the facility provided by the RDBMS, we can create forms to enter data in all the above 3 tables.

ADVANTAGES OF USING RDBMS

There are various advantages of using RDBMS, some of them are listed here.

1. It can handle very large data tables, and also provide tools to safeguard and inspect the data.
2. It provides with a set of powerful tools for sorting, retrieving, and presenting data.
3. Its strong organizational concept helps managing databases very efficiently.
4. Multiple databases can be linked together to give rise to a pyramid structure of database system.
5. Queries can be made on user's request on the basis of select criteria's either from single or multiple database files.
6. Reports can be generated by grouping some fields with suitable headings from a single or multiple databases.
7. Its wizards, like those in other Microsoft products, make it easy to create tables, queries, reports, mailing labels, and other types of information.
8. It also adds advanced features such as object oriented programming and database scheme, making it a more powerful tool for application developers.
9. It has its own menu builder to design customized menu system for organizing the whole program. It also provides customized windows for the display of suitable messages and screen activities.

Let us Revise

1. Each office maintain the files of the followings: Personal File, Accounts File and Leave Record File.
2. Primary key is the common key between various files.
3. A database comprises of tables.
4. Maintaining a database involves Adding Records, Querying, Modifying Records and Deleting Records
5. Examples of Relational Database Management Systems are: Microsoft Access, Oracle and Sybase
6. Tables contain data in rows and columns called fields.
7. Queries are used to get result from the database.
8. Reports are generated to print information from tables.
9. Forms are created on screen to fill in the data.
10. Using RDBMS you can handle large volume of data.

Multiple Choice Questions

1. Common field to various tables in the database is called :
   (a) Key (b) Common
   (c) Same
2. Forms are :
   (a) Displayed on screen
   (b) Printed on printer
   (c) Outputted on plotter
3. A database consists of various :
   (a) Tables (b) Chairs
   (c) Stools
4. Full form of RDBMS is :
   (a) Relational Database Management System
   (b) Regional Database Management System
   (c) Relational Database Making System

True/False Questions

1. Primary key is the common key between various files.
2. A database comprises of forms.
3. Maintaining a database involves Adding Records, Querying, Modifying Records and Deleting Records
4. Tables contain data in rows and columns called fields.
5. Queries are not used to get result from the database.
6. Reports are generated to print information from tables.
7. Forms are created on screen to fill in the data.

Matching Columns

Match the text in Column A with the text in Column B.

Column A	Column B
1. Database	a. Displaying on screen to fill in the data
2. Table	b. Common key to various tables in database
3. Query	c. Relational Database Management System

4. Report
5. Form
6. RDBMS
7. Primary key

d. To extract information from table
e. A collection of data in rows and columns
f. Printing information from table
g. A collection of tables pertaining to a kind of data

Fill in the Blanks with Appropriate Words

a. Tables b. Query c. Forms d. Table
e. Report

1. ________ are displayed on screen to fill in the data.
2. A database consists of various ________.
3. A ________ is printed based on information from the tables.
4. A ________ can be generated to get results based on the data in the tables.
5. ________ contains data in rows and columns.

Descriptive Type Questions

1. What is a database?
2. What is Relational Database Management System?
3. What all you need for creating Tables?
4. What sort of queries you can generate from the table?
5. What sort of report can you generate from the table?
6. What are the forms used for?
7. What are the advantages of using RDBMS?

Answers to Objective Type Questions

Multiple Choice Questions

1. a 2. a 3. a 4. a

True/False Questions

1. T 2. F 3. T 4. T
5. F 6. T 7. T

Matching Columns

1. g 2. e 3. d 4. f
5. a 6. c 7. b

Fill in the Blanks with Appropriate Words

1. c 2. a 3. e 4. b
5. d

Recommended Readings

1. Learn to Program Visual Basic—Databases *by John Smiley*.
2. Learn to Program Visual Basic—Objects *by John Smiley*.
3. Learn to Program Visual Basic—Examples *by John Smiley*.

—**Published by Firewall Media (An Imprint of Laxmi Publications Pvt. Ltd.)**

5 Introduction to Visual FoxPro

INTRODUCTION

Visual FoxPro is an extension of the database software which has been in use from dBASE version I to IV, Foxbase+ and so on with FoxPro for DOS and now this version for Windows.

STARTING VISUAL FOXPRO

As you would do in the case of any windows based software, you start this software too either from the Start menu, Programs or in case you have the icon, you start with it. Other way of starting could be from Windows Explorer where you click/double-click at the file named VFP.EXE.

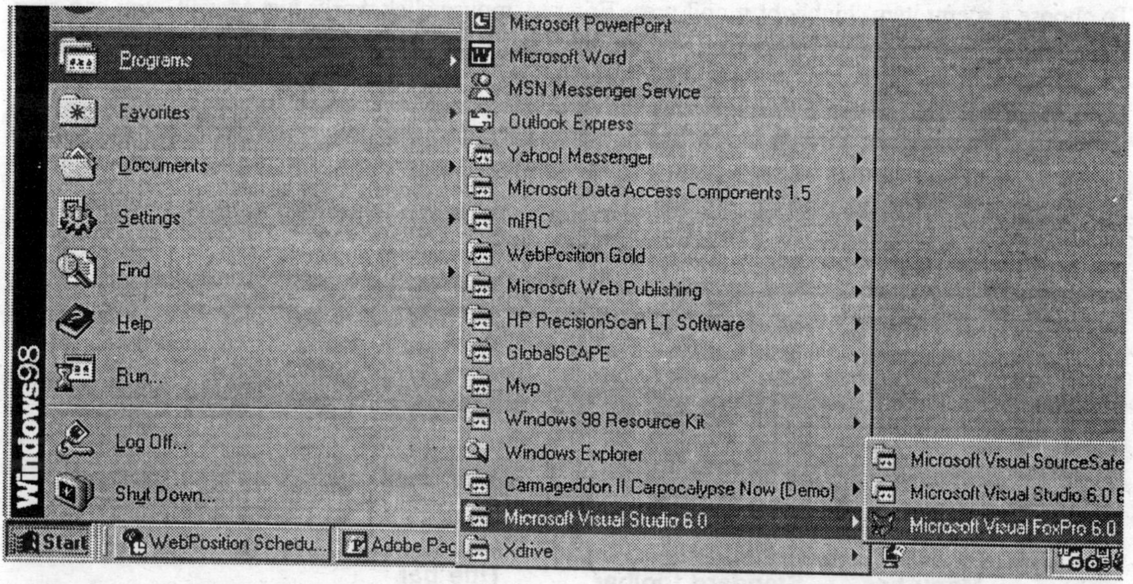

In all cases you would end up having a blank slate for operation, as shown on the next page. As you can see there is also a small Command window on the screen. This is used to write code. For all those who have graduated from DOS based software and quite keen to give commands by writing them. They can do so here.

THE MENU SYSTEM

This bar is there on the screen of most of the windows based software. It is here that you have all the menu options. Under each menu option you have the various commands which can be used to do most of the operations in the software.

You can access these menus either by mouse or by pressing the Alt key and then pressing the letter

underneath the menu. For example Alt+F would open the file menu. Once it is opened, then you can use the arrow keys to move up and down. At a given time, some menu options might appear dimmed, which means that you cannot execute that option now.

To choose a menu item, highlight it and press Enter. A mouse click works just as well. You can even press the underlined letter in the option, if it has one. Notice that in the pop-up menus, you do not press the Alt key with the underlined letter. Some menu options have special key combinations, called shortcut keys, that enable you to jump to that option directly without going through the menu pads. FoxPro displays these shortcut keys along the right side of the pop-up menus. The shortcut key for file, open, for example is Ctrl+O. This means that you can press Ctrl+O any time while you are in Visual FoxPro with the System menu active to open an existing file.

FEATURES OF THE FOXPRO SCREEN

Each software has its own way of representing the various options on the screen. Now that you have seen how the opening screen looks like. Let me show you what these features are:

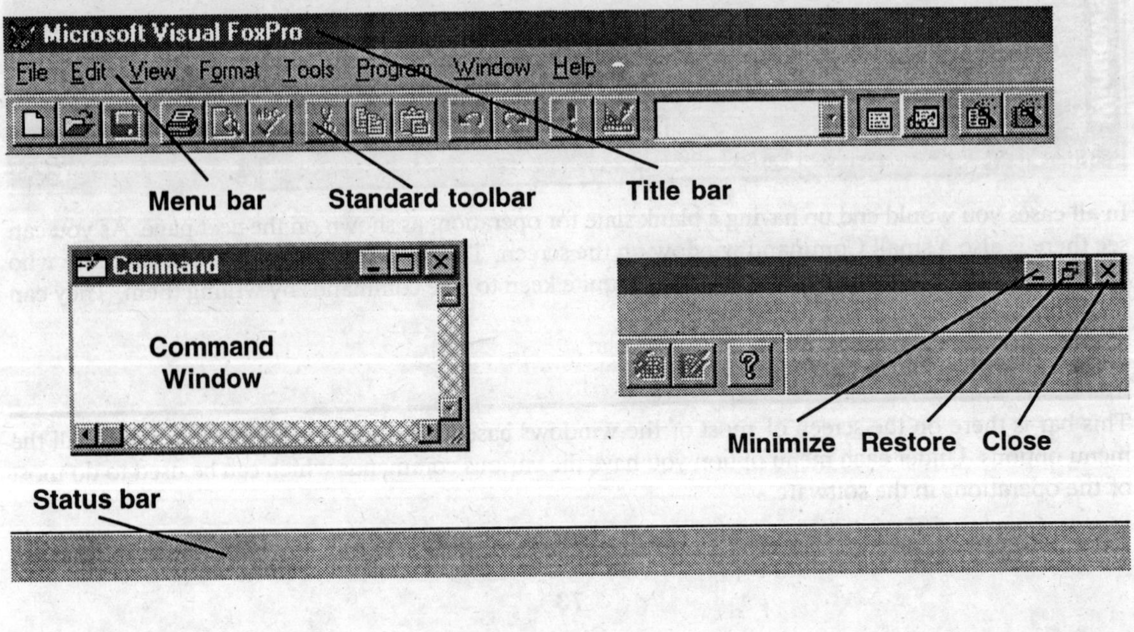

Minimize — It reduces FoxPro to an icon.

Maximize/Restore — It maximize the size of the main FoxPro window. When maximized, a window has no border. It can also be used to restore the window to preceding size after minimization or maximization.

Close — It closes FoxPro.

Command Window — It is normally placed at the bottom right corner of the screen and is used for typing commands.

Title Bar — It is at the top of the screen and displays the name of the program, i.e., Microsoft Visual FoxPro.

Status bar — It displays various kinds of information related to the window that is currently opened.

Standard Toolbar — It contains buttons for performing the most common actions in Visual FoxPro.

You will use them all later in the book.

FILE TYPES

With each software you work on files. Depending upon the software, the files have extensions. In fact from the extension of the files, you can guess from which software it has been created. For example, DOC files are usually the document files and are created using word processing programs. In FoxPro you work on various files. When you opt for creating a new file from the File menu, you come across a dialog box, as shown here.

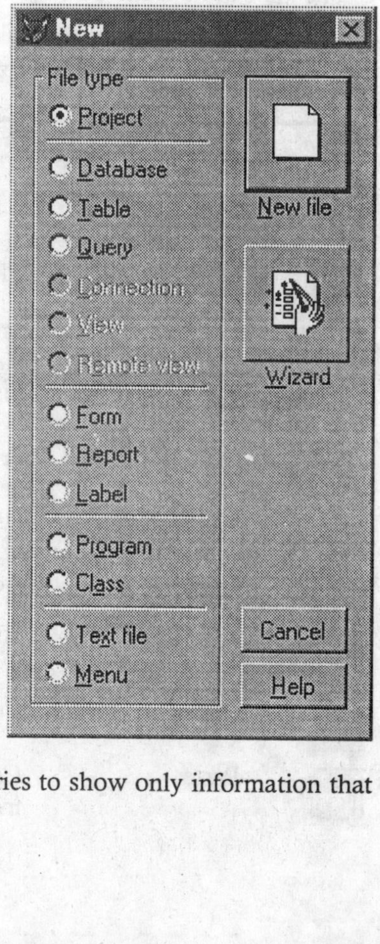

Various options of the dialog box are:

Project — In Visual FoxPro you work on projects which are in turn a combined effort of various files which are executable. It organizes various files to form a single project with extension .pjx.

Database — It is a collection of various data files which have something in common.

Table — It is used to hold the raw data of the database. Your data is entered into the tables. It is then organized into rows and columns.

Query — A query is there to extract information from the table. These can be used to select, change, add or delete records in your database.

Form — You can create forms for entering data for the database. This helps in displaying the data in structural manner and can be entered easily.

Report — These present the data you select in a printed format. Reports can be based on tables to show all the data from the given table, or they can be based on queries to show only information that meets certain criteria.

Label	It enables you to use table data to create mailing labels.
Program	It is a plain text file used to hold Visual FoxPro programming code.
Class	It is used in object oriented programming to hold a class.
Text file	It has a plain text file.
Menu	The file holds the specifications of the menu system for a custom application.

Besides these you have buttons for Connection, View and Remote view. These can be created only when you are using the software. A connection file lets you name and save the specifications used to connect to a server on the network. View and Remote view files let you create updatable queries based on local and remote tables.

THE TOOLBARS

For any software toolbar contains the various tools which help you work fast. They are like the tools which a doctor uses for operation. FoxPro has several toolbars, each of which is customized for the current task. This arrangement eliminates the confusion (and space problems) of having all buttons available at all times. You can experiment with the toolbars in FoxPro 6 by selecting View, which opens the Toolbar dialog box, shown earlier. From this dialog you can select specific toolbars or customize your own selection. You should only keep open the toolbars that you will need because the screen and workspace can become quite cluttered with a lot of toolbars on the screen.

The most important one of the toolbars is the one called Standard toolbar. It has the following commands. These commands are otherwise available under the various menu options too.

Button	*Name*	*Description*
	New	Opens the New File dialog box to create a new file.
	Open	Opens the Open File dialog box to open an existing file.
	Save	Saves changes made to the current file. By default, the button uses the file's original filename, except for a new file that has no name, in which case it prompts for a filename.
	Print	Prints the active file, Command window contents, or Clipboard contents.
	Print Preview	Uses a preview window to show what Print would output.
	Spelling	Activates the spell checker.
	Cut	Cuts the current selected text or object and places it on the Clipboard.
	Copy	Copies the current selected text or object and places it on the Clipboard.
	Paste	Copies the current contests of the Clipboard and pastes it at the current insertion point location.

 **Undo** — Undoes the last action or command, with some limitation.

 **Redo** — Repeats the last command or action.

 **Run** — Appears enabled if Visual FoxPro has an executable file open, such as a screen or program.

 **Modify form** — Switches the currently executing form back into designer mode.

Database — Lists the names of all open databases in a drop-down list. The current database appears in the text box. You can switch to a different database by selecting it from the list.

 **Command Window** — Opens or a pop the View window back into view and makes it the active window.

 **View Window** — Opens or pops the View window back into view and makes it the active window.

 **Form Wizard** — Launches the Form Wizard.

 **Report Wizard** — Launches the Report Wizard.

 **AutoForm Wizard** — Creates a form from the current table.

 **AutoReport Wizard** — Creates a report from the current table.

 **Help** — Displays Visual FoxPro's Help Contents screen.

VISUAL DESIGNER

As mentioned earlier, we work with Tables, Queries, etc., in FoxPro. There are 2 easy way of creating them. One of them is Visual Designer and the other is Wizard. Personally I prefer Wizards. They ask you minimum questions and give you the maximum results. Visual Designer on the other hand lets you design above mentioned files yourself or customize those you have created using the Wizards. Designer are comparatively difficult to use.

WIZARDS

As we have see in quite a number of software, Wizards are the best way to start if you are not very much familiar with the working of the software. Wizards not only create the required files for you but also guide you to the working of the software.

There are as many as 22 wizards in Visual Fox Pro. They are:

Application	Cross-Tab	Database
Documenting	Form	Graph
Import	Label	Local View

Mail Merge
One to Many Form
One to Many Report
Oracle Upsizing
PivotTable
Query
Remote View
Report
SQL Server Upsizing
Setup
Table
WWW Search Page
Web Publishing

These can be accessed from the Tools menu, as shown here.

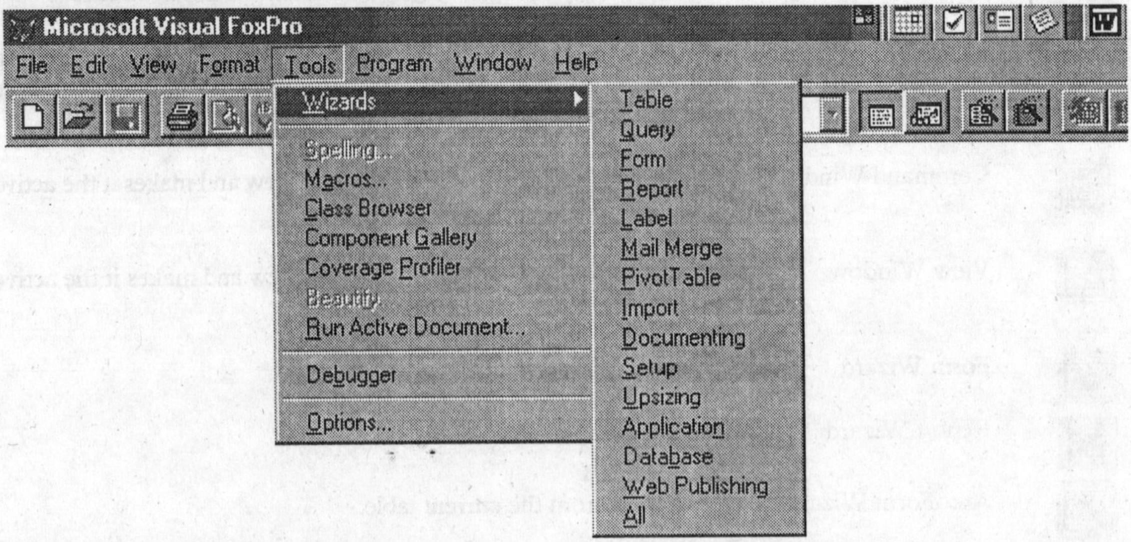

Let us create a project using Application Wizard and understand how this Wizard can help us in building up an application of our choice.

APPLICATION WIZARD AND BUILDER

As expected you would click at Application in the Wizards list selected from the Tools menu. Once clicked it would lead us to the first screen as shown here. You give here the name of the project which you want to run. The associated file would be shown to you. You should initially opt for creation of the project directory too. The wizard will put the application components into the project file, open the Project Manager for this new project, and show you the help file entry for the Developing Applications Using the Application Framework.

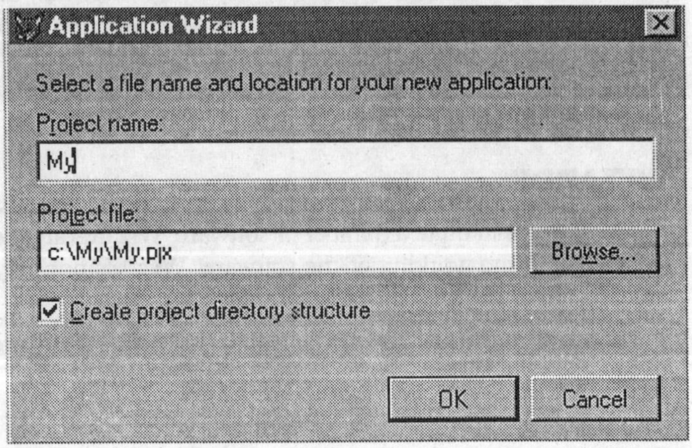

The directory structure will make it easy for your to keep track of the components of your application. Now comes the part of the Application Builder. First of its screen is now shown to you. It has 6 panels, you are given the first panel to work on, i.e., General.

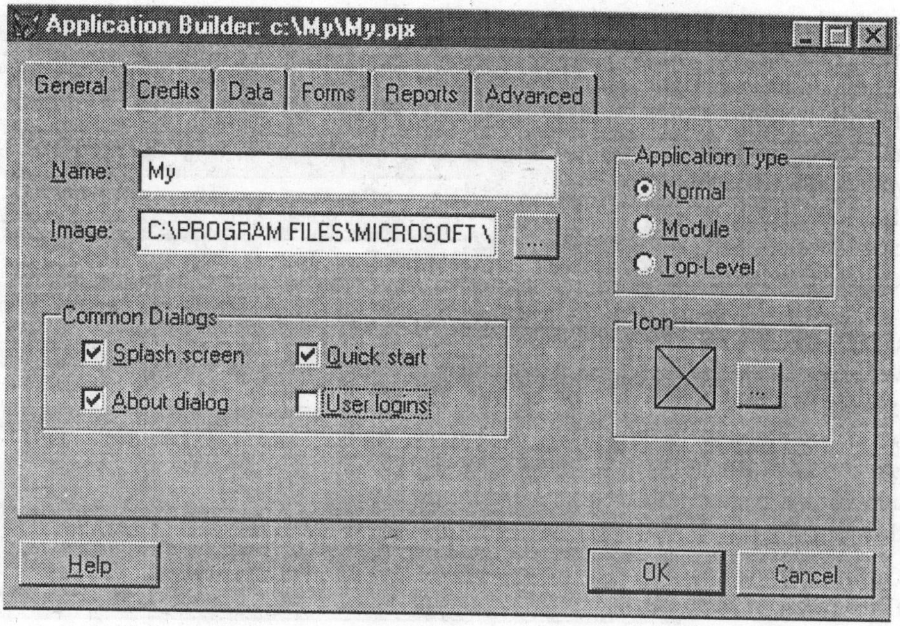

As you can see from the dialog box on the screen, you have to give the name of the project which you are working on, in this case, My. In the Image dialog box, you have to give the name of the file to be used as image. You can type the location of the file or browse by clicking at the button next to the box.

There are other options too on the screen, which are:

Common Dialogs

Splash Screen	If clicked it will create a splash screen that is displayed during the loading process of the application. If left unclicked, it will skip the splash screen.
About dialog	If clicked it includes an About dialog on the help menu. If unchecked it excludes About dialog.
Quick Start	It is a menu form which enables the user to access the forms and reports without using the menu system. If clicked this box includes a quick start form and if unclicked it excludes the quick start form.
User Logins	If clicked this box requires users to log the application using a user name and password. If unclicked it skips this option.

Application Type

Normal	If clicked then the application will run in the Visual FoxPro desktop. The main Visual FoxPro screen will contain the forms for the application.
Module	If clicked then the application will be a module that is called from some other application.
Top-Level	If clicked then the application runs outside of the Visual FoxPro screen as a top-level application under Windows.

Now click at Credit to get the next screen. Credit screen, as shown on the next page, has the following dialog boxes, which you have to fill up according to your requirements.

Next is the Data panel.

As you can see, I have chosen the option of Books from the database. You can choose from the various databases available to you. For this click at first of the 2 boxes on the top right corner of the box. When clicked it will give rise to the various screens of the database wizard and would allow you to create a new database. In this case I have chosen, as said before, Books. The various screen that this Wizard will present to you are shown on the next pages and also allows you to save this database.

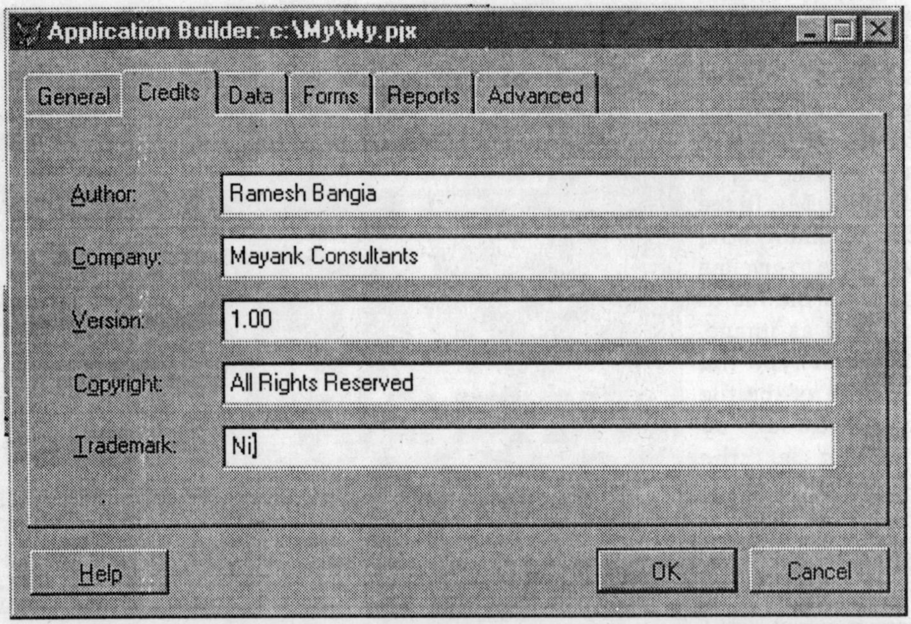

Coming back to Data panel, it has the following options:

Datasource As mentioned I had chosen Books, so this will show the various datafields of the Book database. It will generally include all the tables of the database.

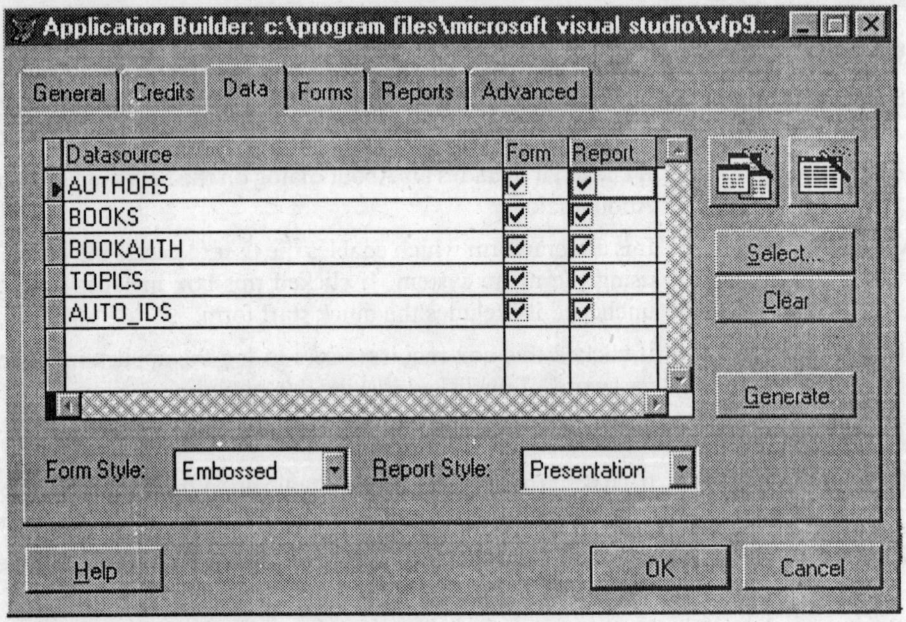

Form If clicked against any of the table name, it will create a form for the same using the Form Wizard.

Report As above, it will create a report format using the Report wizard.

Form Style The various styles to choose from are: Standard, Chiseled, Shadowed, Boxed, Embossed, Fancy, Stone, Flax, and Colorful. This would effect the way the forms created would look.

Report Style Various styles for report are: Presentation, Ledger, Executive, Banded, and Casual. Choose the one which you want for your report generated here.

Select If clicked it produces the File Open dialog box to enable you to search for tables or databases on the disk drive and include them in the list of tables.

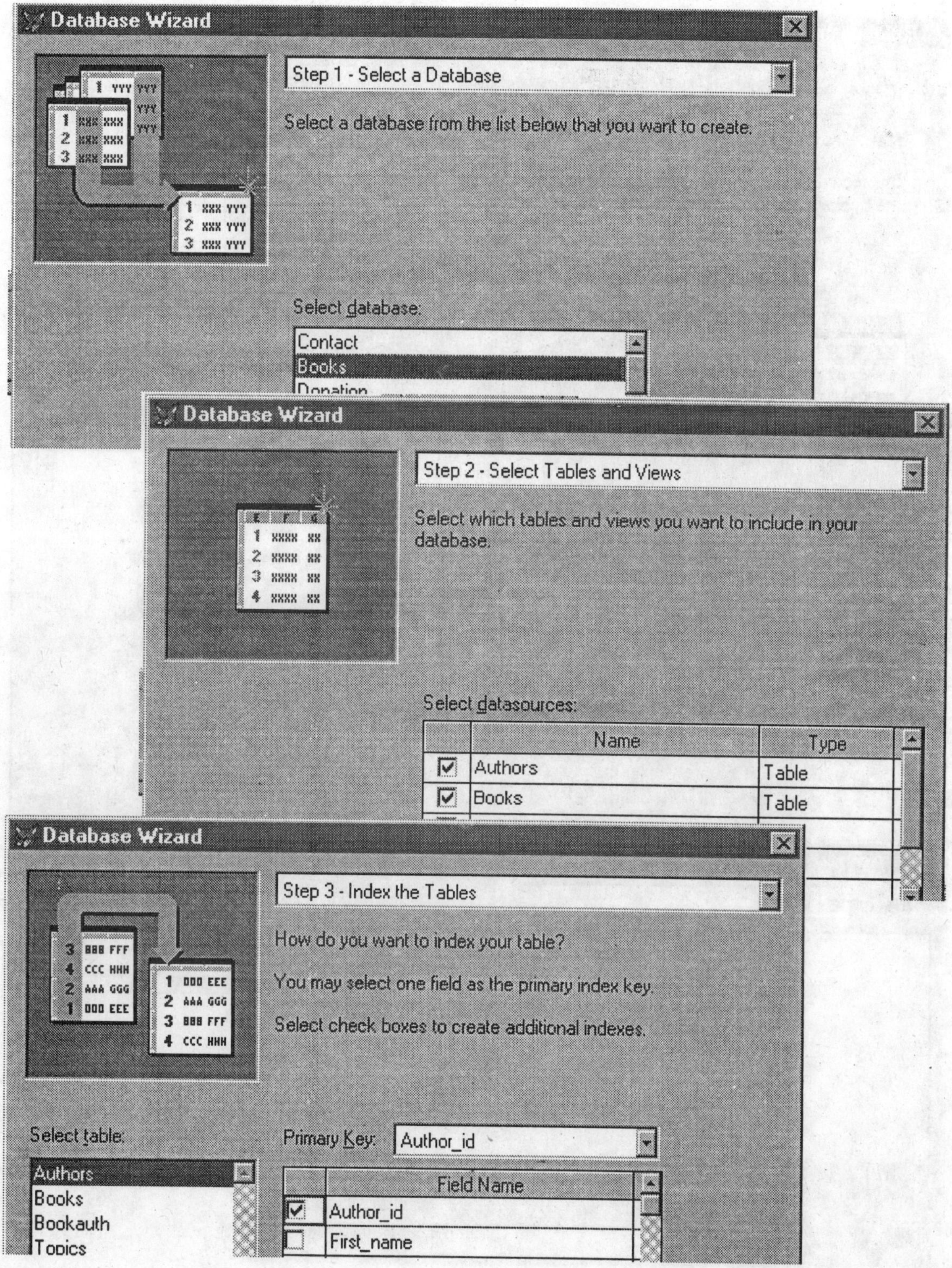
Database Wizard
Step 1 - Select a Database
Select a database from the list below that you want to create.
Select database:
Contact
Books
Donation
Database Wizard
Step 2 - Select Tables and Views
Select which tables and views you want to include in your database.
Select datasources:
Name
Type
Authors
Table
Books
Table
Database Wizard
Step 3 - Index the Tables
How do you want to index your table?
You may select one field as the primary index key.
Select check boxes to create additional indexes.
Select table:
Authors
Books
Bookauth
Topics
Primary Key:
Author_id
Field Name
Author_id
First_name

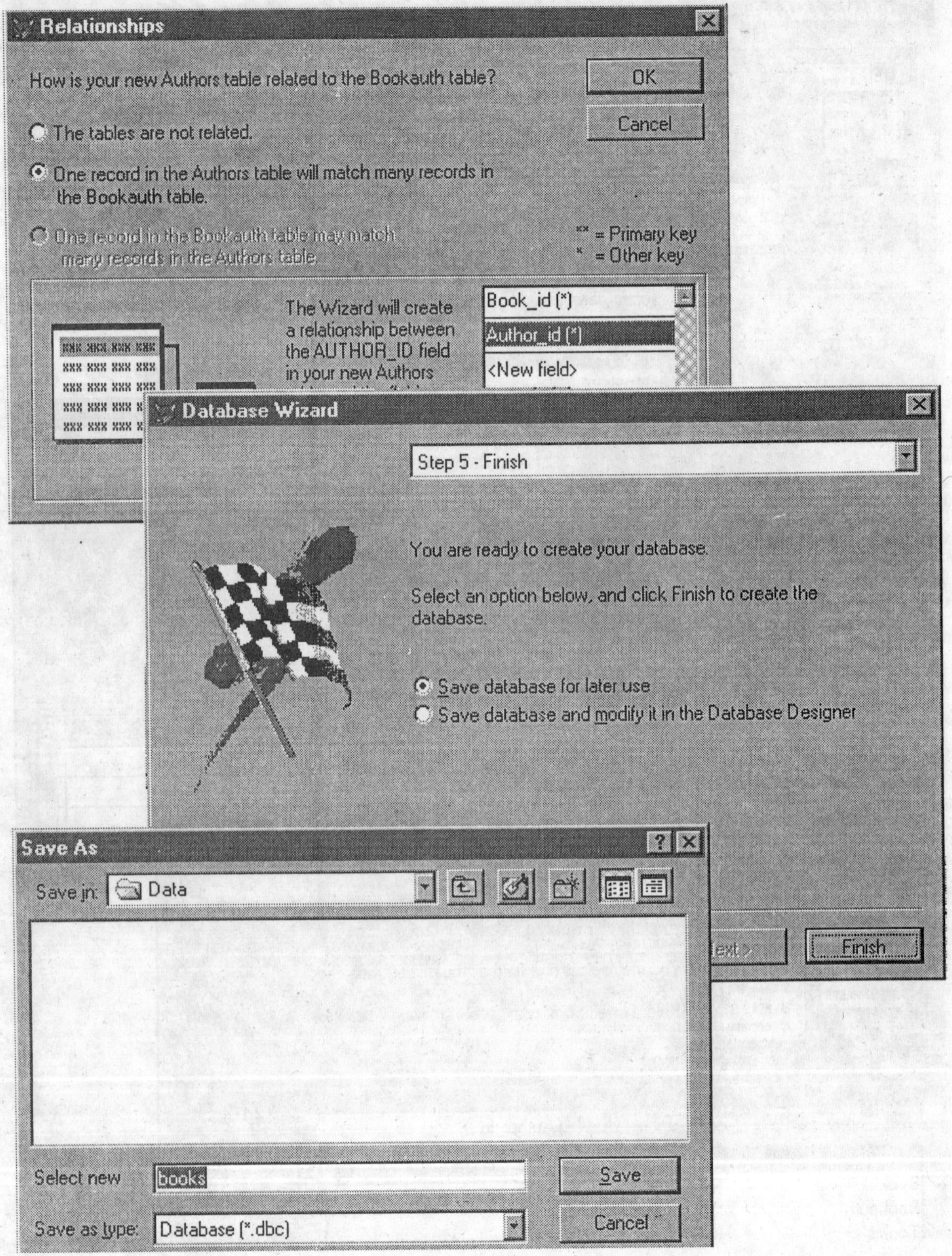
Relationships
How is your new Authors table related to the Bookauth table?
OK
Cancel
The tables are not related.
One record in the Authors table will match many records in the Bookauth table.
One record in the Bookauth table may match many records in the Authors table.
** = Primary key
* = Other key
The Wizard will create a relationship between the AUTHOR_ID field in your new Authors
Book_id (*)
Author_id (*)
<New field>
Database Wizard
Step 5 - Finish
You are ready to create your database.
Select an option below, and click Finish to create the database.
Save database for later use
Save database and modify it in the Database Designer
Finish
Save As
Save in: Data
Select new
books
Save
Save as type: Database (*.dbc)
Cancel

Clear It clears out the list of tables from the screen to allow you to search for tables or databases on the disk drive and include them in the list of tables.

Generate It generates a form or report for the selected table in the grid using the Form Style and/or Report Style selected with the combo boxes.

Next in line is the Forms panel, it has the following options:

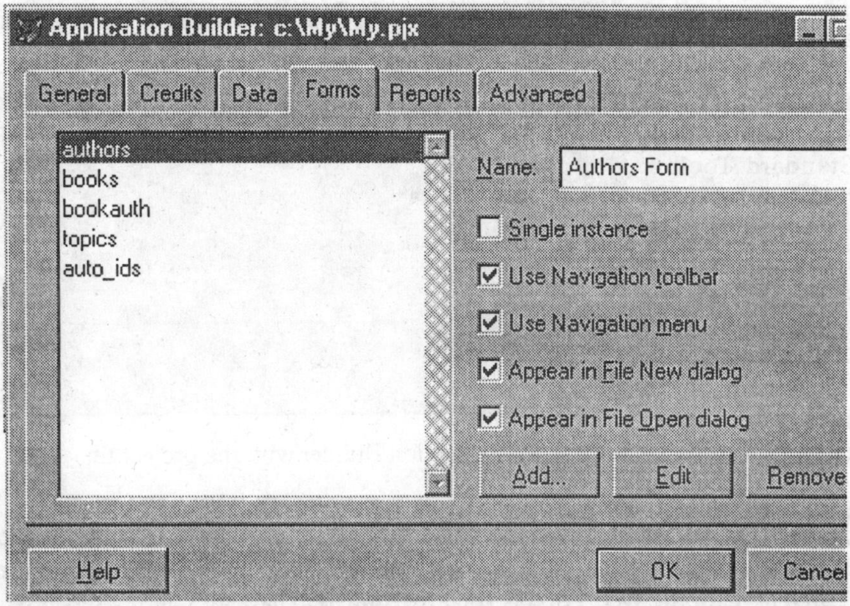

Single Instance If clicked it enables only one instance of the form to be open at a time, if unclicked it enables multiple instances of the form to be open.

Use Navigation Toolbar If clicked it will include a navigation toolbar for the highlighted form, if unclicked it omits the navigation toolbar.

Use Navigation Menu If clicked it includes a navigation menu for the highlighted form, if unclicked it omits the navigation menu.

Appear in File New Dialog If clicked it causes the form's name to appear in the application's New dialog.

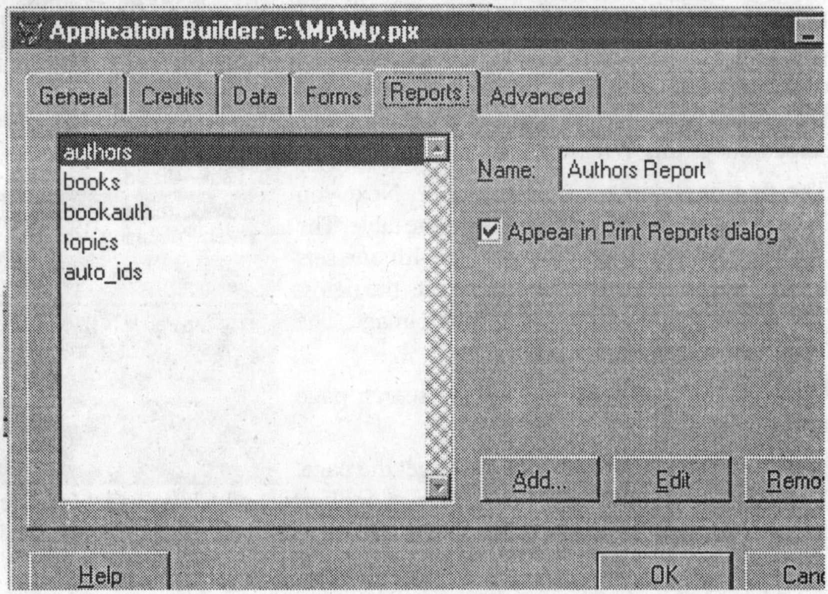

Appear in File Open Dialog If clicked it causes the form's name to appear in the application's Open dialog.

The next panel is Reports.

It is similar to the Forms panel except that it deals with reports rather than with forms. It is used to include existing reports in the application. The Add, Edit and Remove buttons function the same way as they on the Forms panel.

The last is Advanced panel.

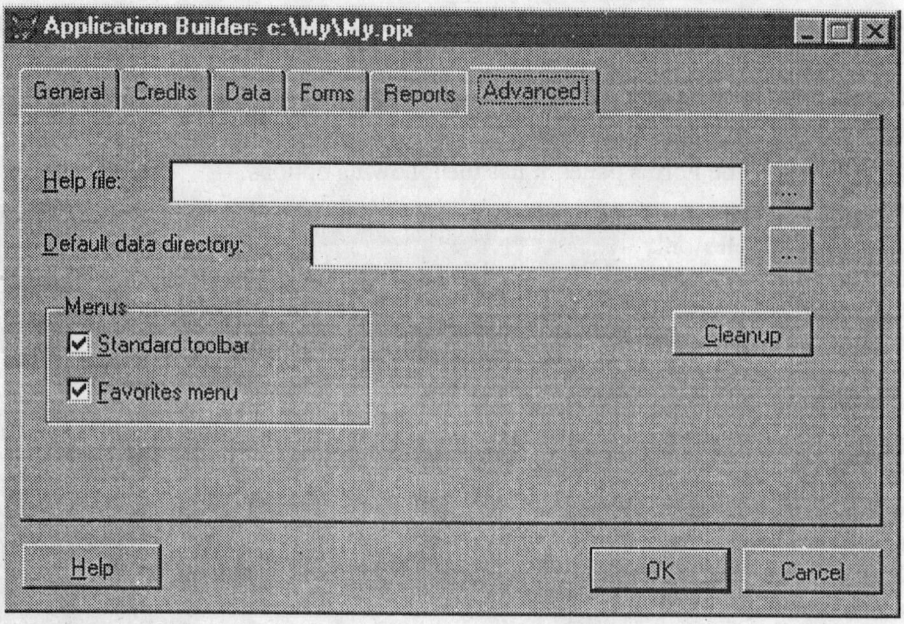

Here the Default Data Directory text box enables you to provide a path to the data that the application will use. The button alongwith allows you to browse for the directory you want. The menus: Standard Toolbar and Favorites Menu allow options to be included in their respective components. The Cleanup button runs a routing to reconcile any changes you have made in the Application Builder with the project file.

WWW SEARCH PAGE WIZARD

Next we will study the WWW Search Page Wizard. This allows you to create a Visual FoxPro based search page for the Web. For this you are required to have an Internet server set up to use the search page which is created. This will create 3 files with extensions, .HTM, .HTX and .IDC. You will need to copy these files into the WWW root directory for your Internet server application.

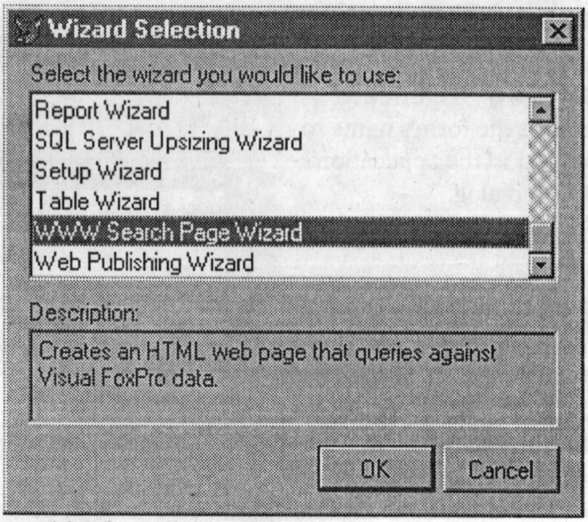

We will start this with the usual WWW Search Page from Tools menu and Wizards submenu. If you want you can select All to have the following dialog box and then select the one wanted by you. On the following pages, you will see the various screen under this Wizard.

The first one is just a welcome page. Next you have to choose the Search table from the table. The 3rd one asks you to set options. The 4th one sets up the Search page. The 5th one selects the fields. The 6th one allows set up background image. The 7th one is just the Finish one.

Once created you have to save the search page under a name.

Now you have to apply the search to get the page. For this you run the Visual FoxPro server application which is available under the Server subdirectory of Inetwzi and Tools directory. The file is named as

```
server.app
```

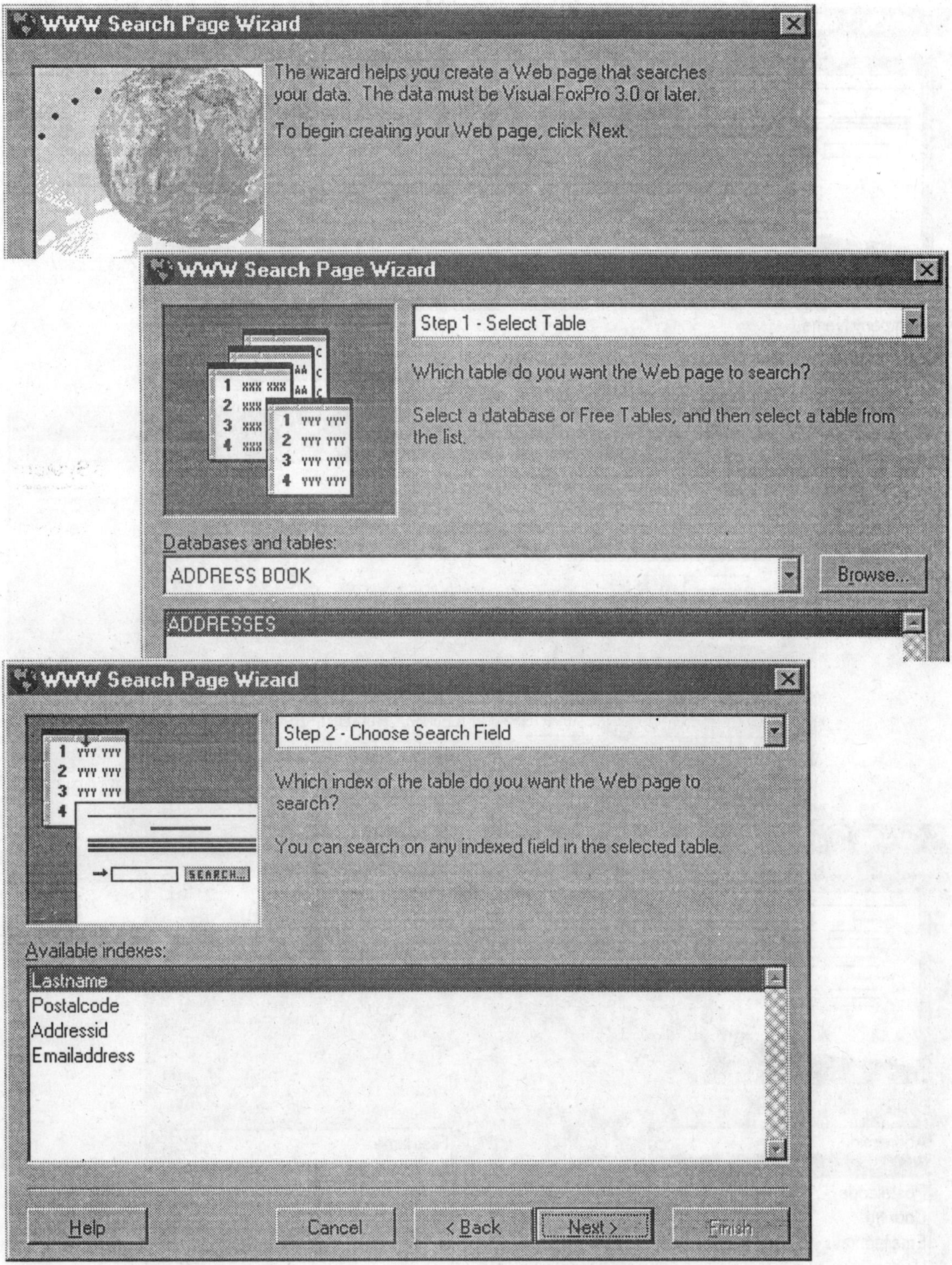
WWW Search Page Wizard
The wizard helps you create a Web page that searches your data. The data must be Visual FoxPro 3.0 or later.
To begin creating your Web page, click Next.
WWW Search Page Wizard
Step 1 - Select Table
Which table do you want the Web page to search?
Select a database or Free Tables, and then select a table from the list.
Databases and tables:
ADDRESS BOOK
Browse...
ADDRESSES
WWW Search Page Wizard
Step 2 - Choose Search Field
Which index of the table do you want the Web page to search?
You can search on any indexed field in the selected table.
Available indexes:
Lastname
Postalcode
Addressid
Emailaddress
SEARCH...
Help
Cancel
< Back
Next >
Finish

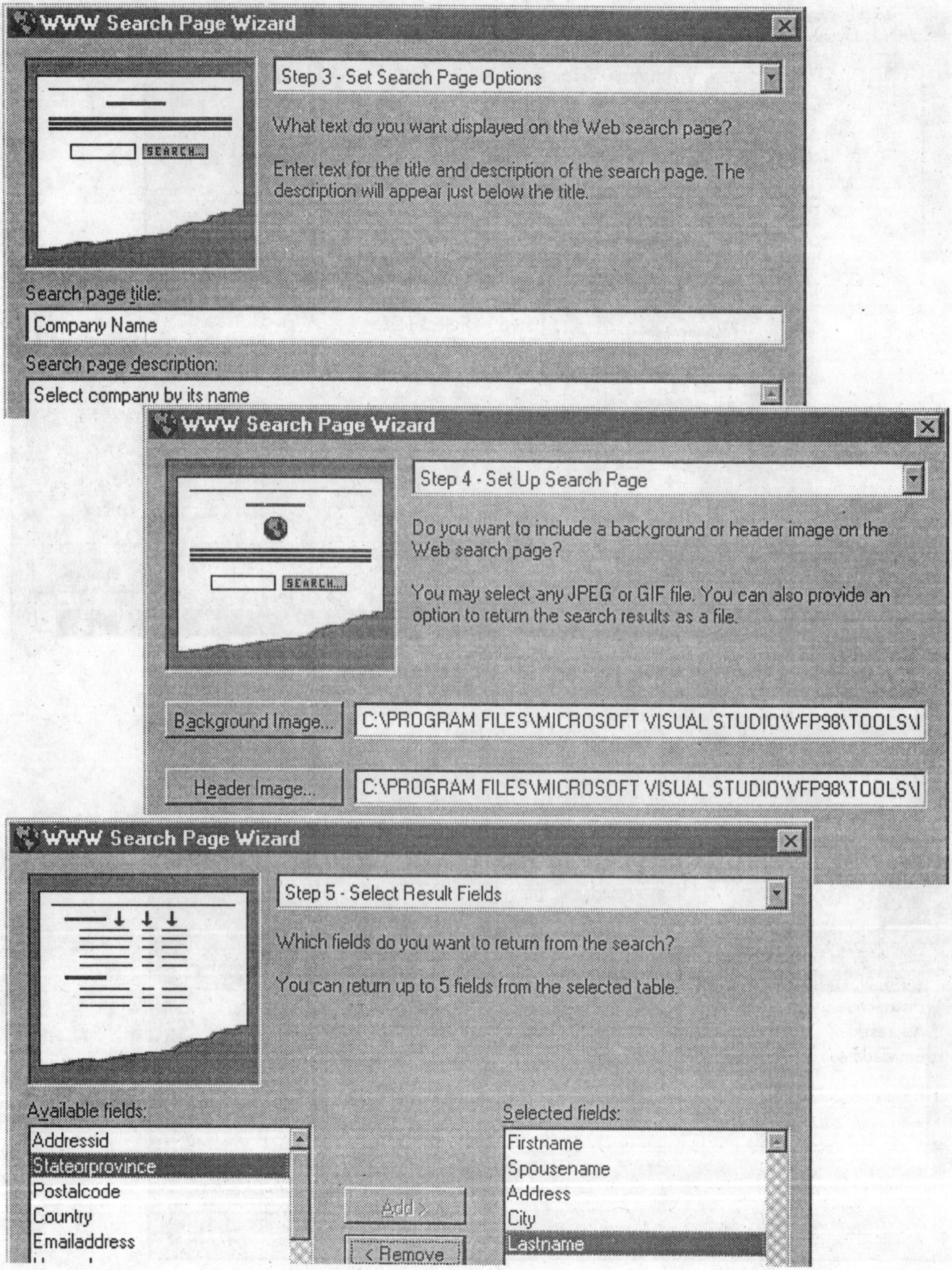
WWW Search Page Wizard
Step 3 - Set Search Page Options
SEARCH...
What text do you want displayed on the Web search page?
Enter text for the title and description of the search page. The description will appear just below the title.
Search page title:
Company Name
Search page description:
Select company by its name
WWW Search Page Wizard
Step 4 - Set Up Search Page
SEARCH...
Do you want to include a background or header image on the Web search page?
You may select any JPEG or GIF file. You can also provide an option to return the search results as a file.
Background Image...
C:\PROGRAM FILES\MICROSOFT VISUAL STUDIO\VFP98\TOOLS\I
Header Image...
C:\PROGRAM FILES\MICROSOFT VISUAL STUDIO\VFP98\TOOLS\I
WWW Search Page Wizard
Step 5 - Select Result Fields
Which fields do you want to return from the search?
You can return up to 5 fields from the selected table.
Available fields:
Addressid
Stateorprovince
Postalcode
Country
Emailaddress
Add >
< Remove
Selected fields:
Firstname
Spousename
Address
City
Lastname

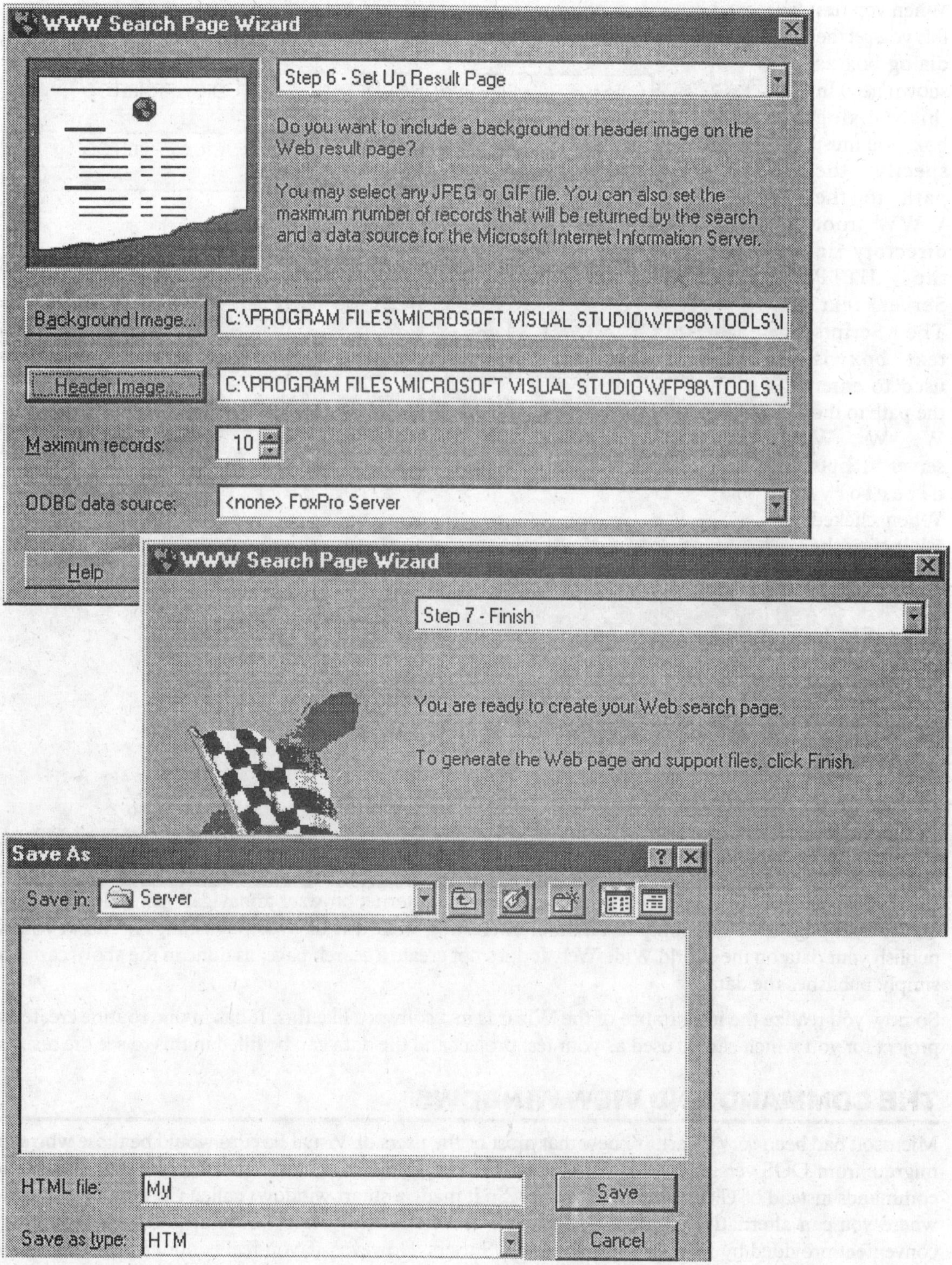
WWW Search Page Wizard
Step 6 - Set Up Result Page
Do you want to include a background or header image on the Web result page?
You may select any JPEG or GIF file. You can also set the maximum number of records that will be returned by the search and a data source for the Microsoft Internet Information Server.
Background Image...
C:\PROGRAM FILES\MICROSOFT VISUAL STUDIO\VFP98\TOOLS\I
Header Image...
C:\PROGRAM FILES\MICROSOFT VISUAL STUDIO\VFP98\TOOLS\I
Maximum records:
10
ODBC data source:
<none> FoxPro Server
Help
WWW Search Page Wizard
Step 7 - Finish
You are ready to create your Web search page.
To generate the Web page and support files, click Finish.
Save As
Save in:
Server
HTML file:
My
Save
Save as type:
HTM
Cancel

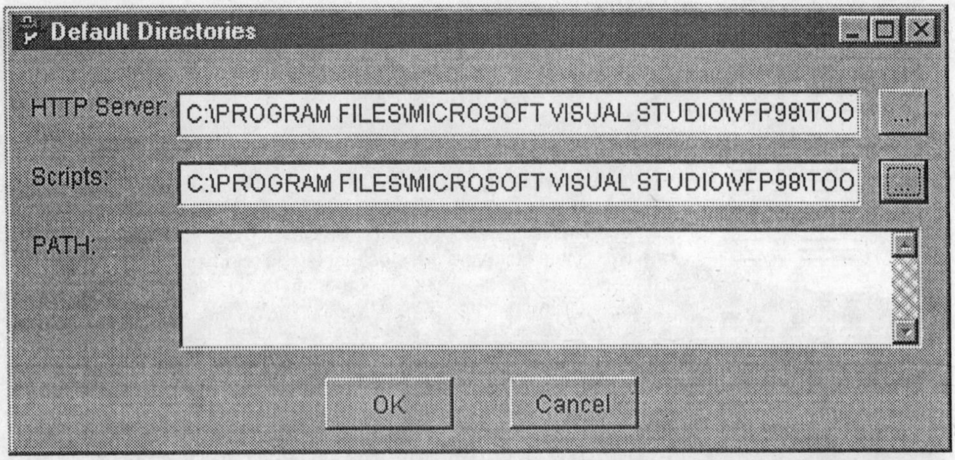

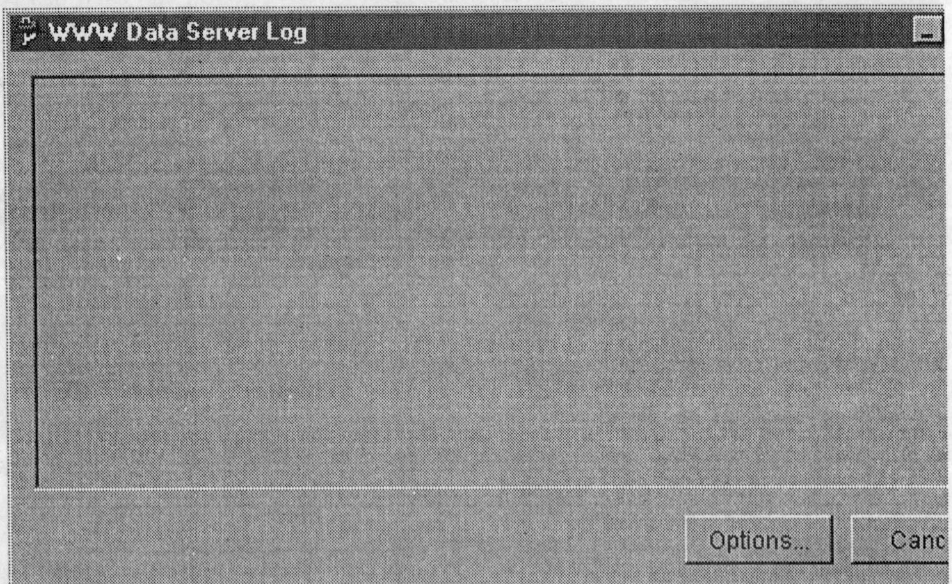

When you run this you get the dialog box as shown here. In this dialog box, you must specify the path to the WWW root directory in the HTTP Server text. The Scripts text box is used to enter the path to the W W W server's scripts directory. When clicked Ok it gives the box as shown above.

This box looks blank at this stage but will be filled up when you use the search page. To use your search page, you must have an Internet server running. You can then use your favorite Internet browser to navigate your file. Well look on the next page to see the output. Another interesting wizard is of Web publishing. It allows you to publish your data on the World Wide Web. It does not create a search page, as done in the above case but simply publishes the data.

So now you realize the importance of the Wizards in a software like this. It has in one routine created a project for you which can be used as your test project and the data can be filled in this to see the results.

THE COMMAND AND VIEW WINDOWS

Microsoft had been very smart. It knew that most of the users of Visual FoxPro would be those who will migrate from DOS version of dBASE or FoxPro. So it knew of the users who very happy typing the commands instead of clicking them by mouse. So it made a smart windows called Command Windows where you can alternatively type the command as would do in the DOS based software. It is just a convenient provided by Microsoft for those DOS users. However, if you feel confident of clicking the

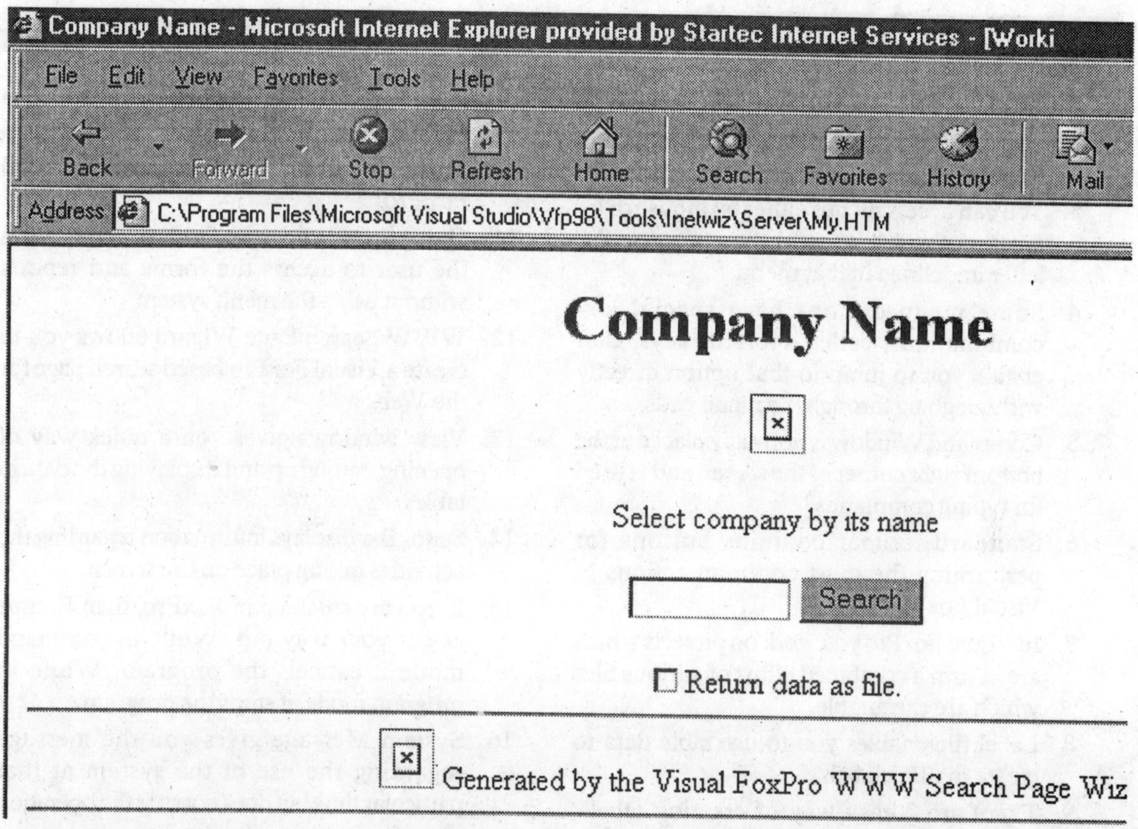

commands with mouse, you may not even this window. What's more you can even hide it you feel that it is disturbing your view.

View windows gives you a quick way of opening, setting up and displaying the data in tables. It also lets you control table properties and open multiple tables at the same time and relate them.

OTHER FEATURES OF VISUAL FOXPRO INTERFACE

While working with FoxPro you would come across various features of the software which are very useful for working. Some of them are listed here.

Status Bar: It displays information regarding the activities taking place on the screen. It does give you the short description of the menu command being used.

Alert Message: Nobody is perfect. It is possible that you will give some command at some stage which is not acceptable to the software, in that case it will give you the Alert message, very politely saying that it is possible to accept such command.

Escape Key: If you are stuck up in FoxPro, then Escape key is your way out. While in command mode it cancels the program. While in program mode, it stops the program.

System Message: It gives you the message regarding the use of the system at that particular time but does not stop the operation as such.

Let us Revise

1. Visual FoxPro is a database software.
2. You can click/double-click at the file named VFP.EXE to start Visual FoxPro.
3. You can access menus either by mouse or by pressing the Alt key and then pressing the letter undelined in that menu.
4. Some menu options have special key combinations, called shortcut keys, that enable you to jump to that option directly without going through the menu pads.
5. Command Window is normally placed at the bottom right corner of the screen and is used for typing commands.
6. Standard toolbar contains buttons for performing the most common actions in Visual FoxPro.
7. In Visual FoxPro you work on projects which are in turn a combined effort of various files which are executable.
8. Label file enables you to use table data to create mailing labels.
9. There are 2 easy way of creating tabels, reports, forms, etc., one of them is Visual Designer and the other is Wizard.
10. There are as many as 22 wizards in Visual Fox Pro.
11. Quick Start is a menu form which enables the user to access the forms and reports without using the menu system.
12. WWW Search Page Wizard allows you to create a Visual FoxPro based search page for the Web.
13. View windows gives you a quick way of opening, setting up and displaying the data in tables.
14. Status Bar displays information regarding the activities taking place on the screen.
15. If you are stuck up in FoxPro, then Escape key is your way out. While in command mode it cancels the program. While in program mode, it stops the program.
16. System Message gives you the message regarding the use of the system at that particular time but does not stop the operation as such.

Multiple Choice Questions

1. Visual FoxPro is a :
   (a) Database software
   (b) Word Processing software
   (c) Spreadsheet software
2. Command Window is for :
   (a) Seeing the window
   (b) Typing commands
   (c) Giving command to the operator
3. In Visual FoxPro the main aim is to create :
   (a) Tables (b) Forms
   (c) Projects
4. How many wizards are there in Visual FoxPro:
   (a) 20 (b) 22
   (c) 21
5. You can extract information from table and work on it by using :
   (a) Query (b) Table
   (c) Form
6. You can create tables, forms, etc., using :
   (a) Visual Designer
   (b) Label Designer
   (c) Menus
7. Application Wizard is used for developing the :
   (a) Project (b) Application
   (c) Table

True/False Questions

1. Visual FoxPro is a database software.
2. You can click/double-click at the file named VFP.EXE to start Visual FoxPro.
3. Some menu options have special key combinations, called shortcut keys, that enable you to jump to that option directly without going through the menu pads.
4. Command Window is normally placed at the top right corner of the screen and is used for typing commands.
5. In Visual FoxPro you work on projects which are in turn a combined effort of various files which are executable.
6. Label file enables you to use table data to create mailing labels.
7. There are as many as 32 wizards in Visual Fox Pro.
8. Quick Start is a menu form which enables the user to access the forms and reports without using the menu system.
9. View windows gives you a quick way of opening, setting up and displaying the data in tables.
10. Status Bar displays information regarding the activities taking place in the hard disk.
11. System Message gives you the message regarding the use of the system at that particular time but does not stop the operation as such.

Matching Columns

Match the text in Column A with the text in Column B.

Column A	Column B
1. Visual Designer	a. Used for extracting information from table
2. Wizard	b. Used to create report format using table
3. Table	c. Used to display on screen for filling data
4. Query	d. Collecting of various related tables
5. Form	e. Faster way of creating tabels, etc.
6. Report	f. Collection of various executable files
7. Database	g. Used for creating tables, etc.
8. Projects	h. Collection of data

Fill in the Blanks with Appropriate Words

a. Command b. Title Bar c. Standard toolbar d. Status Bar
e. Minimize f. Close

1. To reduce Visual FoxPro to an icon, we use the ___________ button.
2. To close Visual FoxPro, we use the ________ button.
3. Window that is used for typing commands is called the __________ Window.
4. ___________ is at the top of the screen and displays the name of the program, i.e., Microsoft Visual FoxPro.
5. ___________ displays various kinds of information related to the window that is currently opened.
6. _________ contains buttons for performing the most common actions in Visual FoxPro.

Descriptive Type Questions

1. What is Visual FoxPro?
2. How would you start Visual FoxPro?
3. What all the various features of FoxPro screen?
4. Which kind of files are used in Visual FoxPro?
5. Which are the various tools used in Visual FoxPro?
6. What is Visual Designer?
7. How are Wizards used?
8. What are Application Wizard and Builder?
9. How would you use WWW Search Page Wizard?
10. Describe the other features of Visual FoxPro Interface.

Answers to Objective Type Questions

Multiple Choice Questions

1. a	2. b	3. c	4. b
5. a	6. a	7. b	

True/False Questions

1. T	2. T	3. T	4. F
5. T	6. T	7. F	8. T
9. T	10. T	11. T	

Matching Columns

1. g	2. e	3. h	4. a
5. c	6. b	7. d	8. f

Fill in the Blanks with Appropriate Words

1. e	2. f	3. a	4. b
5. d	6. c		

Recommended Readings

1. Learn to Program Visual Basic—Databases *by John Smiley.*
2. Learn to Program Visual Basic—Objects *by John Smiley.*
3. Learn to Program Visual Basic—Examples *by John Smiley.*

—Published by Firewall Media (An Imprint of Laxmi Publications Pvt. Ltd.)

6 Working with Tables

CREATING A NEW TABLE

As we learned in the last chapter, the best way of creating anything in Visual FoxPro is through Wizard. So we will also create one using Wizard called Table Wizard and then later on we will create a table using Table Designer. But, before this we must understand what a Table is. Those of you who have used databases earlier are familiar with the word. But, in general, it can be said that a table is a compilation of data kept in records having various fields which are common to all records.

Let us create a table using the Wizard.

TABLE WIZARD

You can access the Wizards from the Tools menu. Here you select Table wizard for creation. The various steps here are:

Step1 asks you to select either Personal and Business. Based upon this it will show you the various tables it has in store for you. Select one and the respective fields of the same.

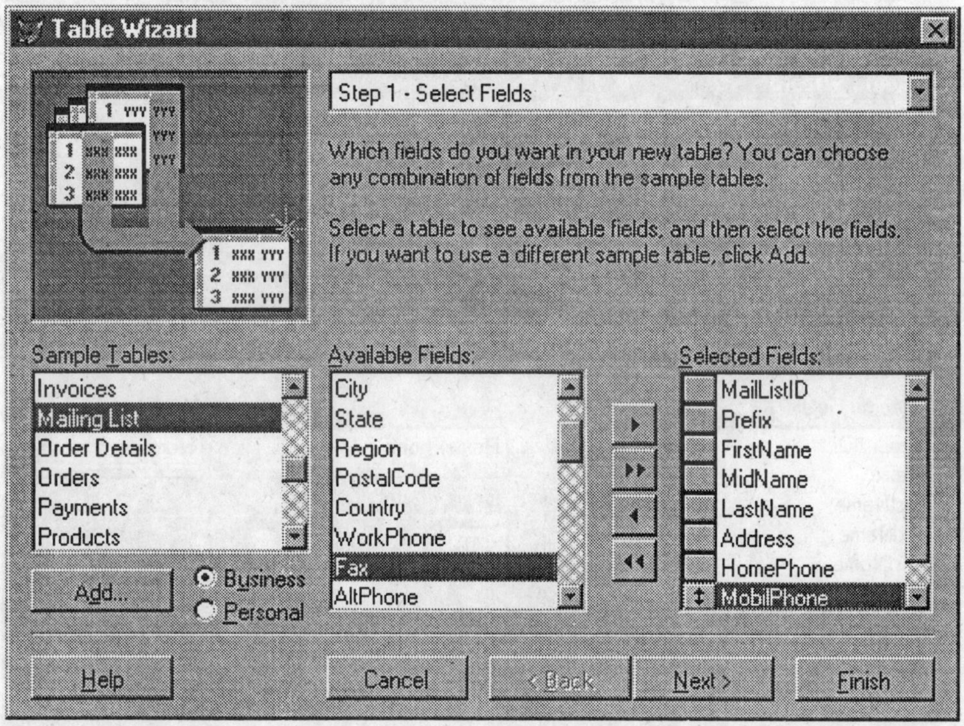

Step1a asks you whether you want this table to be stand alone or as an add on to another database.

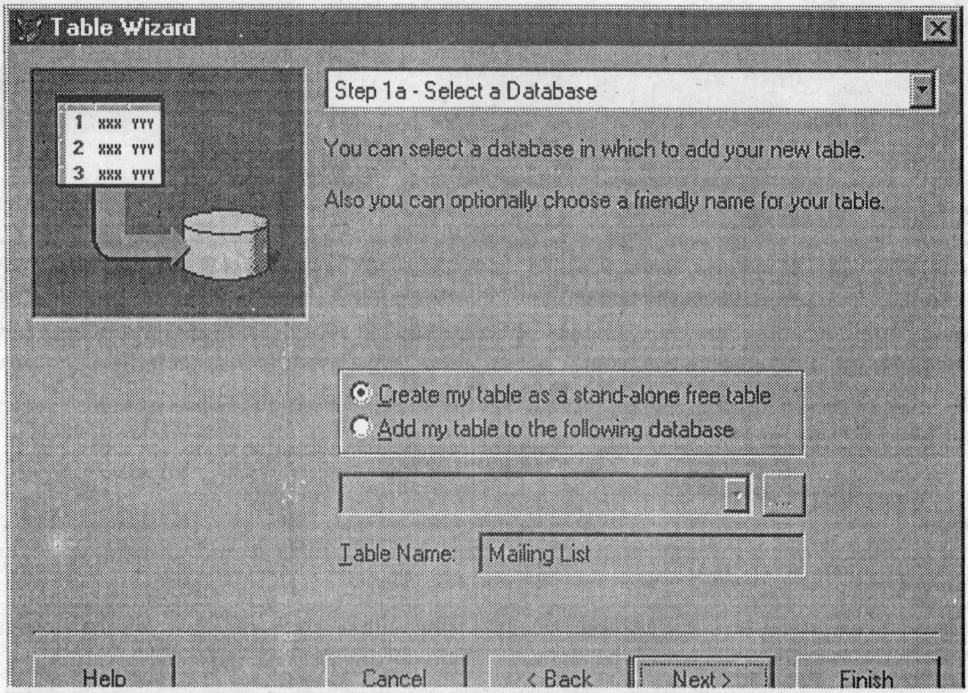

Step2 allows you to modify any of the above mentioned fields.

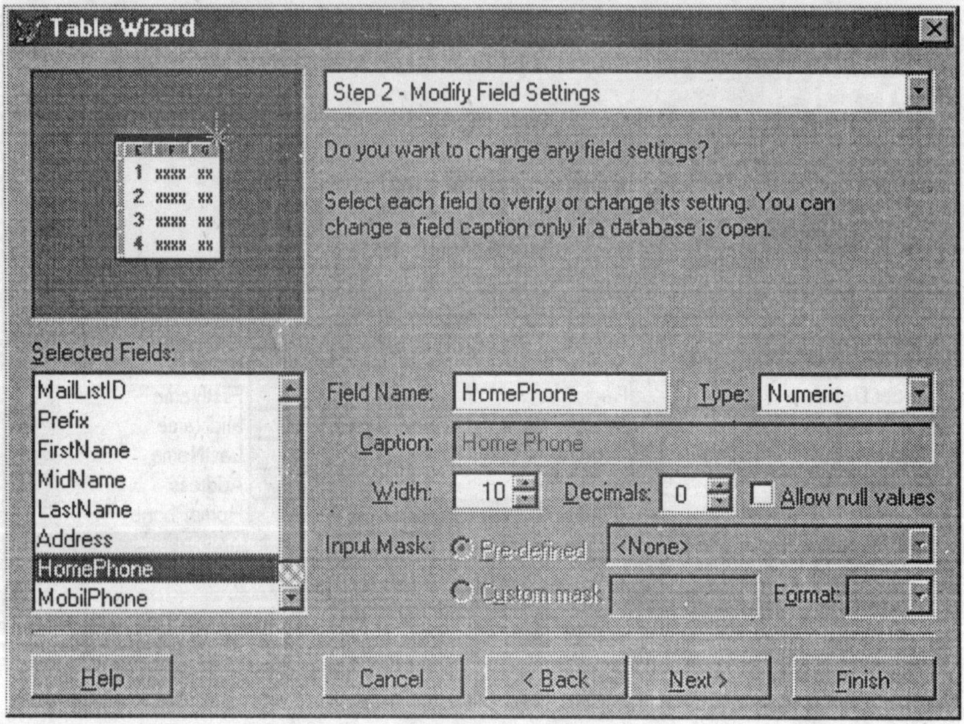

Step3 allows you to index the Table in particular fields.

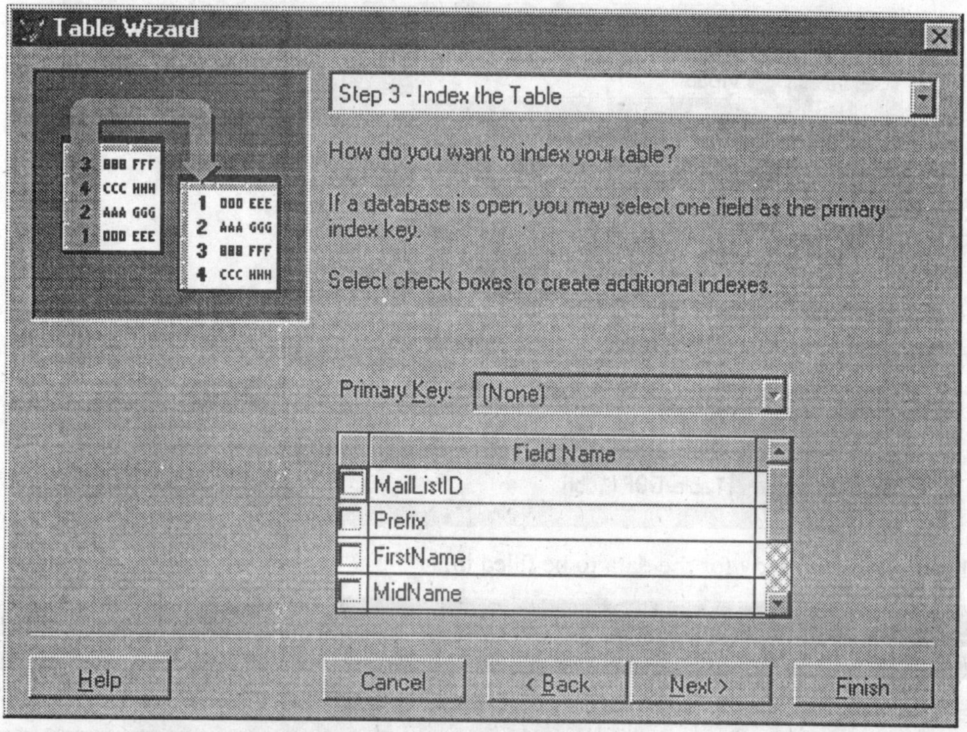

Step4 finishes the table and asks you to save with a name.

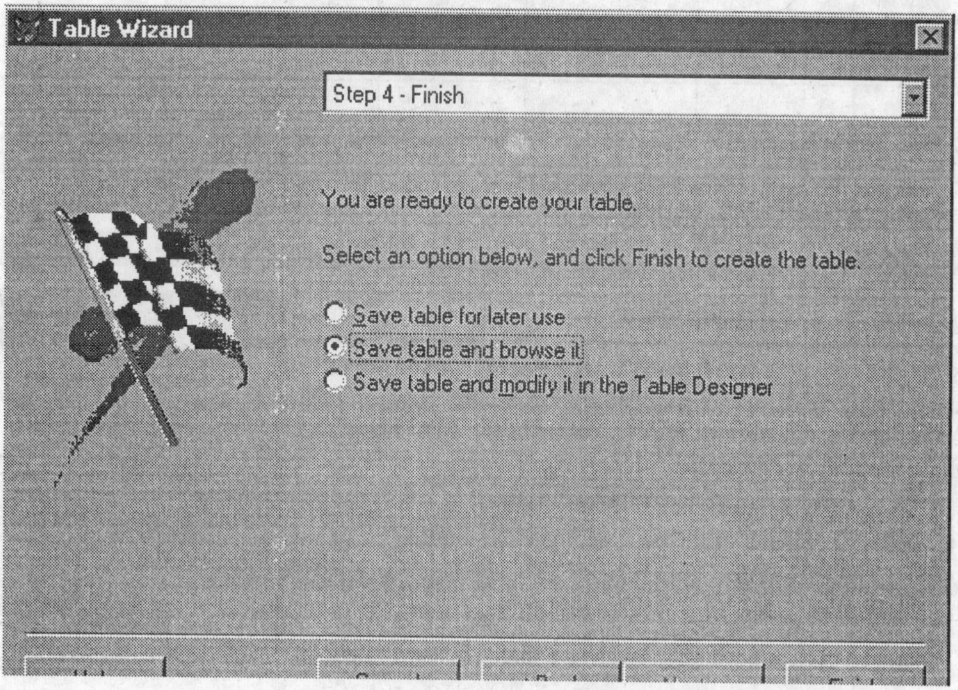

I have saved it with a name m_list and the format for this has been displayed in the next screen.

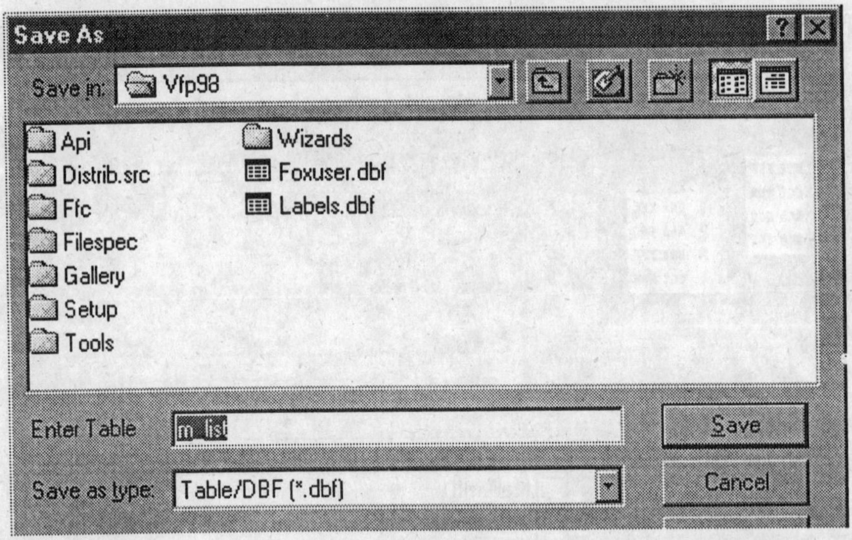

With this our table is ready for the data to be filled in.

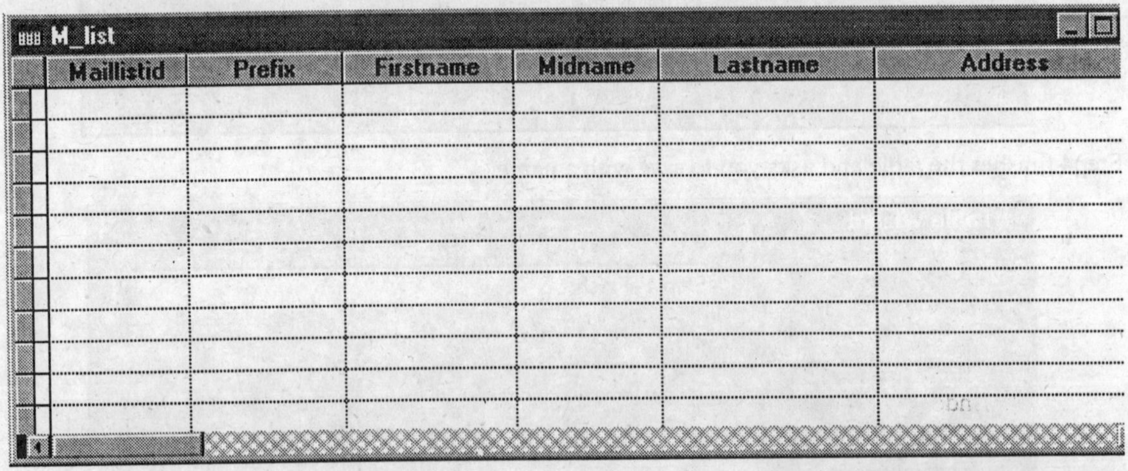

USING TABLE DESIGNER

This is the method where you have to have the complete information about the various fields before proceeding further for creation of a table. As usual we will start with the New from the File menu and then follow the following steps:

1. In the dialog box, given here, select the Table option by clicking at the box next to it and then clicking at New File.
2. You would be asked to allot a name to the table or by default you would be given a name with table1, etc.
3. When you click at Save, you are given a dialog box with options

to select the various fields which you are going to have in your table.

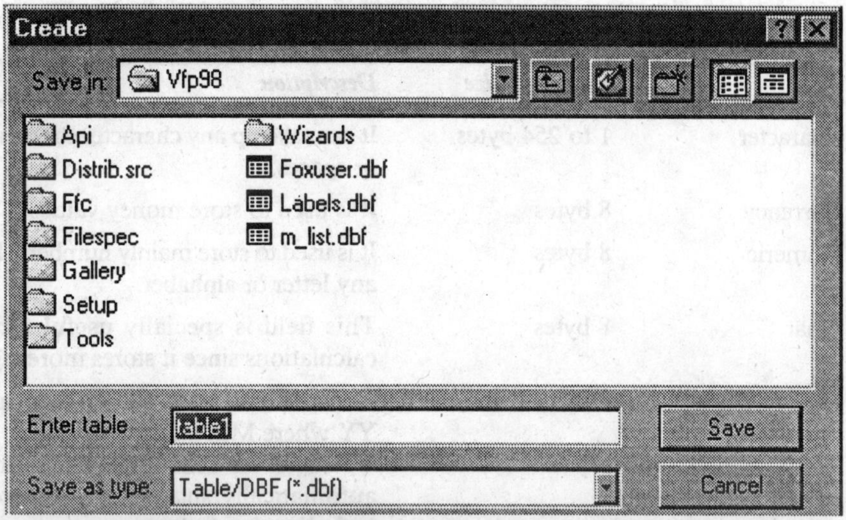

4. You would be given a Table Designer dialog box, in which you will type out the fields which you want to have in your table.
5. You can press Tab key to reach one field to another.

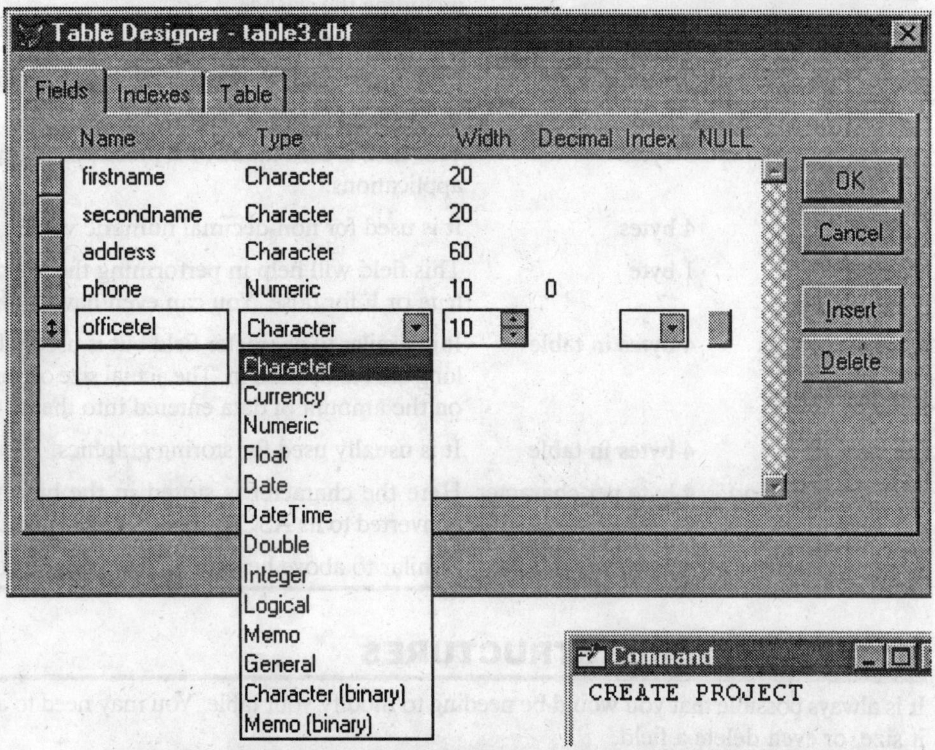

6. When you have made all the required entries of the fields, click Ok.
7. You would be given another dialog box, in which you would be given the option of filling up the data.

8. For filling up the data, the fields are defined and space is left for filling.

Before going further let me tell you about the various type of fields which you can have in your table.

Type	*Permitted Size*	*Description*
Character	1 to 254 bytes	It can take up any character such as letters, numbers, symbols or spaces.
Currency	8 bytes	It is used to store money values.
Numeric	8 bytes	It is used to store mainly numbers. If defined it will not accept any letter or alphabet.
Float	8 bytes	This field is specially useful for scientific and statistics calculations since it stores more significant digits internally.
Date	8 bytes	Here the date is stored in American format, i.e., MM/DD/YY where MM stands for month, DD stands for Date, and YY stands for Year. When you select date type, Visual FoxPro automatically shows the standard width for 8 characters including the slashes.
DateTime	8 bytes	It is a combination of date and time. The format for this is yyyy/mm/dd/hh/mm/ss. You can store date, time or both, as there is not Time field type.
Double	8 bytes	This field is used mainly for precise scientific and engineering applications.
Integer	4 bytes	It is used for non-decimal numeric values.
Logical	1 byte	This field will help in performing the logical part, i.e., T for true or F for false. You can even have Y/N.
Memo	4 bytes in table	It is similar to character field but is used when you have very long data to be filled in. The actual size of memo fields depends on the amount of data entered into them.
General	4 bytes in table	It is usually used for storing graphics.
Character (binary)	1 byte per character	Here the character is stored in the binary format and not converted to its ASCII character as would be done otherwise.
Memo (binary)	4 bytes in table	Similar to above here also the data is stored in binary.

MODIFYING TABLE STRUCTURES

It is always possible that you would be needing to modify your table. You may need to add a field, change it size, or even delete a field.

Adding Fields

Adding new fields to an existing table is one of the safes changes you can make. In fact, problems occur only if you attempt to use the same field name twice. Even in that situation, FoxPro responds automatically. FoxPro will not enable you to exit the name column if it is a duplicate of an existing field name. Rather, FoxPro displays an information box with the message Invalid or duplicate field name and enables you to edit it.

Deleting Fields

At some point, one or more fields in a table might become obsolete. Rather than waste space, you might decide to remove them from the table. To delete a field, simply display the table in the Table Designer dialog box, highlight the obsolete field, and click the Delete button. You delete a field and save the structure, it is gone forever, including any indexes that reference the deleted field. Make a backup copy of your .DBF before deleting a field.

Renaming Fields

Renaming fields might require only rewriting the .DBF header with the new field name. To change a field name, simply open the Table Designer dialog box, highlight the name, edit the name, and then save the structure. As long as an open index does not reference the field, FoxPro renames the field when you save the structure.

Correcting Mistakes

If you need to correctt a mistake, use the mouse or the insertion point to the field parameter you wish to correct and use Backspace or Del key to make the desired correction. To insert a new character between existing characters, place the insertion point at the desired location and then type the correction.

The following keys can be used for editing in Visual FoxPro.

Key	Actions
Left Arrow	Move insertion point left one character
Right Arrow	Move insertion point right one character
Up Arrow	Move insetion point up one line or one field
Down Arrow	Move insertion point down one line or one field
Ins	Toggle insert mode on/off
Del	Delete character at cursor
Backspace	Delete character to the left of the cursor
Esc	Abort operation
Tab	Move insertion point right one field
Shift + Tab	Move insertion point left one field
Ctrl + W	Save changes and exit

USING TABLES

Tables are integral part of the databases. They can be used for various purposes like modifying the data in it, generating queries based on the data in them. You can print the data in it or even create totals of the fields in it. You can even Find a particular data and Replace it with another.

You can Add, Delete records in the tables. You can even Modify the structure of the table at a later stage, if you find any field short for the data to be entered. It is not that you will always add the records in the end of the table, you can even add records in between the two records.

OPENING A TABLE

As you would open any file in any software, you would open a table in Visual FoxPro. Follow the following steps for it.

1. Choose Open from the File menu.
2. Open dialog box appears.
3. In the file types, click at Table (*.dbf)
4. You would be shown only the table files.
5. Click at the one to be opened by you.

WORKING ON A TABLE

Data is the main thing as far as the table is concerned. You can work on a table by working on the data within it. There are ways of adding and editing data. Some of them are discussed here.

Appending Data

There are two ways of adding records, one is adding to the last, which is called Appending. Second is adding in between the two records which is called Adding. This adding can be done using the commands Browse or Edit. Let us first see how you can add a new record.

Adding a Single Record

Just follow the following steps to do this:

1. Choose Browse command from the View menu.
2. Click on Append New Record in the Table menu. In doing so you will add a new blank record at the end of the Browse/Edit window in which the data for the new record can be entered.

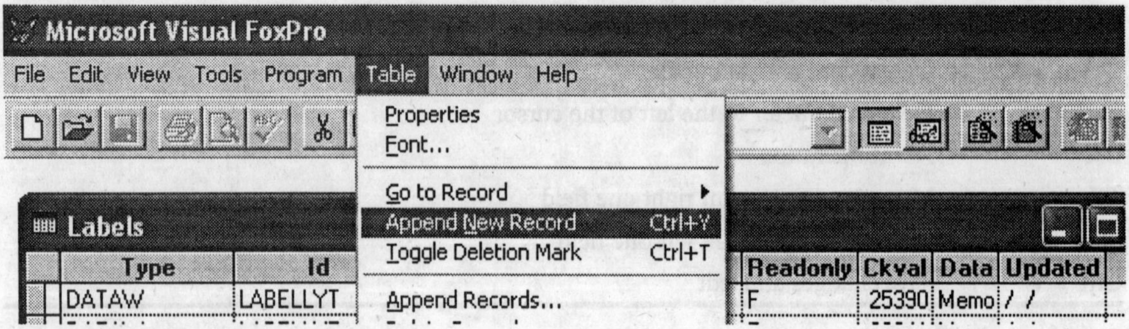

Adding Multiple Records

To add multiple records, do this:

1. As earlier choose the browse mode.
2. Click on Append Mode in the View menu to add series of records to the table. When you select this option, a new blank record is added to the end of the table.
3. Type the desired data. As soon as you add data to this record, Visual FoxPro adds another record to the end of the table. In this way you can continue to add data as long as you remain in Append mode.

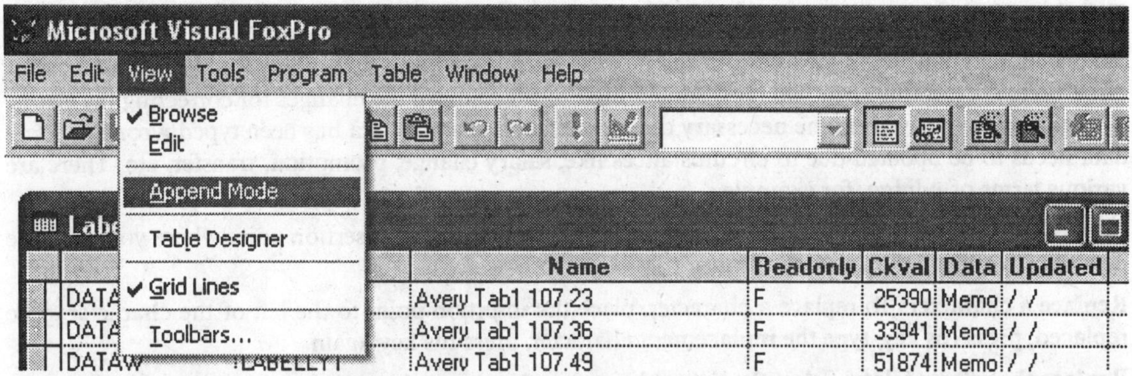

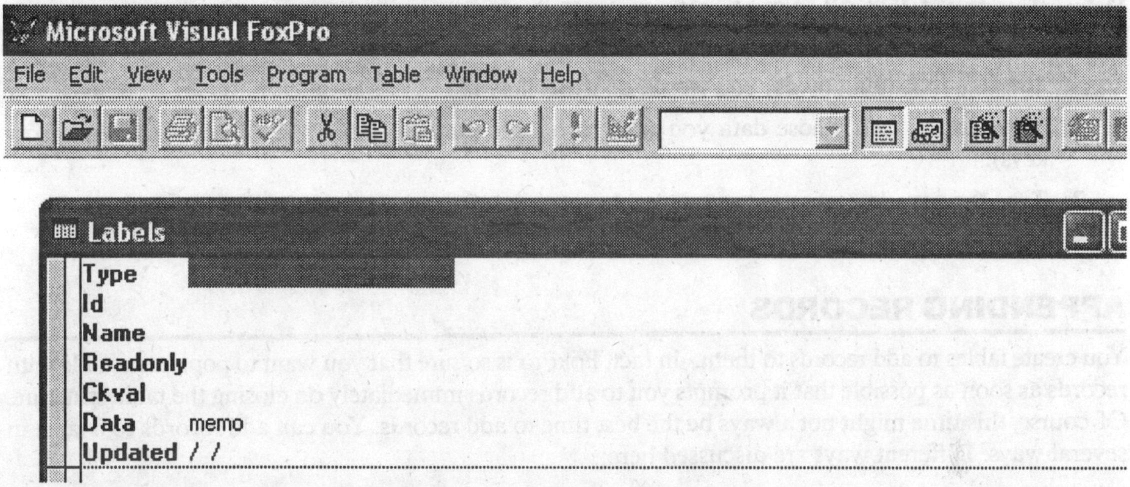

SWITCHING FROM BROWSE TO EDIT MODE

Using the View menu, you can switch from browse mode to Edit mode, as shown above. For some of you, Edit mode may be better choice than Browse mode. You can do editing in both the modes mentioned above, i.e., Browse and Edit. In Browse mode, records are listed in a horizontal format with one record per line. In Edit mode, because the records are displayed in a vertical format with one field per line, you can see more of the fields without scrolling the window. This feature makes Edit mode preferable for data entry in tables with many fields.

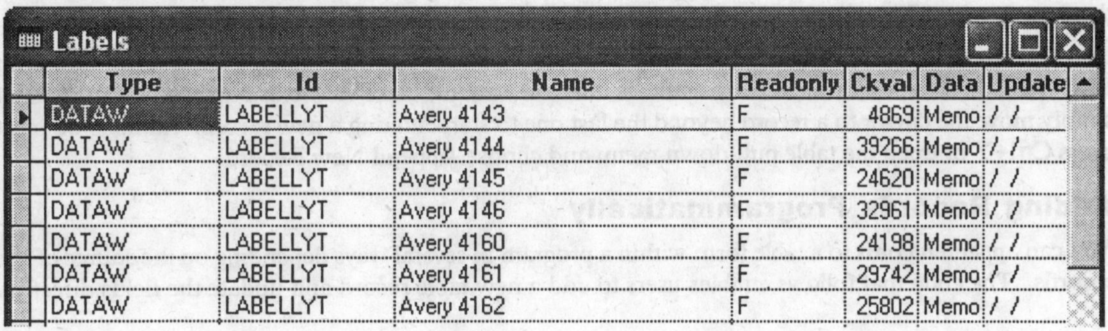

Editing Data

Whenever data is entered into the records there is every possibility that there would be some kind of error. So to correct this error you need something Editing to make the changes for correcting the errors. This change may have become necessary due to the fact that some data has been typed wrong or some data needs to be updated due to circumstances like, salary change, promotion, transfer, etc. There are various terms of editing, for example,

Insert Data: To insert data click the mouse button to the place of an insertion point where you want the new data to appear, then type the data.

Replace a character: To replace a character, place the insertion point to the left of the character to be replaced, press Ins key, type the replacement character, press Ins key again.

Replace the selected data: Select the data to be replaced and type the new data.

Delete the selected data: Select the data then press Del or Backspace key to delete the data and retype the entry.

To edit the data in Editing mode, you would do the following:

1. Move to the field whose data you wish to replace (double click on the field or use the arrow keys).
2. Type the new data
3. Press Enter key.

APPENDING RECORDS

You create tables to add records to them. In fact, FoxPro is so sure that you want to populate a table with records as soon as possible that it prompts you to add records immediately on closing the table structure. Of course, this time might not always be the best time to add records. You can add records to a table in several ways. Different ways are discussed here:

Through BROWSE or EDIT Screens

Once you have the database open on the screen. You can give the following commands in the command window and append the record.

```
USE table3
APPEND
```

These commands open an edit window, add a blank record, and place the cursor in the first field. After you enter data in the fields of the first record, FoxPro automatically adds another blank record and places the cursor in it. This process continues until you close the window.

You also can open the Edit window directly with the EDIT command or open a Browse window with BROWSE. In these windows, FoxPro assumes that you want to edit or view existing records. You cannot simply move the cursor to a record beyond the last one to start entering a new record. Rather, you must press Ctrl+Y or open the table pull-down menu and choose Append New Record.

Adding Records Programmatically

You can append records to a table form within a program in several ways depending on the source of the records. The code that follows enables users to add a new table record and update the fields directly.

```
*Code appends record to table and updates fields directly
SELECT <table>
APPEND BLANK
*Call a previously created form that allows the user
*to enter fields
DO FILLForm
```

Appending Data from Other Tables

Suppose that you want to append records to the current table from a another table. You could read through one record at a time, store the fields in memory variables, and then append these values to a record in the second table.

MOVING THROUGH A TABLE

In both modes, Edit and Browse, you move record to record. This can be very cumbersome, specially if you have a table with large number of records. So Visual Fox Pro provides options wherein you can go to particular record quickly. First among them is the command called GoTo.

GO TO COMMAND

As mentioned you can go to a particular record using this command. There are various options of the command, among which are:

Top:	Positions the pointer on the first record in the table.
Bottom	Positions the pointer on the last record in the table.
Next	Positions the pointer on the record immediately after the current record.
Previous:	Position the pointer on the record immediately before the current record.
Record #	Displays a Go to Record dialog box, in which you specify a record number.
Locate:	Displays the Locate Record dialog box, in which you can find an indexed or unindexed field or locate more than one record in a table.

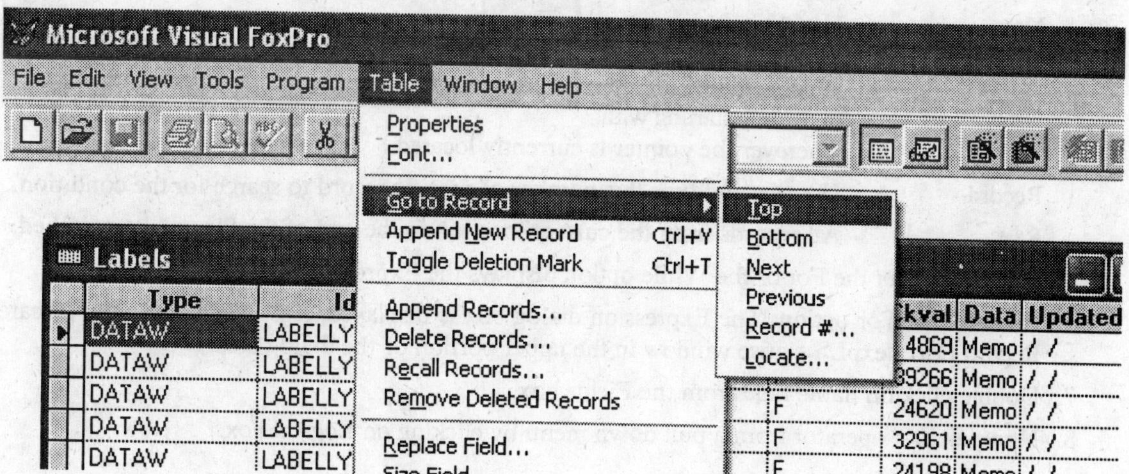

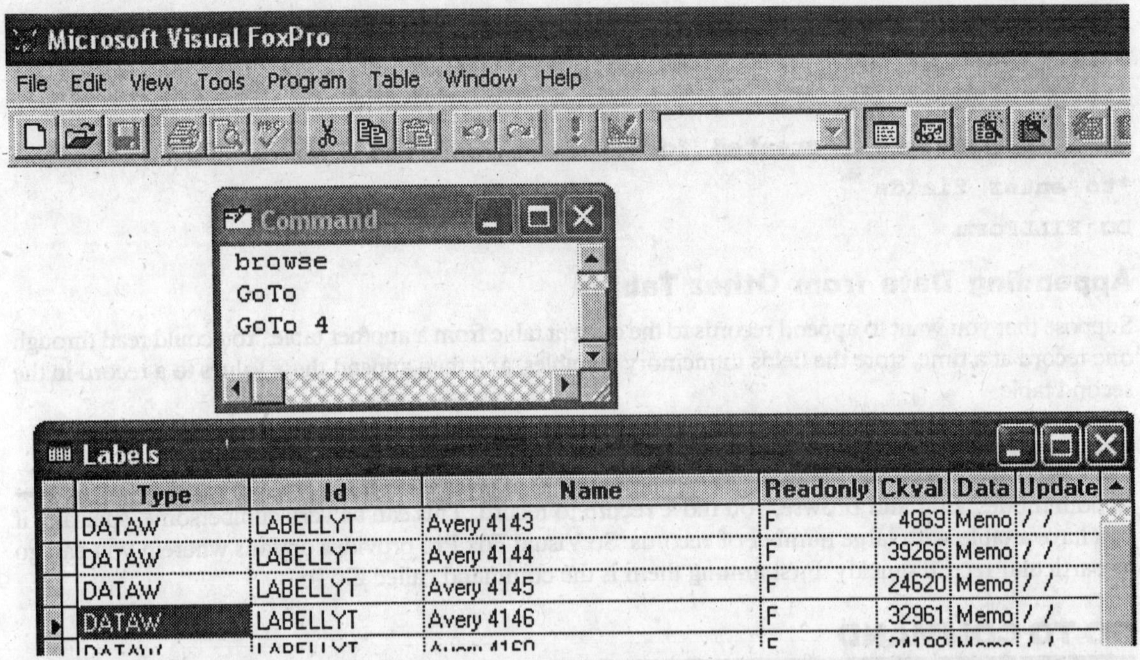

Of these Locate is probably the most commonly used one. Here is how it is used.

1. From the View menu choose to have the Browse mode.
2. Open the Table menu and click at Go To and then Locate.
3. You will get the dialog box, as shown here.

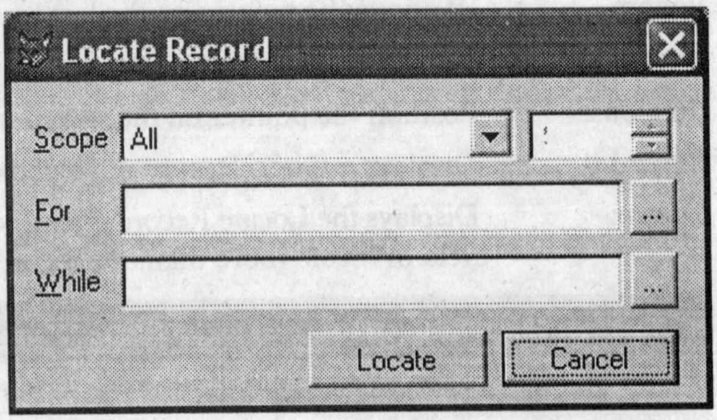

4. In the scrope option specify the record or choose any one of the following options which have the following meanings:

All	It is used to specify and Locate all records
Next	Use this option and then enter a number, which specifies a group of records starting with, wherever the pointer is currently located.
Record	Use this and type this number of specific record to search for the condition.
Rest	All records from the current location to the end of the file will be searched.

5. Selecting either the For or the While option displays the Expression Builder.
6. Click on the For option. The Expression dialog box is displayed; it is indicated by the Locate Record For: <expL> clause window in the upper portion of the dialog box.
7. Double click on name field from the Fields box.
8. Now select = operator from a pull down menu by clicking on Logical box.

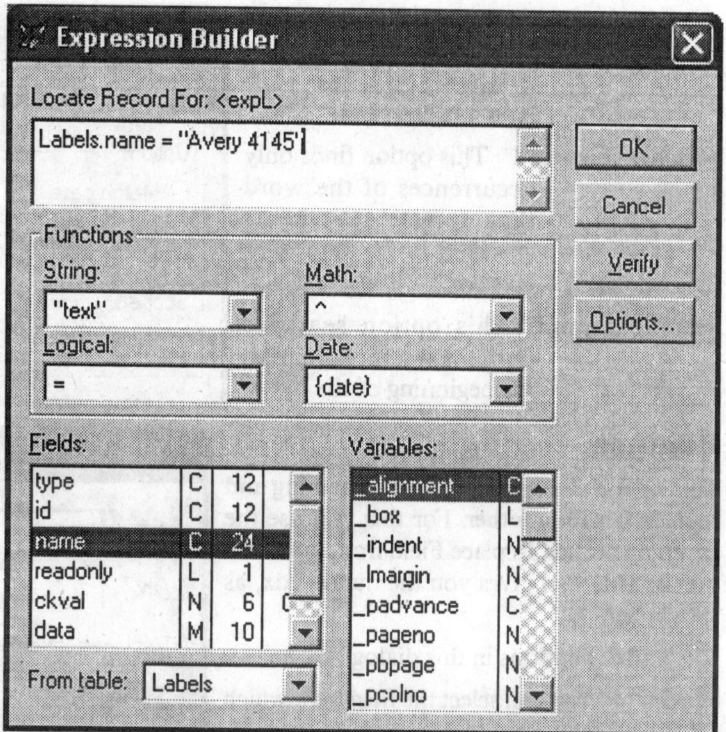

9. Give a space and type the actual text which you want to locate.
10. Here I have used Avery 4145 and do not forget to have the expesion within quotes.
11. Click on the Ok button to finish the entry. The Locate Record dialog box will reappear with the For option now selected.
12. Finally, select the Locate button in the Locate Record dialog box to start the search process.
13. When Visual FoxPro finds the matched record, it displays the same.
14. To find the next occurence of the same search click at the Command Window and type continue.
15. Now it starts the search again. Again if the match is found, it will be displayed.
16. If no match is found, you will get the mesage, End of Locate scope, at the Status bar.

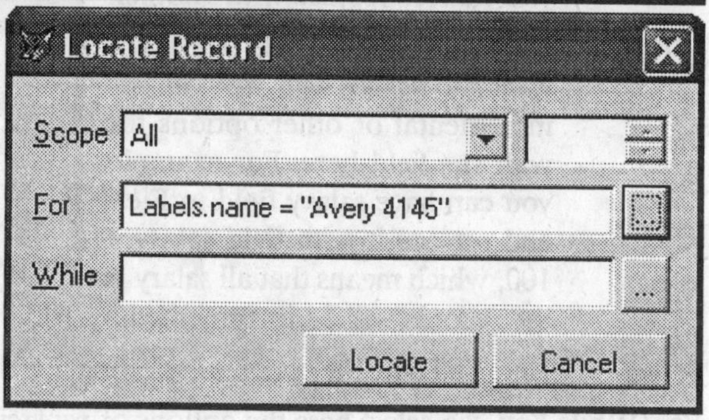

Next option of working with data in the records is the option of Finding something and Replacing it with another.

FIND AND REPLACE

Those of you who are familiar with Word Processing know how useful is this combination of Find and Replace command. You can find anything and replace it with another. Even Visual FoxPro has the same option which can be applied to the data in the records. Let us first see the command Find.

Find

This command can be called from Edit menu. This will give you a dialog box as shown on the next page. This dialog box has the following options:

Match case — This option finds the word specified in the Look for text: box with the exact combination of uppercase and lowercase letters.

Wrap around — This option searches from the position of the insertion point to the end of the file and then from the beginning of the file back to the insertion point, so that you can search the entire table, regardless of where the insertion point is when you begin your search of the Find.

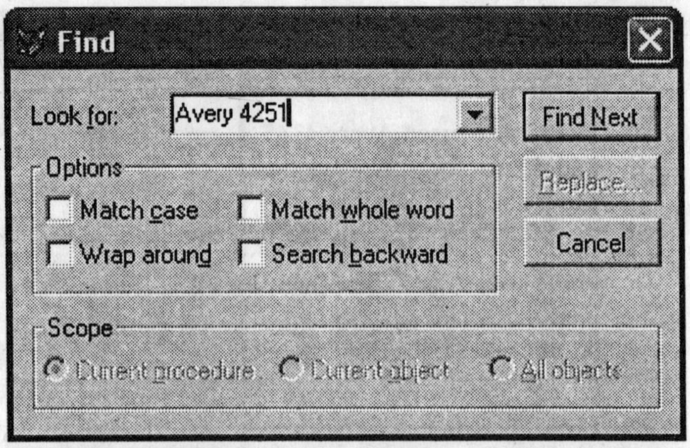

Match whole word — This option finds only occurrences of the word that appear exactly as specified in the Look For text box.

Search backward — This option searches from the insertion point to the beginning of the file.

Replace

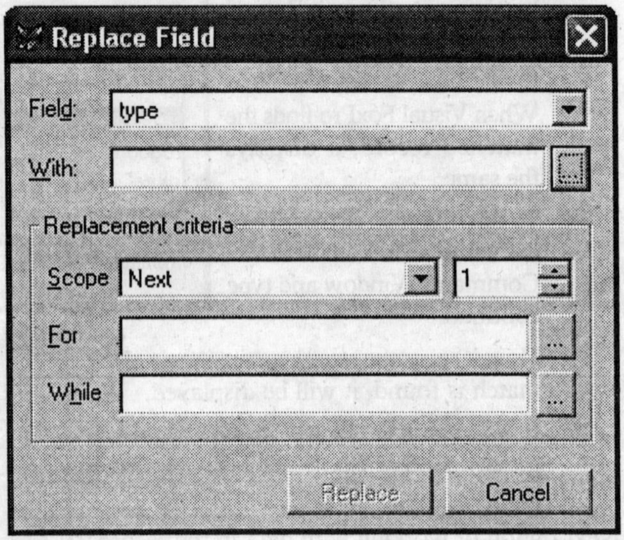

This option allows you to find something and replace it with another. For this you use the command called Replace Field from the Table menu. This also gives you the dialog box, as shown here.

The various options in this dialog box are:

Field — You can select the field here which you want to replace with another.

With — Here you select the field which you want it to replace with. You can add incremental or other options too with the field here. For example, you can have salary field in Field and replace it with field salary + 100, which means that all salary in the records will be incremented by 100.

Scope — Here you have the option of selecting the Next record or All records or even records by number.

For/While — You can select here the options of replacing for a certain criteria.

Deleting Record

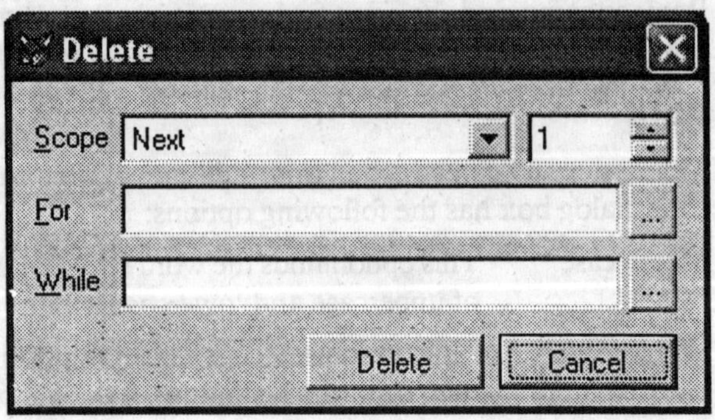

You can get rid of the records not needed by you. There is no option of recalling them back after deleting them. So make doubly sure that the records are not needed again before deleting them. Like most of the database programs, in Visual FoxPro too, the deletion is done in 2 two steps. In the first step the software marks the records for deletion without outrighting deleting them. In this case these records are not taken into account as far as totalling of fields are concerned. So when you are taking the total of salaries of all employees in the table, the salaries of the records which are marked for deletion is counted. In fact, till this stage you can recall these marked records, by using the command called Recall Records.

In the second step, the records are actually removed. For this you choose the option of Remove Deleted Records from the Table menu.

ALTERING THE SCREEN DISPLAY

There are various ways you can change the display of various options on the screen. First among them is Grid.

Grid Off/On

This option hides vertical lines that normally appear between columns. This option is a toggle switch; so selecting it will alternately hide and display the vertical lines. From View menu, select Grid lines. Selecting Grid lines hides both vertical and horizontal lines. You can reselect it to display the lines using same commands again.

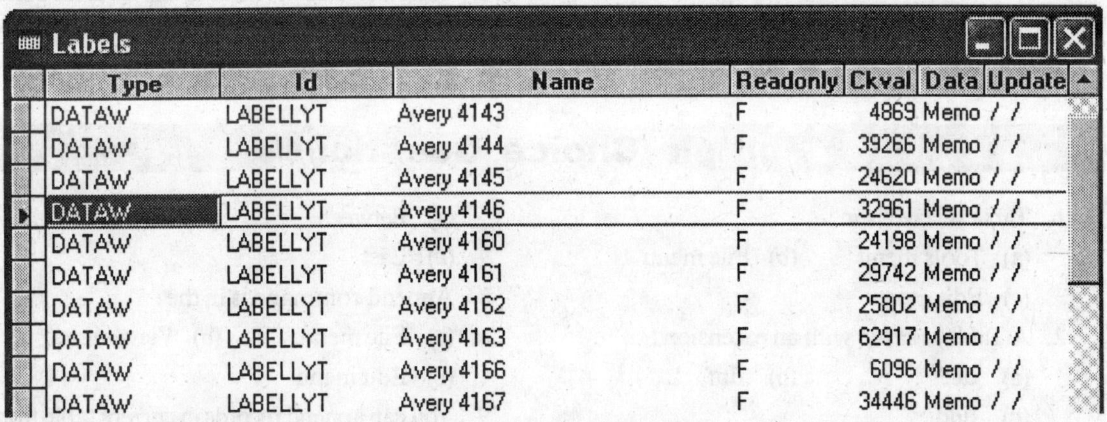

Type	Id	Name	Readonly	Ckval	Data	Update
DATAW	LABELLYT	Avery 4143	F	4869	Memo	/ /
DATAW	LABELLYT	Avery 4144	F	39266	Memo	/ /
DATAW	LABELLYT	Avery 4145	F	24620	Memo	/ /
DATAW	LABELLYT	Avery 4146	F	32961	Memo	/ /
DATAW	LABELLYT	Avery 4160	F	24198	Memo	/ /
DATAW	LABELLYT	Avery 4161	F	29742	Memo	/ /
DATAW	LABELLYT	Avery 4162	F	25802	Memo	/ /
DATAW	LABELLYT	Avery 4163	F	62917	Memo	/ /
DATAW	LABELLYT	Avery 4166	F	6096	Memo	/ /
DATAW	LABELLYT	Avery 4167	F	34446	Memo	/ /

Resizing Fields

If you feel that your screen is not able to show all the fields you want to see on the screen. For this you place the mouse pointer to the grid line to the right of the field's name, you want to resize. Note that the mouse pointer becomes a cross with arrowheads pointing left and right. Drag the gridlines (border) in or out until the columns is in the size you want. Using the mouse, resizing a field is very simple. Just click on the vertical grid line to the left or right of the field to be resized and drag the mouse to resize the field. Release the left mouse button when the field is of the desired size.

Moving Fields

By Moving Field you can move a field in a record of a table to a new location. Press tab key to the desired field. Select the Move Field in Table menu option and press left or right arrow keys to relocate the field and press Enter key. For interchanging the fields using mouse, move the pointer to the grid line to the right of the field's name. Hold down the left button and drag to left or right.

Let us Revise

1. A table is a compilation of data kept in records having various fields which are common to all records.
2. Table designer allows you to design a table from scratch.
3. Various type of fields you can have in Type of table structure.
4. You can modify the structure of the table.
5. You can add, delete, change data fields in the table.
6. For correcting mistakes you can use the arrow keys too.
7. You can work on a table by working on the data within it.
8. You can add a single record or multiple records in the table.
9. You can view a table in Edit or Browse mode.
10. You can edit the data in the table.
11. You can append records using Edit or Browse.
12. Using GoTo command you can go to a particular record.
13. Using Find you can find a particular data in the table record.
14. Using Replace you can find a particular data and replace it with another.
15. The Grid option hides vertical lines that normally appear between columns.
16. You can resize the fields of the table for better view on the screen.

Multiple Choice Questions

1. Table wizard is in :
   (a) Tools menu (b) File menu
   (c) Edit menu
2. A Table is saved with an extension :
   (a) .dcf (b) .dbf
   (c) .ddd
3. Logical field can take up value T or :
   (a) S (b) F
   (c) U
4. Can you use the same field name twice :
   (a) Yes (b) No
5. A field can be renamed :
   (a) Yes (b) No
6. In Edit mode a Del key would :
   (a) Delete a character
   (b) Delete a record
   (c) Delete a field
7. In Appending the records are added in :
   (a) Between (b) First
   (c) Last
8. Append command is in the :
   (a) File menu (b) View menu
   (c) Edit menu
9. You can append records in current table from an existing table :
   (a) Yes (b) No
10. Find command is under :
    (a) File menu (b) Edit menu
    (c) Tool menu
11. Grid lines are :
    (a) Vertical lines between columns
    (b) Lines between rows
    (c) Lines between characters
12. You can resize fields on the screen using the mouse and then :
    (a) pushing (b) dragging
    (c) pulling

True/False Questions

1. A table is a compilation of data kept in records having various fields which are common to all records.
2. Table designer allows you to design a table from scratch.
3. Various type of fields you can have in Type of table structure.
4. You cannot modify the structure of the table.
5. You can add, delete, change data fields in the table.
6. For correcting mistakes you can use the arrow keys too.
7. You can work on a table by working on the data within it.
8. You cannot add a single record or multiple records in the table.
9. You can view a table in Edit or Browse mode.
10. You cannot edit the data in the table.
11. You can append records using Edit or Browse.
12. Using GoTo command you can go to a particular record.
13. Using Find you can find a particular data in the table record.
14. Using Replace you can find a particular data and replace it with another.
15. The Grid option hides vertical lines that normally appear between columns.
16. You can resize the fields of the table for better view on the screen.

Matching Columns

Match the text in Column A with the text in Column B.

Column A	Column B
1. Character	a. It is stored as American format mm/dd/yy
2. Currency	b. Used for non-decimal numeric values
3. Numeric	c. Combination of date and time
4. Float	d. Logical value such as T or F
5. Date	e. Used to store money values
6. Date Time	f. Used for scientific and statistics calulations
7. Integer	g. Such as letters, numbers, symbols or spaces
8. Logical	h. Stored as numbers

Fill in the Blanks with Appropriate Words

a. General b. GoTo c. Arrow d. Character (binary)
e. Modify Structure f. Memo

1. For storing character is binary format you have to use ________.
2. When you have very long data to be filled in, you use the field called ________.
3. For storing graphics in tables, you use the type as ________.
4. ________ command will take the curser to a particular record.

5. For correcting mistakes, you use the ________ keys.
6. You can modify the structure of a table using the command __________.

Descriptive Type Questions

1. What is a table?
2. How will you create a table using Table Wizard?
3. How would you create a table using Table Designer?
4. How would you modify the structure of the table?
5. How would you add, delete and rename the fields of the table?
6. How would you append records in the table?
7. How would you add records through program?
8. What is the function of GoTo command?
9. How is Find command used?
10. What is the function of Replace command?
11. How would you alter the screen display?
12. How would you use the option of Grid?

Answers to Objective Type Questions

Multiple Choice Questions

1. a	2. b	3. b	4. b
5. a	6. a	7. c	8. b
9. a	10. b	11. a	12.b

True/False Questions

1. T	2. T	3. T	4. F
5. T	6. T	7. T	8. F
9. T	10. F	11. T	12. T
13. T	14. T	15. T	16. T

Matching Columns

1. g	2. e	3. h	4. f
5. a	6. c	7. b	8. d

Fill in the Blanks with Appropriate Words

1. d	2. f	3. a	4. b
5. c	6. e		

Recommended Readings

1. Learn to Program Visual Basic—Databases *by John Smiley*.
2. Learn to Program Visual Basic—Objects *by John Smiley*.
3. Learn to Program Visual Basic—Examples *by John Smiley*.

—Published by Firewall Media (An Imprint of Laxmi Publications Pvt. Ltd.)

7 Working with Queries

INTRODUCING QUERY

So far I have talked about creations. Its time I talk about taking the results out of Visual FoxPro. This is mostly done by Query which is the short name of question. Here query means asking question to the software and getting the result from it. The questions are based on the database which is in use.

For example, in a school database, you can ask the following questions:

— How many students are there who live in Noida

— How many students have their height more than 170 cms

— How many students have taken up computer as additional subject

This way you can think of the various questions and get the result from system using the queries as mentioned above. The best part of queries is that they can be saved and run whenever required.

As usual we will first learn to create query using the Wizards.

CREATING QUERY WITH WIZARD

You can call the query wizard from the Tools menu and Wizards submenu. But before that you have to open the database based on which you want to create the queries. The query wizard dialog box shown on the next page gives you the choice of creating queries of various types. Since our query is of simple type, we would click at the Query Wizard and go ahead.

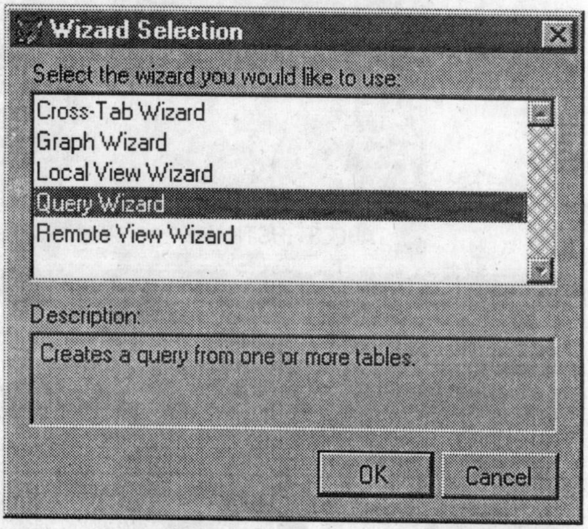

The following screens will appear.

Step1 will ask you about the fields from the database to be used.

Step2 is reserved for some other option.

Step3 will ask you about the filler records.

Step4 will ask you about the sequence in which to sort the records.

Step4a will ask you whether you want to limit your records to first or last records.

Step5 will finish the query wizard and ask you to save the query

Save the query with a name as shown in the Save As dialog box.

This way you create a query and save it under a given name. You can now run it anytime you need.

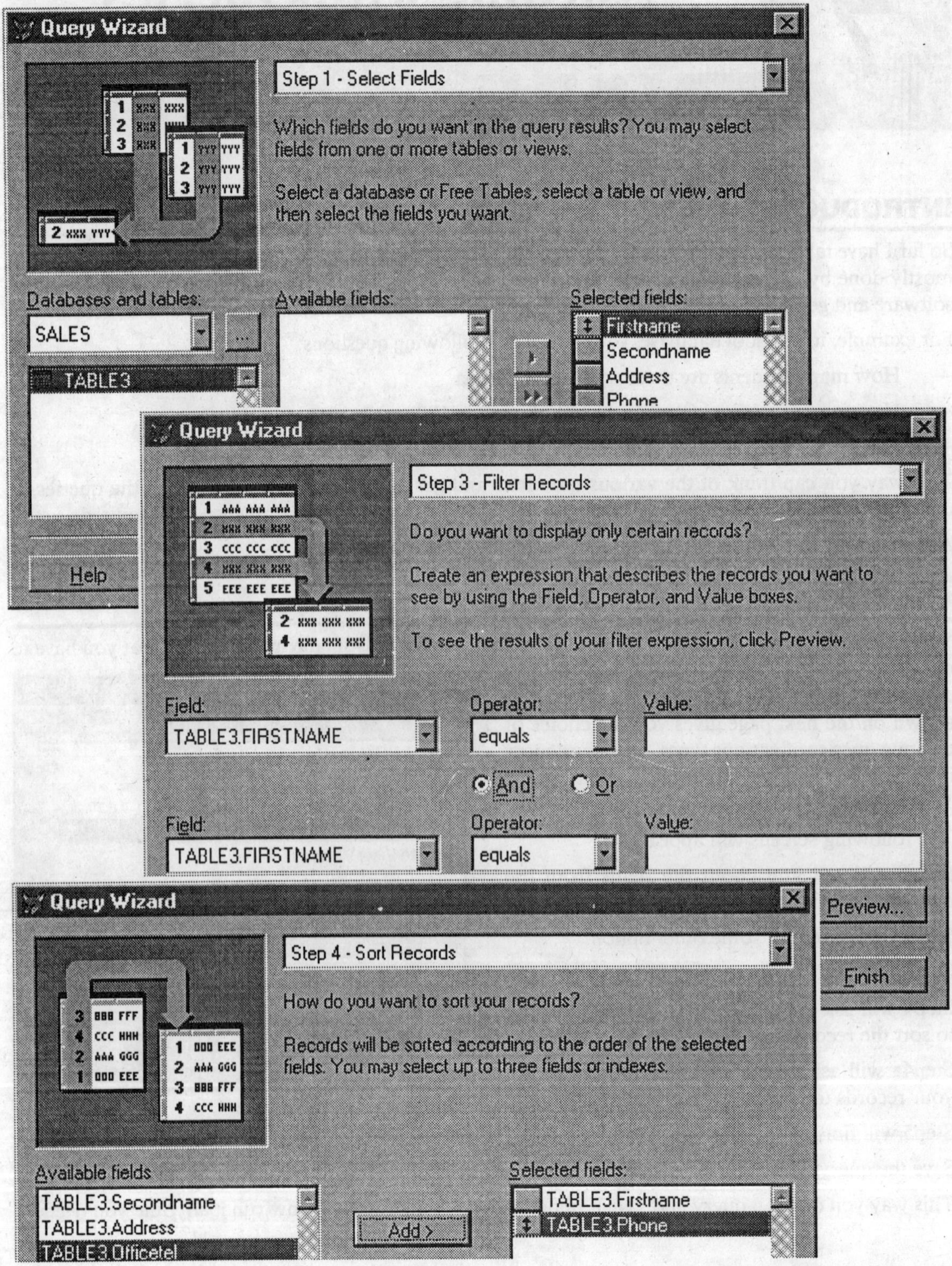
Query Wizard
Step 1 - Select Fields
Which fields do you want in the query results? You may select fields from one or more tables or views.
Select a database or Free Tables, select a table or view, and then select the fields you want.
Databases and tables:
SALES
TABLE3
Available fields:
Selected fields:
Firstname
Secondname
Address
Phone
Help
Query Wizard
Step 3 - Filter Records
Do you want to display only certain records?
Create an expression that describes the records you want to see by using the Field, Operator, and Value boxes.
To see the results of your filter expression, click Preview.
Field:
TABLE3.FIRSTNAME
Operator:
equals
Value:
And
Or
Field:
TABLE3.FIRSTNAME
Operator:
equals
Value:
Preview...
Finish
Query Wizard
Step 4 - Sort Records
How do you want to sort your records?
Records will be sorted according to the order of the selected fields. You may select up to three fields or indexes.
Available fields
TABLE3.Secondname
TABLE3.Address
TABLE3.Officetel
Add >
Selected fields:
TABLE3.Firstname
TABLE3.Phone

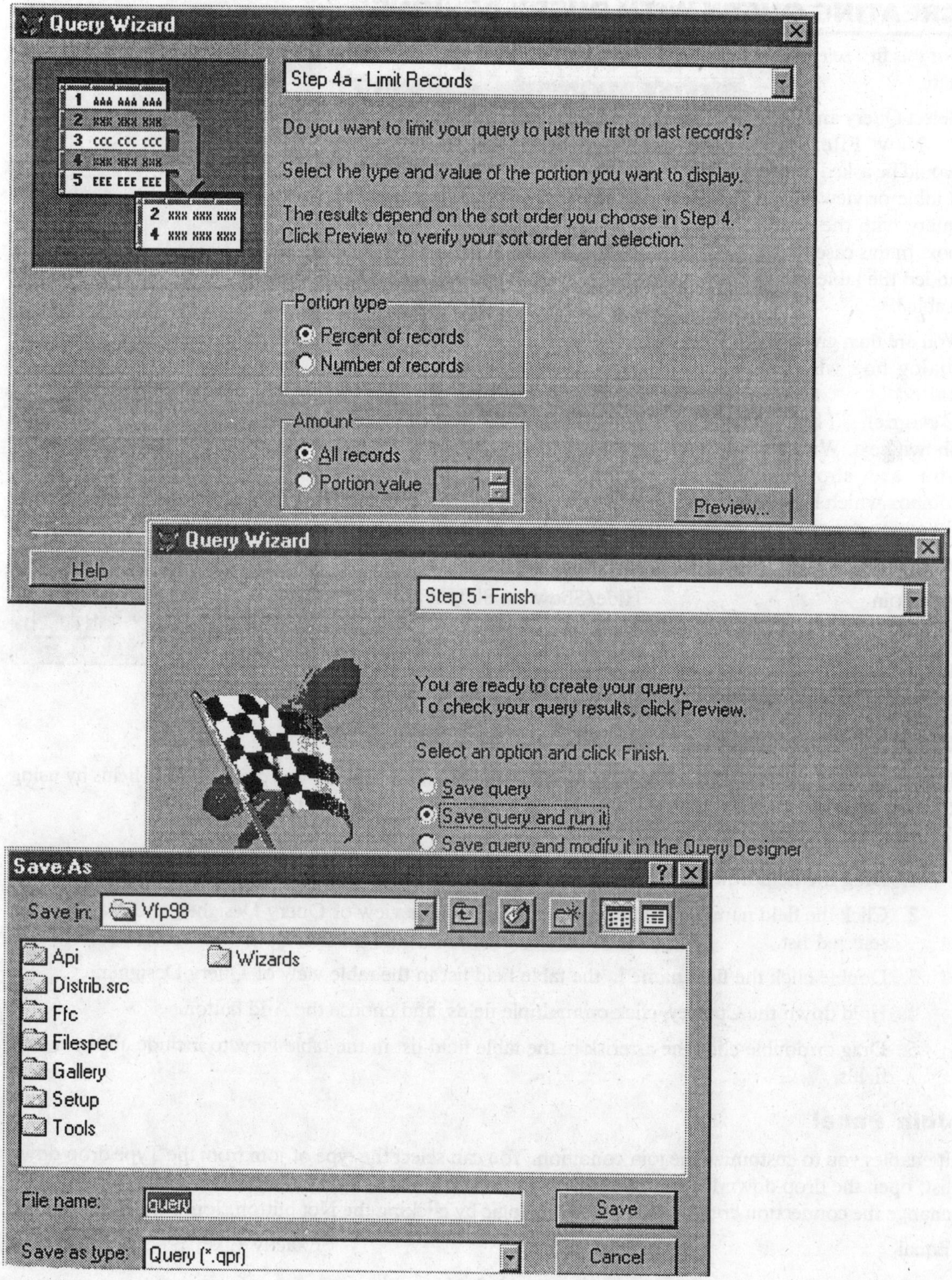
Query Wizard
Step 4a - Limit Records
Do you want to limit your query to just the first or last records?
Select the type and value of the portion you want to display.
The results depend on the sort order you choose in Step 4.
Click Preview to verify your sort order and selection.
Portion type
Percent of records
Number of records
Amount
All records
Portion value
Preview...
Help
Query Wizard
Step 5 - Finish
You are ready to create your query.
To check your query results, click Preview.
Select an option and click Finish.
Save query
Save query and run it
Save query and modify it in the Query Designer
Save As
Save in: Vfp98
Api
Wizards
Distrib.src
Ffc
Filespec
Gallery
Setup
Tools
File name: query
Save
Save as type: Query (*.qpr)
Cancel

CREATING QUERY WITH QUERY DESIGNER

For this first select New from the file menu to get the dialog box shown here.

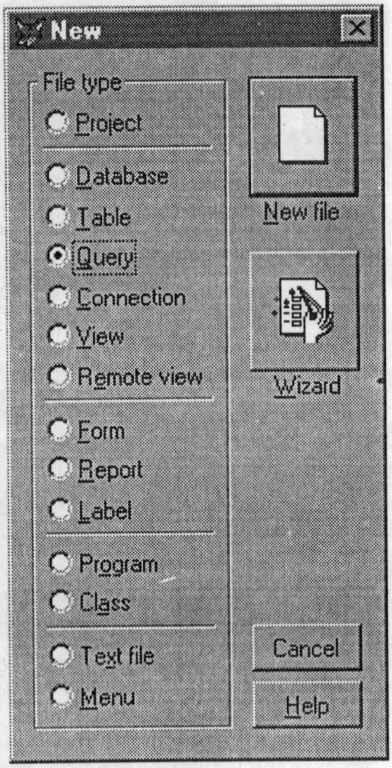

Select Query and click at New File. You would be asked to add a table or view to the query with the dialog box. In this case I have added the table called Table3.

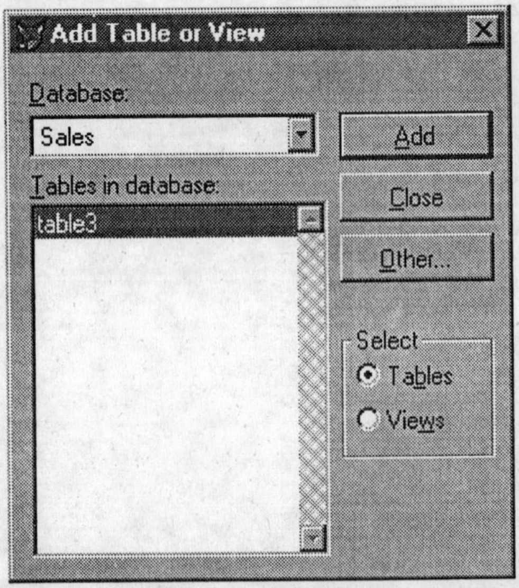

You are then given the dialog box which is called Query Designer. This is shown next. With this you are shown a toolbox which has the following options:

Add Table	Delete Table
Add Join	Hide/Show the SQL Window
Maximize the Table view	Query Destination

Besides these you have the various panels on the bottom. You can select anyone of them and respond to the query of them.

Fields in the Query

Now that you have the fields in the table available to you on the screen, you can add these fields by using the Add button. You can also use Add All in case you are planning to use all the fields.

To move a field, you do the following:

1. Drag the field from the Available list to the Selected list.
2. Click the field name in the table field list in the table view of Query Designer, and drag it to the selected list.
3. Double click the field name in the table field list in the table view of Query Designer.
4. Hold down the Ctrl key, click on multiple fields, and choose the Add button.
5. Drag or double-click the asterisk in the table field list in the table view to include all the table's fields.

Join Panel

It enables you to customize the join condition. You can select the type of join from the Type drop-down list, open the drop-down list for either field, and select fields to define the join relations. You can also change the connection criteria and reverse the logic by clicking the Not button. Join supports 5 criteria:

Equal	Like	Exactly Like

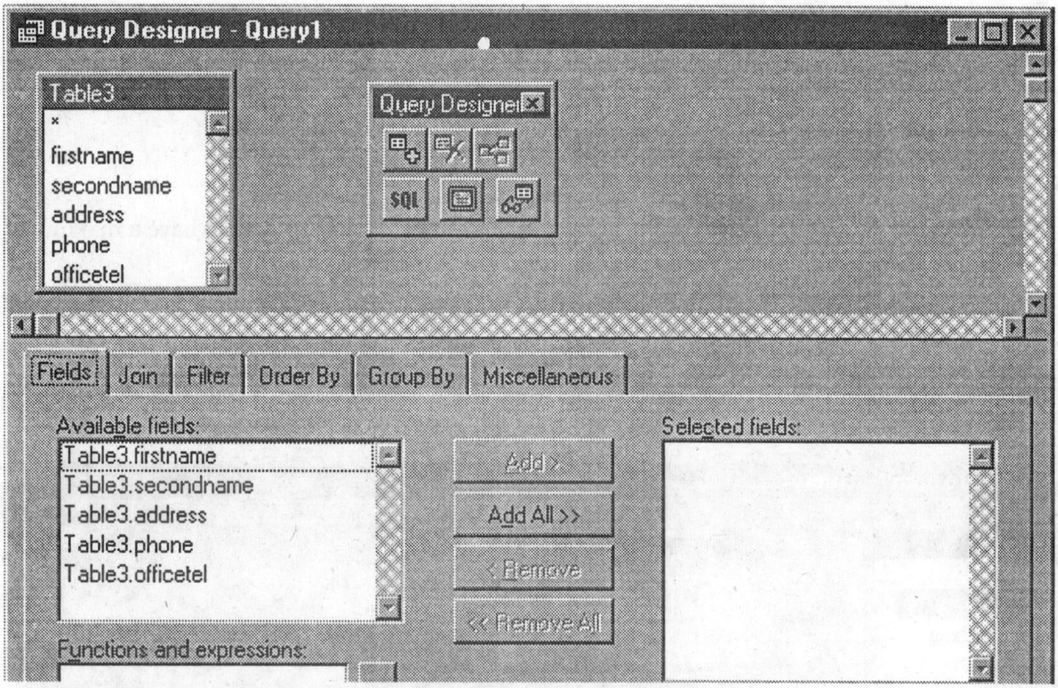

More Than Less Than

This dialog box enables you to select the type of join and describes each condition. The four types of joins are:

1. Inner join, which includes only the records from both tables that match the join condition.
2. Left outer join, which includes all records from the table on the left and records that match the join condition from the table on the right.

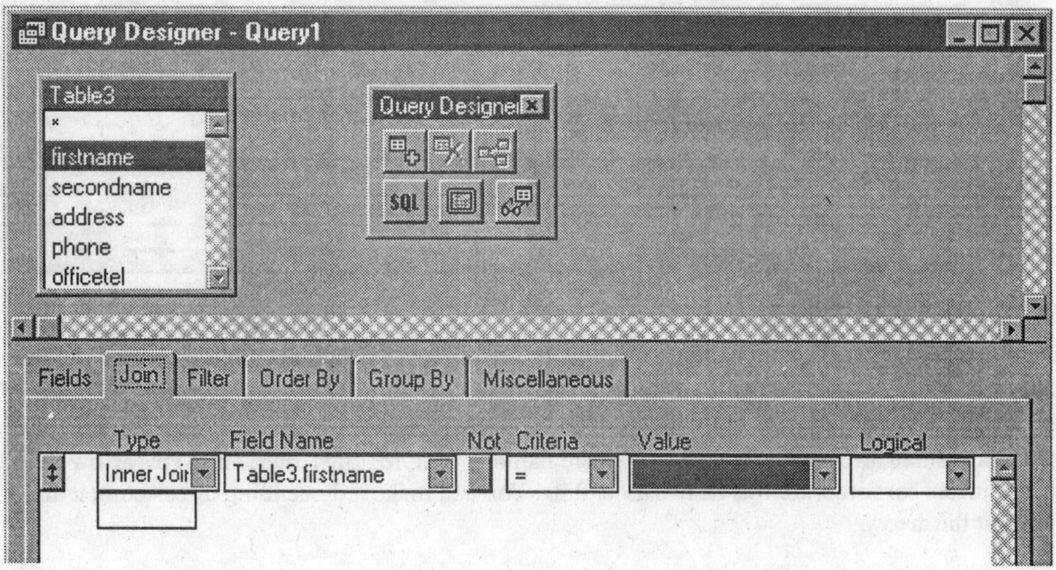

3. Right outer join, which includes all records from the table on the right and those records that match the join condition from the table on the left.
4. Full outer join, which includes all records from both tables and combines those that match the join condition into one record in the result set.

Filter Conditions

This allows you to put conditions on the fields. For example, you would like to field to have a maximum or a minimum value.

You may set a particular value for the field too. Clicking at criteria leads to Expression builder dialog box in which you can create any valid FoxPro expression.

So when you run this query the result will shown according to their value and the criteria chosen by you.

You can run this query even from the database which is a combination of various tables stored together.

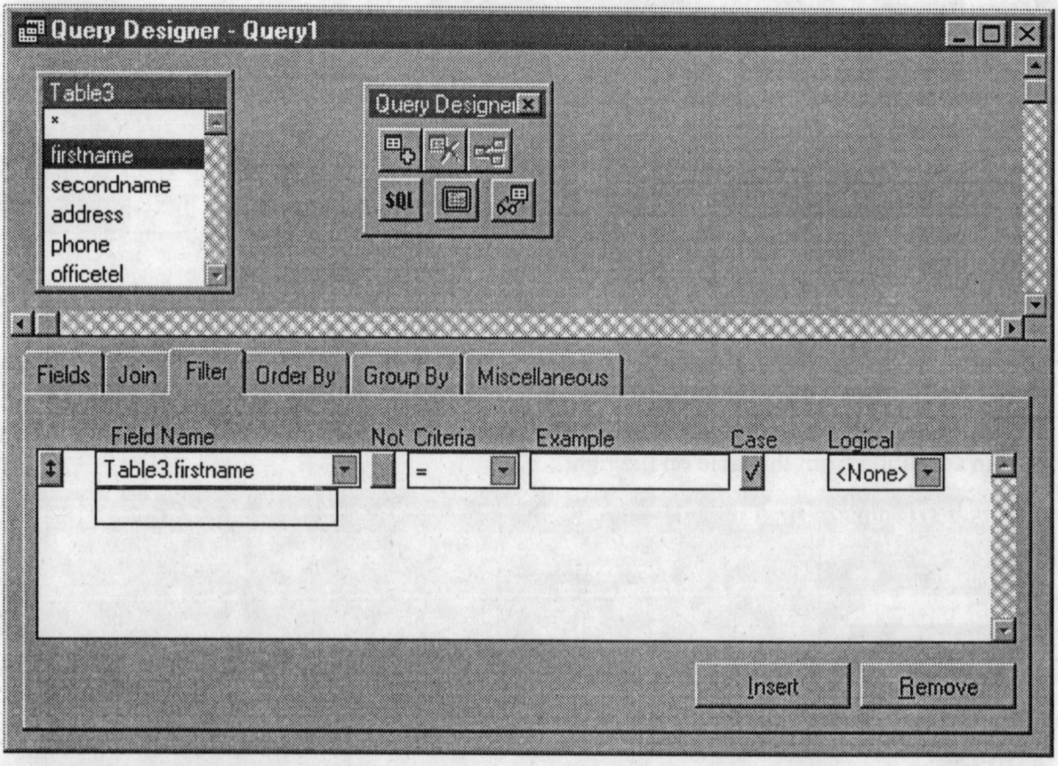

Order By Conditions

This option displays two list boxes that contain fields. The left box contains only the Selected fields. To begin the sort with the supplier's company name, click it and then click Add. As with adding fields, this action moves the selected field to the right list box.

Notice that a small arrow appears next to the field name in the Ordering Criteria list. This arrow indicates that the current sort order for this field is ascending. You can make it descending by selecting it and then clicking at the arrow.

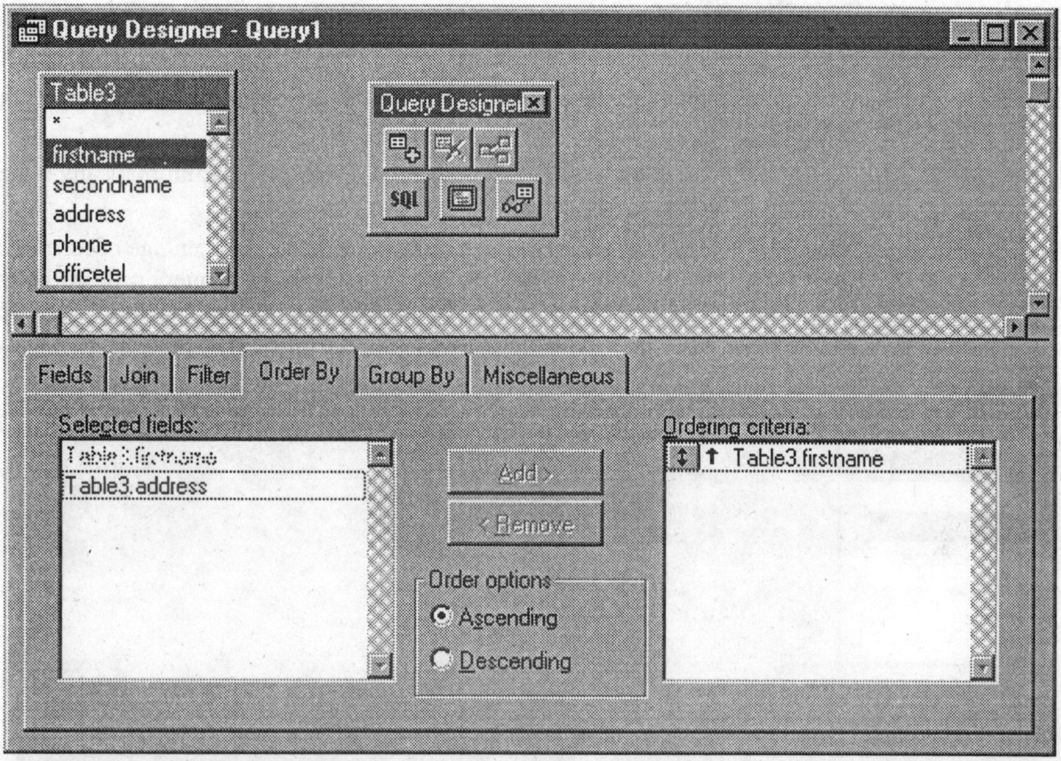

Group By Conditions

This allows you to group various fields into a group. So that when you take the total of the fields it does not give the total of individual fields but gives the total of the whole group as a single identity.

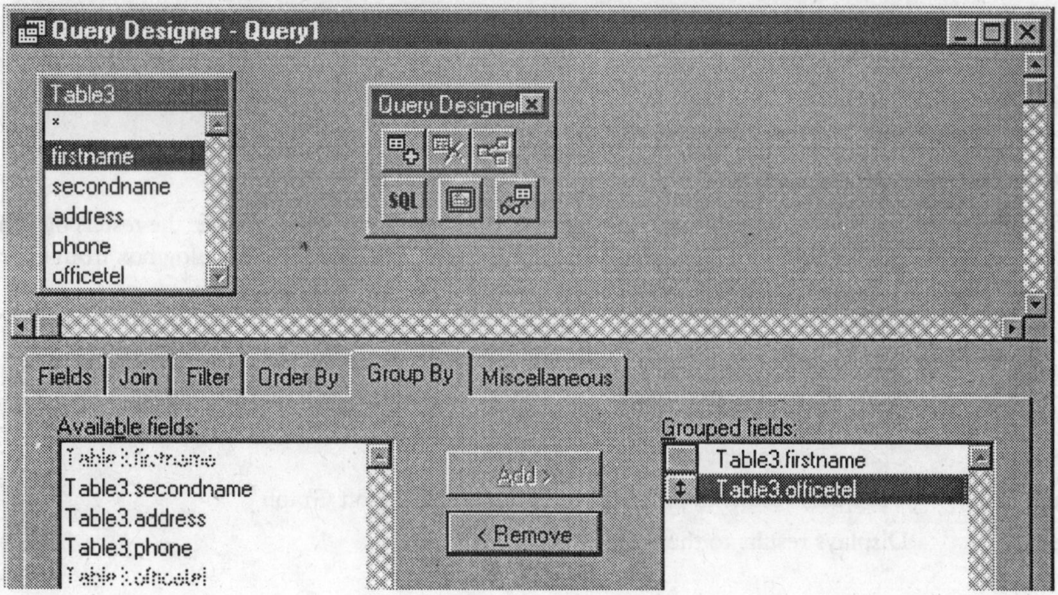

Miscellaneous Conditions

This option provides for additional record-selection criteria:

No Duplicates — This condition enables you to show or to exclude duplicate records from your selection.

Cross-Tabulate — This outputs the result set into a cross-tabular format. It also automatically selects the Group and Order By fields.

Top — It enables you to select all records, several records, or a percentage of records to be returned. If you want to show the top 10 sales items, a query ordered by the units sold and limited to the top 10 would provide your top 10 items. Changing the order option from ascending to descending provides the bottom 10 sales items.

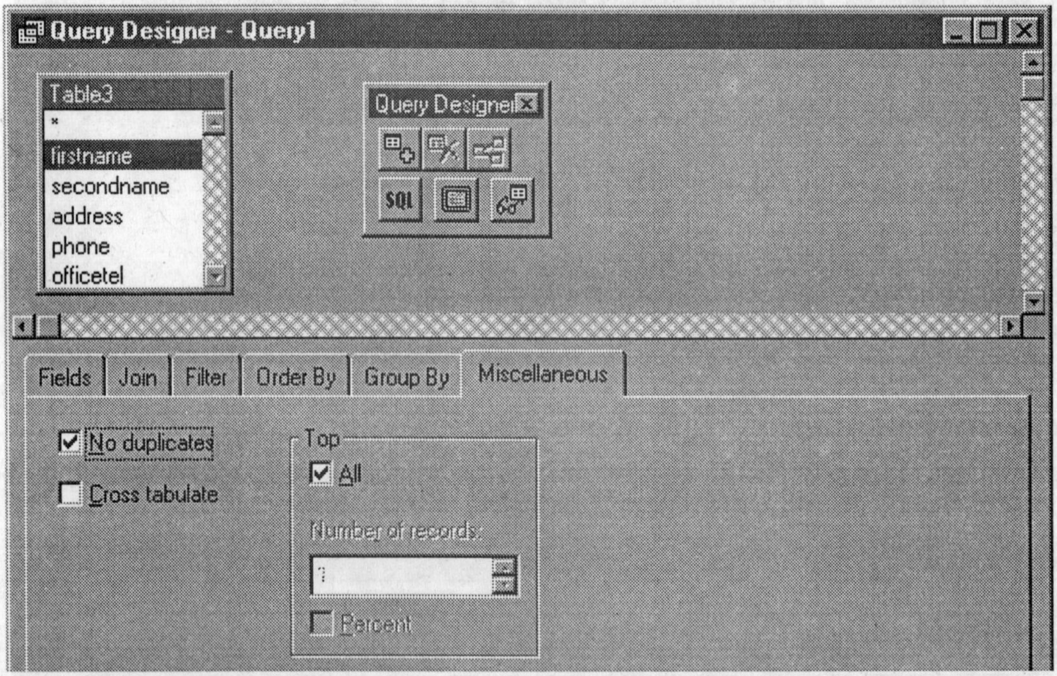

Outputting the Results

So far you have studied to see the queries on the screen. But, this is not all you can see the results on other too by changing the destination. To change it you open the Query Destination dialog box from Query toolbar.

As you can see there are various options on the screen. These are:

Browse	View query results in a Browse window only
Cursor	Create a temporary table or cursor with query results
Table	Crate a permanent table
Graph	Use query results to produce a graph with Microsoft Graph
Screen	Displays results to the screen only

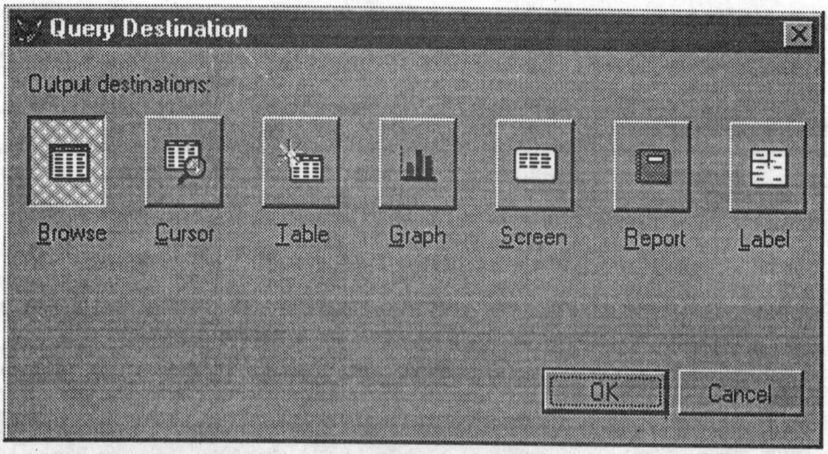

Report Uses query results as a data source for a report

Label Uses query results as a data source for labels

A few of them are discussed here.

Output to the Screen

This is used since the query results after writing on the screen fade away. So you must create a more permanent copy by selecting To Print or To Text File. Later on these can be used for sending to the printer.

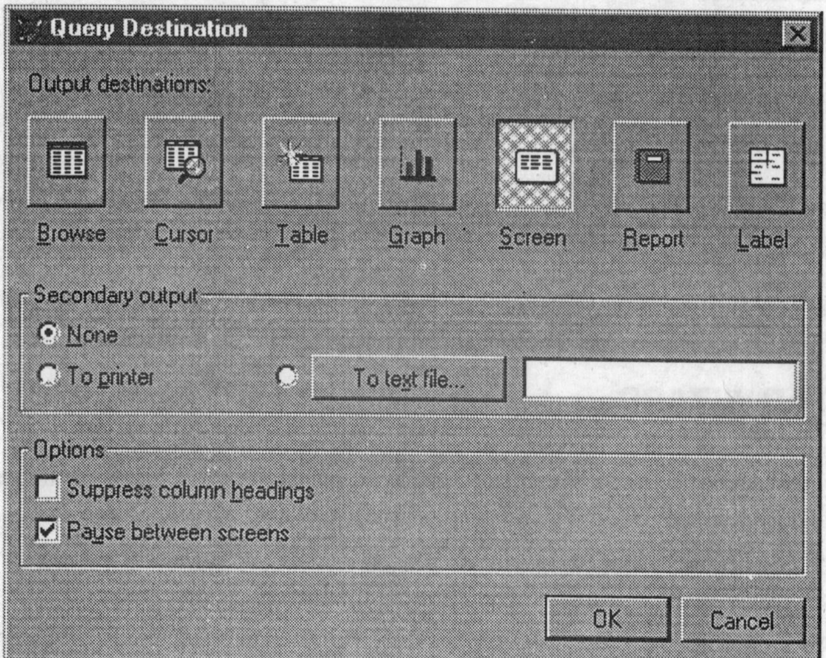

Output to a Report

Using this open you can club the results of the query with an existing report available under Open Report. By clicking Page Preview you can see the results before printing.

Output to a Label

Similar to the report option, here you can club the results of the query with an existing label format.

RUNNING THE QUERY

You can run the query in one of the following four ways:

1. You can select the Run Query from the Query menu.
2. You can also press Ctrl + Q keys together to run the query.
3. You can right click on table window in the query window and select Run Query option from the menu. By default the result will be displayed in Browse window.
4. You can click on ! mark on the Standard toolbar to run the query.

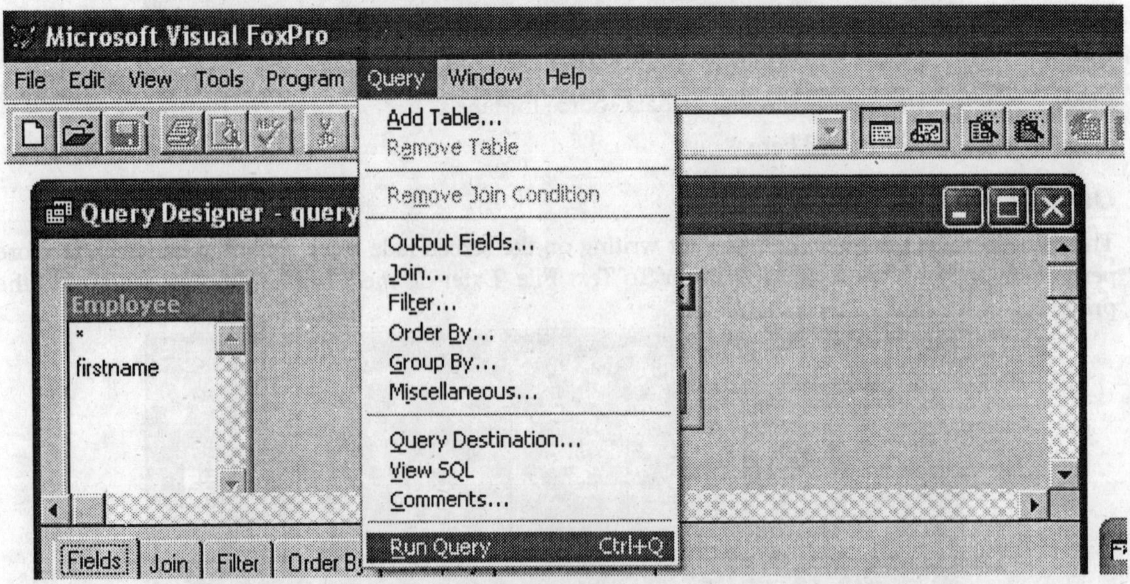

The resulting Browse window will show the selected fields. Notice that the output is in Browse mode, unless you have selected a different format.

CROSS TAB WIZARD

As we all know that the data in the tables is shown in the form of rows and columns. This wizard is a powerful tool which allows you to change the positioning of the data. You can show the data in rows and columns as per your needs. Let us see how it is created and used.

Let us now first create the following table, with the structure as you will see next.

1. Click on New in the File menu. The New dialog box will be displayed.
2. Click on Table and choose the option of New file button to create a new table file. This will give rise to another dialog box know as Create dialog box.
3. Type Table3.dbf in the enter table list box and then click Save button.
4. Table Designer dialog box appears; create the structure as shown here.

5. Click on OK button to save the structure of table3.dbf file.
6. A message box is displayed "Input data records now?".
7. Click on Yes. Visual FoxPro opens the table3 table in Append mode so you can begin adding records.
8. After adding these records press Ctrl + W keys together to save these records.
9. From the View menu choose Browse "Table3.dbf" to see the table records.
10. Again from View menu, choose Browse. Now records are displayed in browse mode.

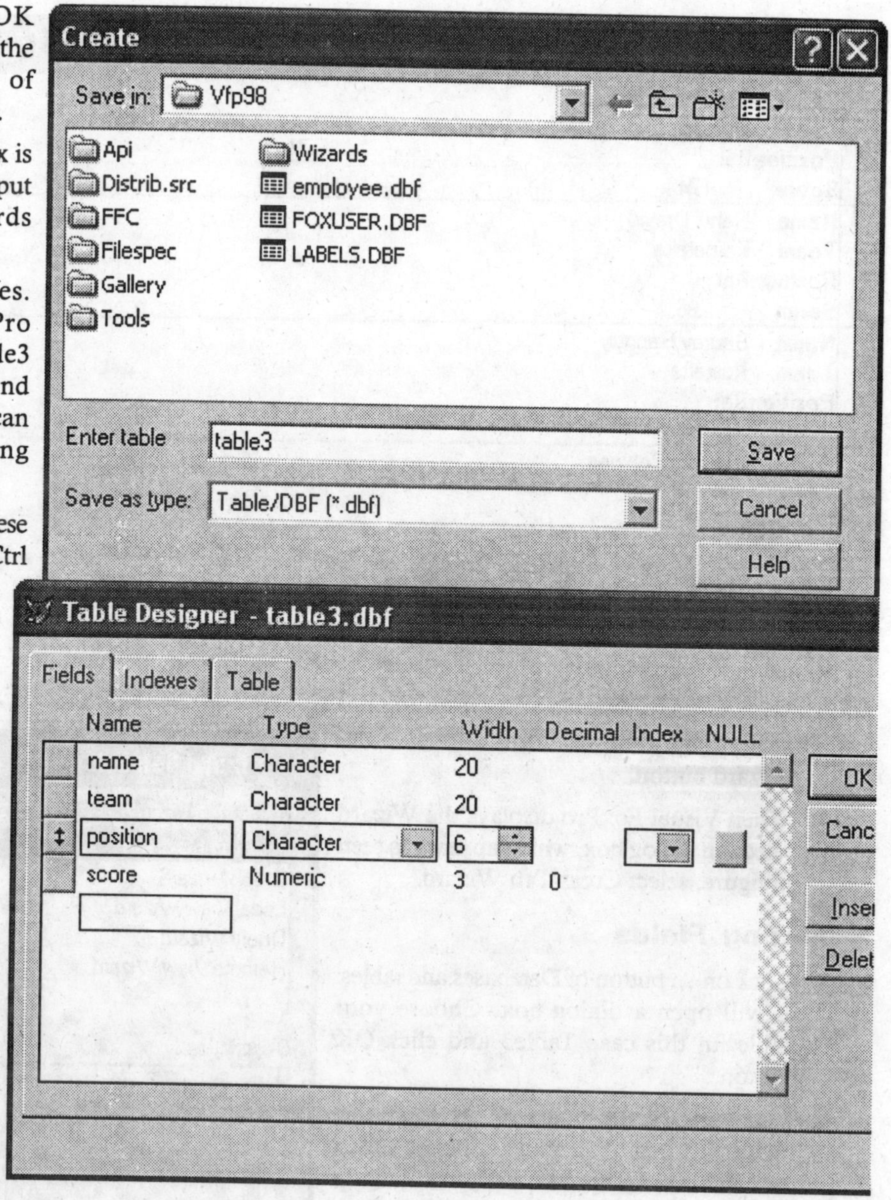

Now we will create a cross-tab of the table.

Creating a Cross-Tabs

This can be done if the following method:

1. From the Wizards submenu on the Tools menu choose Query.
2. In the Wizard Selection dialog box, choose Cross-Tab Wizard.

   Or

   From the File menu select New…option.

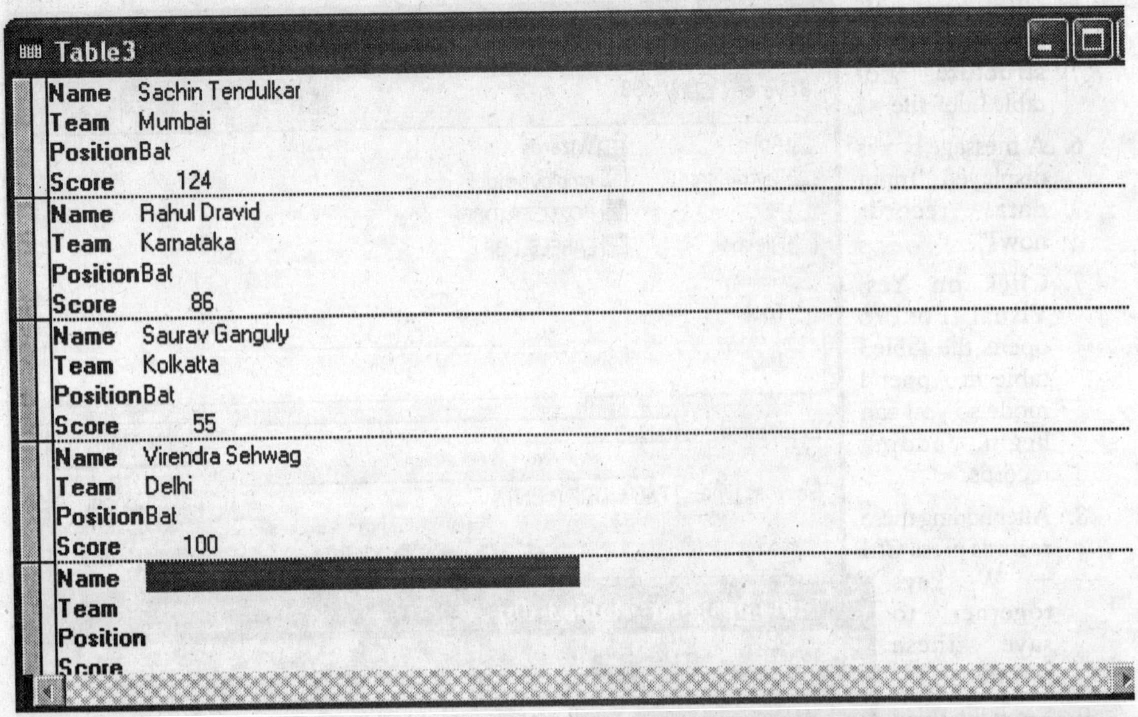

2. Select Query radio button and click the Wizard button.
3. When Visual FoxPro displays the Wizard selection dialog box, which appears as seen in figure, select Cross-Tab Wizard.

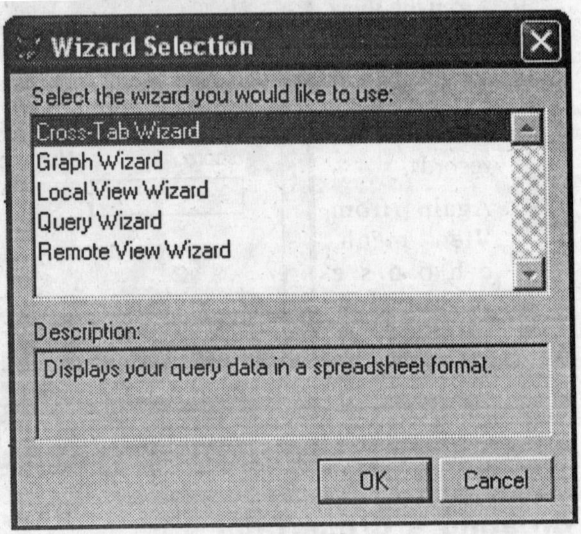

Selecting Fields

1. Click on ... button of Databases and tables: it will open a dialog box. Choose your table, in this case Table3 and click OK button.
2. You can see the fields in the Available fields: list box. You must choose at least one field, since we have only one field in our Table3 table, so click (>>) button to move all the fields into the selected fields: box.
3. Click Next> button to move to next step.
4. The next step lets you lay out the Cross-Tab by clicking and dragging fields – one for the column headings, one for the row headings and one that is used as the basis of the calculations in the cells.
5. Your Cross-Tab query results will display a column for each unique value that exists for the table field that you drag to the Data box.
6. Click on Next> button to move to next step.

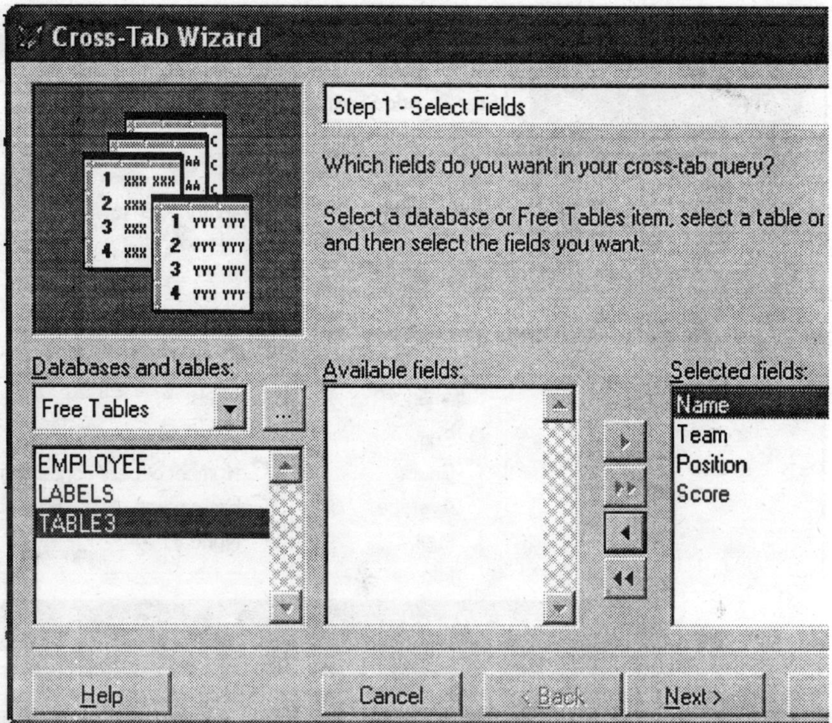

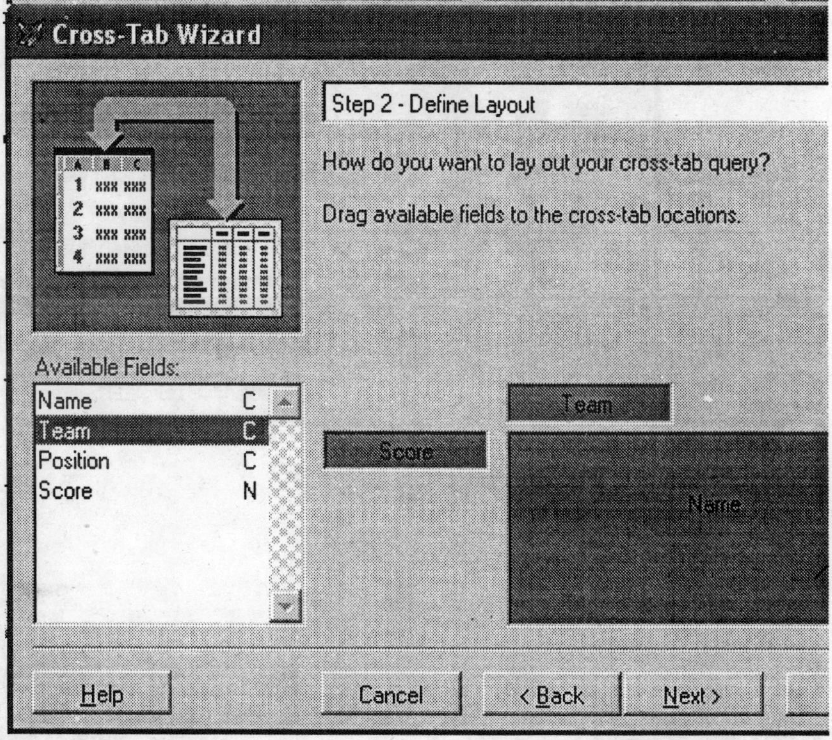

7. You can add a column that contains summary information add subtotals by selecting the appropriate radio button from the summary and subtotals areas. The totals will appear in the rightmost column of your Cross-Tab Query result.
8. Quick on Next> button to move to the next step.
9. The next step lets you create the query and is similar to the Finish step of other wizards. Use the radio button to save the query for later use, to save and run the query or to save the query and modify it in the Query Designer. You can also click on Preview button to view the result of the query in a preview window.
10. Now press the Esc key to close the Browse window.
11. Click on Save and run cross-tab query radio button to save the query and run it.

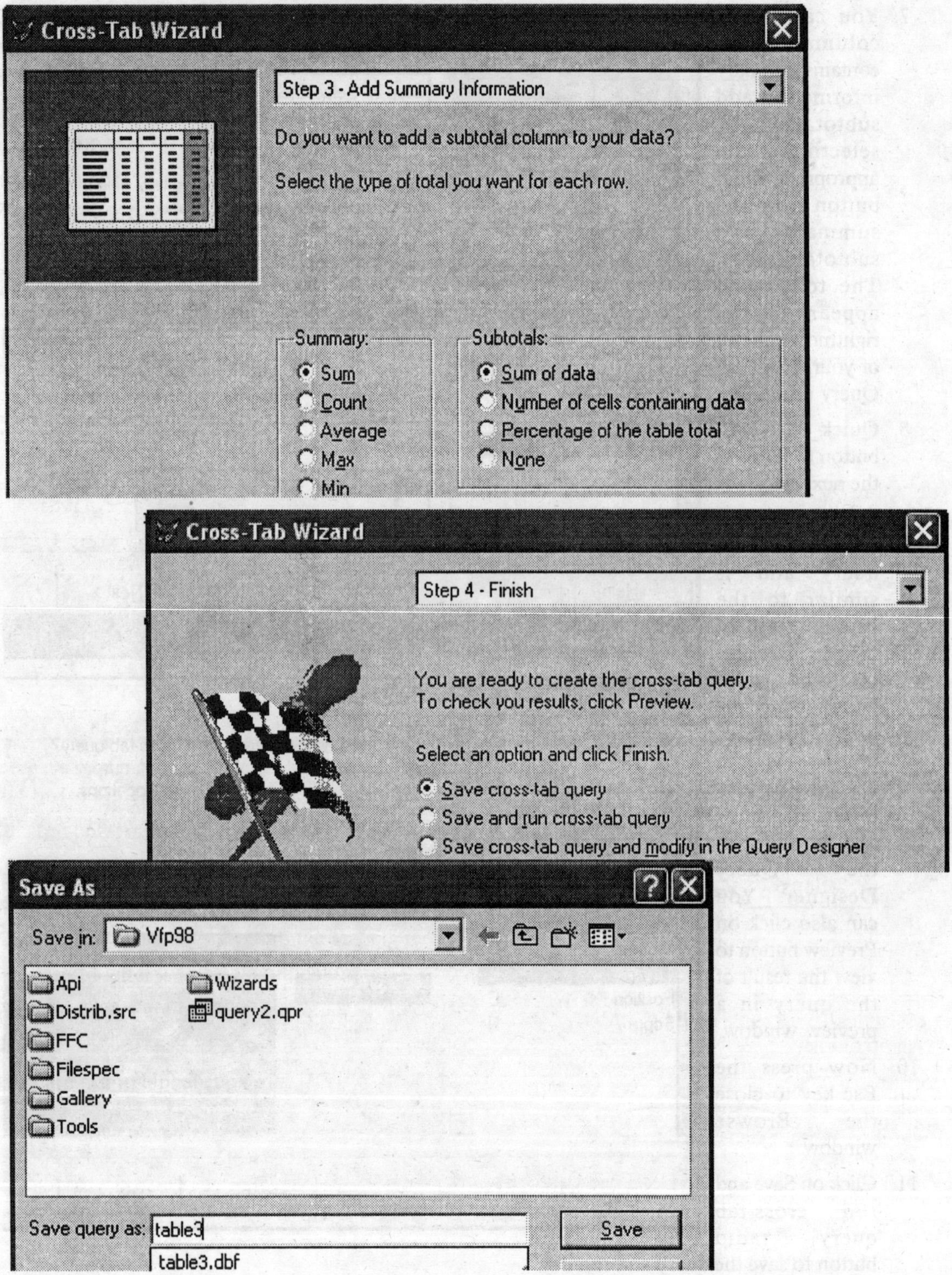
Cross-Tab Wizard
Step 3 - Add Summary Information
Do you want to add a subtotal column to your data?
Select the type of total you want for each row.
Summary:
Sum
Count
Average
Max
Min
Subtotals:
Sum of data
Number of cells containing data
Percentage of the table total
None
Cross-Tab Wizard
Step 4 - Finish
You are ready to create the cross-tab query.
To check you results, click Preview.
Select an option and click Finish.
Save cross-tab query
Save and run cross-tab query
Save cross-tab query and modify in the Query Designer
Save As
Save in: Vfp98
Api
Distrib.src
FFC
Filespec
Gallery
Tools
Wizards
query2.qpr
Save query as: table3
table3.dbf
Save

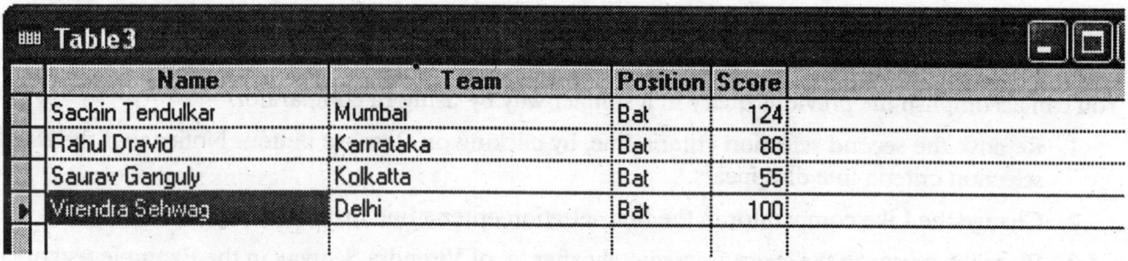

Table3

Name	Team	Position	Score
Sachin Tendulkar	Mumbai	Bat	124
Rahul Dravid	Karnataka	Bat	86
Saurav Ganguly	Kolkatta	Bat	55
Virendra Sehwag	Delhi	Bat	100

12. Click on Finish button. It will display a Save dialog box. Type the name of the query as Table3 and click on the save button.
13. Browse the table and see the difference.

USING THE QUERY

There are various options which can be used in the query. Some of them are listed here.

Using OR Condition (OR/IN Comparators)

You can create queries with multiple condition using OR and AND logical operators. Use the following simple procedure to display data.

1. Click on Field Name drop down list and select Table3.name in the drop down list.
2. Click in the Not Criteria drop down list and select Like.
3. Click in the Example text box and type Virendra Sehwag.
4. Click in the Logical drop down list and select OR.
5. Click on the empty Field Name box to open the Field Name drop down list and select Table3.name.
6. Select Like from the Not Criteria drop down list.
7. Type Sacchin Tendulkar in the Example box.

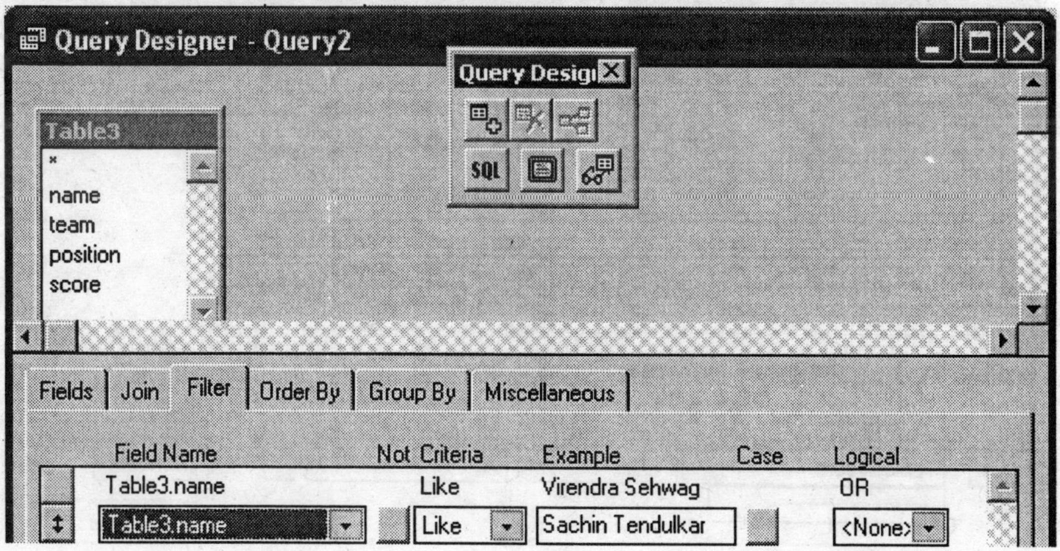

8. Click on the Run ! button to run the query.
9. Press Esc key to close the Browse window.

You can accomplish the previous query in a simpler way by using In comparator.

1. Remove the second selection criteria line, by clicking on Remove button. Notice that the third selection criteria line disappears.
2. Change the Like comparator in the first selection criteria line to an In comparator.
3. Place the cursor to the space immediately after 'g' of Virendra Sehwag in the Example text area and type Sachin Tendulkar.
4. From the Logical drop down list select <None>.
5. Select Run Query button and your result should be same as the previous one using the OR comparator.
6. Press Esc key to close the Browse window.
7. Click on the Remove button to remove existing selection criteria line.

Using more than (>) or less than (<) Comparators

Visual FoxPro allows you to compare using > (more than) or < (less than) comparators, while performing query. For example, suppose you want to extract all the records with score more than 90 from table3.dbf.

1. From Field Name drop down list, choose table3.dbf.
2. Choose > from the Comparison in the criteria drop down list.
3. In the Example text box, type 90.
4. Click on the Run (!) button from the Standard toolbar to run the query. Visual FoxPro will show all the records matching the criteria in Browse window.
5. Press Esc key to return to the Query Designer window.
6. Click on Remove button to remove the existing selection criteria line.

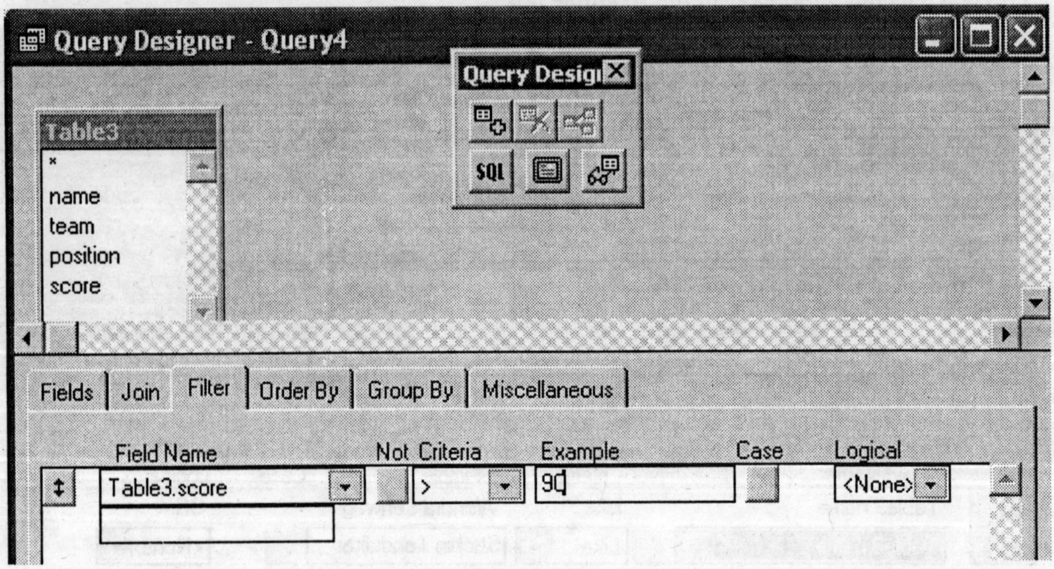

Using AND Condition

You can also create conditions that need to satisfy more than one criterion. Suppose that you are interested only in the records of employees whose team is Delhi and score should be less than 110. This can be done using AND condition, as detailed in the following;

1. Click on the Field Name drop down list, select Team.
2. Click on the Field Name drop down list, select Like.
3. Click in the Example text box and type Delhi.
4. From the Logical drop down list box select AND condition.
5. Now to specify second condition, click on the Field Name drop down list below table3 and select Score from the pull down list.
6. Click in the Criteria drop down list, Select < (less than) comparator.
7. Click in the Example text box and type 110.
8. Click on the Run ! button to run the query.
9. This will give you the only records which meets both the options.

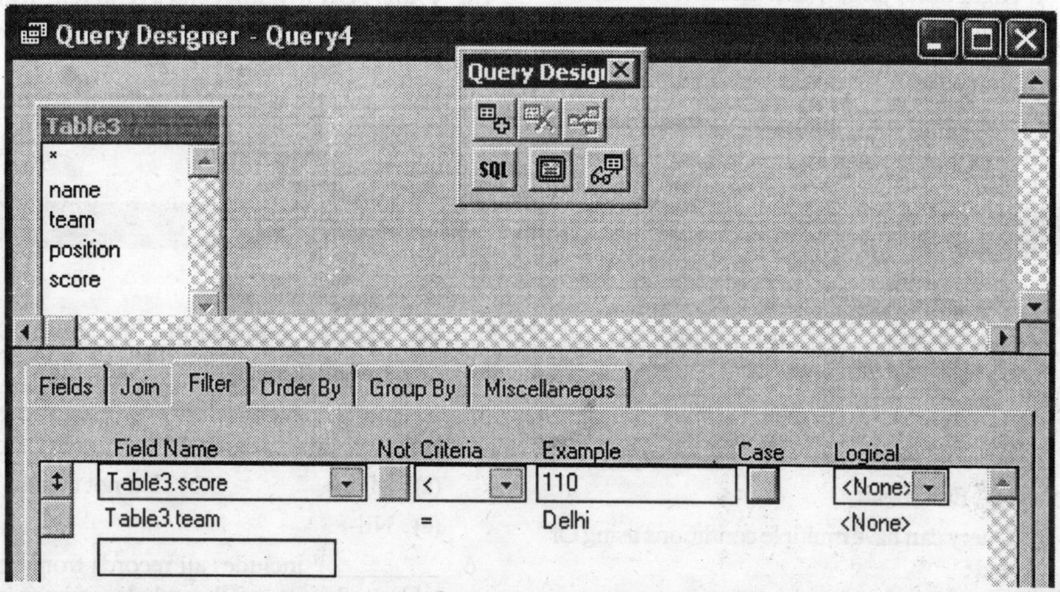

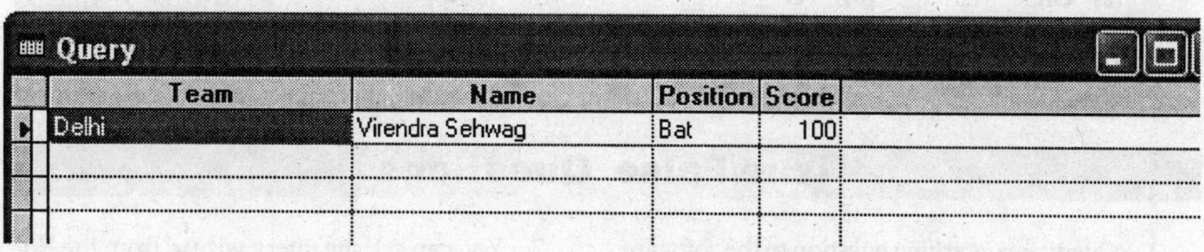

Let us Revise

1. Query means asking question to the software and getting the result from it.
2. You can call the query wizard from the Tools menu and Wizards submenu.
3. For creating a Query, after clicking at New in the File menu, Select Query and click at New File.
4. Inner join, which includes only the records from both tables that match the join condition.
5. Left outer join, which includes all records from the table on the left and records that match the join condition from the table on the right.
6. Right outer join, which includes all records from the table on the right and those records that match the join condition from the table on the left.
7. Full outer join, which includes all records from both tables and combines those that match the join condition into one record in the result set.
8. Expression builder dialog box allows you to create any valid FoxPro expression.
9. The Query Destination dialog box from has following options: Browse, Cursor, Table, Graph, Screen, Report and Label.
10. You can run your query from Query menu.
11. Cross Tab wizard is a powerful tool which allows you to change the positioning of the data.
12. You can create queries with multiple condition using OR and AND logical operators.
13. Visual FoxPro allows you to compare using > (more than) or < (less than) comparators, while performing query.
14. You can also use AND condition in the Query.

Multiple Choice Questions

1. Query works on :
   (a) Table (b) Forms
   (c) Reports
2. You can run Query from :
   (a) File menu (b) Query menu
   (c) Edit menu
3. Query can have multiple conditions using Or and :
   (a) OR (b) TO
   (c) AND
4. FoxPro expression can be created using :
   (a) Query Builder
   (b) Expression Builder
   (c) Design Builder
5. Inner join, which includes only the records from two tables that fulfill the condition of:
   (a) Match (b) Do not match
   (c) Nil
6. __________ includes all records from both tables and combines those that match the join condition into one record in the result set.
   (a) Right outer join (b) Left outer join
   (c) Full outer join

True/False Questions

1. Query means asking question to the software and getting the result from it.
2. You can call the query wizard from the Edit menu and Wizards submenu.

3. For creating a Query, after clicking at New in the File menu, Select Query and click at New File.
4. Inner join, which includes only the records from both tables that match the join condition.
5. Left outer join, which includes all records from the table on the left and records that match the join condition from the table on the right.
6. Right outer join, which includes all records from the table on the right and those records that match the join condition from the table on the left.
7. Full outer join, which includes all records from both tables and combines those that match the join condition into one record in the result set.
8. Expression builder dialog box does not allow you to create any valid FoxPro expression.
9. The Query Destination dialog box from has following options: Browse, Cursor, Table, Graph, Screen, Report and Label.
10. You cannot run your query from Query menu.
11. Cross Tab wizard is a powerful tool which allows you to change the positioning of the data.
12. You can create queries with multiple condition using OR and AND logical operators.
13. Visual FoxPro allows you to compare using > (more than) or < (less than) comparators, while performing query.
14. You can also use AND condition in the Query.

Matching Columns

Match the text in Column A with the text in Column B.

Column A	Column B
1. Query	a. For creating valid expressions
2. Query Wizard	b. Wizard which allows you to change positioning of the data
3. Inner Join	c. Box which allows you to send queries
4. Expression Builder	d. All records from table on the left
5. Query Destination Box	e. Easier way to create query
6. Cross Tab Wizard	f. All records from the table on the right
7. Left Outer Join	g. Getting information from the table
8. Right Outer Join	h. Joining of two tables for matching fields

Fill in the Blanks with Appropriate Words

a. Query Wizard   b. Query Destination Box   c. Inner Join   d. Queries
e. Cross Tab Wizard   f. Expression Builder

1. To get information from the table we use ___________.
2. ______________ allows you to build valid expressions.
3. Wizard which allow you to change the positioning of the data is called ________________.
4. You can create query using ___________.

5. The dialog box which allows you to select the destination of a query is called ______.
6. When two tables are joined on matching fields the join is called the ______.

Descriptive Type Questions

1. What is a Query?
2. How would you create a query using Query Wizard?
3. What all the different panels on the dialog box?
4. What do you understand by Order By and Group By conditions?
5. Describe the various possible destinations of the query.
6. How would you run the query?
7. What does the Cross Tab Wizard do?
8. How would you use a query?
9. How would you use OR condition in the query?
10. How is AND condition used in the query?

Answers to Objective Type Questions

Multiple Choice Questions

1. a	2. b	3. c	4. b
5. a	6. c		

True/False Questions

1. T	2. F	3. T	4. T
5. T	6. T	7. T	8. F
9. T	10. F	11. T	12. T
13. T	14. T		

Matching Columns

1. g	2. e	3. h	4. a
5. c	6. b	7. d	8. f

Fill in the Blanks with Appropriate Words

1. d	2. f	3. e	4. a
5. b	6. c		

Recommended Readings

1. Learn to Program Visual Basic—Databases *by John Smiley*.
2. Learn to Program Visual Basic—Objects *by John Smiley*.
3. Learn to Program Visual Basic—Examples *by John Smiley*.

—Published by Firewall Media (An Imprint of Laxmi Publications Pvt. Ltd.)

8 Working with Forms

Generally, a form is used to fill in the data which forms part of a table. Each application in Visual FoxPro has atleast one form. Some may have more than one. Creating a Form is very easy. Since it is related to a table, you must have the table opened before you proceed further for creating of a form. The best way to create form as usual is the Wizard method.

CREATING A FORM USING WIZARD

From the Tools menu, select Wizards and Form to get a dialog box. This asks you whether you want to create a one to many form wizard or just form wizard. We would simply use a form wizard. This would lead to various screens of the wizards.

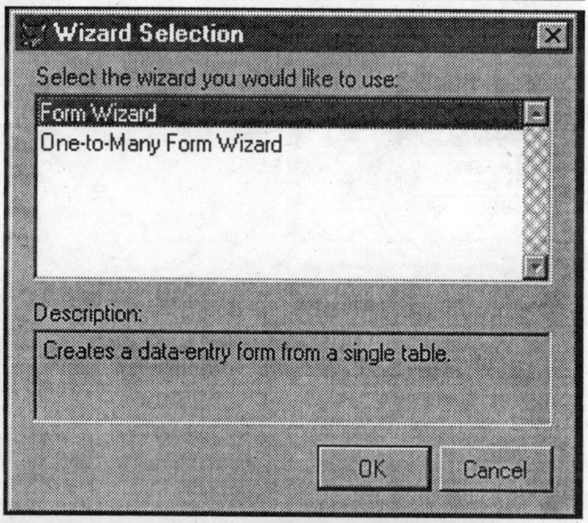

Step1 asks you to select fields which you want to use in the form from the table.

Choosing Fields

In the Available fields: list box, click Add All (>>) button (the one with two right pointing arrows) to select all the fields. The selected fields are now listed in the Selected fields: list box. Scroll through the list. Your screen should be as shown in the following figure.

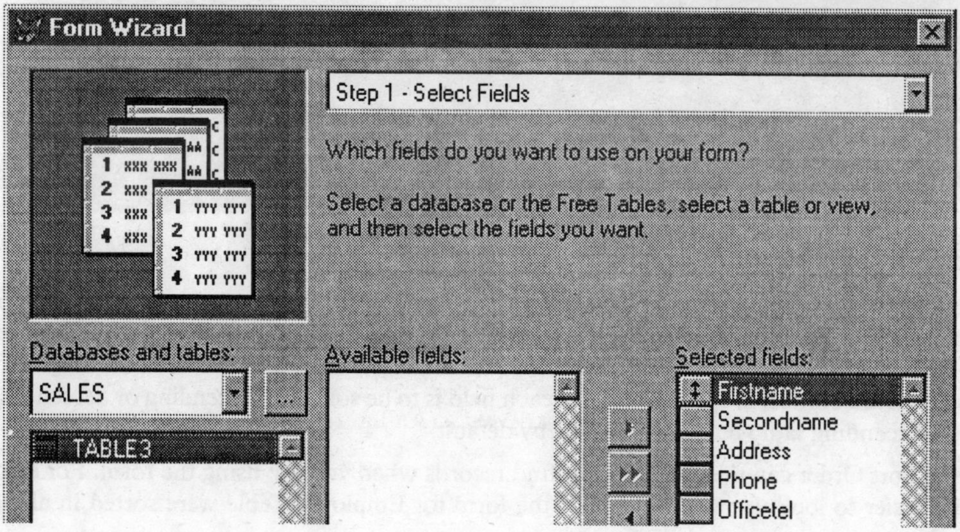

Choosing a Style

Next you have to select the style which you want to use on your form. Here you are given different styles to choose from: Standard, Chiseled, Shadowed, Boxed or Embossed.

The other options on the screen are: Standard colored area; Chiseled with three-dimensional lower border, Shadowed with the area having a shadowed line below and to the right; Boxed which is quite different because it puts both the prompt and the edit area into a box and changes the font to a bold typeface and finally Embossed, which has a classy three-dimensional look.

The magnifying glass view at the top of the screen will change with each selection to show you an example of the style you have just selected.

Button type options are: verify that text buttons is selected. In this screen, you also choose which style navigation buttons you prefer or whether you would like to use scrolling grid to navigate through your table.

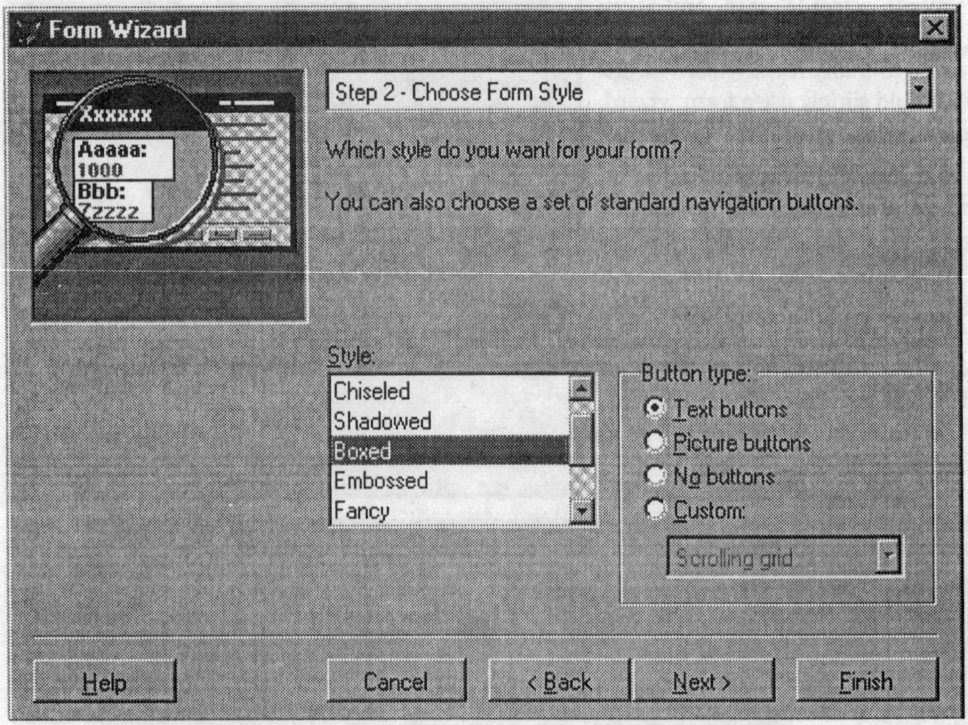

Choosing Sort Order

Next you are prompted to specify the Sort order to the table's records. You can add up to three fields on which to sort by clicking each desired field in the Available fields: list box. From the lists of fields, double click on Name field to move this field from Available field: list box to the Sort order or records list. Use the radio buttons to specify whether each field is to be sorted in Ascending or descending order. Note that Ascending radio button is selected by default.

Specifying Sort Order can make it easier to find records when you are using the form. For example, it would be easier to look up on Employee if the form for Employee Table were sorted in alphabetical order by Name.

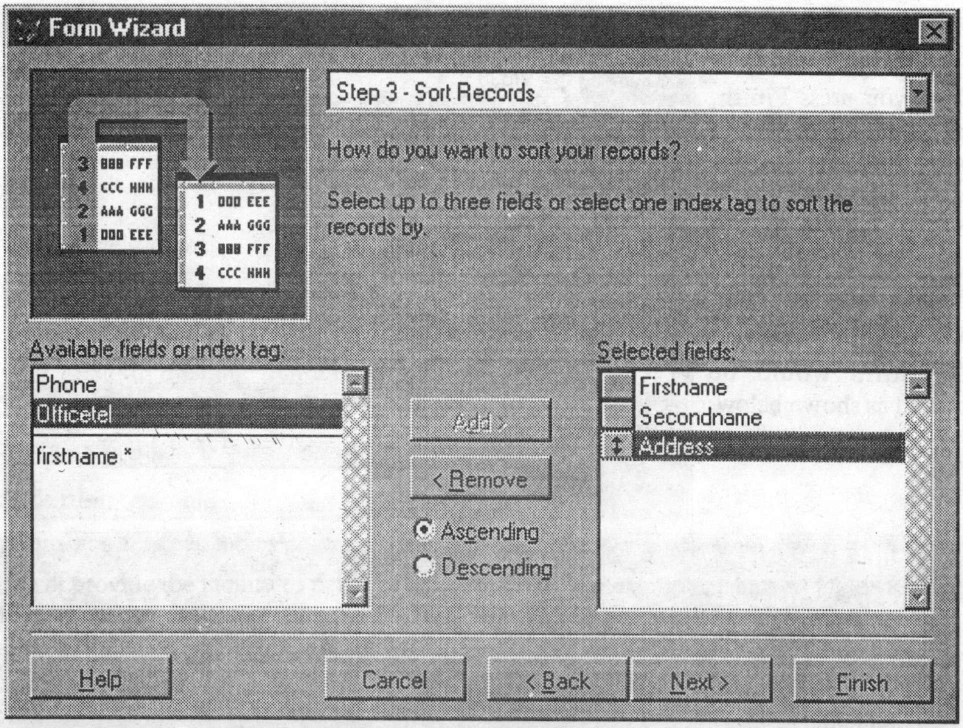
Form Wizard
Step 3 - Sort Records
How do you want to sort your records?
Select up to three fields or select one index tag to sort the records by.
Available fields or index tag:
Phone
Officetel
firstname *
Selected fields:
Firstname
Secondname
Address
Add >
< Remove
Ascending
Descending
Help
Cancel
< Back
Next >
Finish

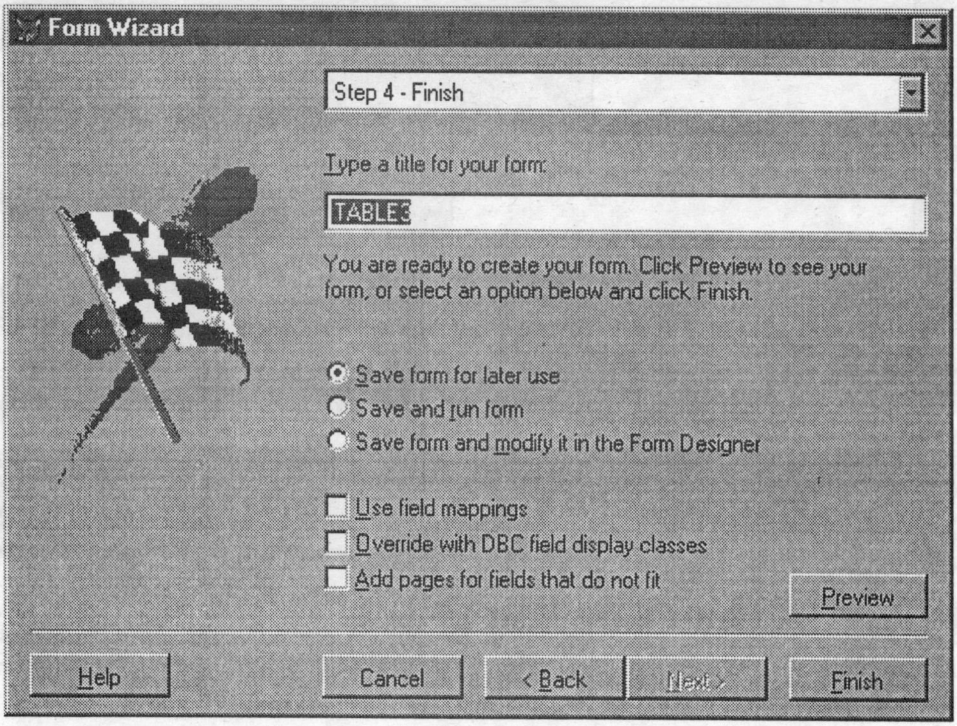
Form Wizard
Step 4 - Finish
Type a title for your form:
TABLE3
You are ready to create your form. Click Preview to see your form, or select an option below and click Finish.
Save form for later use
Save and run form
Save form and modify it in the Form Designer
Use field mappings
Override with DBC field display classes
Add pages for fields that do not fit
Preview
Help
Cancel
< Back
Next >
Finish

Generating the Form

Once you press Finish, the system asks you to save the form with a name.

This name should preferable be linked with the table. It will be saved with extension .SCX.

The form would be created as shown below.

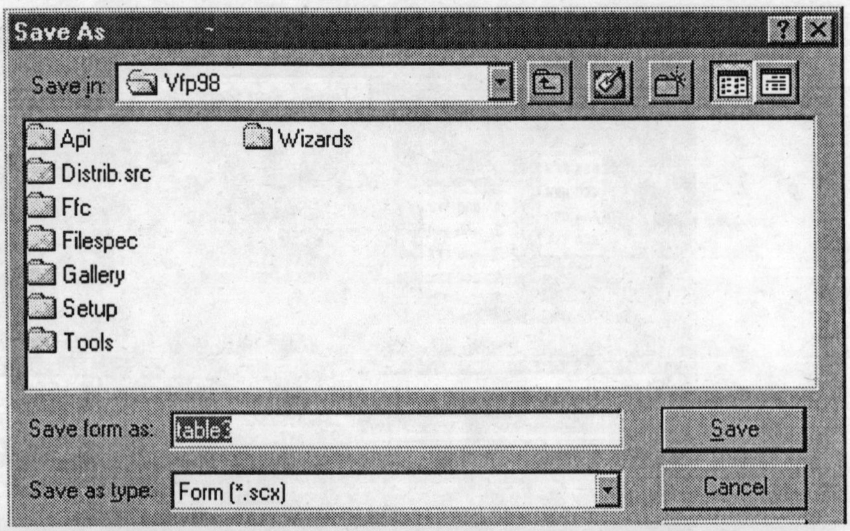

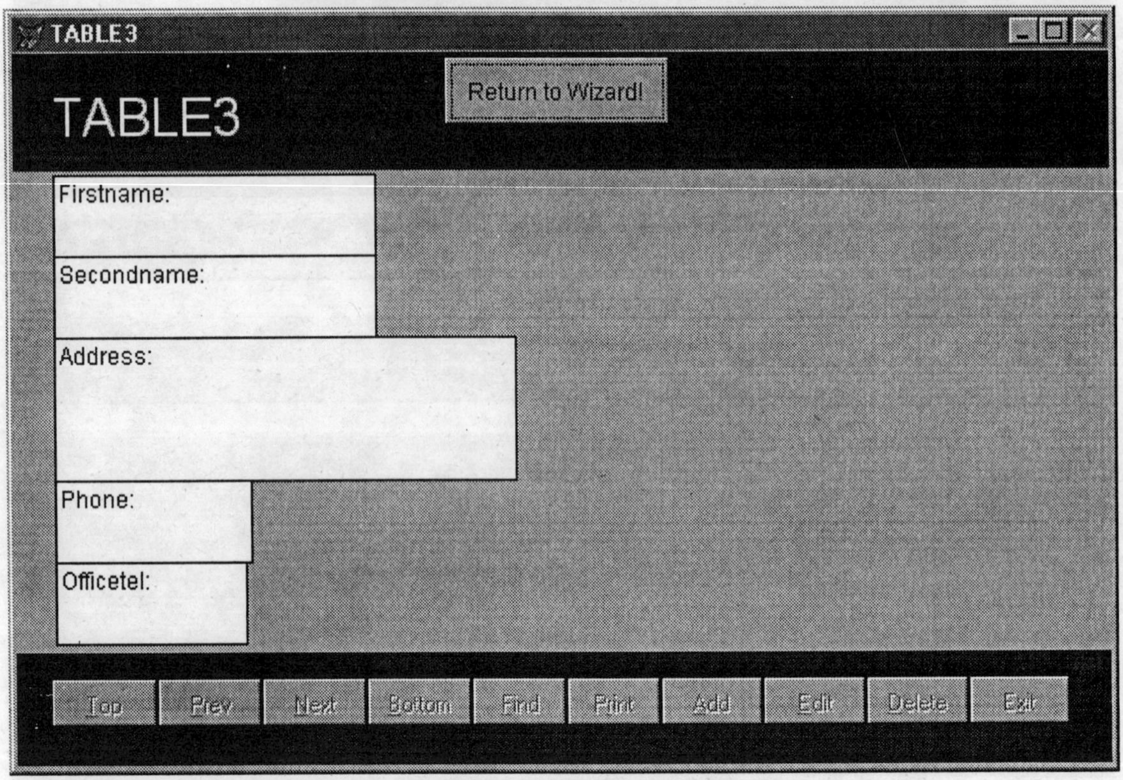

USING THE FORM'S CONTROL PANEL

The set of buttons at the bottom of the form are also called its Control panel. These buttons make it easy to work with the form.

These buttons are explained in the following table.

Button	*Description*
Top	Moves record point to first record
Prev	Moves record point back one record
Next	Moves record pointer forward one record
Bottom	Moves record pointer to last record
Print	Prints a report
Find	Displays the Search dialog box.
Add	Adds a new record to the end of the table.
Edit	Allows user to change values in current record.
Delete	Deletes current record
Exit	Closes form.

CREATING FORM USING FORM DESIGNER

Another method of creating Form is through the Form Designer which can be accessed by clicking New from the File menu. This would lead to the common dialog box from where you click at the Form and New File. Remember, you table must be open at this stage.

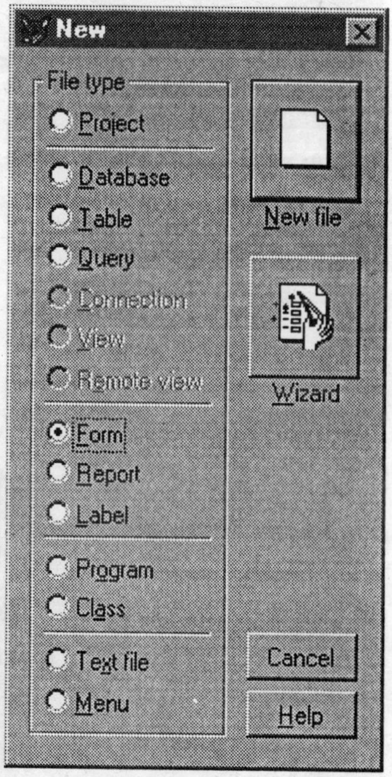

This would open up the Form Designer dialog box. Also it will give you the Form designer toolbox. On the toolbox click the one which opens the Data Environment form. This form, as shown here, has all the fields of the table.

Pick these fields one by one and place them on the form where you want to place them. Each field will make two boxes. One for the data and the other for the heading of the field. You may have to make some adjustments before reaching the final form.

A rough layout of the form is shown on the next page.

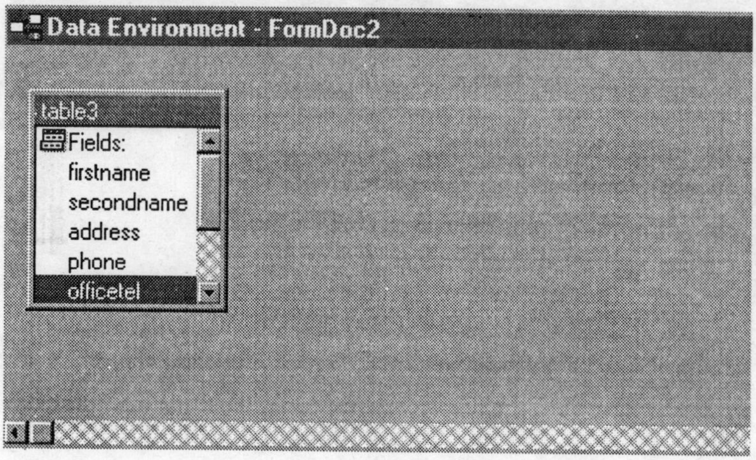

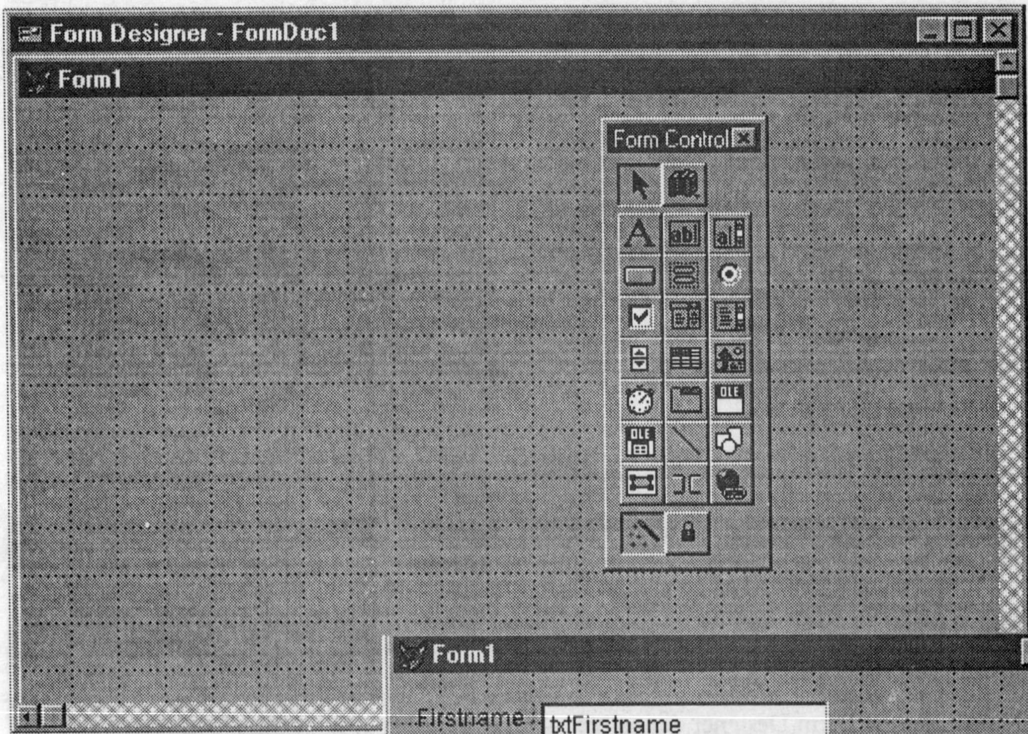

As you must have noticed that a Form Designer form has a properties dialog box alongwith it. This has various panels. The panels are:

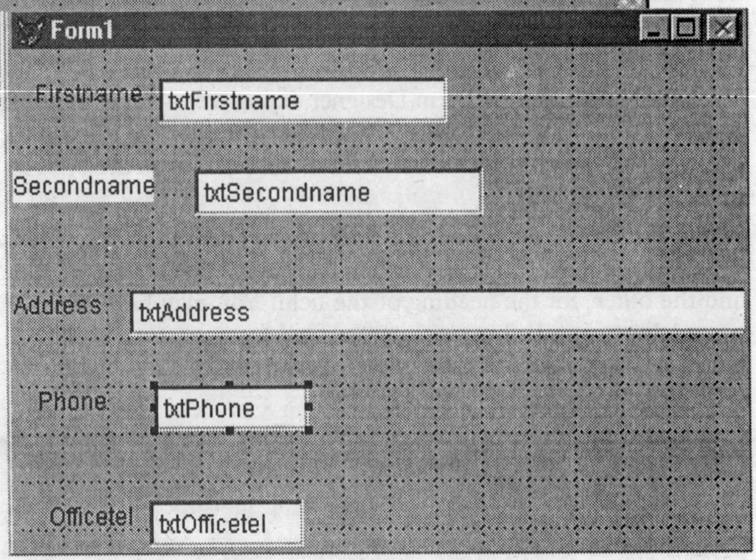

All

It has all PEM setting for the object specified, including user-defined properties and objects.

Data

This shows only those properties related to the data for the control.

Methods

This shows all methods and events, including user-defined methods.

Layout

This shows all the native Visual FoxPro properties related to the physical apperance of the obect.

Other

This shows all the native Visual FoxPro properties that do not fit logically into the Data or Layout categories.

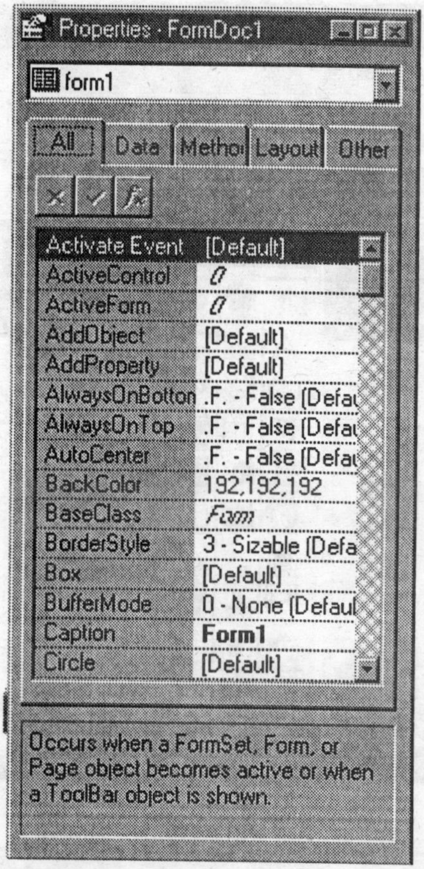

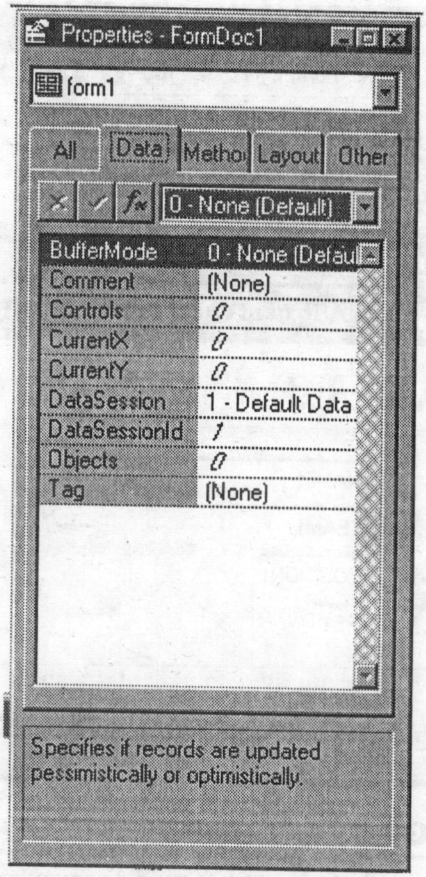

AUTOFORMS

You can create AutoFom by clicking at the AutoForm button on the Standard toobar. Rest everything is done by the software and in a flash you will see the form on the screen.

The form shows the field names and a text box to let you enter data in every field.

For memo fields, it includes a scrollable text box. If the memo field is too large to fit in the box, the scroll bar is activated so you can view it completely.

The form also includes buttons that make it easy to perform such basic operations as viewing, editing, and adding data.

RUNNING A FORM

Now that you have created a form, using it is quite easy. Just type the following command in the command window, or include it in your code:

```
DO FORM FROM1
```

This way you can run the form.

The other way of running is to double the form icon in the Open dialog box.

You can also Run Form from the Form menu. Form generated for Table3 is shown on the next page.

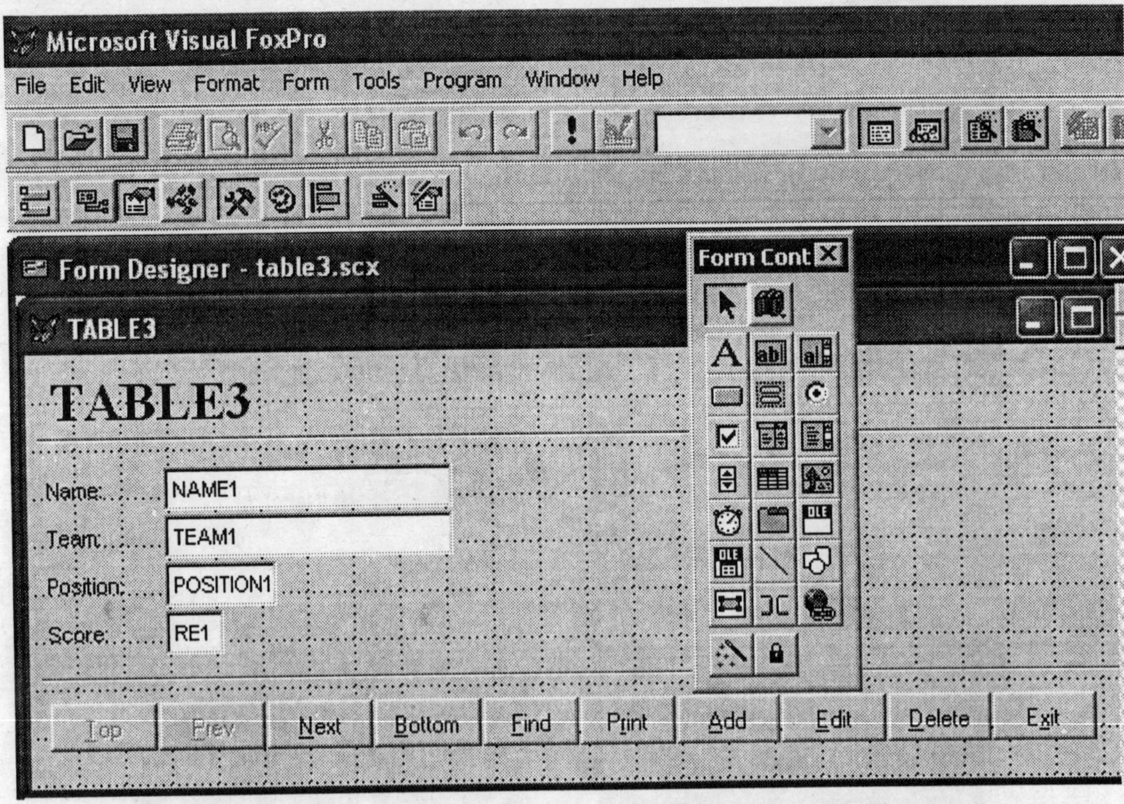

USING FORMS

You can use the form as you would do any other similar form. Mostly using the arrow and tab keys. Tab would allow you to go to the next field and arrow keys would allow you to move from one field to another. You can click on Next record to display next record. Click on Previous record to see the last record. Click on Exit to close the form.

What's more you can change form's design any time. You can resize, move, and delete field objects. But, remember, if you change and omit a field, all the data in that field would be lost and there is no way of retrieving that data.

USING BUILDERS

You can use various builders to build forms too. A builder is like a wizard which enables you to quickly and easily define some of the basic behaviours and formats of a form and its controls.

The following builders can be made using the Form Designer.

AutoFormat Builder
Command Group Builder
Form Builder
List Box Builder
Text Box Builder
ComboBox Builder
Edit Box Builder
Grid Builder
Option Group Builder

For creating any builder right-click at object with the mouse and the respective builder dialog box would come up.

This dialog box would have panels which would ask for various data to be filled up. Fill up the required data in the suggested location or click at the desired button and press Ok.

The various screens of the Text Box Builder are shown here and on the next page.

You can similarly create various other builders.

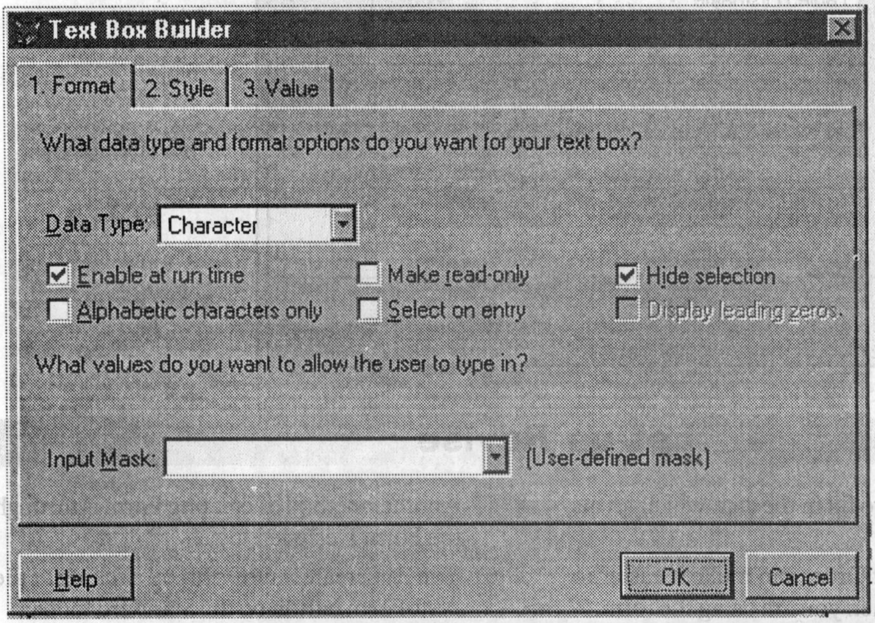

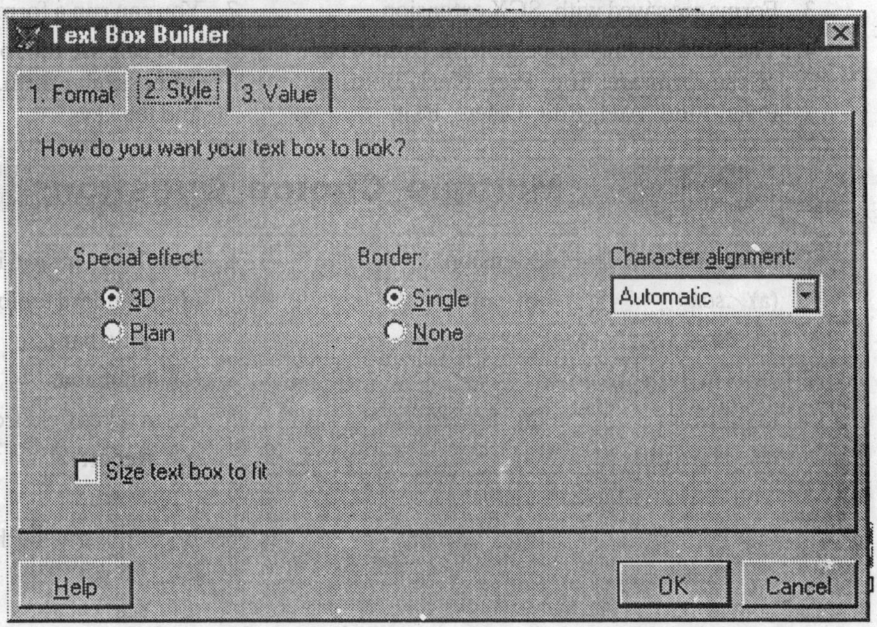

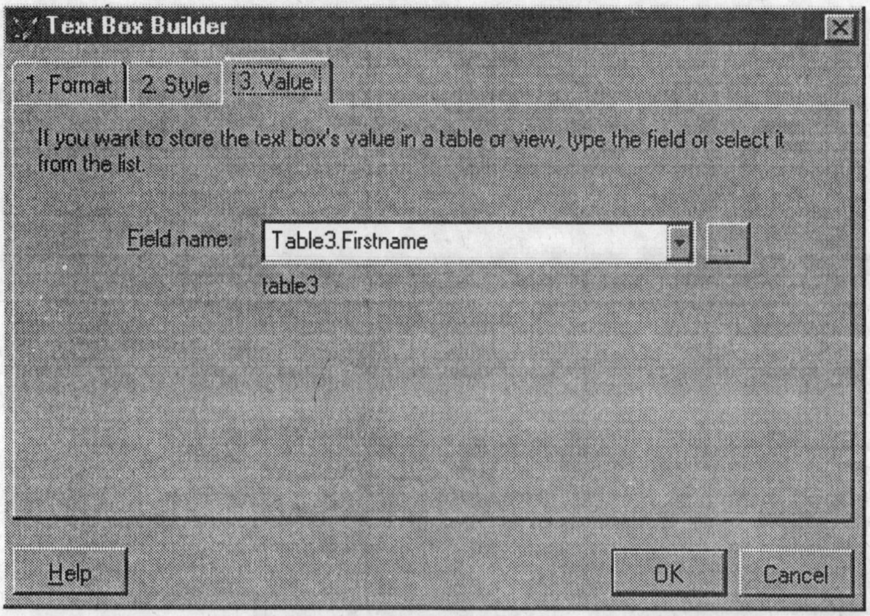

Let us Revise

1. A form is used to fill in the data which forms part of a table.
2. Specifying Sort Order can make it easier to find records when you are using the form.
3. Forms are saved with .SCX extension.
4. The buttons which appear on the control bar of the form are: Top, Prev, Next, Bottom, Print, Find, Add, Edit, Delete, Exit.
5. Another method of creating Form is through the Form Designer.
6. You can create AutoForm by clicking at the AutoForm button on the Standard toobar.
7. You can run a form from Form menu.
8. You can use the form as you would do any other similar form. Mostly using the arrow and tab keys.

Multiple Choice Questions

1. Forms are saved with extension:
   (a) .scx (b) .dbf
   (c) .frm
2. A form is displayed on :
   (a) Printer (b) Screen
   (c) Hard disk
3. You can run a form using the :
   (a) Form menu (b) File menu
   (c) Edit menu
4. AutoForm button is on :
   (a) Standard toolbar
   (b) Title bar
   (c) Menu bar
5. Form takes field from :
   (a) Report (b) Table
   (c) Wizard
6. Bottom is one of the buttons on the control bar of the form.
   (a) Yes (b) No

True/False Questions

1. A form is used to fill in the data which forms part of a table.
2. Specifying Sort Order can make it easier to find records when you are using the form.
3. Forms are saved with .DOC extension.
4. The buttons which appear on the control bar of the form are: Top, Prev, Next, Bottom, Print, Find, Add, Edit, Delete, Exit.
5. Another method of creating Form is through the Report Designer.
6. You can create AutoForm by clicking at the AutoForm button on the Standard toobar.
7. You can run a form from Edit menu.
8. You can use the form as you would do any other similar form. Mostly using the arrow and tab keys.

Matching Columns

Match the text in Column A with the text in Column B.

Column A	Column B
1. Form	a. Designing a form yourself
2. Form Wizard	b. Extension of form file name
3. AutoForm	c. Faster way of creating a form
4. Form Designer	d. From the Form menu
5. .SCX	e. Used to fill in data on the screen
6. Running the Form	f. A way of creating form

Fill in the Blanks with Appropriate Words

a. Print b. Add c. Find d. Next
e. Delete f. Top

Following buttons which are there on the form control bar are used for following purposes.

1. To move record point to the first record, you will use ________.
2. To move record pointer one record forward you will use _______.
3. To print a report, you will use the button ________.
4. To display the Search dialog box, you will use __________.
5. To add a new record at the end of the table, you will use the button _______.
6. To delete the current record, you will use the button ________.

Descriptive Type Questions

1. How would you create a form using the Form Wizard?
2. How would you use the Form's control panel?
3. What is AutoForms?
4. How would you run the Form?
5. How would you use the builders?
6. Describe the process of creating a form using the Form Designer.

Answers to Objective Type Questions

Multiple Choice Questions

1. a	2. b	3. a	4. a
5. b	6. a		

True/False Questions

1. T	2. T	3. F	4. T
5. F	6. T	7. F	8. T

Matching Columns

1. e	2. c	3. f	4. a
5. b	6. d		

Fill in the Blanks with Appropriate Words

1. f	2. d	3. a	4. c
5. b	6. e		

Recommended Readings

1. Learn to Program Visual Basic—Databases *by John Smiley*.
2. Learn to Program Visual Basic—Objects *by John Smiley*.
3. Learn to Program Visual Basic—Examples *by John Smiley*.

—Published by Firewall Media (An Imprint of Laxmi Publications Pvt. Ltd.)

9 Working with Reports

INTRODUCTION

Reports are the ways of presenting your table in any required form. It should be in such a way that it looks more presentable and is accurate. If possible the numeric fields should be totalled as grand total or group totals as the case maybe.

As usual we would first go through the Wizard method of creating the Report. It can be accessed from Tools menu and Wizard submenu. A number of wizard steps will appear on the screen from which you have to select the various options before moving further.

Once you have filled in the required information, press Next to go to the next screen.

Step1 will ask you to select the table and fields.

Step2 will ask you to group records.

In Step2, both the screens of Grouping and Summing options are also shown.

Step3 will ask you select the report style.

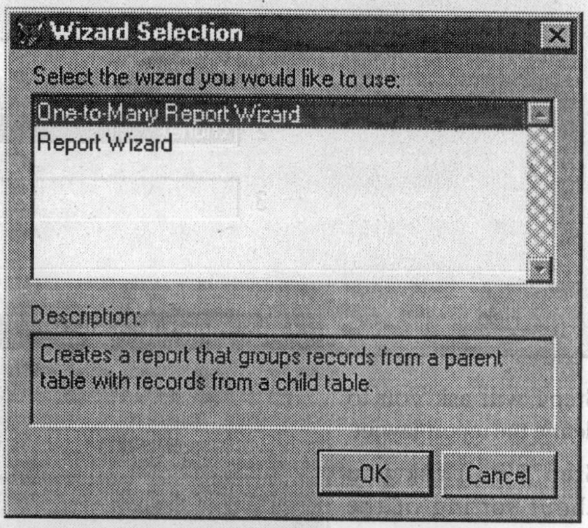

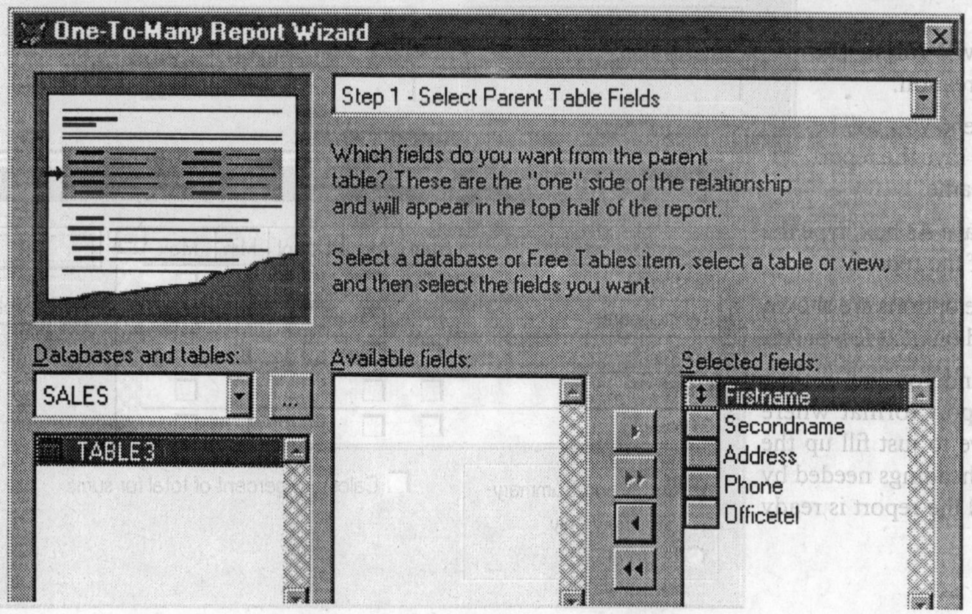

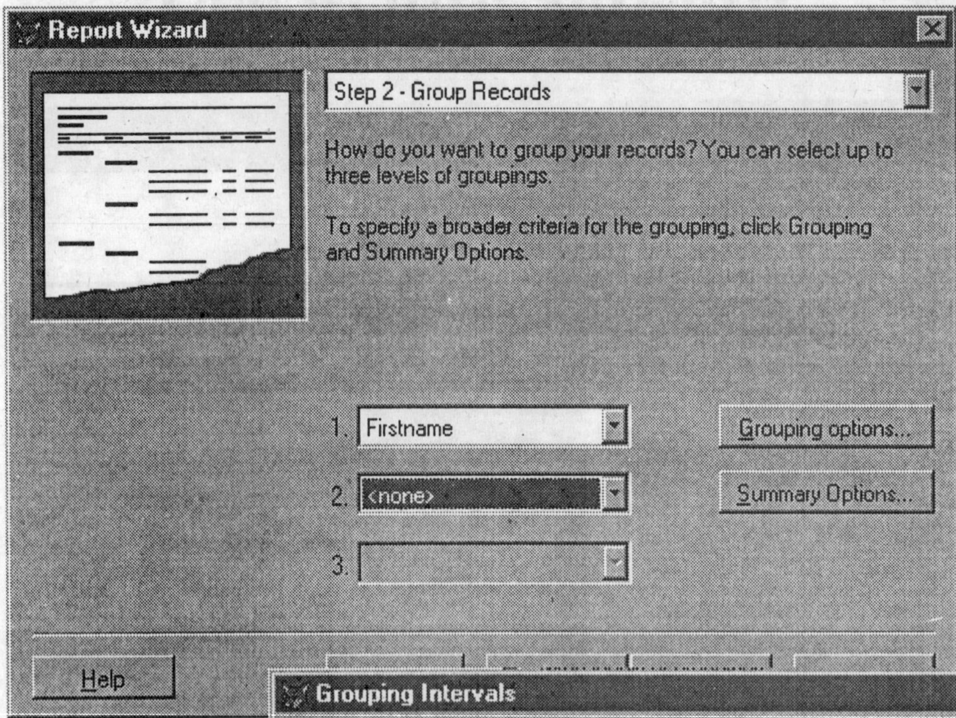

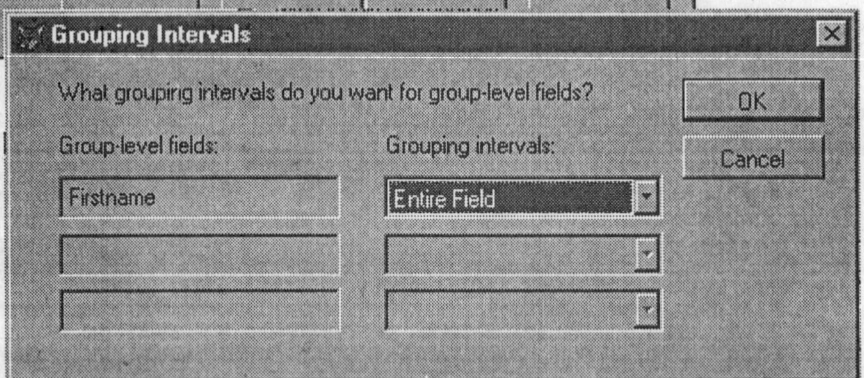

Step4 will ask you to define the report layout.

Step 5 will ask you about sorting of the records.

Step6 will finish the report creation.

After Step6 you will be asked to save the report with a name.

In the Save As box, type the name of the report.

All these options are shown here and on next few pages.

In the end you will get the final report format where you have to just fill up the type of headings needed by you and the report is ready for you.

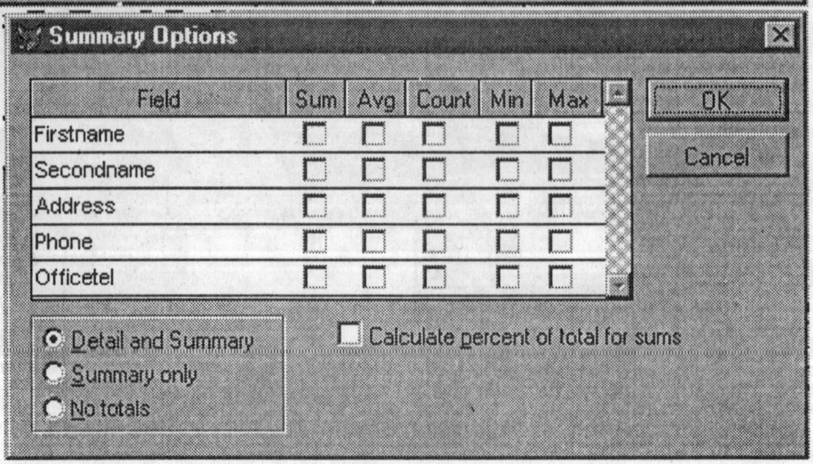

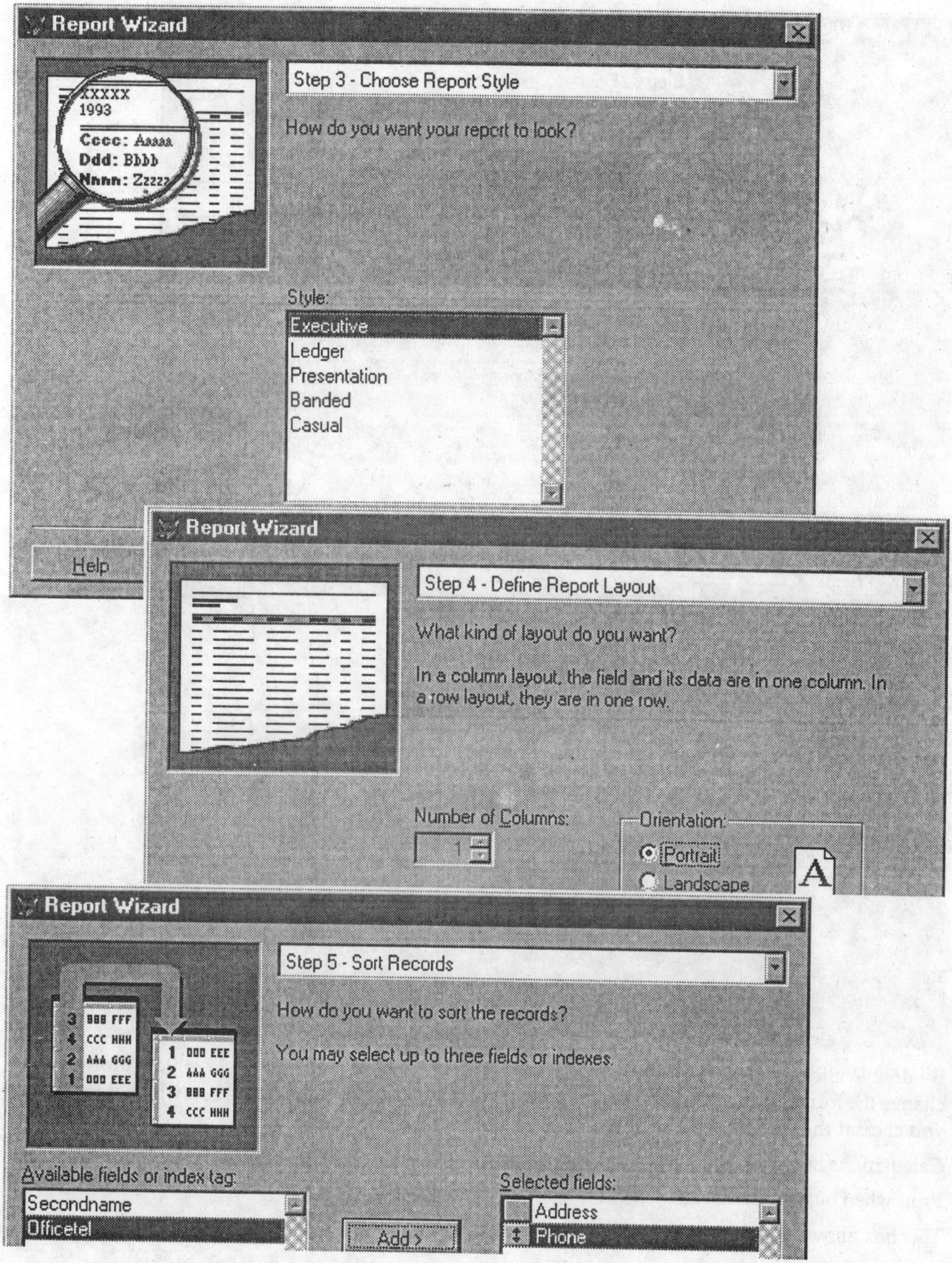
Report Wizard
Step 3 - Choose Report Style
How do you want your report to look?
Style:
Executive
Ledger
Presentation
Banded
Casual
Help
Report Wizard
Step 4 - Define Report Layout
What kind of layout do you want?
In a column layout, the field and its data are in one column. In a row layout, they are in one row.
Number of Columns:
1
Orientation:
Portrait
Landscape
Report Wizard
Step 5 - Sort Records
How do you want to sort the records?
You may select up to three fields or indexes.
Available fields or index tag:
Secondname
Officetel
Add >
Selected fields:
Address
Phone

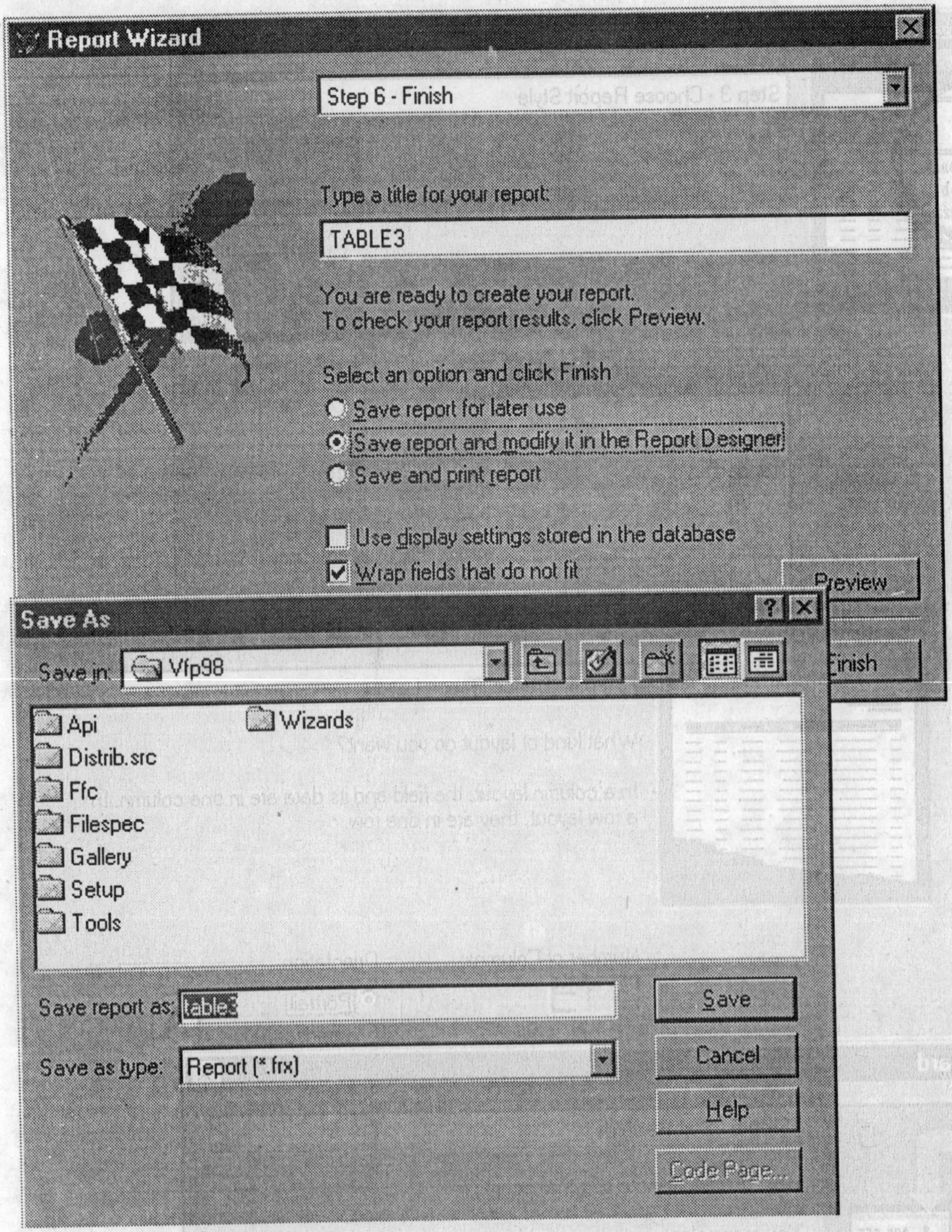

By double clicking at the fields you can get the Report Expression of that field which allows you to change the format from any of the format which you may select from the dialog box which it leads once you click at the ellipses.

Calculations button would lead to a dialog box which allows you to take average, etc. of the field.

Print when button when clicked leads to another dialog box.

This box allows you to use the various options, as shown above.

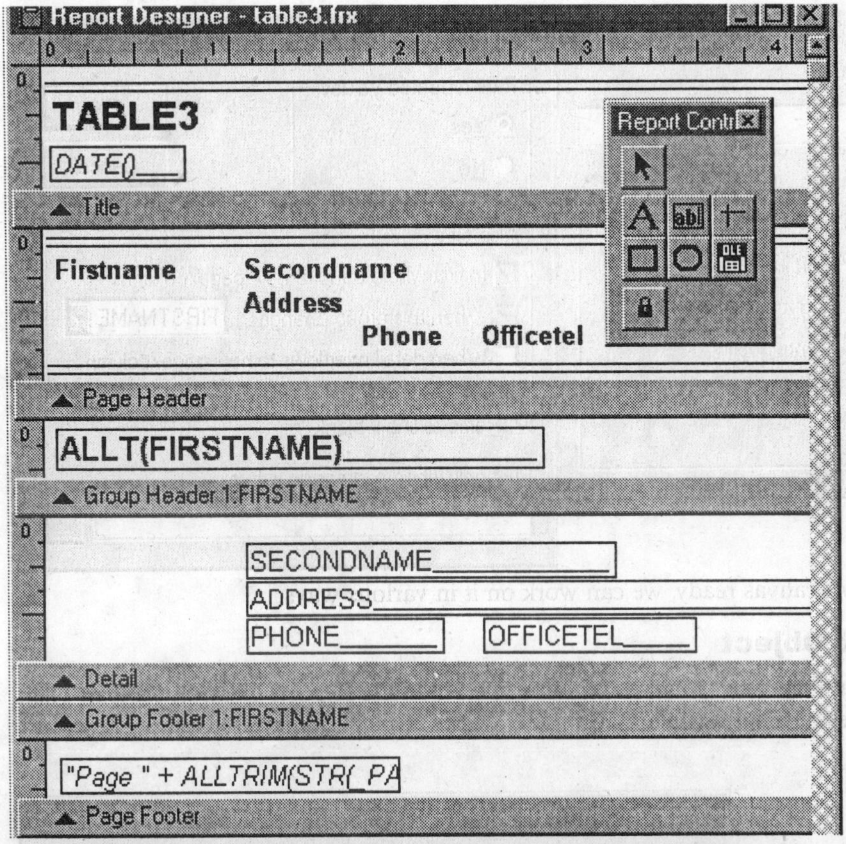
Report Designer - table3.frx
TABLE3
DATE()
Title
Firstname
Secondname
Address
Phone
Officetel
Page Header
ALLT(FIRSTNAME)
Group Header 1:FIRSTNAME
SECONDNAME
ADDRESS
PHONE
OFFICETEL
Detail
Group Footer 1:FIRSTNAME
"Page " + ALLTRIM(STR(_PA
Page Footer
Report Contr

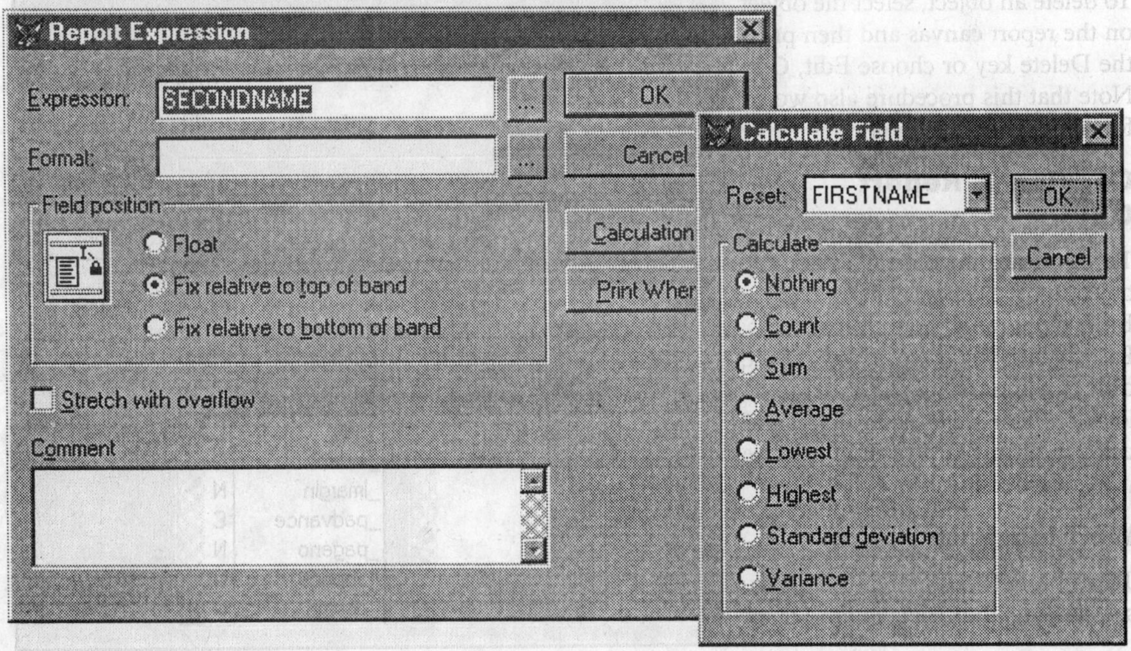
Report Expression
Expression:
SECONDNAME
Format:
OK
Cancel
Calculation
Print Wher
Field position
Float
Fix relative to top of band
Fix relative to bottom of band
Stretch with overflow
Comment
Calculate Field
Reset:
FIRSTNAME
OK
Cancel
Calculate
Nothing
Count
Sum
Average
Lowest
Highest
Standard deviation
Variance

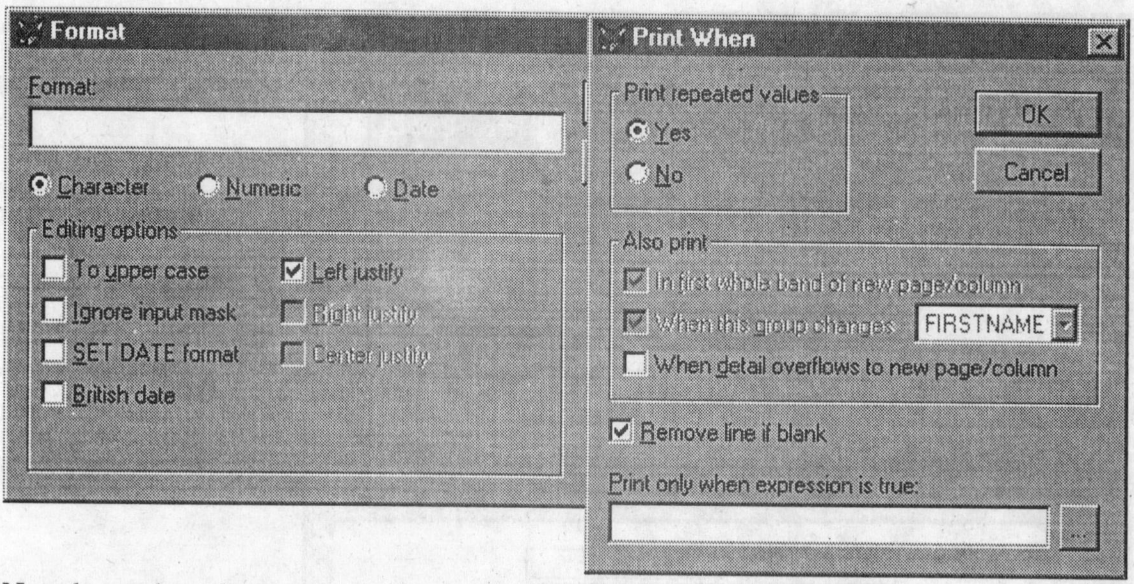

Now that we have the report canvas ready, we can work on it in various ways.

Selecting a Report Object

To select an object, make sure the Select Objects button is selected in the Reports Controls toolbar. Then point to and click on the desired type of object.

Deleting a Report Object

To delete an object, select the object on the report canvas and then press the Delete key or choose Edit, Cut. Note that this procedure also works for multiple selected items.

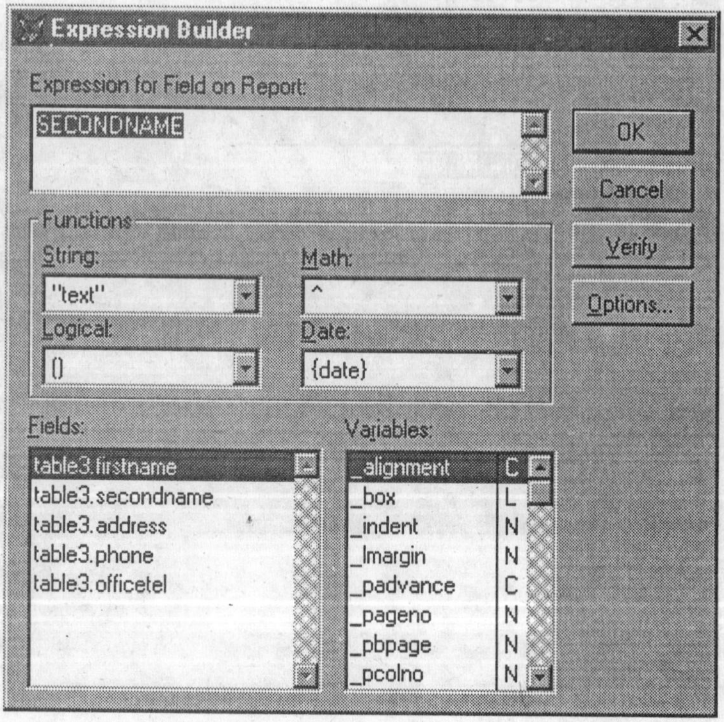

Copying a Report Object

To duplicate an object, select the object on the report canvas, choose Edit, Copy and then choose Edit, Paste. When you do so, a copy of the object appears near its original location. You can click the object and using the arrow keys or mouse, move it to a desired location.

Working with Fields

To add a field to the report canvas, select the textbox/field control from the Report Controls toolbar. When you click on the report canvas to add the control, the Report Expression dialog box appears, where you can specify several key properties, as follows:

Changing Field Expressions

The Expression text box includes the expression, field name, or function call that will evaluate to the data you want to show. You can type a field or expression into the box yourself, or you can use the ellipsis at the right to bring forward the Expression Builder, which includes a number of tools for helping you add data to your report, including a list of available fields.

Changing Field Formats

In the Format field of the Report Expression dialog box, you can enter formatting guidelines for the resulting text or numeric data. Clicking the ellipsis for this property accesses the Format dialog box. You can use this dialog box to quickly format the data you are showing on your report and then return to the Report Expression dialog box.

CREATING REPORT USING REPORT DESIGNER

As in the case of Table and Forms, you can create report too using the Designer. But, here you will have to mention everything yourself. For this do the following:

1. Open an existing table, in this case table3.dbf.
2. Type BROWSE in the command window to see the details of the records.
3. Press Esc to close the browse window.
4. Now type Create Report in the command window to have the Report Designer window on the screen.
5. Since the name has not been specified, it is giving the name as Report1.

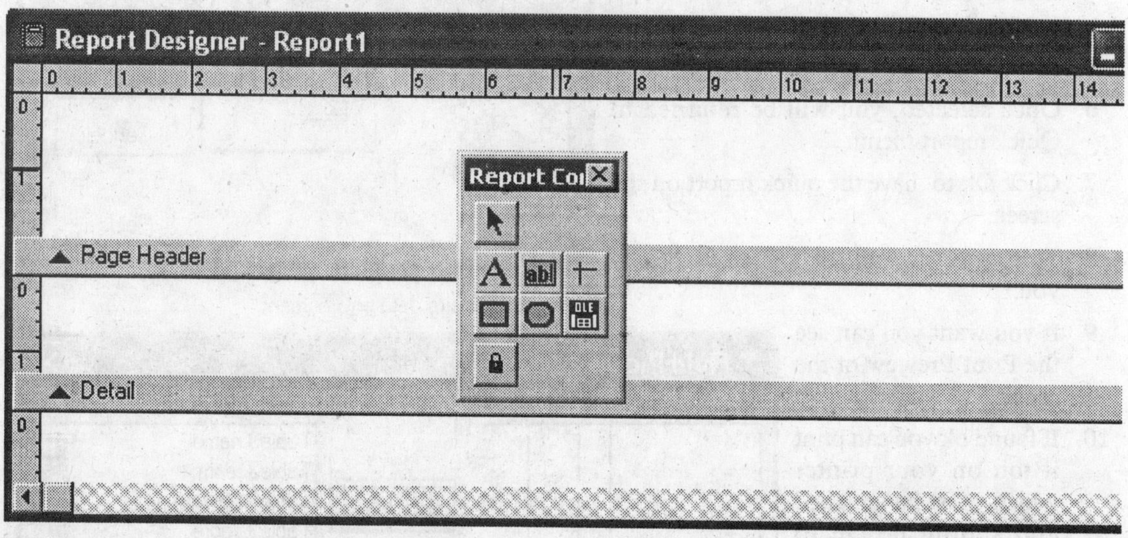

This screen as you can see is divided into 3 parts, Page Header, Detail and Page Footer (it is hidden here). We will fill up all 3 of them one by one. But, first let us see what each one of them should have.

In the Page Header, you will define the header of the report, or simply called the Report Heading. It should contain the name of the company, report name, various column heads, etc. Details will be used as the body of the report. Page Footer is similar to Page Header with the difference that it appears at the bottom instead of top. You can include it to have totalss, date, time, page number, etc.

GENERATING A QUICK REPORT

This is another method of creating a report quickly. Visual FoxPro does everything and creates the report for you, whether you like it or not. This is how it is done.

1. With the table open click at Report button on the toolbar.
2. You will get the Report Designer window on the screen.
3. From the Report menu, click at Quick Report.

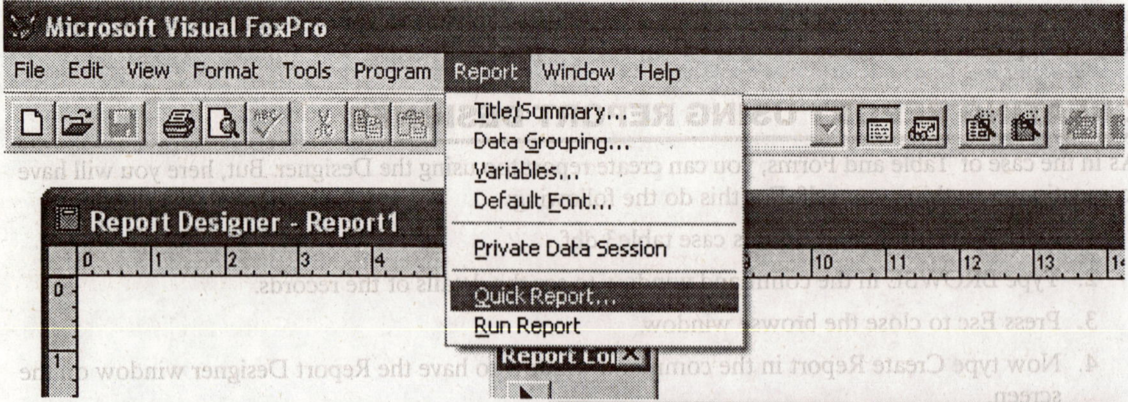

4. The first dialog box asks you to select the field layout.
5. If you click at Fields you get the Field Picker dialog box for selecting the fields.
6. Once selected, you will be returned to Quick report menu.
7. Click Ok to have the quick report on the screen.
8. This report has all the fields selected by you.
9. If you want you can see the Print Preview of the report.
10. If found ok you can print it too on your printer which must be attached and should be On to receive the report.
11. Preview of the report is shown on the next page.

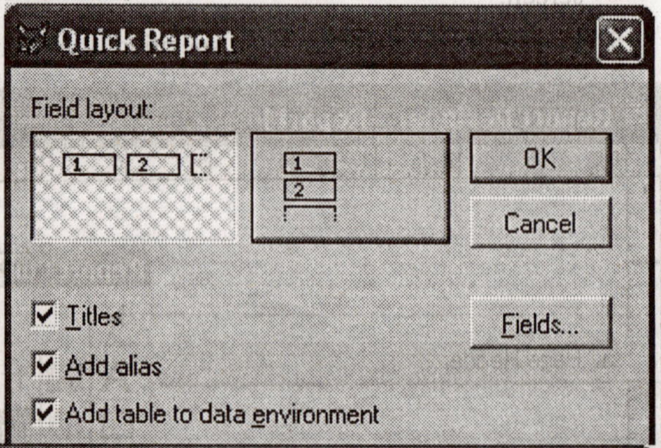

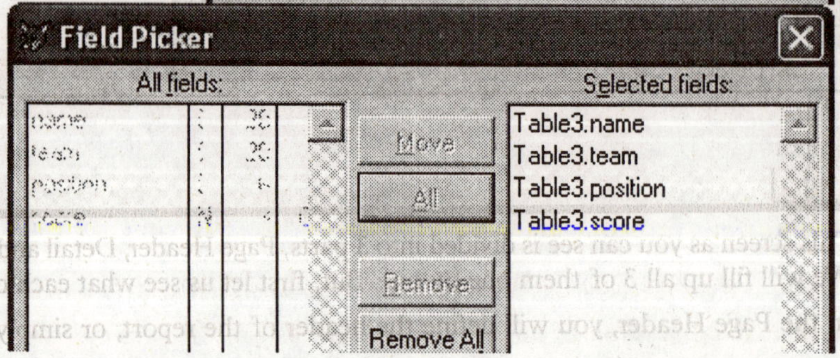

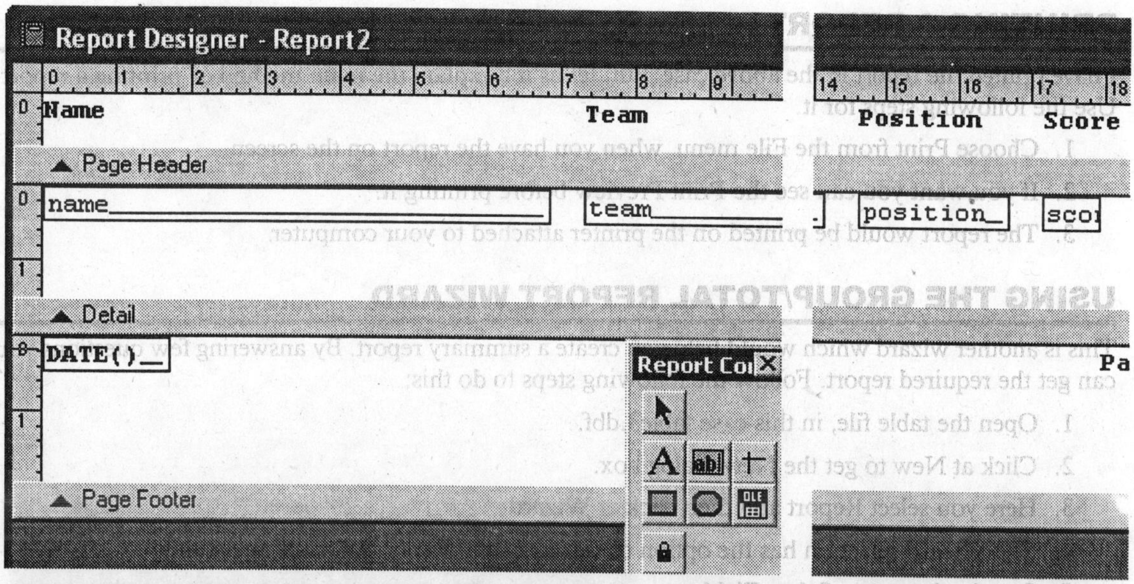

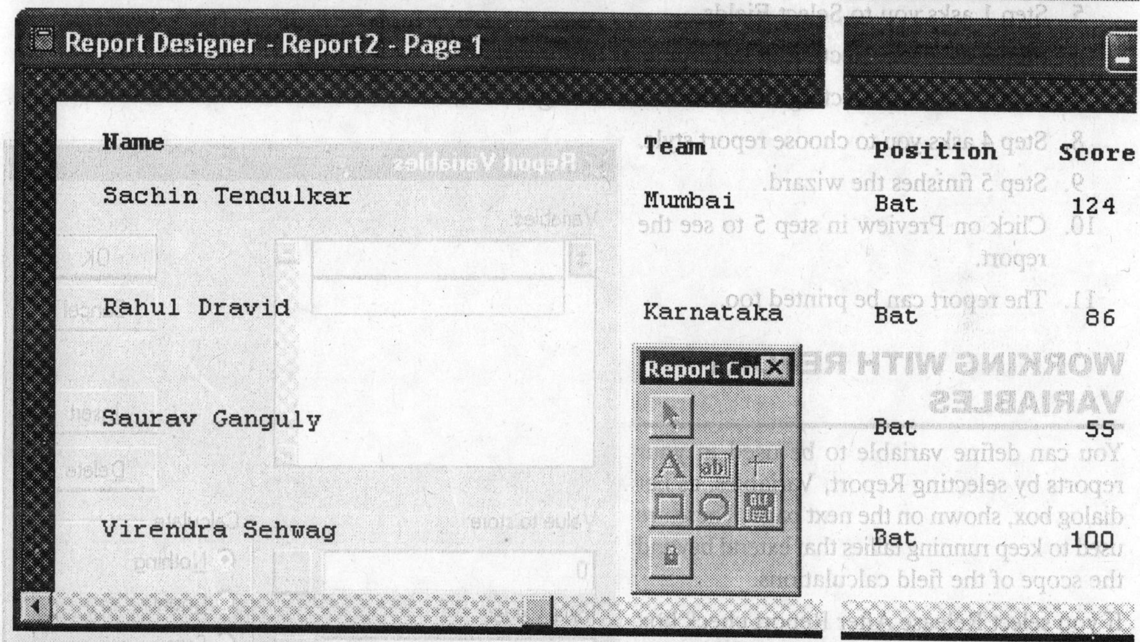

SAVING THE REPORT

Report is saved in Visual FoxPro with an extension .FRX. You can give a name of your choice to the report file. To save the report do the following:

1. Click on Save/Save As on the File menu.
2. Type the name.
3. Specify the desired drive and/or directory in which you wish to save the report.
4. Click on Save.

PRINTING A REPORT

I have printed the report in the above case. But, let us me explain the main method of printing a report. Use the following steps for it.

1. Choose Print from the File menu when you have the report on the screen.
2. If you want you can see the Print Preview before printing it.
3. The report would be printed on the printer attached to your computer.

USING THE GROUP/TOTAL REPORT WIZARD

This is another wizard which would help you create a summary report. By answering few questions you can get the required report. Follow the following steps to do this:

1. Open the table file, in this case table3.dbf.
2. Click at New to get the New dialog box.
3. Here you select Report and then click at Wizard.
4. The Wizard selection has the option of Group/Total Report Wizard. Select this.
5. Step 1 asks you to Select Fields.
6. Step 2 asks for selecting of Grouping of Records.
7. Step 3 asks for selecting the records for sorting.
8. Step 4 asks you to choose report style.
9. Step 5 finishes the wizard.
10. Click on Preview in step 5 to see the report.
11. The report can be printed too.

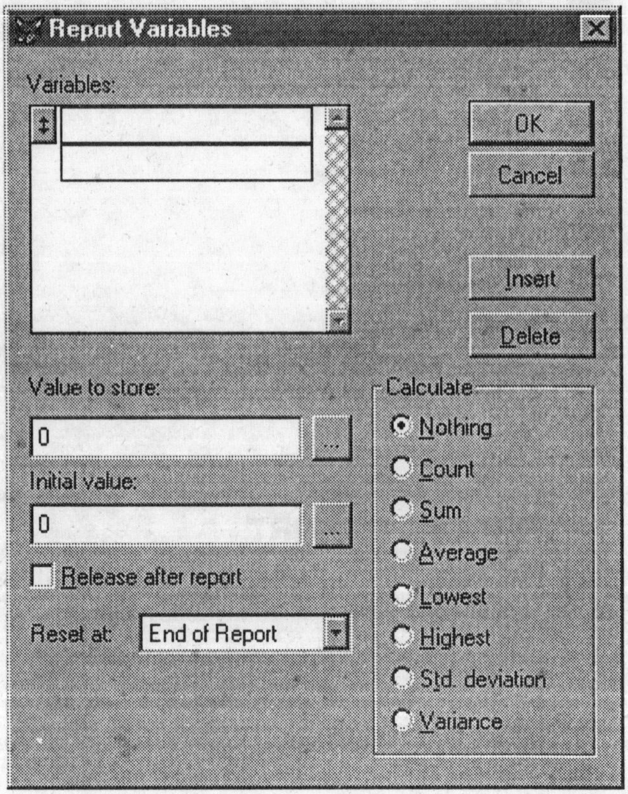

WORKING WITH REPORT VARIABLES

You can define variable to be used in your reports by selecting Report, Variables, as per dialog box, shown on the next page. These are used to keep running tallies that extend beyond the scope of the field calculations.

If you select Release After Report check box in the dialog box, the Report variables are scoped privately, which means that any user-defined function you call can access them. If you do not check this box, the variables will remain in memory as public variables. It is unlikely you would ever need to retain the variables in such a global scope.

WORKING WITH GRAPHICS AND PICTURES

Add text and shape objects is useful, but when your really want to decorate your report, attract attention to a particular piece of information, or just include a company logo, you can turn to a full-fledged graphics.

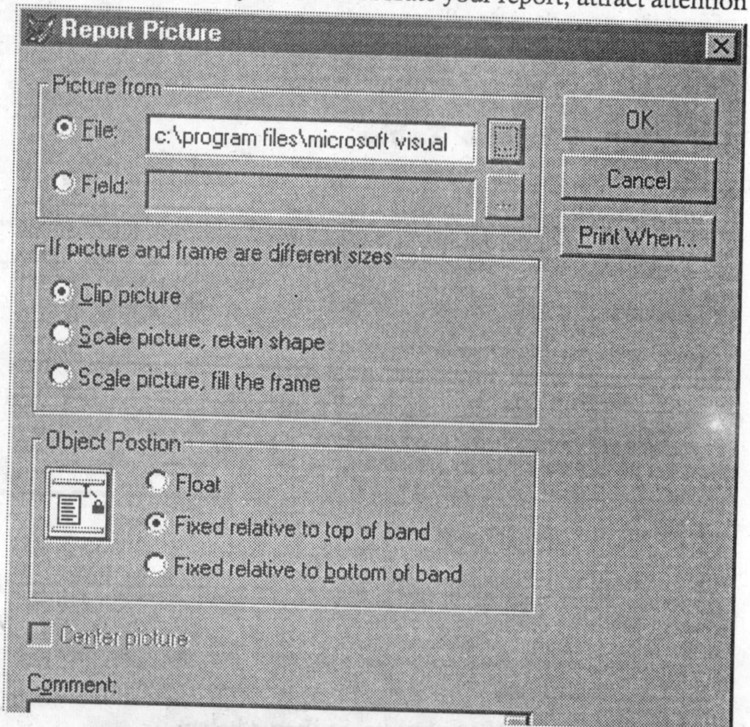

You can add graphics to a report from the general field of a Visual FoxPro table or from a file or from a file on disk.

You can add a picture to a report in the following manner:

1. Select the Pictures icon on the Report Controls toolbar.
2. Click at the staring point for the graphics and drag until the frame reaches the desired size for the picture. When you release the mouse, Report Picture dialog box appears.
3. Set the options to tell where to find the picture and how to size it relative to the band it is in.
4. Click Ok. The picture will appear in the report.

WORKING WITH SHAPES

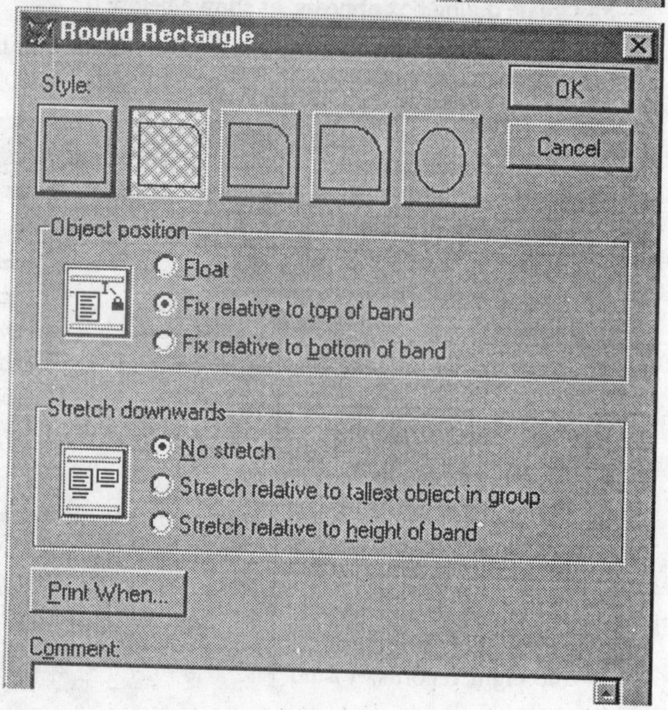

You can easily add a shape or a line of text to a report. Just select it and drop it, as you would any of the controls. But you can also determine the behaviours of shapes and text on a report.

Double click on the object in a report, and the dialog box appears. In this case I have taken the rounded rectangles option. As you can see there are 5 different options to choose from.

Click at one of them and you have the same in the report.

MAILING LABELS

FoxPro is very useful for creating and printing labels, specially the address labels. Because of its capabilities of arranging the data in different orders you can sort the data in different fields and print the labels, town wise, pin wise, name wise, etc. What's more you can design the size of your labels according to your choice. Let us create and print some labels.

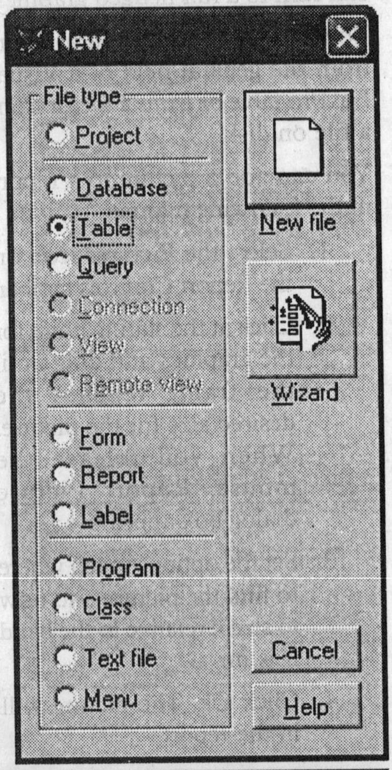

Creating Address Table

Let us create one table, table1.dbf with structure as given below:

Name	*Type*	*Width*
Code	N	4
Name	C	20
Address	C	20
City	C	8
Pin	N	6

Let us now create the table.

1. From the File menu choose New .... Option. A new dialog box appears.
2. Select Table button and click on New File option at the top of the dialog box.
3. Create dialog box appears, as shown below.
4. Type the file name as table1 in the Enter table text box and click on Save button. A table Designer dialog box appears as shown on the next page.
5. Now fill the structure.
6. Click on OK button. Visual FoxPro shows a dialog box and ask if you want to input data records now.
7. Press Y to select Yes button or click with the mouse on yes button.

   Visual FoxPro displays a blank record for data entry. Now enter the following records into the table.

   After you have entered all the eight records, Visual

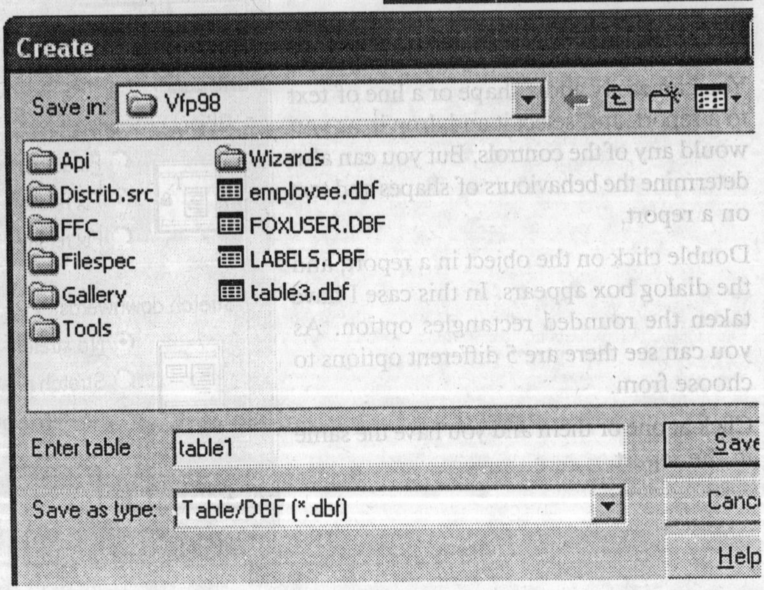

FoxPro displays the next empty record on the screen. Press Ctrl + W to save the data entered.

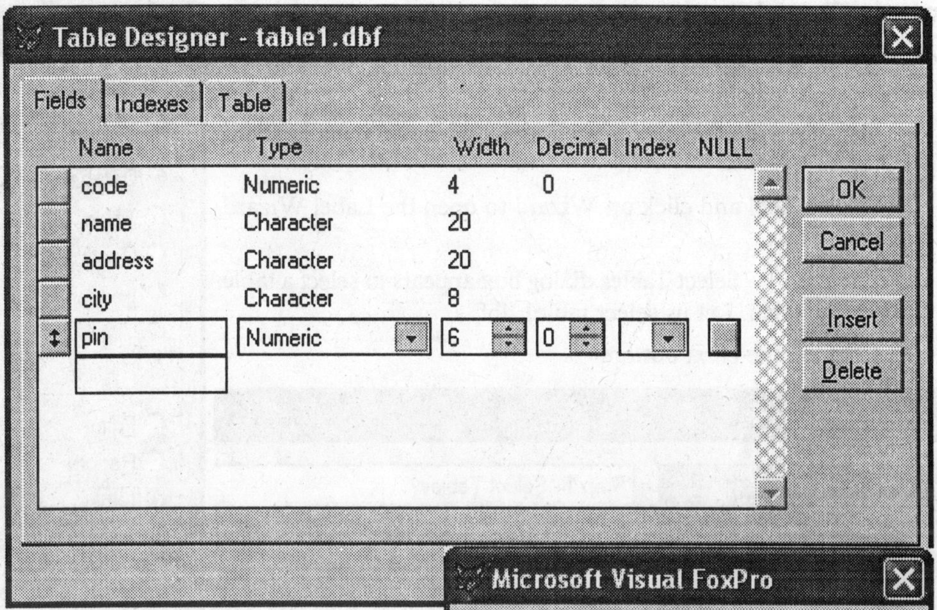

If you want you can view the data by choosing Browse from the View menu.

10. Press Esc key to close the Browse mode.

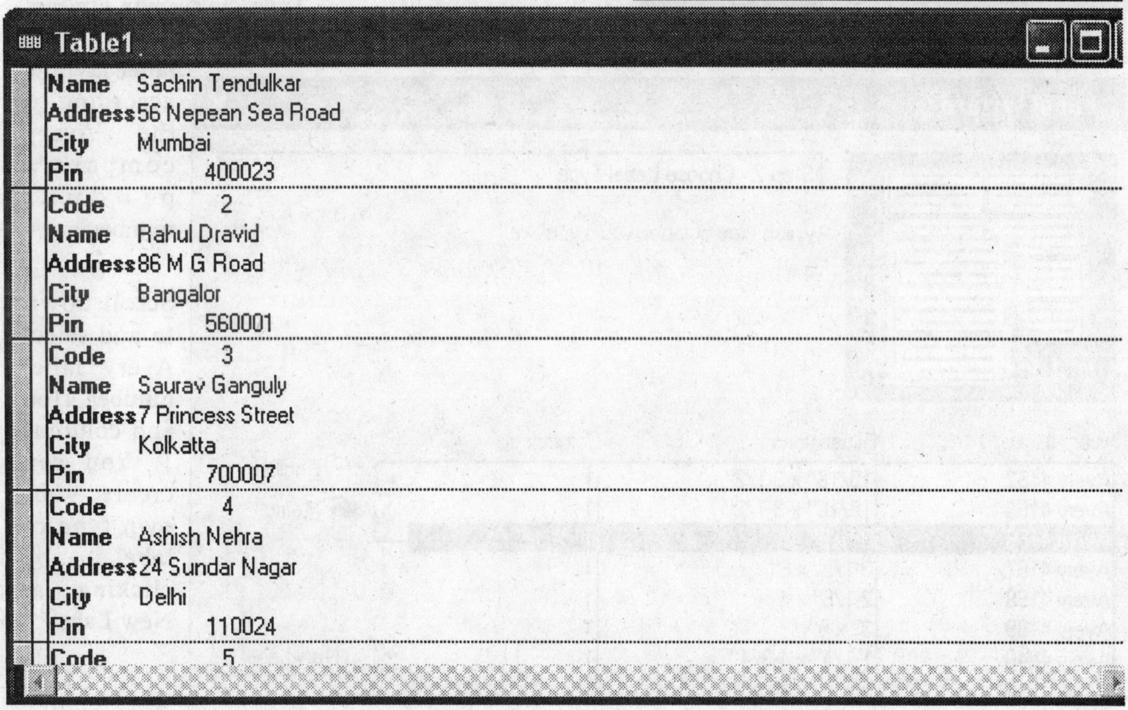

Label Wizard

Now, we come to the other part, i.e., creating labels using Label Wizard.

1. Open the New dialog box by clicking on New icon on Standard toolbar.
2. Select Label and click on Wizard to open the Label Wizard dialog box.
3. The Step 1 – Select Tables dialog box appears to select a table for the label. Let us select table1.dbf
4. Click on the Next button.

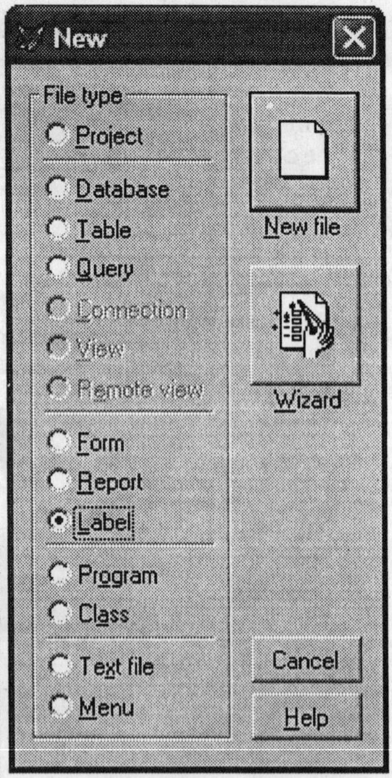

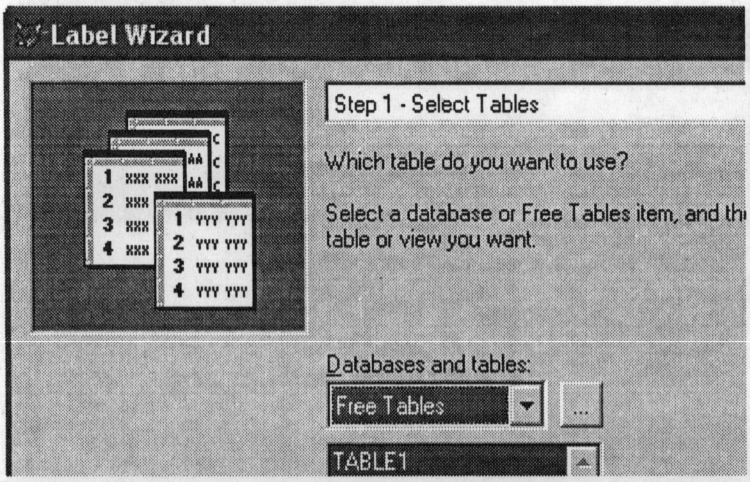

5. The Step 2 – Choose Label Type dialog box appears with listing of various label layouts according to the Avery company's product numbers.
6. Scroll down to and select Avery label number 4166 and columns 1. You can create your own type of label by clicking at New Label.

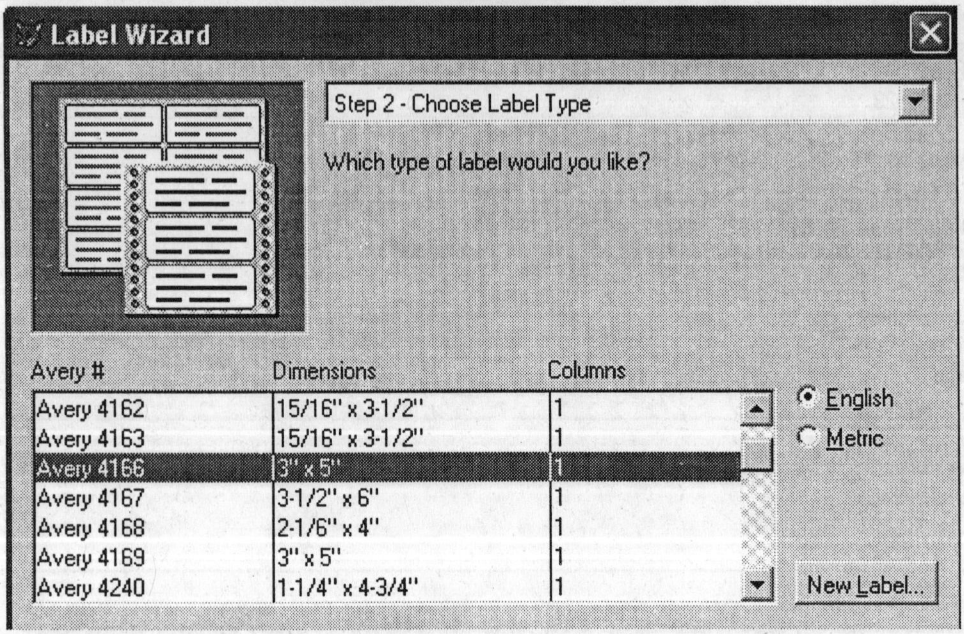

7. Click on Next > button.
8. The Label Step – 3 Define Layout window opens.
9. In the Step – 3 Define Layout dialog box, add the Fields in the order you want them to appear on the Label. You can use the punctuation, space and newline buttons to format the label. Use the Text box to add text.

   Here I have moved all the fields with comma (,) in between and a space.

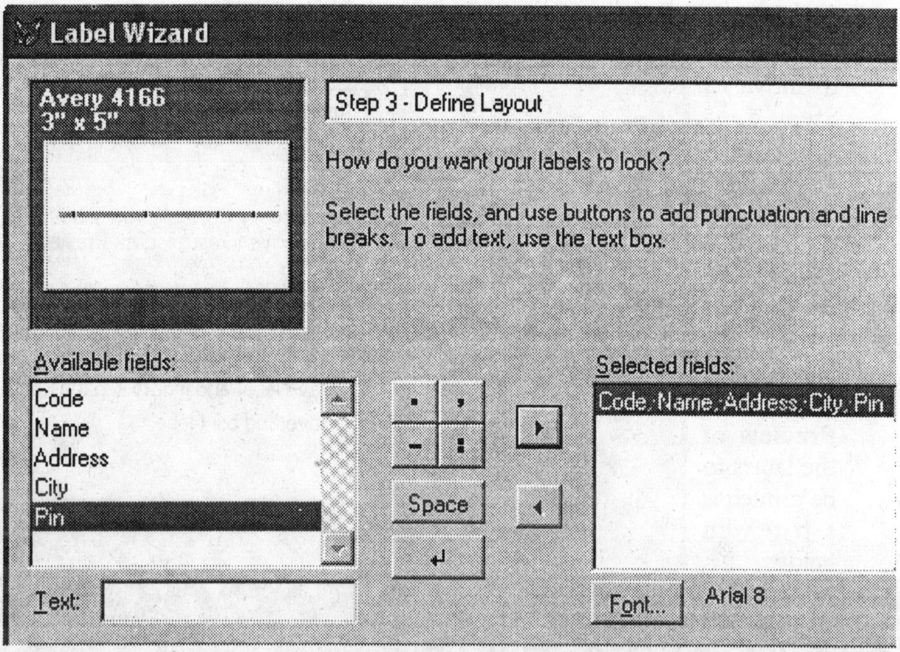

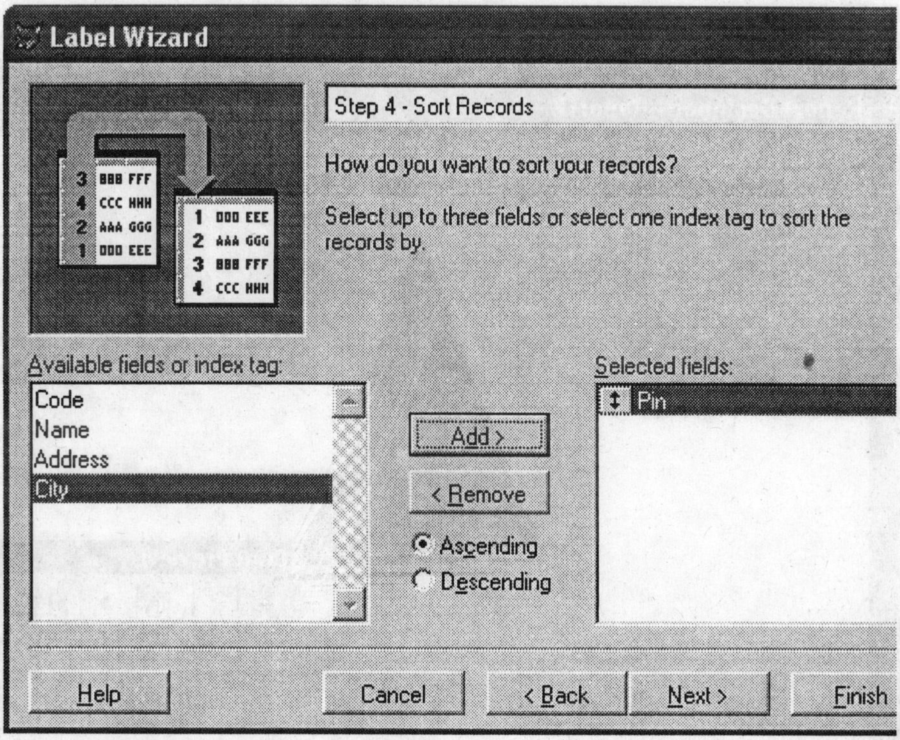

10. Click on Next button to move to Step 4 – Sort records dialog box.

Here you can select the fields or index tag in the order that you would like to sort the records. Now let us sort the records pin wise. Double click on pin field to move it to Selected Fields. Note that by default Ascending radio button is selected.

11. Click on Next button to move to Step 5 – Finish dialog box. You can choose Preview to verify your choices before finishing. Preview of the labels to be printed is shown below.

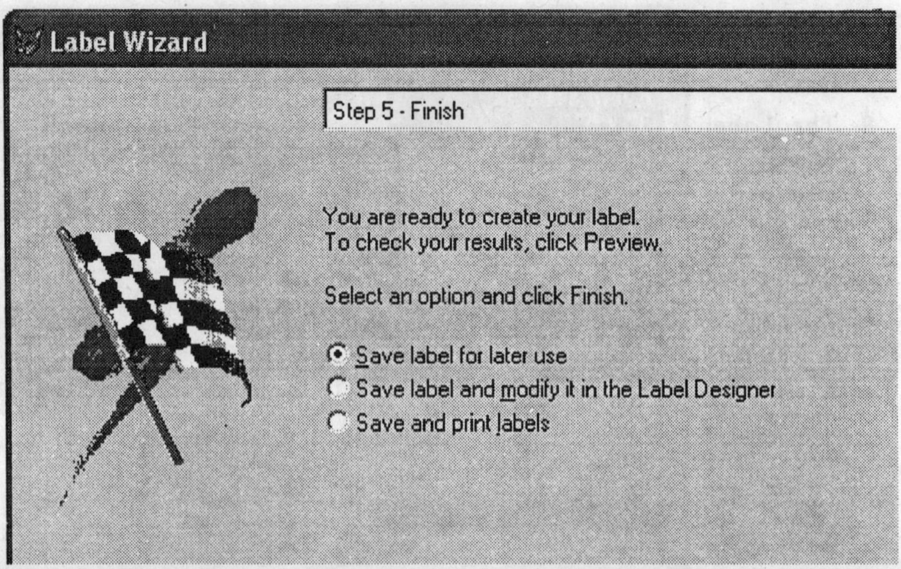

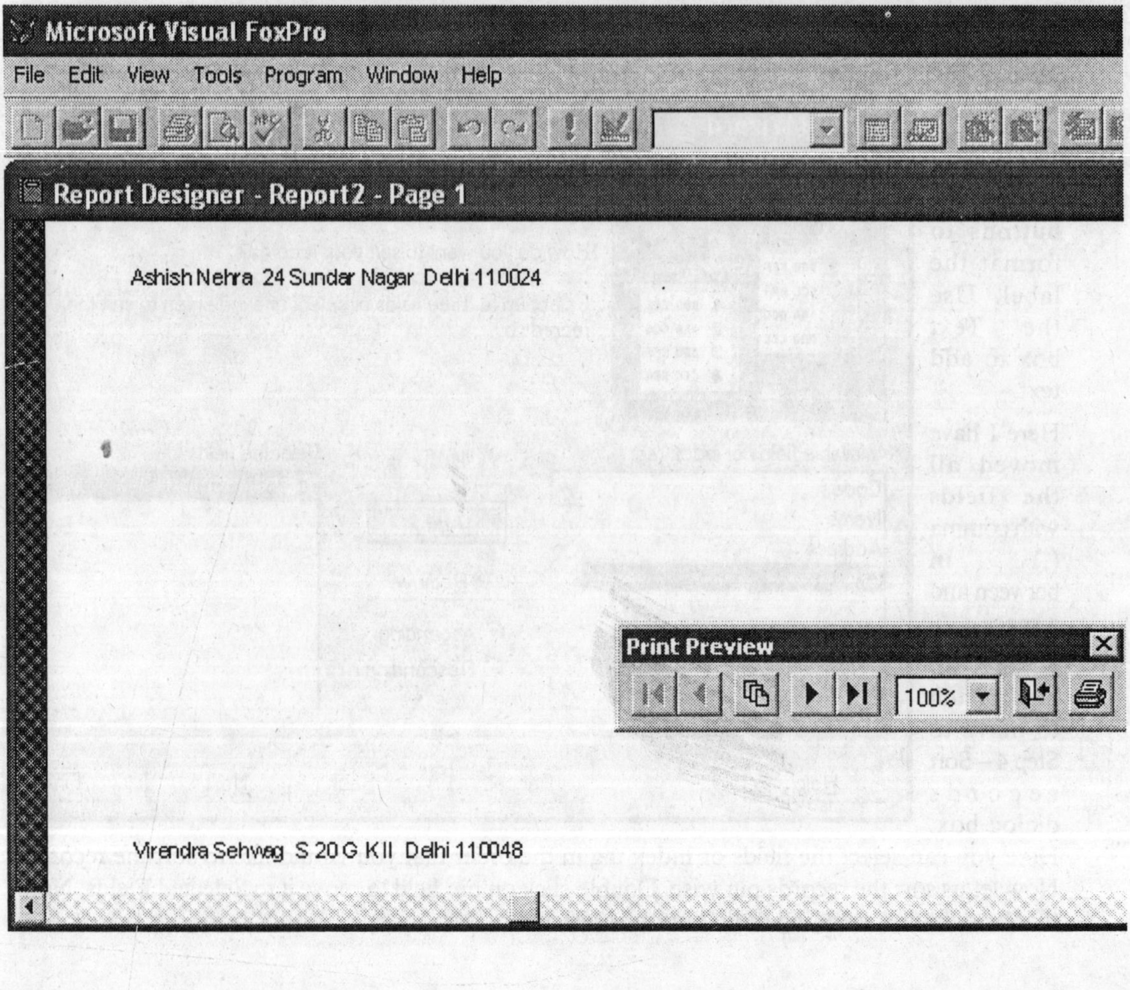

12. Press Esc key to close the Preview window and return to Finish dialog box.
13. Click on Finish button. The Save As dialog box appears. Type the name as table1 in the Save Label and click on Save button.
14. Label file is saved as table1.lbl.

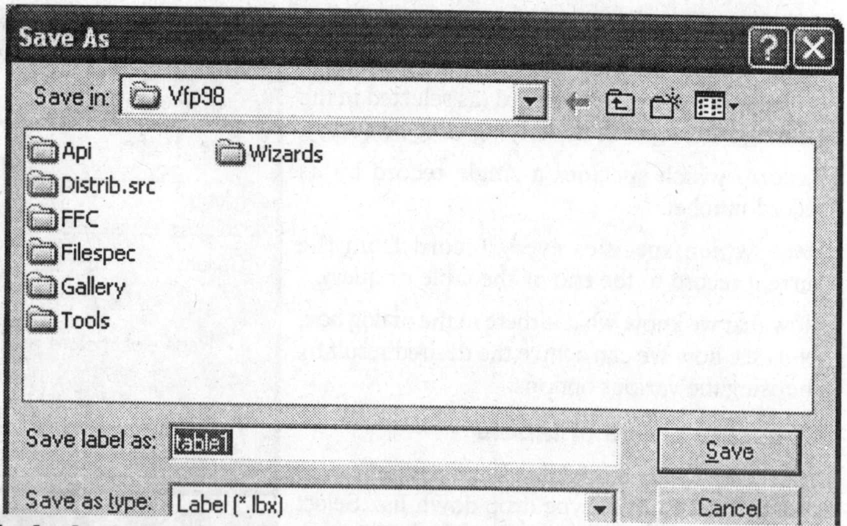

Printing Mailing Label

Now that we have created the labels, naturally we would like to print them too.

1. Open the required label file, in this case table1.lbl.
2. Insert the appropriate mailing labels stationery in the printer's paper tray.
3. Click on the Print button from the Standard toolbar.

Printing Selective Records

If you want you can select and print a selective number of records in the form of labels. For this we have the option of Scope in Visual FoxPro. To get to this select Print from the File menu. It displays a print dialog box, as shown here. Choose Options button from here.

A new dialog box named Print Options will be displayed. Choose Options again from this dialog box.

It displays Report and Label Print Option dialog box. Click on the Scope drop down list.

The Scope dialog box contains four options.

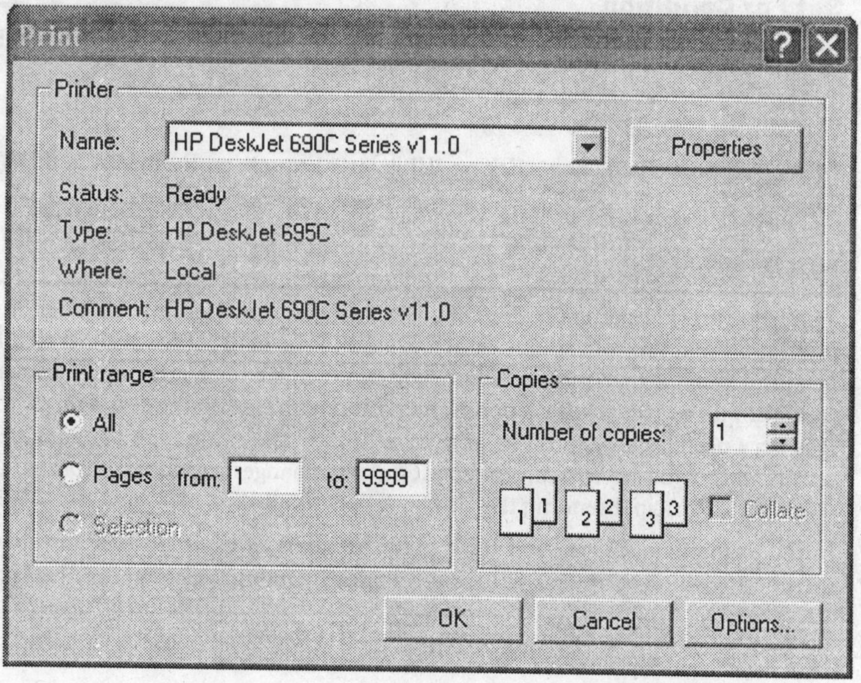

All which specifies all records.

Next, which specifies any number of records, starting with the current record (as selected in the mailing-label report's underlying table or query).

Record, which specifies a single record by its record number.

Rest, which specifies every record from the current record to the end of the table or query.

Now that we know what is there in the dialog box, let us see how we can achive the desired result by choosing the various options.

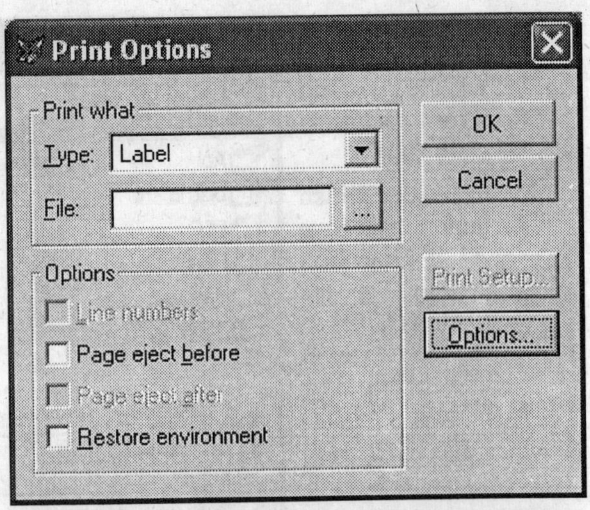

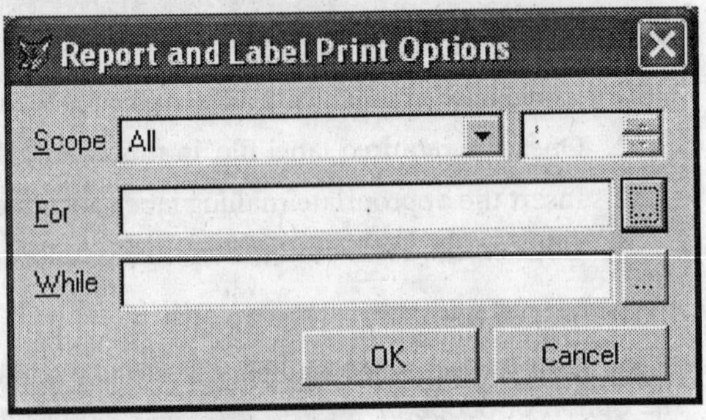

Generate range of labels

Select table query record that starts desired range; choose File, Print in type drop-down list. Select Labels. Click on button to the right of File box and double-click on desired label-layout file name; click on Options; click on Scope; click on Next or Rest. If you clicked on Next, type desired number of records. Click on OK.

Generate single label

In Scope dialog box, click on Record; type desired record number. Click on OK.

Set For Condition

In Print Options dialog box, click on For; use Expression Builder to build For condition expression. Click on OK.

Set While Condition

In Print Options dialog box, click on While; use Expression Builder to build While condition expression. Click on OK.

MAIL MERGE

This is the most important feature of a word processing program. But, what is it doing here in a database program. Well, the data source which is used in the mail merge is generated here, that is why it is used here. But, what is mail merge. Simply you can merge a mail letter with various name and addressess and create copies of letters with different name and addresses but the content of the letter remains the same. It is very useful specially when you have to mail the same type of letter to various people, like your clients whom you have to inform about the rate changes, creditors whom you have to send the payment remindors, Principal sending the similar letters to all staff members, etc. There can be many usuage.

In the example given below, I have used the same letter of Best Wishes to most of our cricket team members wishing them best of luck for the forthcoming series against the New Zealand.

Let us see how this is done.

Mail Merge uses two files:

1. a data file that contains a listing of data items (or fields) arranged in some specific order.
2. a master file that contains the standard text as well as the data variables which are replaced with specific data items from the data file during the merge operation. This file may be available in a Word processor say MS-Word.

The first file is called the Data Source and the second one is called the Main Document. This data source is created in Visual FoxPro. The Main document can be created in any word processing program, MS Word, WordPerfect or any other. This letter can be created in advance before starting the actual Mail Merge procedure from Visual FoxPro. If the letter is short, then you can do it at the same time too.

Mail merge is done in the following steps:

1. Create a data source
2. Create the main document
3. Insert data fields into the main document
4. Merge one record to see that everything is ok.
5. Merge the data source document and the main document.
6. Finally print the merged documents.

Mail Merge Process

To do this follow the following steps very carefully. The following steps are performed using the Wizard.

1. Click the Tools menu and choose Wizard and select Mail Merge.
2. The first Step dialog box appears, as shown here. Click on button to select table. Note that it displays your table and the fields in the Available fields.
3. Select first field and click on > to move to the selected fields. Similarly select other fields one by one. If you want to select all of them then click >> in the beginning itself.
4. Click on Next button to go to the next step.

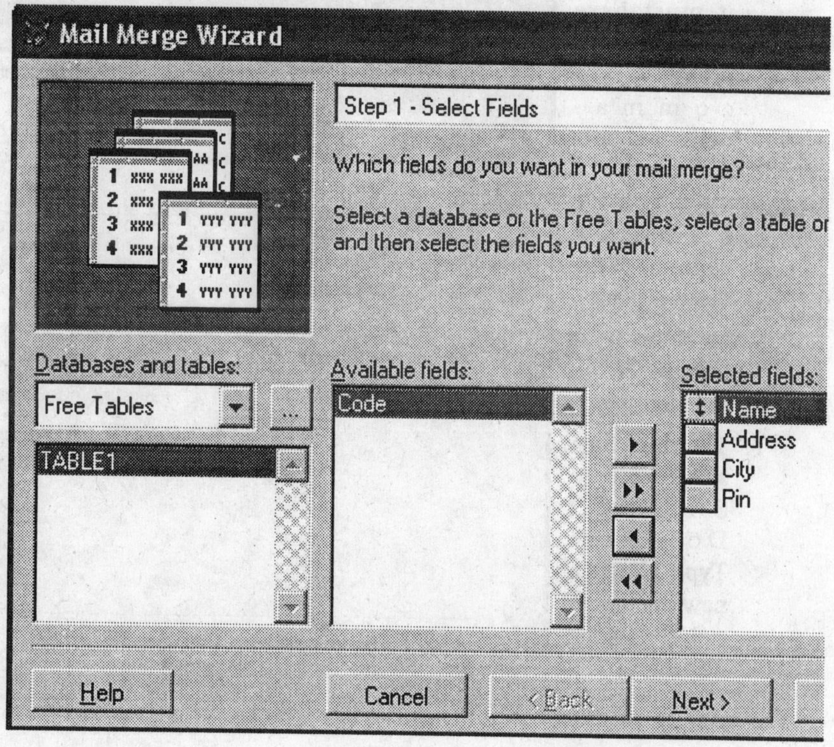

5. The second Step asks you to Choose Word Processor. Since here we have to create a document for merging, so your computer must have a word processor installed in your computer. Mostly Microsoft Word is used. If you are using any other word processing software, then it must have the capacity to create a comma-delimited text file, which is a plain text file having commas at the desired places.

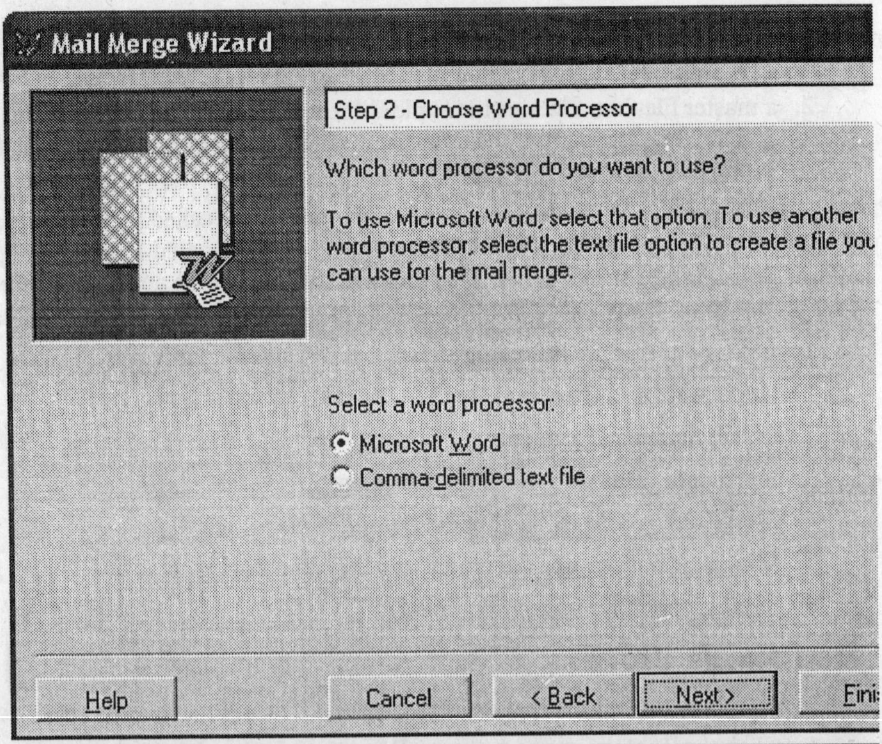

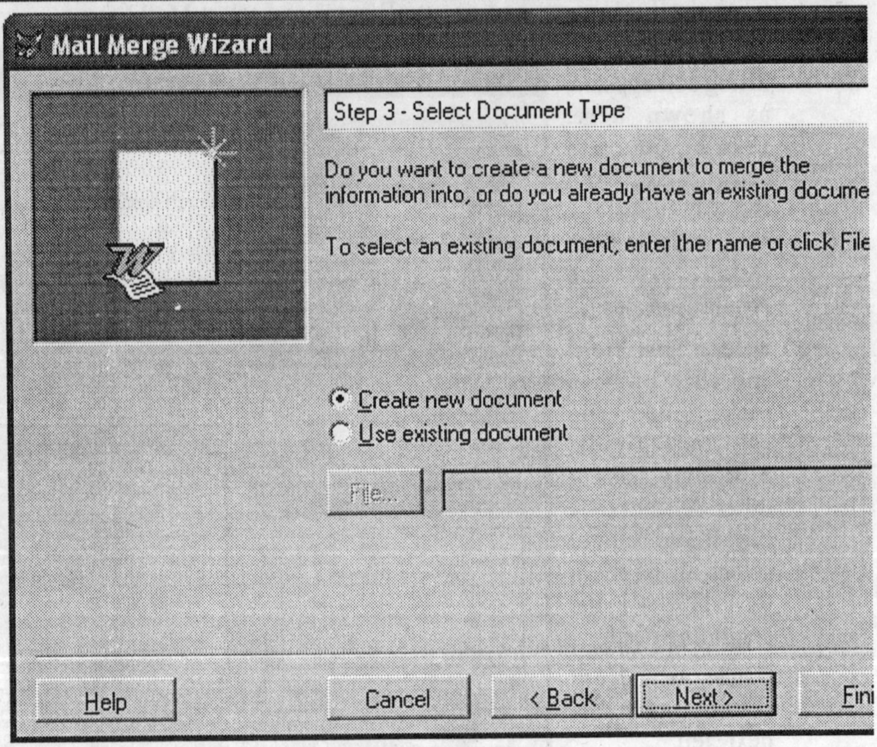

6. Click on Next button to go the next step.
7. The third Step asks you to Select Document Type, Create a new document or Use existing document. Let us choose to Create a new word processing document radio button.

8. Click on Next button to go the next step.
9. The fourth Step aks you to Choose Document Style, which allows you to select one of the Microsoft Word image document types. Here, select a document type: as a Form letter.
10. Click on Next button to go the next step.
11. The fifth and last Step asks you to Finish.

    If you have chosen to create a Microsoft Word document, the wizard will open the document in Microsoft Word.

    If you have chosen to create a text file, the Wizard will prompt you to save. Since we have chosen Microsoft document, clicking on Finish button open a MS-Word blank doucemnt.

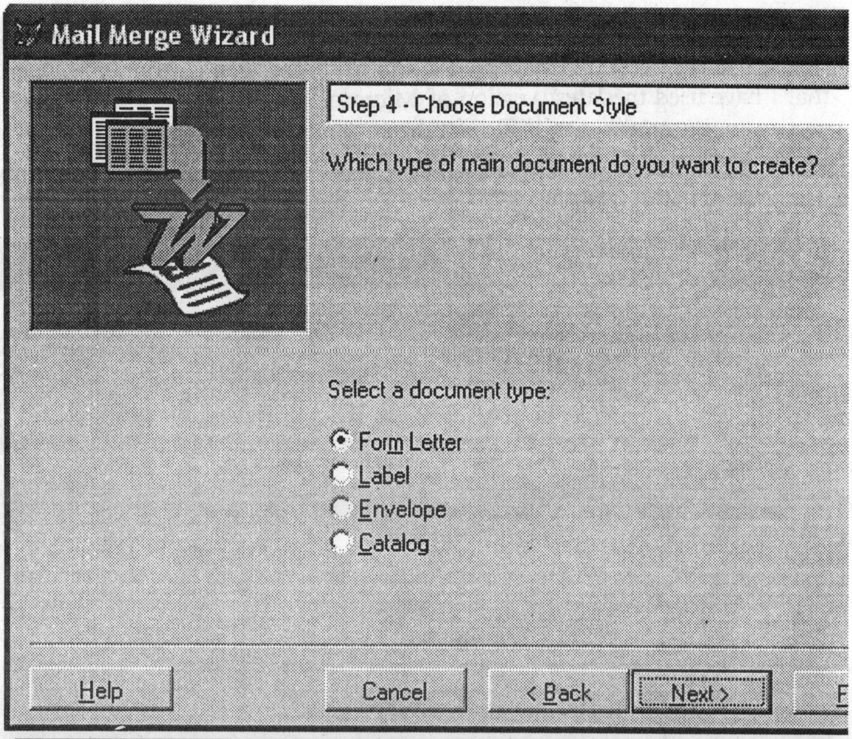

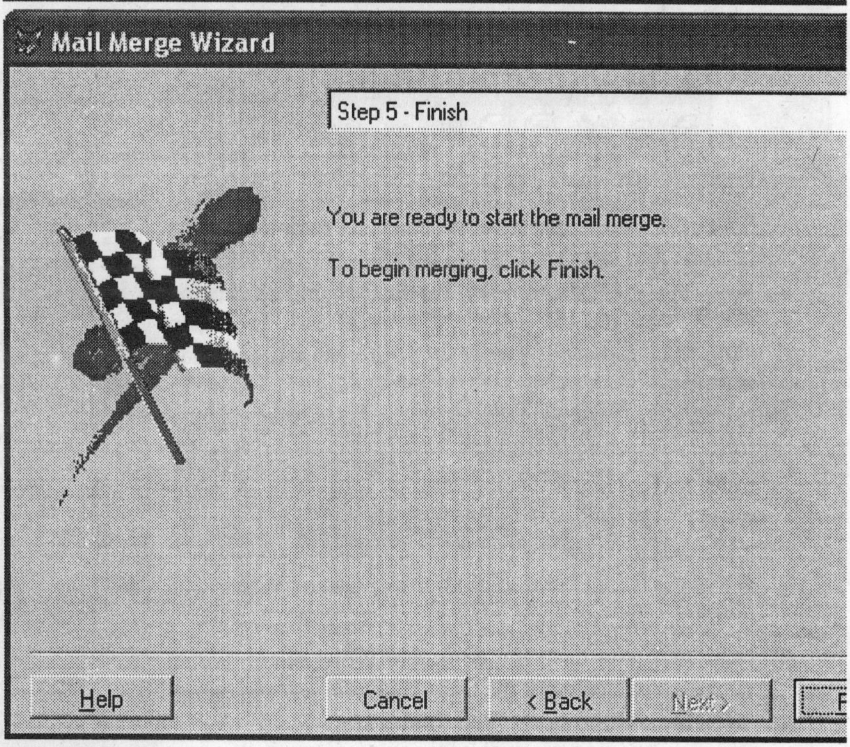

Now the control shifts to the Word Processor, i.e., Microsoft Word.

The following steps are performed in the word processing program, i.e., Microsoft Word. Please note that I have used the latest version of Microsoft Word which is Word 2002. If you are using the other version, your screens may differ but the concept remains the same.

1. Since the control has been transferred from FoxPro, the Word shows the MailMerge Wizard option with the tool bar already there for the actions, as seen below.

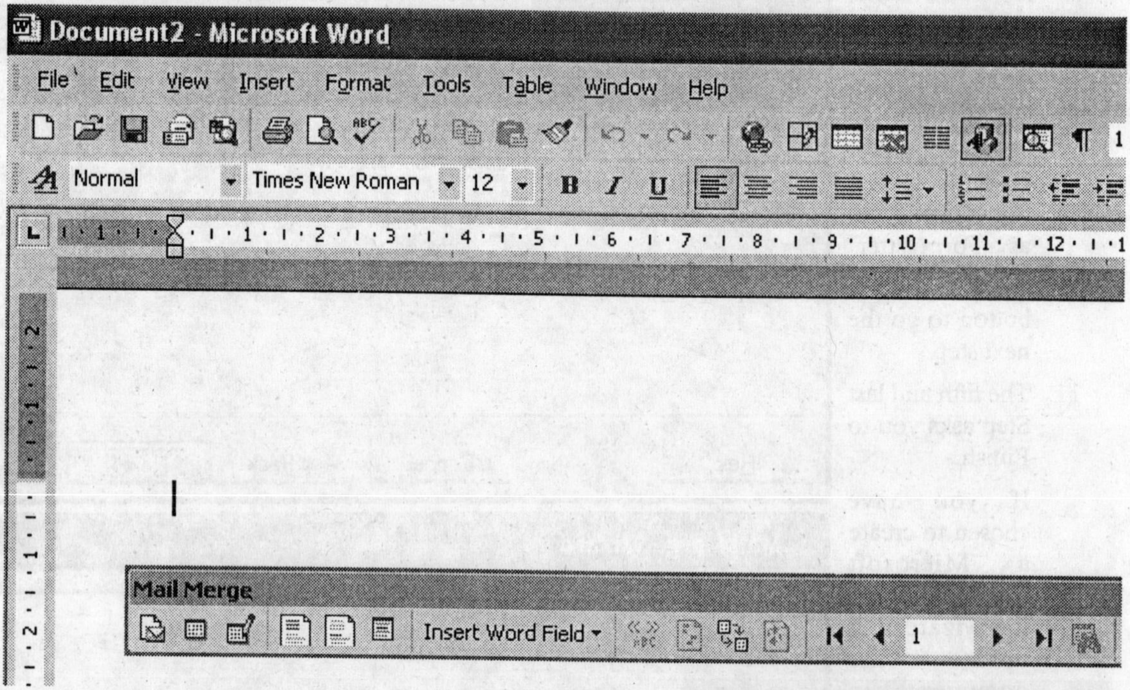

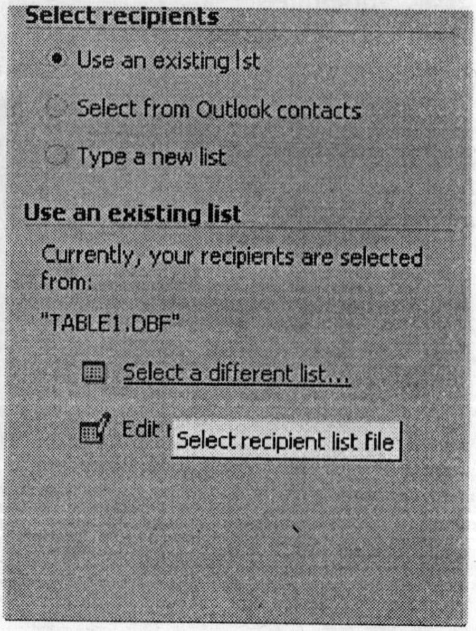

2. The next step it asks you to select the recipients. The options are: Use an existing list, Select from Outlook contracts or Type a new list. If you are using an existing list, it gives you the list of the table already in use, in this case TABLE1.DBF or any other which you may select.

3. Since you have the table to be used is already selected, click at Next to go to the option of Write your letter.

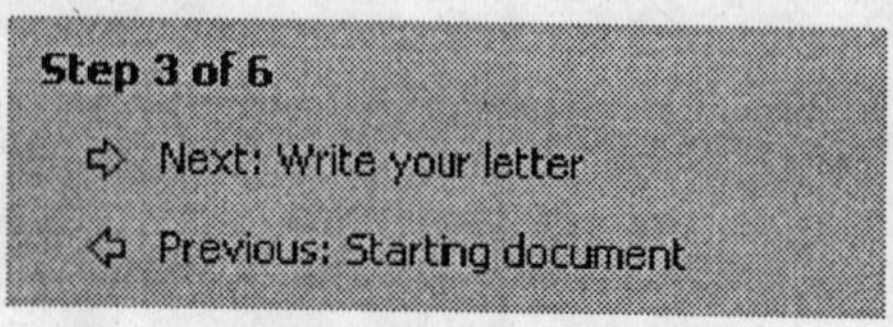

4. Now here you have the complete Word document at your disposal, type out the text which you want to merge using the data source called Table1.dbf.

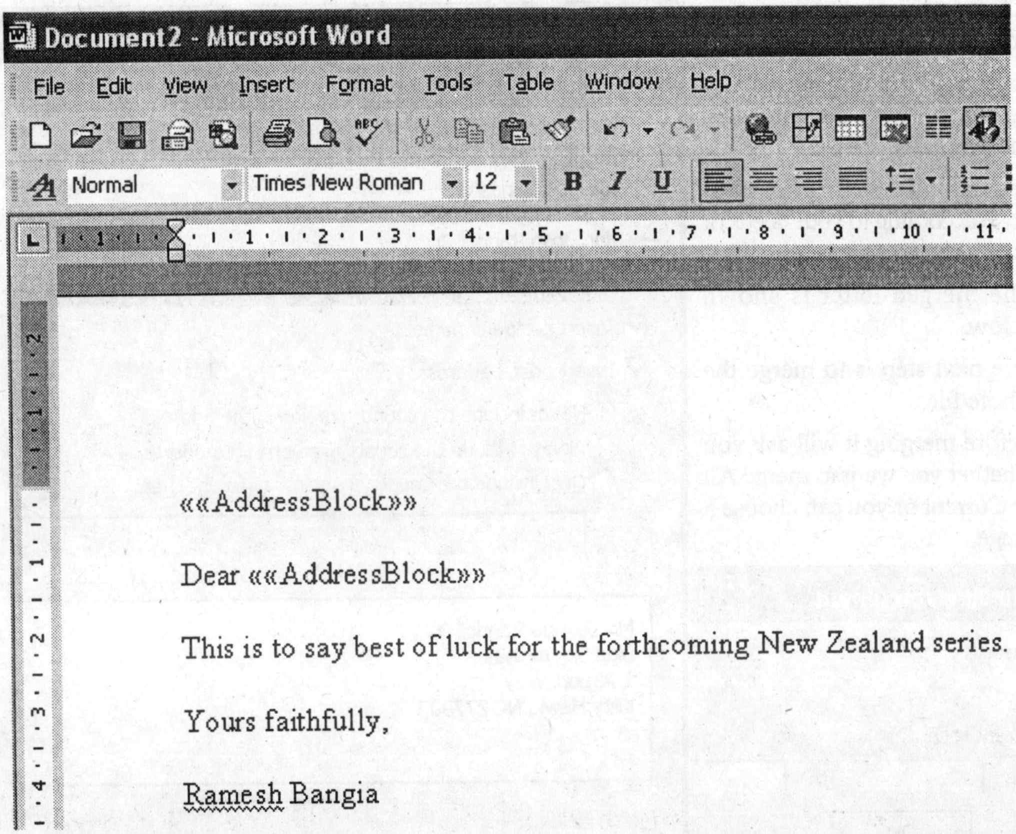

5. See above the text which I have typed. Now wait, where did I get the Address Block from. See you must be very sure in the beginning itself where you want what. So in the beginning of the letter, I want to put the name and address of the player from the source. So what do I do, I click at the option called Addresss block. It gives rise to another dialog box called Insert Address Block, which is shown on the next page.

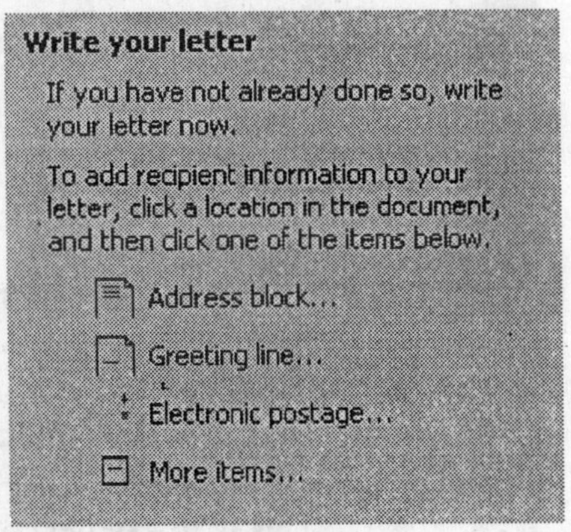

6. In the Insert Address Block select the option of Insert Company Name and Insert Postal Address and Ok it.
7. You will see the << <<Address Block>> >> in your document which means that here the actual address will be merged.
8. Next I have typed Dear and then again I have used Address Block.
9. This will again give rise to the dialog box. But this time I will select only the Company Naame and not its postal address. Since I want to address the person and not the address.
10. The next text is simple to understand.

11. Click on Next to get the option of previewing your lettter.
12. Here only the first record will be merged with the letter and shown on the screen.
13. See that the merging has been done according to your needs or not.
14. The merged letter is shown below.
15. The next step is to merge the whole file.
16. Before merging it will ask you whether you want to merge All or Current or you can choose a range.

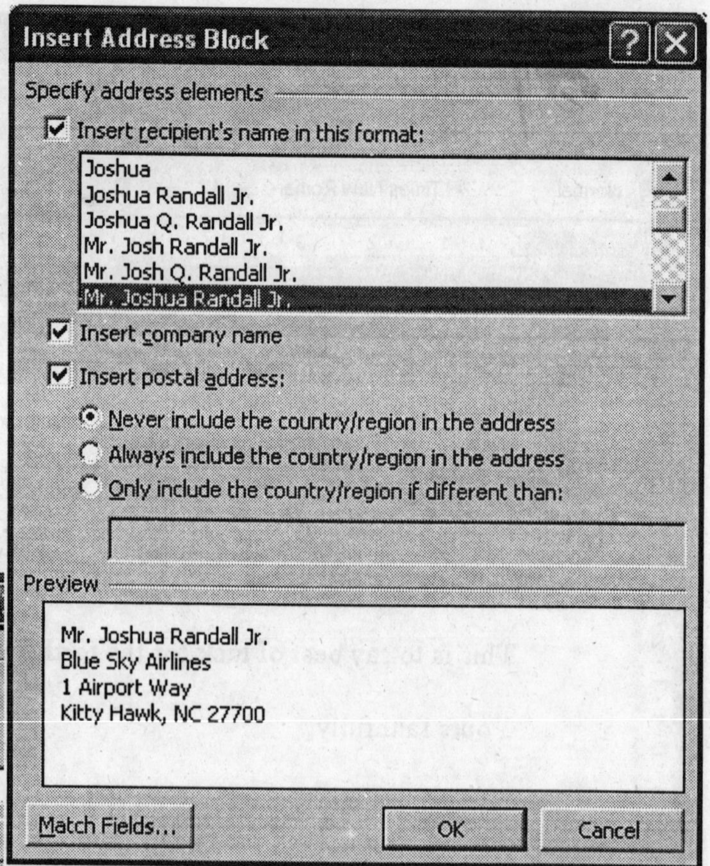

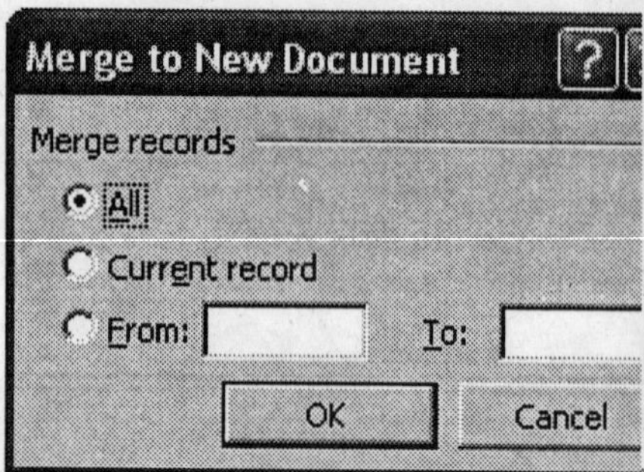

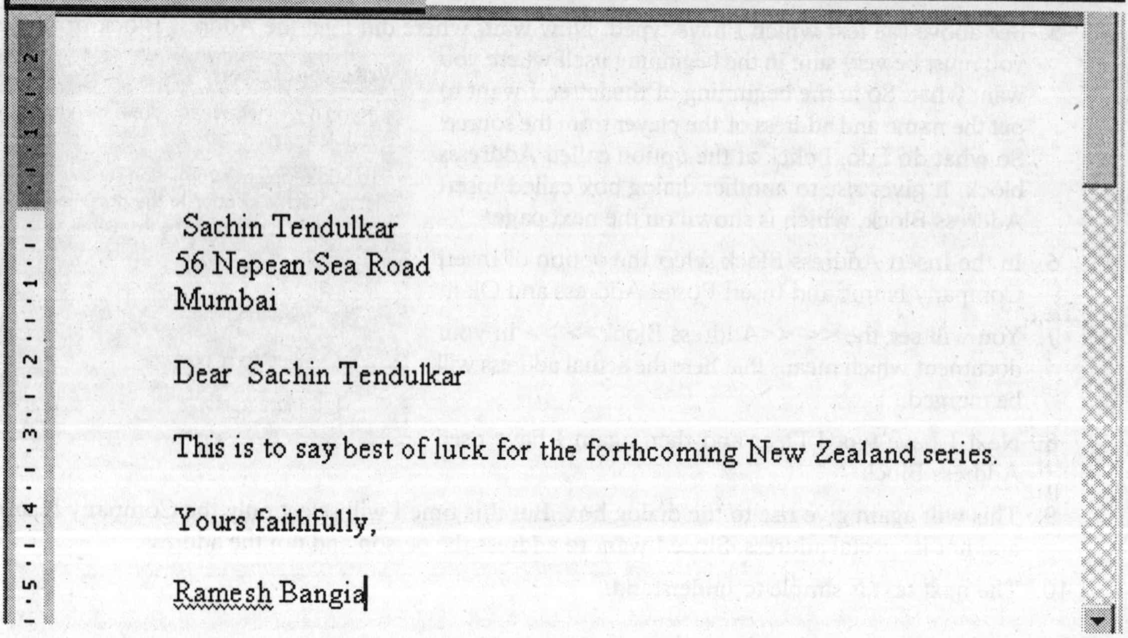

17. Well choose All and see that the whole range of letters created using the name and addresses from the file called table1.dbf.
18. If you want you can save the merged letter file.

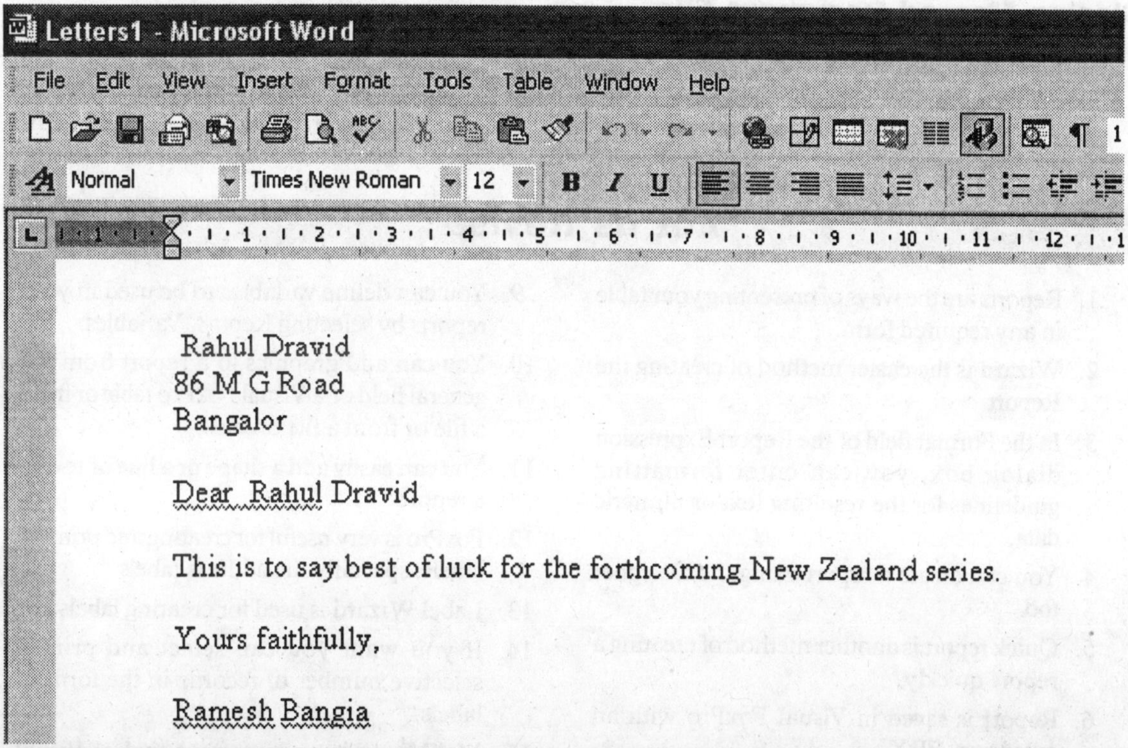

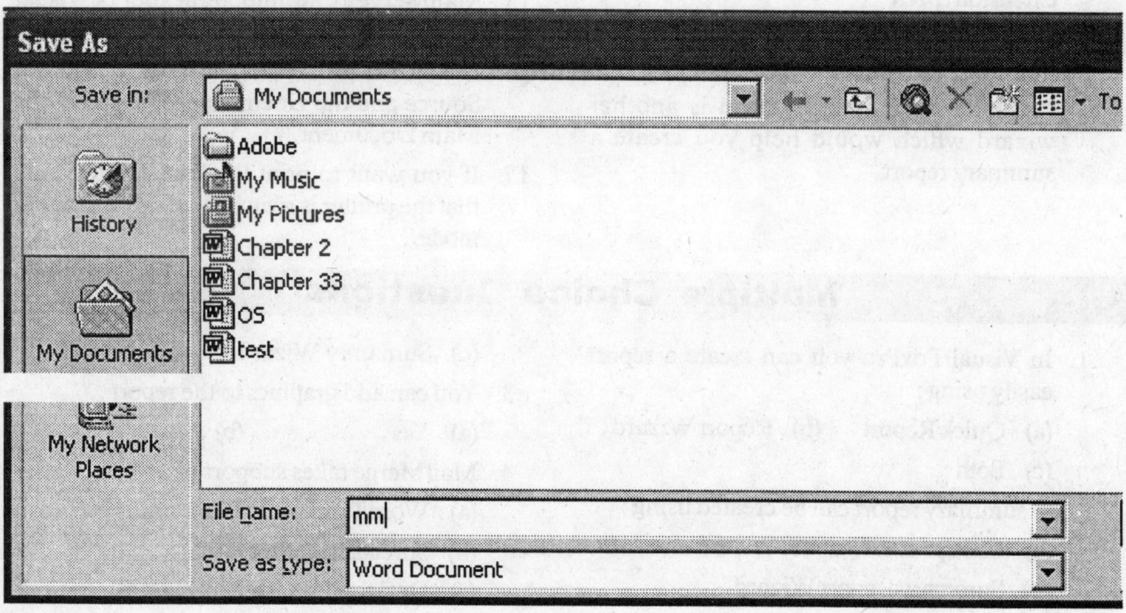

Printing Merged Letters

If you want to print the letters, make sure that the printer is switched on and is in ready mode. Then click at the Print command in the File menu or click at the Print button on the Standard toolbar.

Closing Merged Document File

1. Click the File menu and choose Close.
2. When a message appears asking whether you want to save this document, you have a choice to save it or click the No button to ignore it. In that case you will have to go through the method of mail merge again.

Let us Revise

1. Reports are the ways of presenting your table in any required form.
2. Wizard is the easier method of creating the Report.
3. In the Format field of the Report Expression dialog box, you can enter formatting guidelines for the resulting text or numeric data.
4. You can create a report using the Designer too.
5. Quick report is another method of creating a report quickly.
6. Report is saved in Visual FoxPro with an extension .FRX
7. You can print a report using Print command from the File menu.
8. Group/Total Report Wizard is another wizard which would help you create a summary report.
9. You can define variables to be used in your reports by selecting Report, Variables.
10. You can add graphics to a report from the general field of a Visual FoxPro table or from a file or from a file on disk.
11. You can easily add a shape or a line of text to a report.
12. FoxPro is very useful for creating and printing labels, specially the address labels.
13. Label Wizard is used for creating labels.
14. If you want you can select and print a selective number of records in the form of labels.
15. MailMerge is an important tool of Visual FoxPro.
16. In MailMerge the data file is called the Data Source and the Document file is called the Main Document.
17. If you want to print the letters, make sure that the printer is switched on and is in ready mode.

Multiple Choice Questions

1. In Visual FoxPro you can create a report easily using :
   (a) Quick Report (b) Report Wizard
   (c) Both
2. A summary report can be created using :
   (a) Group/Total Report Wizard
   (b) Summary Report Wizard
   (c) Sumamry Wizard
3. You can add graphics to the report :
   (a) Yes (b) No
4. MailMerge takes support of a :
   (a) Word Processing Program
   (b) Spreadsheet Program
   (c) Desktop Publishing Program

5. You can add shapes to the report :
   (a) Yes (b) No
6. You can create mailing labels in Visual FoxPro using :
   (a) Label Wizard (b) Mail Wizard
   (c) Label Maker
7. Report file in Visual FoxPro is saved with extension :
   (a) .scf (b) .scx
   (c) .frx

True/False Questions

1. Reports are the ways of presenting your table in any required form.
2. Wizard is the easier method of creating the Report.
3. You cannot create a report using the Designer too.
4. Quick report is another method of creating a report quickly.
5. Report is saved in Visual FoxPro with an extension .FPX
6. Group/Total Report Wizard is another wizard which would help you create a summary report.
7. You can define variables to be used in your reports by selecting Report, Variables.
8. You cannot add a shape or a line of text to a report.
9. FoxPro is very useful for creating and printing labels, specially the address labels.
10. Label Wizard is used for creating labels.
11. If you want you cannot select and print a selective number of records in the form of labels.
12. MailMerge is an important tool of Visual FoxPro.
13. If you want to print the letters, make sure that the printer is switched on and is in ready mode.

Matching Columns

Match the text in Column A with the text in Column B.

Column A	Column B
1. Report	a. Method of creating labels
2. Report Wizard	b. File extension of reports
3. Quick Report	c. Merging document with address labels
4. Label Wizard	d. Wizard to create summary report
5. MailMerge	e. Easier method of creating report
6. .FRX	f. Quicker method of creating a report
7. Group/Total Report Wizard	g. Data from table in presentable format

Fill in the Blanks with Appropriate Words

a. Group/Total b. Label c. MailMerge d. .FRX
e. Preview f. Report Wizard

1. Before printing the report, you can see its ___________.
2. Report can be easily created using ___________.
3. Report file is saved with extension _______.
4. Summary report can be created using ___________ Wizard.
5. In ______________ you merge the document with the data from a FoxPro table.
6. You can easily create address labels using ___________ Wizard.

Descriptive Type Questions

1. What is a Report?
2. How would you create a report using Report Designer?
3. How would you create a report using Quick Report method?
4. How would you save and print a report?
5. What is Group/Total Report Wizard and how it is used?
6. How would you add graphics and shapes into reports?
7. How would you create labels using Label Wizard?
8. How would you print selective labels?
9. What is Mail Merge?
10. Describe the Mail Merge process.

Answers to Objective Type Questions

Multiple Choice Questions

1. c 2. a 3. a 4. a
5. a 6. c

True/False Questions

1. T 2. T 3. F 4. T
5. F 6. T 7. T 8. F
9. T 10. T 11. F 12. T
13. T

Matching Columns

1. g 2. e 3. f 4. a
5. c 6. b 7. d

Fill in the Blanks with Appropriate Words

1. e 2. f 3. d 4. a
5. c 6. b

Recommended Readings

1. Learn to Program Visual Basic—Databases *by John Smiley.*
2. Learn to Program Visual Basic—Objects *by John Smiley.*
3. Learn to Program Visual Basic—Examples *by John Smiley.*

—Published by Firewall Media (An Imprint of Laxmi Publications Pvt. Ltd.)

10 Working with Command Window

INTRODUCTION

I remember that when I was a child, the most popular proverb was that you can do the same thing in two ways depending upon the option which you like. Since your interest would be more in the method which you feel convenient with, your result in this case would be of better quality.

So far I have talked about the way of using Visual FoxPro which would be used by someone who is using the software for the first time and specially those who have started using the computer after the evolution of Windows operating systems. But, what about those, who have graduated from Disk Operating System and have used the earlier version of FoxPro and are quite happy to write commands instead of clicking them with mouse. For them we have the concept of Command Window. This window is for those who want to write the command. It is very similar to the command prompt which was there in the DOS version of the software. Just type the command press Enter and you have the result on the screen.

In this chapter we will see how the commands can be given from the Command Window. Let us start from the very basic, i.e., creating a table and then we will use various commands on this table.

CREATING A NEW TABLE

For this the simple command is CREATE. You can use this giving the name of the file you want to create. So the command would become:

```
CREATE STUDENT
```

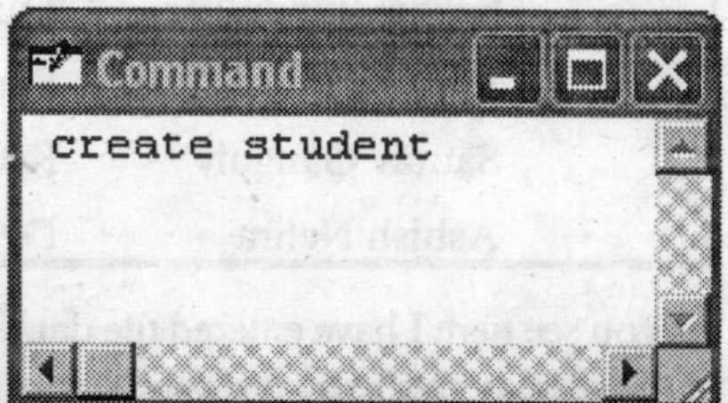

I have type in caps, but you can do otherwise too. This would give rise to a blank table creation dialog box, as shown here. Now that this is the blank structure of the table. You will have to fill it up with the type of data which you are going to have in this.

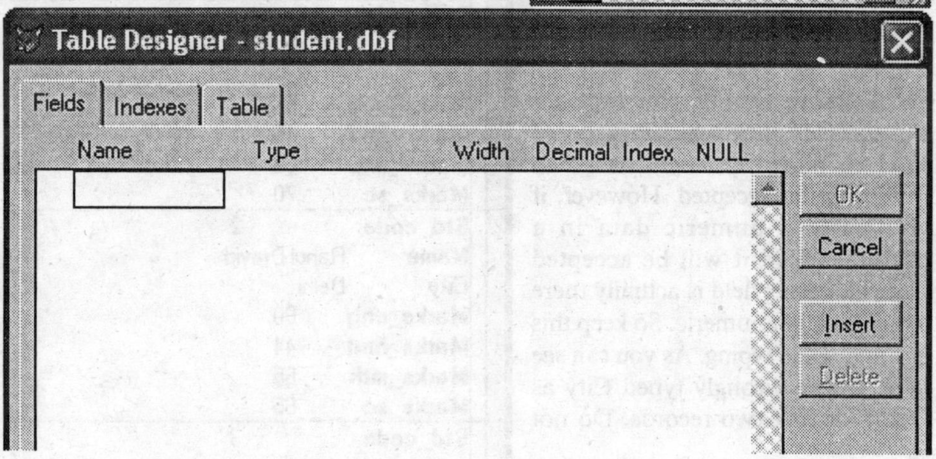

I am taking here the data of a student, with his student code named as std_code of 4 numeric, name of 20 characters, city as 10 characters, then the various marks of 3 numeric values each of English,

Hindi, Maths and Science, termed as marks_eng, marks_hnd, marks_mth and marks_sc, respectively. Once you fill up the structure, your Table Designer dialog box would look like the one shown here.

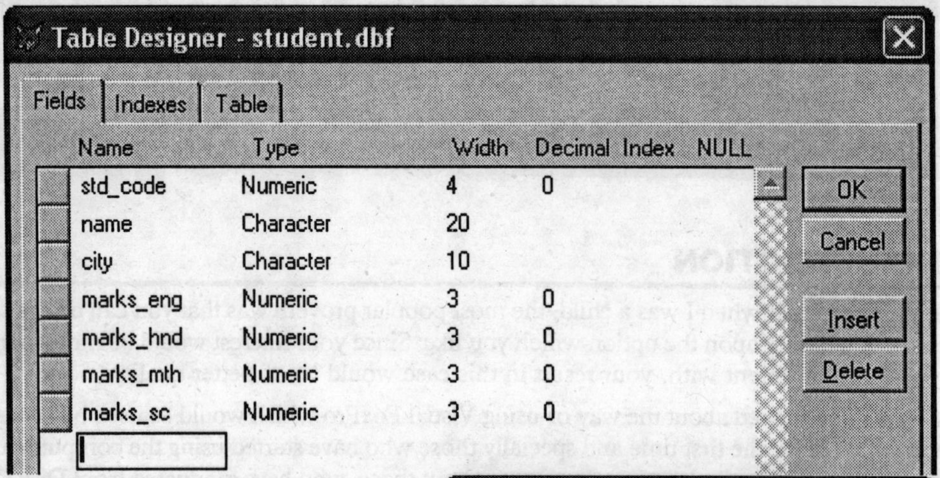

Now that you have the structure ready, what next, just fill up the data. So when you press Ok, the system asks you whether you want to enter the data now or would you do it later.

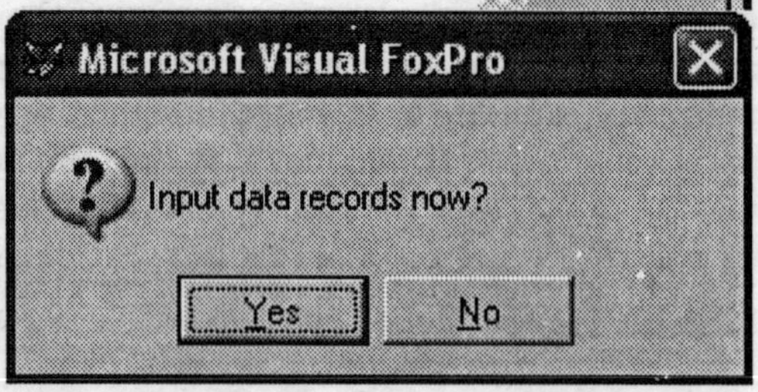

Say Yes to enter the data and fill up the following data. This is just a dummy data so you enter it and follow it up with Ctrl + W to save the data.

std_code	*name*	*city*	*marks_eng*	*marks_hnd*	*marks_mth*	*marks_sc*
1	Sachin Tendulkar	Mumbai	55	45	60	70
2	Rahul Dravid	Bangalore	60	44	65	65
3	Saurav Ganguly	Kokatta	55	60	50	45
4	Ashish Nehra	Delhi	70	66	55	44

As you see here I have entered the data in the display mode by just typing one entry after the another in the space provided for.

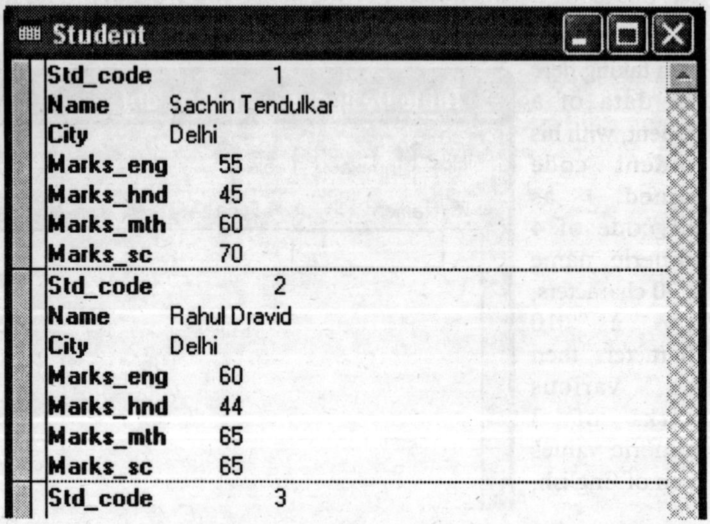

Please note that if you type an alphabet in the field which is supposed to accept only the numeric data then it will not be accepted. However, if you write a numeric data in a character filed it will be accepted since character field is actually there to accept alphanumeric. So keep this in mind while typing. As you can see here, I have wrongly typed City as Delhi for first two records. Do not worry since I am going to change them later, when I will come for correcting data. Once you have entered the data and saved with Ctrl + W, type browse in the command window and you will have the total data there on the screen in the form you would probably wanted to see.

Supposing after looking at the displayed data, you think that you should have made the name field more than 20, let us say 25. So what will you do. For this we have the command called Modify Structure.

MODIFYING THE STRUCTURE

The command for this is very simple, MODIFY STRUCTURE. Give this in the command window and you have the structure of the file in front of you. Now using the arrow keys or mouse change the field you want to change. Here I have changed the std_code from 4 to 5.

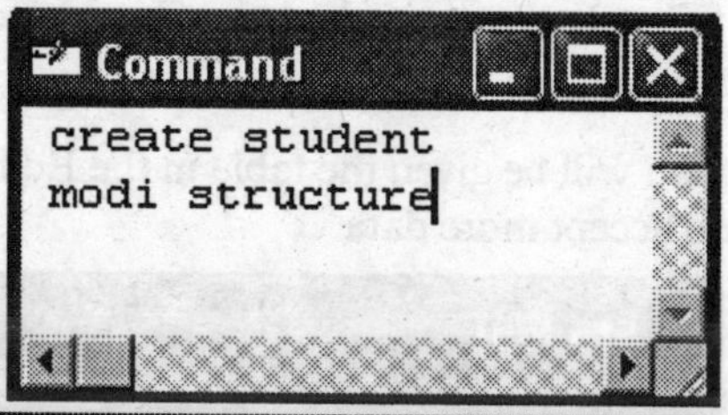

The immediate response from the system would be in the form of a dialog box, which asks you whether you want this change to be permanent. Say Yes, and the structure would be changed.

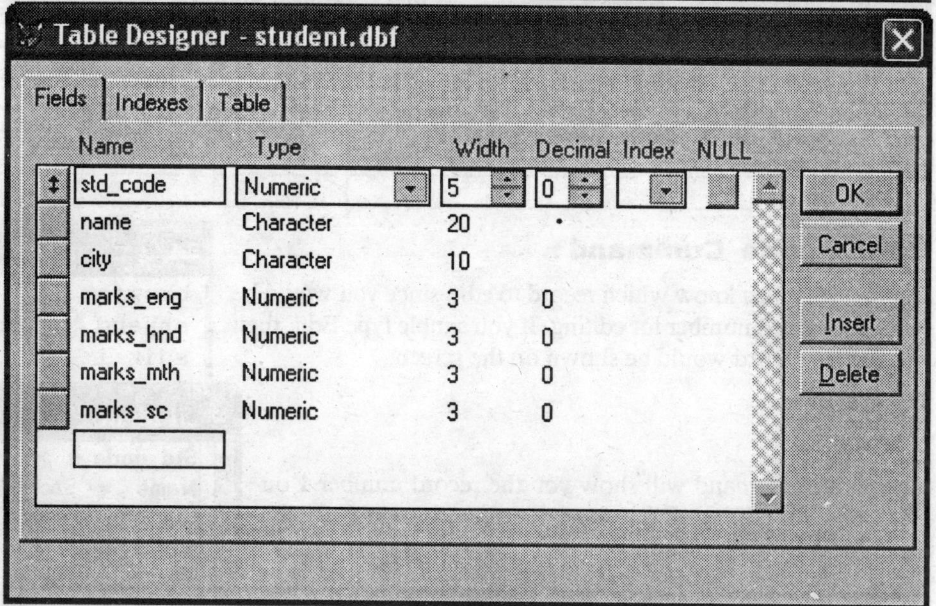

It is not that you can make changes only in the fields, you can even add a new field or delete a field.

Adding a new field would be easy since, you have to just click at Insert and a new field row would be available for you.

Deleting a field is a bit tricky. If you delete a field which already contains data, then you have it. Since this data cannot be retrieved by any method. So make sure what you have to do and then do it.

Now we come to editing of the data.

EDITING DATA

Editing of the data can be done using one the following commands:

APPEND	Append to add records in the .
EDIT	Edit or Change to display the table in Edit mode.

BROWSE Browse to display the table in Browse mode.

REPLACE Replace to change the contents in more than one record.

Let us study them one by one.

Append Command

Using this command you can enter more data then what it has. This command will add data at the end of the existing data in the form of new records. For this, you can use Command window. Assuming that the table is open, type the following commands in the Command window:

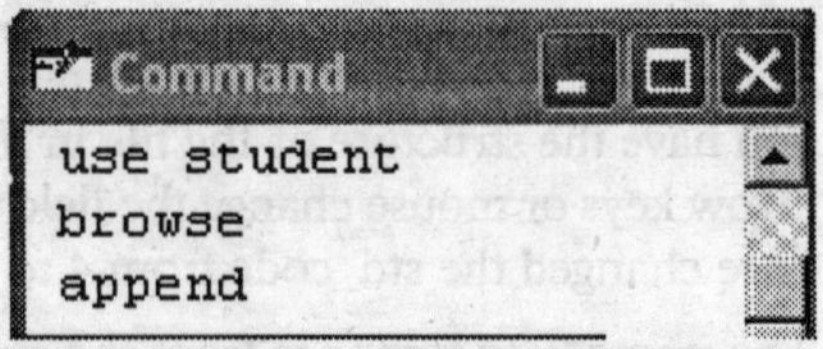


```
APPEND
```

You will be given the table in the Edit mode and would be ready to accept more data.

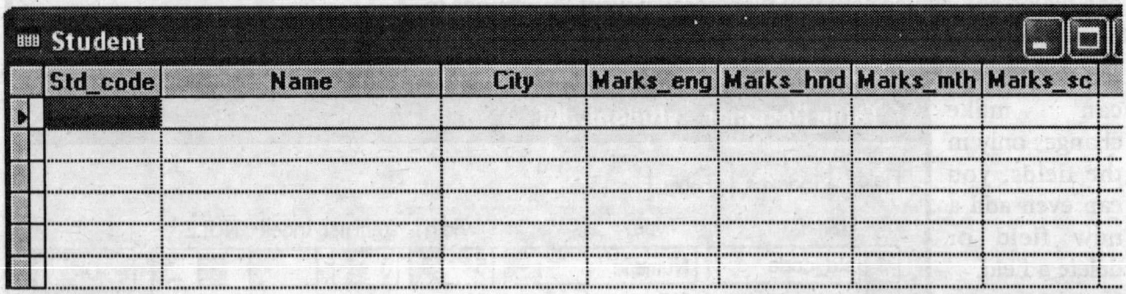

Edit/Change Command

For this you must know which record to edit, since you would be using the record number for editing. If you simple type Edit, then the current record would be shown on the screen.

For example:

```
EDIT 1
```

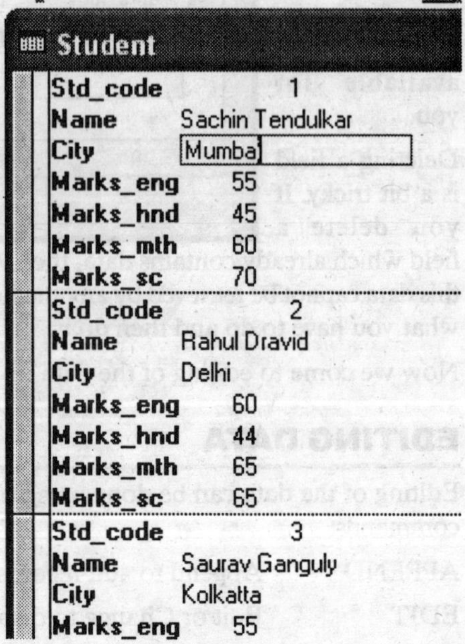

The above command will show you the record number 1 on the screen for editing. Of course other records would also be there for editing them later.

You may also specify the field list, conditions and scope while giving EDIT command. For instance, the following commands show only Std_code and name field for editing:

```
EDIT FIELDS STD-CODE, NAME

CHANGE FIELDS STD_CODE,NAME
```

If you want to edit only the Name, and Marks_hnd of the table for the City Delhi only, then you will give the following command:

```
EDIT FIELDS NAME, MARKS_HND FOR CITY =
"DELHI"
```

Browse Command

Browse is a powerful command in Visual FoxPro. It enables you to scroll through table horizontally as well as vertically. In addition, the Browse command shows records in a tabular format, displaying one record in one row. At the same time, fieldnames are placed at the top of the columns a headers. Browse command displays as many fields and records as will fit on one screen at a time. You can position the cursor at the data item you want to make changes to. You can also use Browse command for locating errors, like spelling mistakes in the table.

The command is very simple, just type BROWSE with table already opened:

```
BROWSE
```

There are various ways in which the browse command can be used. One of them is to browse few fields only. For example in the following display, I have browsed only the name and marks. See below:

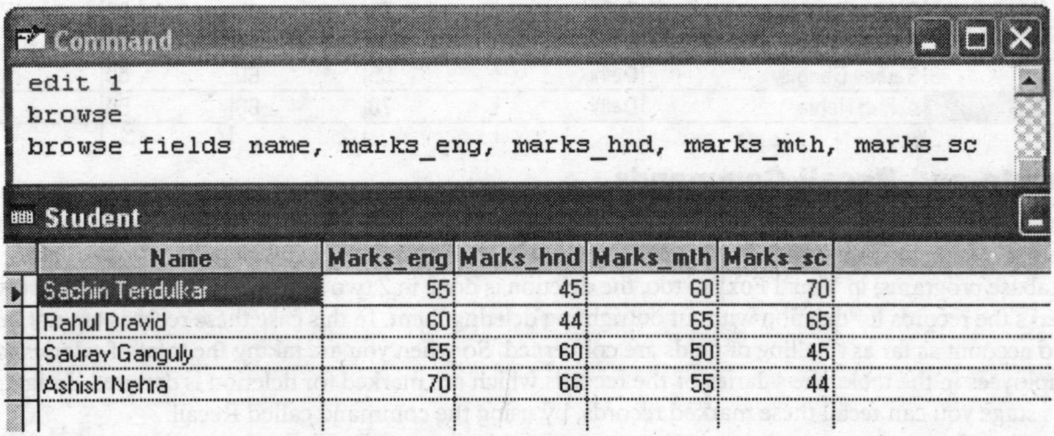

You can see only the Name and the various marks. You may use the option NOEDIT or NOMODIFY with Browse command that disables any changes in the table. Thereafter, you cannot change data in any of the records. This option will also not allow you to add or delete any record accidently.

Enter the following command in the Command window:

```
BROWSE FIELDS NAME, CITY NOEDIT
```

You will now see the two fields in Browse window, but you will not be able to edit or change any of the fields. If you want to make changes, give the following command again:

```
BROWSE FIELDS NAME, CITY EDIT
```

Now you can edit the fields

Replace Command

Replace is a very powerful command and can replace any field data with another depending upon the command given. But, make sure that the command is given is right, since once replaced data cannot be called back.

The syntax of the Replace command is:

```
REPLACE[SCOPE] FIELDNAME WITH FIELD-REPLACEMENT FOR CONDITION
```

The scope parameter is optional and is used to determine the number of records that replace command will look at. The fieldname is that field for which the change will be made. Field-replacement is the expression with which the field will be replaced.

In the following example, I have changed all City values to Delhi. See the result.

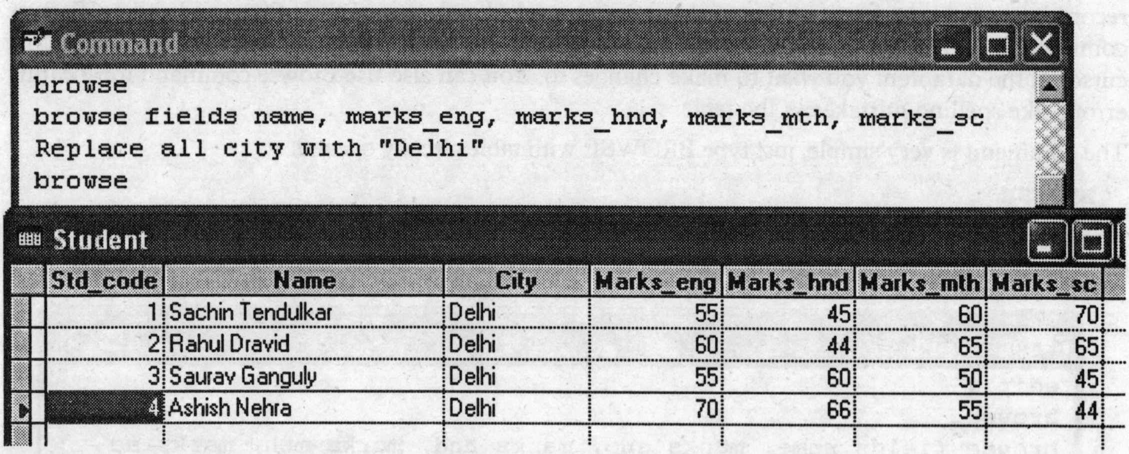
Command

```
browse
browse fields name, marks_eng, marks_hnd, marks_mth, marks_sc
Replace all city with "Delhi"
browse
```

Student

Std_code	Name	City	Marks_eng	Marks_hnd	Marks_mth	Marks_sc
1	Sachin Tendulkar	Delhi	55	45	60	70
2	Rahul Dravid	Delhi	60	44	65	65
3	Saurav Ganguly	Delhi	55	60	50	45
4	Ashish Nehra	Delhi	70	66	55	44

Delete and Recall Commands

You can get rid of the records not needed by you. There is no option of recalling them back after deleting them. So make doubly sure that the records are not needed again before deleting them. Like most of the database programs, in Visual FoxPro too, the deletion is done in 2 two steps. In the first step the software marks the records for deletion without outrighting deleting them. In this case these records are not taken into account as far as totalling of fields are concerned. So when you are taking the total of salaries of all employees in the table, the salaries of the records which are marked for deletion is counted. In fact, till this stage you can recall these marked records, by using the command called Recall.

In the second step, the records are actually removed. Let us see how it is done.

In the Edit or Browse mode mark the record for deletion by clicking in the far left column. With the command window, you can mark the record for deletion by using the record number. For example,

```
DELETE RECORD RECORD_NUMBER
```

In the other case, you go to that particular record which you want to delete by giving the command.

```
GOTO RECORD_NUMBER
```

Now you give the command as:

```
DELETE
```

Delete command puts a physical marker to the record, which you want to delete, but it does not actually remove the record form the file. They will remain in the table and they can be brought back with the Recall command at any time. In other words, the records with physical mark can be reclaimed.

The command for Recall is very simple:

```
RECALL RECORD N
```

Where n is the record number you want to recall. Once you have recalled the record then the physical marker from the record will be removed.

Next we come to the process of deleting the record permanently using the Pack command.

Pack Command

Pack Command permanently deletes the records marked for deletion from the table. The command can be given as:

```
PACK
```

There is another command in this category called Zap, read about it next.

Zap Command

Supposing you have created a student file as mentioned earlier for the 1st semester marks. Now you want to create a new semester file without changing the structure. What you will do is give the command as Zap and all the records with their data would be lost expect for the structure. The command for this is given as:

```
ZAP
```

Deleting Records by Set Deleted Command

Visual FoxPro, by default can use the records even though marked for deletion. Since records marked for deletion are still in the table, operations such as Sum, Total, Count, etc., can still use the marked records for such calculations. You can handle this problem in many ways. One method is to use Pack command before you use any other command. But this method is time consuming specially when you are working with a large table. If you delete records frequently and use these commands frequently, you will have to pack marked records table many times.

Another way to handle this problem is to use Set Deleted command. This command would hide records marked for deletion for doing some other operations on the table and thus, make them unavailable for most of the table operations. As an example, enter the following command:

```
GO TOP
DELETE NEXT 3
LIST STD_CODE, NAME
```

You will see first three records are marked for deletion with * mark at record 1, 2 and 3. Now if you enter the command Set deleted on, it will not include any records that are marked for deletion. If you enter the command Set Deleted Off and type List Std_code, Name again the records marked for deletion will be visible with the asterisk marking. Use Recall command to unmark records which were marked for deletion earlier. To do so, enter:

```
GO TOP
RECALL NEXT 3
LIST EMP_CODE, NAME
```

Records 1, 2 and 3 will now be unmarked for deletion.

Erase Command

This command is used to erase a file from the disk. The syntax of ERASE command is:

```
ERASE FILENAME \? [RECYCLE]
```

Filename specifies the file to be erased, including the path drive or directory if the file is on a different from the current drive or directory. Filename can contain wildcard characters such as * and ? For example, you can erase backup file with Erase *.back command. ? displays the delete box containing names of the files. From this, you can choose a file to erase. Recycle specifies that the file is not immediately deleted from disk and is placed in the Windows operating system's Recycle bin.

ADDITIONAL COMMANDS OF VISUAL FOXPRO

Following are some more commands which will be very useful to learn.

Run Command

Using this command you can run any DOS based command. Of course after running the command you can come back to Visual FoxPro. The result of a DOS Command appears in a separate Visual FoxPro Run command window. The command is stopped automatically when the command has finished its action.

Set Default Command

Visual FoxPro uses its default drive and directory for creating files, unless you specify the path separately. However, you can specify the default drive and/or directory by using the command Set Default To. For example:

```
SET DEFAULT TO C:
```

You can specify the full pathname of a directory by using:

```
SET DEFAULT TO C:\VISUALFOX
```

Display and List Command

Both these commands are used to see the records in the table. Of course, you can see the selected part of the table too.

Display command shows the contents of the current directory or file on the screen, unless you specify the number of records to be displayed whereas List displays the contents on the screen. Both Display and List commands display records on the screen behind any open Visual FoxPro window. If any window is opened you might move them to see the records.

To view the contents of the records in the file student.dbf enter the following command from the Command window:

```
LIST
```

The records of the file student.dbf will be displayed as shown on the next page.

However, you can limit the display to certain fields by including the required field names after List. For example,

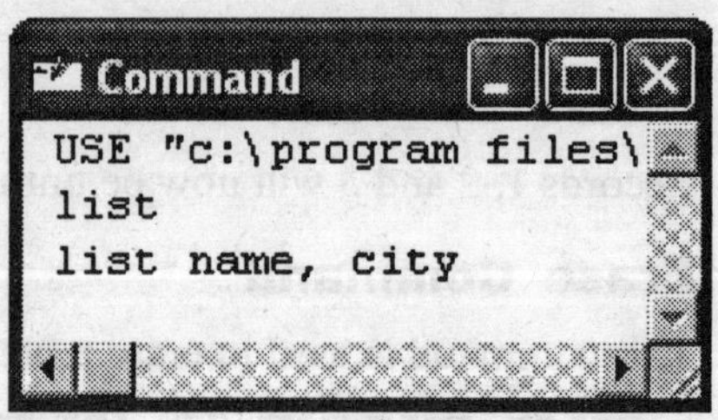


```
LIST NAME, CITY
```

This display a list of 2 fields namely Name and City as seen in second figure on the next page. To change the order of the fields, type the following in the Command window.

```
LIST NAME, STD_CODE
```

Thus, using this method of writing commands, you can display the records with the required fields. You can also use To Print at the end of List command to send the listing to the printer as well as to the screen. If you do not want record numbers to be displayed, add off option with the List command. For example:

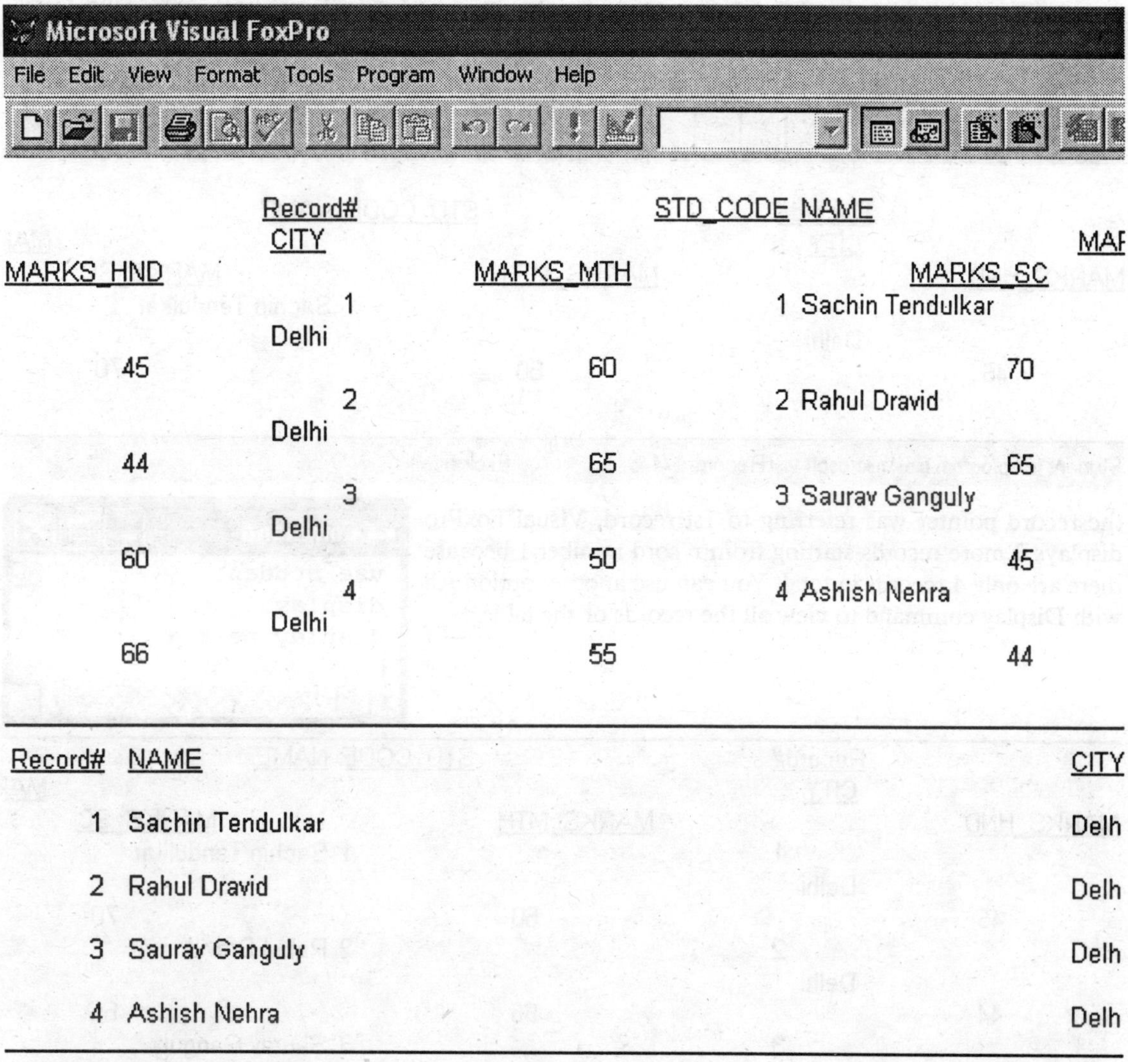


```
LIST TO PRINT OFF
```

The Display command is different from the List command. By default, it allows you to view the current record only. The record you marked last is the current record. Visual FoxPro keeps track of the record where the cursor was. Visual FoxPro uses a pointer which remains move or close the Table. Whenever, a table is in use (open) it always points to one record at a time. When you open the file with Use Visual FoxPro command, it points to the first (top) record. The command for this is very simple, just type:

```
DISPLAY
```

You will find the Display command showing the contents of the first record, as shown on the next page, and status bar showing Rec: 1/4. It suggests that there are a total of 4 records in the table file in use and Visual FoxPro is pointing to the first record.

How about seeing all the records. To view more than one record with DISPLAY command, you must add an option clause such as All or Next. Let us type Display Next 4 in the Command window. Since

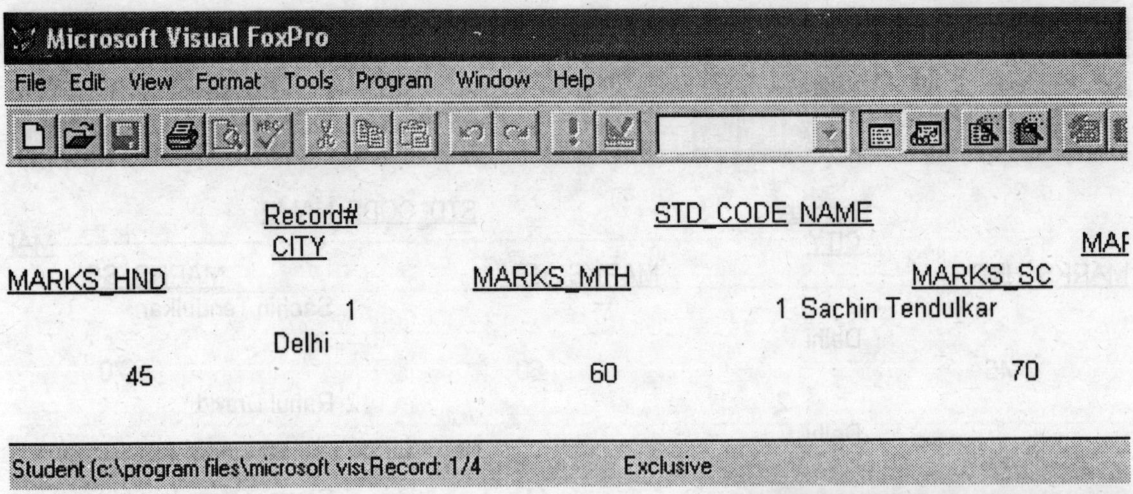

the record pointer was referring to 1st record, Visual FoxPro displays 3 more records starting from record number 1 because there are only 4 records in total. You can use another option All with Display command to view all the records of the table.

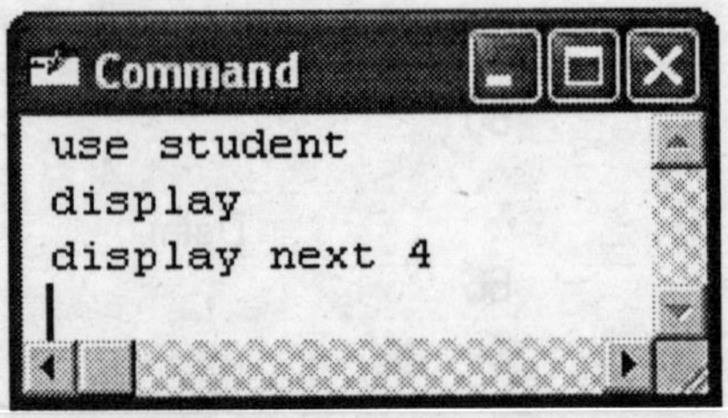

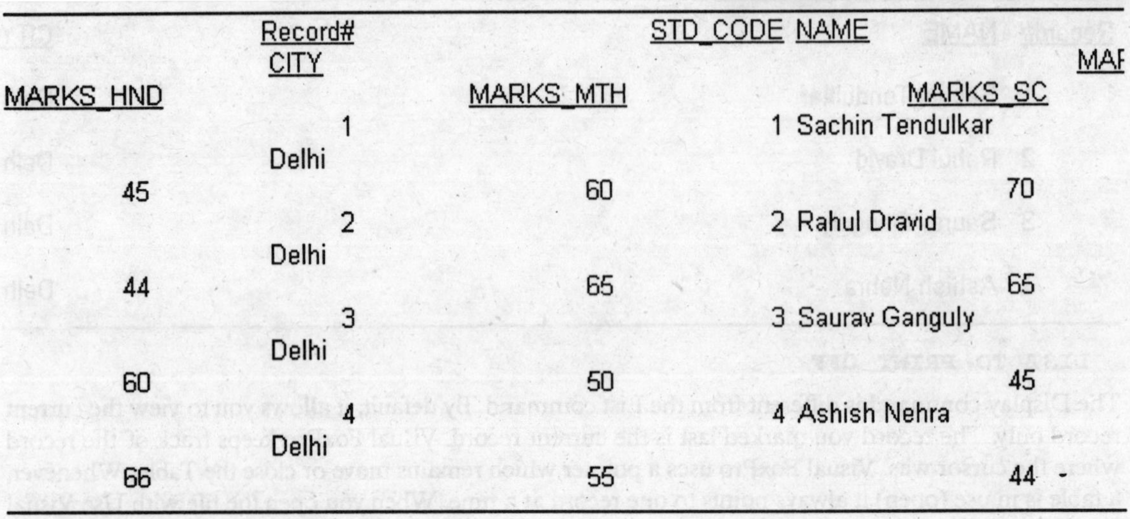

Options with List Command

Let us now see the various options which can be used with the List command. On the next page, you will see the options which I have used. They are:

```
LIST FOR NAME = "SACHIN TENDULKAR"

LIST FOR MARKS_MATH > 50

LIST FOR MARKS_ENG = 50
```

Record#	STD_CODE	NAME	CITY	MARKS_HND	MARKS_MTH	MARKS_SC	MAF
1	1	Sachin Tendulkar	Delhi	45	60	70	

Record#	STD_CODE	NAME	CITY	MARKS_HND	MARKS_MTH	MARKS_SC	MAF
1	1	Sachin Tendulkar	Delhi	45	60	70	
2	2	Rahul Dravid	Delhi	44	65	65	
4	4	Ashish Nehra	Delhi	66	55	44	

Record#	STD_CODE	NAME	CITY	MARKS_HND	MARKS_MTH	MARKS_SC
3	3	Saurav Ganguly	Delhi	60	50	45

All the 3 results are shown above.

A Relational operators such as <, =, >=, <=, etc., allow you to compare two (or more) values or expressions. Typical relational operators are:

Operator	*Description*
=	Equal to
>	Greater than
<	less than
<> or # or !=	not equal to
>=	greater than or equal to

<=	less than or equal to
$	substring (contained within)
= =	equal to and equal in length (exact match)

You can also use the logical operator And, Or and Not to combine two or more conditions (logical expressions) to obtain a compound logical value. (The query that contains an expression that results in either true or false is a logical expression).

Operation	*Meaning*
And	Both operands of the expression must be true for the entire expression to be evaluated as true.
Or	Either operands of the expression must be true for the entire expression to be evaluated as true.
Not or !	The expression that follows must be untrue for the entire expression to be evaluated as true.
()	Used for grouping.

Options with Display Command

Like List you can use Display command to search for specific information such as:

```
DISPLAY FIELDS STD_CODE, NAME FOR CITY = "DELHI"
```

This command will display the code and name only for those cases where the city is Delhi. In the following example, I have use the command as:

```
DISPLAY FIELDS NAME, CITY, MARKS_ENG FOR MARKS_ENG > 50
```

```
display fields name, city, marks_eng for marks_eng > 50
```

The displayed result is:

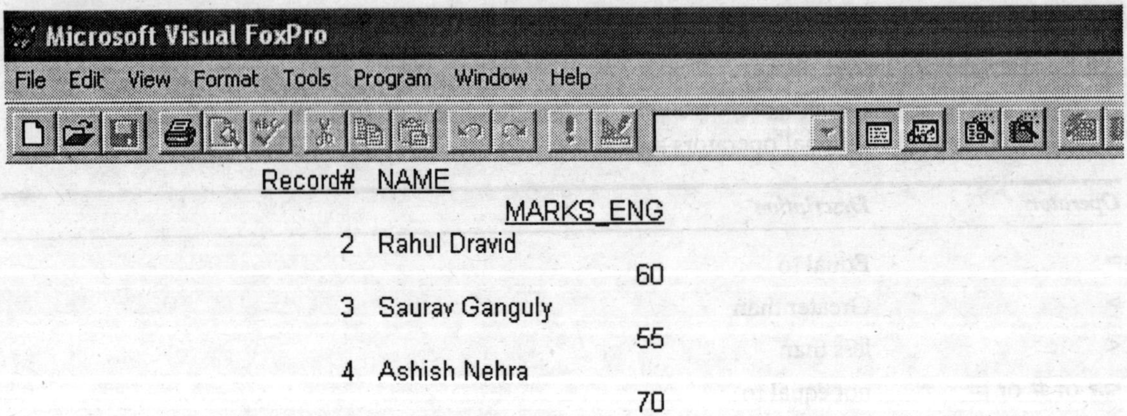

Query with Locate For Command

The Locate command is used for finding the position of a record in a table as per the required criterion. The criterion can be applied for one or more than one fields. Locate command does not show the record on the screen. It gives you only the record number(s) in the status bar, if a match is found. You can then use Display command to see the searched record or records on the screen.

In the following example I have used the command as:

```
LOCATE FOR NAME = "RAHUL DRAVID"
```

Visual FoxPro has found the record and waits for your next command, which I have given as Display. See the result.

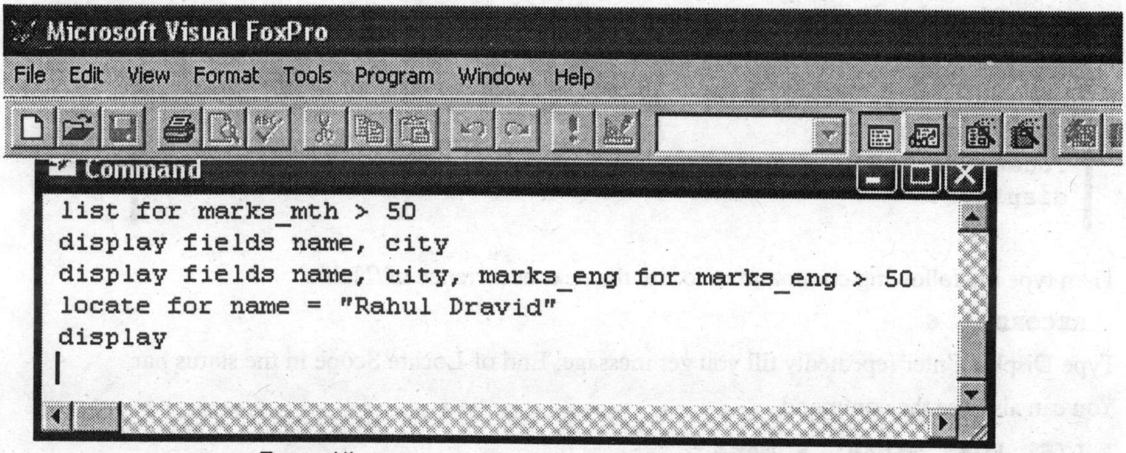

Record# STD_CODE NAME
CITY MAF
MARKS_HND MARKS_MTH MARKS_SC
2 2 Rahul Dravid
Delhi
44 65 65

Word Embedded in Text

Suppose you want to search for records whose Name field contains Nehra. The command Locate for Name = 'Nehra' will not be able to find any record because the word Nehra is embedded in the middle of the Name field. To retrieve this record, we need to give a command that asks similar to "Display all records that have the word Nehra embedded in the name field." Visual FoxPro can do so by means of the string operator ($) which finds the embedded word in the text. So, to locate such a record containing 'Nehra' in the Name field type the command:

```
LOCATE FOR 'NEHRA' $ NAME
```

The following is displayed

```
RECORD = 4
```

Then type the following command to display record 4.

```
DISPLAY
```

The record would be displayed as shown on next page.

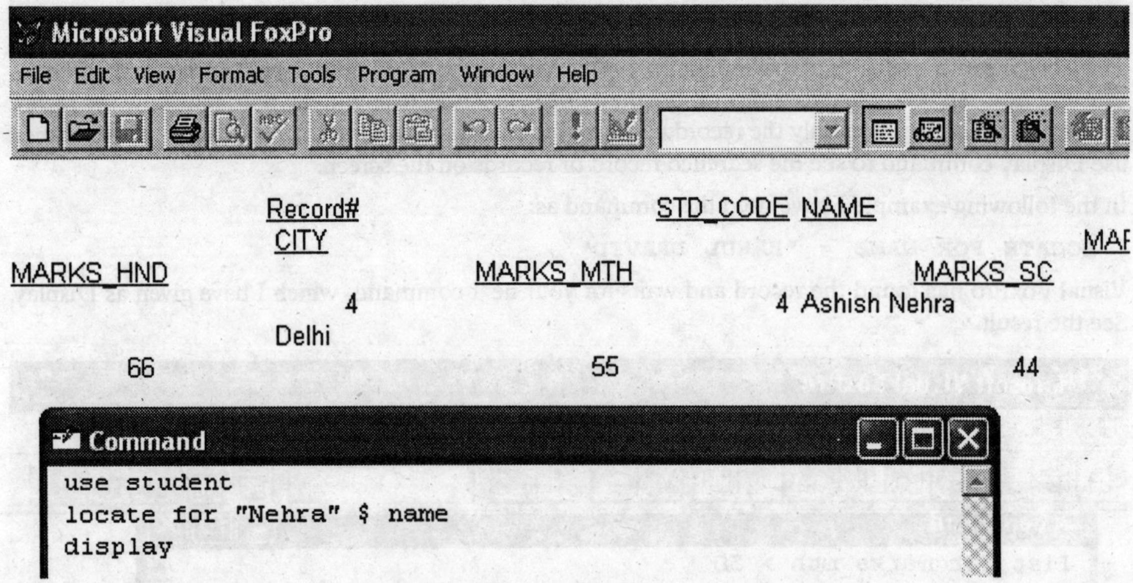

Then type the following command to locate the next occurrence of 'Nehra'

```
RECORD = 6
```

Type Display Enter repeatedly till you get message: End of Locate Scope in the status bar.

You can also use the command

```
LIST FOR 'NEHRA' $ NAME
```

This command will list and show all the records with 'Nehra' embedded in the Name field.

Multiple Conditions in Single Command

Another approach would be to ask for the desired record more specifically, that is using a logical operator. The various logical operators were defined earlier. Let us use the AND Operator. Now enter the command:

```
LOCATE FOR NAME = 'SACHIN TENDULKAR' AND CITY = 'DELHI'
```

The two statements connected with the operator And must be true to get the record. That is, the Name must be "Sachin Tendulkar" and the City must be "Delhi". The result after the first search will be:

```
RECORD = 1
```

Now use display command to view the record. So type:

```
DISPLAY
```

The result is shown on the next page. On using the command continue, you get the following message in the status bar.

```
END OF LOCATE SCOPE
```

There is so because there is no other record which satisfies the two conditions at the same time. The AND operator gives a result only when both the search conditions are true otherwise it does not give any output. If you require a listing of all employee records where name is either Sachin or Nehra embedded in the field Name, then type the following command:

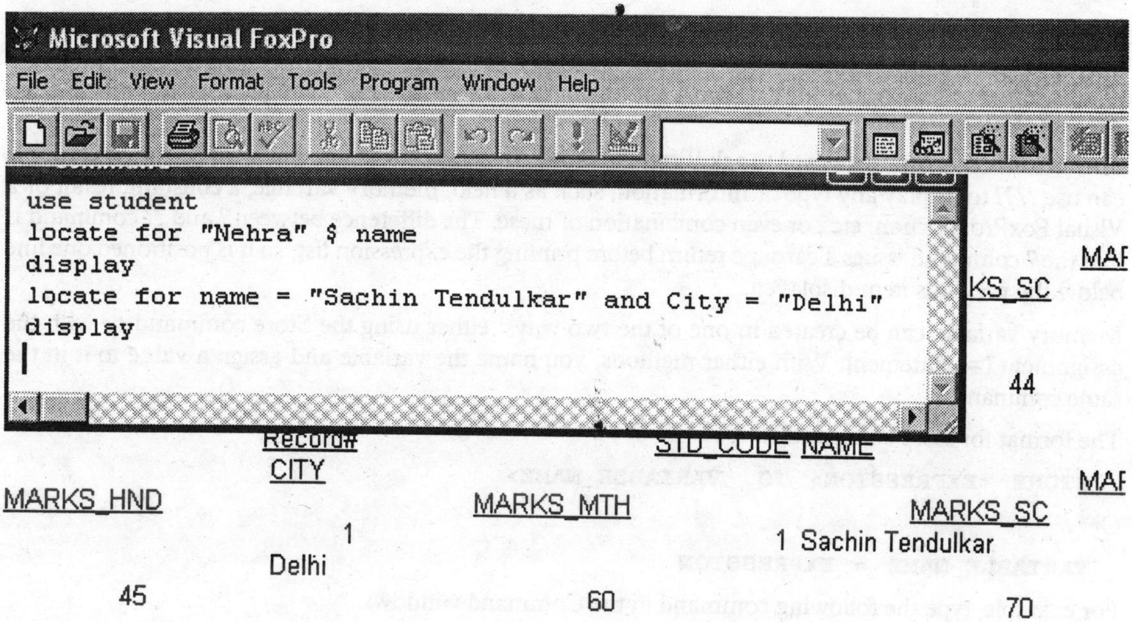


```
LOCATE FOR 'NEHRA' $ NAME OR 'SACHIN' $ NAME
```

Type Display Enter, Continue Enter repeatedly until you get the message: End of Locate scope. You can also use List For command to give similar result by using Locate, Continue command:

```
LIST FOR 'NEHRA' $ NAME OR 'SACHIN' $ NAME
```

The result will be seen in figure.

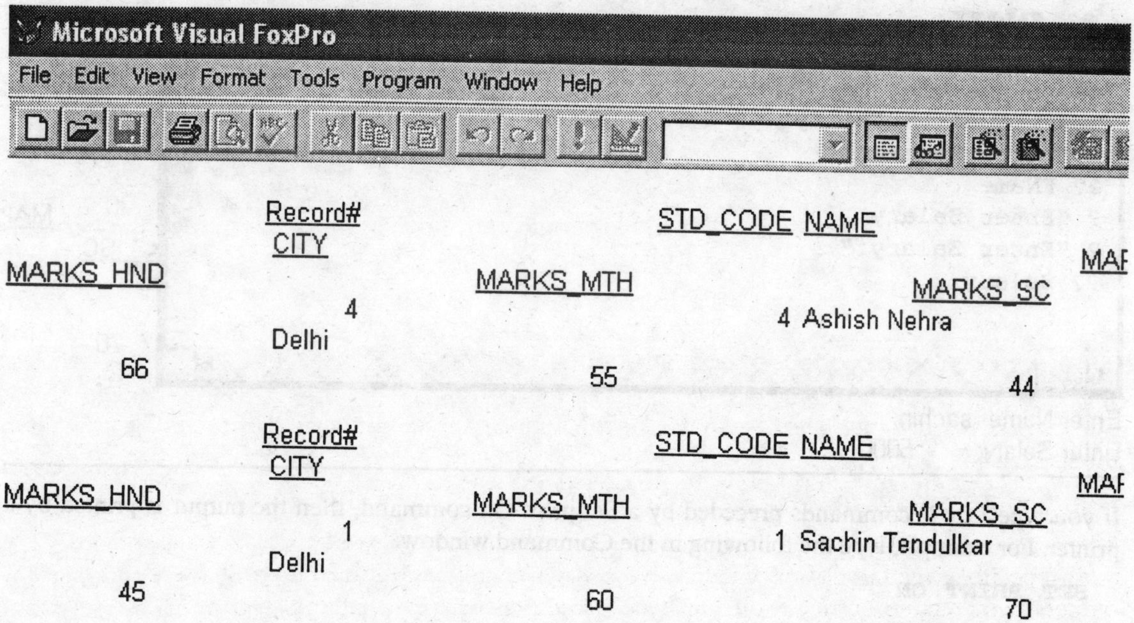

Note that by using And Operator in the above command would not display any output. It is so because there is no record which contains both Nehra and Sachin in the fieldname.

The ? Command

The ? and ?? commands are used to ask Visual FoxPro to display a particular data item on the screen. You can use ?/?? to display any type of information, such as a field, memory variable, a constant, result of a Visual FoxPro function, etc., or even combination of these. The difference between ? and ?? command is that the ? command issues a carriage return before printing the expression list, so it is positioned one line below the previous item displayed.

Memory variable can be created in one of the two ways: either using the Store command or with the assignment (=) statement. With either methods, you name the variable and assign a value to it in the same command.

The format for store command is:

```
STORE <EXPRESSION> TO <VARIABLE_NAME>
```

Or

```
VARIABLE_NAME = EXPRESSION
```

For example, type the following command in the Command window:

```
STORE "SACHIN" TO FNAME
STORE 5000 TO SALARY
? "ENTER NAME:"
?? FNAME
? "ENTER SALARY:"
?? SALARY
```

```
store "sachin" to FName
Store 5000 to Salary
? "Enter Name: "
?? FName
? "Enter Salary
? "Enter Salary:"
?? Salary
```

```
Enter Name: sachin
Enter Salary:      5000
```

If you type ? or ?? commands preceded by a Set print On command, then the output is printed by a printer. For example, type the following in the Command window:

```
SET PRINT ON
? "ENTER NAME:"
```

```
?? FNAME
? "ENTER SALARY:"
?? SALARY
SET PRINT OFF
```

USING EXPRESSION BUILDER

Expression is a concept. Using it you can create building blocks, like constants, fields, variables and functions and can use increasingly complex logical expressions that use the Boolean operators, like And, OR and NOT. Expressions are used in Visual FoxPro to communicate specifications and instructions for many commands and functions.

An expression can include several components. These are:

Field names

Variables

Constants (or literals)

Functions

Operators

You can either type directly in the Expression box of Expression Builder or select them using the Expression Builder controls as follows;

- Use the four drop-down controls at the top of the Expression to select functions and operators of different data types.
- Use the fields list to select Field names.
- Use the variables list to select variables. The Expression box shows the expression you have constructed with your selections. You can also type the expression or parts of it directly into this box. You can click the Verify button to check whether the Expression box holds a valid expression – i.e. one that does not contain any errors in syntax.

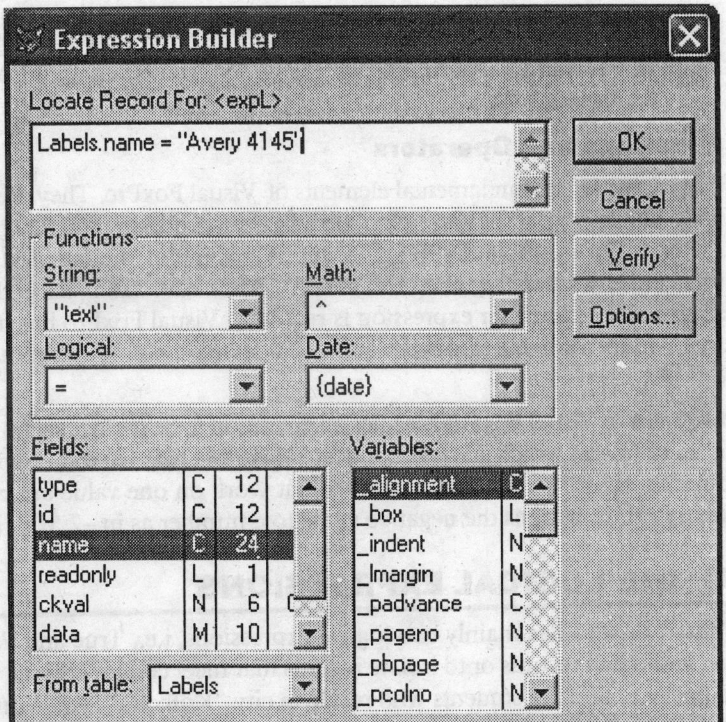

Fieldname

They are the names of fields of your table as std_code, name, city, etc. By default the names of all the fields in a table can be selected from the Fields list in the Expression Builder.

Variables

A variable is a named space in the Random Access Memory (RAM) of your computer where Visual FoxPro stores values. The name is given to the variable when you assign it a value. For example, Name = "Sachin". A variable is one of the Visual FoxPro's expressions and an important building block for the programming language. There are mainly two type of variables.

System Variables are built in, always beginning with the underscore character and always have the same meaning. For example, _PAGENO represents the current page of a report and it can be included in an expression added to the report Designer.

Memory variables are created by the user and are used in advanced expressions, used in Visual FoxPro programming.

Constant

It remains fixed throughout the use. Its value does not change. Constants may be letters, numbers or data that are used with their literal meaning. For example, if you wanted an expression to actually include the Word name: before each student's name, you would use the constant "Name" as part of that expression. Constant, that is used in an expression must include the following delimiters to indicate their data type:

Character constants Character constants must be enclosed in double quotation marks (" "), single quotation mar (' ') or square brackets ([ ]). For example, you could use "Hello" or 'Hello' or [Hello] in an expression to make an expression include the actual word Hello.

Date and DateTime constants These constant must be enclosed in curly brackets ({ }). For example, {12/23/99}

Number constant It is used without any delimiter. Simply use the number itself.

Logical constants There are two logical constants, enclosed by dots - .T. represents True and .F. represents False.

Functions and Operators

Functions are the fundamental elements of Visual FoxPro. They are, small programs that perform certain tasks like testing, information lookup and even processing. A function is identified by the parentheses at the end. For example the function upper(). Some of the functions have commas in their parentheses, showing how many arguments then need. Some have examples in their prarentheses such as expc, which shows that a character expression is required. Visual FoxPro has more than 300 in-built functions with many more available through commercial sources, plus you can make your own. These are called user-defined functions.

Operator in Visual FoxPro specifies an operation to be performed on operands to give a value. An operand is an entity on which an operator acts. Operators that work on two operand are called binary operators such as +, -, *, /, etc. The operators that work on one value are called unary operators. For example, unary minus assigns the negative value to a number as in –2.5.

USING LOGICAL EXPRESSIONS

Visual FoxPro has mainly two logical expressions, i.e., True and False. They are generally used to find an individual records or to isolate records that meet certain criteria. For example, if you wanted to make a query to find the students who reside in city "Kolkotta", you would have to use the expression City = "Kolkotta". Visual FoxPro looks at each record to see letters Kolkotta. If they are, the expression City = "Kolkotta" is evaluated as True. If not, the expression is evaluated as False.

LOGICAL FUNCTIONS

Some functions also return .T. true or .F. i.e., False although they are generally used in programming. Common examples of Logical functions are EOF(), i.e., End of File and BOF(), i.e., Beginning of File. Let us see them in details.

EOF()

End of File means the logical end of the file, i.e., the system has reached the last record of the file. The normal format of the function is simply EOF(). The function EOF() returns a logical True (.T.) value when the record pointer is at the end of a file and is then moved forward by one more record. The SKIP command can move the record pointer forward one record at a time. The syntax for this is:

```
EOF ((<NUMERIC EXPRESSION>/<CHARACTER EXPRESSION>))
```

Type the following in the Command window:

```
USE STUDENT
GO BOTTOM
SKIP 1
?EOF()
GOTO TOP
? STD_CODE, NAME
SKIP 1
```

As you can see from the figure below, in the first case, i.e., when ?EOF() was given the system response was .T. and when ? std_code, name was given, it responded by giving the std_code and name of the first record.

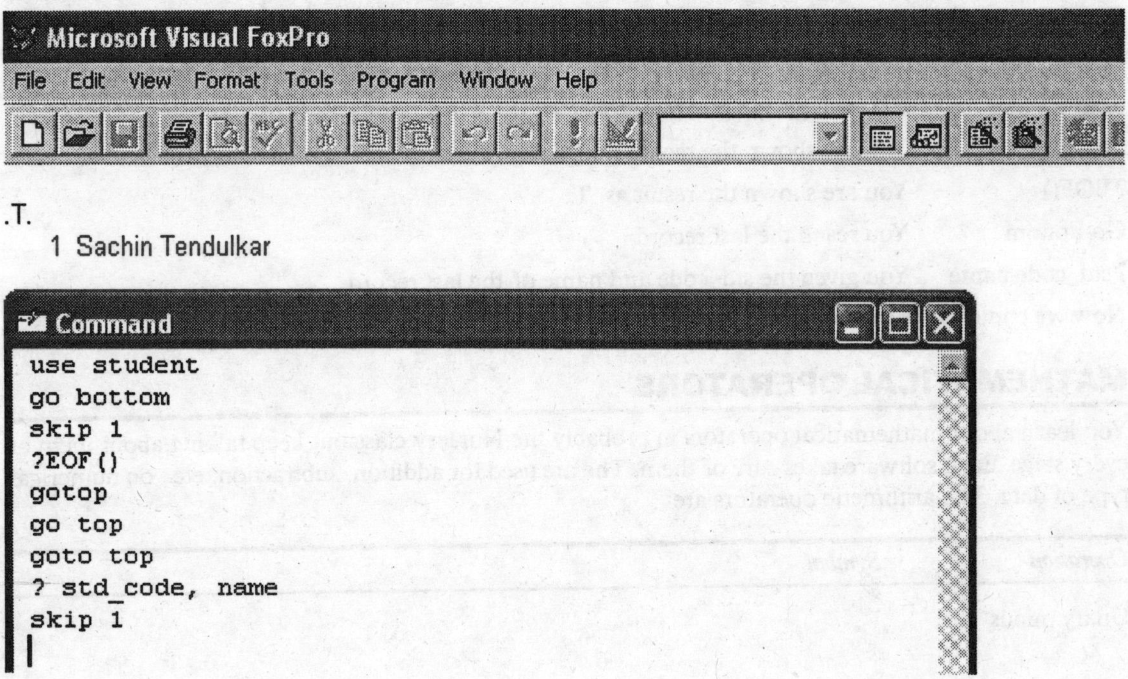

Now we come to Beginning of the File.

BOF()

It gives a logical value of .T. when an attempt has been made to push the record pointer above the first record in the file. Otherwise, it returns a logical value of .F. If the record pointer is positioned at the first record of a table, the Skip 1 command sets BOF() to True. The syntax for this is:

```
BOF ((<NUMERIC EXPRESSION>/ <CHARACTER EXPRESSION>))
```

Type the following the command window:

```
USE STUDENT
GOTO TOP
?RECNO ()
? BOF()
.F.
SKIP 1
? RECNO()
? BOF()
GO BOTTOM
? STD_CODE NAME
```

The above expressions can be explained as follows:

Use Student	The file student is put into memory.
GOTO top	Your control is transferred to the first record.
?Recno ()	You are shown the record number on the screen, i.e., 1.
? BOF()	It will given you the result as .F.
Skip 1	You will go the record number 1
? REcno()	You are shown the record number as 1.
? BOF()	You are shown the result as .T.
Go Bottom	You reach the last record
? std_code name	You given the std_code and name of the last record.

Now we come to the mathematical expressions, operators.

MATHEMATICAL OPERATORS

You learn about mathematical operators in probably the Nursery class but keep talking about them at every stage. Each software takes care of them. The are used for addition, subtraction, etc., on numerical type of data. The arithmetic operators are:

Operation	*Symbol*
Unary minus	

Exponentiation (raising to a power)	^ or **
Division	/
Multiplication	*
Subtraction	-
Addition	+

RELATIONAL OPERATORS

Relational operators determine the relation among different operands. In other words, relational operators are used to test the relation between two expressions or values. It may be used for comparing numerical variables. The values your compare can be constant or variables. Visual FoxPro provides six relational operators for comparing number and characters. Any comparison of values result in logical value of True or False. If the compression is True, the relational expression results into the .T. and .F. if the comparison is False. The $ symbol is used to search for a substring. The == operator which (means is identical to) is not the same as = (which means is equal to).

LOGICAL OPERATORS

Logical operators combine the results of one or more expression and it is called a logical expression. The logical operators are And, Or Not and () are explained in an earlier table.

STRING OPERATORS

These operators are used to combine two or more character strings, known as Concatenation. The Plus (+) sign is used to combine strings including blanks. The minus (-) sign is used to concatenate strings eliminating embedded blanks between them. For example,

```
? TRIM(FNAME)+ " " + TRIM(MNAME)
```

would now display Sachin Tendulkar, if FNAME has Sachin and MNAME has Tendulkar. The minus(–) sign is used to eliminate the blanks. It is generally used as a shortcut. The command:

```
? FNAME-MNAME
```

is similar to

```
? TRIM(FNAME)+ TRIM(MNAME)
```

Order of Precedence

I remember the class IX of mine where I was first taught about order of precedence. That was the time when we were studying so called Algebra and this was required since we did not know what would be solved first + or –. The confusion was solved when our teacher gave us him Guru Mantra and this was called BODMAS rule. This can be explained as follows:

B Bracket

O Overhead line

D Divide

M Multiply

A Add

S Subtract

Another interesting thing which I want to share with you is the expression:

2 + 3 * 4 + 5

If you solve this on a very ordinary calculator the result would be 25. And if you do this on a scientific calculator then the result would be 17. Guess which one is true. Apply the above BODMAS rule and you will understand what I am talking about. The result 17 is true since 3 * 4 would be solved first and then all additions will take place.

Similarly in Visual FoxPro we have the following order of precedence.

1. Expression enclosed in parenthesis, starting with the innermost set of parenthesis and bound to the rules of precedence within each set.
2. Functions
3. Mathematical operations, in the following order.
   a. Exponentiation
   b. Multiplication and division, form left to right
   c. Modules calculations
   d. Addition and subtraction from left to right.
4. Character string concatenation
5. Relational operators, from left to right
6. Logical operators, in the following order:
   a. Not
   b. And
   c. Or

SORTING AND INDEXING

The major difference between the two is that in the case of sort, a new file is created with the sorted records while in the case of indexing, the table remains the same but each record is marked for indexing. Sorting and indexing of the files can be done from the command window as shown below.

Sort

Sorting means grouping records in a particular order say ascending or descending based on a key field of the records. Ascending order means that the names in records of a table will be arranged beginning with the letter A at the top and Z at the bottom. On a numeric field, the smallest number comes first and on a date field, the record with the earliest date comes first. The descending order is just the reverse of it. This means, that names in a table will be arranged with the letter Z at the top and A at the bottom. This is particularly useful for date fields, where you often want the most recent date to come first.

A practical example of sorting of words is the arrangement of numbers and words in a dictionary where thousands of words are arranged in ascending order. Telephone dictionary is another familiar example where names of subscribers are arranged in alphabetical order. Sorting helps us in locating required records such as names of subscribers quickly. The different users of a table may need records in different sequences.

Sorting a Table

Visual FoxPro creates a new table using the sort command and stores the sorted records. From the command window, the format for the Sort command is

```
SORT TO <NEW FILE> ON <FIELD /A/D/C>, <FIELDS...>
```

The option /A specifies an ascending order for the field name. This order for the field name. This order places character field in alphabetical order (A to Z) numeric fields in numerical order (0 to 9) and date fields in chronological order (earliest to latest).

The option /D specifies a descending order, i.e., character fields are sorted in descending order (Z to A) numeric fields from highest to lowest (largest number to lowest numbers) and Date fields in reverse chronological order (from latest to earliest).

If you include /C option after the name of a character field, then uppercase and lowercase letters are treated equally in the sorting order. Otherwise upper case letter Z comes earlier to lower case letter a. you can thus use (/AC or /DC) after the name of a character field to ignore the distinction of upper case and lower case letters in either order i.e. Ascending or Descending..

Let us sort on marks_hnd field in student.dbf table using the Sort command. We will save the sorted data to a file called std2.dbf. The command will be given as:

```
USE STUDENT
SORT TO MARKS_HND TO STD2
USE
USE STD2
BROWSE
```

The result is shown below.

Std2

Std_code	Name	City	Marks_eng	Marks_hnd	Marks_mth	Marks_sc
2	Rahul Dravid	Delhi	60	44	65	65
1	Sachin Tendulkar	Delhi	55	45	60	70
3	Saurav Ganguly	Delhi	55	60	50	45
4	Ashish Nehra	Delhi	70	66	55	44

The records are sorted in the sequence of marks_hnd in ascending order i.e., from 44 to 66.

If the similar command is given to sort the records in the ascending order of name, then the command set would be :

```
USE STUDENT
SORT ON NAME TO STD1
USE
USE STD1
BROWSE
```

You will get result as shown in the figure on the next page.

Std1

	Std_code	Name	City	Marks_eng	Marks_hnd	Marks_mth	Marks_sc
▶	4	Ashish Nehra	Delhi	70	66	55	44
	2	Rahul Dravid	Delhi	60	44	65	65
	1	Sachin Tendulkar	Delhi	55	45	60	70
	3	Saurav Ganguly	Delhi	55	60	50	45

Using FOR Clause to Sort Selected Records

You can create a sorted file to include only the selected records by giving specific command which would include suitable Scope and Condition. To produce such a sorted file that should contain only specific records from the table, you will use the "FOR" scope with the Sort command. The syntax for the Sort command when used in this manner is:

```
SORT TO <NEW FILE> ON <FIELD LIST> FOR <LOGICAL EXPRESSION>
```

For example, if you need to include records for students who belong to Delhi and put them in alphabetic order of name too then you give the following command at Command window:

```
USE STUDENT
SORT TO STD3 ON NAME FOR CITY = "DELHI"
USE
USE STD3
BROWSE
```

The following figures show both the results before and after sorting.

Student

	Std_code	Name	City	Marks_eng	Marks_hnd	Marks_mth	Marks_sc
	1	Sachin Tendulkar	Mumbai	55	45	60	70
	2	Rahul Dravid	Delhi	60	44	65	65
	3	Saurav Ganguly	Kolkotta	55	60	50	45
▶	4	Ashish Nehra	Delhi	70	66	55	44

Std3

	Std_code	Name	City	Marks_eng	Marks_hnd	Marks_mth	Marks_sc
▶	4	Ashish Nehra	Delhi	70	66	55	44
	2	Rahul Dravid	Delhi	60	44	65	65

Sorting Table on Multiple Fields

It is possible that you may need to sort a table on two fields instead of one. One will be the major field and the other would be minor field. The general format for the command is:

```
SORT TO NEWFILE ON FIELD1 [/A/C/D], FIELD2 [/A/C/D],....... LAST FIELD
[/A/C/D]
```

The above mentioned table Student can be sorted on City and Name to give the following result:

Std4

Std_code	Name	City	Marks_eng	Marks_hnd	Marks_mth	Marks_sc
4	Ashish Nehra	Delhi	70	66	55	44
2	Rahul Dravid	Delhi	60	44	65	65
3	Saurav Ganguly	Kolkotta	55	60	50	45
1	Sachin Tendulkar	Mumbai	55	45	60	70

INDEXING A FILE

I had talked about Indexing while defining Sort. It is a process of arranging the records. In indexing, original record numbers do not change. However, here the records are indexed in the alphabetic order of name. To get a better understanding of an index file, consider the index at the back of this book. If you wish to find information on a specific subject, just refer to the page number given along with the subject and you would find the detail of the subject on that page. Visual FoxPro supports two type of index files: These are:

a. Single Index files

b. Compound index files

Let us see them in details.

Single Index Files

The index file here is kept with the extension .IDX. This index can be kept up to date by opening the index everytime you do some editing, i.e., adding, altering, etc., you will have to open this index file too. In other words, if you keep the index files open (active), they automatically get updated regardless of the operation you perform. This type of index files can be two types:

Compact: These files are faster to access and occupy less disk space due to reduced size.

Non-compact: Here the files are slower to access and are use more space.

The command for Compact type is:

```
INDEX ON <EXPR> TO <.IDX FILE> COMPACT
```

For non compact one you will use the command:

```
INDEX ON <EXPR> TO <.IDX FILE>
```

Compound Index Files

These are identified by the .CDX extension. Unlike the IDX files, each of which can hold only one Index, compound index files can hold multiple indexes in a single file, which are identified by names called tags. The exact number of tags you can include in a .CDX index file is limited only by the available main memory of the machine you are using. Here also you have two types: Structural and Independent. Let us see what they mean.

Structural: It is opened automatically whenever you open the table. A structural compound index is automatically given the same name as the table file with the extension .CDX. To create a structural compound index file the syntax is:

```
INDEX ON <EXPR> TAG <TAGNAME>
```

When Visual FoxPro opens a table, it looks for a structural compound index file (a compound index file having the same name as the table with the extension .CDX). If such a file is found, Visual FoxPro opens it and updates it automatically as and when changes are made in the table.

Independent: Compound Indexes other than Structural Compound Index are called independent compound indexes. These can have any name with extension .CDX. however, these files cannot be given the same name as the table. To create an independent compound index file the syntax is:

```
INDEX ON <EXPR> TAG <TAGNAME> OF <.CDX FILE>
```

For most of the database applications, a structural compound index file serves well. However, if you have a group of indexes that you use only once in a year or so as to produce reports, keep them as a separate, independent index file. Then you can specifically use that file and reindex it once in a year before producing the reports.

Deleting Tags

When you put tag in an index file, there must be a way to delete them too. You can delete one or more tags from a compound index file by using the Delete Tag compound. If a tag is in a non-structural index file, you must open the index file before you execute the Delete tag command. The syntax is:

```
DELETE TAG <TAG NAME> OF <.CDX INDEX NAME>
```

you can also delete more than one tag at a time by specifying a list of tag names rather than a single tag in the Delete Tag command. The syntax is:

```
DELETE TAG <TAGNAME1> {OF <.CDX FILE1> [, <TAGNAME2>] [OF <.CDX FILE2]
```

you can also delete all the tags from compound index by adding keyword All to Delete Tag command.

```
DELETE TAG ALL [OF <.CDX FILE>]
```

Note the use of [OF <.cdx file>] clause implies reference to an independent compound index file.

CREATING INDEX

Index command is used to create an Index file or tag for the current table. Records in a table that has an index file are displayed and accessed in the order specified by the index expression. The physical order of the records in the table is not changed by an index file. The Index command in Visual FoxPro arranges records more efficiently from the command level.

The general format for index command is:

```
INDEX ON <FIELD EXPR> TO <.IDX FILE> \ TAG <TAG NAME> [OF <CDX FILE>]
[FOR <CONDITION>] [COMPACT] [ASCENDING/DESCENDING] [UNIQUE] [ADDITIVE]
```

The above command creates an index file for the table that is open in the current work area. The index command arranges records in an apparent order based on the field expression, but actual order of the records in the table file does not change. You can create an .idx index file by including file To <idx file> clause. The index file is given the default extension .Idx.

```
TAG <TAG NAME> [OF <CDX FILE>]
```

You can also create a compound index file by including Tag <tag name>. A tag of a compound index file (.cdx) contains multiple index tags within one file. If you do not specify a filename Visual FoxPro makes this a tag of the structural compound index file, which has the same name as the table file and is automatically opened whenever the table file is opened.

The optional For clause makes the index include only those records for which the logical expression is true. The compact option directs Visual FoxPro to create compact Idx index files. The compact option reduces the size of the index files and make them more efficient. The **Ascending** and **Descending** options allow you to tell Visual FoxPro whether to index the file according to ascending or descending values of the particular field. However, ascending option is the default. The **Unique** option makes the index file include the records with the first occurrence of a given value for the field expression only. This option will eliminate the duplicate data records from the index file. The **Additive** option allows previously opened index files to remain open while you create a new index file. We shall now use the index command to index Employee.dbf file on Name field.

For this, we just need to open student.dbf file and enter the following command:

```
INDEX ON NAME TO NAMES
```

The index command creates an index file (Names.idx) on name field and displays the following message:

```
4 RECORDS INDEXED
```

At this stage if you give the command as List you will find the screen as shown below.

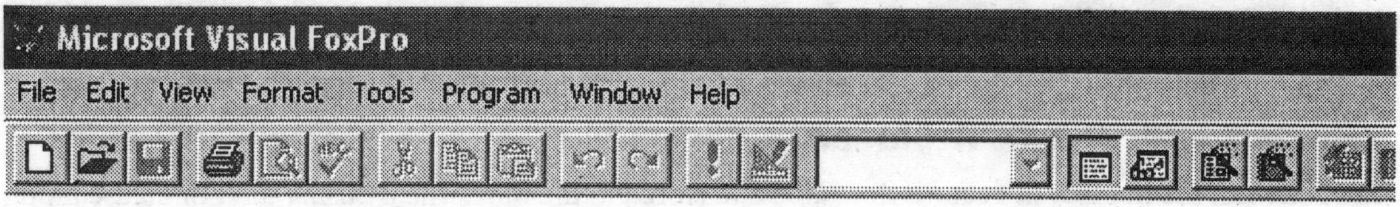


```
          Record#                    STD_CODE NAME
          CITY                                                  MAI
MARKS_HND                  MARKS_MTH                  MARKS_SC
                4                    4 Ashish Nehra
          Delhi
   66                         55                         44
                2                    2 Rahul Dravid
          Delhi
   44                         65                         65
                1                    1 Sachin Tendulkar
          Mumbai
   45                         60                         70
                3                    3 Saurav Ganguly
          Kolkotta
   60                         50                         45
```

You see that there is no change in the order of the records. Each of the record is at the same place where it was.

We can also index records on another field say marks_eng. I am doing this deliberately since this field is numeric while name was character. Enter the following command in the Command window:

```
INDEX ON MARKS_ENG TO ENG
```

It displays message in status bar as:

```
4 RECORDS INDEXED
```

now type the command :

```
LIST STD_CODE, NAME, MARKS_ENG
```

Visual FoxPro displays the records in the ascending order of marks_eng.

Student

Std_code	Name	City	Marks_eng	Marks_hnd	Marks_mth	Marks_sc
1	Sachin Tendulkar	Mumbai	55	45	60	70
3	Saurav Ganguly	Kolkotta	55	60	50	45
2	Rahul Dravid	Delhi	60	44	65	65
4	Ashish Nehra	Delhi	70	66	55	44

Thus, you have two index files for student.dbf. One which contains sorted name, i.e., (names.idx) and other which contains sorted marks-eng, i.e., (eng.idx). At one time you can use only one of them. However you can select other index files either by opening the table file with the desired index file or by specifying the index filename with Set index command. For example,

```
SET INDEX TO NAMES
```

Indexing with the FOR clause

You can limit the number of records in a table and stored in the index file by using the For clause along with the Index on command. You can also do so by using the <for…> expression window of the Index On dialog box. If used from the command window, the syntax for the index command is as follows:

```
INDEX ON EXPRESSION TO FILENAME FOR CONDITION
```

Where the condition used with For is any expression that evaluates to a logical true or false. This is a powerful Visual FoxPro option that can, in effect, filter the table of the unwanted records but placing the records in order at the same time. The set filter command alongwith a simple use of the index command would also accomplish the same result. Assuming that an updated index already exists, then using for with index on is faster method is compared to using set filter.

Indexing a File and Adding Records using Append

Suppose you want to display data from the student table in order of name, enter the following command:

```
USE STUDENT INDEX NAMES
```

You can now add new records with the append command. Visual FoxPro adds a blank record at the end of a file and then you can enter data in the newly added record. After adding the new record to the table, press Ctrl + W to save it. If we type List or Browse command to view the records, then all the records including newly added record will be listed alphabetically by name. Thus there is no need to carry out indexing procedure again.

Indexing on Multiple Fields

You may index file on more than one fields similar to the case of sorting. But, you cannot directly index on multiple fields if the fields are not of the same type. For example, you can not index by Name and other fields in student.dbf table, because name is a character field whereas marks-eng is a numeric field. However, you can index student.dbf on City and the Name fields because both are character fields. Visual FoxPro will first index the file on City field and for records with the same city, it will rearrange them in alphabetic order.

Indexing on Multiple Fields of Different Types

I had talked about the multiple field indexing in the last step. But, what we can do is to change the type of the field using the string function called STR. Thus, in order to sort records on marks_eng and name fields, first you need to convert the field marks_eng which is numeric to string type using, STR() function. The STR() function converts the contents of a numeric field into a string of characters. For example:

```
INDEX ON STR(MARKS_ENG) + NAME TO MULNED
LIST NAME, MARKS_ENG
```

See that the records are in the order of name since there is no duplicate field of the name, if it had been then the one record with less marks in eng would have been given the priority.

Opening Tables and Index Files

You may open a table file with one or more index files simultaneously by adding the word "Index" and filenames after the <Use fielname> portion of the command. However only one index file is active at a time. The syntax for the use command, when taken with the index option would be:

```
USE FILENAME INDEX INDEXNAME1 [,INDEXNAME2]
```

For example, you could open the student table file simultaneously attaching the names and marks_eng index files with the following command:

```
USE EMPLOYEE INDEX NAMES, MARKS_ENG
```

INDEXING COMMANDS

For an index to control the order of the records, it must be active. You can easily tell which indexes are in use at any time by using the list status or list display commands.

Set index

An index that has just been created in active. But by using the Set index command, you can activate any of the indexes.

Set order

To activate an index file use the set order command. With set order, you use numbers such as, set order to 2. The number 2 here indicates the order in which the index file was originally opened.

Reindex

Reindex command recreates all the open index (.idx and .cdx) files. It rebuilds all open index files in the current work area. If any changes have been made to the table while the index file was closed, you can update it with the Reindex command. Index files must be reindexed specially if they were not closed properly, i.e., when PC is turned off or reset without using the Exit. Index files also need to be reindexed if they are not open when the records are appended or edited in the table.

Close index

When you decide not to use any index file, use close index command to close the index files but keeping associated table files open.

SETTING A FILTER CONDITION

Specifying, or setting a filter condition is an efficient way of selecting a group of records from a table. For example, by using filter, you can display all records where city is Delhi or those records with marks_eng more than 50. After you set a filter, you need not worry about adding the criterion to each command. Records that do not meet your criterion are filtered out indefinitely, until you remove the filter. You can create a filter from the Command window by entering:

```
SET FILTER TO <LOGICAL EXPRESSION>
```

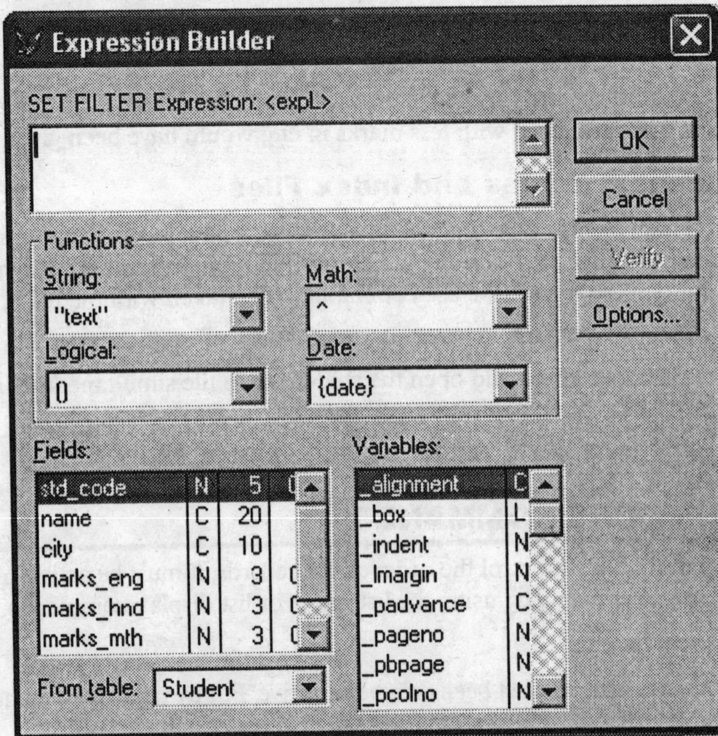

After you use a filter, it remains in effect until you change it or remove it. Before you can view the entire table again, you must remove the filter. If you want to remove the filter just enter Set filter to command without any logical expression. You can also create filter conditions in a special dialog box called the Expression Builder. You can use this dialog box when you need to provide an expression or condition to complete a command. To create a filter condition, do this:

1. Open the table in the Browse window and click table menu. Choose Properties to open the Work Area Properties dialog box.
2. Click on the Data filter button.
3. Double-click on the field to be affected.
4. Type the remainder of the expression; or choose an operator from the Logical drop-down list, choose the type of string from the String drop-down list and type the condition.
5. To verify that the expression is valid, click on Verify.
6. Click OK button to return to the Work Area Properties dialog box.

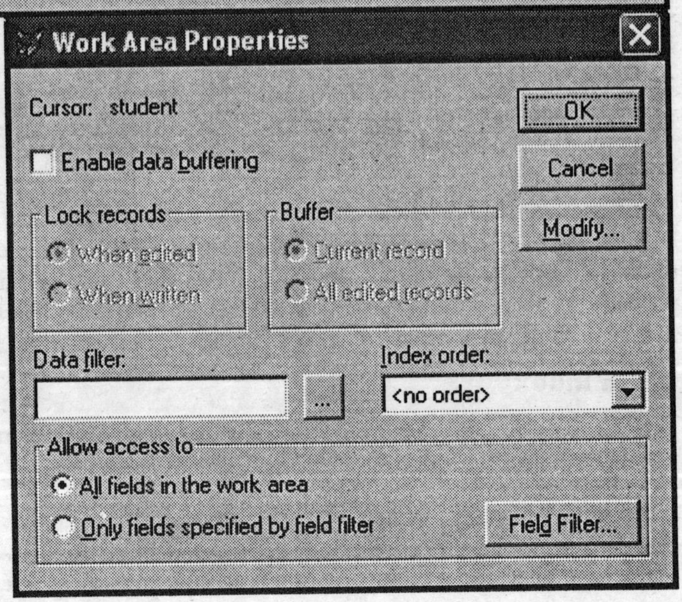

A mathematical operator is a symbol or sequence of symbols, such as +, * and = that tell the program to perform an operation to calculate a result. A function is a preprogrammed calculation that is performed by the program on request.

Changing a Filter Condition

To change an existing filter condition do this:

1. Open the Expression builder dialog box again.
2. In the Fields list box, double-click on the desired field.
3. Type the new expression; or choose the desired parameters from the Functions drop-down lists and type the new condition.
4. Click OK.

Removing a Filter Condition

You can remove a filter condition to display all the records in a table. To remove a filter condition do the following:

1. Select Table menu and choose Properties option. The Work Area Properties box will be displayed.
2. Click all fields in the work area radio button below the Allow access to box.
3. Click Field Filter... button. A Field Picker dialog box appears.
4. Select Remove All button to move the selected fields back to All fields: box.
5. Click OK twice.

MACRO(S)

The macro is just like an ordinary memory variable, but has an ampersand (&) in front of it namely, &Name, &Fld etc. When Visual FoxPro encounters a macro in a command file, it replaces that macro with the contents of the memory variable. For example, if you have a memory variable, called Fld and you have the word Pin_Code stored to that name, every time the &Fld macro is encountered in the program, Visual FoxPro automatically substitutes the word Pin_Code. A memo field can store any type of data namely, keyboard symbols, graphics or special symbols. Memo fields can also store data such as scanned image, digitized sound, binary objects, executable programs and any other data as well. You treat the data in a Memo field like variable length database character fields. The only limitation in using Memo fields is the amount of disk space available in your computer. Data stored in Memo fields do not form part of the database and are not stored in the file with extension .Dbf. FoxPro stores them in a separate file with the same name as original database file but with an extension of .FPPT.

Creating Table with Memo Field

You will now create a table self.dbf with the structure as shown here.

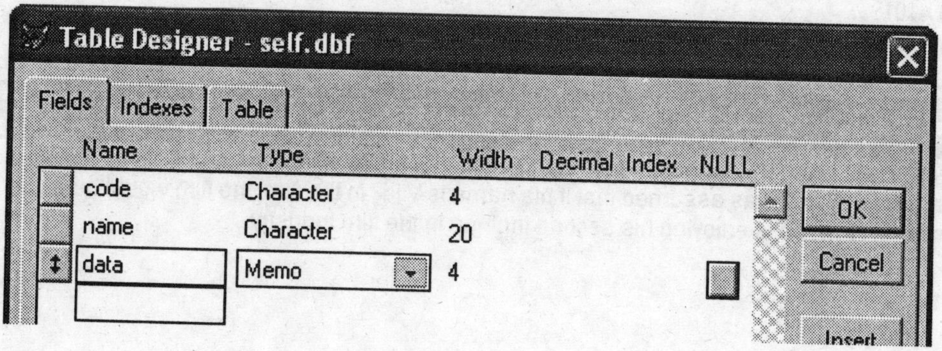

After defining the structure of self.dbf when you see the message "Input data records now?" select Yes and Visual FoxPro displays a blank record for data entry, as shown below.

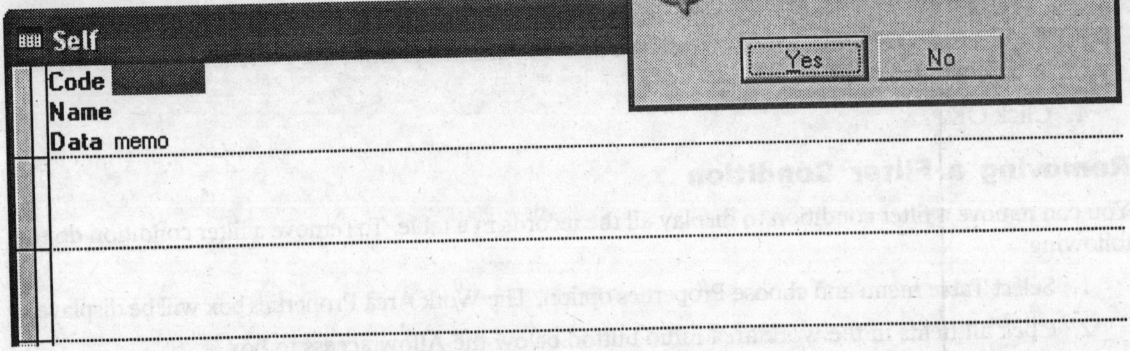

You can enter the following records in the table:

1. A101 Amitabh An excellent actor, has acted in more than 100 films to date. In more than 17 films, his name was Vijay. It was assumed that if his name is Vijay in the film, the film would be a success. Now, he is enjoying his second innings in the film industry.
2. S101 Shah Rukh Coming from Delhi and making a modest start, this actor has had an excellent run in the film industry in the last decade. He is still the number one choice of most of the producers, specially Chopra and Johars. They cannot think of making a film without him.

In the code field type the code of the first entry i.e., A101. Next enter Amitabh in the Name field. So far so good. Now comes the main part.

Entering Data into Memo Fields

Now we come the memo field and to enter data into it, double click the memo field with mouse. You would be shown a Visual FoxPro editor. Enter your complete text into it. This word editor works with Word wrap facility, so you do not have to enter the Enter key after every line. See how the data looks in the editor, below.

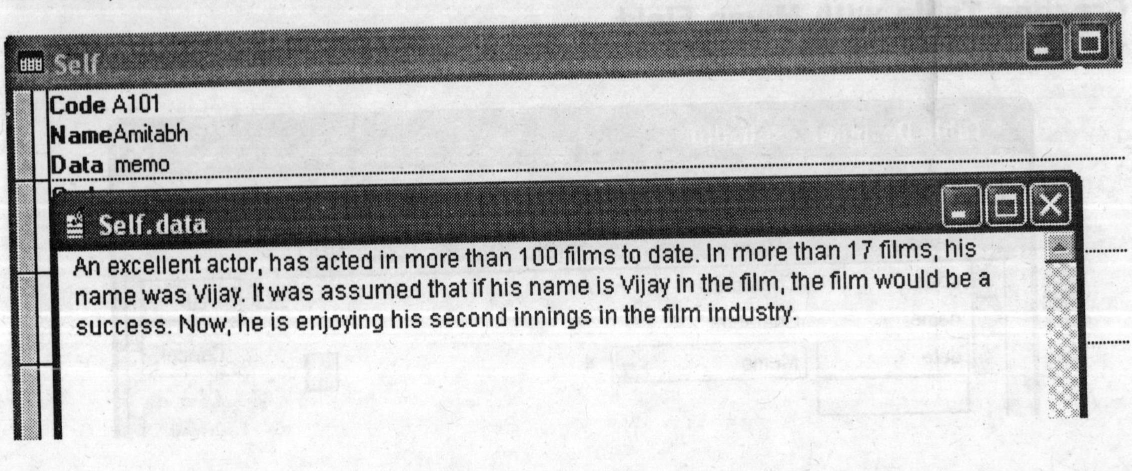

Similarly enter the data for the second record. After entering the information in memo field press Ctrl + W to save text in memo file or select File, and then Close from the Visual FoxPro. You can also click the Close (x) button, located on the top left corner of the window. Finally press Ctrl + W to save the records and click on close (x) button to return to Command Window. You can use the following keys to edit the data in the memo field. Most of you who are familiar with working of word processing would find them similar.

Key	*Description*
Ctrl + PgDn	Activate the Memo Editor when the cursor is in the memo field
Ctrl + Home	Move cursor to the top-left corner of the window
Ctrl + End	Move the cursor to the bottom-right corner of the window
Ctrl + left arrow	Move cursor left one word
Ctrl + right arrow	Move cursor right one word
Ctrl + W	Save changes and exit
Ctrl + A	Select all text within the window
Ctrl + U	Undo
Ctrl + R	Redo
Ctrl + X	Cut
Ctrl + C	Copy
Ctrl + V	Paste
Ctrl + F	Find
Ctrl + G	Find again
Ctrl + E	Replace and find again
Up arrow	Move cursor up one line
Down arrow	Move cursor down one line
Left arrow	Move cursor left one character
Right arrow	Move cursor right one character
Ins	Turn Insert mode on/off
Del	Delete character at cursor
Backspace	Delete character to the left of the cursor
Esc	Close memo field after prompting you to save changes
Shift + Arrow	Select a block text

Viewing Information in Memo Field

Once that you have added data to the memo field, you would like to see it too. Visual FoxPro does not display contents of memo field. Instead it displays the word Memo under the Detail field. To see the contents of Memo field, type the following command at the Command window and watch the output at the screen.

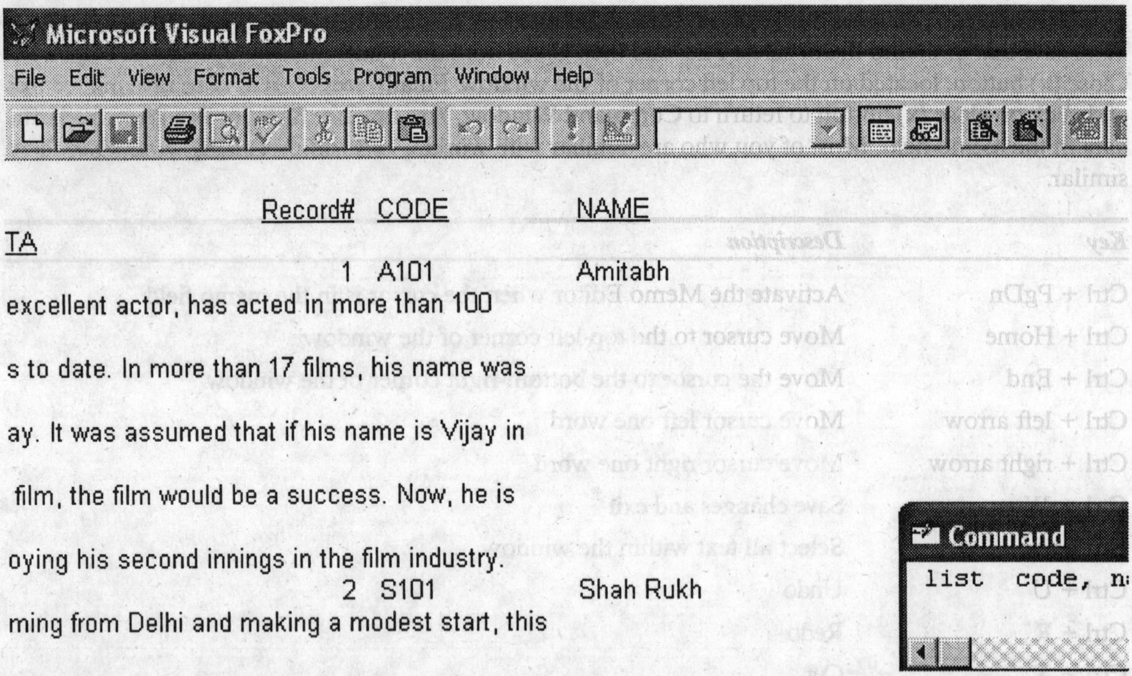


```
LIST CODE, NAME, DATA
```

When you use list command, it uses 50 characters (default) to display the contents of a Memo field. However you can use the Set Memowidth command to control the width of Memo field when displaying contents using list or display command. This may result in more convenient display of information contained in the Memo field. Type the following commands in Command window and watch the screen:

```
SET MEMOWIDTH TO 50 LIST NAME, DATA
```

See if you can find some difference.

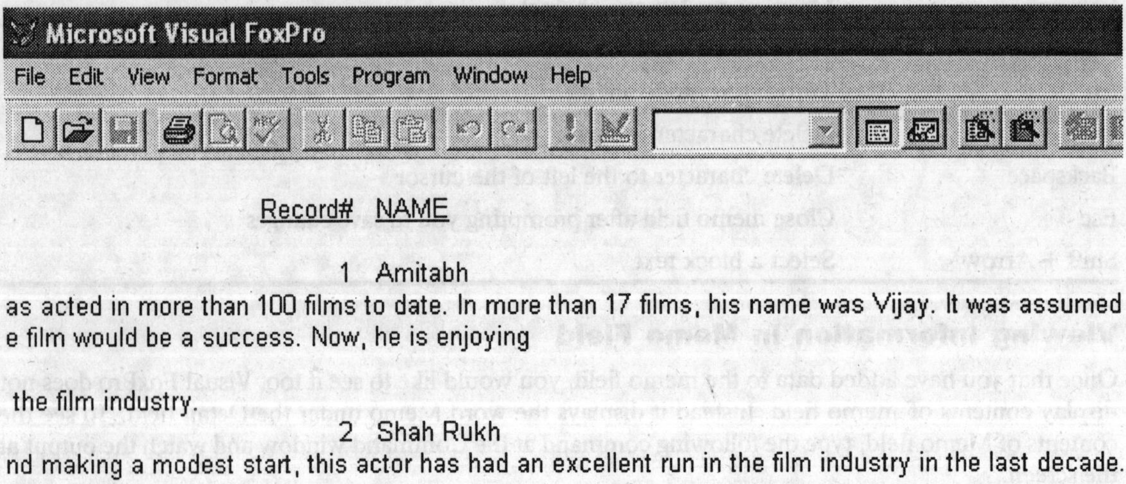

Modifying Memo Field

Modify memo command opens editing window for changing Memo fields in the current table. This command also allows you to view a Memo field's contents or make and save changes in it. If a record has more than one Memo field, then you can open a window for each Memo field. In the above case if you want to edit the memo field, just type:

```
MODIFY MEMO DATA
```

The data in the data field would be on screen for you to edit.

Date and Time Functions

Visual FoxPro offers several data and time functions. The following sub sections describe these with examples.

Date ()

This function reads the computer's system date and then supplies a date-type value representing it. The display will be in the default format mm/dd/yy or in some other as specified by the Set Date command. The syntax is:

```
DATE ()
```

The command ? DATE() would result in the current system date.

CDOW()

The character day of week function converts the date expression into the day of the week expressed in the text form, i.e., Sunday through Saturday. The syntax is:

```
CDOW(DATE)
```

The command cdow(Date) would give you the day of the week, i.e., Friday.

CMONTH()

The character month of year function converts the date expression into the month of the year expressed as a name. The syntax is:

```
CMONTH(DATE)
```

The command ?CMONTH(DTE) would result in the current month, i.e., September.

CTOD()

The character to date function converts the date expressed as a text string into a standard date type expression. The syntax is:

```
CTOD(CHARACTER_STRING)
```

DAY()

The day of month function converts the date expression into the day of the month. The syntax is:

```
DAY(DATE)
```

DMY()

This function returns a date expression in European Day Month Year format for the given date. It always returns the Month with a full spelling. The syntax is:

DOW()

The day of week function converts the dates expression into the day of the week expressed as a number. For example since 03/05/03, was the Wednesday and Wednesday is the fourth day of the week, so DOW({03/05/03}) returns 4. The syntax is:

```
DOW(DATE_EXPRESSION)
```

DTOC()

This function returns a character string containing the date corresponding to a date expression. The syntax is:

```
DTOC(DATE_EXPRESSION, 1)
```

DTOS()

This function returns an eight-digit character string in the format YYYYMMDD for a given date expression. The syntax is:

```
DTOS(DATE_EXPRESSION)
```

GOMONTH()

This function returns the date which is a certain number of months after or before a date expression. The syntax is:

```
GOMONTH(DATE_EXPRESSION, NUMBER_OF_MONTHS)
```

MDY()

This function returns a Month Day Year Character string for a given date expression. It always returns the month with a full spelling. The syntax is:

```
MDY(DATE_EXPTRESSION)
```

MONTH()

The month function converts the date expression into the month of the year expressed as a number. The syntax is:

```
MONTH(DATE)
```

Seconds()

This function returns the system time in seconds, thousandths format, with a resolution of 1 millisecond. The syntax is:

```
SECONDS()
```

SYS(1)

This function returns the current system date as a Julian day number expressed as a character string. The syntax is:

```
SYS(1)
```

SYS(2)

This function returns the number of seconds elapsed since midnight as a character string. The syntax is:

```
SYS(2)
```

SYS(10)

This function converts the numeric day number of a character string. The syntax is:

```
SYS(10, NUMBER)
```

SYS(11)

This function converts a date expression or a character string in date format to a Julian day number returned as a character string. The syntax is:

```
SYS(11, DATE_EXPRESSION/CHARACTER_EXPRESSION)
```

TIME()

The Time() function is eight characters long and is presented in the HH:MM:SS format. HH stands for hours, MM stands for minutes, SS stands for seconds. The time function gives you access to the system time. You can use this function to store the system time to a memory variable or table field. The syntax is:

```
TIME()
```

Year(0)

The year function converts the date expression into a year expression. The syntax is:

```
YEAR(DATE)
```

CONCEPT OF MULTIPLE TABLES

So far, you have worked only with single-table database, which are sufficient for some simple business applications. Visual FoxPro is a relational database manager and hence gives you the choice one or more than one table at a time. It also enables you to define relationships between two or more table.

Relating Files

Earlier, you found that the current table in use is automatically closed as soon as you open a new file. However, using visual FoxPro relational power, you can create a relation to connect or join records from different tables and thus you can access their information at the same time. In a relation, one table is called the parent table and the other is called as child table. The parent table controls the child so that when you move the record pointer (select a record) in the parent table, Visual FoxPro automatically moves the record pointer to the first corresponding record in the child table. If a matching record cannot be traced in the child table, then record pointer moves to the end of the last record in a child file. Visual FoxPro is quite flexible in the ways in which it lets you draw relationships between tables.

You will read more about these relative databases in a later chapter.

Let us Revise

1. Command Window is used to write the command.
2. Create command is used to create a table.
3. Modify Structure command is used to change the structure of the table.
4. Append command adds data at the end of the table.
5. Edit command allows you to change data.
6. Browse is a powerful command enables you to scroll through table horizontally as well as vertically.
7. Replace command can replace any field data with another depending upon the command given.
8. Delete command puts a physical marker to the record, which you want to delete, but it does not actually remove the record form the file.
9. Pack Command permanently deletes the records marked for deletion from the table.
10. ZAP command deletes all the data in the table and retains the structure.
11. Erase command is used to erase a file from the disk.
12. Run command allows you to run any DOS based command.
13. Display command shows the contents of the current directory or file on the screen.
14. List displays the contents on the screen.
15. The Locate command is used for finding the position of a record in a table as per the required criterion.
16. The ? and ?? commands are used to ask Visual FoxPro to display a particular data item on the screen.
17. Expressions are used in Visual FoxPro to communicate specifications and instructions for many commands and functions.
18. A variable is a named space in the Random Access Memory (RAM) of your computer where Visual FoxPro stores values.
19. Functions are the fundamental elements of Visual FoxPro, they are, small programs that perform certain tasks like testing, information lookup and even processing.
20. Visual FoxPro has mainly two logical expressions, i.e., True and False.
21. End of File means the logical end of the file, i.e., the system has reached the last record of the file.
22. BOF() gives a logical value of .T. when an attempt has been made to push the record pointer above the first record in the file.
23. Relational operators determine the relation among different operands.
24. Logical operators combine the results of one or more expression and it is called a logical expression.
25. String operators are used to combine two or more character strings, known as Concatenation.
26. Sorting means grouping records in a particular order say ascending or descending based on a key field of the records.
27. You can create a sorted file to include only the selected records by giving specific command which would include suitable Scope and Condition.
28. In Indexing records are indexed in the alphabetic order of name.
29. Index command is used to create an Index file or tag for the current table.
30. You may open a table file with one or more index files simultaneously.
31. To activate an index file the set order command is used.
32. Reindex command recreates all the open index (.idx and .cdx) files.
33. The macro is just like an ordinary memory variable, but has an ampersand (&) in front of it namely, &Name, &Fld, etc.
34. Visual FoxPro does not display contents of memo field.
35. Set Memowidth command is used to control

the width of Memo field when displaying contents using list or display command.

36. Date () function reads the computer's system date and then supplies a date-type value representing it.
37. CDOW()displays character day of week function converts the date expression into the day of the week expressed in the text form.
38. CMONTH() converts the date expression into the month of the year expressed as a name.
39. CTOD() converts the date expressed as a text string into a standard date type expression.
40. DAY() converts the date expression into the day of the month.
41. DMY() returns a date expression in European Day Month Year format for the given date.
42. DOW() converts the dates expression into the day of the week expressed as a number.
43. DTOC() returns a character string containing the date corresponding to a date expression.
44. DTOS() returns an eight-digit character string in the format YYYYMMDD for a given date expression.
45. GOMONTH() returns the date which is a certain number of months after or before a date expression.
46. MDY() returns a Month Day Year Character string for a given date expression.
47. MONTH() converts the date expression into the month of the year expressed as a number.
48. Seconds() returns the system time in seconds, thousandths format, with a resolution of 1 millisecond.
49. SYS(1) returns the current system date as a Julian day number expressed as a character string.
50. SYS(2) returns the number of seconds elapsed since midnight as a character string.
51. SYS(10) converts the numeric day number of a character string.
52. SYS(11) converts a date expression or a character string in date format to a Julian day number returned as a character string.
53. TIME() function is eight characters long and is presented in the HH:MM:SS format.
54. Year(0) converts the date expression into a year expression.

Multiple Choice Questions

1. Command Window is used for :
   (a) Writing commands
   (b) Getting to windows
   (c) Going to DOS
2. Append command adds the data to the :
   (a) Beginning (b) Last
   (c) Middle
3. Run command is used to run :
   (a) Windows commands
   (b) FoxPro commands
   (c) DOS commands
4. Locate command is used to :
   (a) finding the position of the record
   (b) finding the data (c) finding the field
5. ? command is used to display :
   (a) table (b) data items
   (c) form
6. FoxPro has two logical expressions True and:
   (a) Bad (b) False
   (c) No
7. String operators are used to combine two or more character strings, known as :
   (a) Combination (b) Strings
   (c) Concotation
8. An indexed file can be activated using :
   (a) Set order (b) Set index
   (c) Set sort
9. Macros have this character in the beginning :
   (a) * (b) &
   (c) %
10. List command displays on :
    (a) Printer (b) Screen
    (c) Plotter

True/False Questions

1. Command Window is used to write the command.
2. Create command is used to create a table.
3. Append command adds data at the begining of the table.
4. Edit command allows you to change data.
5. Replace command can replace any field data with another depending upon the command given.
6. Delete command puts a physical marker to the record, which you want to delete, but it does not actually remove the record form the file.
7. ZAP command deletes all the data in the table and structure.
8. Erase command is used to erase a file from the disk.
9. Display command shows the contents of the current directory or file on the screen.
10. List displays the contents on the printer.
11. The ? and ?? commands are used to ask Visual FoxPro to display a particular data item on the screen.
12. Expressions are used in Visual FoxPro to communicate specifications and instructions for many commands and functions.
13. Functions are the fundamental elements of Visual FoxPro, they are, small programs that perform certain tasks like testing, information lookup and even processing.
14. Visual FoxPro has mainly one logical expression, i.e., True.
15. BOF() gives a logical value of .T. when an attempt has been made to push the record pointer above the first record in the file.
16. Relational operators determine the relation among different operands.
17. String operators are used to combine two or more character strings, known as Concatenation.
18. Sorting means grouping records in a particular order say ascending or descending based on a key field of the records.
19. In Indexing records are indexed in the alphabetic order of name.
20. Index command is used to create an Index file or tag for the current table.
21. To activate an index file the set order command is used.
22. Reindex command recreates all the open index (.idx and .cdx) files.
23. FoxPro displays contents of memo field.
24. Set Memowidth command is used to control the width of Memo field when displaying contents using list or display command.
25. CDOW()displays character day of week function converts the date expression into the day of the week expressed in the text form.
26. CMONTH() converts the date expression into the month of the year expressed as a name.
27. DAY() converts the date expression into the day of the month.
28. DMY() returns a date expression in European Day Month Year format for the given date.
29. DTOC() returns a character string containing the date corresponding to a date expression.
30. DTOS() returns an eight-digit character string in the format YYYYMMDD for a given date expression.
31. MDY() returns a Month Day Year Character string for a given date expression.
32. MONTH() converts the date expression into the month of the year expressed as a number.
33. SYS(1) returns the current system date as a Julian day number expressed as a character string.
34. SYS(2) returns the number of seconds elapsed since midnight as a character string.
35. SYS(11) converts a date expression or a character string in date format to a Julian day number returned as a character string.
36. TIME() function is eight characters long and is presented in the HH:MM:SS format.

Matching Columns

Match the text in Column A with the text in Column B.

Column A	Column B
1. CDOW	a. Returns a Month Day Year Character string for a given date expression.
2. CMONTH	b. Returns the current system date as a Julian day number expressed as a character string.
3. DAY	c. Converts a date expression or a character string in date format to a Julian day number returned as a character string.
4. DMY	d. Converts the date expression into the month of the year expressed as a number.
5. DTOC	e. Returns the number of seconds elapsed since midnight as a character string.
6. DTOS	f. Returns a date expression in European Day Month Year format for the given date.
7. MDY	g. This function is eight characters long and is presented in the HH:MM:SS format.
8. MONTH	h. Converts the date expression into the day of the month.
9. SYS(1)	i. Returns an eight-digit character string in the format YYYYMMDD for a given date expression.
10. SYS(2)	j. Converts the date expression into the month of the year expressed as a name.
11. SYS(11)	k. Returns a character string containing the date corresponding to a date expression.
12. TIME()	1. Displays character day of week

Fill in the Blanks with Appropriate Words

a. ? b. & c. Run d. Pack
e. Browse f. Command Window

1. The window which is used for writing commands is known as ______________.
2. To scroll through the table you use the command called __________.
3. To permanently delete the records from the table, you use the command called _______.
4. To run DOS based commands you use the command called _______.
5. To display the contents of data items you use the _____ command.
6. In Visual FoxPro the macros start with the ______ character.

Descriptive Type Questions

1. What is command window used for?
2. What is sorting and how it is done?
3. Explain Order of Precedence.
4. What is indexing? How does it differ from Sorting?
5. Describe the following with respect to indexing: Set Index, Set order, Reindex and Close Index.
6. Describe the working of following commands:

Append	Change
Browse	Replace
Delete	Recall
Pack	Zap
Erase	Run
Set Default	Display
List	?

7. Write short notes on the following functions:

DATE()	CDOW()
CMONTH()	CTOD()
DAY()	DMY()
DOW()	DTOC()
DTOS()	GOMONTH?()
MDY()	MONTH()
SECONDS()	SYS(1)
SYS(2)	SYS(10)
SYS(11)	TIME()
YEAR(0)	

Answers to Objective Type Questions

Multiple Choice Questions

1. a	2. b	3. c	4. a
5. b	6. b	7. c	8. a
9. b	10. b		

True/False Questions

1. T	2. T	3. F	4. T
5. T	6. T	7. F	8. T
9. T	10. F	11. T	12. T
13. T	14. F	15. T	16. T
17. T	18. T	19. T	20. T
21. T	22. T	23. F	24. T
25. T	26. T	27. T	28. T
29. T	30. T	31. T	32. T
33. T	34. T	35. T	36. T

Matching Columns

1. l	2. j	3. h	4. f
5. k	6. i	7. a	8. d
9. b	10. e	11. c	12. g

Fill in the Blanks with Appropriate Words

1. f	2. e	3. d	4. c
5. a	6. b		

Recommended Readings

1. Learn to Program Visual Basic—Databases *by John Smiley*.
2. Learn to Program Visual Basic—Objects *by John Smiley*.
3. Learn to Program Visual Basic—Examples *by John Smiley*.

—Published by Firewall Media (An Imprint of Laxmi Publications Pvt. Ltd.)

11 Relational Database Concepts of Visual FoxPro

INTRODUCTION

You look at Relational Database in this way that if you create a relation between two databases then you can work not with one database but with two databases at a time. Simply putting, if you have databases of students. One having the marks, the other having name, roll number, etc., then you can work on these databases independently or together too, if you create a common field, which maybe rollno. In a Relational Database, data is organized in the form of rows and columns similar to a table. The tables are referred to as relations in a relational data model. Rows of the table are referred to as tuples and the columns of a table are referred to as attributes.

Table in a relational database is similar to the traditional file system with its records, fields and files. The table's rows, called tuples, contain records and columns, called attributes, contain fields. Each tuple or row, has values for the attributes. The attribute describes some feature or property of the objects.

Advantages of Relational Database

a. You can use it with a PC with small memory too.

b. Relational database is very effective for small databases.

c. Relational database is much easier to use because it enables a computer system to accommodate a variety of enquiries in an efficient manner.

d. Relational database is only concerned with data and not with the structures, which improves the performance. The processing time and storage space is comparatively large in relational database but the user is not required to know the intricacies of the structure design, thus making relational database easy to use and learn.

e. Other traditional databases use pointers to implement record relationship. But, in relational databases record relationship is implemented using primary key or composite key field(s). Hence it is very simple and represents the logical relationship among the data items rather than physical relationship (like hierarchical and network model).

f. Relational model is very useful for representing most of the real world object and the relationship among them.

Relationships among Tables

As mentioned above, you have to have a primary keyfield which establishes the relation between the two tables. This key should be present in the tables involved. As mentioned above in the case of students tables, the roll number of the student becomes the keyfield. The type of relationship that can be established are:

One to One

This is the simplest one. Like above each student has a unique roll number which is there is all the relative tables.

One to Many

In this type of relationship, one record in one table has many corresponding records in the other table. This is why it is called One to Many. One-to-many relationship is the most common relationship used in a relational database. For example, one department has many workers.

Many to Many

In many to many relationship, a record in one table has many corresponding records in a second table and for every record in the second table, there are many corresponding records in the previous table. For example Many students would take Many tests.

CREATING A NEW DATABASE IN VISUAL FOXPRO

We have earlier learned about creating tables. The method of creating a database is very similar. Of course we would be using Wizard or Database Designer, as we had done in the case of tables.

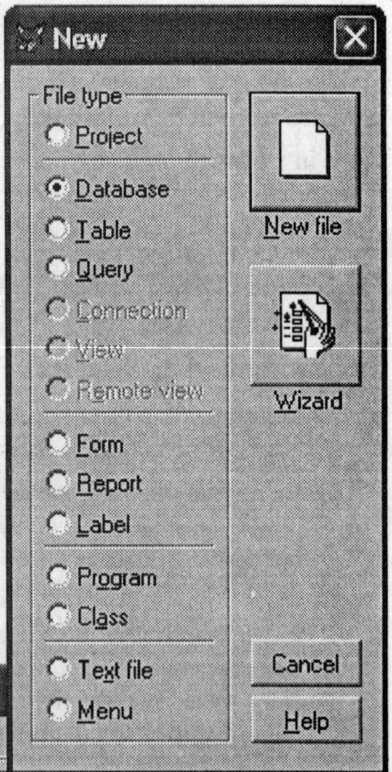

1. Click File menu and choose New… In the New dialog box that appears select the Database radio button and click New File button.
2. Alternatively, you can create a new Database by giving the Create Database command in the Command Window.
3. In the Create dialog box that appears select the directory of your choice and provide a name for the new Database file. We have provided the name "student". Click Save.
4. You will not note that a Database Designer window opens up. If the toolbar is not visible, select it from Toolbars dialog box. This dialog box appears when you click Toolbars… From the View menu. There are different buttons in the Database Designer toolbar. Click the "Add Table button" and add tables "student.dbf" and "table1.dbf" into the database. You will note in figure that one can also create new table or remove existing tables using the Database Designer toolbar.

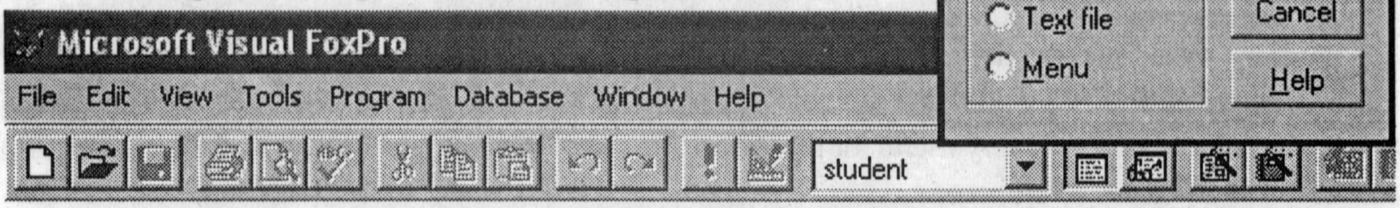

5. Press Ctrl + W keys, when finished.

You have thus created a relational database "student" with the two tables "student.dbf" and "table1.dbf".

ENTERING AND VIEWING DATA USING THE FORM WIZARD

Earlier we had created form for a single table, now we would create a form from two tables which are there in a relation. The One-to-Many Form wizard creates a form from two related tables. One table is considered as the parent table and other as the child table. The fields of child table appear in a grid below the fields of parent table. To do this, we do the following:

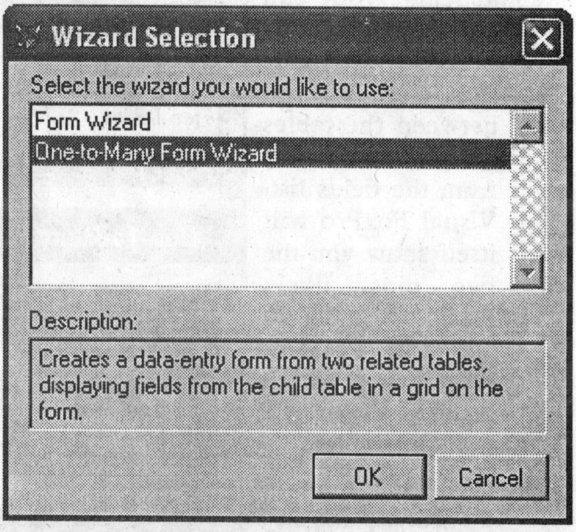

1. Click Tools menu, highlight Wizard and choose Form.
2. The Wizard Selection dialog box will appear. Choose One-To-Many Form Wizard and then click OK.
3. In the dialog box that appears the Databases and Tables: area will show the current Database which is "student" in our case. If you want a table other than this, click on the small button to the right of Databases and Tables: area. The Open dialog box will get opened and you can open the required table using this dialog box. In our case, we have chosen "student.dbf" table. Therefore, this table forms our parent table.

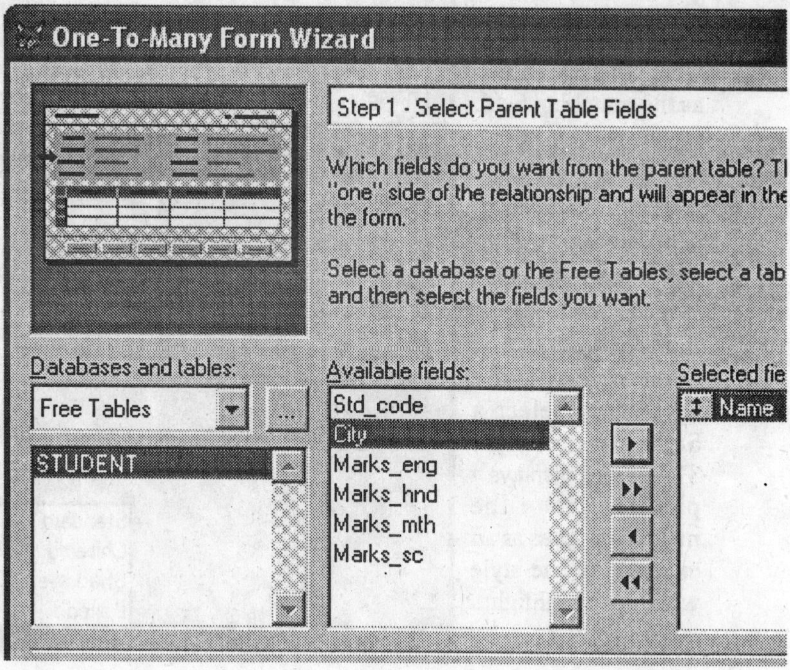

4. From the Available Fields, select the field which you want in your form, then click > button. To select all the fields present in the Available Fields: area click the >> button. I have selected here the filed called Name.
5. To remove a field from the Selected Fields: area click the < button. To remove all the fields, click the << button.
6. Click Next to go to next Step, i.e., Step 2.
7. Similarly, select the fields from the "child"

table in the dialog box that appears. In our case, we have chosen the "table1.dbf" table to be the child table.

8. Click Next.
9. In the dialog box that appears you can accept or select the fields that determine the relationship between the tables (parent and child) from the fields list. Visual FoxPro will itself show you the two most likely fields. If you do not accept the FoxPro's suggestion, select the required related field from the two tables.
10. Click Next to go to the next step, i.e., Step 3.
11. Here it shows that what you have chosen as the matching field. If you want you can change it too.
12. After selecting, choose Next to go to the next step, i.e., Step 4.
13. In the dialog box that appears, from the Style box, select a Style for the form. The wizard displays a picture in the magnifying glass as an example of the style which you highlight.
14. The Button type: area

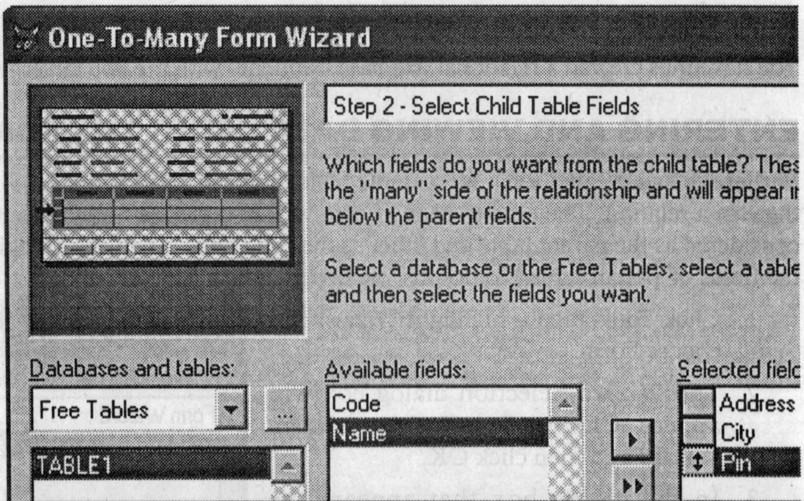

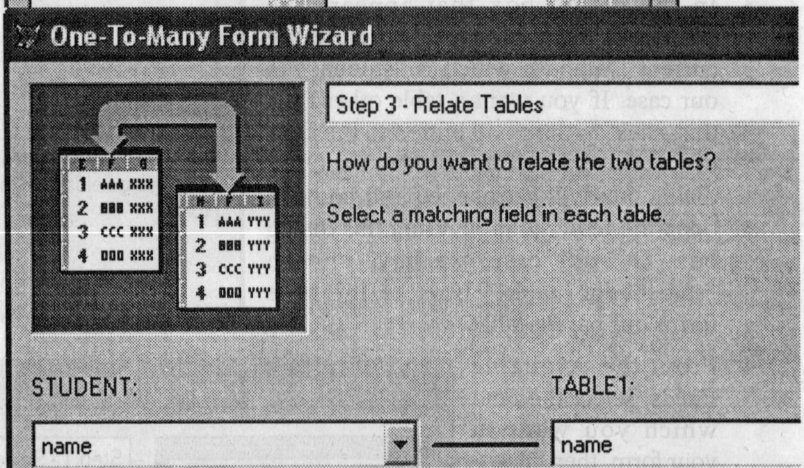

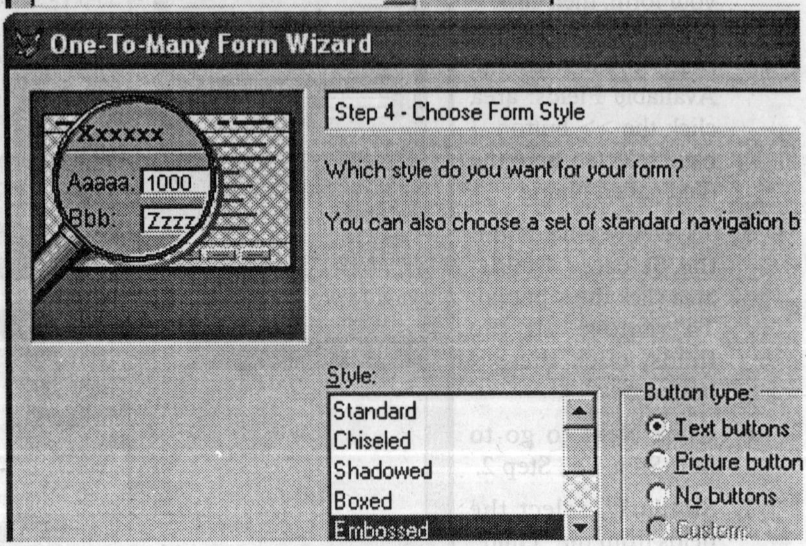

specifies the form's navigation buttons. You will note that this dialog box is same as that of the "form Wizard" you studied in earlier chapter.

15. Click Next to go to the next step, i.e., Step 5.
16. In the next dialog box that appears, select the fields based on which you want to sort the records in the parent table. Here I have chosen Name.
17. Click Next.
18. In the dialog box, click the Preview button to view the form before you exit the One-To-Many Form Wizard. Otherwise, select any of the listed options and click Finish. We have selected "Save and run form". In the Save As dialog box we provided the name "student" and the form appeared as shown here.

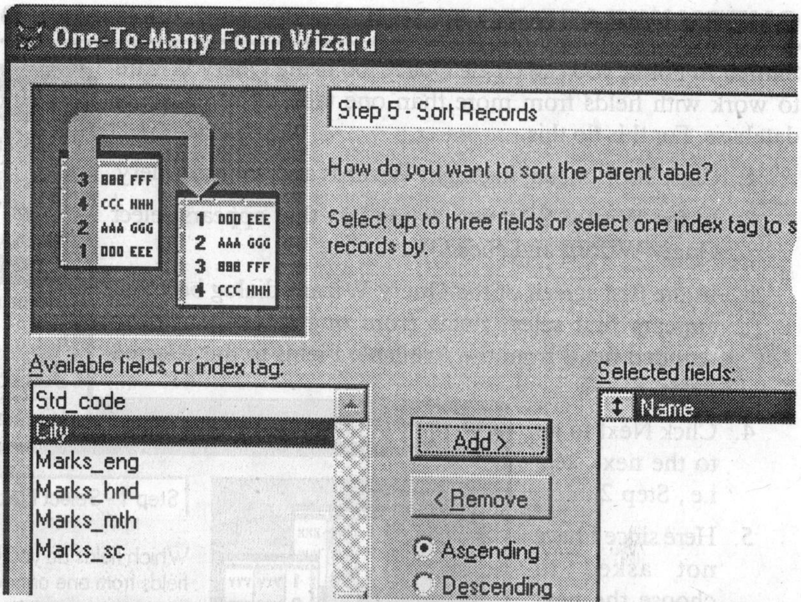

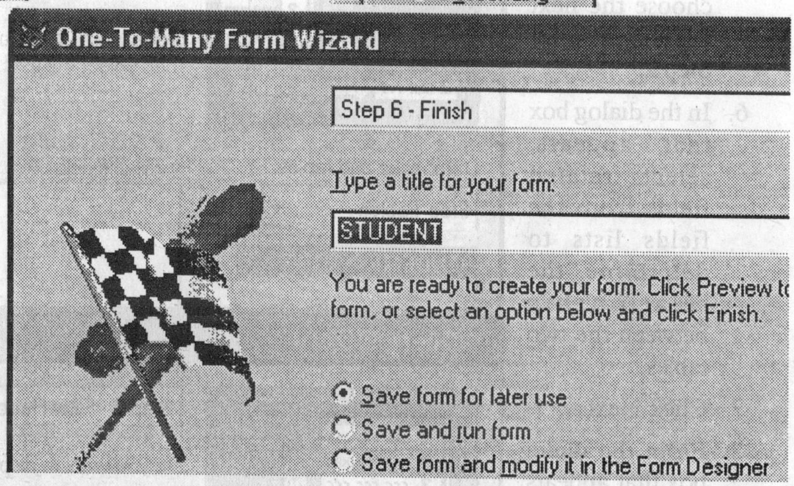

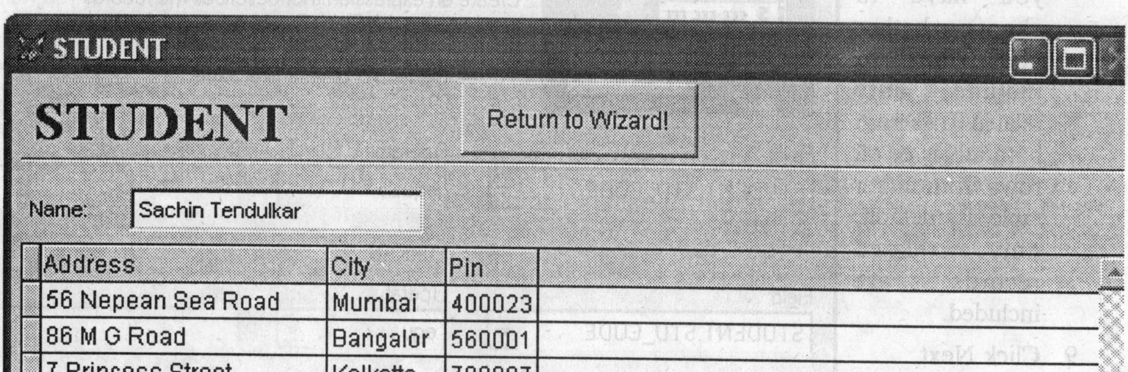

QUERY WIZARD TO WORK WITH RELATIONAL DATABASES

Similar to Form, you can create Query too using Query Wizard to work with fields from more than one table of a relational database. For this do this.

1. Click Tools menu, highlight Wizards and choose Query.
2. In the Wizard Selection dialog box that appears select Query Wizard and click OK.
3. In the first screen of the Query Wizard dialog box that appears first select fields from one table. Move the required fields from the Available Fields to the selected fields.
4. Click Next to go to the next step, i.e., Step 2.
5. Here since I have not asked to choose the next table, there is not Step 2.
6. In the dialog box that appears, select related fields from the fields lists to determine the relationship between the two tables.
7. Click Next.
8. From the dialog box that appears, you have to choose whether you want to include only related rows from both tables or all rows from either table. By default, only related records are included.
9. Click Next.

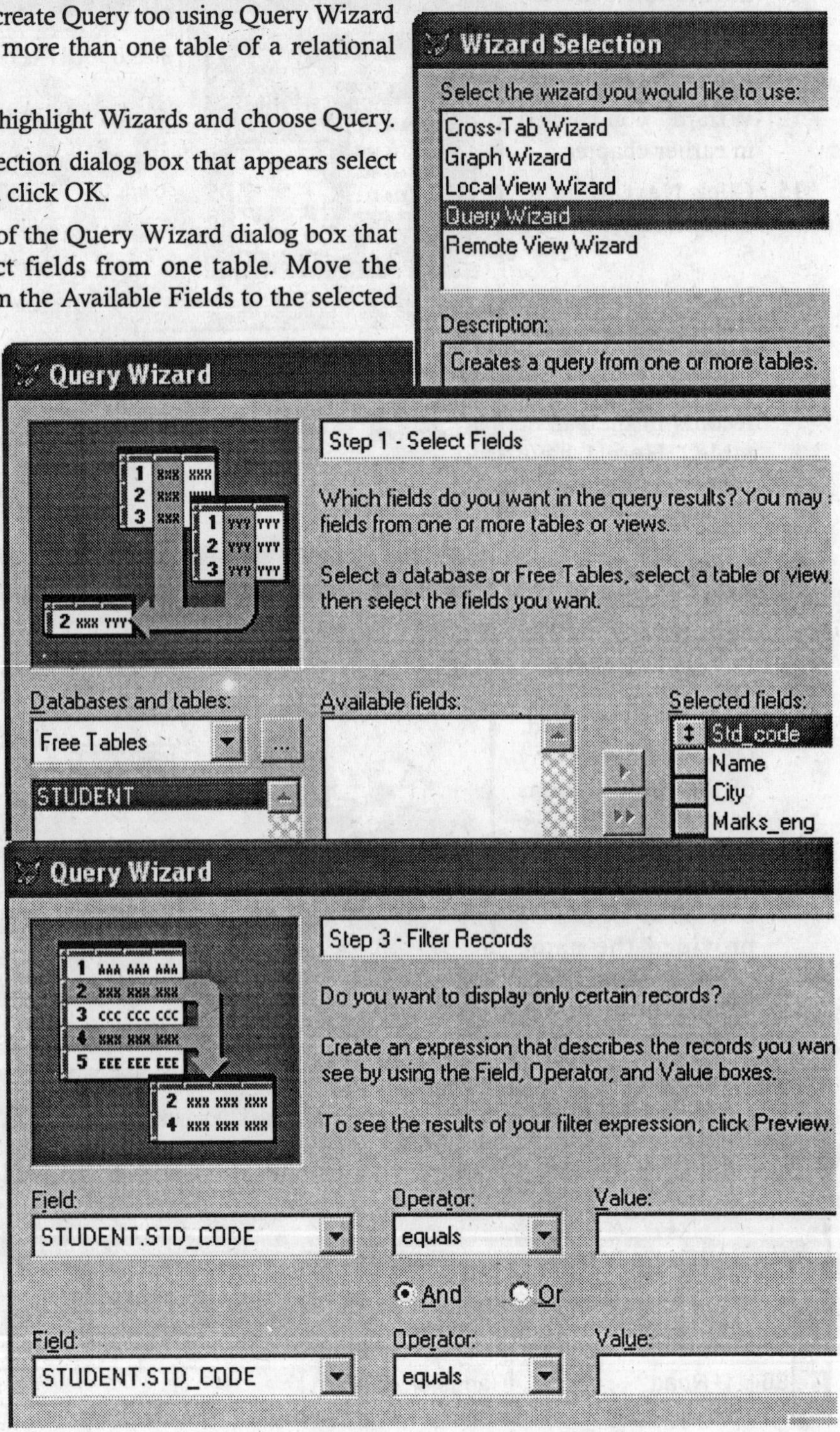

10. The next step is to determine the order in which your query results will be sorted. Select a field from the Available fields and click the Add> button to move it to the Selected fields.

    Select Ascending to sort the results in ascending order, or Descending to sort them in descending to sort them in descending order.

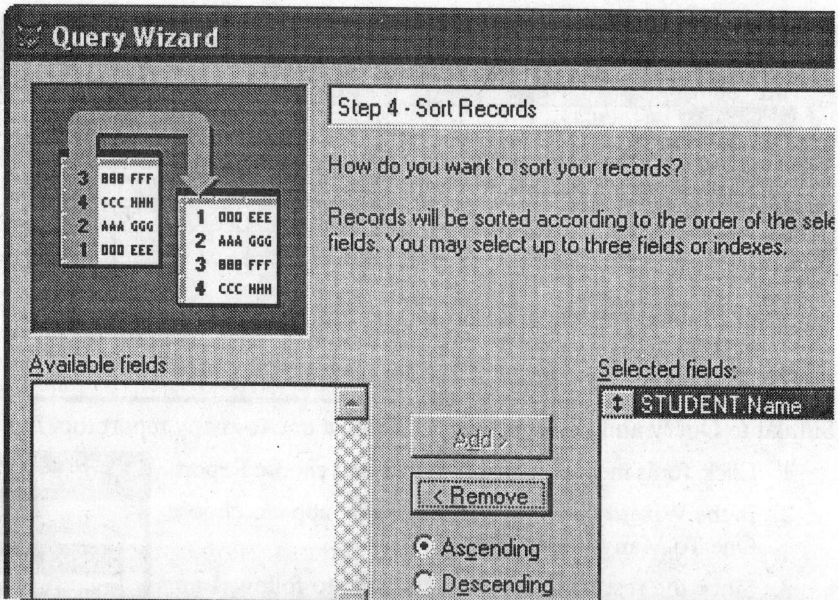

11. Click next.
12. In the dialog box that appears, mention whether you want all the records of only a portion of the records (in percentage). I have chosen to view all the records.

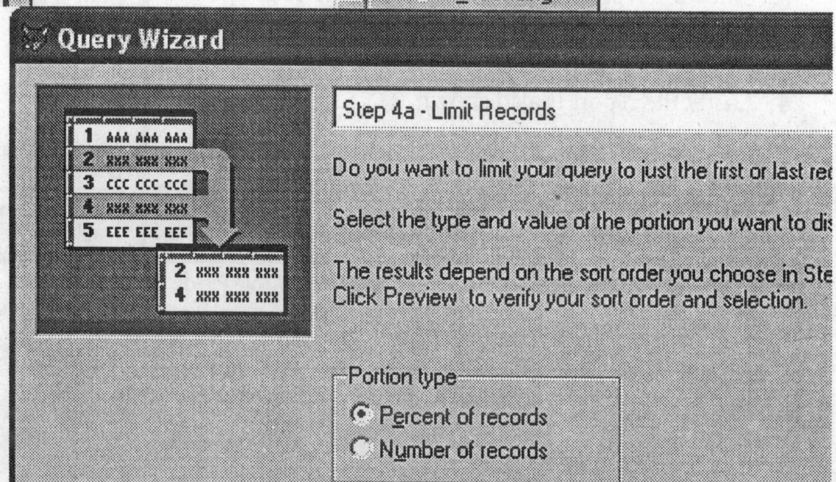

13. Select an option of your choice from the dialog box that appears and click Finish button. I have selected the "Save query" option.

    Click the Preview... button to view the output without existing the wizard.

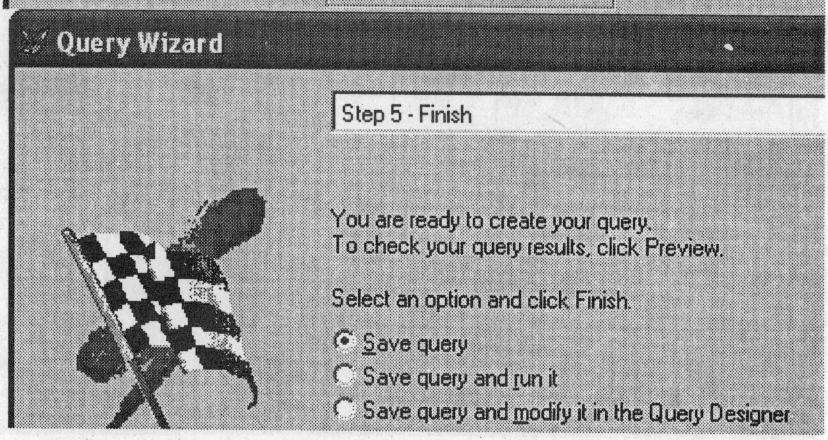

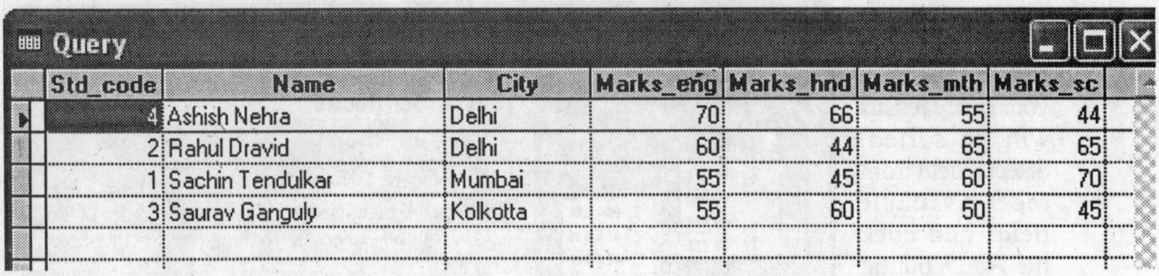

Query

Std_code	Name	City	Marks_eng	Marks_hnd	Marks_mth	Marks_sc
4	Ashish Nehra	Delhi	70	66	55	44
2	Rahul Dravid	Delhi	60	44	65	65
1	Sachin Tendulkar	Mumbai	55	45	60	70
3	Saurav Ganguly	Kolkotta	55	60	50	45

The query output is shown above.

USING ONE-TO-MANY REPORT WIZARD

Similar to Query and Form, we would create a one-to-many report too. For this do the following:

1. Click Tools menu, highlight Wizard and choose Report.
2. In the Wizard Selection dialog box that appears choose One-To-Many Report Wizard.
3. Since the rest of the steps are simple to follow, I am not writing details about them, but, just showing the figures.
4. Lastly the report is also shown.

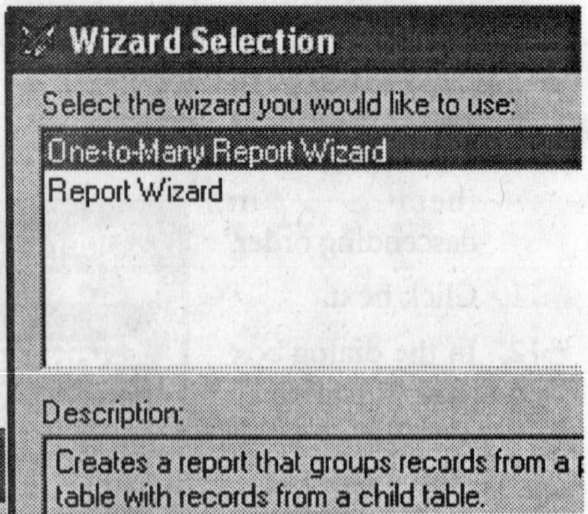

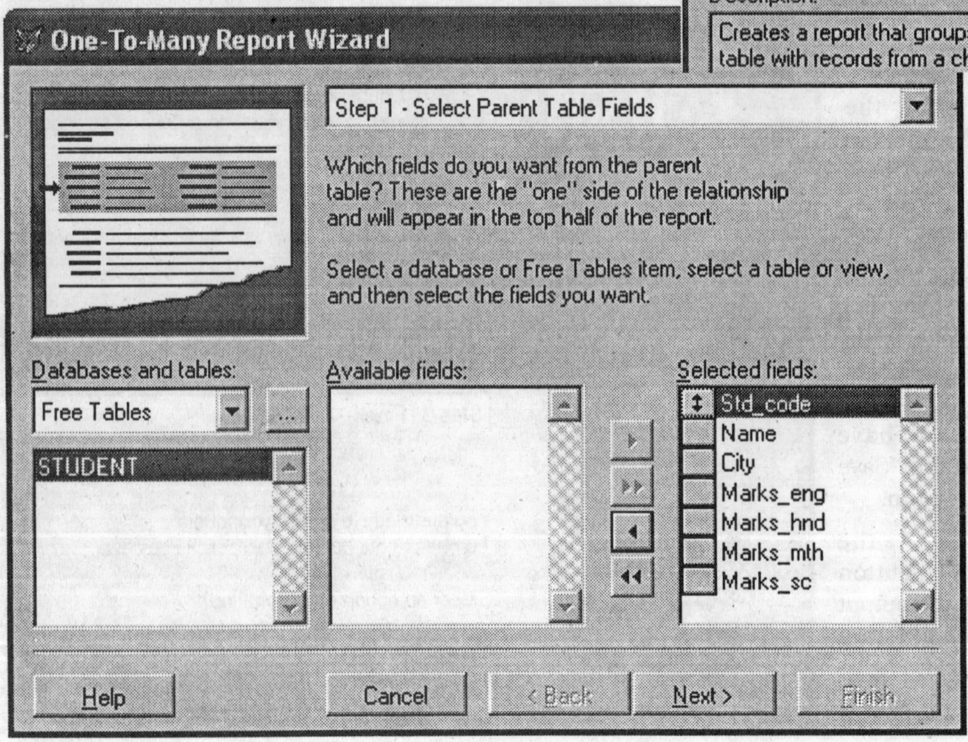

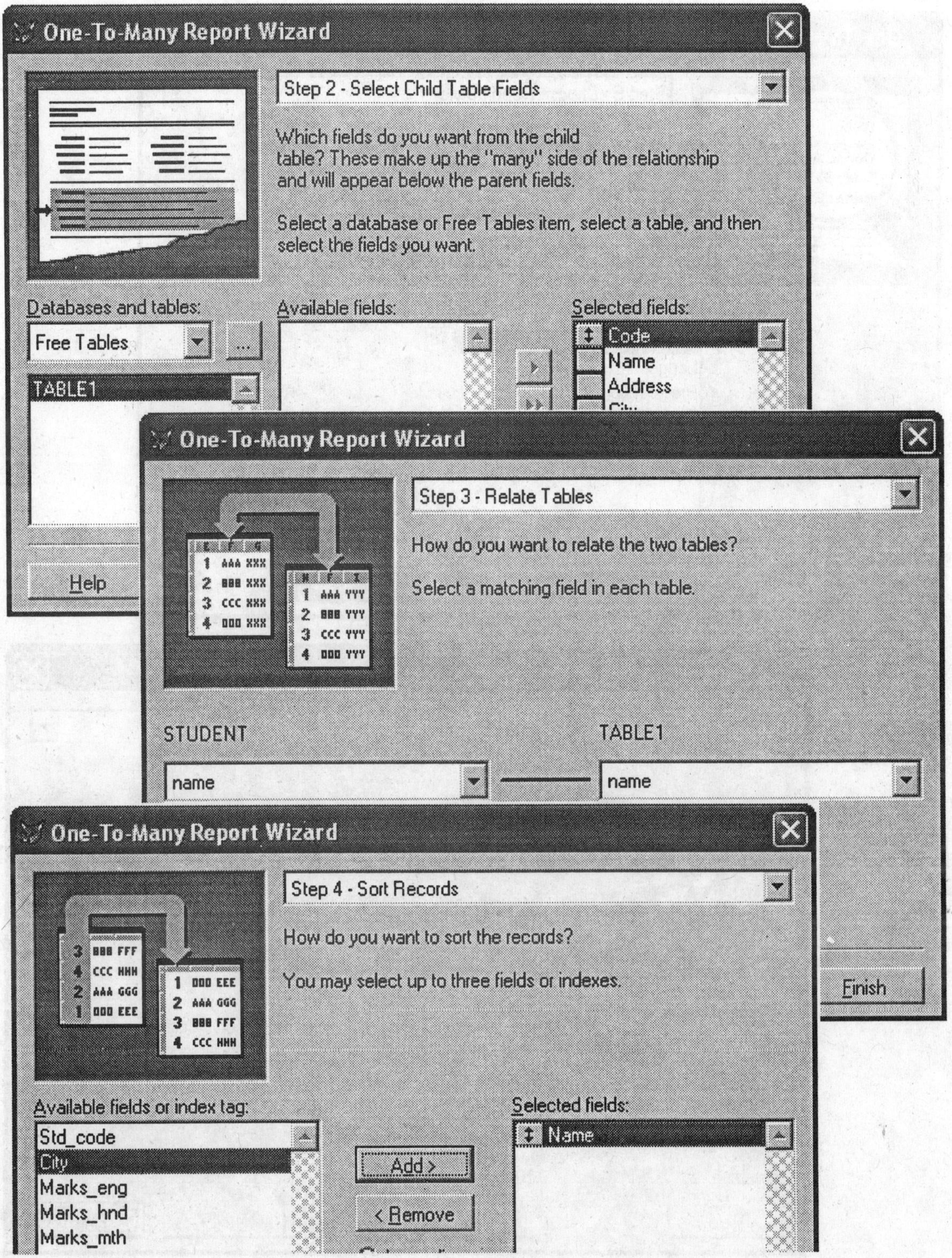
One-To-Many Report Wizard
Step 2 - Select Child Table Fields
Which fields do you want from the child table? These make up the "many" side of the relationship and will appear below the parent fields.
Select a database or Free Tables item, select a table, and then select the fields you want.
Databases and tables:
Free Tables
TABLE1
Available fields:
Selected fields:
Code
Name
Address
Help
One-To-Many Report Wizard
Step 3 - Relate Tables
How do you want to relate the two tables?
Select a matching field in each table.
STUDENT
TABLE1
name
name
Finish
One-To-Many Report Wizard
Step 4 - Sort Records
How do you want to sort the records?
You may select up to three fields or indexes.
Available fields or index tag:
Std_code
City
Marks_eng
Marks_hnd
Marks_mth
Add >
< Remove
Selected fields:
Name

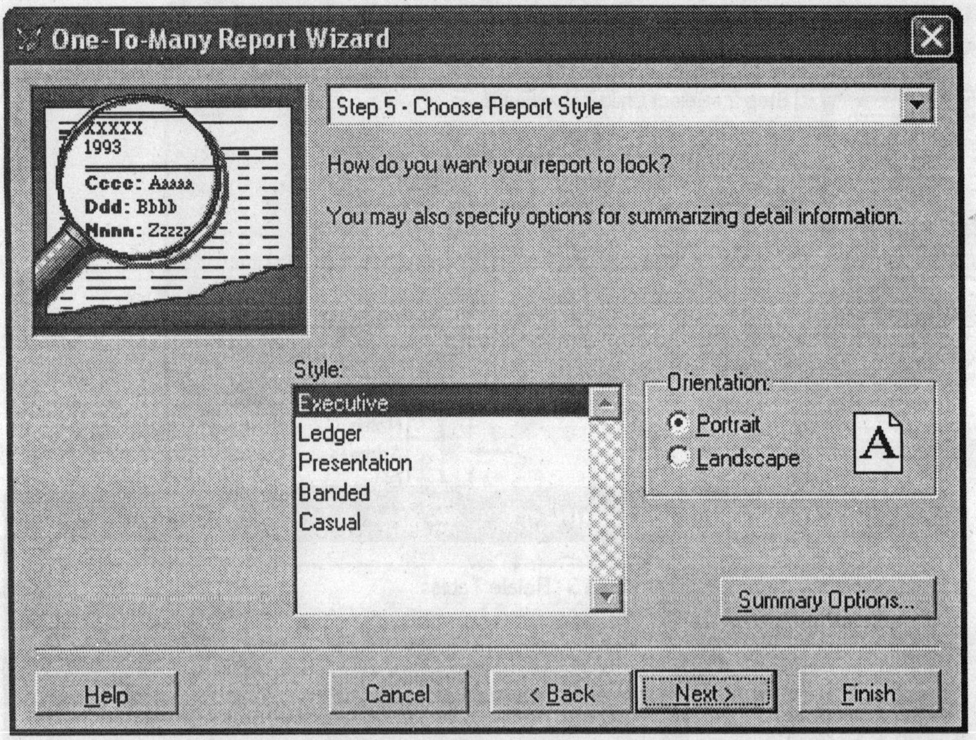
One-To-Many Report Wizard
XXXXX
1993
Cccc: Aaaaa
Ddd: Bbbb
Nnnn: Zzzzz
Step 5 - Choose Report Style
How do you want your report to look?
You may also specify options for summarizing detail information.
Style:
Executive
Ledger
Presentation
Banded
Casual
Orientation:
Portrait
Landscape
A
Summary Options...
Help
Cancel
< Back
Next >
Finish

One-To-Many Report Wizard
Step 6 - Finish
Type a title for your report:
STUDENT
You are ready to create your report.
To check your report results, click Preview.
Select an option and click Finish
Save report for later use
Save report and modify it in the Report Designer
Save and print report
Use display settings stored in the database
Wrap fields that do not fit
Preview
Help
Cancel
< Back
Next >
Finish

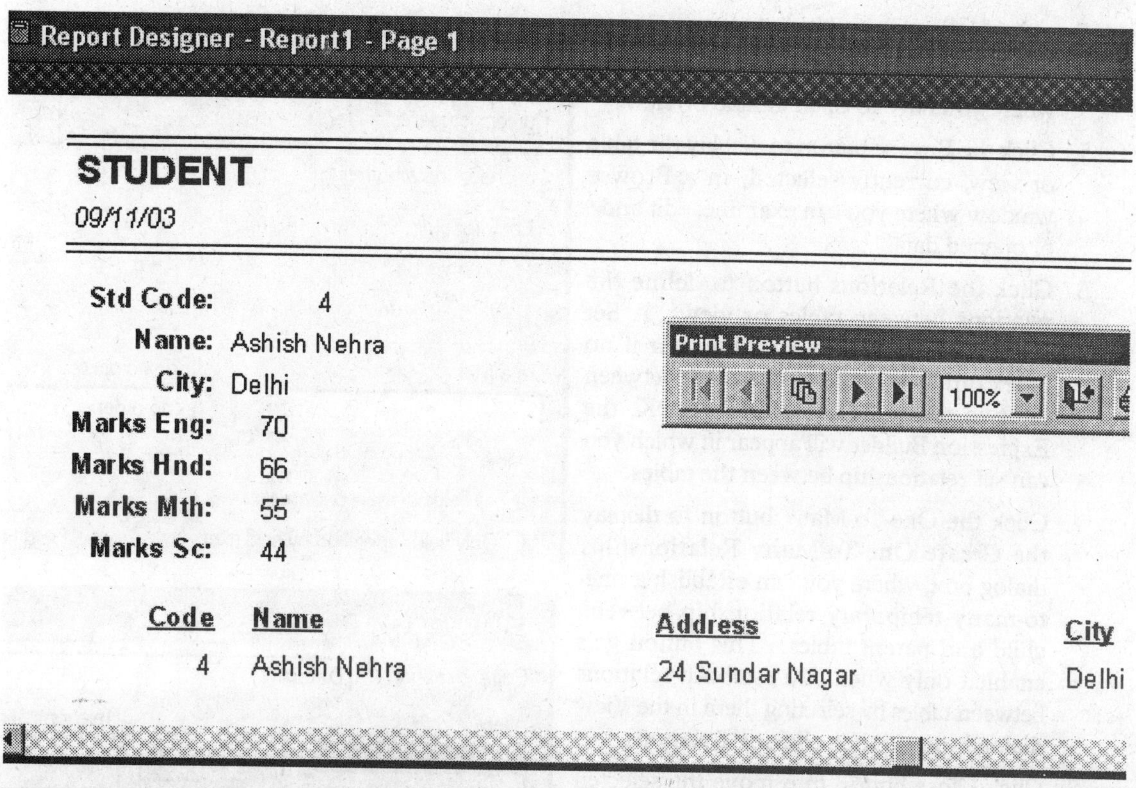

WORKING WITH VIEW WINDOW

This window can be used to open and display tables, to establish temporary relationships and to set work area properties. Let us see how this is done:

1. Click Window menu and choose Data Session. The Data Session window that appears is known as the View window.

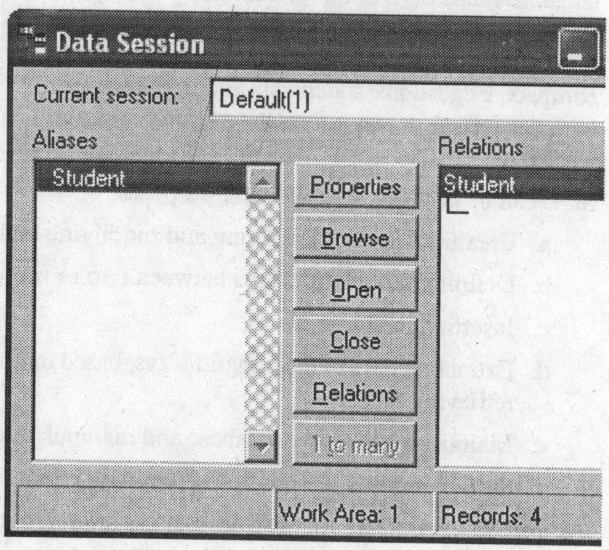

2. The Current session: drop down list displays the name of the current data session. The Aliases area displays the view name or table name without the file extension. The Relations area indicates any temporary relationship established between the tables or vies listed in the Aliases box.
3. Click the Open button, to add a table or view to the Aliases list.
4. Click Properties button to see the Work Area Properties dialog box. In this dialog box, you can modify the structure of a table, select index files and fields and define data filters.

If no tables or views are listed in the Aliases box, an Open dialog box will appear from where you have to open a table or view.

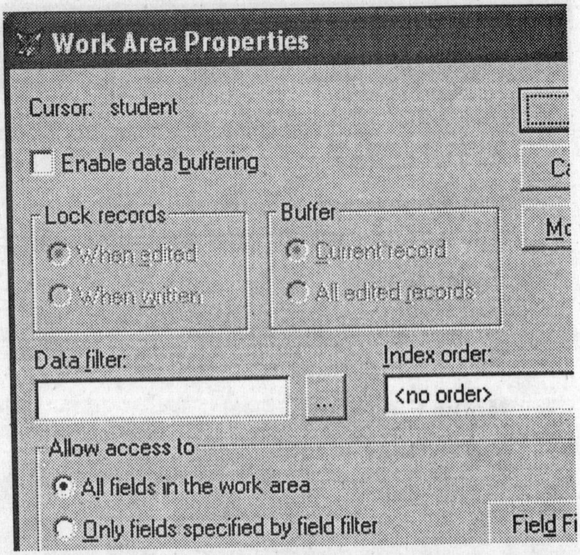

5. Click the Browse button to display the table or view, currently selected, in a Browse window where you can examine, edit and/or opened data.
6. Click the Relations button to define the relations between tables or views. A Set Index Order dialog box will appear if no index orders has already been set between the two tables. When you click OK, the Expression Builder will appear in which you can set relationship between the tables.
7. Click the One-To-Many button to display the Create One-To-Many Relationships dialog box, where you can establish a one-to-many temporary relationship between child and parent tables. This button gets enabled only when you establish relations between tables by selecting them in the View dialog box and then clicking Relations.
8. Click Close button to remove the selected table or view from the Aliases list.

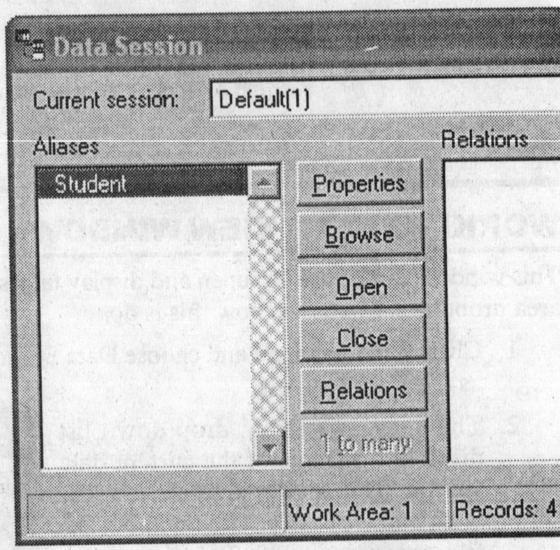

USING QUERIES AND SQL

Let us now read about another programming language called SQL or Structured Query Language. It is a simple high level language that enables us to utilize a database completely and easily. It uses compact, English-like statements and performs very complex jobs to access information from very large sized databases.

SQL can be used for the following purposes:

a. Creating (defining), deleting and modifying table structure.
b. Defining the relationships between two or more tables.
c. Inserting data into tables.
d. Extracting data in meaningful ways, based on the tables' defined relationships, that is accessing or retrieving data.
e. Maintaining data in a database and manipulating the stored values to keep the information current.
f. System security and authorization which must be controlled and maintained.

We will be learning about the SQL Select statement in detail in a later section.

QUERY DESIGNER

You have already worked with the Query Designer in an earlier chapter. In this section, we will learn how to work with multiple tables in Query Designer. The top pane of the Query Designer displays the table in the query. The Query Designer in that figure showed only the "Employee" table. The table is represented by a resizeable window that lists the table's fields. Let us add one more table to the query.

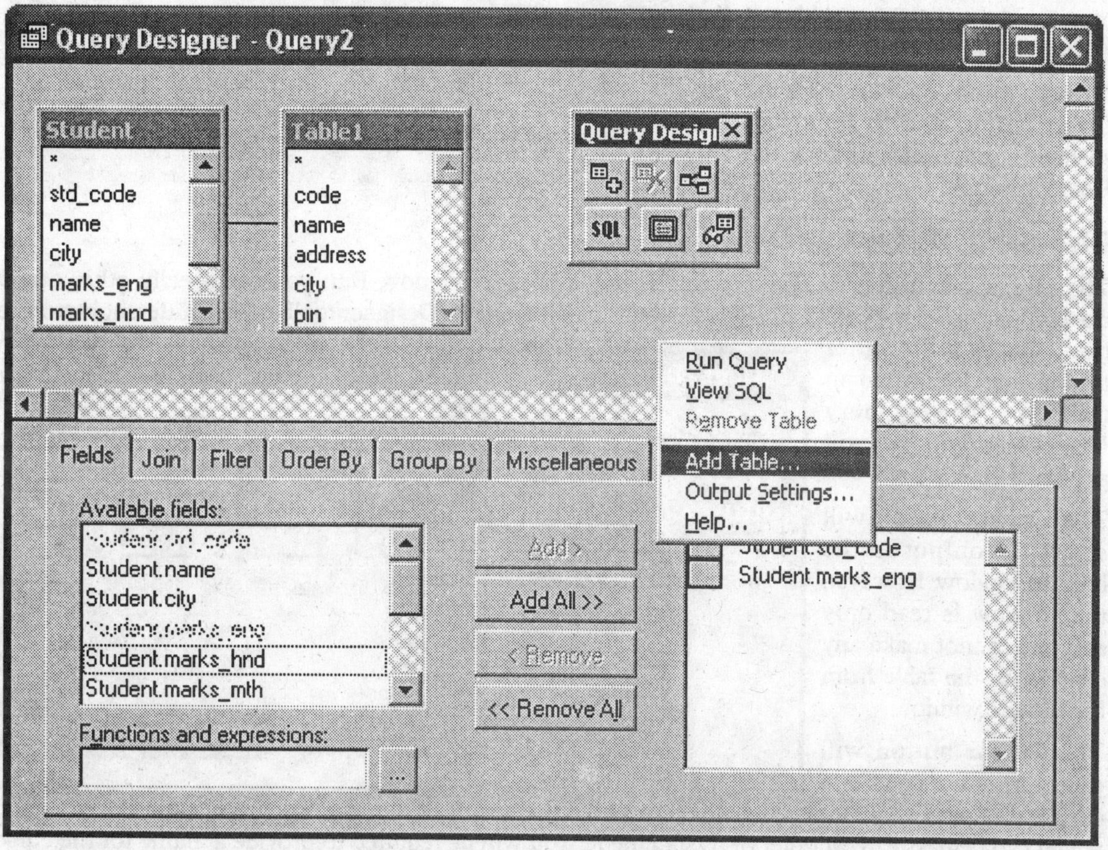

1. Right click the top pane of the designer. Form the menu that appears, select Add Table... In the Add Table or View dialog box that appears, select the table which you want to use and click Add button.
2. A Join Condition dialog box will appear. Select the matching fields from the two tables and specify whether you want Inner, left, Right or Full join. Click OK.
3. You will note that now the top pane of the Query Designer displays two tables. The designer shows join conditions by displaying lines that connect the matching fields between the two tables. You can drag a field from one table to the matching field in the other table to create further join conditions.

The different tab options in the Query Designer window are:

Join

In this tab, you have to specify join type, field name and criteria. For specifying the criteria, you can use relational operators = (like), == (exactly like), > (more than) and < (less than). These relational operators can be used with the NOT operator to negate the logic. Note, the addition of a new line between the two tables, with the addition of a join condition.

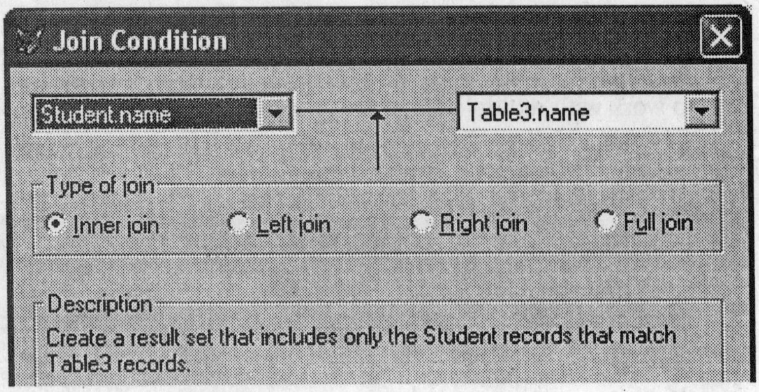

To insert a join condition, click the Insert button and to remove a selected join condition click the Remove button.

Directing Output

The default output for the Query designer is the browse window. But, you can specify other output destinations using the Query Designation button in the Query Designer toolbar (The different buttons of the Query Designer toolbar are identified in figure). The Query Destination window will appear as shown here.

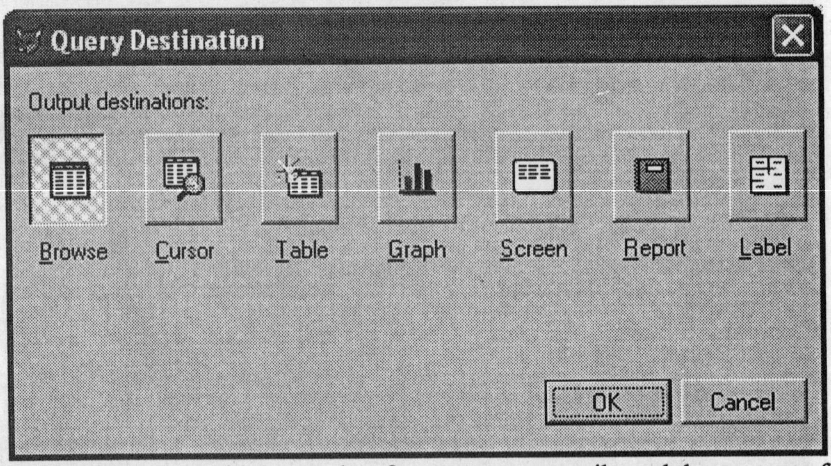

The **Browse** button will direct the output to the browse window. However, the window is read only and one cannot make any changes in the table from the browse window.

The **Cursor** button will direct the output to a cursor. Cursor is a temporary file which can hold the results of a query temporarily and the content of which can be passed to another SQL statement. You will be required to provide a name for the cursor in the Cursor name: text box. You can also choose an existing file by clicking the button with three dots.

The **Table** button will direct the output to a DBF file. You will be required to provide a name for the table in the Table name: text box. You can also choose an existing file by clicking the button with three dots(…). The **Graph** button will connect the output with the Microsoft Graph wizard. It will guide you through the process of creating a rudiment graph. The **Screen** button will connect the output to an input/edit screen (created in the Forms Designer). The **Report** button will direct the output into a Visual FoxPro report or will create a quick report immediately. The **Label** button will direct the output to a Label Form.

After selecting the output destination, click OK.

Running the Query

To run your query, choose Run Query from the Query menu. This will execute the SQL query you have built and sends the results to the output destination which you have specified. Alternatively, press Ctrl + Q keys to run the query. You can also use the Run button in the standard toolbar to run the query.

SQL Select Command

SQL Select command retrieves data from a table. For example, suppose you want to retrieve all the data stored in student table, then type the following statement, in the command window:

```
SELECT * FROM DEPARTMENT
```

From

It is the keyword in SQL, which must be present in every select query. It is followed by a space and then the name of the table being used as the source of the information. The syntax is:

```
SELECT <COLUMNNAME(S)> FROM <TABLENAME>
```

The Select clause is followed by the column list, and from clause specifies the table from which the columns are to be extracted. To select all the columns in a table, a star (*) is used in place of the column list.

Where

Suppose we want to see only a certain number of rows that contain specific values. For this, we would need to place where clause along with the Select statement. The syntax is:

```
SELECT <COLUMNNAME(S)> FROM <TABLENAME> WHERE <COLUMNNAME> <OPERATOR>
<VALUE>
```

All comparison operators, namely >, <, =, >=, <=, <> (not equals) are supported by SQL. Moreover, SQL also supports Boolean operators NOT, AND and OR. The order of evaluation of different operators can be carried out by using parentheses.

Aggregate Functions

SQL aggregate functions produce a single value for the entire group of table entries. Aggregate or column functions can also be used with the Select command. These functions are sum, avg, max, min and count. These aggregate functions are similar to the Functions and expressions: textbox in the Field tab of Query Designer.

Sum: Sum function calculates the arithmetic sum of all selected values of a given column. For example, to find the Sum of basic salary from the Employee table, we would enter the following query:

```
SELECT SUM(MARKS_ENG) FROM STUDENT
```

The output of the sum of the marks_eng calculated by this command will be shown.

Avg: AVG function calculate the average (mean) of all selected values of a given field. For example, to find the average of marks_eng enter the following query:

```
SELECT AVG (MARKS_ENG) FROM STUDENT
```

Max: Max function calculates the largest of all selected values of a given column. For example, using the student table, the following command displays the maximum marks_eng in the column marks_eng. For this, enter the following query:

```
SELECT MAX (MARKS_ENG) FROM STUDENT
```

Min :MIN function calculates the smallest of all selected values of a given column. For example, using the student table, the following command displays the minimum salary value in the column marks_eng. For this, enter the following query:

```
SELECT MIN (MARKS_ENG) FROM STUDENT
```

Count: This function counts the number of rows in the output table. The function Count with the asterisk (*) counts the number of rows in the resulting table. Count (Distinct) eliminates rows containing duplicate field values before counting them in the output table. For example, to find how many students are there in the student table, type the following query:

```
SELECT COUNT(*) FROM STUDENT
```

Order by

In general, the rows displayed from a query do not have any specific order either ascending or descending. But if you want them to be in ascending or descending order in a particular field, then you can control this order for the selected rows. This is done by adding order by to the Select command. The syntax is as follows:

```
SELECT <COLUMNNAME(S)> FROM <TABLENAME> WHERE <CONDITION)> ORDER BY
<COLUMN TO ORDER> [<ASC/DESC>]
```

Group by

Suppose you want to know the total marks, in each city which are groups in the student table, then the clause GROUP BY will be used. The GROUP BY clause allows you to form groups based on the specific condition. The syntax for using this command is:

```
SELECT <COLOUM>, FUNCTION (<COLUMN>), FUNCTIONS (<COLUMN>) FROM TABLE
GROUP BY <COLUMN>
```

Having

You might not always want or need to see all the sub-groups in a table in a single report. Suppose you want to see the list of only those cities where the total marks are greater than 200. In such a case, you cannot use the aggregate functions, namely SUM, etc., in the WHERE clause. The command for this would be:

```
SELECT CITY, SUM(MARKS_ENG) FROM STUDENT GROUP BY CITY HAVING
SUM(MARKS_ENG + MARKS_HND + MARKS_SC + MARKS_MTH) > 200
```

Extracting Data from Multiple Tables

Using the SQL SELECT command, you can retrieve data from several related tables at the same time. But this is possible only if the tables are related with one other. Join operation is used to combine columns from multiple tables. In a join, tables to be included in the query are specified in the FROM clause, separated by commas. The condition required for specifying the relationship between the tables is given in the WHERE clause. The syntax for SELECT statement where we join two tables is mentioned here:

```
SELECT <COLUMNNAME(S)> FROM <TABLE1>, <TABLE2>, ...., <TABLEN> WEHRE
<TABLE1.COLUMN1> = <TABLE2.COLUMN1> AND <TABLE3.COLUMN2> =
<TABLE2.COLUMN4> AND ...... AND <TABLE2.COLUMN3> = TABLEN.COLUMNN>
```

Other SQL Commands

Other than retrieving data, SQL provides commands are used to update the data in a table. This involves commands such as Insert, Update, Delete, etc. SQL can also be used to define security, mechanism or scheme for protecting data in a system from unauthorized access, the commands for such operations are Grant, Revoke, etc.

INSERT INTO command: This command adds (appends) new rows (records) to a table. The syntax of INSERT INTO is

```
INSERT INTO <TABLE NAME> VALUES (<VALUE>, <VALUE>, ....)
```

INSERT INTO can also be used to insert only particular values into a table.

UPDATE command: This command is the SQL verb that changes or modifies data values in a table. The syntax is:

```
UPDATE <TABLENAME> SET <COLUMN NAME = NEW COLUMN VALUE> [WHERE
<CONDITION>]
```

DELETE command: You can remove rows from a table with the command DELETE. This command removes specific rows meeting the condition and not the individual field values.

```
DELETE FROM <TABLENAME> WHERE <CONDITION>
```

GRANT command: SQL is normally used in multiuser environments. The GRANT command is used to permit users access to the database. The syntax for GRANT command is:

```
GRANT <PRIVILEGE_NAME> | ALL ON <OBJECT> TO <USER | PUBLIC> [WITH
GRANT OPTION]
```

Here <privilege_name> specifies the actions such as INSERT, DELETE, UPDATE, SELECT, etc., the user can perform on the <object>. ALL indicates all privileges. <user> specifies the name of the user to whom the privileges have been granted. To grant the privileges to all the users PUBLIC option can be used. <WITH GRANT OPTION> is optional.

REVOKE command: This command is used to cancel database privileges from user(s). The syntax for revoke command is:

```
REVOKE <PRIVILEGE_NAME> | ALL ON <OBJECT> FROM <USER | PUBLIC>
```

Opening a Database

You can open an existing Visual FoxPro database in the same way as you open other files.

1. Click the File menu, and choose Open.
2. In the Open dialog box that appears from the Files of type: drop down list select "Database (*.dbc)".
3. The from the Look in: drop down list, select the folder where the database is located.
4. Your database will get listed in the blank rectangular area. Double click the database.
5. Alternatively, you can also open a database, by entering Open Database <database_name> in the command window.

One can open multiple databases at a time. The names of all the open databases are added to the Database drop down list in the standard toolbar. The currently selected database forms the current active database.

Closing a Database

To close all open databases, type the following command in the command window:

```
CLOSE DATABASES
```

The above command will close all databases and all open tables. There is another command as:

```
CLOSE ALL
```

That will close all open databases, all open tables, form designer, report designer, etc.

Deleting a Database

If you no longer require a database, you can delete it by giving the following command in the command window:

```
DELETE DATABASE <DATABASE_NAME> <DELETE TABLES>
```

All the tables in the database will also get deleted permanently.

Let us Revise

1. A primary keyfield establishes the relation between the two tables.
2. One record in one table has many corresponding records in the other table is called One to Many.
3. In many to many relationship, a record in one table has many corresponding records in a second table and for every record in the second table, there are many corresponding records in the previous table.
4. The One-to-Many Form wizard creates a form from two related tables.
5. You can create Query using Query Wizard
6. View window can be used to open and display tables, to establish temporary relationships and to set work area properties.
7. Structured Query Language is a simple high level language that enables us to utilize a database completely and easily.
8. The default output for the Query designer is the browse window.
9. The Browse button in the Query destination dialog box will direct the output to the browse window.
10. The Cursor button in the Query destination dialog box will direct the output to a cursor.
11. The Table button in the Query destination dialog box will direct the output to a DBF file.
12. The Graph button in the Query destination dialog box will connect the output with the Microsoft Graph wizard.
13. The Screen button in the Query destination dialog box will connect the output to an input/edit screen.
14. The Report button in the Query destination dialog box will direct the output into a Visual FoxPro report or will create a quick report immediately.
15. The Label button in the Query destination dialog box will direct the output to a Label Form.
16. To run your query, choose Run Query from the Query menu.
17. SQL aggregate functions produce a single value for the entire group of table entries.
18. Sum function calculates the arithmetic sum of all selected values of a given column.
19. AVG function calculate the average (mean) of all selected values of a given field.
20. Max function calculates the largest of all selected values of a given column.
21. MIN function calculates the smallest of all selected values of a given column.
22. Count function counts the number of rows in the output table.
23. Using the SQL SELECT command, you can retrieve data from several related tables at the same time.
24. INSERT INTO command adds (appends) new rows (records) to a table.

Multiple Choice Questions

1. In Relational Database Management System two tables are related upon :

   (a) Primary field (b) Main field

   (c) Secondary field

2. One To Many Form Wizard creates Form using:
   (a) One Table (b) Two Tables
   (c) Two Forms
3. Query in RDBMS can be created using:
   (a) Form (b) Query
   (c) Query Wizard
4. Query can be run from:
   (a) Query menu (b) Form menu
   (c) File menu
5. Function which calculates the average of all selected values of a given field is:
   (a) MAX (b) AVG
   (c) MIN

True/False Questions

1. A primary keyfield establishes the relation between the two tables.
2. One record in one table has many corresponding records in the other table is called One to Many.
3. The One-to-Many Form wizard creates a Form from two related tables.
4. You cannot create Query using Query Wizard
5. Structured Query Language is a simple high level language that enables us to utilize a database completely and easily.
6. The default output for the Query designer is the browse window.
7. The Cursor button in the Query destination dialog box will direct the output to a printer.
8. The Table button in the Query destination dialog box will direct the output to a DBF file.
9. The Screen button in the Query destination dialog box will connect the output to an input/edit screen.
10. The Report button in the Query destination dialog box will direct the output into a Visual FoxPro report or will create a quick report immediately.
11. To run your query, choose Run Query from the File menu.
12. SQL aggregate functions produce a single value for the entire group of table entries.
13. AVG function calculate the average (mean) of all selected values of a given field.
14. Max function calculates the lowest of all selected values of a given column.
15. Count function counts the number of rows in the output table.
16. Using the SQL SELECT command, you can retrieve data from several related tables at the same time.

Matching Columns

Match the text in Column A with the text in Column B.

Column A	Column B
1. Sum	a. Calculates the smallest of all values
2. AVG	b. Counts the number of rows in the table
3. MAX	c. This command adds new rows to a table
4. MIN	d. Calculates the average of all selected values
5. Count	e. Creates query for related tables
6. Insert Into	f. Calculates the arithmetic sum of all values
7. Query Wizard	g. Calculates the largest of all values

Fill in the Blanks with Appropriate Words

a. Report b. Graph c. Label d. Cursor
e. Table f. Browse

1. The __________ button in the Query destination dialog box will direct the output to the browse window.
2. The __________ button in the Query destination dialog box will direct the output to a cursor.
3. The __________ button in the Query destination dialog box will direct the output to a DBF file.
4. The __________ button in the Query destination dialog box will connect the output with the Microsoft Graph wizard.
5. The __________ button in the Query destination dialog box will direct the output into a Visual FoxPro report or will create a quick report immediately.
6. The __________ button in the Query destination dialog box will direct the output to a Label Form.

Descriptive Type Questions

1. What are the advantages of Relational Databases?
2. How are relationships among tables developed?
3. Describe the various type of relationships: One to One, One to Many and Many to Many.
4. How would you create a new relational database using Visual FoxPro?
5. How would you use One-to-Many Report Wizard?
6. How would you run the Query?
7. Describe the following SQL functions: Order By and Group By.

Answers to Objective Type Questions

Multiple Choice Questions

1. a	2. b	3. c	4. a
5. b			

True/False Questions

1. T	2. T	3. T	4. F
5. T	6. T	7. F	8. T
9. T	10. T	11. F	12. T
13. T	14. F	15. T	16. T

Matching Columns

1. f	2. d	3. g	4. a
5. b	6. c	7. e	

Fill in the Blanks with Appropriate Words

1. f	2. d	3. e	4. b
5. a	6. c		

Recommended Readings

1. Learn to Program Visual Basic—Databases *by John Smiley.*
2. Learn to Program Visual Basic—Objects *by John Smiley.*
3. Learn to Program Visual Basic—Examples *by John Smiley.*
4. Keeping Ahead—SQL Server 7.0 *by Joelle Mosset.*
5. MCSE—Administering SQL Server 7.0 *by Jerome Gabillaud.*

– Published by Firewall Media (An Imprint of Laxmi Publications Pvt. Ltd.)

12 Visual FoxPro Utilities

IMPORTING TEXT USING IMPORT WIZARD

Visual FoxPro allows you to import and export data files from various other software into it. To import a file called Progress in a new table, we do the following:

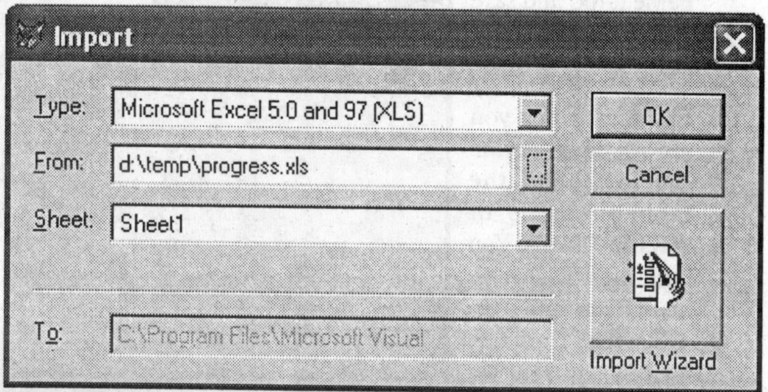

1. Click at Import in the File menu.
2. An import dialog box opens, as shown here.
3. In the Type drop down list, specify the type of file to import. Here I have chosen Microsoft Excel 5.0 and 97(XLS)

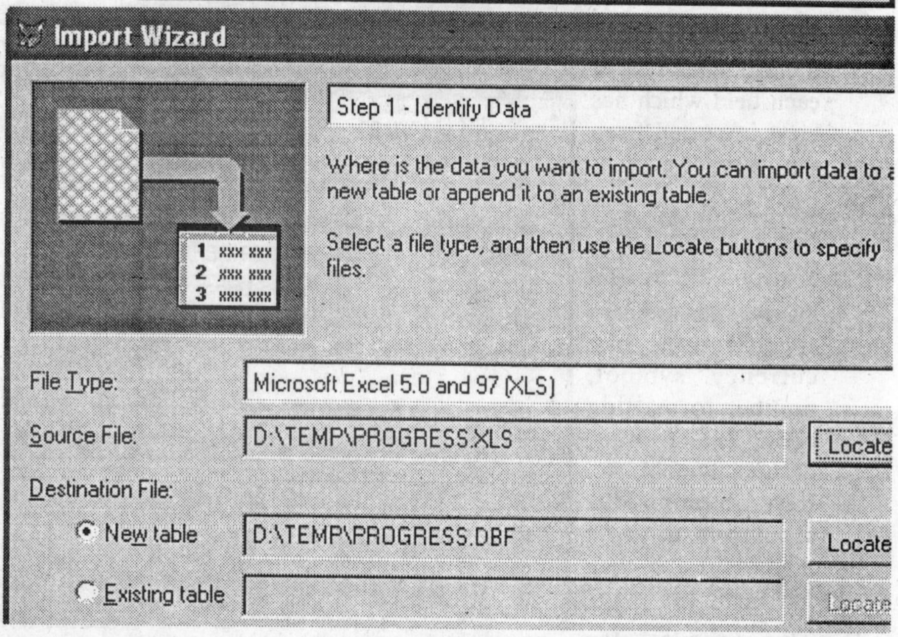

4. Click at Import Wizard to start the importing process.
5. In the first step, you have to identify the data. File Type you have already given. You have to locate and tell the system, which file you want to import, i.e., the source file. About the destination, you can have an existing table or create a new table, which would be done for you by the wizard.
6. Click Next.

7. Here you can select the database to which you want to add the data.
8. If you opt for creating a table as a stand-alone free table, then you would be asked to name it too and save it with a name.
9. Click Next.
10. In the next step you are asked to define the format of the table in terms of rows and sheets. You can mention it to start from row 1 or otherwise.
11. Click Next.
12. Here you can define the width and type of each field which has been imported from the other software.
13. Click Next.
14. This step asks you to define the international standard specifications like currency symbol, number formatting code, data format, decimal symbol, etc. If you have no idea about them, just leave them as it and click Next.
15. This is the last step where you have to just click at Finish and the data would start importing.
16. You can see the data in your table by using the Browse command.
17. All the steps and the result in the table are shown on the next pages.

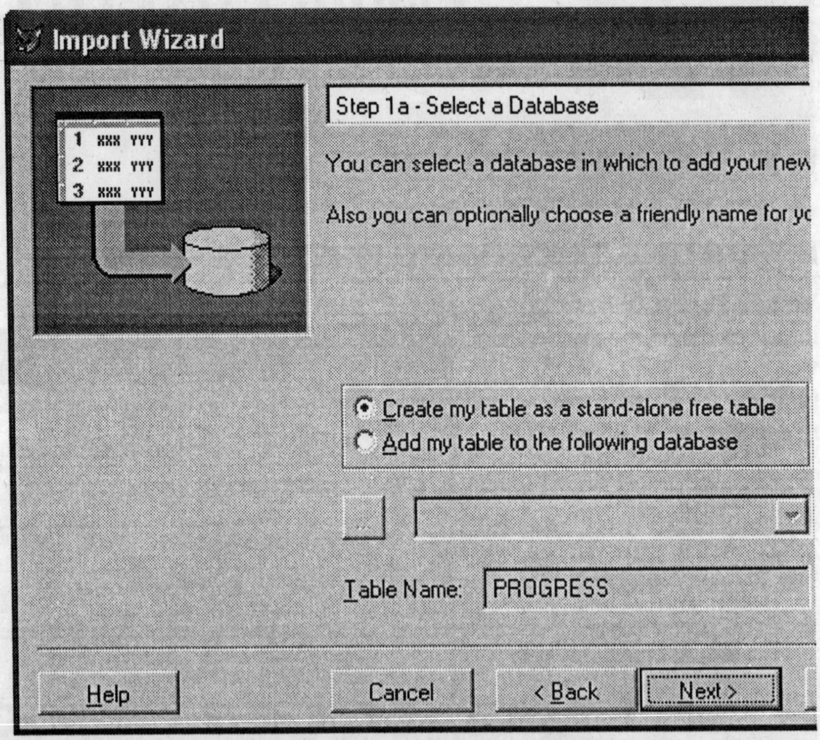

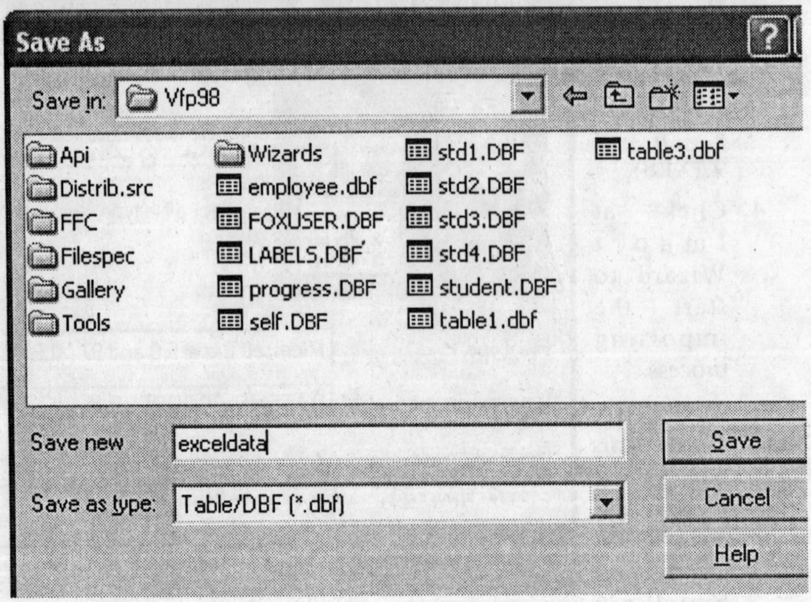

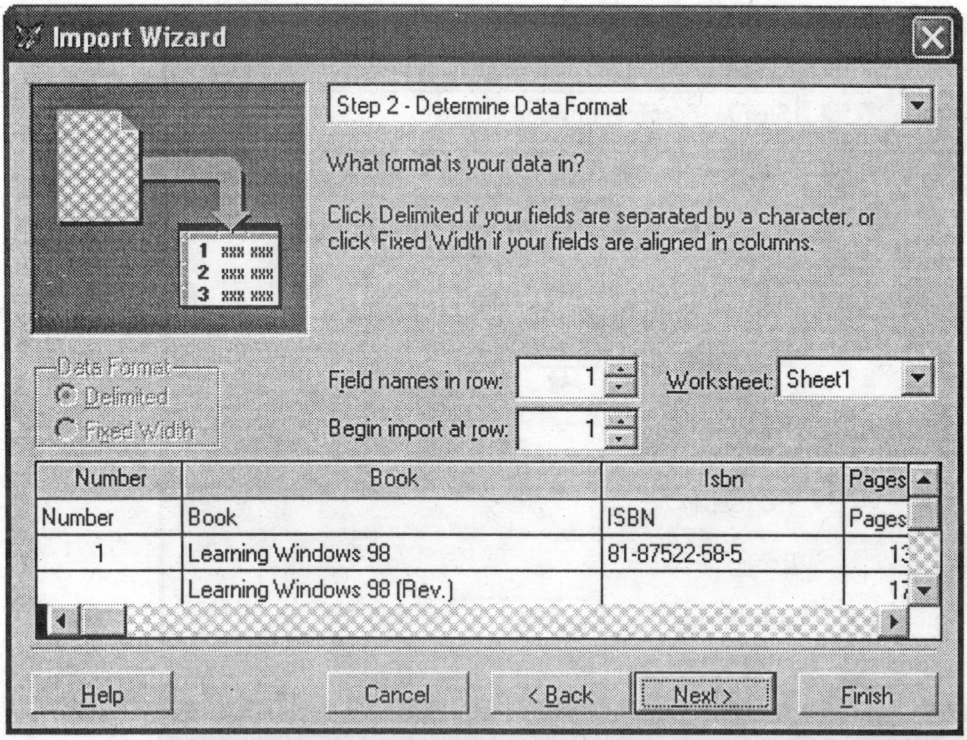
Import Wizard
Step 2 - Determine Data Format
What format is your data in?
Click Delimited if your fields are separated by a character, or click Fixed Width if your fields are aligned in columns.
Data Format
Delimited
Fixed Width
Field names in row: 1
Worksheet: Sheet1
Begin import at row: 1
Number
Book
Isbn
Pages
Number
Book
ISBN
Pages
1
Learning Windows 98
81-87522-58-5
Learning Windows 98 (Rev.)
Help
Cancel
< Back
Next >
Finish

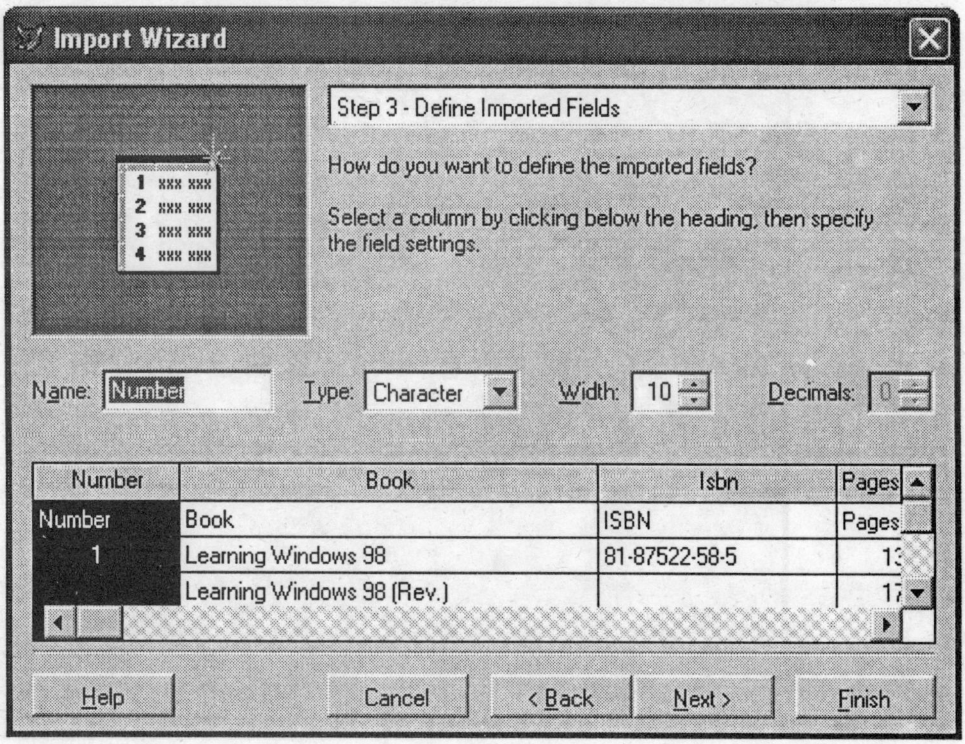
Import Wizard
Step 3 - Define Imported Fields
How do you want to define the imported fields?
Select a column by clicking below the heading, then specify the field settings.
Name: Number
Type: Character
Width: 10
Decimals: 0
Number
Book
Isbn
Pages
Number
Book
ISBN
Pages
1
Learning Windows 98
81-87522-58-5
Learning Windows 98 (Rev.)
Help
Cancel
< Back
Next >
Finish

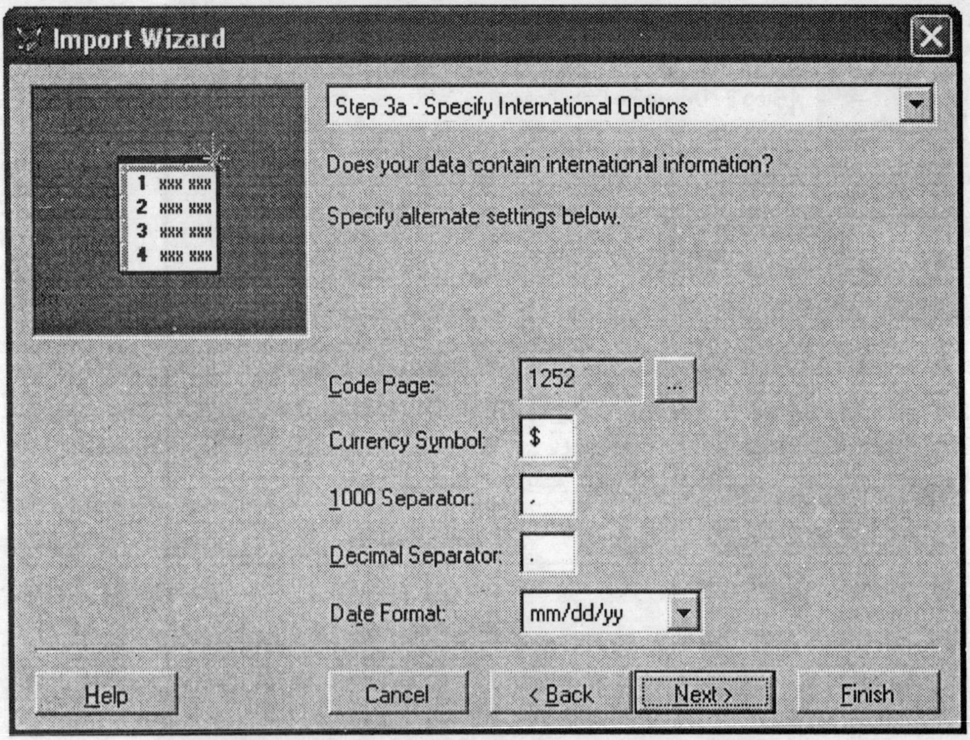
Import Wizard
Step 3a - Specify International Options
Does your data contain international information?
Specify alternate settings below.
Code Page:
1252
Currency Symbol:
$
1000 Separator:
Decimal Separator:
Date Format:
mm/dd/yy
Help
Cancel
< Back
Next >
Finish

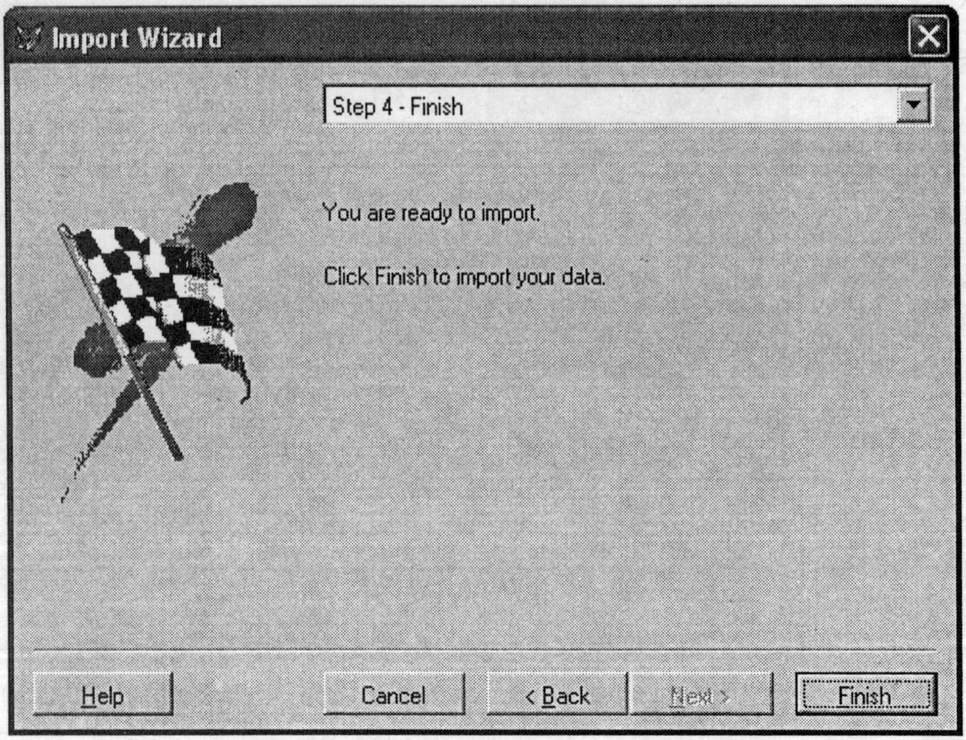
Import Wizard
Step 4 - Finish
You are ready to import.
Click Finish to import your data.
Help
Cancel
< Back
Next >
Finish

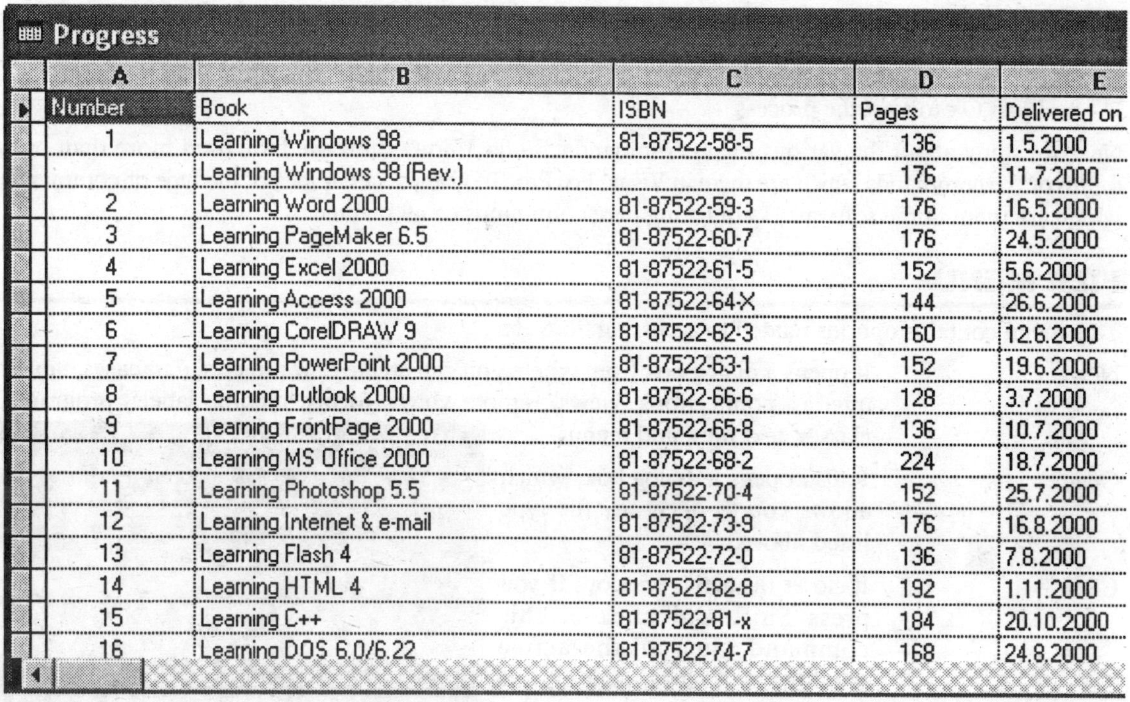

Progress

	A	B	C	D	E
	Number	Book	ISBN	Pages	Delivered on
	1	Learning Windows 98	81-87522-58-5	136	1.5.2000
		Learning Windows 98 (Rev.)		176	11.7.2000
	2	Learning Word 2000	81-87522-59-3	176	16.5.2000
	3	Learning PageMaker 6.5	81-87522-60-7	176	24.5.2000
	4	Learning Excel 2000	81-87522-61-5	152	5.6.2000
	5	Learning Access 2000	81-87522-64-X	144	26.6.2000
	6	Learning CorelDRAW 9	81-87522-62-3	160	12.6.2000
	7	Learning PowerPoint 2000	81-87522-63-1	152	19.6.2000
	8	Learning Outlook 2000	81-87522-66-6	128	3.7.2000
	9	Learning FrontPage 2000	81-87522-65-8	136	10.7.2000
	10	Learning MS Office 2000	81-87522-68-2	224	18.7.2000
	11	Learning Photoshop 5.5	81-87522-70-4	152	25.7.2000
	12	Learning Internet & e-mail	81-87522-73-9	176	16.8.2000
	13	Learning Flash 4	81-87522-72-0	136	7.8.2000
	14	Learning HTML 4	81-87522-82-8	192	1.11.2000
	15	Learning C++	81-87522-81-x	184	20.10.2000
	16	Learning DOS 6.0/6.22	81-87522-74-7	168	24.8.2000

Similar to Importing we have the Exporting.

EXPORTING A TABLE

You can export a table to any file format which it defines. Mostly you would be converting the tables to text format for using it in word processors. Let us see how it is done.

1. Click at Export in the File menu.
2. An Export dialog box will be shown you.
3. From the Type drop down list, select the type of text which you want to create. I have selected here the Delimited Text.

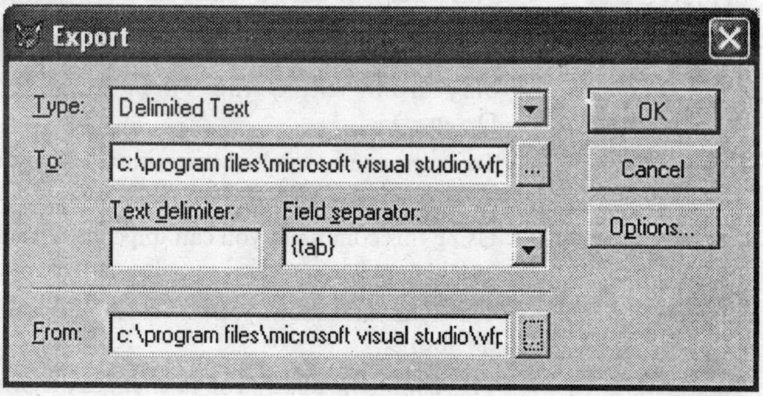

4. In To you have to select a file name where the data would go. If not there, you can create a new file and name it too.
5. You can choose a Text delimiter, if you want to. In most of the text for word processing, a comma (,) delimiter is used.

6. Mostly {tab} is used as Field separator.
7. Lastly you have to define the location of the table from where the data is to come.
8. Press Ok to start the process.

Next we study about the various menu commands. So far I don't think we have used more than one-fourth of the commands which are there in Visual FoxPro. To give you a fair idea of the type of commands which are there in the software, I am listing here commands of all menus.

FILE MENU

This menu contains options related to accessing files, etc.

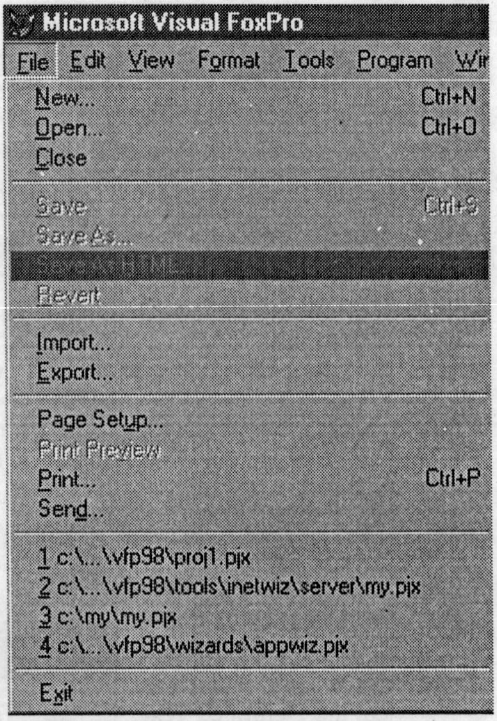

New	It opens a dialog box from where you can create new projects, databases, tables, queries, connections, views, remote views, forms, reports, labels, programs, classes, text files, and menus.
Open	It also opens a dialog box, which allows you to open any file type listed above.
Close	It closes the active window. If you press Shift and click at this command, then all the active windows will close, making this command as Close All.
Save	This command saves the file in the active window with its current name. For a new file that has no name, the option prompts the user to give it a name and then save.
Save As	This command allows you to save the current file under a new name or overwrite the existing file.
Save As Class	This command allows you to save the current form or selected controls as a class definition (active only from within the Form Designer).
Revert	This command cancels changes made in the current file during the current editing session.
Import	Using this command you can import a Visual FoxPro file or a file formatted by another application. You can also use this option to start the Import Wizard.
Export	This command allows you to exports a Visual FoxPro file in another application's file format.
Page Setup	This command allows you to changes the printer setting for reports.
Page Preview	This command displays pages in a window as they will appear when printed.

Print — This command prints the contents of the current window, a file, or Visual FoxPro's Clipboard.

Send — This command enables you to send email from the desktop of Visual FoxPro.

<files> — It provides quick access to reopen any of the last four opened projects.

Exit — It allows you to exits from Visual FoxPro. Choosing this option is the same as typing quit in the Command window.

EDIT MENU

This menu has options for editing programs, forms, and reports, etc.

Undo — This command allows you to reverse an unlimited number of changes made in the current edit session. Changes made before the last save, even if made during the same session, are not reversible.

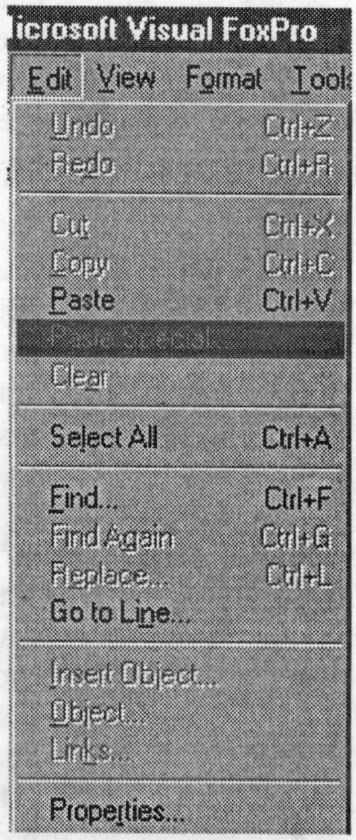

Redo — You can perform a reversed change again using this command.

Cut — This command removes the selected text or object form current document and places it on the Clipboard.

Copy — This command makes a copy of the selected text or object and places it on the Clipboard.

Paste — This command copies the current contents of the Clipboard to the current insertion point.

Paste Special — This command is used to insert OLE objects from other applications into a general files. You can embed objects or merely link them. Visual FoxPro stores a copy of embedded objects in the current object. When an object is linked, FoxPro stores a path and name reference to the original object only.

Clear — This command removes selected text without copying it to the Clipboard.

Select All — This command selects all objects in the current window. This option is used often in form and report design to move or format all objects at the same time.

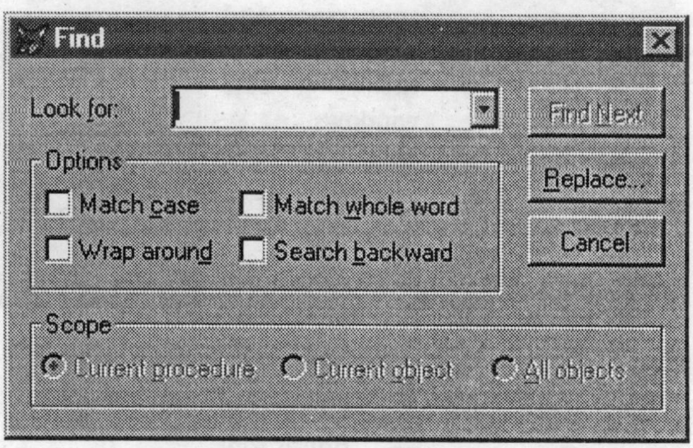

Find — This command displays the Find dialog box, which is used to locate text strings in files. Find options include the capability to ignore case, wrap around lines, match entire words, and search forward or backward.

Find Again — This command repeats the last Find starting at the current insertion point position rather than the beginning of the document.

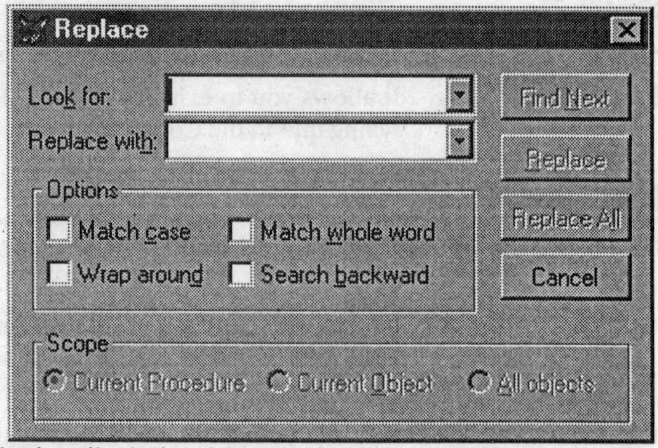

Replace — This command displays the Replace dialog box, which is used to locate and replace text strings in files.

Go to Line — This command is used primarily during debugging to go to a specific line number in a program file. This option cannot be used when word warp is on.

Insert Objects — This command is similar to Paste Special, except that it does not assume that the object already exists and is stored on the Clipboard. The option embeds objects in general type fields. When chosen, Insert Objects opens the other application without exiting Visual FoxPro. After creating the object in the other application, Insert Object returns to Visual FoxPro and inserts the linked or embedded object.

Object — This command provides options for editing a selected OLE object.

Links — This command opens linked files and enables you to edit the link

Properties — This command displays the Edit Properties dialog box, which enables you to affect the behavior, appearance, and save options of the edit windows.

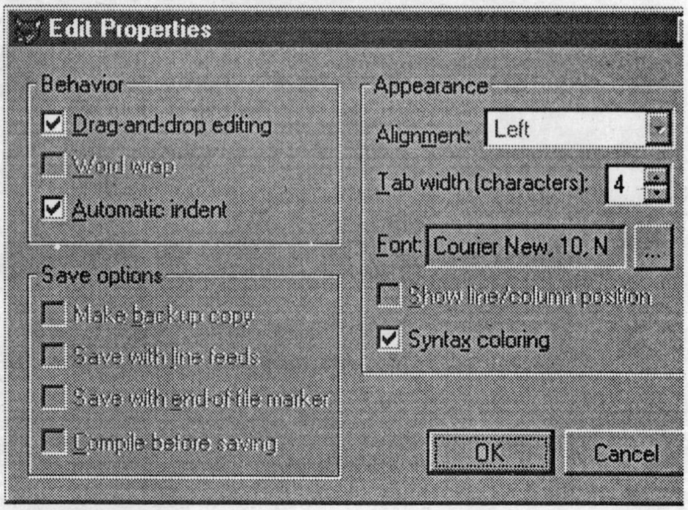

You can also specify the following:

- Alignment of text (usually left for programs)
- Number of spaces in a tab
- Editor font

— Use of syntax coloring (a helpful enhancement)

— Display of the column and row position of the insertion point

VIEW MENU

The view menu displays options that are appropriate for viewing the current table, if one is open. If you are not currently viewing a file, the menu displays a single option (Toolbar) that opens the Toolbar dialog box, which lists the available toolbars used by Visual FoxPro 6.

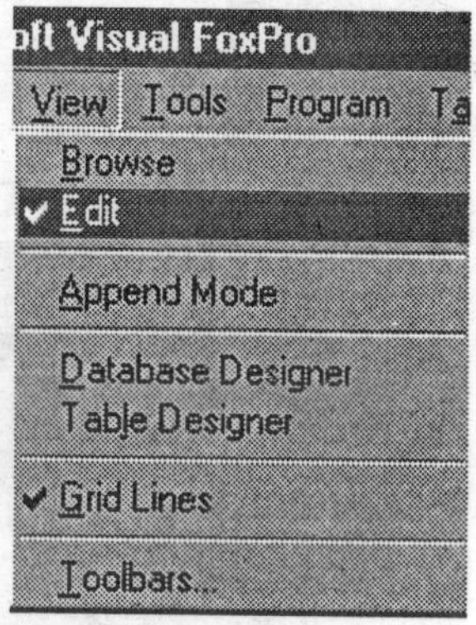

If you are browsing a table or editing a form, menu, or additional options appear as described below:

Edit	This command changes to an Edit layout style for viewing and changing records. The option displays fields vertically, and a horizontal line separates records (if grid lines are active).
Browse	This command changes to a Browse layout style for viewing and changing records. The option displays fields horizontally; rows represent records and columns represent fields.
Append Mode	This command appends a blank record to the end of the table and moves the record pointer to the first field in it.
Design	This command displays the Form, Label, or Report Designer.
Tab Order	This command enables you to set the tab order in forms.
Preview	This command shows a preview of labels or reports onscreen.
Data Environment	This command defines tables and relations used in a form, form set, or report.
Properties	This command displays the Properties dialog box for forms and controls.
Code	This command opens the code windows when you are editing object methods.
Form Controls Toolbar	This command opens the Form Controls toolbar while you are in the Form Designer.
Report Controls Toolbar	To displays the Report Control toolbar, which enables you to add controls to a report, you use this command.
Layout Toolbar	Opens the Layout toolbar, which helps you align controls.
Color Palette Toolbar	Opens the Color Palette toolbar, which enables you to select foreground and background colors for a control.
Report Preview Toolbar	Provides buttons that move between pages of the preview change the zoom factor, print the report, and exit preview mode.
Database Designer	It opens the Database designer, which maintains tables, view, and relationships stored in a database.
Table Designer	It opens the Table Designer, as shown on the next page, which enables you to make structure modifications to associated and free tables and to their indexes.
Grid Lines	This command toggles the display of grid lines on and off.

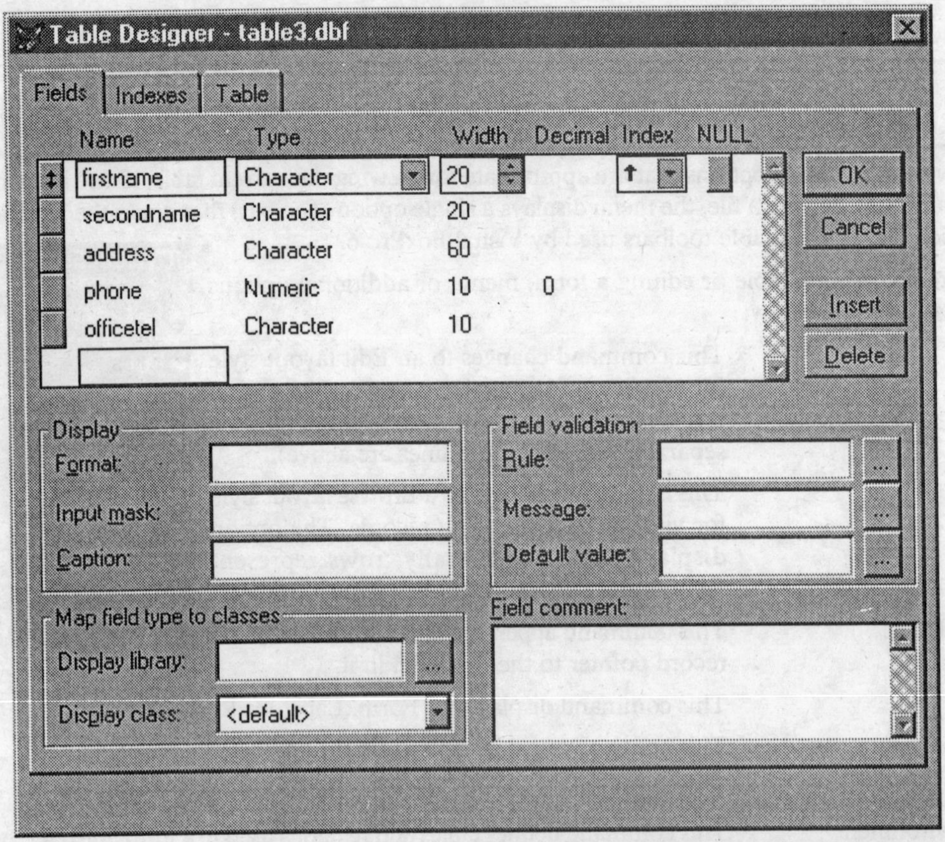

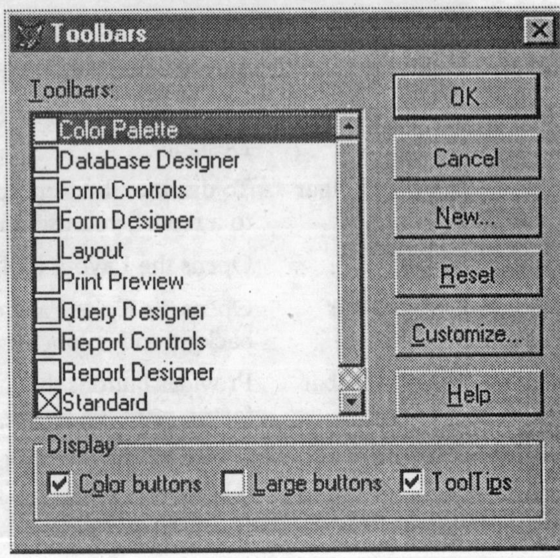

Show Position — This command displays the position, height, and width of the selected object or form in the status bar.

General Options — By using this command you can add code in a menu when you are using the Menu Designer.

Menu Options — This command adds code to specific menu options.

Toolbars — Displays a dialog box, as shown above, that lists every toolbar used by FoxPro, enabling you to customize the buttons in toolbars and to create your own.

FORMAT MENU

This menu normally consists of options that control font characteristics, text indentation, and spacing.

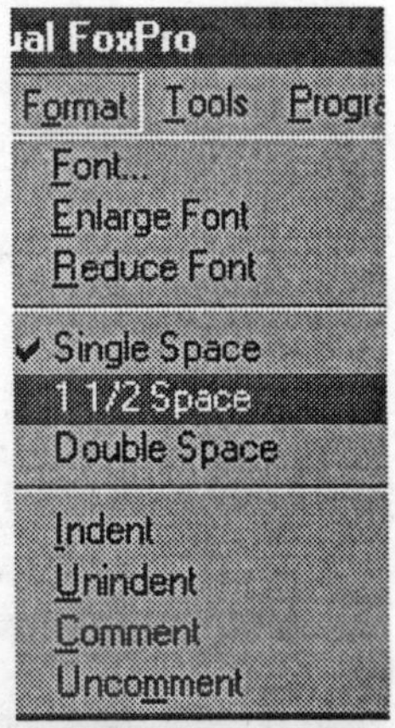

Font	It selects a font and its characteristics.
Enlarge Font	It enlarges the font used in the current window.
Reduce Font	It reduces the font size used in the current window.
Single Space	This command single-spaces the text in the current window.
1½ Space	This command uses 1½-line spacing for the text in the current window.
Double Space	Double-spaces the text in the current window.
Indent	Indents the current or selected lines in the current window.
Unindent	It removes the indent of the current or selected lines in the current window.
Comment	This command comments out selected lines.
Uncomment	It removes comments from the selected lines.
Align	It opens options that align selected objects.
Size	It opens options that size selected objects.
Horizontal Spacing	It provides options that adjust horizontal spacing between selected objects.
Vertical Spacing	It provides options that adjust vertical spacing between selected objects.
Bring to Front	It moves the selected object to the top of the objects in a form.
Sent to Back	It moves the selected object to the back of the objects in a form.
Group	It associates a selected of objects in reports and enables you to work with them as a group.

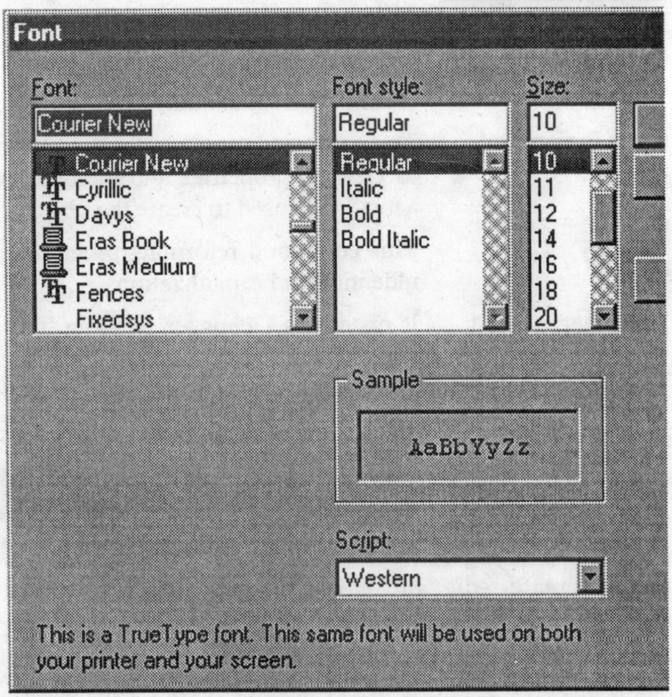

Ungroup — It breaks a group definition into individual objects again.

Snap to Grid — When you are moving objects, repositions and top-left corner to the nearest grid intersection when the mouse button is released.

Set Grid Scale — This command determines how far apart the vertical and horizontal grids are.

Text Alignment — This command aligns text in the selected object.

Fill — This command defines a fill pattern for shapes.

Pen — This command defines a pen thickness and style for shapes.

Mode — This command defines whether the background of an object is opaque or transparent.

TOOL MENU

The Tools menu provides a variety of programmer tools, ranging from wizards to the debugger.

Wizards — As you would see in the next chapter, these wizard are the best to start with the various options of the software.

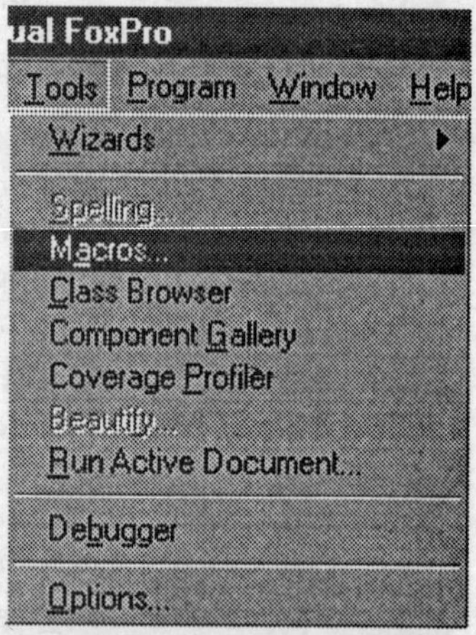

Spelling — It spell-checks text fields and memos.

Macros — It defines and maintains keyboard macros.

Class Browser — This command examines the contents of any class to view its properties and methods or even the actual code used to create the object.

Beautify — This command reformats program files to add indenting and capitalization.

Debugger — It opens the Debugger window. This improved replacement for the Debug and Trace window adds windows for watch variables, locals, call stack, and capability to track events and analyze coverage during testing.

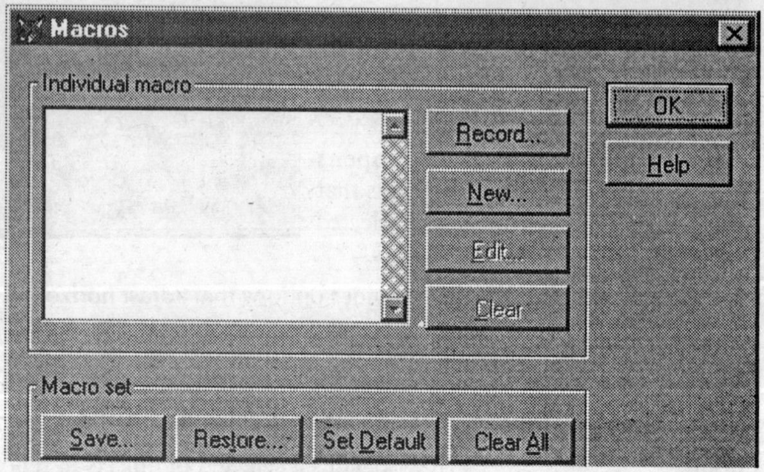

The macro dialog box enables you to create, edit, and view macro definitions. A macro definition consists of a series of Visual FoxPro commands that you can store and execute with a single keystroke. Previously FoxPro provided eight default macro definitions, which are assigned to function keys F2 through F9. Pressing F5, for example, executes the command DISPLAY STRUCTURE, which lists the structure of the current table.

Key	Command	Description
F2	SET	It opens the View window.
F3	LIST	It lists records from the current table; opens the GETFILE window if no table is being used.
F4	DIR	It lists all tables in the current directory.
F5	DISPLAY STRUCTURE	It shows the fields definitions of the current table; opens the STRUCTURE GETFILE window if no database is being used.
F6	DISPLAY STATUS	It shows the table open in each area. If an index is also open. F6 displays its expressing. The key also shows the setting of SET COMMANDS and other system information.
F7	DISPLAY MEMORY	It displays the values stores in all memory variables, including system variables. F7 also shows the definitions of all menus, pads, pop-up lists, and windows.
F8	DISPLAY	It displays the current record; opens the GETFILE window if no table is being used.
F9		It enters append mode for the current table. Opens the GETFILE window if no database is being used.

In addition to these eight macros, you can define your own. In fact, because you can use a variety of key combinations to name macros, you can define more than 250 macros at one time.

PROGRAM MENU

This menu has six options that are related to compiling and running a program.

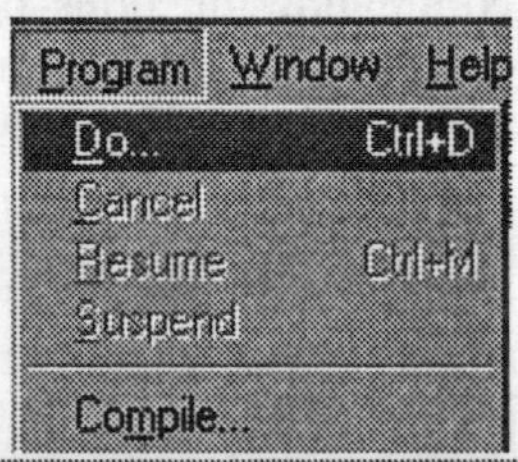

Do This command runs a program selection from a dialog box.

Cancel This command cancels the current program.

Resume This command resumes the current program from a suspended state.

Suspend It stops the current program form executing but does not remove it from memory.

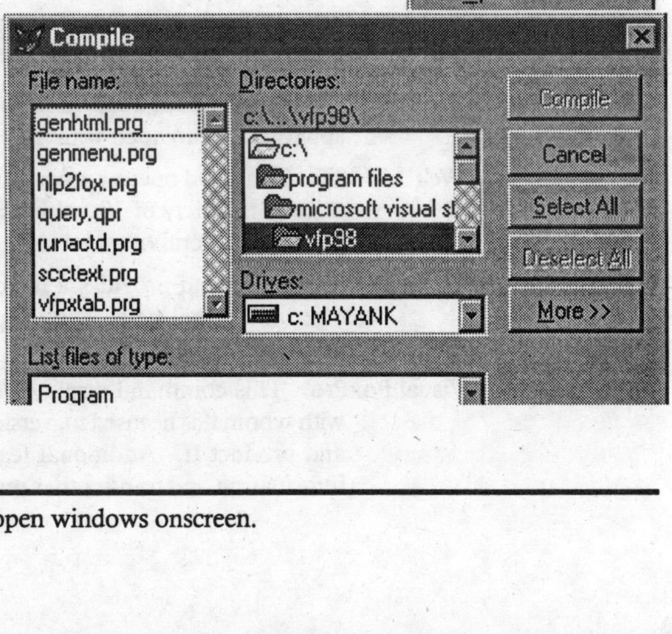

Compile This command translates a source file into object code.

Run This command runs the current program. (The options appears in the menu as DO, followed by the name of the PRG.)

WINDOW MENU

This menu contains options that manage open windows onscreen.

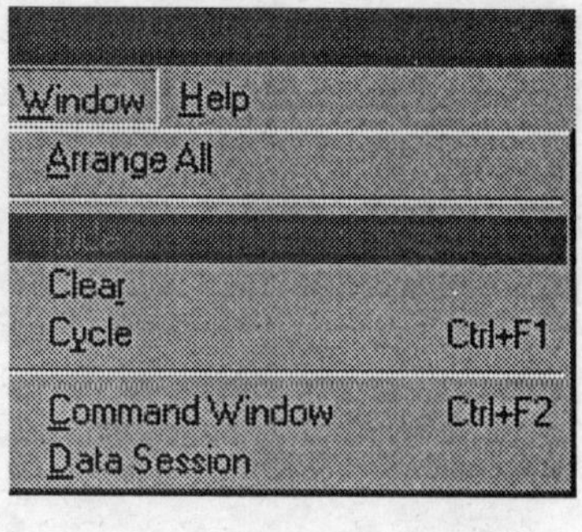

Arrange All This command arranges open windows as non-overlapping tiles.

Hide This command hides the active window but does not remove it from memory.

Show All This command displays all defined windows.

Clear This command clears text from the application workspace or current output window.

Cycle This command moves from one open window to the next, making the next window the active one.

Command Window This command makes the Command window active and brings it to the top, opening it if necessary.

Data Session This command makes the Data Session window active and brings it to the top, opening it if necessary.

<Window List> It displays the first nine defined windows. If more than nine windows have been defined, a final option – More Windows – appears. To change focus to any window, simply click its name.

HELP MENU

The first two options on this menu present different ways to access the help file to get information on commands, functions, or features. The third options lists support options that area available from Microsoft. The last option opens the typical copyright screen for the product; it adds additional functionality by providing system information and allowing the user to run other applications from within FoxPro.

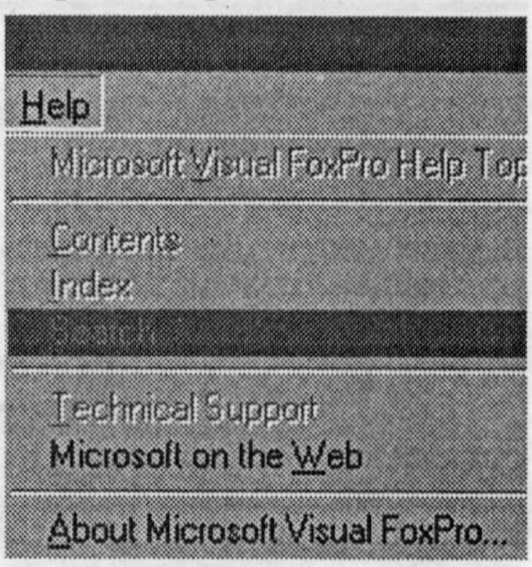

Contents This command displays help information via an outline format.

Documentation This command opens the FoxPro online documentation.

Sample Applications This commend describes the sample applications provided with Visual FoxPro.

Microsoft on the Web This command opens a second menu with options to use your Web browser to go to a variety of Visual FoxPro pages on the Web, the Microsoft home page, and several other locations.

Technical Support This command provides a list of available resources from Microsoft that offer additional help. The list includes a section that answers common questions.

About Microsoft Visual FoxPro This command displays the copyright screen for the product, along with whom it is licensed to, version date, resource filename, default directory, and product ID. Additional features include the capability to list system information and to run other programs.

SPELLING TOOL

It was mentioned briefly while talking about the Tools menu. Let us go into details of it. Using this tool you can spell check the data of your program or of the memo field. Those of you who are familiar with the working of Spell Checker in work processing would find it easier to use since it is very similar. Do the following for spell checking:

1. With the program file or memo field open, click at Spelling in the Tools menu.
2. The spell checking process will start and stop at any wrong spelling.
3. Like in the following case it has stopped at Johars, which I feel is right. But, this is a proper word and is not there in the dictionary of the software, because of which it is given as error.
4. The dialog box shown here has the following options:

Change To	FoxPro usually suggests a word which you can change to. It is the perception of the software, which you may not agree. If you by any chance agree to this, just click at Change. The word would be replaced and the spell checker would move further.
Suggestions	FoxPro would list out a number of similar words out of which you can choose the word which would be the right word according to you. It is not necessary that you would find the correct word here.
Ignore	Like in the case shown here, we know that the word is correct, since it is the name of a person. So you can overrule the system and click at Ignore to accept the word as it is.
Ignore All	Clicking at this would mean that if this word is found again in the remaining text, it would again be ignored.
Change	This button is pressed when you are planning to replace the word.

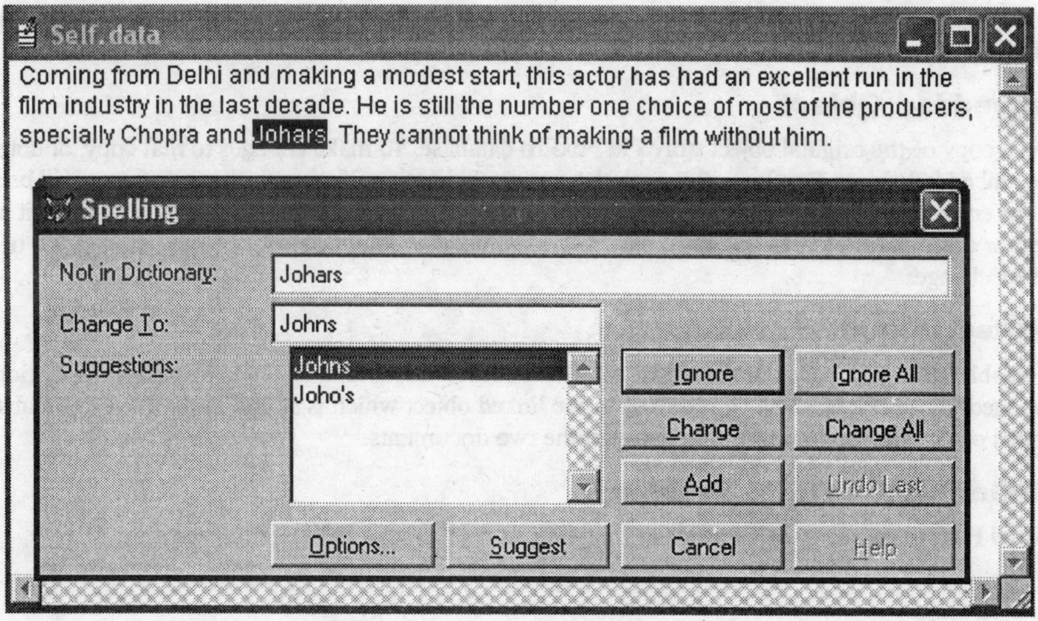

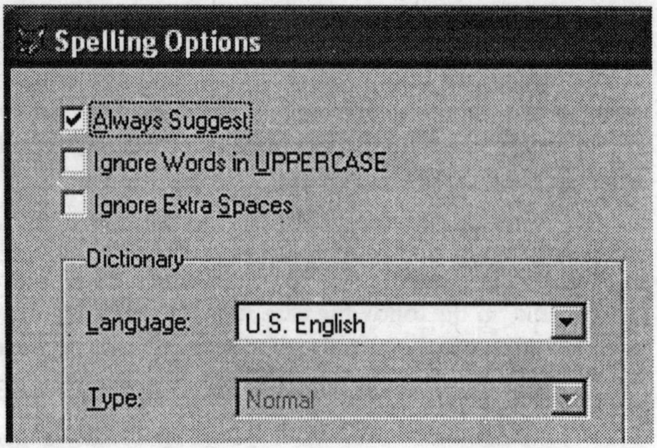

Change All	Pressing this button would mean that all similar words would be changed similarly in the remaining text.
Add	Sometime you feel that you are going to use this particular word many a times and do not want this to be seen as an error everytime. So add this word in the dictionary of the system and the word would be accepted everytime it occurs.
Options	This leads to another dialog box, where you can fix the option for the spell checking. For example, you can opt for always suggesting the other words, Ignoring Extra Spaces, etc. You can also pick up the dictionary to be used.
Suggest	It suggests the word which is similar to the word for your selection.
Cancel	This would stop the spell checking process.

OBJECT EMBEDDING AND LINKING

It is a method by which FoxPro shares with other software an object created in that software. There are two methods by which you can insert an object into a table. One is copying the object and placing it in table and the other is linking the object. So both type of objects can be defined as below:

Embedded Object

It is a copy of the original object stored in FoxPro database. To make changes to that copy, double click the embedded object, FoxPro will launch the source application. However, changes if any, will be made to the embedded copy in FoxPro, and not to the original information. Once the copy is inserted it has no further association with the original object. The embedded copy does not change even if the original object changes

Linked Object

It establishes a link between the destination and source document. If later, original information gets changed, those changes will be reflected in the linked object which is stored in the FoxPro database. A linked object maintains connection between the two documents.

Adding OLE Data to Database

Visual FoxPro support two methods of inserting an object into a field in database.

First method

1. Open the source or its application and copy the object to the clipboard. In this case, I have taken an object of CorelDRAW.
2. Open the database where you want to embed or link the object.
3. Modify the structure of the table to include a field having type as General.
4. Select the record and general field.
5. Open the general field by double clicking on it or by pressing Ctrl + Home.
6. A new window like the memo window comes on screen to accept the picture.
7. From edit menu, click at Paste.
8. Picture would be pasted in the window.
9. Close the window.
10. See how the Gen field is shown having a picture.

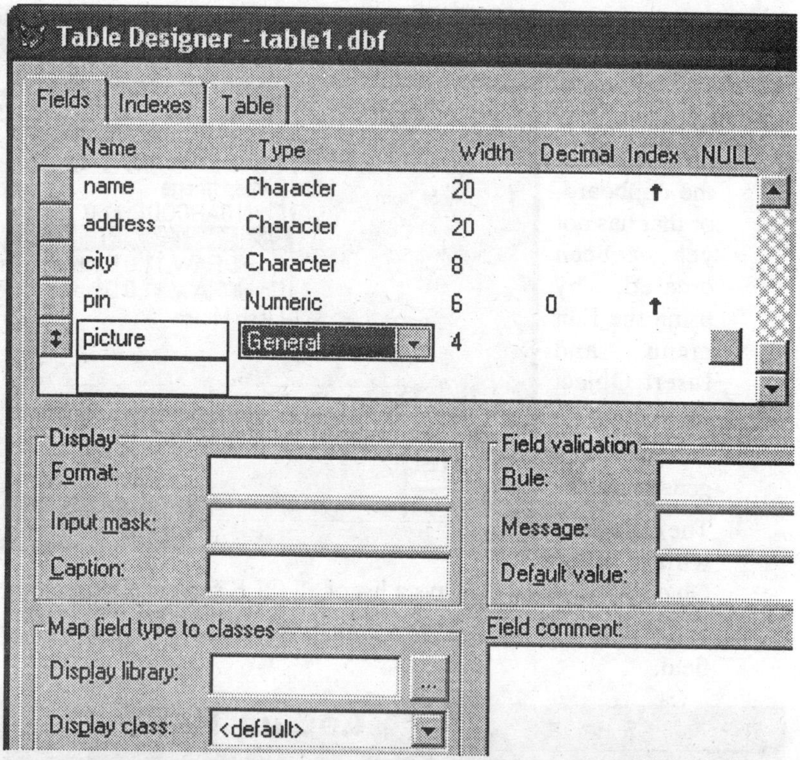

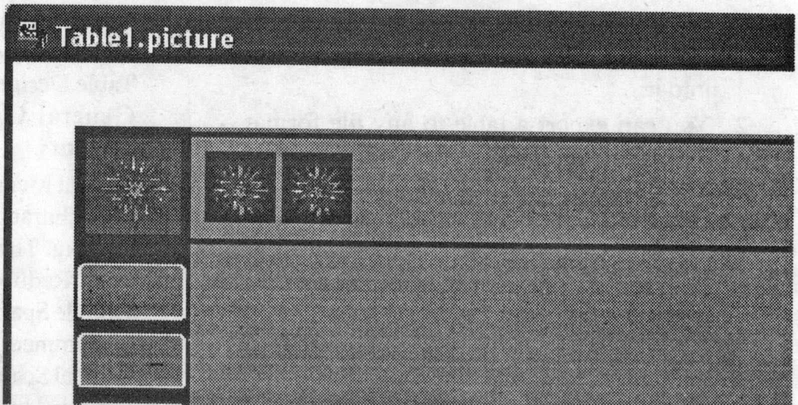

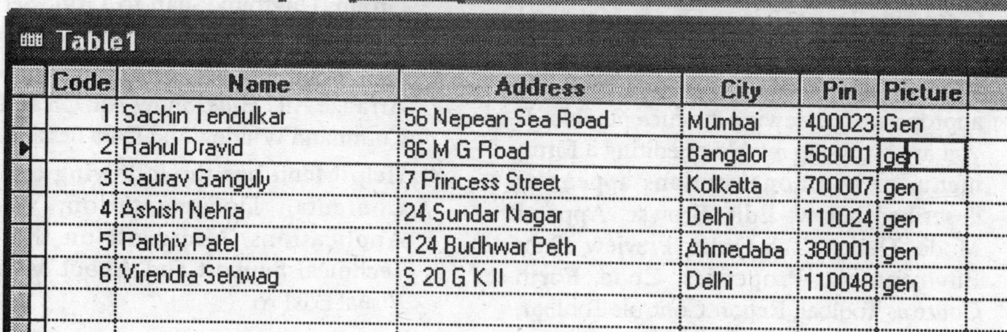

Second Method

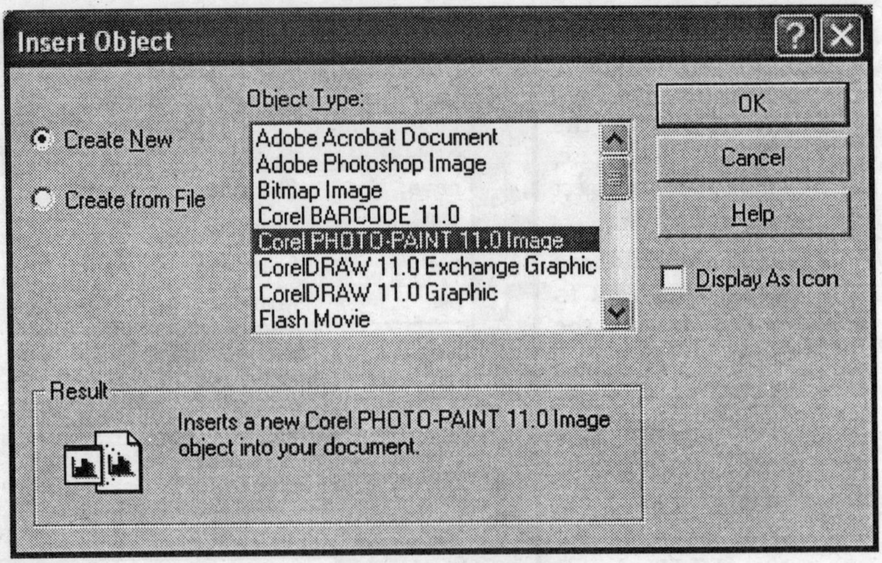

1. You can also embed an object that is not stored in the clipboard, or that has not yet been created, by using the Edit menu and Insert Object command.
2. Open the general field.
3. The dialog box which Insert Object has opened displays a list of all OLE servers. Choose one and create object.
4. When done, exit and FoxPro automatically embeds the entire object file and includes in the general field.

Let us Revise

1. Visual FoxPro allows you to import and export data files from various other software into it.
2. You can export a table to any file format which it defines.
3. File Menu has the following commands: New, Open, Close, Close All, Save, Save As, Save As Class, Revert, Import, Export, Page Setup, Page Preview, Print, Send and Exit.
4. Edit Menu has the following commands: Undo, Redo, Cut, Copy, Paste, Paste Special, Clear, Select All, Find, Find Again, Replace, Go to Line, Insert Objects, Object, Links and Properties
5. View Menu displays options that are appropriate for viewing the current table. If you are browsing a table or editing a form, menu, or additional options appear as described below: Edit, Browse, Append Mode, Design, Tab Order, Preview, Data Environment, Properties, Code, Form Controls Toolbar, Report Controls Toolbar, Layout Toolbar, Color Palette Toolbar, Report Preview Toolbar, Database Designer, Table Designer, Grid Lines, Show Position, General Options, Menu Options and Toolbars.
6. Format Menu consists of options that control font characteristics, text indentation, and spacing. The commands are: Font, Enlarge Font, Reduce Font, Single Space, 1½ Space, Double Space, Indent, Unindent, Comment, Uncomment, Align, Size, Horizontal Spacing, Vertical Spacing, Bring to Front, Sent to Back, Group, Ungroup, Snap to Grid, Set Grid Scale, Text Alignment, Fill, Pen and Mode.
7. Window Menu has the following options: Arrange All, Hide, Show All, Clear, Cycle, Command Window and Data Session.
8. Help Menu has the following options : Contents, Documentation, Sample Applications, Microsoft on the Web, Technical Support and About Microsoft Visual FoxPro.

9. Using Spell tool you can spell check the data of your program or of the memo field and even add new words to the dictionary.
10. FoxPro can share with other software an object created in that software.
11. Embedded object is a copy of the original object stored in FoxPro database.

Multiple Choice Questions

1. New file is opened from :
   (a) File menu (b) Edit menu
   (c) Tools menu
2. Using Spell check, you can add a new word to the dictionary :
   (a) Yes (b) No
3. Browse command is available in :
   (a) File menu (b) Edit menu
   (c) View menu
4. Align command is available under :
   (a) Format menu (b) File menu
   (c) Edit menu
5. Replace is part of :
   (a) File menu (b) Edit menu
   (c) Format menu
6. Print command is under :
   (a) File menu (b) Edit menu
   (c) Format menu
7. Double space command is under :
   (a) File menu (b) Edit menu
   (c) Format menu

True/False Questions

1. Visual FoxPro allows you to import and export data files from various other software into it.
2. You can export a table to any file format which it defines.
3. Page Setup command is under File Menu.
4. Tab Order command is under Edit Menu.
5. Code command is under View Menu.
6. Show All command is under Format Menu.
7. Window Menu has the following options: Arrange All, Hide, Show All, Clear, Cycle, Command Window and Data Session.
8. Help Menu has the following options : Contents, Documentation, Sample Applications, Microsoft on the Web, Technical Support and About Microsoft Visual FoxPro.
9. Using Spell tool you can spell check the data of your program or of the memo field and even add new words to the dictionary.
10. FoxPro can share with other software an object created in that software.
11. Embedded object is a copy of the original object stored in FoxPro database.

Matching Columns

Match the text in Column A with the text in Column B.

Column A	Column B
1. Preview	a. Format menu
2. Find Again	b. Window menu
3. Form Controls Toolbar	c. File menu
4. Reduce Font	d. Help menu

5. Cycle	e. Edit menu
6. Microsoft on the Web	f. View menu

Fill in the Blanks with Appropriate Words

a. Ignore b. Window c. File d. Edit
e. Linked f. Copy

1. Embedded object is the _____ of the original object stored in database.
2. Linked object is ________ with the object created in other software.
3. You can also _______ the word shown as wrong by the Spell Checker.
4. Data Session dialog box can be called from __________ menu.
5. Export command is under ________ menu.
6. Links command is under ______ menu.

Descriptive Type Questions

1. Describe the process of importing objects into FoxPro?
2. How would you export a table into other software?
3. What do you understand by Object Linking and Embedding?
4. Write short notes on the commands available under following menus :

File menu	Edit menu
View menu	Format menu
Tool menu	Windows menu
Help menu	

Answers to Objective Type Questions

Multiple Choice Questions

1. a	2. a	3. c	4. a
5. b	6. a	7. c	

True/False Questions

1. T	2. T	3. T	4. F
5. T	6. F	7. T	8. T
9. T	10. T	11. T	

Matching Columns

1. c	2. e	3. f	4. a
5. b	6. d		

Fill in the Blanks with Appropriate Words

1. f	2. e	3. a	4. b
5. c	6. d		

Recommended Readings

1. Learn to Program Visual Basic—Databases *by John Smiley.*
2. Learn to Program Visual Basic—Objects *by John Smiley.*
3. Learn to Program Visual Basic—Examples *by John Smiley.*
4. Keeping Ahead—SQL Server 7.0 *by Joelle Mosset.*
5. MCSE—Administering SQL Server 7.0 *by Jerome Gabillaud.*

—Published by Firewall Media (An Imprint of Laxmi Publications Pvt. Ltd.)

13 Functions in Visual FoxPro

INTRODUCTION

Visual FoxPro supports various type of functions. In this chapter, I list them out alongwith their usages and description.

String Functions

In Visual FoxPro a string is a series of characters and spaces. Using these string functions you can find out the various aspects of these strings. You can even change the form of these strings. Various string functions used in Visual FoxPro are:

$

It returns true (.T.) if a target expression contains a source expression. Its syntax is:

```
SOURCE_EXPRESSION $ TARGET_EXPRESSION
```

For example,

```
? SOURCE_EXPRESSION $ TARGET_EXPRESSION
```

will give the following result if you have "bangia" in source_expression and "ramesh bangia" in target_expression.

```
.T.
```

ACOPY()

This function copies elements from one memory variable array to another location. Its syntax is:

```
ACOPY(SOURCE_ARRAY, TARGET_ARRAY, SOURCE-START, ELEMENTS_TO_COPY,
TARGET_START)
```

ASC()

This function returns the ASCII code equivalent of the leftmost character in a character expression. Its syntax is:

```
ASC(CHARACTER_STRING)
```

For example,

```
? IASC("X")
```

will give the following result,

```
88
```

AT()

This function searches for an occurrence of source_expression in a target_expression. It returns the position where the source expression was found. Its syntax is:

```
AT(SOURCE_EXPRESSION, TARGET_EXPRESSION, NUMBER-OF_OCCURRENCE)
```

For example,

```
? AT(FIND_STR, STRING, 3)
```

will give the following result, if find_str has BBB and string has BBBBBB,

```
3
```

BETWEEN()

This function determiness if an expression lies between two other expressions. It returns a true value (.T.) if the expression is greater than or equal to the lower_limit and less than or equal to the upper_limit. Its syntax is:

```
BETWEEN (SOURCE, LOWER_LIMIT, UPPER_LIMIT)
```

CHR()

This function returns the character whose ASCII code is the same as the value of a numeric expression. Its syntax is:

```
CHR(NUMERIC_EXPRESSION)
```

For example,

```
? CHR(88)
```

will give the following result,

```
X
```

CTOD()

This function converts a character expression to a date expression. Its syntax is:

```
CTOD(CHARACTER_EXPRESSION)
```

DIFFERENCE()

This function returns a relative phonetic difference between two character expressions. Its syntax is:

```
DIFFERENCE(STRING1, STRING2)
```

DTOC()

This function converts a date expression to a character expression. The optional argument returns the date in a form suitable for direct use in INDEXing. This can be particularly useful in combination with the TIME() function to maintain a table in time sequence. Its syntax is:

```
DTOC(DATE_EXPRESSION, 1)
```

For example,

```
? DTOC({09/22/03}, 1)
```

will give the following result,

```
20030922
```

INT()

This function returns the integer portion of a numeric expression. Its syntax is:

```
INT(NUMERIC_EXPRESSION)
```

For example,

```
? INT(-9.4)
```

will give the following result,

```
-9.4
```

ISDIGIT()

This function returns a logical value: true(.T.) if a given character expression begins with a numeric digit; otherwise it returns false (.F.). Its syntax is:

```
ISDIGIT(STRING)
```

For example,

```
? ISDIGIT("65/80 ROHTAK ROAD")
```

will give the following result,

```
.T.
```

ISALPHA()

This function returns true (.T.) if an expression begins with an alpha character. Its syntax is:

```
ISALPHA(EXPRESSION)
```

For example,

```
? ISALPHA("RAMESH")
```

will give the following result,

```
.T.
```

ISLOWER()

This function returns true (.T.) if the first character in a string is a lowercase alpha character. Its syntax is:

```
ISLOWER(STRING)
```

For example,

```
? ISLOWER(RAMESH)
```

will give the following result,

```
.F.
```

ISUPPER()

This function returns true (.T.) if the first character in a string is an uppercase alpha character. Its syntax is:

```
ISUPPER(STRING)
```

For example,

```
? ISUPPER("RAMESH")
```

will give the following result,

```
.T.
```

LEFT()

This function returns a specified number of characters from the left of the string. Its syntax is:

```
LEFT(STRING, NUMBER_OF_CHARACTERS_TO_RETURN)
```

For example,

```
? LEFT("RAMESH BANGIA", 6)
```

will give the following result,

```
RAMESH
```

LEN()

This function returns the length of a character expression. Its syntax is:

```
LEN(CHARACTER_EXPRESSION)
```

For example,

```
? LEN("NAMASTE")
```

will give the following result,

```
7
```

LIKE()

This function compares twwo character expression's pattern and a target expression and returns a true (.T.) or false (.F.). If the target contains the pattern string. Its syntax is:

```
LIKE(PATTERN, TARGET_STRING)
```

For example,

```
? LIKE (PATTERN, TARGET)
```

will give the following result, if target has "Ramesh" and pattern has "Ram".

```
.T.
```

LOWER()

This function returns a specified character expression in lowercase. Its syntax is:

```
LOWER(CHARACTER_EXPRESSION)
```

For example,

```
? LOWER(STRING)
```

will give the following result, if the string has "RAMESH"

```
ramesh
```

LTRIM()

This function returns a character string resulting from removing leading blanks from a character expression.

Its syntax is:

```
LTRIM(CHARACTER_EXPRESSION)
```

For example,

```
? CITY LTRIM(STATE)
```

will give the following result, if city contains "Hyderabad" and state contains AP,

```
HYDERABAD AP
```

PROPER()

This function returns a character expression capitalized as appropriate for proper names. Its syntax is:

```
PROPER(CHARACTER_EXPRESSION)
```

For example,

```
? PROPER(STRING)
```

will give the following result, if the string has "ramesh" in it,

```
Ramesh
```

REPLICATE()

This function returns a character resulting from repeating a character expression to a specified number of times. Its syntax is:

```
REPLICATE(CHARACTER_EXPRESSION, NUMBER_OF_TIMES)
```

For example,

```
? REPLICATE("TEN", 4)
```

will give the following result,

```
TEN TEN TEN TEN
```

RIGHT()

This function returns the rightmost portion of a character string or memory variable. Its syntax is:

```
RIGHT(STRING, NUMBER_OF_CHARACTER_TO_RETURN)
```

For example,

```
? RIGHT("DILIP KUMAR", 5)
```

will give the following result,

```
KUMAR
```

RTRIM()

This function removes trailing blanks from a specified string. Its syntax is:

```
RTRIM(STRING)
```

For example,

```
? RTRIM(STRING)
```

will give the following result, if the string contains, "Delhi   "

```
DELHI
```

SPACE()

This function returns a character string composed of number of specified blanks. Its syntax is:

```
SPACE(NUMERIC)
```

For example,

```
? STORE SPACE(10) TO BLANK
```

This will store 10 blanks to BLANK.

STR()

This function converts a numeric expression to a character expression. Its syntax is:

```
STR(NUMERIC_EXPRESSION, LENGTH_OF_CHARACTER_STRING, DECIMALS)
```

For example,

```
? STR(789.5678, 8, 3)
```

will give the following result,

```
789.567
```

STRTRAN()

This function returns the given expression with one or more occurrences of an old pattern replaced with a new pattern. Its syntax is:

```
STRTRAN(EXPRESSION, OLD_PATTERN, NEW_PATTERN, NUMBER_OF_REPLACEMENTS,
NUMBER_OF_OCCURRENCES)
```

STUFF()

This function returns a specified number of characters from a given expression. Its syntax is:

```
STUFF(OLD_STRING, LENGTH_OF_CHARACTER, NUMBER_OF_CHARACTERS,
NEW_STRING)
```

For example,

```
? STUFF(OLD_STRING, 7, 0, NEW_STRING)
```

will give the following result, if old_string contains "start end" and "added" is there in new_string.

```
START ADDEDEND
```

SUBSTR()

This function returns a specified number of characters from a given expression. Its syntax is:

```
SUBSTR(EXPRESSION, STARTING_POSITION, NUMBER_OF_CHARACTERS)
```

For example,

```
? SUBSTR(STRING, 1, 5)
```

will give the following result, if string contains Ramesh,

```
RAMES
```

TRANSFORM()

This function allows you to format character strings and numeric variables without the use of the @..SAY command. Its syntax is:

```
TRANSFORM(EXPRESSION, PICTURE)
```

For example,

```
? TRANSFORM(AMOUNT,'$$$.99')
```

will give the following result, if the amount contains the figure of 99.99

```
99.99
```

TRIM()

This function trims trailing blanks from an expression. TRIM() is identified to the RTRIM() function. Its syntax is:

```
TRIM(CHARACTER_EXPRESSION)
```

For example,

```
? TRIM(CITY)
```

will give the following result, if the city contains, "Mumbai

```
MUMBAI
```

TYPE()

This function returns character describing the data type of an expression. The values returned include the following:

Value	Description
C	Character string expression
N	Numeric expression
D	Date expression
L	Logical expression
M	Memo expression
U	Undefined type of expression

Its syntax is:

```
TYPE(EXPRESSION)
```

For example,

```
? TYPE("CITY")
```

will give the following result,

```
C
```

For example,

```
? TYPE("NUMBER")
```

will give the following result,

```
N
```

For example,

```
? TYPE("COMPUTER")
```

will give the following result,

```
U
```

For example,

```
? TYPE("DATE()")
```

will give the following result,

```
D
```

UPPER()

This function returns the specified expression in uppercase. Its syntax is:

```
UPPER(STRING)
```

For example,

```
? UPPER("ramesh bangia")
```

will give the following result,

```
RAMESH BANGIA
```

Numeric Functions

These are useful for many mathematical and financial calculations.

ABS()

It returns the absolute value of a numeric expression. Its syntax is:

```
ABS(NUMBER)
```

For example,

```
? ABS(-20)
```

will give the result as

```
20
```

ACOS()

It returns the cosine of a numeric, an angle in radians between 0 and +π (3.141590. The value of the numeric may range between +1 and –1. Its syntax is:

```
ACOS(NUMBER)
```

For example,

```
? ACOS(-1)
```

will give the result as

```
3.14
```

ASIN()

It returns the arc of a numeric value in radians between -π/2 and +π/2. The value of the numeric argument must be between +1 and –1. Its syntax is:

```
ASIN(NUMBER)
```

For example,

```
? ASIN(-20)
```

will give the result as

```
-1.57
```

ATAN()

It returns the arc tangent of a numeric value, an angle in radians between -p/2 and +p/2. The numeric argument can be any value. Its syntax is:

```
ATAN(NUMBER)
```

For example,

```
? ATAN(-1)
```

will give the result as

```
-0.79
```

ATN2()

It returns an arc tangent angle (in radians) for all four quadrants. With the ATN(2) function you specify two arguments, the coordinates, as opposed to specifying the tangent value. The function eliminates errors caused by division by zero. Its syntax is:

```
ATN2(X_COORD, Y_COORD)
```

For example,

```
? ATAN2(1, 0)
```

will give the result as

```
1.57
```

BETWEEN()

The function returns a value of true (.T.) if the first numeric expression is greater than or equal to a second numeric expression and less than or equal to a third numeric expression. Its syntax is:

```
BETWEEN(SOURCE_EXPRESSION, LOWER-LIMIT, UPPER_LIMIT)
```

For example,

```
? BETWEEN(5, 1, 4)
```

will give the result as

```
.F.
```

CEILING()

It returns the nearest integer that is greater than or equal to the numeric argument. It rounds all positive numbers with a decimal portion up to the next highest number and rounds all negative numbers with a decimal portion up to the next number closet to zero. Its syntax is:

```
CEILING (EXPRESSION)
```

For example,

```
? CEILING(10.2)
```

will give the result as

```
11
```

COS()

It returns the cosine of a numeric argument. The result returned by this function ranges between –1 and +1. Its syntax is:

```
COS (NUMBER)
```

For example,

```
? COS(-1)
```

will give the result as

```
0.54
```

DTOR()

It converts a numeric angle from degrees to radians. You must convert to a decimal angle expressed in degree minute:second format. Its syntax is:

```
DTOR (NUMERIC_ANGLE)
```

For example,

```
? DTOR(90)
```

will give the result as

```
1.57
```

EXP()

This is the natural exponent (e) operator. Its syntax is:

```
EXP (NUMBER)
```

For example,

```
? EXP(12)
```

will give the result as

```
162754.79
```

FLOOR()

It returns the nearest integer value that is less than or equal to the numeric argument. This function rounds all positive numbers with a decimal portion down to the next lowest number and rounds all negative numbers with a decimal portion down to the next number farther from zero. Its syntax is:

```
FLOOR(DECIMAL_NUMBER)
```

For example,

```
? FLOOR(10.1)
```

will give the result as

```
10
```

FV()

This is a financial function. It returns the future value of an investiment. You must supply the equal periodic payment, the periodic interest rate, and the number of periods the payments are made. Its syntax is:

```
FV(PAYMENT, INTEREST, PERIOD)
```

For example,

```
? FV(1000, 9.5, 120)
```

will give the result as

```
199080.68
```

INT()

This function evaluates the numeric argument and returns the integer part of the numeric. Its syntax is:

```
INT (DECIMAL_NUMBER)
```

For example,

```
? INT(-1.1)
```

will give the result as

```
1
```

ISDIGIT()

This function returns a true value (.T.) if the first character of a character expression is a digit from 0 to 9. Its syntax is:

```
ISDIGIT (CHARACTER_EXPRESSION)
```

For example,

```
? ISDIGIT(5CHAT)
```

will give the result as

```
.T.
```

LOG()

This is the natural logarithm operator. Its syntax is:

```
LOG (NUMBER)
```

For example,

```
? LOG(10)
```

will give the result as

```
2.30
```

LOG10()

This function returns the common logarithm of the nueric argument. The base for the common logarithm is 10. Its syntax is:

```
LOG10(NUMBER)
```

For example,

```
? LOG10(1)
```

will give the result as

```
0.00
```

MAX()

This function returns the highest value of two numeric expressions. Its syntax is:

```
MAX(NUMERIC_1, NUMERIC_2)
```

For example,

```
? MAX(A, B)
```

will give the following result if A = 11 and B = 15,

```
15
```

MIN()

This function returns the lower value of two numeric expressions. Its syntax is:

```
MIN(NUMERIC_1, NUMERIC_2)
```

For example,

```
? MIN(A, B)
```

will give the following result if A = 11 and B = 15,

```
11
```

MOD()

This function returns the value of the remainder from a division problem. Its syntax is:

```
MOD(NUMBER, DIVISOR)
```

For example,

```
? MOD(25, 5)
```

will give the following result,

```
0
```

PAYMENT()

This function returns the amount of each periodic payment on a loan. You must supply the principal of the loan, the interest rate, and the total number of payments to be made. Its syntax is:

```
PAYMENT (PRINCIPAL, INTEREST, PERIOD)
```

For example,

```
? PAYMENT(PRINCIPAL, INTEREST, PERIOD)
```

will give the following result if Principal = 25000, Interest = 9.5% and for 5 years,

```
525.05
```

PI()

This function returns the numeric constant π(pi). Its syntax is:

```
PI()
```

For example,

```
? PI()
```

will give the following result,

```
3.14
```

PV()

This function returns the present value of an investment. You must supply the equal periodic payment, the periodic interest rate, and the total number of periods the payments are to be made. Its syntax is:

```
PV (PAYMENT, INTEREST, PERIOD)
```

For example,

```
? PV(PRINCIPAL, INTEREST, PERIOD)
```

will give the following result if Principal = 2000, Interest = 9.5% and for 10 years,

```
154562.42
```

RAND()

This function returns aa random number between 0 and 1. Its syntax is:

```
RAND (NUMBER)
```

For example,

```
? RAND (-1)
```

will give the following result,

```
0.55
```

ROUND()

This function rounds a number to a specified number of decimal places. Its syntax is:

```
ROUND(NUMBER, DECIMAL_PLACES)
```

For example,

```
? ROUND(1456.7896, 2)
```

will give the following result,

```
1456.79
```

SIGN()

This function returns a numeric value of 1, –1, or 0 depending on the sign of a numeric expression. If the numeric argument is positive, the function returns 1. If the numeric expression is negative, it returns –1. If the numeric argument is zero, it returns 0. Its syntax is:

```
SIGN(NUMERIC_EXPRESSION)
```

For example,

```
? SIGN(-8)
```

will give the following result,

```
-1
```

SIN()

This function returns the sine of a numeric argument. The value of the argument is an angle measured in radians. The result returned by this function ranges between –1 and 1. Its syntax is:

```
SIN(NUMBER)
```

For example,

```
? SIN(45)
```

will give the following result,

```
0.85
```

SQRT()

This is the square root operator. Its syntax is:

```
SQRT(NUMBER)
```

For example,

```
? SQRT(25)
```

will give the following result,

```
5.00
```

TAN()

This function returns the tangent of a numeric argument. The value of the argument is an angle measured in radians. Its syntax is:

```
TAN(NUMBER)
```

For example,

```
? TAN(45)
```

will give the following result,

```
1.62
```

VAL()

This function returns a numeric value that corresponds to the value of the digits contained in the character string expression. Its syntax is:

```
VAL(CHARACTER_EXPRESSION)
```

For example,

```
? VAL("20G")
```

will give the following result,

```
20.00
```

Logical Functions

In Visual FoxPro you deal with a number of logical functions. They are listed here alongwith their description and example.

BOF()

It finds out whether it is the beginning of the file or not. If it is then a T is returned else F is returned. Its syntax is:

```
BOF(ALIAS)
```

For example,

```
USE TABLE
GOTO TOP
?BOF
```

will give the result as

```
.T.
```

DELETED()

It returns deletion status of one or more records. It returns a logical value such as .T. or .F.. This function supports an optional argument ALIAS which indicates the work area. If you omit the argument, it reutrns the status for the currently selected work area. Its syntax is:

```
DELETED(ALIAS)
```

For example,

```
USE TABLE
DELTE RECORD 2
1 RECORD DELETED
? DELETED
```

will give the result as,

```
.T.
```

EOF()

It is used to determine if the SKIP command moves the record pointer past the last record in a table. If it has, it returns a logical true. The EOF() function supports an optional argument ALIAS which indicates the work area. If you omit the argument, it returns the status for the currently selected work area. Its syntax is:

```
EOF(ALIAS)
```

For example,

```
USE TABLE
GO BOTTOM
? EOF
```

will give the result as,

```
.F.
```

FILE()

It is used to test for the existence of a file. You must explicitly specify any extensions in the filename. Its syntax is:

```
FILE("FILE_NAME")
```

For example,

```
IF FILE("STUDENT.DBF")
DO MARKS
```

will run the program marks, if the file is found.

FOUND()

It is used to find a logical true value when it has found the object of the FIND, SEEK, LOCATE, or CONTINUE commands. If it does not find the object, it returns a logical false. The FOUND() function supports an optional argument ALIAS which indicates the work area. If you omit the argement it returns the status for the currently selected work area. Its syntax is:

```
FOUND(ALIAS)
```

For example,

```
USE TABLE
LOCATE FOR CITY = "DELHI"
? FOUND
```

will give the result as,

```
.T.
```

IIF()

It is used in place of an if, else, endif expression. The function checks the logical expression for a logical true or false value. If it is true, it returns the expression. If it is false, it returns the false expression. Its syntax is:

```
IIF(LOGICAL_EXPRESSION, TRUE_EXPRESSION, FALSE_EXPRESSION)
```

For example,

```
CHECK = IIF(NUM, A, B)
? CHECK
```

will give the following result if NUM is the numeric expression and A and B contain YES and NO,

```
YES
```

ISALPHA()

If the argument begins with an alphabeticaal character, this function returns a logical true. Its syntax is:

```
ISALPHA(EXPRESSION)
```

For example,

```
? ISALPHA(DETAILS)
```

will give the following result if DETAILS contains TEXT DONE,

```
.T.
```

ISCOLOR()

If you are using a colour display, this function returns a logical true value. Its syntax is:

```
ISCOLOR()
```

ISLOWER()

The function returns a logical true value if the first character in an expression is a lowercase alphabetic character. Its syntax is:

```
ISLOWER(EXPRESSION)
```

For example,

```
? ISLOWER("RAMESH")
```

will give the following result,

```
.F.
```

ISUPPER()

This function returns a logical true value, if the first character in an expression is an uppercase alphabetic basic character. Its syntax is:

```
ISUPPER(EXPRESSION)
```

For example,

```
? ISUPPER("RAMESH")
```

will give the following result,

```
.T.
```

PRINTSTATUS()

This function returns true (.T.) value if the printer or print device is ready to print. It returns false (.F.) if it is not. Its syntax is:

```
PRINTSTATUS()
```

SEEK()

It is used to return the true value if a SEEK was successful. The SEEK() function searches an indexed table for the first occurrence of a record whose index key expression matches a specified expression. If a match is found, it returns a logical true (.T.) value and moves the record pointer to the matching record. If it is not found, it returns a logical false (.F.) value and positions the record pointer at the end of the file. Its syntax is:

```
SEEK(EXPRESSION, ALIAS)
```

Let us Revise

1. $ returns true (.T.) if a target expression contains a source expression.
2. ACOPY() function copies elements from one memory variable array to another location.
3. ASC() function returns the ASCII code equivalent of the leftmost character in a character expression.
4. AT() function searches for an occurrence of source_expression in a target_expression.
5. BETWEEN() function determiness if an expression lies between two other expressions.
6. CHR() function returns the character whose ASCII code is the same as the value of a numeric expression.
7. CTOD() function converts a character expression to a date expression.
8. DIFFERENCE() function returns a relative phonetic difference between two character expressions.
9. DTOC() function converts a date expression to a character expression.
10. INT() function returns the integer portion of a numeric expression.
11. ISDIGIT() function returns a logical value: true(.T.) if a given character expression begins with a numeric digit; otherwise it returns false (.F.).
12. ISALPHA() function returns true (.T.) if an expression begins with an alpha character.
13. ISLOWER() function returns true (.T.) if the first character in a string is a lowercase alpha character.
14. ISUPPER() function returns true (.T.) if the first character in a string is an uppercase alpha character.
15. LEFT() function returns a specified number of characters from the left of the string.
16. LEN() function returns the length of a character expression.
17. LIKE() function compares twwo character expression's pattern and a target expression and returns a true (.T.) or false (.F.).
18. LOWER() function returns a specified character expression in lowercase.
19. LTRIM() function returns a character string resulting from removing leading blanks from a character expression.
20. PROPER() function returns a character expression capitalized as appropriate for proper names.
21. REPLICATE() function returns a character resulting from repeating a character expression to a specified number of times.
22. RIGHT() function returns the rightmost portion of a character string or memory variable.
23. RTRIM() function removes trailing blanks from a specified string.
24. SPACE() function returns a character string composed of number of specified blanks.
25. STR() function converts a numeric expression to a character expression.
26. STRTRAN() function returns the given expression with one or more occurrences of an old pattern replaced with a new pattern.
27. STUFF() function returns a specified number of characters from a given expression.
28. SUBSTR() function returns a specified number of characters from a given expression.
29. TRANSFORM() function allows you to format character strings and numeric variables without the use of the @..SAY command.
30. TRIM() function trims trailing blanks from an expression.
31. TYPE() function returns character describing the data type of an expression.
32. UPPER() function returns the specified expression in uppercase.

33. ABS() returns the absolute value of a numeric expression.
34. ACOS() returns the cosine of a numeric, an angle in radians between 0 and +π (3.14159).
35. ASIN() returns the arc of a numeric value in radians between -π/2 and +π/2.
36. ATAN() returns the arc tangent of a numeric value, an angle in radians between -π/2 and +π/2.
37. ATN2() returns an arc tangent angle (in radians) for all four quadrants.
38. BETWEEN() function returns a value of true (.T.) if the first numeric expression is greater than or equal to a second numeric expression and less than or equal to a third numeric expression.
39. CEILING() returns the nearest integer that is greater than or equal to the numeric argument.
40. COS() returns the cosine of a numeric argument.
41. DTOR() converts a numeric angle from degrees to radians.
42. EXP() is the natural exponent (e) operator.
43. FLOOR() returns the nearest integer value that is less than or equal to the numeric argument.
44. FV() is a financial function. It returns the future value of an investment.
45. INT() function evaluates the numeric argument and returns the integer part of the numeric.
46. ISDIGIT() function returns a true value (.T.) if the first character of a character expression is a digit from 0 to 9.
47. LOG() is the natural logarithm operator.
48. LOG10() function returns the common logarithm of the nueric argument.
49. MAX() function returns the highest value of two numeric expressions.
50. MIN() function returns the lower value of two numeric expressions.
51. MOD() function returns the value of the remainder from a division problem.
52. PAYMENT() function returns the amount of each periodic payment on a loan.
53. PI() function returns the numeric constant π(pi).
54. PV() function returns the present value of an investment.
55. RAND() function returns a random number between 0 and 1.
56. ROUND() function rounds a number to a specified number of decimal places.
57. SIGN() function returns a numeric value of 1, –1, or 0 depending on the sign of a numeric expression.
58. SIN() function returns the sine of a numeric argument.
59. SQRT() is the square root operator.
60. TAN() function returns the tangent of a numeric argument.
61. VAL() function returns a numeric value that corresponds to the value of the digits contained in the character string expression.
62. BOF() finds out whether it is the beginning of the file or not.
63. DELETED() returns deletion status of one or more records.
64. EOF() is used to determine if the SKIP command moves the record pointer past the last record in a table.
65. FILE() is used to test for the existence of a file.
66. FOUND() is used to find a logical true value when it has found the object of the FIND, SEEK, LOCATE, or CONTINUE commands.
67. IIF() is used in place of an if, else, endif expression.
68. ISALPHA(), if the argument begins with an alphabeticaal character, this function returns a logical true.
69. ISCOLOR(), if you are using a colour display, this function returns a logical true value.

70. ISLOWER() function returns a logical true value if the first character in an expression is a lowercase alphabetic character.

71. ISUPPER() function returns a logical true value, if the first character in an expression is an uppercase alphabetic basic character.

72. PRINTSTATUS(), this function returns true (.T.) value if the printer or print device is ready to print. It returns false (.F.) if it is not.

73. SEEK() is used to return the true value if a SEEK was successful.

Multiple Choice Questions

1. RTRIM() function removes ______ blanks:
   (a) trailing (b) leading
   (c) Workers
2. BETWEEN() function determines if an expression lies between two other:
   (a) strings (b) expressions
   (c) characters
3. ABS() retuns which type of value:
   (a) negative (b) true
   (c) absolute
4. Which type of operator is LOG()?
   (a) logarithm (b) logic
   (c) logo
5. File() tests for the existence of a:
   (a) Table (b) File
   (c) Document
6. IIF is used for if, else and .
   (a) endif (b) iff
   (c) alsoif

True/False Questions

1. $ returns true (.T.) if a target expression contains a source expression.
2. ASC() function returns the ASCII code equivalent of the rightmost character in a character expression.
3. BETWEEN() function determiness if an expression lies between two other expressions.
4. CTOD() function converts a character expression to a date expression.
5. DTOC() function converts a date expression to a numeric expression.
6. ISDIGIT() function returns a logical value: true(.T.) if a given character expression begins with a numeric digit; otherwise it returns false (.F.).
7. ISLOWER() function returns true (.T.) if the first character in a string is a lowercase alpha character.
8. LEFT() function returns a specified number of characters from the left of the string.
9. LIKE() function compares twwo character expression's pattern and a target expression and returns a true (.T.) or false (.F.).
10. LTRIM() function returns a numeric string resulting from removing leading blanks from a character expression.
11. REPLICATE() function returns a character resulting from repeating a character expression to a specified number of times.
12. RTRIM() function removes trailing blanks from a specified string.
13. STR() function converts a character expression to a character expression.
14. STUFF() function returns a specified number of characters from a given expression.
15. TRANSFORM() function allows you to format character strings and numeric variables without the use of the @..SAY command.
16. TYPE() function returns numeric describing the data type of an expression.

17. ABS() returns the absolute value of a numeric expression.
18. ASIN() returns the arc of a numeric value in radians between -π/2 and +π/2.
19. ATN2() returns an arc tangent angle (in radians) for all four quadrants.
20. CEILING() returns the nearest integer that is greater than or equal to the numeric argument.
21. DTOR() converts a numeric angle from degrees to radians.
22. FLOOR() returns the nearest integer value that is greater than or equal to the numeric argument.
23. INT() function evaluates the numeric argument and returns the integer part of the numeric.
24. LOG() is the natural logarithm operator.
25. MAX() function returns the lowest value of two numeric expressions.
26. MOD() function returns the value of the remainder from a division problem.
27. PI() function returns the numeric constant π(pi).
28. RAND() function returns a random number between 0 and 1.
29. SIGN() function returns a numeric value of 1, −1, or 0 depending on the sign of a numeric expression.
30. SQRT() is the square root operator.
31. VAL() function returns a numeric value that corresponds to the value of the digits contained in the character string expression.
32. DELETED() returns deletion status of one or more records.
33. FILE() is used to test for the existence of a file.
34. IIF() is used in place of an if, else, endif expression.
35. ISCOLOR(), if you are using a colour display, this function returns a logical true value.
36. ISUPPER() function returns a logical true value, if the last character in an expression is an uppercase alphabetic basic character.

Matching Columns

Match the text in Column A with the text in Column B.

Column A	Column B
1. CHR()	a. Returns the integer portion of a numeric expression.
2. DTOC()	b. Returns a specified character expression in lowercase.
3. LEN()	c. Returns True (.T) if an expression begins with an alpha character.
4. INT()	d. Returns a character expression capitalized as appropriate for proper names.
5. LOWER()	e. Removes trailing blanks from a specified string.
6. ISALPHA()	f. Returns the character whose ASCII code is same as the value of a numeric expression.
7. PROPER()	g. Returns the length of a character expression.
8. RTRIM()	h. Converts a date expression to a character expression.

Fill in the Blanks with Appropriate Words

a. LEN() b. STR() c. SPACE() d. TRIM()
e. BETWEEN() f. CTOD()

1. The function which convers a character expression to a date expression is called ________.
2. The function which determines if an expression lies between two other expressions is called ________.
3. The function which returns the length of a character expression is called ________.
4. The function which converts a numeric expression to a character expression is called
5. The function which returns a character string composed of number of specified blanks is called________.
6. The function which trms trailing blanks from an expression is called ________.

Descriptive Type Questions

1. Describe various type of String functions.
2. Describe Numeric functions.
3. What all Logical functions?

Answers to Objective Type Questions

Multiple Choice Questions

1. a	2. b	3. c	4. a
5. b	6. a		

True/False Questions

1. T	2. F	3. T	4. T
5. F	6. T	7. T	8. T
9. T	10. F	11. T	12. T
13. F	14. T	15. T	16. F
17. T	18. T	19. T	20. T
21. T	22. F	23. T	24. T
25. F	26. T	27. T	28. T
29. T	30. T	31. T	32. T
33. T	34. T	35. T	36. F

Matching Columns

1. h	2. f	3. g	4. a
5. b	6. c	7. d	8. e

Fill in the Blanks with Appropriate Words

1. f	2. e	3. a	4. b
5. c	6. d		

Recommended Readings

1. Learn to Program Visual Basic—Databases *by John Smiley.*
2. Learn to Program Visual Basic—Objects *by John Smiley.*
3. Learn to Program Visual Basic—Examples *by John Smiley.*
4. Keeping Ahead—SQL Server 7.0 *by Joelle Mosset.*
5. MCSE—Administering SQL Server 7.0 *by Jerome Gabillaud.*

—Published by Firewall Media (An Imprint of Laxmi Publications Pvt. Ltd.)

14 Programming and Developing Applications

AN OVERVIEW OF PROGRAMMING

In the earlier chapter we read about the various aspects of programming and the features supported by Visual FoxPro. In this chapter, we will learn more about programming in Visual FoxPro. We know that the programming is based upon commands which are given to the computer to do something. A command file (or program file) created by the programmer in Visual FoxPro contains a group of commands. When required, we can use this file containing group of commands without retyping them. Moreover there are some very powerful control commands such as IF-ELSE-ENDIF, DOWHILE-ENDDO, DO CASE-ENDCASE and FOR-ENDFOR. These can be used in a command file and not in the command window. A command file can be stored on a floppy or hard disk. You record commands in a file because it is more convenient to execute a batch of commands rather than typing every command at the Command window, whenever the program is to be run. Once the commands are saved in a command file, you can execute all such commands as a group.

CREATING COMMAND FILES

For this do the following:

1. Click File menu and choose New… From the New dialog box that appears, choose Program radio button and click on the New file button.
2. A program editor as shown below will appear.
3. Type your program in this editor.
4. After you have entered the commands, invoke File menu and select Save As.. When Visual FoxPro displays the Save As dialog box, type the filename to save the current document.
5. Click save button.

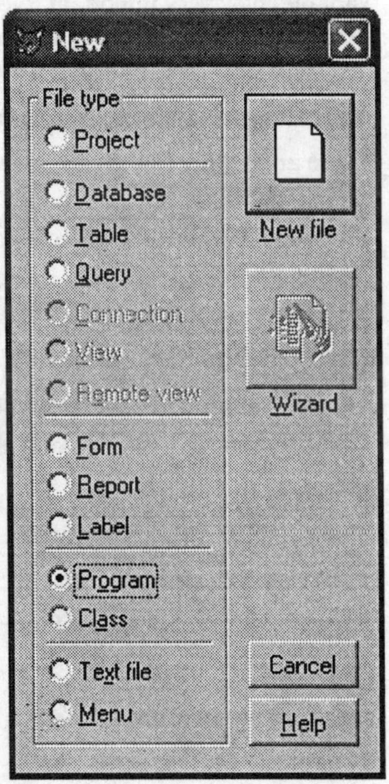

Running the Program

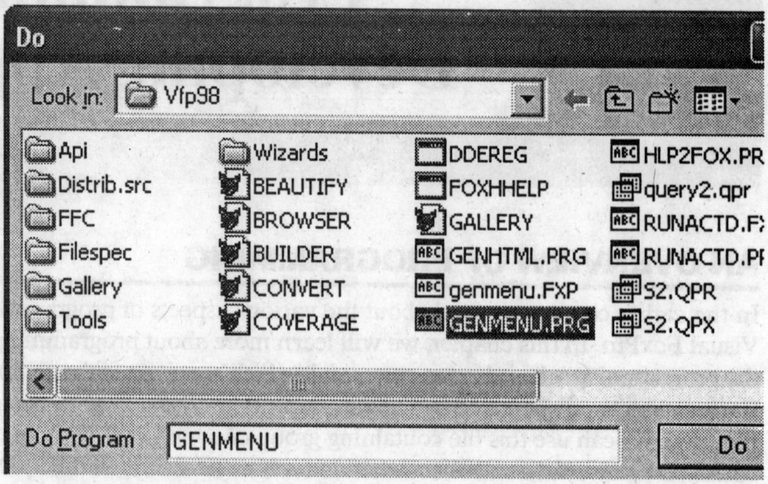

You can run the program by selecting DO from the Program menu and selecting a program from the DO dialog box (which works just like the open dialog box).

If you use the program file without the extension .prg then it is assumed that the program has the extension .prg

INPUT/OUTPUT

Variables

A variable is a memory location within the computer that is used to store data temporarily. Variables are referred to by their assigned names so that you can refer to the required variable by name and use it in calculations or for some other application. For naming a variable, follow the same rules as are used for naming a field. Variable names must contain only letters, numbers and underscores and must begin with a letter. You cannot use spaces and punctuation marks in variable names. Visual FoxPro is not case sensitive when it comes to variable names. For example WAGE and wage would refer to the same variable.

Variables play very important role in programming by collecting and storing inputs; preserving data from a table record; storing the results of calculations for future use and storing individual items of information that must be globally available throughout an application

Creating and Using Variables

There are mainly four types of variables used in Visual FoxPro. These are character, numeric, data and logical variables.

Character Variables: Character variables store strings of characters, which can be letters, numbers or a combination of both.

Numeric Variables: Numeric variables are used to store numeric values such as whole or decimal numbers.

Data Variables: Data variables store data values written in MM/DD/YY format as (03/25/97).

Logical Variables: Logical variables contain a logical value of T (true) or (false) or Y (yes) or N (no).

Variables can be created in one of the following two ways:

Storing the Variable

The format for store command is;

```
STORE <EXPRESSION> TO <VARIABLE_NAME>
```

For example, the following Store command assigns a numeric value 0 to the variable ZERO:

```
STORE 0 TO ZERO
```

Assigning the Variable

The format for this is:

```
VARIABLE = EXPRESSION
```

For example, the following statement assigns a numeric value 0 to the variable ZERO:

```
ZERO = 0
```

Variables can also be created using single (') or double (") quotation marks or square brackets. For example, you can use any of the following commands to create a variable Mname and store "Amitabh Bachchan" in it

```
STORE 'AMITABH BACHCHAN' TO MNAME
STORE "AMITABH BACHCHAN" TO MNAME
STORE [AMITABH BACHCHAN] TO MNAME
```

The same can be accomplished using the statement like following:

```
MNAME = "AMITABH BACHCHAN"
MNAME = 'AMITABH BACHCHAN'
MNAME = [AMITABH BACHCHAN]
```

A logical variable contains a single true or false value and it can be created with the .T. (TRUE) or the .F. (FALSE) symbol. The following command would assign a logical value True to the variable Test:

```
STORE .T. TO TEST
```

Or

```
TEST = .T.
```

You can store date to variables in Visual FoxPro using various methods. For example, it can be done by surrounding the date value with curly braces as given below:

```
STORE {09/19/03} TO B_DAY
```

Or

```
B_DAY={09/19/03}
```

This would store 01/19/03 in a date variable named B_Day.

Creating Array Variables

You must have read about arrays at various stage of your reading. It is a storage option of storing variables. There are rows and columns in it for storing data. There are one-dimensionald and two-dimensioal arrays. Visual FoxPro lets you create a special type of memory variable. Each items in an array is called an element and the total number of elements is always equal to the number of rows multiplied by the number of columns.

To create an array variable in Visual FoxPro, we use Declare or Dimension statement. The syntax for this is:

```
DECLARE ARRAY NAME [NUMBER OF ROWS[, NUMBER OF COLUMNS]]
```

Or

```
DIMENSION ARRAY NAME [NUMBER OF ROWS[, NUMBER OF COLUMNS]]
```

Number of columns is optional, i.e. you may or may not specify them. If you specify the number of columns you are creating a two-dimensional array and if you specify only the number of rows and not the number of columns, you are creating a one-dimensional array. You can identify elements in the array by the use of subscripts. Note that the subscript in an array always start with 1. To declare an array, we must specify two things: its name and its size. We need not specify the type of data it will hold, as each element can contain a different datatype. For example, you could declare a one-dimensional array containing 31 elements and named MONTH as shown below;

```
DECLARE MONTH[30]
```

Or

```
DECLARE MONTH[30]
```

Or

```
DIMENSION MONTH[30]
```

In the above declaration, 30 refers to the size of the array, i.e., the MONTH memory variable array will have the elements – month(1), month(2), month(3)..... month(30). After you create an array variable, Visual FoxPro makes all its elements as logical variable and stores .F. in them. You can use command:

```
DISPLAY MEMORY LIKE MONTH
```

To enter data in memory variable make use of the command Store. For example:

```
STORE 12 TO MONTH(1)
```

The above example stores a value of 12 in the month(1). You can also store any data such as character, logical, data etc. in any element of the declared array.

Storing Two Dimensional Variable

Visual FoxPro also lets you create two-dimensional array. For example:

```
DIMENSION TEST(3,2)
```

The above statement creates an array memory variable called TEST with the dimension command and you can store values to the array elements with the store or assignment statements. For example:

```
STORE 33 TO TEST(1,1)
STORE "RESULT" TO TEST(2,2)
STORE .F. TO TEST(3,1)
```

Now to view the contents of array variable speed type the following command in the Command window:

```
DISPLAY MEMORY LIKE TEST
```

And press Enter key, you will see the screen as shown in figure.

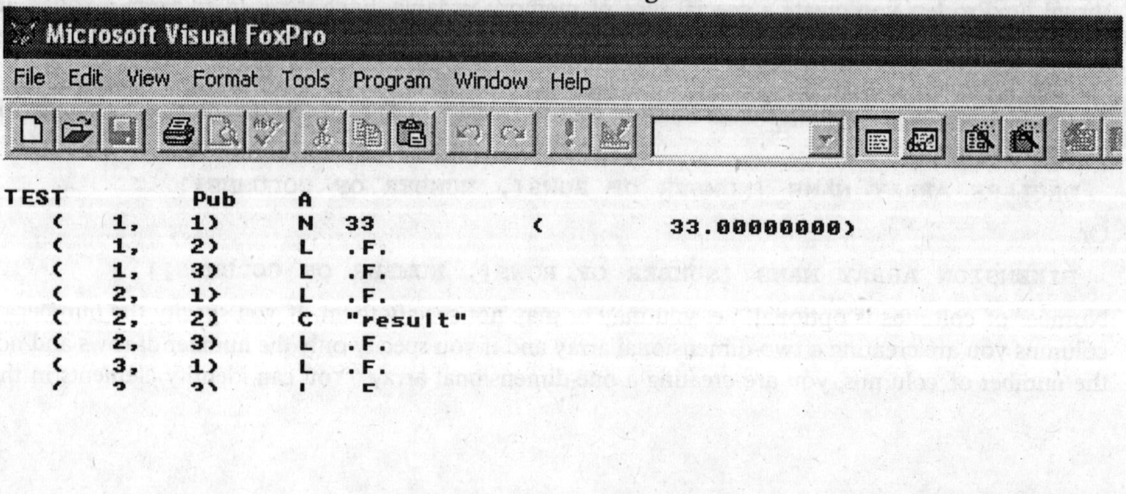

Visual FoxPro allows you to change the size and dimensions of an array. You do this by using the command Dimension in the program. When you need to increase or decrease the number of elements in the array you created, you can increase the size of one-dimensional array or change it to two dimensional array or reduce the size of a two-dimensional array to one dimension. For example:

```
DIMENSION A(3)
STORE 'X' TO A(1)
STORE 'Y' TO A(2)
STORE 'Z' TO A(3)
DISPLAY MEMORY LIKE A
```

This would give you the following result.

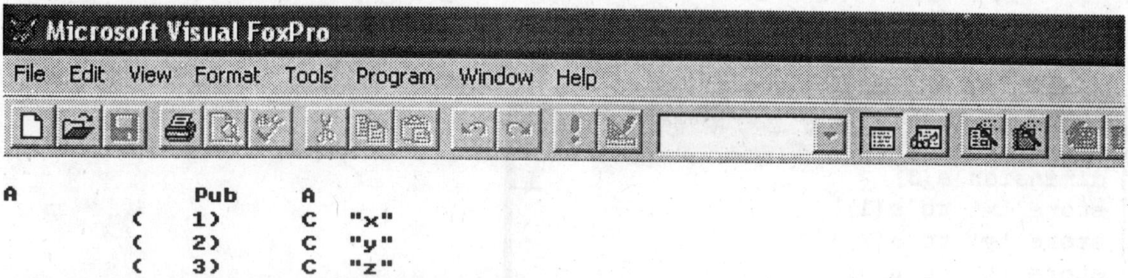

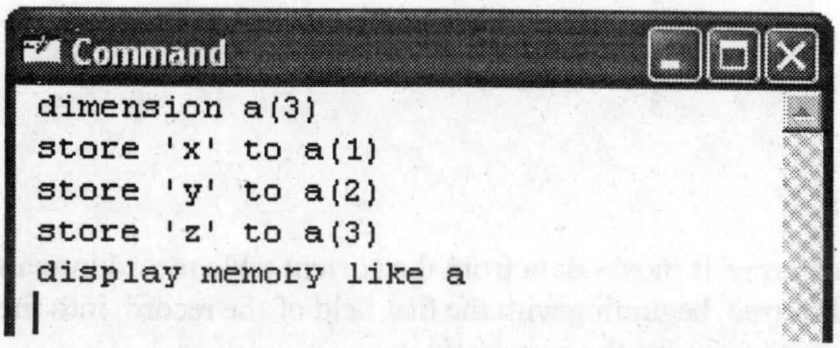

Next we change the dimension to make it a two-dimensional array with the following commands:

```
DIMENSION X(2,3)
DISPLAY MEMORY LIKE X
```

This will show the result as shown on the next page.

When you change from one dimensional array to two dimensional array, Visual FoxPro places data from the elements in the original array into the first row of two-dimensional array. Visual FoxPro initializes the remaining elements in the array as Logical elements and store a logical .F. (False) values.

Using Arrays with Table Files

A common use of array is to move fields to or from a table file. The following Visual FoxPro commands can be used to do so:

a. SCATTER

b. COPY to ARRAY

c. COPY from ARRAY

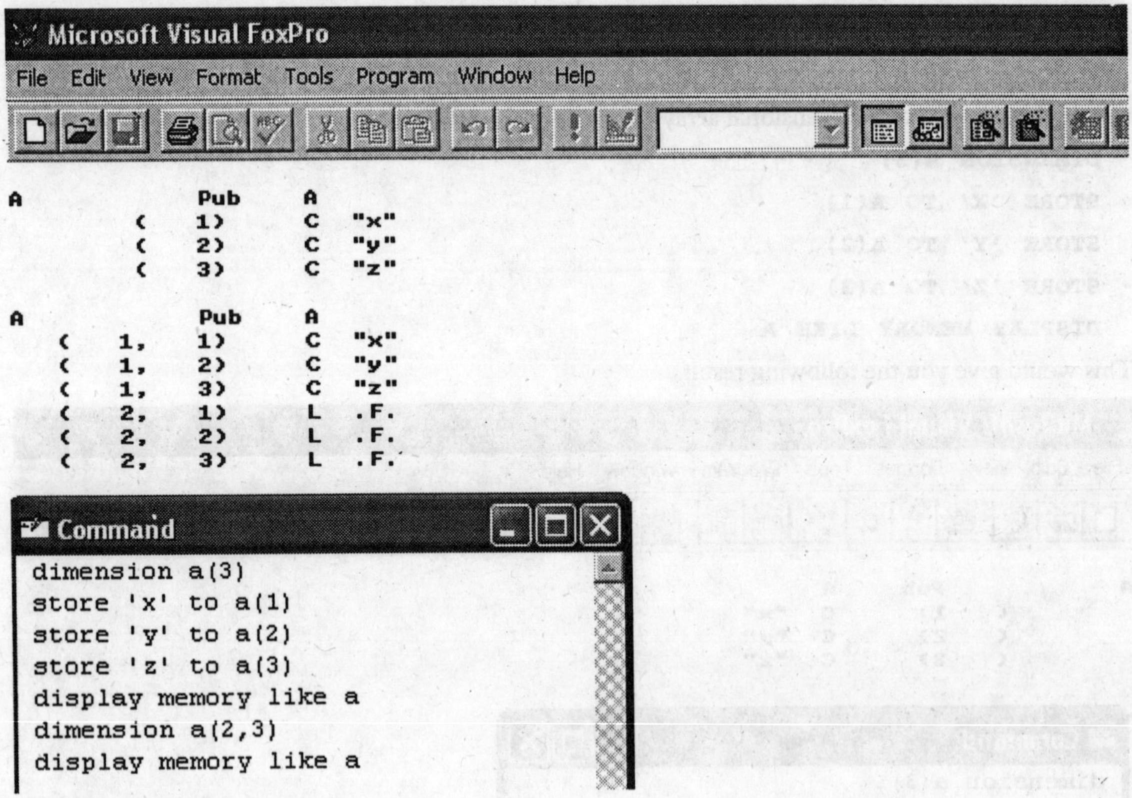

d. GATHER

Using Scatter Command

This command also creates a one-dimensional array. It moves data from the current table record into an array. The fields of the current record are transferred, beginning with the first field of the record, into the corresponding elements of the array. The general form for the command is:

```
SCATTER TO ARRAY
```

For example

```
USE TABLE1
SCATTER TO XYZ
DISPLAY MEMORY LIKE XYZ
```

In the above case the data from the table1 is scattered into an array called zyz. See the result on the next page. If the array xyz does not exist, scatter command automatically creates it.

If you want to transfer selected fields, use the field clause. For example:

```
SCATTER FIELDS NAME, ADDRESS, CITY TO XYZ
```

Above command transfers or copies only name, address and city fields to the array xyz.

Displaying Using '?' Command

The syntax for this is;

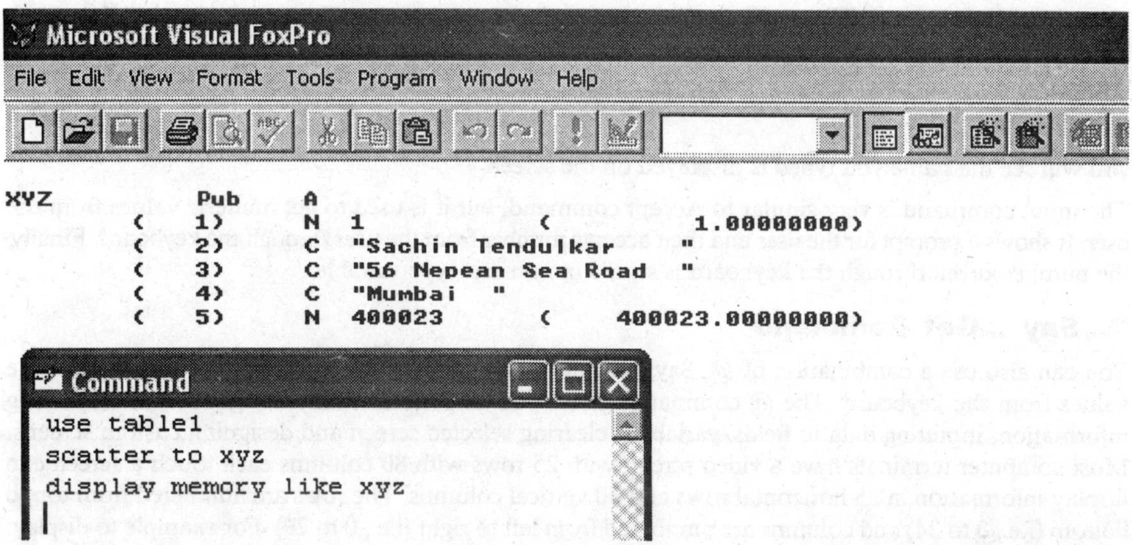


```
? MNAME, ABC, XYZ
```

The ? displays the specific values that had been stored in the memory variables. However, you can use Display memory or List memory commands to show existing memory variable values. Enter the following command to display active memory variable.

```
DISPLAY MEMORY
```

Accepting from User

Variables can be accepted from the user in Visual FoxPro using two commands, mainly, Accept and Input. When you use either Accept or Input commands, you enclose the prompt to be asked in apostrophes (') or double quotes ("). You also need to provide a variable to store the answer to the question. For example, if you type the following commands:

```
ACCEPT "ENTER YOUR NAME:" TO MYNAME
```

You will see the prompt on the screen as shown in figure below.

Visual FoxPro will leave the prompt on the screen until you type a name. Type any name and then press Enter. After you press enter, the Command window appears because the program is over. If you now type:

```
?MYNAME
```

you will see the name you typed is displayed on the screen

The input command is very similar to Accept command, but it is used to get numeric values from the user. It shows a prompt for the user and then accepts number from the user through the keyboard. Finally, the number keyed through the keyboard is stored in numeric type variable.

@...Say ...Get Command

You can also use a combination of @, Say, Get and Read commands to prompt the user to enter the values from the keyboard. The @ command allows you to perform many things such as displaying information, inputting data in fields/variables, clearing selected screen and designing custom screens. Most computer terminals have a video screen with 25 rows with 80 columns each. Such a screen can display information in 25 horizontal rows and 80 vertical columns. The rows are numbered from top to bottom (i.e., 0 to 24) and columns are numbered from left to right (i.e., 0 to 79). For example to display:

```
"ENTER YOUR NAME"
```

message in row 3 and column 8, type the following command in command file:

```
MYNAME = SPACE(20)
CLEAR
@ 3,8 SAY "ENTER YOUR NAME" GET MYNAME
READ
```

In the above example the following takes place:

Myname = space(20)	Creates a variable called Myname containing 20 blank spaces
Clear	Clears the screen
@ 3,8 say.....	Displays the message beginning from row 3 and column 8
Read	It puts the cursor into the prompt for the variable Myname and waits for the user to type some data. Type a name, say Sachin and press enter.

To verify that Myname variable now contains the data you typed, enter the command:

```
?MYNAME
```

Clearing Screen with @ Command

You can clear your screen using the @ ...clear statement. This command is very useful for clearing unwanted information from part of the screen before a new information is presented on it. Now use the following command and see the screen.

```
@15,35 CLEAR
```

you will notice that Visual FoxPro has blanked the screen below the 14th row and to the right side of the 34th column. Similarly, use another @..clear command:

```
@10,25 CLEAR
```

and Visual FoxPro blanks more portion of the screen.

Drawing and Clearing Box using @ Command

The @ command can also be used to draw lines and boxes on the screen. Boxes can be drawn with a single or doubleline border. For drawing a box, you need to specify the top-left and bottom-right co-ordinates of the box. First clear the screen with Clear command and then draw two boxes one with single border and the other with double border. For this, type the following in the Command window:

```
@1,5 TO 4,25
@3,30 TO 8,50 DOUBLE
```

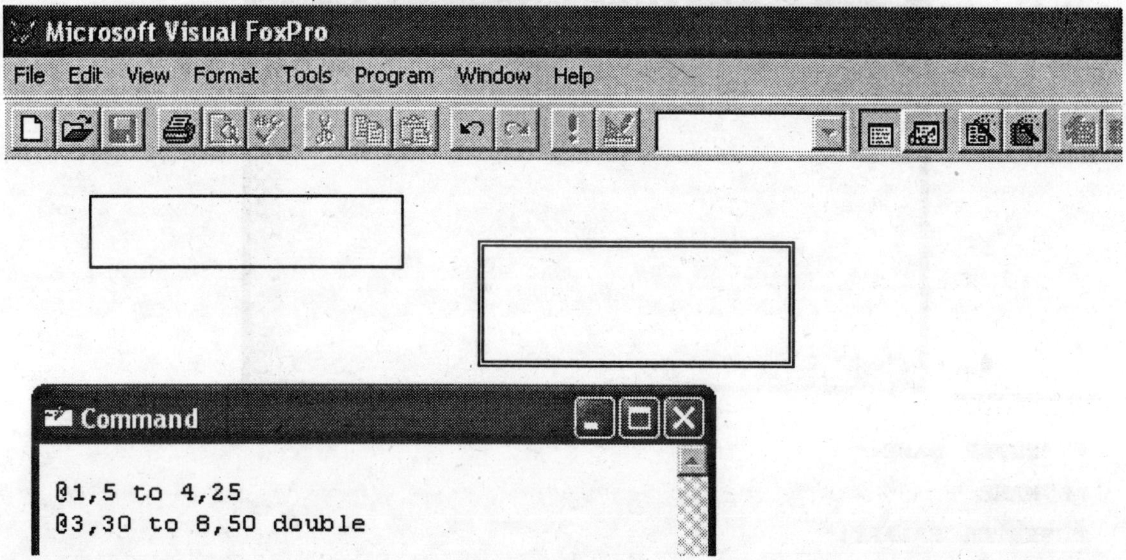

See the result above. Now if you want you can give the command in a specific way, the result would however, remain the same.

```
@2,6 SAY "SINGLE LINED BOX"
@6,32 SAY "DOUBLE LINED BOX"
```

For drawing lines at least one of the variable in the above cases would reamain the same. Look at the following example and you would notice the difference. For example to draw a horizontal line on the screen, type the following in the Command window:

```
@1,5 TO 5,5 DOUBLE
```

similarly, to draw vertical line on the screen, type: the following in the Command window:

```
@20,1 TO 20,10 DOUBLE
```

The result is shown on the next page.

Displaying and Manipulating Information with ?/?? Commands

Both ? and ?? can be used to display data on the screen. The difference between ? and ?? command is that the ? command issues a carriage return before printing the expression list, so it is positioned one line below the previous item displayed. The ?? command does not include a linefeed and carriage return before the display, so the subsequent value is displayed on the current line.

For example, type the following in the Command window:

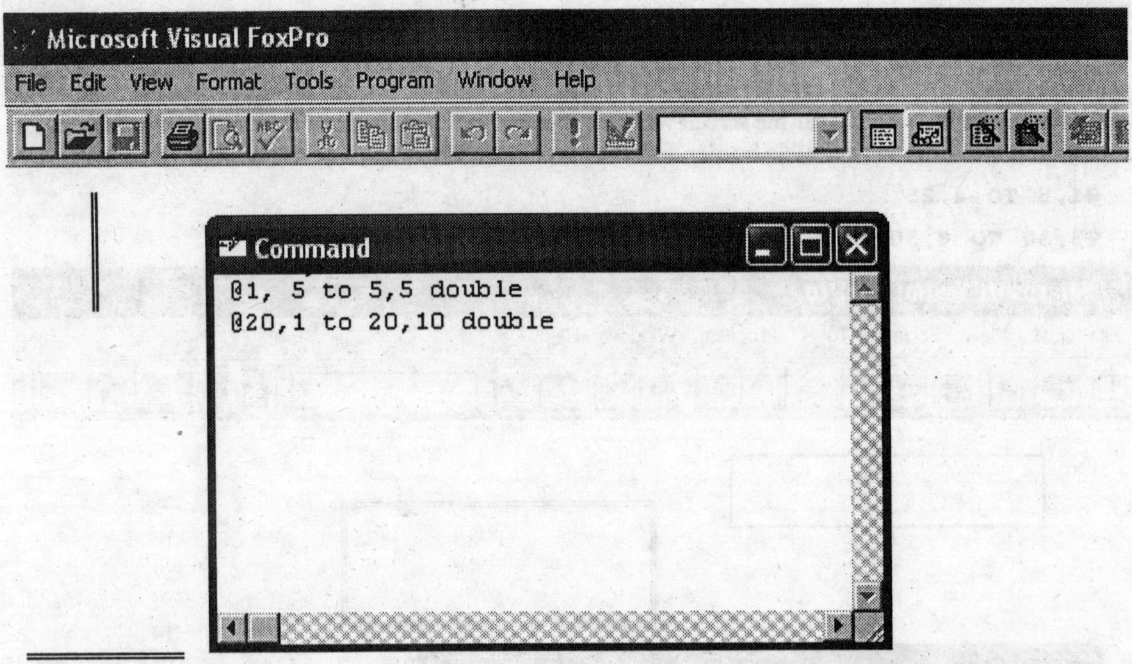


```
? "ENTER NAME:"
?? NAME
? "ENTER SALARY:"
?? SALARY
```

PICTURE CLAUSES

The picture clause restricts entry to specific characters and it validates formats but not values. The following table lists the different picture clause codes.

Symbol	*Meaning*
A	Accepts only alphabetic characters
L	Accepts on Y (yes) or N (no)
N	Accepts letters and digits
X	Accepts any character
9	Accepts only digits or sign
#	Accepts digits, blanks nad sign
!	Converts lowercase letters to uppercase
$	Display currency symbol
.	Specifies decimal point precision
.	Left of the decimal

For example, if you want to get std_code that must begin with an alphabet and has three digits then you can write Picture 'A999'.

CONTROL FLOW

Visual FoxPro like all other programming languages support the various logical commands where you can control the operations depending upon the options given. These operations can be performed whenever needed and how many times needed. The commands in this category are:

Looping statements

Selection Statements

Looping

It means that you do the things again and again. Or for a specified number of times. Visual FoxPro provides three loop commands. These are:

a. Do While…Enddo

b. Scan…Endscan

c. For …Endfor

Let us first take up Do While ... Enddo

Do while...Enddo

There will be many times when your program will need to perform the same task repeatedly. FoxPro has two commands, DO WHILE and ENDDO, that are used as a matched pair to repeat a series of commands as many times as necessary. The commands that you want to repeat are enclosed between the DO WHILE and the ENDDO commands.

The DO WHILE command always begins the loop, and the ENDDO command normally ends it. The commands inside the loop will continue to execute until the condition that you've specified, as a part of the DO WHILE command, is no longer true. The condition that you specify will determine when the loop should stop; otherwise, the loop could go on indefinitely. The format is

```
DO WHILE CONDITION
    [COMMANDS...]
ENDDO
```

As long as the condition within the DO WHILE command is true, the commands between the DO WHILE and the ENDDO commands are executed. Whenever ENDDO is reached, FoxPro returns to the top of the loop and reevaluates the condition. If the condition is still true, FoxPro executes the commands within the loop again; if the condition is not true, FoxPro jumps to the command following the ENDDO command. If the condition is false when the DO WHILE command is first encountered, none of the commands in the loop will be executed, and the program proceeds to the first command that follows the ENDDO command.

As an example, you could use the DO WHILE and ENDDO commands to create a command file that will print all the names and addresses in the Dayal Videos database, with triple line-spacing between them. Go to the Command window and open a new command file named TRIPLE, by entering

```
MODIFY COMMAND TRIPLE
```

When the FoxPro Editor comes up, enter the following command file:

```
SET TALK OFF
USE MEMBERS
SET PRINT ON
DO WHILE .NOT. EOF()
   ? FIRSTNAME + LASTNAME
   ? ADDRESS
   ? CITY + STATE + " " + PINCODE
   ?
   ?
   ?
   SKIP
ENDDO
? "TRIPLE REPORT COMPLETED."
SET PRINT OFF
EJECT
```

Before you save this command file, take a brief look at its design. After such preliminaries as activating the MEMBERS file and routing the output to the printer, the program begins the DO WHILE loop. The condition for DO WHILE is .NOT. EOF(), which simply means, "As long as the end of the file-EOF()-is NOT reached, continue the DO WHILE loop." The first three statements inside the loop print the name and address from the current record. Next, three question-mark symbols print three blank lines between each pair of records.

The SKIP command moves the pointer down one record, each time the body of the DO WHILE loop is executed. (If this command were absent, the pointer would never reach the end of the file, the condition would never become false, and the program would never leave the loop. It would, in fact, simply continue printing the same record over and over again!)

The ENDDO command is then reached, so FoxPro returns to the DO WHILE statement to re-valuate the condition. If the pointer hasn't reached the end-of-file, the loop is repeated. Once the end-of-file has been reached, FoxPro proceeds past the ENDDO command. The final two commands in the program are executed, and control is returned on the Command window.

Indenting the commands between DO WHILE and ENDDO is a convention that can help you identify the body of the loop. This is especially helpful if you have nested DO WHILE loops-that is, placed a DO WHILE loop within a DO WHILE loop.

After typing the above commands, press Ctrl + S to save the command file to disk, and close the window. Then make sure your printer is on, and enter the command DO TRIPLE. The command file will print the names and addresses on your printer, with three blank lines between each pair.

Scan...Endscan

Another set of commands you may encounter in working with FoxPro programs are the SCAN and ENDSCAN commands. These commands, like DO WHILE and ENDDO, are a matched pair. Also like DO WHILE and ENDDO, the SCAN and ENDSCAN commands let you create a repetitive loop in which operations are performed for a group of records in a database.

The syntax for these commands is

```
SCAN[SCOPE] [FOR CONDITION][WHILE CONDITION]
  [COMMANDS...]
ENDSCAN
```

The SCAN and ENDSCAN commands are simpler alternatives to the DO WHILE and ENDDO commands. If you simply wish to use DO WHILE and ENDDO to perform repetitive processing, you can often use SCAN and ENDSCAN instead, and use slightly fewer lines of programming code.

As an example, perhaps you want to write a program that, using a DO WHILE loop, would print the name and tape limit for every person in the database who has a tape limit of more than three. You could accomplish the task with a program like this:

```
USE MEMBERS
SET PRINT ON
DO WHILE .NOT. EOF()
  IF TAPELIMIT > 3
    ? LASTNAME, FIRSTNAME
    ?? TAPELIMIT
  ENIF
  SKIP
ENDDO
```

By comparison, you could use the SCAN and ENDSCAN commands to accomplish the same task. An example of the program code using SCAN and EDSCAN is shown here;

```
USE MEMBERS
SET PRINT ON
SCAN FOR TAPELIMIT > 3
  ? LASTNAME, FIRSTNAME
  ?? TAPELIMIT
ENDSCAN
```

Because the SCAN command combined the WHILE and IF clauses to specify the condition (a tape limit greater than three), you can use fewer lines of program code to accomplish the same task.

FoxPro automatically skips to the next successive record when it encounters ENDSCAN, unless you are at the end of the file. Once the end of the file is reached, program control drops out of the loop and moves on to the next command. Note that program control may exit from the loop before the end of the file is reached if you include a WHILE clause as a part of the SCAN statement.

If...else...endif

In many command files, FoxPro needs to perform different operations depending on a user's response to an option, a previous calculation or operation, or different values encountered in a database. For example if a program's main menu gives the user a choice of editing or printing a record, the program must be able to check which choice the user makes, and then start the appropriate operation. FoxPro can use the

IF, ELSE, and ENDIF commands to branch to the part of the program where the chosen operation is performed. Much like the DO WHILE-ENDDO loop, the IF and ENDIF commands are used as a matched pair, enclosing a number of commands. The ELSE command is optional, and is used within the body of IF-ENDIF as another decision step. The IF and ENDIF commands can be used to decide between actions in a program.

The format of the command is

```
IF CONDITION
    [COMMANDS...]
ELSE
    [COMMANDS...]
ENDIF
```

This decision-making command must always start with IF and end with ENDIF. The commands that you place between the IF and ENDIF statements determine exactly what will occur if the condition is true. (Again, indenting the commands within the body of IF-ENDIF makes the flow of the program easier to understand.) The optional ELSE statement can be used to specify an alternate set of commands that will be carried out only if the condition in the IF statement is not true. A good way to build IF and ELSE structures is to write them first in pseudocode, then in the FoxPro command language, and then compare them to make sure your commands specify what you originally intended. For example:

Pseudocode	**FoxPro**
If last name is Sharma, then display last name.	IF LASTNAME = "Sharma" ? LASTNAME ENDIF
If monthly rent is less than Rs. 300, then display "Reasonably priced."	IF RENTMONTH < 300 ? "Reasonably priced." ENDIF

Using IF and ENDIF alone works fine for making a single decision, but if you wish to add an alternative choice, you need the ELSE statement:

Pseudocode	**FoxPro**

If last name is Cook,e then print last name; or lese print "There is no one by that name in this database."	IF LASTNAME = "Sharma"
	?LASTNAME
	ELSE
	? "There is no one by that name in this database."
	ENDIF

FoxPro evaluates the condition following the IF command to see if any action should be taken. If no action is necessary (that is, the condition is false), FoxPro looks for an ELSE statement. If it fins one, it executes the commands following the term ELSE; otherwise, control simply passes to the next command after the ENDIF command. In the following example, if SALARY is not 10 then the STORE command will not be executed, and FoxPro will proceed to the command following ENDIF:

```
IF SALARY = 10
  STORE SALARY TO MATCH
ENDIF
```

You can also use multiple IF-ENDIF commands if you need to have the program make more than one decision. Consider this example:

```
? "ENTER 1 TO PRINT MAILING LABELS OR 2 TO EDIT."
INPUT "WHAT IS YOUR CHOICE?" TO CHOICE
IF CHOICE = 1
  DO TRIPLE
ENDIF
IF CHOICE = 2
  DO CHANGES
ENDIF
```

The answer that the user types is stored in a memory variable called CHOICE. One of three things can happen then, depending on whether the user has typed a 1, 2, or something else in response to the question. If CHOICE equals 1, the TRIPLE program is run from disk.

If CHOICE equals 2, then CHANGES program is run. If CHOICE equals neither 1 or 2, then the program proceeds to the next command after the ENDIF command.

Nesting IF-ENDIFs

You can use nested IF-ENDIF statements, which are IF-ENDIF statements placed inside of other IF-ENDIF statements. For the innermost IF-ENDIF statement to be processed, the condition tested by the outermost IF-ENDIF statement must be true.

The following is an example of a nested IF-ENDIF statement:

```
INPUT "DISPLAY REPORT ON (S)CREEN OR (P)RINTER?" TO ANS
IF UPPER (ANS) = "P"
   INPUT "READY PRINTER, PRESS ENTER, OR TYPE C THEN;
   PRESS ENTER TO CANCEL REPORT." TO ANS2
      *USER CANCELED PRINT RUN.
      RETURN
   ENDIF
   REPORT FORM MEMBERS TO PRINT
   EJECT
ENDIF
```

In this example, whether the innermost IF-ENDIF will ever be processed is determined by the response supplied to the outermost IF-ENDIF statement. If the user does not type P for printer, FoxPro skips ahead to the outermost ENDIF statement. If the user does respond with P for printer, FoxPro displays the "Ready printer" message, and the innermost IF-ENDIF tests for the user's response and takes appropriate action.

Tip If you are going to nest IF-ENDIF statements, then indenting your commands will help you keep track of whether you have matching statements (that is, an ENDIF for each IF). It is very important to make sure that nested IFs and ENDIFs match up, or else your program will incorporate serious (and often hard-to-find) errors.

IIF()

Within programs, you may want to make use of the IIF (Immediate IF) function. The syntax for the function is

```
IIF(CONDITION, EXPRESSION1, EXPRESSION2)
```

If the condition specified is true, FoxPro returns the first expression; if the condition is false, FoxPro returns the second expression. As an example, the statement

```
CREDITOK = IIF (INCOME>=15000, "YES", "NO")
```

would, when processed in a program, store a character expression of "YES" to the CREDITOK variable if the amount in INCOME was equal to or greater than 15,000. Otherwise, it would store the character expression "NO". In effect, this statement performs the same task as the following commands:

```
IF INCOME >= 15000
   CREDITOK = "YES"
ELSE
   CREDITOK = "NO"
ENDIF
```

The advantage of the Immediate IF function is that it takes fewer lines of code to accomplish the same task, and it is executed slightly faster.

Using the IF-ENDIF Statement

You can use the IF-ENDIF statement in a command file to search for and display data from a specific record in your database. For example, if you want to find a member named Verma, you can use the ACCEPT and IF-ENDIF commands to search for the record. (This operation can be done faster with SEEK, but for demonstration purposes, a combination of IF and DO WHILE is used here.)

First, let's use pseudocode to outline what needs to be done:

USE MEMBERS database.

ACCEPT the last name.

BEGIN the DO-WHILE loop.

IF the Lastname field = the ACCEPT variable,

PRINT (on the screen) name, address, tape limit, and expiration date.

END the IF test.

SKIP forward one record.

END the DO-WHILE loop.

RETURN to the command window.

Now create a command file by entering

```
MODIFY COMMAND SHOWMEMB
```

When the FoxPro Editor appears in a window, enter the following;

```
*THIS PROGRAM FINDS AND SHOWS DATA IN THE MEMBERS FILE.
USER MEMBERS
SET TALK OFF
CLEAR
*BEGIN LOOP THAT CONTAINS COMMANDS TO DISPLAY RECORD.
ACCEPT "SEARCH FOR WHAT LAST NAME? "TO SNAME
DO WHILE .NOT. EOF()
  IF LASTNAME = SNAME
     ? "LAST NAME IS: "
     ?? LASTNAME
     ? "FIRST NAME IS: "
     ?? FIRSTNAME
     ? "ADDRESS IS: "
     ?? ADDRESS
     ? CITY + STATE + " " + PINCODE
     ?
     ? "TAPE LIMIT IS: "
     ?? TAPELIMIT
     ? "EXPIRATION DATE IS: "
     ?? EXPIREDATE
     ?
  ENDIF
  SKIP
ENDDO
WAIT
RETURN
```

After saving the file with CTRL+S, try running the program by entering DO SHOWMEMB in the Command window. In response to the lastname prompt that appears on the screen, enter Verma, and FoxPro will search the database for the record containing this name. Run the program again, and enter Dayal. You will see the records for both Dayal displayed.

In the search you used the ACCEPT, IF, and ENDIF commands. The ACCEPT command stored the name that you entered into the memory variable SNAME. The IF loop began a decision-making process that stated the condition, "If the memory variable SNAME contains the same name as the Lastname field, then execute the commands that follow the IF command." There is no limit to the number of commands that you can place between IF and ENDIF in the loop. You can also link multiple IF-ENDIF and ELSE commands if multiple choices are needed within a program.

Do Case...Endcase

Your program may need to make more than two or three decisions, based on a single-response. A series of IF-ENDIF statements could do the job, but using more than three IF-ENDIFs to test the value of one field (or memory variable) is unwieldy. There is an easier way: use the CASE statement. With the CASE statement, the IF-ENDIF tests are made into alternative cases of one long conditional statement, and FoxPro then chooses the first case, the second case, or whichever other case matches the user's response.

The CASE statement is framed by a matched pair of terms: DO CASE and ENDCASE. All conditional choices are declared between DO CASE and ENDCASE. The OTHERWISE term functions exactly like the ELSE in an IF-ENDIF statement. The general format is

```
DO CASE
   CASE CONDITION
   [COMMANDS...]
   [CASE CONDITION...]
   [COMMANDS...]
   [OTHERWISE]
   [COMMANDS...]
ENDCASE
```

Whenever FoxPro encounters a DO CASE command, it examines each CASE term until it finds a condition that is true; then it executes the commands below that line, until it encounters either the next CASE term or the ENDCASE term (whichever comes first).

If you want to create a simple menu that offers a choice of displaying a record, printing labels, editing a record, or adding a record, you could write a command file like this:

```
CLEAR
? "1. DISPLAY A MEMBERSHIP RECORD"
?
? "2. PRINT THE MEMBERSHIP DATABASE"
?
? "3. CHANGE A MEMBERSHIP RECORD"
?
INPUT "CHOOSE A SELECTION " TO SELECT
DO CASE
  CASE SELECT = 1
    DO SHOWMEMB
  CASE SELECT = 2
    DO TRIPLE
```

```
  CASE SELECT = 3
     DO EDITMEMB
ENDCASE
```

In this example, the INPUT statement queries the user for selection. When the user's response has been entered, it is stored in the SELECT variable. Then, in the DO CASE series, FoxPro compares the value of the SELECT variable against the test value in each CASE. If it finds a match, it executes the command file named within that CASE statement, and no other CASE statement is evaluated.

If no match is found, FoxPro proceeds to the next statement after the ENDCASE command. Like IF-ENDIF, the DO CASE and ENDCASE commands are used in pairs. You must always end a CASE series with an ENDCASE command. You should use DO CASE to process menu selections if you have more than three choices. For example, if you wanted to offer the same three selections from the last program using IF-ENDIF and ELSE, the command file might look like this:

```
CLEAR
? "1. DISPLAY A MEMBERSHIP RECORD"
?
? "2. PRINT THE MEMBERSHIP DATABASE"
?
? "3. CHANGE A MEMBERSHIP RECORD"
?
INPUT "CHOOSE A SELECTION" TO SELECT
IF SELECT = 1
   DO SHOWMEMB
ENDIF
IF SELECT = 2
   DO TRIPLE
ENDIF
IF SELECT = 3
   DO EDITMEMB
ENDIF
```

Using IF-ENDIF becomes more complex than DO CASE as the number of choices increases.

Let's use a CASE statement to create a main menu for the Dayal Videos database. (Note that FoxPro provides much better and more attractive ways to create menus, but this technique is used here for the sake of simplicity.) In the Command window, enter the statement MODIFY COMMAND MENU1, and when the FoxPro Editor appears, enter the following command file:

```
USE MEMBERS
SET TALK OFF
STORE 0 TO CHOICE
DO WHILE CHOICE <> 5
```

```
CLEAR
 * DISPLAY THE MENU.
 ? " DAYAL VIDOES MEMBERSHIP SYSTEM MENU"
 ?
 ? "1. ADD A NEW ENTRY TO THE DATABASE."
 ? "2. CHANGE AN EXISTING ENTRY."
 ? "3. PRODUCE THE MEMBERSHIP REPORT."
 ? "4. DISPLAY DATA REGARDING A PARTICULAR MEMBER."
 ? "5. EXIT THIS PROGRAM."
 INPUT "ENTER SELECTION:" TO CHOICE
 DO CASE
   CASE CHOICE=1
     APPEND
   CASE CHOICE=1
     DO EDITMEMB
   CASE CHOICE=3
     REPORT FORM SAMPLE
   CASE CHOICE=4
     DO SHOWMEMB
   CASE CHOICE=5
     CLOSE DATABASES
     SET TALK ON
     RETURN
   ENDCASE
 ENDDO
```

The menu offers five choices, and the INPUT command stores the user's response in the CHOICE variable. If FoxPro finds a matching choice, it executes the command or commands that follow that choice.

Save this command file by pressing Ctrl + S, and close the window. When the prompt reappears, enter DO MENU1. Try some of the menu choices on your own to see how the system operates. The simple menu created by the above example does the job, but is not very appealing from a visual standpoint. In the next chapter, you will learn how you can create menus that resemble the menus used by FoxPro.

EXIT AND LOOP COMMAND

The EXIT command can be used within a DO WHILE-ENDDO programming statement; it lets FoxPro exit from the DO WHILE-ENDDO loop to the first command below ENDDO. Note that an EXIT command arbitrarily placed within a DO WHILE loop will prevent FoxPro from ever reaching the commands between the terms EXIT and ENDDO; thus, EXIT makes sense only if it is executed conditionally. For this reason, you will frequently find EXIT commands inside IF-ENDIF and CASE statements. Consider the following example, in a program that lists a name based on a desired address. The same task could be accomplished with a LOCATE command, but to demonstrate the EXIT command, this program uses a DO WHILE loop.

```
USE MEMBERS
SET TALK OFF
GO TOP
ACCEPT "WHAT IS THE ADDRESS- " TO CHOICE
DO WHILE .NOT. EOF()
  IF ADDRESS = CHOICE
    ? LASTNAME, FIRSTNAME
    EXIT
    SKIP
ENDIF
```

If the contents of Address (a field) match CHOICE (a variable), the EXIT command will cause the DO WHILE loop to terminate. Otherwise, the SKIP command below the ENDIF statement will advance the pointer by one record, and the comparison will be repeated. If no match is found at all, control will finally pass out of the loop after the last record is read. Use EXIT commands conservatively: a program that is always jumping out of loops-and around the program, for that matter-is difficult to follow and debug, and is contrary to good program design. Most DO WHILEs that have EXITs can be redesigned to omit them.

CANCEL

The CANCEL command halts execution of a FoxPro command file and returns you to the Command window. It can be useful when you are testing command files. However, using CANCEL in a completed FoxPro program may be unwise. CANCEL simply drops the user into the Command window, and the inexperienced user may not know how to restart the program or exit FoxPro. QUIT is an alternative command, which will exit both the command file and FoxPro, and return the user to the Windows desktop. You can include an option on your command file's mainmenu that invokes the QUIT command.

WAIT

The WAIT command halts execution of a FoxPro program until a key is pressed. WAIT can also display a message or prompt and store the value of the pressed key to a character variable. The normal format of the command is

```
WAIT [PROMPT] [TO MEMORY-VARIABLE]
```

Both prompt and memory-variable are optional. If a prompt is not specified, FoxPro supplies the message "Press any key to continue..." as a default prompt.

As an example, to display a message, halt execution of a program until a key is pressed, and store that key as a variable named ANSWER, you could use the following command:

```
WAIT "ENTER Y TO BEGIN PROCESSING TRANSACTIONS, ANY OTHER KEY TO
CONTINUE:" TO ANSWER
```

You could then use an IF-ELSE-ENDIF structure to test the value of ANSWER and take different actions depending on the result.

ZAP

The ZAP command is a one-step command for erasing all records from a database while leaving the structure of the database intact. Using ZAP is functionally equivalent to entering **DELETE ALL** and then entering **PACK**. However, ZAP operates considerably faster than a DELETE ALL command followed by a PACK command. If you include the ZAP command in a program, you may want to place the SET SAFETY OFF command above it; this tells FoxPro not to ask for confirmation before erasing all records from the database. If so, make sure to SET SAFETY ON again afterwards. Also, since the ZAP command is destructive, be very careful in using it. If the database file which you are ZAPping is anything more important than a temporary scratch database, be sure to make a backup copy of the file before testing the ZAP command.CANCEL

The CANCEL command halts execution of a FoxPro command file and returns you to the Command window. It can be useful when you are testing command files. However, using CANCEL in a completed FoxPro program may be unwise. CANCEL simply drops the user into the Command window, and the inexperienced user may not know how to restart the program or exit FoxPro. QUIT is an alternative command, which will exit both the command file and FoxPro, and return the user to the Windows desktop. You can include an option on your command file's mainmenu that invokes the QUIT command.

PROCEDURES AND PARAMETERS

A procedure is a set of instructions that work as a unit. It is a sequence of Visual FoxPro commands that is functionally equivalent to a program, except that it resides in another program file. You can create procedures in the same way as you create programs, using the Modi Comm command [Visual FoxPro assumes the extension .PRG if you do not include the extension in the file name]. The only difference is that you have to create the procedure by giving the following command:

```
PROCEDURE <PROCEDURE_NAME>
    <COMMANDS>
    [RETURN]
ENDPROC
```

Where procedure_name is the name of the procedure that you create. Procedure name must begin with a letter or underscore(_) and it may contain any combination of letters, numbers and underscores.

The procedure name is followed by a series of Visual FoxPro commands. The return statement is used to return control to the calling program or to another program. The return statement is optional. If you do not write it, the function, by default returns to the calling program when it quits. The endproc statement signifies the end of the procedure.

You can make any number of procedures and functions in a procedure file – a text file that contains only procedures and user-defined functions. Once can also place procedures within the programs that call them. They are placed after the Return command that ends the main portion of the program (sometimes called the mainline routine).

The procedure file is opened with the following command:

```
SET PROCEDURE TO <PROCEDURE_NAME>
```

Once a procedure file is open, you can execute any procedure or function it contains from the Command window.

You can call a procedure located in the same file or in some other file using a simple do command. You can execute a procedure located in any file by naming this file in the Do command, as follows:

```
DO <PROCEDURE NAME> IN <PROGRAM FILE>
```

Visual FoxPro closes any procedure file previously opened before opening a new procedure file. To close a procedure file, without opening another, you can use:

```
SET PROCEDURE TO
```

Or

```
CLOSE PROCEDURE
```

Visual FoxPro does not allow you to edit an open procedure file, although you can open the file in an editing window to view its contents. However, if you begin to edit the text, Visual FoxPro closes the procedure file and displays a message window in the upper-right corner of the screen informing you of this fact. Once the procedure file is closed, you can proceed with the editing session. Remember to reopen the file with a new Set Procedure command after you have made your changes. The Set Procedure command causes Visual FoxPro to recompile the procedure file.

Scope of Variables

A variable's scope specifies the variable makes its value known to other procedures and functions. Visual FoxPro offers two commands, Private and Public that are used to classify variables. These commands let you control the application of variable from one Visual FoxPro command file to another. If you have created a variable in one command file and you need to use it in other command file then you should declare them public. However, if you want the variable you are declaring should be available only to the program that has created the variable and also to programs that are called by that specific program, then declare it as private.

Declaring a variable as public requires two steps:

a. Public <variable_name>

b. declaring the actual variable with the Store command or with an assignment symbol (=).

For example:

```
PUBLIC ABC
ABC = 124.4
```

You can also declare several variable as public by typing a list, such as:

```
PUBLIC X,Y,Z
STORE 'HIM' TO X
STORE 'MOTOR' TO Y
STORE '58.45' TO Z
```

A private variable can be visible to all procedures called by the command file. You do this by not declaring the variable in the Procedure file. For example:

```
* NAME.PRG
PRIVATE NAME
```

```
NAME="RAMESH"
DO NEWNAME
? NAME
RETURN
* PROCEDURE NEWNAME
PROCEDRUE NEWNAME
  ? NAME
RETURN
```

In the above example, the procedure newname displayed "Ramesh" while the main program also displayed "Ramesh". Thus you see that even though you declare the variable Private in the name.prg command file, it is visible to the procedure file newname.

You can use the ALL, LIKE and EXCEPT options with PRIVATE to cover more than one variable at a time. Examples of ALL, LIKE and EXCEPT options with PRIVATE would include:

Command	*Meaning*
PRIVATE ALL	Declares all variables or arrays private
PRIVATE ALL EXCEPT X, Y, Z	Declares variables or arrays private unless they match the list
PRIVATE ALL LIKE M?	Declares variables or arrays Private that match the skeleton.

Passing Parameters

A parameter is a value passed to a function or procedure. A procedure that requires that the calling program should pass parameters to it, must use the command PARAMETER <MEMVAR LIST> as the first command after PROCEDURE <PROCEDURE_NAME>. Enclose the list of parameters in a set of parentheses and separate the parameters with commas. Then, the simplest say of passing the value to a procedure, when you call it, is to use the command Do…with <exp list>. The expressions in the list following Do…with are assigned in order, to the variables in the list following PARAMETER.

The procedure can be run by giving the following command in the Command Window:

```
DO OUTPUT IN MYPROC.PRG WITH 10, "TEN", .T.
```

Note that we have passed a numeric, string and logical value to the procedure. The arguments that appear in procedure definition are formal arguments. For example, suppose we call the "output" procedure as follows:

```
X = 10
Y = "TEN"
Z = .T.
DO OUTPUT IN MYPROC.PRG WITH X, Y, Z
```

Here, x, y and z are the actual or dummy arguments and take the value (a, b, c) from the calling procedure.

Pass by Value

It is a means of passing a variable to a procedure or function. A copy of the value of the variable is created and passed to the called routine. The procedure or function can change the value of this copy but cannot change the value of the argument in the calling procedure.

In pass by value method, the formal argument is a copy of actual argument. To understand it clearly take one real life example. Suppose your English teacher has given you one printed passage with grammatical errors and spelling mistakes on a sheet of paper and wanted you to note down the same passage in your notebook and then do corrections wherever you find any grammatical error or spelling mistake. Here, printed sheet with error represents the actual parameter and your test notebook, where you copied down the passage represents the formal parameter; what ever the changes you made in your notebook would not reflect any change to your teacher's original sheet.

Thus, in pass by value method, the values of actual parameters are passed on to formal parameters and the changes made in the values in the formal parameters are not reflected back into the actual parameters of the calling procedure.

Pass by Reference

If the programmer desires that the changes made to the formal parameter(s) be reflected on the corresponding actual parameter(s) then he/she should use call by reference method for parameter passing. In this method, the calling routine passes the address of the variable to the called routine, which can then use that address to retrieve or modify the variable. When the procedure changes the value of the passed variable, the variable's original value in the calling program is also changed.

In the call by reference method, the actual and formal arguments refer to the same memory location or area. Remember that a reference is an alias, i.e., a different name for a predefined variable. That means the same variable's value can be accessed by one of the two names, i.e., the original variable's name and the reference name. Take again a real life situation to understand this situation. Suppose in your college, all the labs are numbered as 1 for chemistry lab, 2 for physics lab, and 3 for biology lab and 4 for computer lab. Now to refer to any lab you can either say the lab number or call it by its name. For example you can refer to the 'Computer lab' by either giving the original name as 'Computer lab' or by its reference "No. 4 lab".

User-Defined Functions

Apart from the built-in library functions of Visual FoxPro, users can also define and write small programs as functions to do a task relevant to their programs. Such functions are called User-Defined Functions (UDFs). These are procedures that return a value. These functions should be codified by the user, so that such functions can perform the task as desired by the user. Suppose we write a user-defined function to search for a database. If the function finds the database, it returns .T. and otherwise returns .F. The Syntax for using functions is:

```
FUNCTION <FUNCTION_NAME>
COMMANDS
[RETURN [EXPRESSION]]
ENDFUNC
```

The FUNCTION <FUNCTION_NAME> statement designates the beginning of a function in a program and identifies the function by name. This is followed by a series of commands that make up the function. You can include RETURN anywhere in the function to return control to the calling program or to another program and to the calling program or to another program and to define the value to be returned by the user-defined function. If you do not include a RETURN command, an implicit RETURN is automatically executed when the function reaches the last statement. If the RETURN command does not include a return value (or if an implicit return is executed), Visual FoxPro assigns .T. (True) as the return value.

The function ends with the ENDFUNC command. This command is optional. If you do not include this command the function will automatically quit when it encounters another function command or a procedure command or a procedure command or the end of the program file.

Difference in Parameter Passing to Functions and Procedures

By default, Visual FoxPro passes parameters to procedures by reference, which means that only one copy of the variable exists in memory. When you pass a variable to a procedure, the called procedure receives not a specific value, but a reference to this memory location, which the called routine can examine to determine the value of the variable. Because the calling program and the procedure are operating on a single copy of the variable, any changes made to the value of the variable in the procedure are passed back to the calling program.

In contrast, Visual FoxPro passes parameters to user defined functions by value. The UDF (User Defined Function) makes local copies of the all parameters and gives them the values passed by the calling program. Thus, if the UDF changes the values of variables passed as parameters, these changes are local to the function, even if the variables have the same names as variables specified by the calling program. One significant implication of this default behavior is that you do not have to declare as private the variables in the parameters list, in order to protect identically named variables in the calling program. (Other variables defined in the UDF are not given any special treatment and must be declared private if there names might coincide with variables names used in the calling program).

The most likely reason for the difference in the default treatment of parameters in procedures and user defined functions is the context in which you are expected to use these two types of routines. A procedure, like a program, can do anything – open and close databases, manipulate records, perform calculations, display or print data or carry out any other operations that you can describe with the Visual FoxPro programming language. Some of these operations are general, whereas others are tightly linked to the specific requirements of one application. In contrast, a user-defined function receives input from the calling program, processes the input and returns a single value of a particular datatype. You can view all functions as block boxes – the manner in which the return value is calculated should make no difference and any variables required to carry out its calculations should remain hidden. In practice, of course, you can decide whether to write a particular routine as a function or a procedure based primarily on the context in which you intend to call it.

USING THE MENU DESIGNER

In Visual FoxPro, the menu designer is used to create menus, menu items, submenus of menu items, etc. Using menu designer you can design menus for applications. To use the menu designer, do the following:

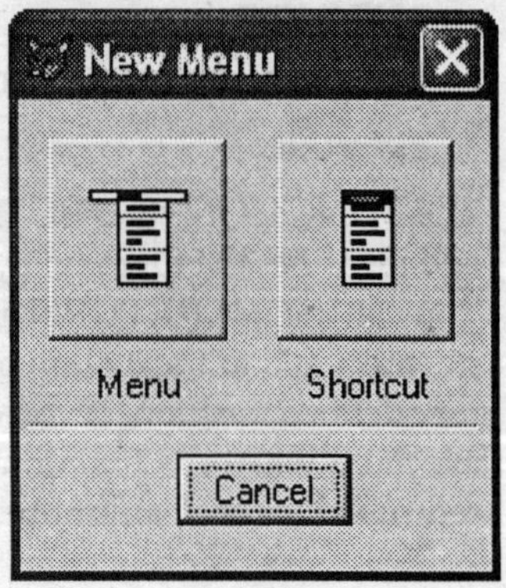

1. Enter the following command in the Command Window;

```
CREATE MENU <MENU-FILE>
```

   Menu-file is the filename for the menu table. We have named it as "Test".

2. The menu designer window will open as shown on the next page.
3. Under the Prompt column, specify the menu titles or menu items in your menu system. For example, I have specified the File menu system. I have also chosen Close All, Close, Open, and New.
4. You will notice a double-headed arrow button to the left of the Prompt column. This is known as the Mover Control and it allows

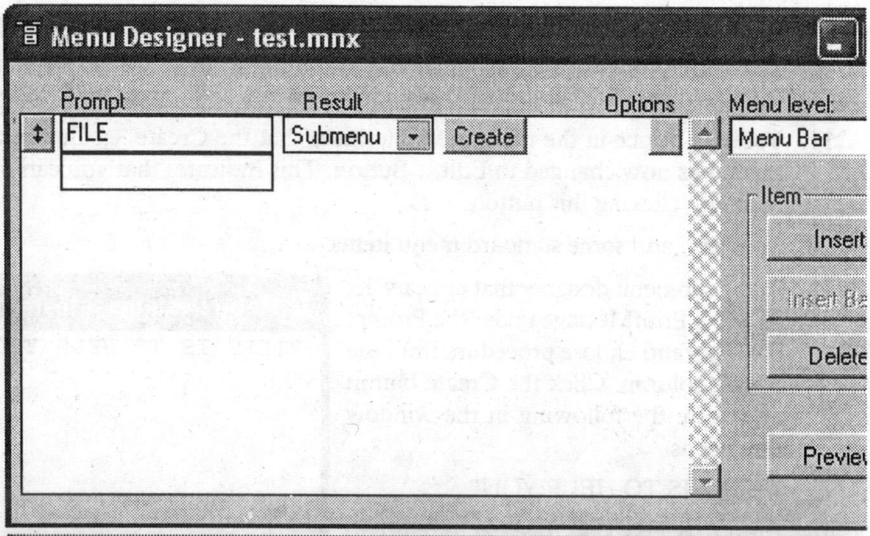

you to arrange the menu items in a certain order. Move this up and down to arrange the menu items.

5. Under the Result column, specify the action that occurs when you choose a menu title or menu item. For example, you can execute a command, open a submenu or run a procedure.
6. For the File and Edit menu items, we have chosen submenu. You will notice that a Create... Button appears to the right of the Result column. Click this button and a sub-menu-designer window appears.

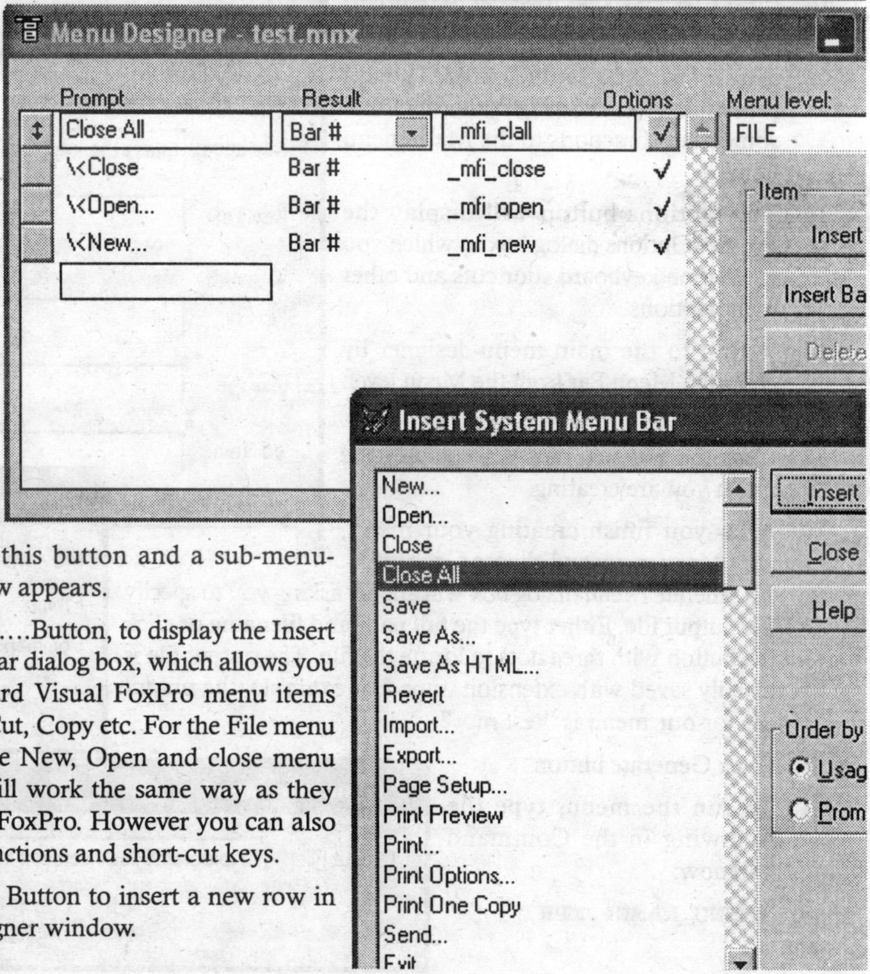

7. Click Insert Bar....Button, to display the Insert System Menu Bar dialog box, which allows you to insert standard Visual FoxPro menu items such as Open, Cut, Copy etc. For the File menu item, we choose New, Open and close menu items. These will work the same way as they work in Visual FoxPro. However you can also change their functions and short-cut keys.
8. Click the Insert Button to insert a new row in the Menu Designer window.

9. Click the Delete button to remove the current row from the Menu Designer window.
10. To return to the main designer, choose Menu Bar from the Menu level: list box. The Menu level: list box allows you to choose the menu, submenu or shortcut with which you want to work.
11. You will notice in the main menu-designer that the Create .... Button associated with the File menu has now changed to Edit... Button. This indicates that you can make changes to the File menu by clicking this button.
12. Similarly, add some standard menu items.
13. In the submenu-designer that appears, let us add a PrintMessage under the Prompt columns and choose procedure from the Result column. Click the Create button and write the following in the window that opens.
    ?"THIS IS TO HELP YOU"
14. Press Ctrl + W keys together to return to Menu Designer.
15. Similarly, add some more string procedures to the String menu item and some math functions to the Math menu item.
16. The Options button will display the Prompt Options dialog box in which you can define keyboard shortcuts and other menu options.
17. Return to the main menu-designer by choosing Menu Bar from the Menu level: list box.
18. Click the Preview button to display the menu you are creating.
19. After you finish creating your menu, click Menu menu and choose Generate.... A Generate Menu dialog box will appear asking you to specify the output file. Either type the full path and filename or click the button with three dots to locate the file. The output file is usually saved with extension .mpr. For example, the output file for our menu is "test.mpr".

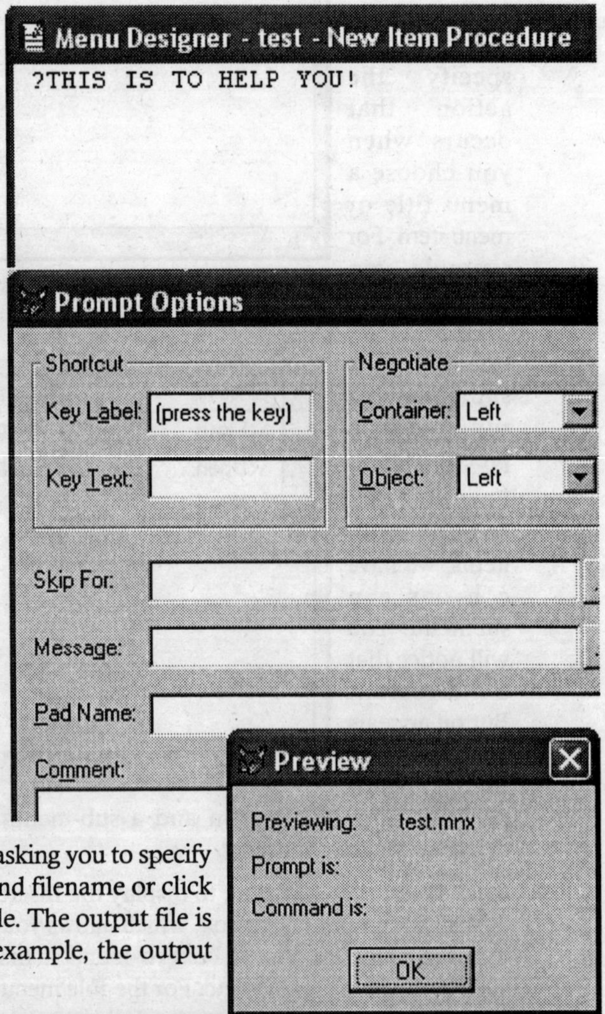

20. Click Generate button.
21. To run the menu, type the following in the Command Window:

```
DO <MENU_NAME>.MPR
```

USING THE PROJECT MANAGER

The Project Manager is used to organize and manage all your files in projects. To open the project manager, do the following:

1. Click File menu and choose new…. In the New dialog box that appears select the Project radio button and click New File button.
2. In the Create dialog box that appears, select the directory of your choice and provide a name for the new Project file. We have provided the name "Proj1". Click Save.

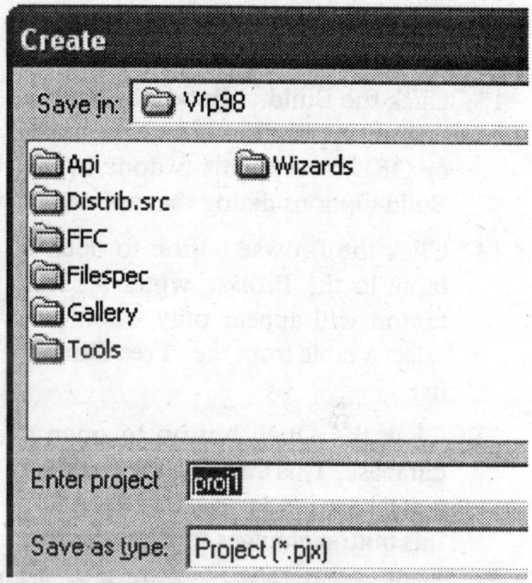

3. The Project Manager window will appear as shown next.
4. When the Project Manager window is active, Visual FoxPro displays the Project menu on the menu bar.
5. You will notice that the items in the Project Manager window are organized in a manner that you can expand or collapse. A plus sign appears to the left of items if there are further items of that type in the project. Once clicked, the plus sign changes to a minus sign, which you click to collapse the expanded list.

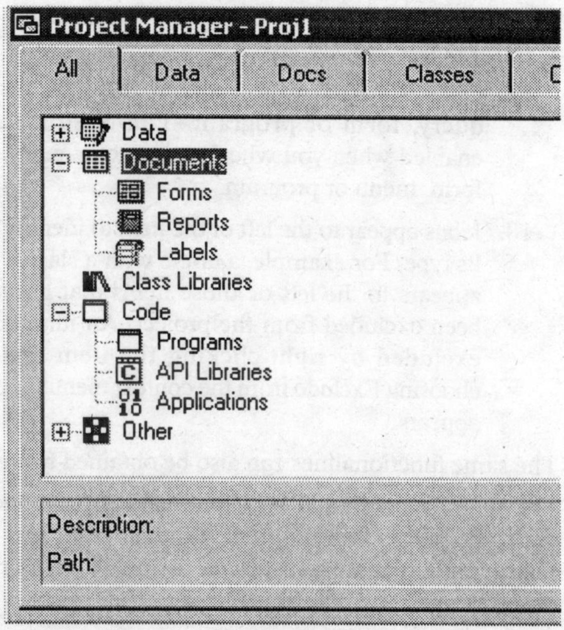

6. The project manager window can be docked to the top of your Visual FoxPro. This can be down by either dragging to the menu bar or by double-clicking the title bar of the Project manager window.
7. When the window is docked click these tabs to display their contents. You can tear off a tab by dragging them away from the menu bar. To replace it, just drag it back to its original position or click the Close box.
8. You may see a list of items in the Project manager window such as tables, Forms, reports, Queries, Labels etc. Clicking the plus (+) sign to the left of an item will display the sub-items. For example, if you click the Forms item, all the forms added to this project will be displayed.
9. Click the Add… Button to add an existing item to the currently selected item.
10. Click the New … Button to add a new file or object. The new file or object will get added to the currently selected item.
11. Click the Modify button to make any changes to the added item. This button gets enabled only when you select an item.

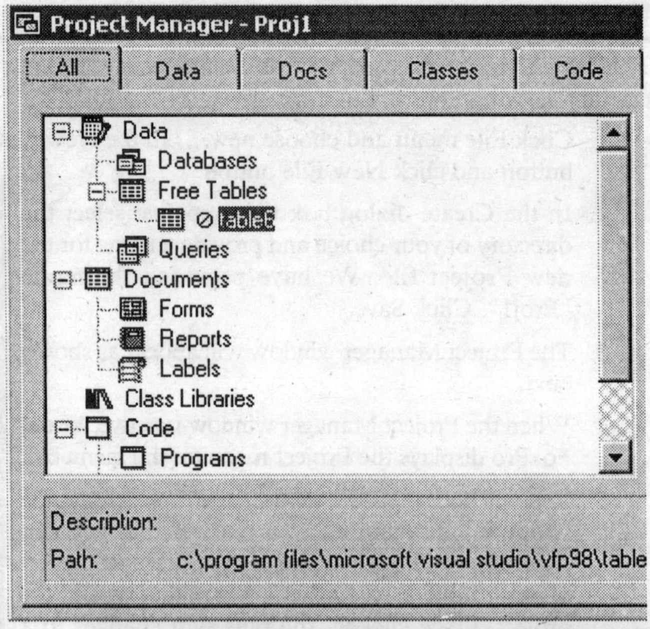

12. Click the Remove... Button to eliminate the selected file or object from the project. A window will appear asking whether you want to just remove the file from the project or you want to delete it from the disk.
13. Click the Build... Button to build a project, application or an executable or OEL server. This is done in the Build Options dialog that appears.
14. Click the Browse button to open a table in the Browse window. This button will appear only when you select a table from the "Free Tables" list.
15. Click the Open button to open a database. This button appears when a database is selected. Once opened, this button changes to Close button.

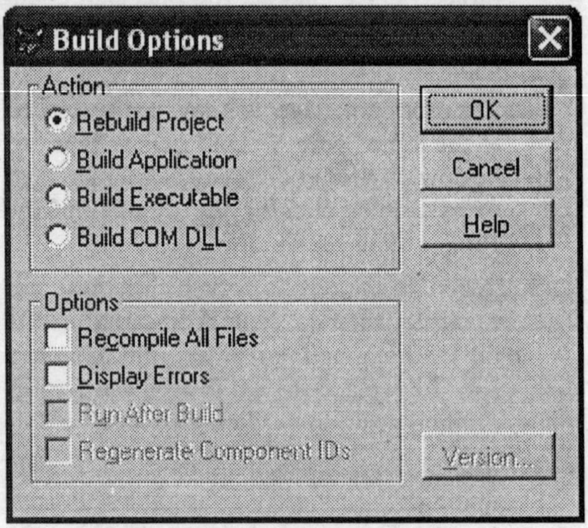

16. Click the Preview... Button to display the selected report or label in Print Preview mode.
17. Click the Run button to run the selected query, form or program. This button is enabled when you when you select a query, form, menu or program.
18. Icons appear to the left of the item to identify its type. For example, a circle with a slash / appears to the left of those items that have been excluded from the project. An item is excluded by right-clicking the item and choosing Exclude from the context menu that appears.

The same functionalities can also be obtained from the Project menu.

The Set main command is used to make the selected program, menu, query or form as the application's main program. Main program is the program that is initially executed in a compiled application. The main program name is displayed in bold letters in the Project Manager window.

The Refresh option refreshes the project. The Clean Up Project option runs the Pack command to decrease the size of the project (.PJX) file by permanently removing files that have marked for deletion. When you remove a file from a project using the Remove button, the associated record remains in the project's .PJX file but is marked for deletion.

Such files get permanently removed when you choose Clean Up Project from the project menu.

TECHNIQUE OF WRITING EFFICIENT FOXPRO PROGRAMS

You should refer to chapter number 3 for writing good program. This chapter covers in details the various aspects of writing a good program. It also discusses the various other aspects of programming like, designing, coding and flow writing. Data handling, Data input and Data verification is also discussed in it.

Let us Revise

1. Programming is based upon commands which are given to the computer to do something.
2. Once the commands are saved in a command file, you can execute all such commands as a group.
3. You can run the program by selecting DO from the Program menu and selecting a program from the DO dialog box (which works just like the open dialog box).
4. A variable is a memory location within the computer that is used to store data temporarily.
5. Character variables store strings of characters, which can be letters, numbers or a combination of both.
6. Numeric variables are used to store numeric values such as whole or decimal numbers.
7. Date variables store date values written in MM/DD/YY format as (03/25/97).
8. Logical variables contain a logical value of T (true) or (false) or Y (yes) or N (no).
9. Visual FoxPro also lets you create two-dimensional array.
10. Visual FoxPro allows you to change the size and dimensions of an array.
11. Scatter command moves data from the current table record into an array.
12. You can also use a combination of @, Say, Get and Read commands to prompt the user to enter the values from the keyboard.
13. You can clear your screen using the @...clear statement.
14. The @ command can also be used to draw lines and boxes on the screen.
15. Both ? and ?? can be used to display data on the screen.
16. FoxPro has two commands, DO WHILE and ENDDO, that are used as a matched pair to repeat a series of commands as many times as necessary.
17. You can use nested IF-ENDIF statements, which are IF-ENDIF statements placed inside of other IF-ENDIF statements.
18. You can use the IF-ENDIF statement in a command file to search for and display data from a specific record in your database.
19. The EXIT command can be used within a DO WHILE-ENDDO programming statement.
20. The CANCEL command halts execution of a FoxPro command file and returns you to the Command window.
21. The WAIT command halts execution of a FoxPro program until a key is pressed.
22. The ZAP command is a one-step command for erasing all records from a database while leaving the structure of the database intact.
23. A procedure is a set of instructions that work as a unit.
24. Visual FoxPro offers two commands, Private and Public that are used to classify variables.
25. A parameter is a value passed to a function or procedure.
26. Apart from the built-in library functions of Visual FoxPro, users can also define and write small programs as functions to do a task relevant to their programs.
27. The User Defined Function makes local copies of the all parameters and gives them the values passed by the calling program.

28. Menu designer is used to create menus, menu items, submenus of menu items, etc.
29. Project Manager is used to organize and manage all your files in projects.
30. The Set main command is used to make the selected program, menu, query or form as the application's main program.

Multiple Choice Questions

1. For running a Visual FoxPro program, you use the command :
   (a) Run (b) Do
   (c) Program
2. Date value is stored in the format of :
   (a) DD/MM/YY (b) MM/DD/YY
   (c) YY/DD/MM
3. To move data from table to an array you use the command :
   (a) Move (b) Array
   (c) Scatter
4. Lines and boxes are drawn on the screen using which command :
   (a) Draw (b) @
   (c) Line
5. Program can be restarted after WAIT command by :
   (a) Any key (b) Enter
   (c) Esc
6. For erasing all records and keeping the structure intact, the command is :
   (a) Cancel (b) Wait
   (c) ZAP

True/False Questions

1. Once the commands are saved in a command file, you can execute all such commands as a group.
2. You can run the program by selecting DO from the Program menu and selecting a program from the DO dialog box (which works just like the open dialog box).
3. Character variables store strings of characters, which can be letters, numbers or a combination of both.
4. Numeric variables are used to store alphabetic values such as whole or decimal numbers.
5. Logical variables contain a logical value of T (true) or (false) or Y (yes) or N (no).
6. Visual FoxPro also lets you create two-dimensional array.
7. Scatter command moves data from the current form into an array.
8. You can also use a combination of @, Say, Get and Read commands to prompt the user to enter the values from the keyboard.
9. The @ command can also be used to draw lines and boxes on the screen.
10. Both ? and ?? can be used to display data on the screen.
11. You can use nested IF-ENDIF statements, which are IF-ENDIF statements placed inside of other IF-ENDIF statements.
12. You can use the IF-ENDIF statement in a command file to search for and display data from a specific record in your database.
13. The CANCEL command stops execution of a FoxPro command file and returns you to the Command window.
14. The WAIT command halts execution of a FoxPro program until a key is pressed.
15. Visual FoxPro offers two commands, Private and Public that are used to classify variables.
16. Apart from the built-in library functions of

Visual FoxPro, users can also define and write small programs as functions to do a task relevant to their programs.

17. The User Defined Function makes local copies of the all parameters and gives them the values passed by the calling program.
18. Project Manager is used to organize and manage all your files in projects.
19. The Set main command is used to make the selected program, menu, query or form as the application's main program.
20. Menu designer is used to create menus, menu items, submenus of menu items, etc.

Matching Columns

Match the text in Column A with the text in Column B.

Column A	Column B
1. ZAP	a. Exits from a DO WHILE loop
2. CANCEL	b. END DO
3. WAIT	c. END IF
4. EXIT	d. Halts execution and returns to command window
5. DO WHILE	e. Used to create menus, menu items, etc.
6. IF	f. Deletes all data from records but keeps the structure intact
7. User Defined Functions	g. Functions defined by the users
8. Menu Designer	h. Halts the program

Fill in the Blanks with Appropriate Words

a. @ b. Variable c. Scatter d. ??

e. Set f. Project Manager

1. ______________ is used to organize and manage all your files in projects.
2. The ________ main command is used to make the selected program, menu, query or form as the application's main program.
3. Both ? and ________ can be used to display data on the screen.
4. The ___________ command can also be used to draw lines and boxes on the screen.
5. A __________ is a memory location within the computer that is used to store data temporarily.
6. ____________ command moves data from the current table record into an array.

Descriptive Type Questions

1. How do you create command files?
2. How do you run the programs?
3. What are the methods of creating arrays?
4. How do you use the @..Say...Get command?
5. Describe the various picture clauses.
6. Which commands form the looping?
7. How would you use Nested if?

8. How is the combination Do while and End do used?
9. How would you use the combination of Scan and Endscan.
10. How is EXIT command used?
11. How is CANCEL command used?
12. What does ZAP command do?
13. What are Procedures?
14. What do you understand by passing parameters?
15. How is menu designer used?
16. What is Project Manager?

Answers to Objective Type Questions

Multiple Choice Questions

1. b	2. a	3. c	4. b
5. a	6. c		

True/False Questions

1. T	2. T	3. T	4. F
5. T	6. T	7. F	8. T
9. T	10. T	11. T	12. T
13. F	14. T	15. T	16. T
17. T	18. T	19. T	20. T

Matching Columns

1. f	2. d	3. h	4. a
5. b	6. c	7. g	8. e

Fill in the Blanks with Appropriate Words

1. f	2. e	3. d	4. a
5. b	6. c		

Recommended Readings

1. Practical Project Management *by Ivan Bayross.*
2. Programming and Problem Solving Through "C" Language *by Harsha Priya, R. Ranjeet.*
3. Learning Computer Programming : It's not about languages *by Mary Farrell.*
4. Learn to Program Visual Basic—Databases *by John Smiley.*
5. Learn to Program Visual Basic—Objects *by John Smiley.*
6. Learn to Program Visual Basic—Examples *by John Smiley.*
7. Keeping Ahead—SQL Server 7.0 *by Joelle Mosset.*
8. MCSE—Administering SQL Server 7.0 *by Jerome Gabillaud.*

—Published by Firewall Media (An Imprint of Laxmi Publications Pvt. Ltd.)

15 Design, Analysis and Development of Business Applications

COMPUTERIZED ACCOUNTING

Accounting is an important part of any company's computerization. This is so because this is the department which effects everyone from employees to employers. A well maintained accounting setup with capabilities of the quick production of reports and summaries is an asset to any business activity in that the management is aware of the latest up to date financial standing of the business thereby facilitating right decision making. Using computerization, the accounts are mostly up-to-date and finalization at the end of the year does not take much time.

Accuracy is the most important as regards accounting data is concerned which is often lost in a manual system. Also the type of accounting data are of simple numerical in nature involving large volumes and laborious calculations. Using computerized accounting, it has become possible to prepare profit and loss figures monthly or if necessary even on a daily basis. To understand a computerized accounting system it is imperative that one should have a clear background to this field of study as otherwise when talking to the accounting personnel, he would be faced with terminologies like debits and credits which would be rather incoherent to a software personnel.

Computerization

The first step in computerizing an accounting system is to identify the heads of accounts required and code them as appropriate. In an actual business environment there would be many more heads of accounts and these should be studied in detail and classified into major and minor groups, such as Fixed Assets and within fixed assets, Land and Buildings, Plant & machinery, etc. A suitable coding structure should then be designed. A typical coding structure is given below.

The account heads in a business can generally be classified as follows:

Balance Sheet Heads

Within this major grouping, we can have various subgroups as under.

1. ASSETS
2. LIABILITIES

Within ASSETS, minor grouping can be done as

1. FIXED ASSETS: Within which sub grouping can be done as
    1. Land
    2. Building
    3. Plant & Machinery
    4. Furniture etc.

2. CURRENT ASSETS: sub groups within as
    1. Stocks
    2. Cash
    3. Bank
    4. Debtors etc.

Similarly within liabilities, there can be Capital a/c and Current liabilities with in which Creditors, Loans, etc., can be classified.

Profit & Loss Account Heads

These are classified into

1. Income – Account Heads representing income within which there could be
    1. Direct income Heads like
        1. Sales A/c – Coconuts
        2. Sales A/c – Other agricultural products.
    2. Indirect Income Heads like
        1. Interest gained from deposits
        2. Refunds received
        3. Sale of Assets, etc.
2. Expenditure – Account Heads representing expenditures within which there could be
    1. Direct Expenditure like
        1. Salaries & Allowances
        2. Travelling expenses
        3. Cost of Raw materials consumed, etc.
    2. Indirect Expenditure like
        1. Depreciation of an Asset
        2. Bad debts written off, etc.
3. Debtors : All debtors are given a Head of account like
    1. ABC traders
    2. Metro Trading Co.
    3. Global Enterprises, etc.

Sometime debtors can be classified as

1. Customers who are regular buyers of your product.
2. Individual debtors with whom you have occasional transactions
3. Staff members of the organization etc.

4. Creditors: All creditors are also given a Head of account like
    1. Varkey's Super Market

2. Delhi Hardware Stores
3. S.K. & F
4. Fertilisers & Chemicals of Travancore
5. Mr. Pramod Kumar, etc.

Creditors can also be classified as

1. Suppliers of Raw materials
2. Suppliers of Machinery and Space parts
3. Machinery Maintenance companies
4. Sundry creditors, etc., depending on the type of creditors in any organization.

Classification of account heads as above is not a very difficult job as you can seek the help of the Accountant who are quite familiar with the specific requirements of an organization. After such classifications, codes can be allotted using any of the coding technique.

For example:

BL/01/01/01 -	could represent Land under fixed assets under ASSETS head under Balance Sheet a/c heads.	
	BL –	Balance Sheet – Major Group
	BL01	Balance Sheet - Asset – Inter-Group
	BL0101 -	Balance Sheet - Fixed Assets Minor Group
	BL010101 –	Balance Sheet – Land etc.
BL010102 -	can represent Buildings	
BL020104 -	Creditors etc.	
	BL – Balance Sheet	
	02 – Liabilities	
	01 – Current Liabilities	
	04 – Creditors	

Similarly PL/01/02/03 – Can represent Sale of assets under indirect income under Income head of P & L Account.

A good coding system, needless to say, goes a long way in efficient computerisation of an accounting function.

After the codes are thus allotted, the next step is to design the Master Files. In a typical accounting system, thee are two Master Files.

1. Account Master File
2. Budget Master File – used in Budgetory control system which will be discussed later.

Accounts Master File

This master file is designed depending on whether you are going to do batch processing or on line processing. In a batch processing the master files are updated only periodically, normally once in a month. In an on line processing environment, the master file are updated immediately on a transaction taking place and will always reflect the latest financial position of the organization.

Master File Layout

Sl No.	*Description*	*Width*	*Dec*	*Type*	*Remarks*
1.	Account Number	8		Character	Code allotted
2.	Description of the account	30		Character	Name of account
3.	Financial Year ending	8		Date	Year ending date, e.g. 31/03/03
4.	Current Balance	10	2	Numeric	
5.	Todate debits	10	2	Numeric	
6.	Todate credits	10	2	Numeric	
7.	Opening Balance – April	10	2	Numeric	
8.	Opening Balance – May	10	2	Numeric	
9.	Opening Balance – June	10	2	Numeric	
10.	Opening Balance – July	10	2	Numeric	
11.	Opening Balance – August	10	2	Numeric	
12.	Opening Balance – September	10	2	Numeric	
13.	Opening Balance – October	10	2	Numeric	
14.	Opening Balance – November	10	2	Numeric	
15.	Opening Balance – December	10	2	Numeric	
16	Opening Balance – January	10	2	Numeric	
17.	Opening Balance – February	10	2	Numeric	
18.	Opening Balance – March	10	2	Numeric	
*19.	Closing Balance for the year	10	2	Numeric	

We have assumed here that the financial year of the organization is April to March of the succeeding year, which also happens to be the Tax year. Some organization do have a separate financial year, e.g., July to June of next year or the Calender year itself.

Current Balance

This is the latest balance up to the last transaction entered into the computer. This can be a positive or negative figure. Negative figures are preceded by a minus sign, e.g., –6325.00. In other words, the current balance represent the sum total of all debits and credits of all transactions that has occurred in the current financial year plus any opening balance for the respective financial year.

In computers, credits are considered as negative figures and debits as positive ones, normally. There is no harm done even if you enter a debit as a negative figure as when balancing is done, usual mathematical rules of addition or subtraction are followed.

To date Debits/Credits

These fields are used to store the total of all debit transaction and credit transactions that has occurred in a financial year in respect of the given account number contained in the file layout.

Opening Balance

This is the balance in respect of the account number as at the beginning of every calendar month. The usage of this is primarily for selective printing of a ledger for a given month, which will be explained later in this chapter.

Closing Balance for the Year

This is the balance as at the end of the financial year which can again be positive or negative in respect of the account number.

The above master file is usually maintained in the account number order. At the beginning of the financial year, To date debits/credits fields as well as opening balances from May through March are initialized to Zero. The closing balance for the year also is set to zero. The fields current balance and opening balance for April would be the closing balance of the account for the previous year in respect of all balance sheet, Debtors & Creditors account heads. In Profit & Loss accounts, these are also initialized to zero.

At any point of time, the current balance would be equal to (Opening balance for April + To date Debits – To date Credits). Similarly the Closing balance for the year would be the same figure as that of the current balance at the end of the year. So this field is strictly superfluous and can be removed. If you have understood this, you are doing well with the comprehension of the accounting system.

The first program to be written in an accounting system thus would be to create, maintain and query the Accounts Master File. Normally, the data contained in this file should never be modified except at the beginning of a financial year when the Numeric fields of the file would be initialized to zero.

You can use the following screen layout for writing the above program.

ACCOUNTS MASTER FILE MAINTENANCE

No. CB/102/2003 Date: [/ /]

Account Number: [ ] Name of Account: [ ]

Year Ending: [/ /]

Current Balance: [ ]

Todate Debits: [ ] Todate Credits [ ]

<u>OPENING BALANCES</u>

April: [ ] May: [ ]

June: [ ] July: [ ]

August: [ ] September: [ ]

October: [ ] November: [ ]

December: [ ] January: [ ]

February: [ ] March: [ ]

The Program should check that when modifications are done, the current balance and opening balance for April should be the only fields where data other than zero can be entered in respect of non P & L accounts. For all other fields if the data is 1st April of any year, you can zeroise the fields. For any other month, no changes to data should be permitted. In other words, data in the above file should never be manually changed except at the beginning of every financial year to initialize the file. Querying this file is always allowed.

When the master file creation is complete we should next prepare the transaction files. Any for of expenditure or income is entered into this transaction file. In a manual system, transactions which are authenticated through any one of the source documents described earlier are first posted into a journal. In the computerized system, this is not necessary. Records are created and appended to the transaction file direct from the source documents. Often transaction records are generated automatically when the source document is itself prepared on a computer. For example, when an invoice is printed, the corresponding transactions are appended to the accounting transaction file by the sales system. Thus we see that all other systems computerized in an organization is ultimately linked to the accounting system. We will discuss this aspect a little more in detail later.

We will now look at a transaction file layout.

Transaction File Layout

Sl No.	*Description*	*Width*	*Dec*	*Type*	*Remarks*
1.	Date of transaction	8		Date	
2.	Source document Number	8		Character	e.g. I/94/032
3.	Document Date	8		Date	
4.	Document Code	3		Character	
5.	Narration	30		Character	
6.	Account Number	8		Character	
7.	Amount	10	2	Numeric	(Minus for Credit amount)
8.	Cost Centre code	2		Numeric	
9.	Bank Code	2		Numeric	(For cheque payments and receipts)
10.	Cheque Number	8		Character	

All transactions emanate from a source document and it is this source document number and date of document which are entered into Fields 2 & 3. For e.g. I/94/032 may be an invoice number representing sale of items to a specific customer.

All document are coded as under

INV	Invoices
CM	Cash Memos
RPT	Receipts – Cash
CSH	Cash payment Voucher
RPQ	Receipts – Cheque
CQP	Cheque Payment Voucher

DN Debit Note
CN Credit Note
JV Journal Voucher etc.

While a debit mount is entered as such, a credit amount is prefixed by a minus sign. Expenses and income are sometimes analyzed department wise or cost centre wise. A cost centre is a department or section which directly contributes to the cost of production of an item. Accounts department, Personnel department etc. are generally non profit earning departments and expenses incurred by them do not directly affect the cost of production. These cost centres are coded and keyed in into the last field of the transaction record.

Data are entered into the transaction file either through a data entry program or directly from linked computerized systems like Payroll, Inventory, Sales or Purchase systems. We will first concentrate on a data entry procedure done in line. A typical screen for data entry is given below.

ACCOUNTS TRANSACTION DATA ENTRY

Date of Transaction:	[/ /]	Name of Account:	[ ]
Source Document Number :	[ ]	Document Date:	[/ /]
Narration:	[		]
Account No.:	[ ]	Amount:	[ ]
Bank Code:	[ ]	Cost Center Code:	[ ]
Reverse Account No :	[ ]	Cheque No.:	[ ]
Confirm Recording:	[ ] Enter Y or N	Any more Records (Y/N) :	[ ]

< Message Line>

We had earlier mentioned that for every transaction there will a debit and credit entry. That is for every transaction two heads of accounts are affected. The 'Reverse Account Number; shown in the screen layout is to generate the second transaction.

When after data entry, you respond with a "Y" to the prompt "Confirm Recording", two records will be generated, the first one charged to the account number and the second one charged to the reverse account. The amount in the first record if a debit, in the second record, it will be created as a credit (with a minus sign prefixed) or vice versa. These two records are appended to the transaction file which is generally maintained in Account Number, date of transaction order. Apart from this the accounts Master File would be updated to reflect the latest current balances and todate debits and credits in respect of the two account numbers affected in the transaction. This result in some amount of duplication of data which can be eliminated by using certain short cuts which will be described later. However, with storage space becoming cheaper with technological advances in the field of computers, this draw back can easily be ignored. Needles to mention, data entered should be well validated and visually verified before recording and updating.

Data Entry through Linked Systems

From Sales System

When an invoice is printed, it represents a sales activity. The customer to whom the invoice is being sent in a debtor to the organization, if the sale is done on credit basis. Therefore the grow value of the invoice is debited to the 'customer's personal account' and credited to 'Sales account'. These transactions automatically generated and appended to the accounts transaction file and the master updated.

Similarly when a cash Sale is made to a customer, a cash bill is prepared. The amount of the bill has been received in cash and therefore debited to 'Cash account' and credited to 'Sales Account' and suitable transactions are generated and appended to the transaction file and the corresponding master record updated.

From Payroll System

Salaries and allowances are calculated in this system and when department wise earnings summary is being prepared, the total salaries and allowances of the employees in the departments are computed and transaction records created by debiting such amount to the head 'Salaries and allowances' and credited to 'Cash account' when salary payments are made in cash. If payments are being made by cheque, the amount will be credited to the 'Bank account'. Accounts master file is then updated as appropriate.

From Inventory Control System

Whenever an issue is made form the stores, the value of items issued is credited to stock account and debited to the corresponding account pertaining to the usage of the items. For examples if raw materials are issued from stores to the production department, the value of issues is debited to 'Cost of raw materials' Master records are also updated automatically.

From Purchase System

When purchases are made from suppliers on credit, the supplier sends an invoice showing value of items supplied. The value of goods thus received is debited to Stock account and credited to the suppliers account (Creditor). If purchases are made against cash, the value of items purchased is credited to 'Cash account' and debited to 'Stock account' and master records are automatically updated.

Similarly when debit notes or credit notes are prepared consequent to purchase returns or issue / sales returns, the corresponding transactions are generated by the system and appended to the transaction file while updating the accounts master file.

Subsidiary Book of Accounts

In the manual accounting system, the main journal of accounts is subdivided into many subsidiary journals like

1. Cash Book
2. Bank Book
3. Sales Journal/Register
4. Purchase Journal/register
5. Debit note Journal or Goods Returns Outward Book.
6. Credit note Journal or Goods Returns Inward Book.

These subsidiary books of accounts can easily be prepared in a Computerized accounting system periodically. Cash book is prepared on a day to day basis for reconciliation of the cash balances, to find out whether there has been under/over payments or whether a transaction has been omitted to be entered into the transaction file.

Let us now see how cash reconciliation is done. The input to this program is the account transaction file.

The documents codes CSH and RPT representing Cash payments and receipts are only selected for this purpose. The opening balance of cash at the beginning of the day is keyed in as a parameter or retrieved from a file, specially kept to store daily cash opening and closing balances.

The format of the cash book would be as follows:

CASH BOOK

Date: 20th September, 2003

Voucher Ref. No.	*Particulars*	*Debit a/c.*	*Debit*	*Credit*
	Opening Balance	BL006		5000.00
CSH/132/03	By travelling exps. paid to XYZ	PL015		250.00
CSH/156/03	Cash purchase of 3 bulbs	PL027		25.00
RPT/10/02	Cost of goods received back	PL001		3000.00
CSH/05/03	Salary paid to peons	PL008		4000.00
-	-	-	-	
-	-	-	-	
	Total Cash Receipts	....	3000.00	
	Total Cash Payments	....		4275.00
	Closing Balance	BL006	3725.00	

We thus see that all cash transactions made during a day are listed in this Cash book together with the opening balance of cash at the beginning of the day. When the last transaction is printed, the total cash receipts for the day and total cash payments are printed and the closing cash balance is computed and given as the last entry of the cash book. If this cash closing balance does not tally with the cash in the cash box, an error has occurred in either the receipts or payments or in data entry which must be investigated and the errors corrected. The cash closing balance will be the opening cash balance for tomorrow.

Similar to Cash book preparation, Bank books and other subsidiary books of accounts can also be prepared on the computer periodically usually at the end of the month. Observe that the opening balances of each account head is provided in the Accounts Master for each month of the financial year. This figure together with the related transactions in respect of Sales a/c, Purchase a/c etc. are used to prepare tne relevant journals, at the end giving the total debits and credits of all transactions and the closing balance of the month computed in respect of the account. These books can also be prepared either quarterly, half yearly or annually as desired.

In an online accounting system, the transactions are entered as and when they take place and this provide an upto date recotd of the financial position of the organization. Let us now see what other reports are prepared form the data thus stored to make meaningful analysis and consequent decision making or strategical finance planning.

Ledger

This is the main book of accounts and is the final book of accounting entries. All transactions are posted into the ledger from either the source documents or from the journal book in such a manner that every account head and transactions pertaining to the account appears in the ledger separately and independent of each other, together with their debit and credit effects to provide summarized information of all heads of accounts in respect of all associated transactions.

In a computerized accounting system, the ledger is prepared monthly when all the transactions pertaining to the month are data entered into the accounts transaction file. Together with the Accounts master file, the ledger is printed.

The following is a paint layout of a computerized Ledger.

LEDGER FOR THE MONTH OF MARCH 2003

Page: 1

Date Printed: 15th June, 2003

A/c No.	*Account Name*	*Date*	*Voucher No.*	*Particulars*	*Debit*	*Credit*
BL001	Land & Buildings			B/F Balance	5,00,000	-
		3.11.03	CQP/1300	Cost of land purchased	50,000	
				Balance	5,50,000	
BL002	Plant and Machinery			B/F Balance	8,00,00	
		12.11.02	INV/06/03	Cost of old grinder sold	-	5,000
		8.11.02	CQP/1826	New roller purchased	1,00,000	
				Balance	8,95,000	
-	-	-	-	-	-	-
-	-	-	-	-	-	-
PL001	Sales Account			B/F Balance	-	12,00,00
		3.11.02	INV/04/02	Goods sold to ABC	-	3,00,000
		5.11.02	INV/06/02	Goods sold to XYZ	-	1,00,000
		8.11.02	INV/08/02	Goods sold to DEF	-	1,50,000
				Balance		17,50,000
-	-	-	-	-	-	-
-	-	-	-	-	-	-
				Total Debits	37,40,000	
				Total Credits		37,40,000

End of Ledger

The details given in the above layout are jut dummy figures only to understand the format of a ledger.

From the above format, you can see that a ledger is printed account headwise with all the transactions listed datewise with the document reference numbers, particulars of transaction and a debit or credit amount as appropriate. The ledger account details for the 'month are preceded by the opening balance figure for the respective account and at the end of all transactions listed, the closing balance figure is computed by adding up all debit amounts and credit amounts separately and the difference calculated by subtracting credit total from the debit total and if this total is positive the net balance is printed under the debit column and if other wise the balance printed under the credit column. The closing balance for the month is entered into the Accounts Master record as the opening balance for the succeeding month.

At the end of the ledger, total of all debit and credit transactions excluding the closing balance figures are printed in respect of all account heads put together. Obviously these two figures would be the same since in a double entry book keeping system, for every debit there is a corresponding credit. If it is not, there is some mistake somewhere and it has to be localised and corrected and the ledger reprinted.

This ledger can be printed selectively, i.e. either monthly, quarterly or annually and such selections are provided to the program through input parameters at the time of running the program. For e.g. you can give the 'from date' and 'to date' and transactions will be picked out to fall between the dates supplied and the appropriate opening balance extracted from the Accounts Master. You can also print the ledger for selected account heads too. In a manual accounting system, you will hear about the balancing of the Ledger accounts and this is achieved automatically in a computerized accounting system, the method of which is explained above. The user is transparent to such intricacies in a computerized system.

Understanding Ledger Accounts

Personal Accounts

Every personal account showing debit balance (i.e. excess of debit side over credit side) will reveal the amount by which the debit side is more than the credit side. Debit side. Debit balance is recoverable from the person whose account shows a debit balance. A debit balance to a personal account is an asset and therefore the more debit balance to a personal account is an asset and therefore the more debit balances to personal accounts, more the assets are in the form of outstanding recoverables. Similarly a personal account showing credit balance means such balances are payable to the person whose account shows a credit balance. So credit balances to personal accounts are a liability. More the credit balances to personal accounts, more the amounts payable to others.

Property or Real Accounts

All real accounts show a debit balance in the ledger except Sales and Returns outward accounts which show credit balances as they represent goods. A debit balance to every other real account shows the value of the properties in possession of an organisation on any day. It represents the wealth and financial position of the company in the form of properties owned and therefore more the debit balances in such accounts, the more wealthy the organization is.

Nominal or Fictitious Accounts

Nominal accounts which represent non-recoverable expenses will have debit balances and is a loss of the company. More such debit balances, more are the losses of the organization. Nominal accounts with credit balances represent gains to the organization and it is quite welcome to the organization. More the nominal accounts with credit balances, more incomes and gains to the organization. The duty of analysing a ledger is the function of the accounts department and computer users need not normally worry about such things.

Trial Balance

A ledger for a month when printed will run into many pages and it would be very difficult for anyone to go through them in detail. You can imagine what would be the volume when a ledger is printed which could be in the order of 5000 to 10,000 transactions in a medium sized organized in a month. To make this ledger more readable and comprehensible often the summary of all transactions together with the opening balances is computed and an account headwise summary report of the closing balances in respect of all account heads are printed. This is known as Trial Balance in a computerized system. Look at the following format of a trial Balance.

TRIAL BALANCE FOR THE MONTH OF MARCH 2003

Page: 1

Date Printed: 15th June, 2003

A/c No.	*Account Name*	*Debit*	*Credit*
BL001	Land & Buildings	5,50,000	-
BL002	Plant and Machinery	8,95,000	-
PL001	Sales Account	-	17,50,000
PL002	Salaries & Allowances	2,30,000	-
DB001	ABC traders	2,50,000	-
CR001	XYZ Enterprises	-	6,00,000
CR002	Mr. Pramod Kumar	-	500.00
	Total Debits & Credits	37,40,000	37,40,000

Every account head preparing in a ledger is listed in this trial balance. At the end the total of debits and credits in respect of all accounts are also printed. As mentioned before these totals should be the same if we have meticulously entered all transactions into the computer. If they do not tally, the reasons should be investigated in depth.

In a manual accounting system, the trial balance has a different definition. It is a statement of balances of all the ledger accounts, extracted from the ledger at the end of a specific period to determine whether the grand total of debits and credits tally and thus (find out that all transactions have been properly journalised and) posted into the ledger. In contrast, the computer ledger tallies or not. Moreover, in the manual system, Cash and Bank expenses are only posted as debits and the corresponding credits are posted as a total extracted from the cash book or the Bank Book at a later date, may be at the end of the month when the subsidiary books are individually reconciled.

A computerised accounting system is thus less prone to errors in posting and accuracy of accounts can be ascertained, if necessary even on a day to day basis. And the ledger at any point of time is exhaustively maintained and no short cuts are ever to be employed to save posting efforts in contrast to the manual system. When the trial balance tallies, it only means arithmetic accuracy in respect of the double entry book keeping system. It is not a proof of accounting accuracy. Many mistakes could still be there through trial balance be tailed arithmetically. Let us look at them.

Errors of Principles

Where accounts are wrongly debited or credited due to improper application of the golden rules of accounting, we call them an error of principles. For example a Personal account rule is applied to a transaction where it whould have been considered as a Property account. Suppose Rs 500 were paid to Ms. ABC Enterprises for purchase of an electric iron. We had in the transaction debited Ms. ABC enterprises with Rs 500 and credited a similar amount to Cash account. Actually it should have been debited to a Property account 'Plant & Machinery'. The trial balance would tally with this error, but the accounts is still incorrect. Is it not so? How do we correct such a mistake.

Rectification of the entry referred above can be done by creating a Journal Voucher debiting the said amount to 'Machinery account' and crediting it to 'Ms. ABC Enterprises' account which was wrongly debited earlier. This journal voucher should be duly authorised by an officer of the accounts department. Given below is the appropriated journal voucher specimen.

JOURNAL VOUCHER

J.V.No.: JV/AD/01 **Date: 20th September, 2003**

Serial No.	*Particulars*	*Account No.*	*Debit*	*Credit*
1.	To Plant & Machinery A/c.			
	Cost of electric iron purchased	BL002	500.00	
2.	To M/s. ABC Enterprises A/c.			
	By wrong debit of A/c vide			
	ref voucher No. INV/02/37	DB008		500.00

Prepared By: **Passed By:**

This journal voucher is now keyed in into the accounts transaction file and the master records would be updated accordingly to rectify this error of principle.

Error of Commission

This is an error where principles of accounts are not violated, but there has been a transcription error. For example instead of debiting and crediting the affected account heads as above with Rs. 500 only Rs. 50 were debited and credited. In an online accounting system, this type of error is quite common, that we key in the amount only once and the other corresponding account is automatically created by the computer and updated as appropriate by referring to the Reverse Account (Refer the screen layout of transaction data entry).

Now both debit and credit side has a shortfall of Rs 450 and the trail balance will tally. To rectify this error, create a journal voucher debiting the 'Machinery account' by Rs 450 and crediting 'Cash account' by a similar amount with a suitable narration in the Particular column, duly authorised by the Accounts officer. This voucher is then data entered into the transaction file and master updated accordingly.

Errors of Compensation

When an error on one side of an account gets compensated by an error on the other side, they are called 'Compensatory errors' As in the previous example, the shortfall of Rs 450 can be considered as this type of error since the short debit of Rs. 450 compensates short credit of Rs. 450. Another example of this type of error is when goods worth Rs. 5000 was bough from M/s. Varkey's supermarket and by mistake, this was treated as a sales transaction and the following wrong entries were made.

1. Debited Rs. 5000 to M/s. Varkey's supermarket account.

2. Credited Rs. 5000 to Sales Account

Though the trial balance would tally, the entries are not correct, one mistake covers the other mistake. Isn't it? To rectify this error, we have to completely reverse the entries as follows.

1. Credit M/s. Varkey's super market A/c. With Rs. 5000
   Debit Sales a/c with Rs 5000
2. Debit Stock a/c with Rs 5000
   Credit M/s. Varkey's supermarket with Rs. 5000

The journal voucher should be prepared with the above entries, duly authorised and data entered and master updated.

This sort of an error could also happen during data entry by keying in the wrong account code. A transaction a/c number DB004 was wrongly entered as CR004. To correct this type of errors too you should reverse the entries as explained above.

Suitable narrations should be given in the particulars column to explain the transactions as incident to error corrections.

Errors of Omission

When both of the debit and credit aspects in respect of a transaction is omitted while data entry or when a whole document is omitted to be data entered, an error of omission occurs. In such cases, do what should have been done. Enter the data omitted prepare the trial balance once over again. Validation procedures of Hash total checking or Control total checking could eliminate such errors of omission.

Profit and Loss Account

The purpose of preparing the account is to find out the net profit made by the organization, during a particular period. The gross profit or gross loss is not the actual indicator of the net results of the business operation, because while arriving at the gross profit or loss, the indirect expenses are not taken into consideration.

While preparing the P & L account, the first entry on the credit side is the gross profit brought down from the trading a/c. If the trading a/c shows a loss, this would appear on the debit side of the P & L account. Thereafter all expenses of a nominal or fictitious nature are entered into the debit side of the P & L account. Incomes of a nominal nature are entered into the credit side of the account. This account is then balanced and if the credit side is more than the debit side, the excess of credit side over the debit side will be the net profit whereas the excess of debit side over credit side indicate the net loss.

The net profit or loss is eventually transferred into the Balance sheet which will be discussed shortly.

In a computerized accounting system, P & L accounts are coded separately to easily identify them. In our example, of heads of accounts, P & L heads are coded starting with 'PL' for example, 'PL01' shows "salaries & Allowances" etc. These account heads are picked up from the Accounts master and together with the results of the trading accounts, P & L account is printed. Before the certain notional expenditures are computed like depreciation of fixed assets etc. and included in the input data of P & L programs.

Let us now look at the format of P & L statement shown on the next page.

The above format is an extract of an actual P & L account of an organization. This is what normally appears in the company accounts distributed to its shareholders. The figures in this case has been rounded off to thousands. Loss figures (negative figures) are printed in parentheses.

PROFIT AND LOSS ACCOUNT

Period Ending 31st March, 2002

	Period ending 31st March, 2002 Rs. (000's)	Previous Year Rs. (000's)
INCOME:		
Sales/Services Rendered	8,84,960	11,99,658
Dividend received from other companies	685	2,603
Interest Received from deposits	23,684	9,311
Other Income	10,219	20,253
Stock differential	16,778	(21,213)
TOTAL	9,36,326	12,20,612
EXPENDITURE:		
Cost of Goods consumed/sold:		
Opening Stock	31,276	41,881
Purchases/Expenses(Net)	91,936	1,76,135
	1,23,212	2,18,016
Less: Closing stock	35,368	31,276
	87,844	1,86,740
Manufacturing expenses	2,00,516	2,36025
Selling Expenses	52,371	62,201
Salaries, Wages, Other employee benefits	3,51,572	3,95,012
Managerial Remuneration	576	562
Interest paid	40,674	96,561
Depreciation	31,369	32,929
Auditors Fees paid	419	432
Other Expenses	70,343	1,01,279
Provision for Doubtful debts	262	-
Profit before tax	1,00,380	1,08,871
Less: Provision for taxation	40,000	60,000
Profit after tax	60,380	48,871

Data to prepare this report is extracted from the Accounts Master using the P & L account heads file and the heads are groups into Income and Expenditure and printed as above without any rounding off and finally net profit / loss is computed and printed in the end. Rounded off report as shown above is prepared from the above report which would be more meaningful to a Manager or Board of Directors.

Balance Sheet

The entries in the balance sheet are classified as follows

Assets

They are the value of properties in possession of the compan'/ including all the receivables and recoverablles from debtors and other sources. They are further classified:

1. Fixed Assets.
2. Investment in Securities
3. Current Assets
4. Loans and Advances
5. Stocks, Cash and Bank Balances etc.

Liabilities

They are the source or causes of all liabilities which the organization owes to or is indebted to pay to others including the liabilities to the owners of the organization in the form of capital, net profit, reserves, accumulated profits in any form, provisions for various purposes and funds created out of profits. While preparing a balance sheet, assets can be listed on one side and the liabilities on the other side or liabilities can be listed first followed by the assets.

At the end, both the assets and the liabilities are totalled both side totals will be the same if everything is done in order. Those account balances taken in the P & L or trading a/c must not be included while preparing the balance sheet. Only the closing stock shown on the credit side of the trading a/c should be taken into the balance sheet, being assets still in possession of the organization. The net profit or loss from the P & L a/c is taken into the liabilities side for giving effect to the Capital a/c. The Capital of an organization is the asset in excel of all liabilities towards the owners as well as others. We will now look at the format of a balance sheet in a manual accounting system.

BALANCE SHEET

As on 31st March, 2004

Liabilities			*Assets*	
Capital A/c.	1,00,000		Furniture	8,000
Add: Net Profit	24,300		Sundry debtors	7,000
			Cash Balance	3,900
		1,24,300	Closing Stock	27,000
Less: Drawings	12,00			
		1,12,300	Land & Building	1,00,000
Sundry Creditors		15,600	Machinery	15,000
Bank Overdraft		1,500		
Provision for Bad debts		1,500		
Loan taken from ABC		30,000		
Total		1,60,900	Total	1,60,900

Drawings mean withdrawal of funds by the owner from the organization for personal use which should be deducted from the Capital.

The above is a fairly simple balance sheet and a more complex can be prepared on a computer. When a computerized Accounting System is designed, the staff in the accounts department should be consulted to get the full idea about their requirements and the nature of the heads of accounts so that preparation of the final accounts is made easier from the Accounts Master maintained on an up to date basis. Using a properly designed system, it would be possible to take the P & L account and Balance sheet of an organization at any point of time. Usually these are prepared only at the end of a financial year.

INTRODUCTION TO PAYROLL SYSTEM

Payroll is probably the most important application of any company. Why not, it is going to effect all the employees of the company. Well, after all everyone works for earnings and most of those who work in companiés look forward to the pay day. This is the day for which they have already made up the plans. It is true that most of the salaried people distribute 80% of their salary within a week of getting it. All this is mostly planned during rest of the 3 weeks. It is also true that most of the salaried people are short of money in the last of the month, irrespective of their immaculate planning.

Most of the companies prepare payroll whether there are 4 employees or 400 or even 4000. Only thing is that for preparing a payroll of 4000 employees you would need the help of computer. It is not humanly possible. Since payroll is a time bound system, you have to prepare a time bound schedule for it too. Have you ever imagined what will happen if the salary is not distributed in time? Well, nothing less than chaos can happen. So for the preparation of payroll, the most important is timing and strictly adhering to it.

Timing

Well, the officer or the worker takes away the salary slip and salary on the 1st or 7th of the month. For he is not concerned for what goes on in the payroll section during the whole of the month. Obviously, the staff here does not sit idle for the whole month. Their main work is coordination with the various departments, getting all the information from them and putting it to the meaningful form and sending it for computerization.

Following could be the rough schedule for the events to be happening at the payroll section.

Date	*Activity*
5	Receive all corrections to the payroll
7	Send corrections of payroll to computer centre
11	Receive all PF, FPF, and loan registers
12	Receive and send muster roll to various department for filling up the next month data
14	File all FP, LIC, etc., to the respective departments
18	Send all corrections of the muster roll to computer centre
23	Send attendance register for preparing payslips
26	Receive the payslips from the computer centre
29	Distribution of salary to various collection centres for making paypackets

This could again vary from company to company, specially if you have the salary distribution on 7th.

The above dates are subject to the fact that all corrections received from the various collection centres are fed into the computer and a parallel salary run is done to make all the possible corrections. This helps in making the master data up to date and all the monthly reports like PF ledger, Loan registers, etc., are printed only after the corrections have been made.

Well let us see all the above activities in details.

Corrections in Payroll

Well, nobody is perfect. Not even the computer department. When the salary is distributed, the worker or officer would check up the same with his own idea of the salary he was supposed to get. He would immediately point this out to the distributing clerk. He, in turn would check all the possible records and find out where the mistake lies. If the error is human, he would make the necessary correction voucher and make the payment. This voucher is then sent to the payroll department to make the necessary entry before alerting the computer centre for the same.

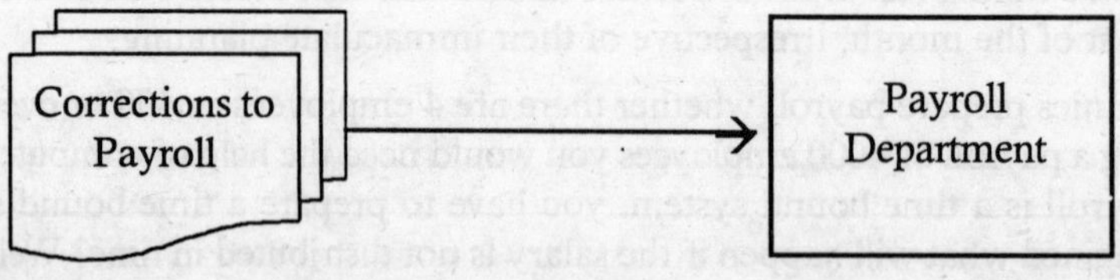

We assume here that by 5th of the month, all the necessary corrections to the payroll are received by the payroll section and sent to the computer centre for amendments.

Parallel run of Salary

Well, this is something which may or may not take place in all the companies. Based upon all the possible corrections mentioned above, the master records of the payroll are corrected. After these changes the related reports of the payroll system are run. This effectively ensures that the ledgers are free from errors.

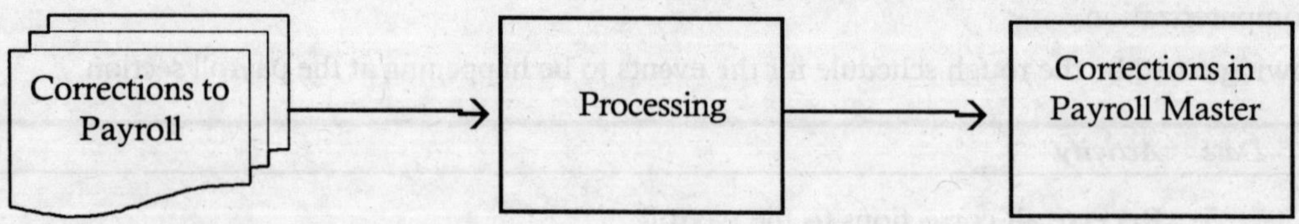

Filing of Ledgers

Once all the ledgers regarding PF, FPF, Various loans, etc., are received, they are sent to the various concerned departments. However, some companies print the ledgers in duplicate and one copy of the same is kept at payroll section too. PF section would need this report for sending the PF amount deducted and the company's contribution cheque to the PF commissioner or to their PF trust, whichever the case maybe.

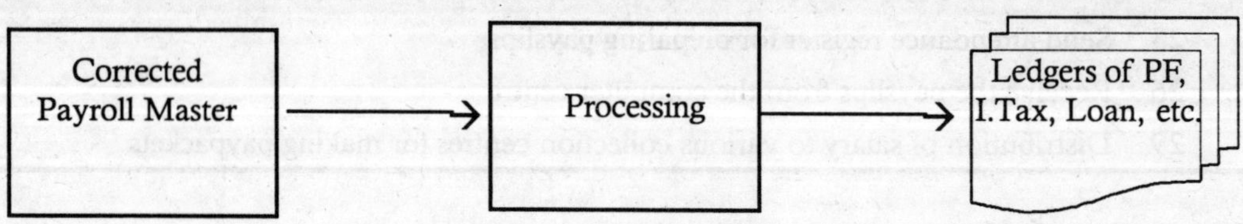

Receiving Muster Roll

The attendance of all the workers is manually entered. For this you need to have the proforma. What is done here is that on the basis of the master information, a blank proforma is printed by the computer centre and sent to the payroll section. This is in turn sent to the various departments who are responsible for filling up the information. This would then become the input for next month's payroll.

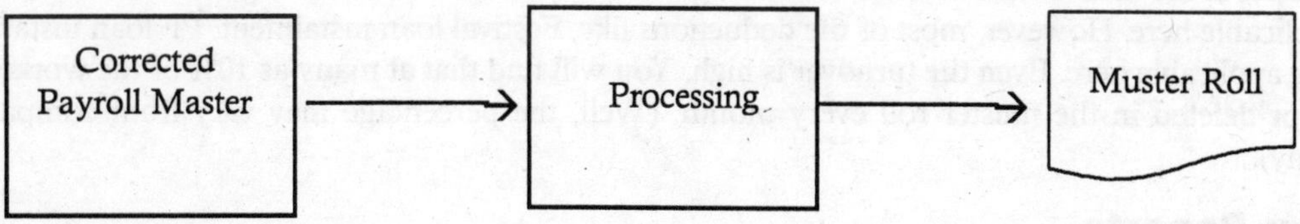

Starting Payroll Process

From this point onwards the process for preparing payroll for the next month starts. The above mentioned muster roll is received back from all the departments alongwith various other variables, like changes in the other master information like Basic, DA, CCA, LIC, Loans payable, etc. This is fed into the computer and the changes made.

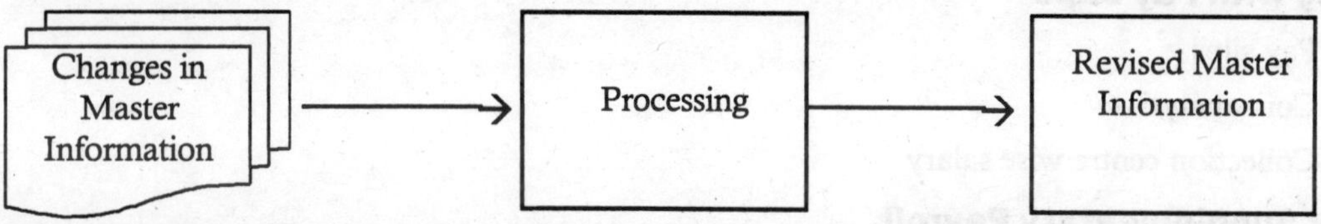

Receiving Payslips

Payslips are received department wise. Usually 4 copies of the payslips are prepared. The original is given to the employee, the 1st copy is given to the finance department for preparing the pay packets with currency notes, the 2nd copy is kept with the individual department as their records, and the last copy is kept at the payroll section.

This can be represented in the tabular form as follows:

Copy	*Disbursement*
Original	Employee
1st Copy	Finance Department
2nd Copy	Concerned Department
3rd Copy	Payroll Section

Styles of Salary

For most of the companies, the salary is divided into 2 styles. One for Officers and the other for workers, which may include daily, weekly or monthly workers, who salary is dependent on the number of days worked. Officers are paid on monthly basis and their leave record is maintained by the Personnel department.

Officers Salary

As mentioned this not dependent on the number of days worked or for that matter their salary is not calculated on the basis of number of days worked in the month. Most of the earnings like House Rent, City Compensatory Allowance, Dearness Allowance, Conveyance Allowance, etc., are applicable here only.

Workers Salary

Attendance is the main factor here for calculating the salary. Most of the earnings mentioned above are not applicable here. However, most of the deductions like, Festival loan instalment, PF loan instalment, etc., are applicable here. Even the turnover is high. You will find that at many as 10% of the workers are added or deleted in the muster roll every month. (Well, the percentage may vary from company to company).

Salary Reports

Various reports are generated from the payroll system. Few of them are generated at the time of pay slips. More of them after making the corrections in the master roll, i.e., after running the supplementary payroll. Some of them are printed on the annual basis.

These reports are:

Along with Pay Slips

- Pay slips
- Coin analysis
- Collection centre wise salary

After Supplementary Payroll

- Master roll
- PF reports
- LIC reports
- I.Tax reports
- Loan reports

Annual Reports

- I.Tax with tax return slips
- PF accounts with confirmation slips
- Bonus processing

All these reports are discussed in the chapter on reports.

Conclusion

Payroll is an interesting system and has no limit to the variations in this. Probably each organization follows its own set of standards. There is no hard and fast rule for system, but few things remain the same, i.e., Earnings and Deductions make the Net Salary and the reports which have to be filed with the respective departments of the Government.

Master Information

Now, we will go through the master information which is needed for creating masters. Most of these items are fixed but can be changed if need arises. For example, the Basic Salary of the employee would remain the same till he gets promotion or an increment. If you are dealing with a payroll of large numbers of employees then this updation becomes necessary every month since even if one employee information is to be changed, this step becomes necessary. On the other hand if the volume is not very high, then it is likely that there may not be any change required in the master information.

Let us go through the various constituents of the master information.

Department

Each organization has various departments in which the employees work. Every employee works in a particular department depending upon the nature of work he has been assigned. If he has been assigned to Finance department, then he must have had experience in accounts or any related department. Some transfers from one department to another do take place.

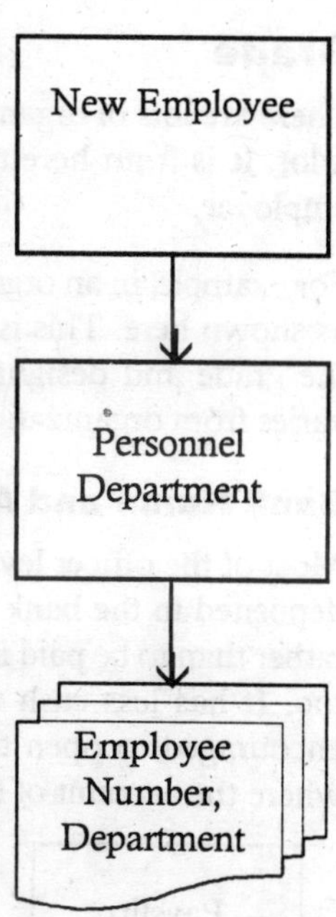

Since it is usually not possible to have the full department name in the master file, usually a 2-digit code is allotted to each department, e.g., Finance department as 01, Sales department as 02, etc. It is this code which is given here and not the full name of the department.

Employee Number

When a employee joins an organization, he is allotted a number. This number is unique and cannot be allotted to anybody else, even if this employee leaves the organization. This number can be of 4 to 5 digits, depending upon the number of employees, the organization has or plans to have.

This number is unique and the master information is kept in the sequence of this number. For all possible processing of the payroll this number is the common factor or the matching factor. Supposing, a Provident Fund Loan deduction, for example, comes with an employee number, then this number is matched with the master information of this number, for making the deduction from the employees gross income.

Employee Name

When we are born, our parents/elders allot us a name, which is sort of allotted to us and we are known by it. We may or may not like it but would have to live with it. This name appears in the masters as per the organizational records, or as the name appears on the appointment letter of the employee.

Father's Name

It is possible that two employees can have the same name. For example, there are many people with the name Mayank. To some extent it is possible that they may not have the same surname. But, if you are living in China, where 65% of the people have surname as Lee, then the confusion becomes more. So to avoid these type of possibilities, this option of father's name is also given. Now, that the son's name and father's name both matching is very very rare case.

Designation

An employee is designated according to his ability and status in the organization. Some people are given the designated designation but most of them earn it. All organizations have various steps of designations. As you rise in the organization, your designation also changes or you are given a new or higher designation. Starting from peon, the designations go up to Managing Director. It is a very rare occasion that an employee's designation is lowered.

Date of Joining

It is the date when the employee joined the organization. No calculation is made from it but it is very essential to mark out the next annual promotion due and seniority. In some organizations, they even keep track of the joining on the basis of forenoon and afternoon.

An employee joining in forenoon has better seniority than the one joining in the afternoon.

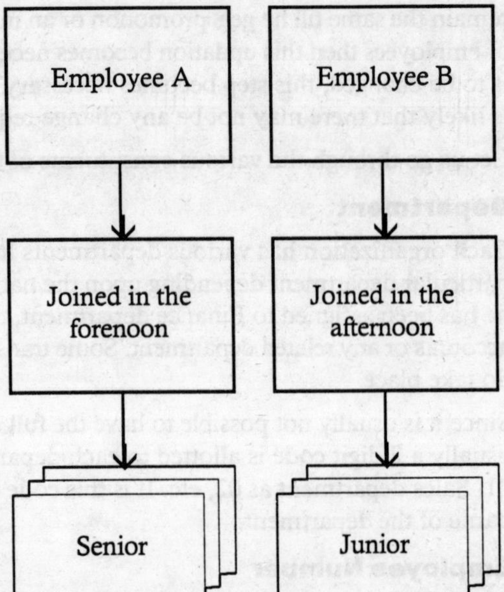

Grade

There are lots of organizations for which the grade means a lot. It is from here that they take out the status of the employee.

For example, in an organization, the grading system can be as shown here. This is just to give you an idea as to how the grade and designations are related. But, again, this varies from organizations to organizations.

Grade	*Designation*
0 - 3	Peon to Helper
4 - 6	Lower Division Clerks
7 - 10	Upper Division Clerks
11-14	Junior Officers
15-16	Officers
17-18	Sr. Officers
19-21	Deputy Manager
22-23	Manager
24-25	Sr. Manager
26-27	Regional Manager
28	Deputy Director
29	Director
30	Managing Director

Bank Name and Account

Most of the officer level employees prefer that their salary is deposited in the bank where they have the savings account, rather than to be paid in cash. In fact, it helps the organization too. It has less cash to handle. Mostly the employees are encouraged to open the account in the same bank/branch where the account of the organization is.

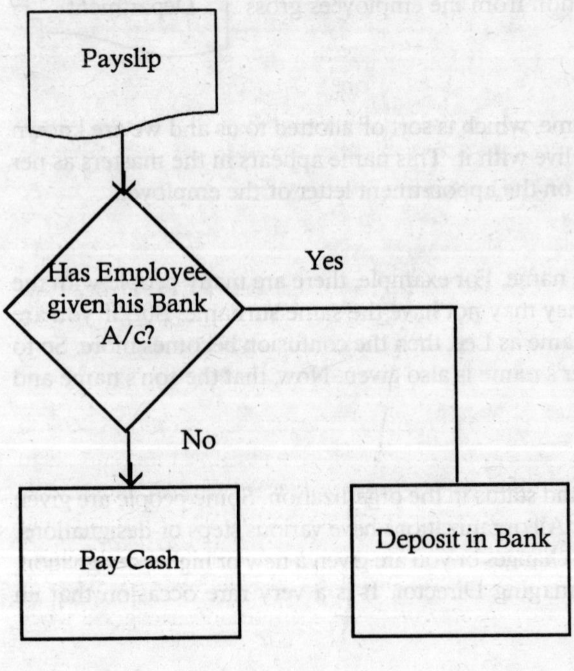

This way the salary payment is cleared immediately within the bank/branch. But, some employees whose account is already in different bank/branch still prefer to keep the same and take the cheque which is then presented for clearance and takes about 2 days.

PF Number

An organization which has a designated number of employees has to introduce Provident Fund scheme in the organization. Under this an equal amount is deducted from the Employee's gross salary and from the organization's funds and this amount in total is deposited with the Provident Fund Commissioner of the State. This is a scheme which forces employees to save a part of their salary with the Government sponsored Provident Funds. If an organization is very big and is based in rural sector, the Government as a special case allows them to have their own Trust to keep the money and give to the employees whenever due.

Since PF is a Government matter, interest on this is given as per the guidelines issued by them. The latest being 10% per annum. Since here the organization is also contributing the same amount as the employee is, the liability of the organization increases per month. So usually some companies try to dodge it by forming small small companies with minimum number of employees so that they do come under the PF network.

Collection Centre

This is another option which is there only when the number of employees is very high. So what the organizations do is that they make various collection centres for delivery of the pay packets. These are opted out by the employees depending upon their work place and the centre nearest to them.

Earnings

Salary as mentioned earlier is divided into 2 parts, i.e., Earnings and Deductions. First, I will discuss the Earnings and then Deductions.

Basic Salary

Probably the most important part of the payroll. This is the most basic salary and all other allowances and deductions are dependent on this. Usually when an employee joins, the basic salary is confirmed to it by means of the appointment letter. Employee on his party gives the confirmation of acceptance by returning back the copy of the appointment letter. This information is then passed on to the Salary department, who then calculate the other allowances and deductions based on this. Most of the organizations have the salary slabs, i.e., you would be given a salary with set number of increments and then you would be given the next slab with new set of increments. Let me explain this with an example. Supposing your basic salary is given as:

750-25-850-75-1000-100-1400

Well, this can be explained like this. Your salary would start at Rs. 750 with an annual increment of Rs. 25. Each year your basic salary would increase by Rs. 25 till you reach Rs. 850 (roughly in 4 years). Then you will enter the next slab and your annual increment would now be Rs.75 instead of Rs. 25. This would again go till you reach Rs. 1000.

It is possible that at the time of joining you are found to quite efficient and organization wants to give you extra incentive but cannot put you into higher grade, then what they do is, give you extra increments in advance. When my friend joined Hindustan Copper Limited in 1979, he was given 3 advance increments and was placed at a basic salary of Rs. 825 and not at Rs. 750 as the grade stipulated. So within one year he was getting increments of Rs. 75. Except for the annual increments, as mentioned above, this salary does not change. You are very unlikely to downgraded. It is however, possible that your boss recommends your increment and you are given 2 increments at a time instead of 1. Well, sometimes the good work does pay, but, alas, not always.

Dearness Allowance

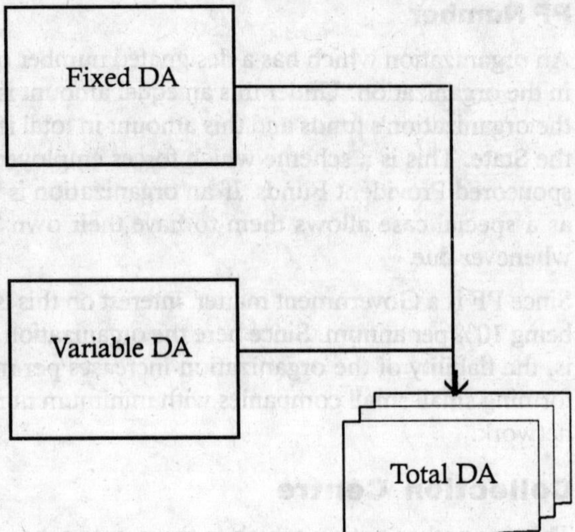

This is linked to the wholesale price index. As the price index rises, employees are given the benefit of this rise in the form of Dearness Allowance. The index has been based on taking the level from one particular year and from that point onward it has been increasing on monthly basis. This is a variable as far as the payroll is concerned. Each month this figure is fed in to calculate the DA.

Some organizations go a step further and divide it into 2 parts. One part which is fixed is called Fixed DA and the other is variable based on the price index. The fixed is derived taking into account the minimum level to be paid and the variable DA is added to it, every month.

House Rent Allowance

There are three types of House Rent Allowance. In both cases here the amount would be fixed by the salary department and is not likely to change every month.

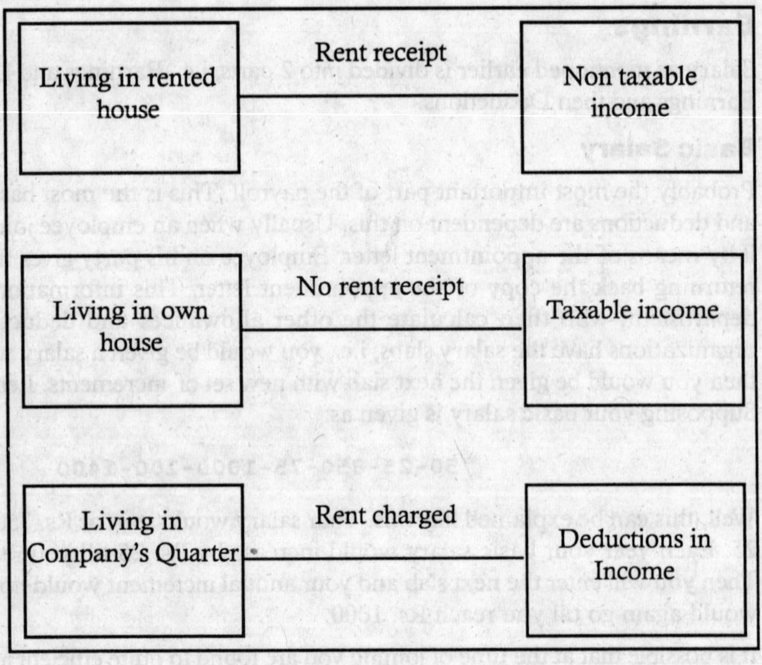

If you are living in a rented house, you have to produce a rent receipt to claim the house rent, which is usually dependent on your entitlement which in turn depends on Basic Salary. In this case this amount is not added to the Net income for computing the Income Tax, since this amount is not taxable then. In second case, if you are living in your own or family home, then you cannot give the receipt of the same. The organization will however, pay you the minimum amount it has stipulated for you, but, it would be taxable. In the third case, where there is a big industrial township of the organization, employees are given quarters to live in. The rent is then charged instead of giving out the house rent allowance. Then this becomes part of the deductions.

City Compensatory Allowance

According to the census of the country, some cities are marked A class cities and some are marked B class and C class. All the metros are considered to be A class. You are paid CCA according to the city you are living in as part of the job. It is not a binding by the Government, but, the organizations decide who is to be given what.

Conveyance Allowance

Companies allow their employee the facility of using their own conveyance for coming to office. For this they are compensated in terms of the petrol they spend. Usually the entitlement is of petrol litres which is multiplied with the current rate of the fuel.

Sometimes a fixed amount is also given, say Rs. 400/-. But, remember, this amount is part of the earnings and is taxable.

Car Allowance

Those of the employees who are maintaining the car are given this allowance. As mentioned above, this is based on the designation of the employee. For example, a clerk having a car would probably not get it. The same goes for the scooter/motorcycle allowance.

Cycle Allowance

Not everybody has a car or scooter, there may be staff having cycle. They too are given allowance for upkeep of the cycle. Of course there is no petrol involved here, only manual labour.

Using Company's Transport

There are time when you would be using the company's car for up and down from home to office. It is like School Bus which picks up the students from home and leaves them home after the school. This is usually possible in the cases where there is big residential complex within the factory area. A jeep is usually provided for this purpose which picks up staff from home and then drops them home. This facility is usually available to the officers only.

Special Allowance

There are various types of special allowance available in various organizations. For example, in banks, the cash counter clerks are paid extra for handling cash. In other cases people are given special allowance called Hill Allowance if they are posted in hilly areas. This may be a fixed amount fed in in the beginning.

Deputation Allowance

This allowance is applicable only when the employee is sent on deputation to other place in connection with the work. This happens in various Government organizations that staff is loaned from one organizations to another. The staff is then paid extra for working under different circumstances.

Split Duty Allowance

This is an interesting one. Take the example of a Bank which is situated in a urban locality. For the convenience of the account holders it is sometimes decided to open the branch in two shifts, i.e., nine to twelve in the morning and five to seven in the evening. The staff has to come to work twice in a day. For this they are paid extra in the form of Split Duty Allowance.

Special Area Allowance

Supposing the company sends you to a place where there is difficult to live and the whole atmosphere is such that some extra incentive has to be given for you to work there. During the troubled times in Jammu & Kashmir, the staff working in various offices where paid this type of allowances.

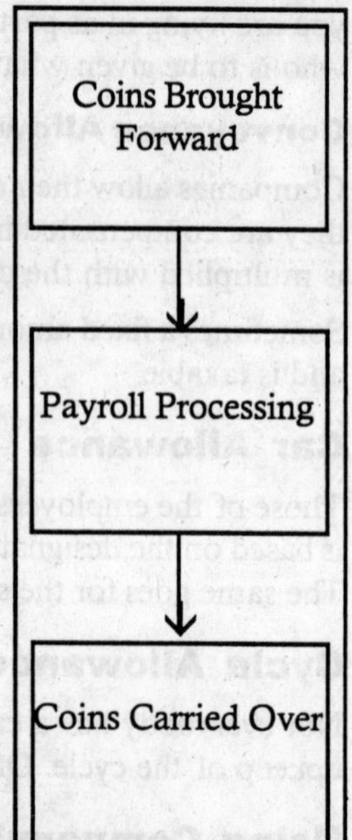

Washing Allowance

If you work in an organization where your clothes are likely to get dirty due to the type of work which you do. For this organizations provide you with the allowance to wash your clothes.

Rotational Allowance

When you reach office at 9, you find that your office is ready for you to work. But, if you reach at 8, it would probably be not. Some members of the staff are called before everyone comes. So for this they are paid extra.

Coins Carried Over

To avoid the distribution of coins at the hands of the collection centre, the net salary is rounded off to the nearest rupee. The coinage due is carried over to the next month when this coinage is added to the net salary before rounding off again. Usually the rounding off is to nearest 5 rupees.

Deductions

Now, we come to the second part of the salary, i.e., deductions. These deductions are both fixed and variables depending upon the options selected by the employees.

Income Tax

Most of the employees in the officer ranks come under the Income Tax net. Mostly a fixed amount is deducted during the first 10 months of the year. The final installments of the tax are calculated during the month of January and usually the final tax is deducted over the last 2 months of the financial year, i.e., February and March. For this end of the year certificate is also issued to the employee.

Provident Fund

While defining PF number, I had mentioned this. The amount here is the calculated amount which is to be deducted every month.

Family Provident Fund

This is part of the Provident Fund. Some portion of the provident fund is reserved for the family provident fund.

Voluntary Contribution

If you have money to spare and would like to invest in Provident Fund, then you can opt for making a voluntary contribution towards the fund through a fixed amount every month. On this you would get the interest as you would get on your contribution towards the PF. Remember, there is no contribution against this from the organization.

Provident Fund Loan

As mentioned under PF, you can withdraw a part of the PF you have deposited while working, as loan. This amount is usually 75% of the contribution made by the employee. You can take loan from the PF, an instalment of which is deducted from your salary every month. This is called Provident Fund Loan Instalment.

Home Loan

Various organizations give their employees loans for constructing houses for themselves. This is at the discretion of the employers and the amount of your tenure with the company. A very reasonable interest is charged on this. An instalment of the this loan is fixed and deducted from the salary. The loan repayment schedule maybe of 5 to 20 years.

Festival Loan

In India there are various type of festivals. If Hindus have Diwali and Holi, then Muslims have Id and Christians have Christmas. Employees are given loan for the festival but the amount is relatively small and is deducted within 6 months at the most. An instalment for the same is calculated and fixed for deduction.

Jewellary Loan

Yes, some organizations do pay you to buy jewellary for maybe, your son/daughter's marriage. For this the jewellery receipt is a must. In no condition this jewellary has to be sold out till the loan is due. The term of this loan is usually not more than 6 months.

Loan Against Securities

For saving Income Tax, employees buy National Saving Certificates. But, for how long you can keep investing the money in NSCs. You are bound to be cash short. So the only option for you is to take loan against these NSCs or on other securities too like Shares. But, it all depends on the organization whether they want to give loan on this or not.

Furniture Rent

It is usually applicable to people who have transferable jobs. On being transferred from one job to another, carrying furniture from one city to another is usually not easy. So what most of the organization do is that they provide senior officers with fully furnished offices and then charge rent for the furniture provided. This amount is usually fixed for the month.

LIC Premium

This is linked with the insurance premium to be paid on the LIC policies taken. Here the policy number is filled up and the amount due date with the mode of payment, i.e., monthly, quarterly, half-yearly and yearly. Once the due date of the first premium is given, the next date is automatically calculated and the amount deducted in that month.

It is possible that the employee may have more than one policies. So the provision has to be made for multiple policy numbers and due dates.

Activity Club Deduction

This is mostly there when the employees are posted in the housing scheme of the organization. There is usually a Club where the families of the employees can use the facilities available there. Most of these clubs are the meeting grounds for the social gatherings. Saturday evenings are usually reserved for the motion picture which is shown on the premises of the club. For this a minimum amount is deducted from the salary as the membership fee.

Union Fee

Which organization does not have a union? Well, if you have to become a member of the union, you have to pay a monthly union fee too. Whether union helps you in your cause or not, but you have to pay its fee.

Calculation of Salary

Now, that we have gone through the various earnings and deductions, let us then go ahead and make the actual calculations. For the purpose of this calculations, I am taking a live example of an employee, who is an officer in a company called ABC Corporation. We would in fact create the payslip while making the calculations. In other words, we would keep on printing the actual details as we calculate them.

As usual we would start with headings first.

Headings

The first part of any payslip is the headings. This contains the name of the company, month, etc., while the second line contains the main information about the employee.

First Line

As mentioned the first line contains the company information. For the company ABC Corporation the payslip for the month of November, 2002 would look like the one shown here.

ABC Corporation **5 Princess Street, Kolkatta - 700 005**	**Salary for the month of November, 2002**

Second Headings

Here the basic information about the employee is provided. We can call it the master information. There has nothing to calculate. The information would all come from the master record of the employee and have the following information.

Employee number

Department

Employee Name

Designation

Collection Centre

Bank/Account Number

All this information can be printed as part of the second heading. I am assuming here that the salary is printed for the employee named Sachin Tendulkar. The salary slip would now look like this.

ABC Corporation **5 Princess Street, Kolkatta - 700 005**			**Salary for the month of November, 2002**	
Emp. No.	Emp. Name	Designation	CC	Bank/Account
1470	**Sachin Tendulkar**	**Sr. Officer**	**Mumbai**	**SB/14097**

Earnings

Now we come to the earnings part and we start with Basic Salary.

Basic Salary

We assume that Sachin is at the basic salary of Rs. 2,200. For this is what is given in the master and needs no calculation.

Fixed Dearness Allowance

Assumingly fixed it is Rs. 400 as per the master records. Again no calculation is needed for it.

Variable Dearness Allowance

Though no calculation is involved here but, it is to be accepted as input from the operator with the help of console. In fact, the date of the processing can also be given from the console.

House Rent Allowance

In this case, we would take the house rent as Rs. 330, which is 15% of the basic salary.

City Compensatory Allowance

Since Sachin is living in Mumbai, he is entitled to CCA of Rs. 300.

Conveyance Allowance

Sachin uses car and the company gives him Rs. 250 as car allowance.

At this stage the payslip looks like this.

ABC Corporation 5 Princess Street, Kolkatta - 700 005				Salary for the month of November, 2002	
Emp. No. **1470**	Emp. Name **Sachin Tendulkar**		Designation **Sr. Officer**	CC **Mumbai**	Bank/Account **SB/14097**
Basic **2200.00**	Fixed DA **400.00**	Variable DA **125.00**	HRA **330.00**	CCA **300.00**	Conveyance **250.00**

Continuing with allowances, we proceed ahead with the calculations of salary. Of the following allowances, some of them are payable to Sachin, as mentioned below:

Special Allowance

There is no special allowance for Sachin.

Deputation Allowance

Since Sachin is at Mumbai, this does not apply to him.

Split Duty Allowance

Sachin is in officer's category, so this does not effect Sachin.

Special Area Allowance

Sachin in not based at any special area, so there is no allowance.

Washing Allowance

Since Sachin plays cricket, he is paid this allowance as a special case. The amount paid to him is Rs. 250.

Rotational Allowance

Sachin is not entitled for this too.

Coins Carried Over

Sachin's last net salary was Rs. 3,567.32. Out of this he was paid Rs. 3,565 and the amount of Rs. 2.32 was carried over for the next month. So this becomes his coinage brought forward.

With the earnings are over and the salary slip looks like this.

ABC Corporation **5 Princess Street, Kolkatta - 700 005**				**Salary for the month of November, 2002**		
Emp. No. **1470**	Emp. Name **Sachin Tendulkar**		Designation **Sr. Officer**		CC **Mumbai**	Bank/Account **SB/14097**
Basic **2200.00**	Fixed DA **400.00**	Variable DA **125.00**	HRA **330.00**		CCA **300.00**	Conveyance **250.00**
Special Al. —	Deputation Al. —	Split Duty Al. —	Special Area Al. —	Washing **250.00**	Rotational Al. —	Coins B/F **2.32**

Deductions

Now we come to the deductions part.

Income Tax

Sachin comes into the bracket and his deduction per month is Rs.100 and during the month of February and March, he is asked to pay more.

Provident Fund

Sachin is a member of provident fund. His PF amount calculated comes to Rs. 214.50, which is calculated as follows:

```
P.F =   Basic Salary x 9.75%
```

Family Provident Fund

This is 10% of the PF. Since Sachin's PF is Rs. 214.50 so his FPF would come to Rs. 21.45.

Voluntary Contribution

Sachin thinks of his future and saves some amount in PF. For this he contributes a partly sum of Rs. 100 towards voluntary contribution.

Provident Fund Loan

At the time of his sister's wedding, he had taken a loan of Rs. 10,000 from the PF. His monthly deduction comes to Rs. 166.66.

Home Loan

Sachin has not planned for home loan so far.

Festival Loan

Last time during Holi, he had taken a loan of Rs. 1,000. His loan instalment for this comes to Rs. 150.

At this stage the salary slip looks like this.

ABC Corporation						
5 Princess Street, Kolkatta - 700 005				**Salary for the month of November, 2002**		
Emp. No.		Emp. Name		Designation	CC	Bank/Account
1470		**Sachin Tendulkar**		**Sr. Officer**	**Mumbai**	**SB/14097**
Basic	Fixed DA	Variable DA		HRA	CCA	Conveyance
2200.00	**400.00**	**125.00**		**330.00**	**300.00**	**250.00**
Special Al.	Deputation Al.	Split Duty Al.	Special Area Al.	Washing	Rotational Al.	Coins B/F
—	—	—	—	**250.00**	—	**2.32**
I.Tax	PF	FPF	Voluntary	PF Loan	Home Loan	Festival Loan
100.00	**214.50**	**21.45**	**100.00**	**166.66**	—	**150.00**

Jewellary Loan

Sachin has not taken any such loan, so there is no deduction.

Loan Against Securities

Again there is no loan.

Furniture Rent

Sachin has not taken loan on furniture.

LIC Premium

Sachin as said earlier has future in mind, so he has taken 2 LIC policies. Since he has to pay them on monthly basis, his monthly contribution is Rs. 112.50. His policy numbers are there in the master information but are not printed here.

Activity Club Deduction

As mentioned that Sachin plays cricket, he is thus an active member of the club and pays Rs. 200 per month as club fee.

Union Fee

He is member of the union and has to pay Rs. 25 as monthly fee.

At this stage the salary slip looks like the one shown on the next page.

At this stage we divide the salary slip into 2 parts. First is for the employees whose salary is not dependent on attendance. The others are those who are paid according to the number of days they have worked in the month.

Since Sachin belongs to first category. The attendance line in his case would be blank and the other categories like Postal Insurance and flood will be blank, as mentioned below.

ABC Corporation
5 Princess Street, Kolkatta - 700 005 **Salary for the month of November, 2002**

Emp. No.	Emp. Name		Designation	CC	Bank/Account	
1470	**Sachin Tendulkar**		**Sr. Officer**	**Mumbai**	**SB/14097**	
Basic	Fixed DA	Variable DA	HRA	CCA	Conveyance	
2200.00	**400.00**	**125.00**	**330.00**	**300.00**	**250.00**	
Special Al.	Deputation Al.	Split Duty Al.	Special Area Al.	Washing	Rotational Al.	Coins B/F
—	—	—	—	**250.00**	—	**2.32**
I.Tax	PF	FPF	Voluntary	PF Loan	Home Loan	Festival Loan
100.00	**214.50**	**21.45**	**100.00**	**166.66**	—	**150.00**
Jewellery	Securities	Furniture	LIC	Club	Union	
—	—	—	**112.50**	**200.00**	**25.00**	

Postal Insurance Premium

Sachin has not taken any postal insurance.

Flood Relief Fund

There is no natural calamity this month, so there is no deduction.

Others

This column has been left blank for making future provisions which may arise from time.

So now the salary slip would look like the one shown below.

ABC Corporation
5 Princess Street, Kolkatta - 700 005 **Salary for the month of November, 2002**

Emp. No.	Emp. Name		Designation	CC	Bank/Account	
1470	**Sachin Tendulkar**		**Sr. Officer**	**Mumbai**	**SB/14097**	
Basic	Fixed DA	Variable DA	HRA	CCA	Conveyance	
2200.00	**400.00**	**125.00**	**330.00**	**300.00**	**250.00**	
Special Al.	Deputation Al.	Split Duty Al.	Special Area Al.	Washing	Rotational Al.	Coins B/F
—	—	—	—	**250.00**	—	**2.32**
I.Tax	PF	FPF	Voluntary	PF Loan	Home Loan	Festival Loan
100.00	**214.50**	**21.45**	**100.00**	**166.66**	—	**150.00**
Jewellery	Securities	Furniture	LIC	Club	Union	
—	—	—	**112.50**	**200.00**	**25.00**	

Now we come to the part where the totals are generated.

Generating Totals

First there is column for Total Earnings.

This is the total of all the columns mentioned in the two rows of earnings in the pay slip, i.e., from Basic to Coins B/F.

In this case it becomes, Rs. 3,857.32

Next is the column for total deductions.

This is the total of the amount mentioned in the next 3 rows, i.e., starting from I.Tax to Others.

In this case it becomes: Rs. 1,090.11

From these two fields the Net Salary can be calculated. This is calculated as Rs. 2,767.21.

Coins carried over field is derived from Net Salary with adjusting the amount to the nearest 5 rupees.

In this case the carry over coins will be Rs. 2.21.

So the net salary then becomes Rs. 2,765.00

The final payslip would look like the one shown below.

ABC Corporation
5 Princess Street, Kolkatta - 700 005 — **Salary for the month of November, 2002**

Emp. No.	Emp. Name	Designation	CC	Bank/Account		
1470	**Sachin Tendulkar**	**Sr. Officer**	**Mumbai**	**SB/14097**		
Basic	Fixed DA	Variable DA	HRA	CCA	Conveyance	
2200.00	**400.00**	**125.00**	**330.00**	**300.00**	**250.00**	
Special Al.	Deputation Al.	Split Duty Al.	Special Area Al.	Washing	Rotational Al.	Coins B/F
—	—	—	—	**250.00**	—	**2.32**
I.Tax	PF	FPF	Voluntary	PF Loan	Home Loan	Festival Loan
100.00	**214.50**	**21.45**	**100.00**	**166.66**	—	**150.00**
Jewellery	Securities	Furniture	LIC	Club	Union	
—	—	—	**112.50**	**200.00**	**25.00**	
Attendance	Underground	Adjustment	Postal Insurance	Flood Relief	Others	
—	—	—	—	—	—	
Total Earnings	Total Deductions	Nett. Pay	Coins C/F	Nett Payable		
3,857.32	**1,090.11**	**2,767.21**	**2.21**	**2,765.00**		

(Rupees Two Thousand Seven Hundred Sixty Five only)

Note: Gross salary includes total of all earnings. Net pay has been credited to Employees Bank A/c after taking into accounts the total deductions.

Now we come to other aspect of the salary where attendance is involved.

Attendance

For this you need to know the number of days in the month too. This variable is taken either from computer date or is fed in through the console. The variable data which is fed, contains the number of days, the employee has worked in the month.

For our calculation purposes, we take that Sachin has worked for 28 days in total. Out of this he has worked underground on 15 days, i.e., has worked in mines, which are below the ground level.

So in fact, he has worked 13 days overground and 15 days underground.

The amount that he has to be paid according to this is calculated as follows:

$$\text{Attendance pay} = \frac{\text{No. of days worked overground} \times \text{Total Pay}}{\text{No. of days in the month}}$$

Where Total Pay is: **(Basic Salary + Fixed DA + Variable DA)**

So for Sachin this becomes, Attendance Pay = 13 x (2200 + 400 + 125) = 13 x 2725 = 35,425 and this when divided by number of days in November, 2002, i.e., 30 becomes 1,180.83. As far as underground attendance is concerned, the calculation goes as follows:

$$\text{Underground pay} = \frac{\text{No. of days underground} \times \text{Total Pay}}{\text{No. of days in the month}}$$

This when calculated becomes: Underground pay = 15 x 2725 = 40,875 and when divided by number of days, i.e., 30, it becomes 1,362.50.

So now the Total Pay according to attendance becomes 1,180.83 + 1,362.30 which is equal to 2543.13. This is infact short of the Total Pay calculated earlier, i.e., Rs. 2,725.00. The shortfall due to attendance thus comes to Rs. 181.87.

This amount is shown in the attendance deduction column.

Similar to the earlier steps of calculating totals, various totals are generated here too.

Total earnings in this case is the same, Rs. 3,857.32

Next total deductions, in this case it is: Rs. 1,271.98

From these two fields the Net Salary can be calculated. This is calculated as Rs. 2,585.34

Coins carried over field is derived from Net Salary with adjusting the amount to the nearest 5 rupees. In this case the carry over coins will be Rs. 0.34.

The final payslip would look like the one shown on the next page.

Salary Reports

I had mentioned about the reports briefly in the first chapter. Now we will see how these reports are created and what they contain.

Along with Pay slips

These reports are printed at the time of printing of the pay slips.

ABC Corporation

5 Princess Street, Kolkatta - 700 005 **Salary for the month of November, 2002**

Emp. No.	Emp. Name	Designation	CC	Bank/Account
1470	**Sachin Tendulkar**	**Sr. Officer**	**Mumbai**	**SB/14097**

Basic	Fixed DA	Variable DA	HRA	CCA	Conveyance
2200.00	**400.00**	**125.00**	**330.00**	**300.00**	**250.00**

Special Al.	Deputation Al.	Split Duty Al.	Special Area Al.	Washing	Rotational Al.	Coins B/F
—	—	—	—	**250.00**	—	**2.32**

I.Tax	PF	FPF	Voluntary	PF Loan	Home Loan	Festival Loan
100.00	**214.50**	**21.45**	**100.00**	**166.66**	—	**150.00**

Jewellery	Securities	Furniture	LIC	Club	Union
—	—	—	**112.50**	**200.00**	**25.00**

Attendance	Underground	Adjustment	Postal Insurance	Flood Relief	Others
28	**15**	**181.87**	—		

Total Earnings	Total Deductions	Nett. Pay	Coins C/F	Nett Payable
3,857.32	**1,271.98**	**2,585.34**	**0.34**	**2,585.00**

(Rupees Two Thousand Five Hundred Eighty Five only)

Note: Gross salary includes total of all earnings. Net pay has been credited to Employees Bank A/c after taking into accounts the total deductions.

Pay slips

Printing of complete payslips has been explained earlier. We would now discuss the various other reports which are printed at the time of printing pay slips.

Coin Analysis

This is an interesting analysis. Once the pay slips reach the finance department, they have to arrange for the money to be distributed. For this they have to draw the money from the Bank, but the problem remains, which type of notes and how many?

He should in fact know how many of each denomination of notes are required. How many of Rs. 500, How many of Rs. 100 and so on. Since all the employees are to be distributed the salary around the same time, there is no room for tendering higher amount and taking back the change. The exact amount should be there in the envelope.

For example, take the salary which we had calculated in the earlier chapter. The net amount comes to Rs. 2,765.00. In fact, the coinage in the form of Rs. 2, Rs. 1 and paisa has already been avoided in the coins carried over. Imagine the problem it would have created. So for Rs. 2,765 you would need the following distribution.

Denomination	*Quantity*	*Amount*
Rs. 500	5	2,500.00
Rs. 100	2	200.00
Rs. 50	1	50.00
Rs. 10	1	10.00
Rs. 5	1	5.00
Total	**10**	**2,765.00**

In the above case if Rs. 5 note is not available, then it can be replaced by a Rs. 5 coin.

Similarly the coinage is calculated for the whole salary and accumulated to get the total denominations required. The cash withdrawal from the bank will be based on this analysis. In fact, the coin analysis is made on the basis of distribution centre and the exact number of notes and coins are sent to the respective distribution centre.

At the distribution centre, each employee's envelope is made with the exact coinage and filled with 2nd copy of the pay slip. This is done much before the actual distribution takes place. Some organizations pay the amount on 1st and some on 7th.

Now we see how this report would look like the one shown below.

ABC Corporation

Coinage Analysis of Salary for the month of November, 2002

Distribution Centre: Finance

Employee Name	Rs. 500	Rs. 100	Rs. 50	Rs. 10	Rs. 5	Total
Sachin	5	2	1	1	1	2765
Rahul	4	3	0	1	1	2315
Saurav	6	4	1	2	0	3470
......	...	...	...	...	...	...
......	...	...	...	...	...	...
Total	**415**	**777**	**450**	**215**	**134**	**310520**

Distribution Centre: Personnel

Employee Name	Rs. 500	Rs. 100	Rs. 50	Rs. 10	Rs. 5	Total
Amitabh	4	3	1	2	1	2375
......	...	...	...	...	...	...
......	...	...	...	...	...	...
Total	**...**	**...**	**...**	**...**	**...**	**...**
Grand Total	**...**	**...**	**...**	**...**	**...**	**...**

Exception Reports

Before arriving at the final pay slips, lots of updation and corrections have been made in the payroll master. Each time a record in the master is corrected/added or some sort of alteration is made, a print out to the effect, showing the previous and new record is printed.

All these exception reports are also sent to the payroll department for their checking. Since at the time of processing of the payroll, there is not enough time to check this time of information, but the records are kept to trace the error, if any.

A sample of this type of report is shown here. You would notice here that the headings for all records are not the same. In fact, this report would only show the records which have been changed with marking Prev and New. Moreover, it will also show only those fields on which some change has taken place. The field which does not appear here means that that field has not been changed. In accordance the headings would also appear as the field is. These reports are very useful in case somebody claims that his payslip is wrong and that he should have got more. Nobody would report if he has got the salary more than what he was supposed to get.

ABC Corporation

Updation of Salary Master for the month of November, 2002

Emp. No.	Employee Name	Designation	CCA	HRA	I.Tax	Washing	Comment
0145	Akshay Kumar	Manager	100	200	100	250	**PREV**
0145	Akshay Kumar	Manager	150	250	150	200	**NEW**
			HRA	Washing	LIC	Voluntary	
0522	Robin Kumar	Officer	150	200	150	150	**PREV**
0522	Robin Kumar	Officer	100	250	100	100	**NEW**

After Supplementary Payroll

The following reports are printed when the supplementary payroll for corrections in the payroll have been pointed out. They are:

Muster roll

It prints out the complete information about the salary master. It is in fact the dump of the salary master file. All the variable fields are left blank for filling up the data for the next month.

As mentioned earlier part of this muster roll is sent to the respective department to fill up the changes for the month and to the pay office for the attendance of the subsequent month.

All changes to the variables like HRA, CCA, Washing, etc., are filled in here and sent to the salary department for processing.

This report is printed department wise.

PF reports

Probably the most important part of salary other than the pay slips. This report is in fact submitted to the PF commissioner or the Trustee of the Trust whichever the case maybe.

Various available variables are PF deduction (Employee contribution and Employer contribution), FPF deduction, Voluntary deduction, etc. A sample report would look like this.

ABC Corporation

Provident Fund Report for the month of November, 2002

Emp. No.	Employee Name	Designation	PF	Contr.	FPF	Vol.	Total
0145	Akshay Kumar	Manager	100	100	10	100	310
...	...	...	...	...	...	...	...
...	...	...	...	...	...	...	...
...	...	...	...	...	...	...	...
Total		...	...	...	...	...	...

LIC reports

As mentioned earlier the LIC premium is deducted from the salary and deposited in the regional office of the LIC.

Those employees who have more than 1 policy is listed accordingly. The report could look like the one shown here.

ABC Corporation

LIC Report for the month of November, 2002

Emp. No.	Employee Name	Policy Number	Due Date	Amount
0145	Akshay Kumar	012345678986	14-11-2002	100.00
...	...	...	...	
...	...	...	...	
...	...	...		
...	...	...	...	
Total		...	...	...

I.Tax reports

Everybody is not covered under I.Tax. So this report is relatively small but is significant. A possible sample of report is given here.

ABC Corporation

Income Tax Report for the month of November, 2002

Emp. No.	Employee Name	Earnings	Deductions	Nett.	I.Tax
1470	Sachin Tendulkar	3857.32	1090.11	2767.21	100.00
...	...	...	...	...	...
...	...	...	...	...	...
Total		...	...	...	...

Loan Reports

These reports are printed for all the loans like PF, Festival, Jewellery, House, etc. In each case the report shows the amount of loan taken, the loan instalment deducted and the balance amount of loan due after the deduction. This is very important for the concerned department to know how much is due from whom. Moreover, it also helps in deciding whether to give more loan or not.

A sample report for PF loan could look like this.

ABC Corporation

PF Loan Report for the month of November, 2002

Emp. No.	Employee Name	PF Loan	Recovery	This month	Balance Due
1470	Sachin Tendulkar	7,000.00	6000.00	166.66	833.34
...	...	...	...	...	...
...	...	...	...	...	...
...	...	...	...	...	...
...	...	...	...	...	...
Total		...	...	...	...

These are the few of the reports which are printed on monthly basis. There are some of them which are made on Annual basis.

Annual Reports

These reports are the usual reports which have been discussed earlier with the difference that here the whole year statement has to be printed and a copy of the same has to be given to the Employee. This applies to both the following reports.

I.Tax with tax return slips

PF accounts with confirmation slips

Bonus Processing

This one has not been discussed earlier. The bonus is calculated on the basis of the amount paid to the employees over the year.

INVENTORY CONTROL

In most of the manufacturing organisations, goods such as raw materials, finished products, spares, consumables, etc., are kept in stock so that whenever need arises these items are available off the shelf and the business does not suffer on account of non availability of the items. The main objectives of a good inventory control system are:

1. To keep the investment on inventory at a minimum so that funds are made available for more productive uses thereby avoiding borrowing and consequent loss on interest.
2. To make sure that items are available in store as and when needed.
3. To minimize losses on account of obsolescence, deterioration and excessive stocking.
4. To bring down the cost of production and maintenance of equipments by optimizing stocking.

5. To maintain proper records for costing and accounting purposes.

Therefore, it is imperative that every organization must have a good inventory control system and computers go a long way in helping to achieve this goal.

The most important task in computerizing the stock system is to allot a code number to each item that is likely to be held in stock. There are many methods of coding the items, but the most commonly accepted one is to classify the items into various categories within which different manufacturers and specifications of the items are incorporated.

The golden rule of coding is that it should be easy to remember, the code should be logical and structured and should be so designed that on experience one should be able to write the code of any item without referring to the master code book.

After the codes are allotted to each item, a code Master Book should be prepared giving details such as category, manufacturer, part number, specifications, usage etc. together with the code number and properly indexed for easy reference and distributed to all departments who are likely to make use of the items in stores. The primary requirement of computerizing the Inventory control system is to create and maintain an item Master File. A typical file design is given below.

Item Master File

Serial No.	*Description*	*Type*	*Width*	*Dec*	*Remarks*
1.	Item Code	Character	6	-	
2.	Category	Character	2	-	e.g. Electrical item
3.	Sub category code	Character	2	-	e.g. Fans
4.	Class of item	Character	1	-	A, B or C
5.	Item name	Character	20	-	
6.	Unit of measure	Numeric	2	-	
7.	Rate per unit	Numeric	8	2	
8.	Quantity on hand	Numeric	8	2	
9.	Maximum Level	Numeric	8	2	
10.	Minimum Level	Numeric	8	2	
11.	Danger Level	Numeric	8	2	
12.	Economic reorder Level	Numeric	8	2	
13.	Expiry date	Date	8	-	
14.	Quantity on order	Numeric	8	2	
15.	Last issue date	Date	8		
16.	Local Status	Character	1		(Y or N)
17.	Bin Location	Character	6	-	Location of the item

From the above, you will note that apart from the item code, we should also suitably design category and subcategory codes for preparation of the master file.

Unit of Measure

Items are stocked in appropriate unit of measures and these also should be coded as below.

Class of Item

Items stocked are usually classified into A, B and C depending on specific criterion for e.g. all item whose issues are above Rs. 10,000 could be classified as A items, below Rs. 1000 as C items and all others into B items. This classification could turn out to be very useful in inventory control.

Maximum, Minimum and Danger Levels

In case of items which are frequently used, a maximum and minimum levels of stock is always desirable. Never the item should be stocked in excess of the maximum level or the level or the stock of the item should never go below the minimum levels. A danger levels is the absolute minimum level of stock, below which the business might suffer losses. For example, in your home, how many match boxes do you keep in stock. A minimum level could be three, a maximum level could be 12. Danger level would be one. It is not?

Economic Reorder Level

Often, when the stock of an item falls below the minimum level, replenishment orders are placed with the Purchase Department. When an order is placed, we should consider that is the most economical quantity to be ordered. For example, suppose the stock of bricks in a construction company has gone below the minimum level and you immediately need a quantity of another 500 bricks for completion of a certain job. If you order for the jut 500 bricks, which has to be procured from say 50 kilometers away, you will have to engage a truck for transportation and pay for a full load as freight charges, which could be rather too costly. So the economic order level would be for a full load of bricks, which may be in the order of 5000 bricks. Thus the cost per brick stocked would be kept to the minimum.

Expiry Date

Certain items, particularly chemicals, provisions, pharmaceutical items etc. are perishable if stored beyond a certain date and this is known as the expiry date. Constant watch of such items could avert avoidable losses. Other fields in the master file layout are self explanatory. If an item is available locally, the local status can be 'yes' and we need only store the absolute minimum of such items.

There could be other fields in the items master file depending on the organization and the nature of business performed.

We must now write the programs required to create and maintain the item master file. As the case of the payroll master file, we need,

1. Program to create and add items in the item master file.
2. Program to modify contents of records in the file.
3. Program to delete a record or records from the file.
4. Checklisting of items with all the details in the file.

This program should be written menu driven and the file should be indexed on item number or item code. A typical menu would be

You can use the following screen layout for Add, Modify and Delete Programs. The column 'Last issue date' will be updated by the system as and when items are issued form the stores. Suitable bottom screen message should be given such as "Confirm Recording", "Any more records to be added/Modified/ Deleted" Etc.

Since all details in the master file cannot be accommodated in a single line, we have used two lines for each item. Or perhaps you could print the details in compressed mode to accommodate the details in a single line.

Transaction File

The transaction possible in an inventory control system are

1. Receipts/Purchase of an item.
2. Issue of an item.
3. Purchase Returns – Return of an item already purchased or received on finding it to be defective, sub standard or for any other reason.
4. Issue Returns – Return of an item already issued for reasons of defect unsuitability or on account of indents of a suspected requirement.

The file layouts for all the above types of transactions can be the same as follows. For this purpose, we will code the type of transaction as below.

RP Purchase / Receipts
IS - Issues
PR - Purchase Returns
IR - Issue Returns

Voucher Reference Number

Every transaction in a stock control system is supported by a voucher duly authorized by an officer of the organization. For purchases, a receipt voucher is prepared and signed by the Stores Officer. For issues, an indent should be prepared and sent to the stores department and on receipt of which, if the material is available, an issue voucher is prepared, duly signed by the stores officer and only after this, the item is physically issued and records updated. All these vouchers will have a document number and this information is stored as the Voucher reference number in the transaction file.

Creation of Transaction Files

Unlike in a payroll system where processing is done at the end of the month, in an Inventory control system, transactions are processed on line. That is to say we do not write programs to create the transaction files and process it in batches. Each transaction is processed immediately on occurrence. When an item is purchased and received into the store, a Receipt Voucher is prepared and authorized by the stores officer and the item master file is updated on line.

Purchases/Receipts

Every batch of receipt of goods in a day will be documented in different receipt vouchers, indicating therein the mode of delivery, registration number of the truck and such other details like the supplier name etc. though these information are not relevant to the Inventory Control system, they are good reference data when needed. Once the receipt vouchers prepared are duly authorized, the inventory control system takes over the document for processing. The entries in the document are appended to the transaction file and item master file updated using a computer program.

The program on accepting the item code should display the description, taken from the item master file. If the item code is not present in the master file, an appropriate message should be displayed and the entry ignored. This will ensure that the item code entered is correct. In case of a new item, a corresponding master record should be created first and only after that the receipt data should be accepted for updating. Validation of date of transaction, range checks of quantity and value are desirable.

While each item purchased is appended to the transaction file, in the item master file, the quantity on hand should be updated by adding the transaction quantity to the now present quantity on hand. The 'rate of unit' field should also be changed using average costing method.

We have here used a YTD balance file. This stores for every item, the opening stock for the beginning of the year and cumulative transaction details (quantity and value) of all types of transactions.

YTD Balance File Layout

YTD stands for Year to Date, i.e., the cumulative totals from the beginning of the financial year.

Serial No.	*Description*	*Type*	*Width*	*Dec*	*Remarks*
1.	Item Code	Character	6	-	
2.	Opening Stock	Numeric	8	2	
3.	Rate per Unit	Numeric	8	2	
4.	Receipts Quantity	Numeric	8	2	Cumulative Receipts
5.	Receipts Value	Numeric	8	2	Cum. Rpts value
6.	Issue Quantity	Numeric	8	2	Cumulative issue
7.	Issue Value	Numeric	8	2	Cumulative value
8.	Purchase Returns Quantity	Numeric	8	2	
9.	Purchase Returns Value	Numeric	8	2	
10.	Issue Returns Qty.	Numeric	8	2	
11.	Issue Returns Val.	Numeric	8	2	

This file is first created when the system is installed by copying the first three fields form the item master file and other fields are initialized to zero. This exercise is repeated yearly on the first day of every financial year beginning. As and when a transaction takes place this file is updated to reflect the cumulative quantity and values of the four different types of transactions at any point of time during the financial year.

Naturally a program has to be written to create this file for the first time as well as the beginning of every financial year. Any new item incorporated in the item master file should also be incorporated in this file. Note that the computer program only copies the item code and opening stock of the Balance YTD files. Other fields are initialized to zero.

Issues

Items are issued from the stores on receipt of a requisition indent from the department who needs them. This indent should also be duly authorized by an officer of the indenting department. When the indenting department prepares the above requisition, it would help very much to query the item master file and ascertain the availability of items, quantity in stock and other details of the item. It should be possible to query the item on item code, description of the item and category code. A query program thus has to be written. If the item queried is not available in the item master file, a suitable message "item not available" should be displayed on the screen. On the other hand if the item is available, all details pertaining to the item are displayed on the screen using the "ITEM MASTER" layout described earlier or as appropriate.

On user response, it should be possible to return to the above screen for querying additional items. When no more items are to be queried, you can press the 'Escape' Key to exit from the program. Often the program can be so designed to block the item record in case of emergency use so that no one else takes the item away in the meantime

On receipt of the stores requisition form, the stores department prepares an Issue Voucher for all items available ex-stock. For items required which are not currently available in stock, a purchase requisition is prepared and sent to the Purchase department for procurement of the items. While preparation of the issue voucher is a manual operation, purchase requisition is prepared on a computer and a file maintained to follow up procurement in time. Let us look at this aspect in detail.

The file layout of purchase requisition file could be as follows.

Serial No.	*Description*	*Type*	*Width*	*Dec*	*Remarks*
1.	Item Code	Character	6	-	
2.	Description of Item	Character	30	-	
3.	Manufacturer's Name	Character	30	-	
4.	Per number of manufacturer	Character	15	-	
5.	Unit of measure	Character	2	-	
6.	Specification of items	Character	25	-	Size, Colour, etc.
7.	Quantity ordered	Numeric	6	2	-
8.	Date of order	Date	8		
9.	Date of receipt of item	Date	8		
10.	Quantity received	Numeric	6	2	
11.	Purchase Requisition status	Character	1		P – Pending C – Completed
12.	From whom the order received	Character	2		

Obviously, we need a program to create and maintain the above file i.e. Add, Modify, Delete and List programs with appropriate Screen layouts and validation of data. On preparation of a purchase requisition record, the 'Quantity on Order' field in the item master file is updated to indicate that an order for the required quantity exists.

When the items ordered are received form the purchase of department, the 9th, 10th and 11th fields of the above file are updated according using the 'Modify' Program or as part of Purchase / Receipt Voucher Processing as indicated in the Receipt Voucher Processing flowchart.

Also on receipt of items ordered, the 'quantity on order' field in the item master file is reduced to the extent of the quantity now received. Using the above file a pending purchase order statement can be prepared periodically to monitor progress of receipts of items ordered.

Orders executed in full can be deleted from the above file periodically. You can also prepare certain management information reports using the above file such as

1. Details of items placed on order and time lag required to complete the order.
2. Details of items ordered on a particular manufacturer and average lead time of receipt of items.
3. Total purchases of an item in a specified quarter, etc.

These reports can be of help in procurement of materials planning which would tell upon the efficiency of the stores department.

Now coming back to the Issue Voucher topic, let us look at a typical issue voucher.

All available items of a requisition are physically issued after preparation of the issue voucher duty verified and signed by the stores officer. The receivers signature is obtained on the issue vouchers. On receipt of the duplicate copy of the issue voucher, the computer operator will enter the details into the computer and are appended to the transaction file and the item master file updated to indicate the outflow of the item from stores. The YTD Balance File is also updated to indicate cumulative issue made in the financial year. Refer to the YTD balance file layout, filed number 6 & 7 titled 'Issue Quantity' and 'Issue Value'.

Purchase / Issue Returns

Items received into stores are sometimes found to be defective or of substandard quality and therefore has to be returned to the supplies. When this sort of a situation arises, a purchase return voucher is prepared indicating therein the quantity being returned, the item code, item description, date of receipt, receipt voucher reference, value of the items returned and the reason for rejection. When the purchase return voucher is prepared and authorized by an officer, the relevant items are physically returned back to the purchase department who takes the responsibility of getting suitable replenishment from the original supplier or compensation thereof.

The inventory control system treats a Purchase Return very similar to an Issue form Stores, except that the transaction type is recorded as PR to later analyze the frequency of such returns and to differentiate them from actual issues made for business purposes. Thus when a Purchase return record is entered into the computer, it is appended to the transaction file, the item master file is updated to show the now quantity on hand, the YTD balance is also updated to show the to date purchase return quantities and value.

Similarly items issued form stores are also returned to the stores by the user departments for various reasons.

1. The items issued are defective, substandard or of wrong specifications.
2. The user department misjudged the requirement of the item.
3. For experimenting purposes, an item may be requisitioned from the store and on diagnosis of the fault in a machine, it is found that this item is no more required to be replaced.
4. Over requisition of items. For example, 5Kgs of Grease had been ordered for servicing a machinery and on completion of the job, there was a balance of 2 Kgs of the item which is then returned to the store.

The computerized stock control system treats all issue returns similar to receipt of an item and prepare an Issue return Voucher with identical details that is contained in a Receipt Voucher except that the transaction type is recorded as IR. This type of transaction is also appended to the transaction file for later analysis. The item master file is updated to the reflect the quantity now on hand and the YTD balance file cumulates the issue return quantities and value. The Processing logic of the above two types of transactions are similar to the receipts/ Issue Voucher processing and therefore are not repeated here.

We have now seen the overall logistics of the functioning of an inventory control system and before discussing the various reports that are prepared for efficient inventory control, let us look at the functions of the stores department without efficient execution of which, a well designed inventory control system would be of little use.

1. Develop improved tools, methods and procedures as aid to effective and efficient receiving, storing, issuing of items from the stores.

2. Improve the equipment and layout of storage.
3. Periodically evaluate the performance of the stores personnel.
4. Never to allow stock of items to fall below the minimum level or to go above the maximum level and to place purchase orders with the purchase department for fresh supply of stock when the stock reaches the reorder level.
5. Check all items on receipts for defect, wrong specifications etc. and store them safely in the allocated place without delay.
6. Ensure proper distribution of items indented and control waste e.g. 5 liters of petrol should be issued on a six litre can to avoid spillage on transportation.
7. Update computer records immediately on completion of a transaction.
8. Avoid wastage, pilferage and deterioration of items by use of bins, bin cards, containers, racks, shelfs and receptacles to accommodate perishable and old stock in such a manner that those longest in stock are issued first.
9. Refuse entry to all unauthorized persons into the stores department and issue of items to be done only against proper item requisitions.
10. Use appropriate methods to symbolize, code and identification of items.

Reports

No planning and control would ever be possible without information. In a computerized system, information is provided in the form of reports either printed on paper or displayed on the screen if one has access to the computer terminal.

For proper inventory control, stock of items should be physically checked periodically and compared with the recorded quantities on hand in the item master file. For this purpose, periodically, a report of items in stock is printed in the bin location order to facilitate checking. Items need not necessarily be stocked in one room and in large organization a warehouse would be available to store all items. Often there would more than one warehouse in large production company. The bin location code thus identifies the exact location of the item and when the reports is prepared in bin location order, it is easy for the checking personnel to carry out the physical verification of the items in stock. This report printing program should be written for selective printing, that is from a given item number to a given item number, or for a specific category of items or for all items in a particular location etc. it would be impractical to check all items in stock periodically and what is usually done is only a random checking. The item master file is sorted on the required key.

Purchase Register

All purchase made during a specified period (weekly, monthly, quarterly, half yearly or annually) are printed and a hard copy maintained for management analysis. The input data for preparing this report is the Transaction file (transaction type RP).

Normally this report is printed date wise, item code wise with total values of items purchased for every date. The description of the item is not contained in the transaction file and it is picked up from the item master file.

As a by-product of the above program, a file containing items that are kept in stock in excess of the maximum level is created and a separate report is printed out. This report is a useful management information and suitable action can be initiated to avoid recurrence of such overstocking.

Issue Register

Similar to the purchase register, issue register is also printed periodically using the transaction file (type IS) and the item master file. Date wise subtotals of value of items issued and grand total at the end of the report should be printed. Description of the item is picked up from the master file. As a by product of this program, a file is created containing items that have fallen below the minimum stock level and an understock report is printed. The report is a very important management tool to take immediate action to replenish the items below minimum level. Sometimes an automatic purchase requisition can be generated to supply items below danger level and consequent 'Quantity on order' field updating in the item master file.

Purchase / Issue Return Register

The above registers are also printed periodically to monitor the frequency of such operations. If there are a high incidence of returns, the reasons thereof should be investigated. Perhaps items supplied by a particular supplier could be substandard and in such cases supplier could be back listed. Certain departments could be very casual in ordering items from the stores and frequently return items issued to them. Such departments can be pulled up to desist.

Adjustment Report

Adjustment done to quantity on hand contained in the item master file due to discrepancies in stock on physical verification are monitored through this report. The management control report could highlighted storage deficiency of items, possible thefts, pilferage and wrong measurements while issuing of items etc. and suitable remedial measures taken. Essentially all the above are routine periodical reports. There are other reports required for Accounting and Costing purposes. They are the Consumption analysis and Stores Ledger which are being discussed below.

Consumption Analysis

Issue register is a detailed list of issues made from the stores datewise and this is just a report keeping report. We must also know itemwise issued data for effective inventory control. This is achieved by production of the following reports.

1. Itemwise quantity and value of stores issue.
2. Categorywise issue of items report.
3. Account headwise issue analysis report.

Itemwise Issue Report

From the transaction file, all 'IS' types of records are selected and sorted on item code. There would be more than one record for each item code and quantities and values of all records for every item code is totalled and printed in this report. The report is also printed periodically from a given date to a given date which is printed in the report. This gives an idea to management which items are being used up more frequently and its value content.

Categorywise Consumption Analysis

Issue transacrion from the transaction file and category, subcagegory information form the item master file are extracted and a separate file created for printing the above analysis. This file is sorted on Category / Subcategory codes and a summarized total of values and count of issues are printed.

Account Headwise Issue Analysis

In the issue transactions, there is a field titled 'To whom Issued'. The department'/ cost centre code is usually entered here. Sometimes the charging account head is given here instead. Items issued are analyzed in this report based on this field and the total value of issues to this head are debited to the user department or the account head. The issue transactions are sorted on the above field to produce the report.

Slow/Fast Moving Items Report

On examining the 'last issue date' column of the item master record which is updated whenever an issue of that item is made, we can find out which items are not moving at all and which are the obsolete items. In conjunction with the 'local status' flag which gives an indication to the availability of the item locally, management decisions could be made as to what should be the minimum, maximum and danger levels of the item. You can consider an item to be slow moving if within a quarter there has been issues of say less than ten units of the item. This criterion could vary from organization to organization to organization and it is the management who defines this term for the respective organizations.

Similarly you can classify an item to be a fast moving one if there are issues of say one hundred units of the item in a quarter. Again, this is organization dependent. The algorithm to be followed for printing these reports periodically (normally quarterly) should be ascertained before writing the Computer Program form the stores department personnel. Occasionally, the criterion varies from item to item too and in such instances, process logic should be suitably designed.

For preparing the above reports once in a quarter, you should use the quarter's transaction file (issues only) and the quarter end item master file. The issue transaction file is used to count the number of times the issues were made of a particular item. The last issue date, quantity on hand and other details are taken from the item master. Items that have moved more than say ten times in a quarter are excluded form this report as these are obviously not slow moving. This is an exception report and should not run into too many pages.

Items that have not moved at least one hundred items in a quarter are excluded from this report. This also is an exception report. Particular care should be taken to have these items in stock in adequate quantities if the items are not available locally. The lead time of procurement of these items should be specially borne in mind when deciding the minimum and danger levels.

A B C Analysis

The value to categorize items into A, B and C are input from the terminal and once in an year, the 'item class' field in the master file is updated after checking the YTD balance file and analysing the cumulative value of issues of the items in the year. The item master file is updated to change the 'item class' based on the total issues in a year which is available in YTD balance file. The updated item master is sorted on item class and together with the year transaction file indexed on item code (only 'IS' type of transactions), the ABC analysis is prepared. Some organizations follow a different criteria in classifying the items. Items with a higher investment value are grouped under class A, items of medium value investment grouped under class B and items of lower investment grouped under class C. For example, items with unit rate of above Rs 1000 can be classified as A, while items with a unit rate of less than Rs 100 classified C. All other items are put under the B class. Stock pilling of A class items should be avoided as it would block a larger investment in stock. To prepare ABC analysis as above, we need the item master file and the transaction files (RP transaction types). As explained earlier, the item master should be updated for the 'item class', sorted on this class and the total purchases accumulated for each class from the receipt/ purchase records of the transaction file.

Stock Leader

This is monthly report where details of all transactions of every item are printed and the closing balance ascertained as per the records maintained in the computer. The purchase and issues are the net figures of the transactions after adjusting for purchase and issue returns. The item master file of the beginning of the month and the month's transaction file are the input data files required to print this report.

Alternatively, the backup of the YTD balance file of the previous month end and the current month end balance file can be used to find out the total of the transaction figures. The item master file to get the opening stock of the month is anyway required.

Year End Processing

The Item Master File is copied as backup to reflect the closing stock of the financial year and safely kept in custody on the last day of the financial year after working hòurs. Similarly the transaction file and the YTD balance files are also backed up and preserved. For the new financial year, we will create an empty transaction file with no records in it by copying the structure of the file only. In the YTD balance file, except for the item code, all other fields are initialized zero. Thereafter the quantity on hand and the unit rate of the item are copied from the year end item master file which would be the opening stock for the current financial year.

Periodic Housekeeping

The item master file, transaction files and the YTD balance files are the backbone of the inventory system when computerized and any damage to these files can be catastrophic to the running of the organization. These files get updated whenever a transaction takes place and reflect and up to date information at any given point of time. Damage to these files can occur due to computer hardware failure, media corruption and deliberate sabotages by disgruntled employees, etc. To safeguard from possible damages, periodic backup of the above files should be taken and kept in safe custody. In the unfortunate even of any of the files getting corrupted, we can thus recreate the file from backup copies and the transactions redone form this point of last backup.

Stores Department of an organization is managed by a Stores Officer. Usually there are three sections within the stores department. Receiving and Issue sections and Warehouses where items are physically stocked and controlled by a Store Keeper. User departments interact with the stores department for their requirements of items. The Stores department liaison with the Purchase department for procurement of materials to be stocked and issued.

COMPUTERIZED INVOICING SYSTEM

An invoice is a bill, which is sent to the customer after the goods have been dispatched. In most of the business concerns the items are sold on credit. When the customer receives an invoice, he verifies the invoices against the goods received by him, verifies the value on a voice and if the invoice is valid, he makes the payment.

When the accounts department receives the payments from the customer, the payments are matched against the respective invoices. In this case, the following points are to be noted.

a. The payment may be for once invoice

b. The payment may be for part of the invoice

c. The payment may be for many invoices

d. There could be an advance from the customer

It is upto the accountant to adjust the payments against the respective invoices. In case of multiple invoices, the older invoice is adjusted first. When the payment for an invoice is complete, the invoice is marked as complete, otherwise it is treated as an outstanding invoice.

Data Entry Screen for Preparation of Invoice

The following figure shows the data entry screen for preparation of invoice. Some validations checks to be made on the invoicing System

INVOICE DATA ENTRY

Date:

Invoice No. *Invoice Date* *Delivery Challan*

Customer code

name

address

Details of items in Invoice

Sr. No.	Iteme Code	Description	Rate	Qty Sold	Value

Some of the validation checks performed in an invoicing system are as follows:

a. Invoice number should be unique

b. Challan number should be unique

c. Customer number should be validated in the customer master file and the customer name and address should be displayed on the screen.

d. At least one item detail should be present.

e. Item Code should be validated in the item master file. If the item code is valid then Qty must be greater than 0.

f. Value is rate (x) qty sold.

g. Sales tax, transportation and discount are not mandatory.

h. Invoice number, Invoice date and cust-id in the invoice detail file should be replaced with details from the invoice date entry screen.

i. Item master file should be updated by decreasing qty sold.

j. If there is not enough quantity on hand, then appropriate error message should be displayed

k. If there is any advance by the customer, then the advance should be adjusted in the final value of the invoice and accordingly the accounts master file should be updated.

Receipt Data Entry

It is very much similar to the Invoice Data Entry form. Only this is that here you have receipt number and details instead of customer.

Validations of Vouchers and Customer Codes

a. Voucher Number should be unique.

b. Customer Code should be validated with the customer master file.

c. When Customer code is valid then the system should check for any pending invoices. If there are no pending invoices then the entire amount should be treated as advance.

d. In case there are pending invoices, a list of these invoices in the form of popup should be displayed. It should be left to the operator to adjust the value of receipt against the invoices.

e. Care should be taken that the same invoice is adjusted twice in the same receipt.

f. Any invoice entered should be checked for from the same customer it should be a pending invoice.

g. In case there is some amount left after the adjustments, then it should be treated as advance.

h. Any advance value should be updated with the advance field in the account master file.

All other invoice numbers should be validated against the appropriate invoice numbers in the invoice file.

Reports

Following reports are created in an Invoicing system

Sales Register

It has the sales done on per day basis. With details of delivery challan number, invoice number, quantity, value and other details.

Party wise Sales

Most of the figures here are the same as sales register, but, they are listed here party wise, for following up with the parties.

Receipt Register

Most of the figures here are the same as shown in receipt voucher and sales register.

Outstanding Invoices

The registe for this could be similar to the one shown here.

OUTSTANDING INVOICES REPORT

Invoice No.	*Date*	*Cust Details*	*Inv. Value*	*Amt. Received*	*Balance*
1.	-	-	-	0..00	0.00
2.	-	-	-	0.00	0.00
-	-	-	-	0.00	0.00

Let us Revise

1. Accounting is an important part of any company's computerization.
2. Accuracy is the most important as regards accounting data is concerned which is often lost in a manual system.
3. The first step in computerizing an accounting system is to identify the heads of accounts required and code them as appropriate.
4. Classification of account heads is not a very difficult job as you can seek the help of the Accountant who are quite familiar with the specific requirements of an organization.
5. Accounts master file is designed depending on whether you are going to do batch processing or on line processing.
6. Current Balance is the latest balance up to the last transaction entered into the computer.
7. Opening Balance is the balance in respect of the account number as at the beginning of every calendar month.
8. While a debit mount is entered as such, a credit amount is prefixed by a minus sign.
9. When an invoice is printed, it represents a sales activity.
10. In the manual accounting system, the main journal of accounts is subdivided into many subsidiary journals like Cash Book, Bank Book, Sales Journal/Register. Purchase Journal/register, Debit note Journal or Goods Returns Outward Book and Credit note Journal or Goods Returns Inward Book.
11. Ledger is the main book of accounts and is the final book of accounting entries.
12. Trial Balance prints only the summary of accounts.
13. The purpose of preparing the account is to find out the net profit made by the organization, during a particular period.
14. Assets are the value of properties in possession of the company including all the receivables and recoverablles from debtors and other sources.
15. Liabilities are the source or causes of all liabilities which the organization owes to or is indebted to pay to others including the liabilities to the owners of the organization in the form of capital, net profit, reserves, accumulated profits in any form, provisions for various purposes and funds created out of profits.
16. Payroll is probably the most important application of any company.
17. Master Information contains information which usually does not change.
18. When a employee joins an organization, he is allotted a number.
19. Probably the most important part of the payroll.
20. Muster roll prints out the complete information about the salary master.
21. Inventory Control is another important computer application of an organization.
22. On receipt of the stores requisition form, the stores department prepares an Issue Voucher for all items available ex-stock.
23. Items received into stores are sometimes found to be defective or of substandard quality and therefore has to be returned to the supplies.
24. Stock ledger is monthly report where details of all transactions of every item are printed and the closing balance ascertained as per the records maintained in the computer.
25. An invoice is a bill, which is sent to the customer after the goods have been dispatched.
26. Sales Register has the sales done on per day basis.
27. Any invoice entered should be checked for from the same customer it should be a pending invoice.
28. Invoice number, Invoice date and cust-id in the invoice detail file should be replaced with details from the invoice date entry screen.

Multiple Choice Questions

1. Land & Building form part of :
   (a) Assets (b) Liabilities
   (c) Both
2. Salaries and Allowances are part of :
   (a) Income (b) Sale
   (c) Expenditure
3. The latest balance up to the last transaction entered into the computer is called :
   (a) Opening Balance
   (b) Closing Balance
   (c) Current Balance
4. The main book of accounts is called :
   (a) Ledger (b) Cash book
   (c) Day book
5. For seeing the profit earned by the organization, we would look into :
   (a) Ledger (b) Cash book
   (c) Profit and Loss Acount
6. Payslips have printed on them :
   (a) Earnings (b) Deductions
   (c) Both
7. Provident Fund is :
   (a) Earnings (b) Deductions
   (c) Both
8. Special Allowance is :
   (a) Earnings (b) Deductions
   (c) Both

True/False Questions

1. Accounting is an important part of any company's computerization.
2. The first step in computerizing an accounting system is to identify the heads of accounts required and code them as appropriate.
3. Accounts master file is designed depending on whether you are going to do batch processing or on line processing.
4. Opening Balance is the latest balance up to the last transaction entered into the computer.
5. While a debit mount is entered as such, a credit amount is prefixed by a minus sign.
6. When an invoice is printed, it represents a purchase activity.
7. Ledger is the main book of accounts and is the final book of accounting entries.
8. Trial Balance prints only the summary of accounts.
9. Payroll is probably the most important application of any company.
10. Master Information contains information which usually change.
11. Probably the most important part of the payroll.
12. Muster roll prints out the complete information about the salary master.
13. Stock ledger is monthly report where details of all transactions of every item are printed and the closing balance ascertained as per the records maintained in the computer.
14. An invoice is a bill, which is sent to the customer after the goods have been received.
15. Sales Register has the sales done on per day basis.
16. Any invoice entered should be checked for from the same customer it should be a pending invoice.

Matching Columns

Match the text in Column A with the text in Column B.

Column A	Column B
1. Dearness Allowance	a. Deductions
2. Home Loan	b. Earnings

3.	Special Allowance	c.	Deductions
4.	LIC Premium	d.	Earnings
5.	Washing Allowance	e.	Deductions
6.	Provident Fund	f.	Earnings
7.	City Compensatory	g.	Deductions
8.	Furniture rent	h.	Earnings

Fill in the Blanks with Appropriate Words

a. Balance Sheet b. Trial balance c. In the beginning d. Payslips
e. Monthly f. Anytime

1. Closing balance in computerized accounting system can be calculated ________.
2. Trial balance is usually printed ________.
3. Assets and Liabilites form part of ________.
4. ________ is printed to tally the accounts.
5. Accounts Master file is created ________.
6. The main output of the Payroll system is ________.

Descriptive Type Questions

1. Describe the various steps involved in Computerized Accounting.
2. What are the various earnings and deductions in payroll system?
3. What does the payroll master contain?
4. How the inventory is controlled in the organizations using computers?
5. How does computer help in printing invoices?
6. Describe the various reports printed in accounting system.

Answers to Objective Type Questions

Multiple Choice Questions

1. a	2. c	3. c	4. a
5. c	6. c	7. b	8. a

True/False Questions

1. T	2. T	3. T	4. F
5. T	6. F	7. T	8. T
9. T	10. F	11. T	12. T
13. T	14. F	15. T	16. T

Matching Columns

1. b	2. a	3. d	4. c
5. f	6. e	7. h	8. g

Fill in the Blanks with Appropriate Words

1. f	2. e	3. a	4. b
5. c	6. d		

Recommended Readings

1. Learn to Program Visual Basic—Databases *by John Smiley.*
2. Learn to Program Visual Basic—Objects *by John Smiley.*
3. Learn to Program Visual Basic—Examples *by John Smiley.*

—Published by Firewall Media (An Imprint of Laxmi Publications Pvt. Ltd.)

16 Visual FoxPro Programming Examples

INTRODUCTION

In this chapter I give few programmes to run and see the results. First study them, then type them and then run. Please note that all database programs allow you to write the commands as only 4 characters the rest of the characters are assumed. So, if in programs you find RETU written instead of RETURN, then do not worry it means the same and the software would readily accept it.

PROGRAM 1

A file R_date.dbf has the following structure:

Field	*Field code*	*Type*	*Width*
Employee Code	Empcode	N	20
Department	Dept	C	
Employee Name	EmpName	C	
Retirement Date	Retdate	D	

Check for retirement dates and print out a report giving details of the employees who are retiring on or before 31st December, 2003. The date in the file is in formate MM/DD/YY but should be printed in DD/MM/YY format.

Program for writing the same would be:

```
* PROGRAM TO PRINT THE DETAILS OF EMPLOYEES WHOSE RETIRE ON OR BEFORE
31ST DEC 2003
SET TALK OFF
SET SAFETY OFF
SET PRINT ON
SET DATE BRITISH
USE RETDATE
INDEX ON RETDATE TO RET
? "DETAIL OF EMPLOYEED WHOSE RETDATE IS ON OR BEFORE 31ST DEC 2003"
LIST EMPCODE, EMPNAME, DEPT, RETDATE FOR RETDATE <= CTOD("12/31/03")
CLOSE DATABASE
SET TALK ON
SET SAFETY ON
```

PROGRAM 2

Here is a very simply library program. The data in the library file is stored using the following structure:

Field Description	*Field Name*	*Type*	*Width*
Title	Title	C	50
Author	Author	C	30
Book Classification no	Class	C	10
Details	Detail	M	10
Quantity instock	Stock	N	3
Quantity Issued	Issued	N	3

Based upon the table, create a query to find out whether a particular book is available. The following program would do the same for you.

```
*  A PROGRAM TO INQUIRING WHETHER PARTICULAR BOOK IS AVAILABLE.
USE LIBRARY INDEX TITLE
*TITLE.IDX IS INDEX FILE ON THE TITLE FIELD
CLEAR
STORE SPACE(50) TO WHICH_BOOK
@3,0 SAY "ENTER BOOK NAME TO SEARCH" GET WHICH_BOOK
READ
SEEK WHICH_BOOK
   IF FOUND()
      LIST WHILE TITLE = WHICH_BOOK
   ELSE
      @ 5,0 SAY "SPECIFIED BOOK NOT FOUND..."
   ENDIF
```

PROGRAM 3

Based upon the same data which you had used in the above program, find out the details of a particular book. The following program would do this for you.

```
*  PROGRAM TO QUERY INQUIRING THE DETAILS OF A PARTICULAR BOOK
USE LIBRARY INDEX FILE
CLEAR
STORE SPACE(50) TO WHICH_BOOK
@ 3,0 SAY "ENTER BOOK NAME TO SEARCH" GET WHICH_BOOK
READ
SEEK WHICH_BOOK
IF FOUND()
   ?" TITLE: ", TITLE
   ?" AUTHOR:   ", AUTHOR
   ?" CLASS NO: ", CLASS
   ?" QUANTITY INSTROCK: ", STOCK
   ?" QUANTITY ISSUED: ", ISSUED
```

```
    ?" DETAILS: ", DETAIL
ELSE
    @ 5,0 SAY "SPECIFIED BOOK NOT FOUND...."
ENDIF
```

PROGRAM 4

Again based on the above file, find out about the books written by the same author. The following program would do the same for you.

```
* PROGRAM TO QUERY INQUIRING ABOUT BOOK WRITTEN BY AN AUTHOR
USE LIBRARY INDEX AUTHOR
* AUTHOR.IDX IS INDEX FILE ON THE AUTHOR FIELD
CLEAR
    WRITER = SPACE(30)
@ 3,0 SAY "ENTER AUTHOR NAME..." GET WRITER
READ
SEEK WRIOTER
IF FOUND()
        LIST WHILE AUTHOR = WRITER
    ELSE
    ? WRITER," - AUTHOR NOT FOUND"
    ENDIF
```

PROGRAM 5

In an organization the master file contains all the information about the employee. Read the master and find out the records which are duplicate, i.e., they have the same emp number. If found print their names and date of birth. The following program would do the same for you.

```
* PROGRAM TO PRINT DUPLICATE RECORDS CONTAINING SAME EMP NUMBER.
SET TALK OFF
SET SAFETY OFF
USE COMPANY
INDEX ON EMP_NO TO EMPMAST
@5,10 SAY "EMP_NO"
@5,30 SAY "EMP_NAME"
@5,50 SAY "EMP_DOB"
?REPLICATE ("_",80)
DO WHILE .NOT. EOF()
    STORE EMP_NO TO CHECK
    SKIP
    IF EMP_NO = CHECK
    SKIP -1
    DO WHILE EMP_NO = CHECK
```

```
* LIST EMPLOYEE NAME AND DATE OF BIRTH
?SPACE(10)+EMP_NO+SPACE(18) +EMP_NAME+SPACE(8)+DTOC(EMP_DOB)
SKIP
ENDDO
   ENDIF
ENDDO
CLOSE DATABASES
SET TALK ON
SET SAFETY ON
```

PROGRAM 6

Write a program to calculate and display the sum of series 4, 8….40, i.e., 10 numbers in the series. The following program would do the same for you.

```
*  PROGRAM TO CALCULATE AND DISPLAY THE SUM OF SERIES 5, 10….50
SET TALK OFF
STORE 0 TO T, RESULT
DO WHILE T < 10
INPUT "ENTER A NUMBER" TO NUM
RESULT = RESULT + NUM
T = T + 1
ENDDO
?" SUM OF NUMBERS = ", RESULT
```

PROGRAM 7

A student file contains student code, name of the student and the courses taken by him. The file is indexed on student code. The following program takes a master code and compares it with the code of the student, if found it prints the name and course, else it skips. The program terminates if the master code is 0.

```
* PROGRAM TO PRINT NAME AND COURSE FOR A STUDENT RECORD WHOSE STCODE
MATCHES MCODE
SET TALK OFF
SET SAFETY OFF
USE STUDENT
INDEX ON STCODE TO CODE
STORE SPACE(3) TO MCODE
DO WHILE .T.
@ 8,5 SAY "ENTER STCODE OR 000 TO END" GET MCODE
READ
IF MODE <> "000"
   FIND &MCODE
IF .NOT. FOUND()
CLEAR
? "CLEAR NOT FOUND:" +MCODE
```

```
ELSE
CLEAR
DISPLAY NAME, COURSE
ENDIF
IF MCODE = "000"
EXIT
ENDIF
ENDDO
ENDIF
CLEAR ALL
SET TALK ON
SET SAFETY ON
```

PROGRAM 8

Create a program file to calculate and display the sum of numbers 5 to 25. The following program would do this for you.

```
*  PROGRAM TO CALCULATE AND DISPLAY THE SUM OF NUMBERS 5 TO 25.
SET TALK OFF
STORE 5 TO NUM
STORE 0 TO RESULT
DO WHILE NUM <=25
RESULT = RESULT + NUM
? NUM
NUM = NUM+1
ENDDO
?" SUM OF NUMBERS 5 TO 25:", RESULT
```

PROGRAM 9

For a school create a student database with the following structure.

Field Name	*Type*	*Width*	*Dec*
Stu_name	C	30	
Age	N	3	
Class	C	5	
Address	C	30	
RollNo	N	4	

Now using this information, create a main menu for student file maintenance modules. The following program would do the same for you.

```
* MAIN MENY FOR ADDING, DELETING, MODIFYING A STUDENT RECORD
SET TALK OFF
```

```
SET SAFETY OFF
CLEAR
USE STUDT
INDEX ON ROLLNO TO STUDT
DO WHILE .T.  && INFINITE LOOP
   MROLL = 0
   MOPTION = 0
   MNAME = SPACE (30)
   MAGE = 0
   MCLASS = SPACE(5)
   MADDR = SPAC(30)
   @ 5, 8 TO 22,45 DOUBLE && DRAW BOX
   @ 8,20 SAY "MAIN MENU"
   @ 9,20 SAY "————————"
   @10,10 SAY "1. ADD A STUDENT RECORD"
   @11,10 SAY "2. DELETE A STUDENT RECORD"
   @12,10 SAY "3. MODIFY A STUDENT RECORD"
   @13,10 SAY "4. EXIT TO PROMPT"
   @20,10 SAY "ENTER YOUR CHOICE" GET MOPTION PICTURE "9"
   READ
   DO CASE
   CASE MOPTION = 1
      DO ADDSTUD
   CASE MOPTION = 2
      DO DELSTUD
   CASE MOPTION = 3
      DO MODSTUD
   CASE MOPTION = 4
      EXIT
   OTEHRWISE
      WAIT WINDOW "INVALID OPTION"
   ENDCASE
ENDDO
CLOSE ALL
CLEAR
RETURN
```

PROGRAM 10

Based upon the information given above, create a module to add students records

```
* PROGRAM TO DISPLAY THE DATA ENTRY SCREEN
```

```
CLEAR
ANS = "Y"
DO WHILE UPPER(ANS) = "Y"
   STORE 0 TO MROLL, MAGE
   STORE SPACE(30) TO MNAME, MADDR
   STORE SPACE(5) TO MCLASS
   @7,7 TO 16,65 DOUBLE
   @8,25 SAY "DATA ENTRY SCREEN"
   @9,25 SAY "―――――――――――――――――"
   @10,10 SAY "ENTER ROLL NO : "
   @11,10 SAY "ENTER NAME        : "
   @12,10 SAY "ENTER CLASS       : "
   @13,10 SAY "ENTER AGE         : "
   @14,10 SAY "ENTER ADDRESS: "
   @10,32 GET MROLL PICTURE "9999"
   READ
   SEEK MROLL
   IF FOUND()
   @22,10 SAY "STUDENT ALREADY EXIST, TRY ANOTEHR"
   @23,10 SAY "PRESS A KEY TO CONTINUE"
   WAIT " "
   @22,0 CLEAR
   LOOP
   ENDIF

   @11,32 GET MNAME PICUTRE "@!"
   @12,32 GET MCLAS PICUTRE "@!"
   @13,32 GET MAGE PICUTRE "999"
   @14,32 GET MADDR PICUTRE "@!"
   READ
   @20,10 SAY "IS THE DATA OK Y/N" GET ANS PICTURE "Y"
   READ
   IF UPPER(ANS) = "Y"
   APEND BLANK
   REPLACE ROLLNOWITH MROLL
   REPLACE STU_NAMEWITH MNAME
   REPLACE AGEWITH MAGE
   REPLACE CLASSWITH MCLASS
   REPLACE ADDRESSWITH MADDR
   ENDIF
```

```
   @22,10 SAY "CONTINUE Y/N" GET ANS PICTURE "Y"
   READ
ENDDO
CLEAR
RETURN
```

PROGRAM 11

Still using the same information, create a module to delete student record

```
* PROGRAM TO DELETE STUDENT RECORD
CLEAR
MROLL = 0
ANS = "Y"
@10,10 SAY "ENTER THE ROLL NUMBER "
@10,32 SAY GET MROLL PICTURE "9999"
READ
SEEK MROLL
IF .NOT. FOUND()
   @22,10 SAY "STUDENT NOT EXIST"
ELSE
   @22,10 SAY "ARE YOU SURE Y/N ? " GET ANS PICTURE "Y"
   READ
   IF UPPER(ANS) = "Y"
      DELETE
   ENDIF
ENDIF
CLEAR
RETURN
```

PROGRAM 12

Still on the same file, create a module to modify students record.

```
* PROGRAM TO EDIT STUDENT RECORD
CLEAR
ANS = "Y"
DO WHILE UPPER(ANS) = "Y"
   STORE 0 TO MROLL
   @7,7 TO 16,65
   @8,25 SAY "DATA MODIFY SCREEN"
   @9,25 SAY "——————————————————"
   @10,10 SAY "ENTER THE ROLL NO : "
   @11,10 SAY "ENTER THE NAME       : "
```

```
@12,10 SAY "ENTER THE CLASS       : "
@13,10 SAY "ENTER THE AGE         : "
@14,10 SAY "ENTER THE ADDRESS: "
@10,32 GET MROLL PICTURE "9999"
READ
SEEK MROLL
IF .NOT. FOUND()
@22,10 SAY "STUDENT NOT EXIST, TRY ANOTEHR"
@23,10 SAY "PRESS A KEY TO CONTINUE"
WAIT " "
@22,0 CLEAR
LOOP
ENDIF
MNAME = STU_NAME
MADDR = ADDRESS
MAGE = AGE
MCLASS = CLASS
@11,32 GET MNAMEPICUTRE "@!"
@12,32 GET MCLASSPICUTRE "@!"
@13,32 GET MAGEPICUTRE "999"
@14,32 GET MADDRPICUTRE "@!"
READ
@20,10 SAY "IS THE DATA CORRECT Y/N" GET ANS PICTURE "Y"
READ
IF UPPER(ANS) = "Y"
REPLACE STU_NAMEWITH MNAME
REPLACE AGEWITH MAGE
REPLACE CLASSWITH MCLASS
REPLACE ADDRESSWITH MADDR
ENDIF
@22,10 SAY "CONTINUE Y/N" GET ANS PICTURE "Y"
READ
ENDDO
CLEAR
RETURN
```

PROGRAM 13

In an organization, the master file contains NAME, BASIC, HRA and TOTAL. Using a program print a report with employee name and total salary for those employees whose total salary is more than 2000, using the formula that Total salary = BASIC + HRA. Lastly, print the total number of employees with total salary more than 2000.

```
* PROGRAM TO PRINT THE TOTAL NUMBER OF EMPLOYEES WITH TOTAL SALARY
MORE THAN 2000
SET TALK OFF
USE PERSON
EMPLOYUEE = 0
@ 2,30 SYA "ABC COMPANY LTD"
@ 3,30 SAY "_______________"
? REPLICATE ("*",80)
@ 5,10 SAY "NAME"
@ 5,40 SAY "TOTAL SALARY"
? REPLICATE ("*",80)
DO WHILE .NOT. EOF()
   IF TOTAL > 2000
? SPACE(10) + NAME + SPACE(10) + STR(TOTAL)
EMPLOYEE = EMPLOYEE + 1
ENDIF
   SKIP
ENDDO
? REPLICATE ("*",80)
? "NO. OF EMPLOYEED WITH TOTAL SALARY > 2000 =", EMPLOYEE
CLOSE DATABASES
SET TALK ON
```

PROGRAM 14

A address file contains: name, address, city and pin. It is also indexed. It is required to accept a name from the user. If the file contains a matching record, it should delete that record. If no matching record is found, it should display a message – "Record not found"

The structure of the file can be:

Name	*Type*	*Width*	*Decimal*
Name	character	20	
Address	character	25	
City	character	10	
Pin	numeric	6	0

The following program would do the same for you.

```
SET STAT OFF
SET CONS OFF
SET TALK OFF
SET SAFE OFF
*** MASTER FILE
SELE A
```

```
USE ADDRESS
INDE ON NAME TAG NAME
SELE A
GO TOP
SET DEVI TO SCREE
STOR SPAC(20) TO G_NAME
DO WHILE NOT EOF()
SELE A
GO TOP
   CLEA
*** INPUT OF NAME
   @ 12,10 SAY "ENTER NAME :"
   @ 12,25 GET G_NAM PICT "! ! ! ! ! ! ! ! ! ! ! ! ! ! ! ! ! ! !
!"
   READ
   IF G_NAME=SPAC(20)
      EXIT
   ENDIF
   SELE A
   SEEK G_NAME
   IF EOF()
      WAIT WIND 'RECORD NOT FOUND....'
      SELE A
      GO TOP
   ENDIF
**** DELETING OF THE RECORD
   IF FOUND()
      RECN=RECNO()
      DELE RECO RECN
   ENDIF
   WAIT WIND
   STOR SPAC(20) TO G_NAME
ENDDO
CLOS DATA
CLEA
RETU
```

PROGRAM 15

The following program finds a telephone subscriber when his telphone number is entered. The following structure can be used:

Field name	*Type*	*Width*	*Description*
Tele_subc	Character	30	Name of the subscriber
Tele_number	Number	07	Telephone number
Address	Character	50	Address of the premises

```
* PROGRAM FOR DISPLAY TELEPHONE SUBSCRIBER INFORMATION
SET STAT ON
SET TALK OFF
SET CONF OFF
SET SAFE OFF
SELE A
USE PHONE
INDE ON TELE_NUMBE TAG TELE_NUMBE
GO TOP
STOR 0 TO PH
DO WHILE NOT EOF()
CLEA
@ 12,10 SAY 'ENTER PHONE NUMBER :'
@ 12,40 GET PH PICT "9999999"
READ
IF PH=0
   CLOS DATA
   CLEA
   EXIT
ENDIF
SELE A
SEEK PH
IF EOF()
   WAIT WIND "PHONE NUMBER NOT AVAILABLE IN RECORDS , TRY AGAIN...."
ENDIF
IF FOUND()
   @ 14,10 SAY 'SUBSCRIBER NAME :'
   @ 14,40 SAY TELE_SUBSC
   @ 15,10 SAY 'SUBSCRIBER ADDRESS :'
   @ 15, 40 SAY ADDRESS
   WAIT WIND
ENDIF
STOR 0 TO PH
ENDDO
CLOS DATA
RETU
```

PROGRAM 16

A pay_roll file contains a number of records. Each record contains among other things, a field called hours_worked and another field called Rate. Each record relates to an individual employee and total_pay is calculated from the table that follows.

Hours_worked	*Total-pay*
Less than or equal to 36	Hours-worked * rate
Greater than 36 but less thanor equal to 45	36 * rate + 1.5 * rate * (hours_worked – 36)
Greater than 45	36 * rate + 13.5 * rate + 2 * rate * (hours_worked – 45)

Write a Visual FoxPro program to read a record from pay-roll calculate total-pay for each employee and to transfer control to a subroutine after each such calculations. You can use the following structure for the master payroll file.

Name	*Type*	*Width*	*Dec*
Emp_no	character	5	
Emp_name	character	30	
Emp_add	character	40	
Hours_work	numeric	3	0
Rate	numeric	2	0
Total_pay	numeric	7	2

The following program would do the same for you.

```
* PROGRAM FOR CALCULATION OF TOTAL PAY ON HOURS WORKED
SET STAT OFF
SET TALK OFF
SET SAFE OFF
SET CONF OFF
SET DATE BRIT
USE PAYROLL
INDE ON EMP_NO TO PAYROLL
USE PAYROLL INDE PAYROLL
GO TOP
STO 0 TO TOT_PAY
DO WHILE NOT EOF()
   IF HOURS_WORK <=36
      TOT_PAY = HOURS_WORK * RATE
   ENDIF
   IF HOURS_WORK > 36 AND HOURS_WORK<=45
      TOT_PAY = 36 * RATE + 1.5 * RATE * (HOURS_WORK - 36)
   ENDIF
   IF HOURS_WORK >45
      TOT_PAY = 36 * RATE +13.5 * RATE + 2 * RATE *
```

```
        ( HOURS_WORK - 45)
    ENDIF
    REPL TOTAL_PAY WITH TOT_PAY
    SKIP
    LOOP
  ENDDO
  CLOS DATA
  RETU
```

PROGRAM 17

Monica & Co. offers trade discount to established booksellers and others for a newly released best seller.

- 20% for private customers and libraries:
- 5% discount is allowed on orders for 6 books or more:
- 10% on orders for 20 books or more;
- 15% on orders for 60 or more
- Trade orders for 20 books and over receive 10% discount in addition to the trade discount.

Monica Madan, the proprietor, wants to create a sales register. She wants the system to use the following information :

Date	6	ddmmyy
Code	1	Alphanumeric (P private, L Library B Booksellers, M Miscellaneous)
Name	40	alphanueirc
Order	4	9(4)
Rate	4 + 2	Rs. 250.00 (Introductory offer for year)
N Disc	6 + 2	999V99
S Disc	6 + 2	9999V99

The reports to be generated are:

A weekly report of sales and discounts of the two types every Monday, Sunday being a holiday. A weekly report on stock balance assuming that she printed 25,000 books for sale, showing a reprint warning when the stock falls to 5,000. The author is to be take a royalty of 5% on net sales every six months and she wants a report for that too.

You can use the following structure for the book traded and the master file.

Name	*Type*	*Width*	*Decimal*
Date	D	8	
Code	C	1	
Name	C	40	
Order	N	4	0
Rate	N	4	0

N_Disc	N	6	2
S_Disc	N	6	2

Name	*Type*	*Width*	*Decimal*
Date	D	8	
Book_Name	C	20	
Balance	N	5	0

```
* PROGRAM FOR PRINTING REGISTER OF SALES AND DISCOUNTS
SET PROC TO BOOK
SET DATE BRIT
SET STAT OFF
SET TALK OFF
SET SAFE OFF
SELE A
USE BOOK_TR
INDE ON DATE TO BOOK_TR
USE BOOK_TR INDE BOOK_TR
SELE B
USE BOOK_MST
INDE ON BOOK_NAME TO BOOK_MST
USE BOOK_MST INDE BOOK_MST
STOR 0 TO CHOICE
CLEA
DO WHILE CHOICE# 6
CLEA
! 1,1 TO 3,78 DOUB
@ 2,22 SAY 'B O O K M A N & C O M P A N Y'
@ 4,1 TO 20,78 DOUB
@ 7,20 SAY 'DATA ENTRY......................................[1]'
@ 9,20 SAY 'SALES REGISTER PRINTING....................[2]'
@ 11,20 SAY 'WEEKLY REPORT - SALES/DISCOUNTS....[3]'
@ 13,20 SAY 'WEEKLY REPORT -STOCK BALANCE......[4]'
@ 15,20 SAY 'ROYALTY REPORT.............................[5]'
@ 17,20 SAY 'EXIT.............................................[6]'
@ 21,1 TO 23,78 DOUB
@ 22,20 SAY "ENTER YOUR CHOICE [ 1 TO 6 ] ...........[ ]'
@ 22,58 GET CHOICE PICT "9"
READ
```

```
IF CHOICE =1
   DO BOOK1
ENDIF
IF CHOICE =2
   DO BOOK2
ENDIF
IF CHOICE =3
   DO BOOK3
ENDIF
IF CHOICE =4
   DO BOOK4
ENDIF
IF CHOICE =5
   DO BOOK5
ENDIF
IF CHOICE =6
   DO BOOK6
   CLOS DATA
   EXIT
ENDIF
ENDDO
PROCEDURE BOOK1
**************
SET PROC TO BOOK
CLEA
STOR DATE() TO SDATE
STOR SPAC(1) TO CCD
STOR SPAC(40) TO CNAMD
STOR 0 TO OQTY,NDIC,SDISC
STOR 250 TO RRATE
STOR 'N' TO ANS
@ 1,1 TO 3,78 DOUB
@ 2,22 SAY 'B O O K M A N & C O M P A N Y'
@ 4,1 TO 20,78 DOUB
@ 6,10 SAY 'ENTER SALE DATE'
@ 6,35 GET SDATE
@ 8,10 SAY 'ENTER CUSTOMER CODE '
@ 8,35 GET CCD PICT '!'
READ
IF CCD=' '
```

```
   RETU
  ENDIF
  @ 10,10 SAY 'ENTER CUSTOMER NAME '
  @ 10,35 GET CNAME PICT "! ! ! ! ! ! ! ! ! ! ! ! ! ! ! ! ! ! ! ! ! ! ! ! ! ! ! ! ! ! ! ! ! ! ! ! ! ! ! ! ! ! ! ! ! ! ! !"
  @ 12,10 SAY 'ENTER ORDER QUANTITY'
  @ 12,35 GET OQTY
  @ 14,10 SAY 'ENTER RATE'
  @ 14,35 GET RRATE
  @ 16,10 SAY 'NORMAL DISCOUNT'
  @ 18,10 SAY 'SPECIAL DISCOUNT'
  @ 22,10 SAY 'UPDATE THE RECORD (Y/N)'
  @ 21,1 TO 23,78 DOUB
  READ
  IF CCD='P' OR CCD='L'
     PDISCR = .20
     SDISCR = 0
  ELSE
     IF CCD='M'
        IF OQTY<6
        PDISCR = 0
           SDISCR = 0
     ELSE
           IF OQTY>=6 AND OQTY<20
                 PDISCR = 0.05
        SDISCR = 0
     ELSE
                 IF OQTY>=20 AND OQTY<60
                    PDISCR = 0.10
                    SDISCR = 0
                 ELSE
                    IF OQTY>=60
                       PDISCR = 0.15
                       SDISCR = 0
                    ENDIF
                 ENDIF
           ENDIF
        ENDIF
     ENDIF
   ELSE
```

```
        IF CCD='B'
           IF OQTY<6
                 PDISCR = 0
                 SDISCR = 0
           ELSE
                 IF OQTY>=6 AND OQTY<20
                       PDISCR = 0.05
                       SDISCR = 0
           ELSE
                 IF OQTY>=20 AND OQTY<60
                       PDISCR = 0.10
                       SDISCR = 0.10
                 ELSE
                       IF OQTY>=60
                             PDISCR = 0.15
                             SDISCR = 0.10
                       ENDIF
                 ENDIF
           ENDIF
        ENDIF
     ENDIF
  ENDIF
  PDISCR = PDISCR * OQTY * RRATE
     SDISCR = SDISCR * OQTY * RRATE
  @ 16,35 SAY PDISCR PICT "9999.99"
  @ 18,35 SAY SDISCR PICT "9999.99"
  @ 22,35 GET ANS PICT '!'
  READ
  OF ANS = 'YS'
     SELE A
     APPEN BLAN
     REPLACE DATE WITH SDATE, CODE WITH CCD, NAME WITH CNAME, ORDER
  WITH OQTY
     REPLACE RATE WITH RRATE, N_DISC WITH PDISCR, S_DISC WITH SDISCR
  ENDIF
  RETU
```

PROGRAM 18

In an organization there are two type of rates for paying to the employees. One called the internal rate and the other as external rate. Each record has both internal and external rate for the employee beside the number of hours worked by him. Using a program you have to print a payroll showing the amounts and other details of the employee. The calculations can be made as below :

Payroll Amount = hours * internal rate

Amount Charged = hours * external rate

Gross Profit = amount charged – payroll amount

The report end should show the various totals.

The table can be created using the following structure:

Emp_code	C	4
Int_rate	N	3
Ext_rate	N	3
Hour_work	N	3

The following program would do the same.

```
* PRINTING PAYROLL REPORT
* PROGRAM PRINTS A REPORT FOR INTERNAL RATE AND EXTERNAL RATE PER
EMPLOYEE AND THE GROSS
* PROFIT EARNED BY THE CONSULTANCY FIRM INDIVIDUALLY AND IN TOTAL.
SET STAT OFF
SET TALK OFF
SET CONS OFF
SET CONF OFF
SET SAFE OFF
USE INT_EXT
INDE ON EMP_CODE TO INT_EXT
USE INT_EXT INDE INT_EXT
GO TOP
STOR 0 TO P_AMOUNT ,AMT_CHG , G_PROFIT
STOR 0 TO TP_AMOUNT ,TAMT_CHG ,TG_PROFIT ,AV_PROFIT

SET PRINT ON
LIN=24
SNO=0
DO WHILE NOT EOF()
*** HEADING
    IF LINE>23
        @ 1,1 SAY 'COMPANY NAME'
        @ 2,1 SAY 'NAME OF THE REPORT'
        @ 3,1 SAY REPLICATE('-',80)
        @ 4,1 SAY 'EMPLOYEE'
        @ 4,10 SAY 'HOURS'
```

```
        @ 4,20 SAY 'INTERNAL'
        @ 4,20 SAY 'INTERNAL'
        @ 4,30 SAY 'PAYROLL
        @ 4,40 SAY 'EXTERNAL'
        @ 4,50 SAY 'AMOUNT'
        @ 4,60 SAY 'GROSS'
        @ 5,10 SAY 'WORKED'
        @ 5,22 SAY 'RATE'
        @ 5,31 SAY 'AMOUNT'
        @ 5,43 SAY 'RATE'
        @ 5,50 SAY 'CHARGED'
        @ 5,60 SAY 'PROFIT'
        @ 6,1 SAY REPLICATE('-',80)
        LIN=8
     ENDIF
  **** REPORT PRINTING AND CALCULATION
     IF LIN<23
        @ LIN,3 SAY EMP_CODE
        @ LIN,13 SAY HOUR_WORK
        @ LIN,23 SAY INT_RATE
        P_AMOUNT = HOUR_WORK * INT_RATE
        AMT_CHG = HOUR_WORK * EXT_RATE
        G_PROFIT = AMT_CHG - P_AMOUINT
        @ LIN,32 SAY P_AMOUNT PICT "999999"
        @ LIN,643 SAY EXT_RATE
        @ LIN,50 SAY AMT_CHG PICT "999999"
        @ LIN,60 SAY G_PROFIT PICT "999999"
        SNO=SNO+1
        TP_AMOUNT = TP_AMOUNT + P_AMOUNT
        TAMPT_CHG = TAMT_CHG + AMT_CHG
        TG_PROFIT = TG_PROFIT + G_PROFIT
        LIN = LIN + 1
        STOR 0 TO P_AMOUNT,AMT_CHG,G_PROFIT
     SKIP
        LOOP
     ENDIF
  ENDDO
  LIN=LIN+1
  @ LIN,32 SAY '————'
  @ LIN,50 SAY '————'
```

```
@ LIN,60 SAY '————'
LIN=LIN+1
@ LIN,10 SAY 'T O T A L'
@ LIN,32 SAY TP_AMOUNT PICT "999999"
@ LIN,50 SAY TAMT_CHG PICT "999999"
@ LIN,60 SAY TG_PROFIT PICT "999999"
LIN=LIN+1
@ LIN,32 SAY '————'
@ LIN,50 SAY '————'
@ LIN,60 SAY '————'
LIN=LIN+1
@ LIN,1 SAY '**** AVERAGE GROSS PROFIT PER EMPLOYEE IS RS.'
AV_PROFIT = TG_PROFIT/SNO
AV_PROFIT = ALLTRIM(STR(AV_PROFIT))
@ LIN,48 SAY AV_PROFIT
SET PRINT OFF
* DEVI TO SCRE
CLOS DATA
RETU
```

PROGRAM 19

Write a procedure to print the name and outstanding balances using the following two data structures.

Structure 1

Field	*Width*	*Type*	*Description*
Emp_code	8	N	Employee's code
Emp_name	30	C	Employer Name

Structure 2

Field	*Width*	*Type*	*Description*
Emp_code	8	N	Employee's Code
Out_bal	13.2	N	Outstanding baqlance
City	30	C	City name

The following program would do the same for you.

```
* PROGRAM FOR PRINTING EMPLOYEE NAME AND BALANCE
* PROGRAM FOR PRINTING THE NAME AND OUTSTANDING BALANCE OF EACH
* EMPLOYEE
SET TALK OFF
SET STAT OFF
SET CONS OFF
SET SAFE OFF
```

```
SET DATE BRIT
***** TRANSACTION FILE

SELE A
USE EMP_TRAN
INDE ON EMP_CODE TO EMP_TRAN
USE EMP_TRAN INDE EMP_TRAN
GO TOP
**** MASTER FILE
SELE B
USE EMP_MST
INDE ON EMP_CODE TO EMP_MST
USE EMP_MST INDE EMP_MST
LIN=24
STOR 0 TO PAGE
DO WHILE NOT EOF()
*** HEADING
   IF LIN>23
      PAGE=PAGE+1
      @ 1,25 SAY 'ABC CO. LTD.'
      @ 2,25 SAY '                        NEW DELHI
      @ 3,1 SAY 'DATE : '
      @ 3,10 SAY DATE()
      @ 3,60 SAY 'PAGE NO:'
      @ 3,70 SAY PAGE PICT"999"
      @ 4,1 SAY REPLICATE ('=',60)
      @ 5,25 SAY ' EMPLOYEE BALANCE REPORT'
      @ 6,1 SAY REPLICATE ('=',60)
      @ 7,1 SAY 'EMPLOYE CODE'
      @ 7,18 SAY 'EMPLOYEE NAME'
      @ 7,65 SAY 'BALANCE'
      @ 8,1 SAY REPLICATE ('=',60)
      LIN=10
   ENDIF
   IF LIN<23
      SELE B
      SEEK A-> EMP_CODE
 **** PRINTING OF NAME & BALANCE
   IF FOUND()
      @ LIN, 1 SAY A->EMP_CODE
```

```
        @ LIN,18 SAY A->EMP_NAME
        @ LIN,60 SAY OUT_BAL
        LIN=LIN+1
    ENDIF
ENDIF
SELE A
LOOP
ENDDO
WAIT WIND
CLOS DATA
RETU
```

PROGRAM 20

In a school the student file each record contains the following information regarding each student:

Field	*Type*	*Width*	
Rollno	C	6	
Name	C	24	(Surname)
Initl	C	4	(Initials)
Sex	C	1	(M/F)
Engmk	N	3	
Mathmk	N	3	
Hismk	N	3	
TotMK	N	4	
Grade	C	1	

You have to write a program to create a file on total marks and within total marks on roll number. The total marks for each student is created by adding all the three subject marks obtained by the student. If total marks, are same, the record will be arranged F first and within sex, alphabetical order of the name. The following program would do the same.

```
*** PROGRAM TO CREATE A STORED FILE
SET TALK OFF
USE STUDENT
REPL ALL TOTMK WITH ENGMK + MATHMK + HISMK
REPL ALL GRADE WITH 'D' FOR (TOTMK/3) > 81
REPL ALL GRADE WITH 'A' FOR (TOTMK/3) > 71 AND (TOTMK/3) <= 81
REPL ALL GRADE WITH 'B' FOR (TOTMK/3) > 61 AND (TOTMK/3) <= 71
REPL ALL GRADE WITH 'C' FOR (TOTMK/3) > 51 AND (TOTMK/3) <= 61
REPL ALL GRADE WITH 'F' FOR (TOTMK/3) < 50
SORT ON TOTMK/A, GRADE/D, SEX,NAME/A TO MARKS
USE
```

```
CLOS DATA
```

PROGRAM 21

In an organization sales personnel information is recorded on a disk file. Each record consists of the salesperson number and amount of sales done by him/her. There can be more than one record for a person. All records pertaining to an individual are grouped together. To mark the end of the data of a salesperson, an additional record, with sales zero, is provided after all the records pertaining to that sales person. You have to write a program to calculate and print saleswise commission and also total sales and total commission for the person. Commission is to be calculated @ 10% of sales.

The following structure can be used for the sales file :

Name	*Type*	*Width*	*Dec*
S_name	C	35	
S_Value	N	10	0

The following program would do this for you.

```
* PROGRAM TO CALCULATE AND PRINT SALESWISE COMMISSION
SET STAT OFF
SET DATE BRIT
SET TALK OFF
SET CONS OFF
SET SAFE OFF
USE SAL_COM
INDE ON S_NAME TO SAL_COM
USE SAL_COM INDE SAL_COM
GO TOP
LIN=24
STOR 0 TO TSALES, TCOMM,SNO
DO WHILE NOT EOF()
STOR 0 TO TSALES, TCOMM
   S_NM1 = S_NAME
   S_NM2 = S_NM1
   SNO = 1
   DO WHILE S_NM1 = S_NM2 AND NOT EOF()
      IF LIN>23
         @ 1,1 SAY 'ABC ENTERPRISES'
         @ 2,1 SAY 'SALESWISE/SALEMANWISE COMMISSION REPORT'
         @ 3,1 SAY REPLICATE ('=',55)
         @ 4,1 SAY 'SR. NO.'
         @ 4,7 SAY 'SALES PERSON'
         @ 4,42 SAY 'SALE VALUE'
         @ 4,60 SAY 'COMMISSION'
```

```
        @ 5,1 SAY REPLICATE ('=',55)
        LIN = 7
     ENDIF
     IF LIN<23
     @ LIN,3 SAY SNO
     @ LIN, 7 SAY S_NAME
     @ LIN, 42 SAY S_VALUE

     COM = S_VALUE*.10
     @ LIN,62 SAY COM PICT "9999999.99"
     TSALES = TSALES + S_VALUE
     TCOMM = TCOMM + COM
     SNO = SNO + 1
     LIN - LIN+1
     SKIP
     S_NM2 = S_NAME
     LOOP
     ENDIF
  ENDO
     @ LIN, 3 SAY 'TOTAL'
     @ LIN,42 SAY TSALES PICT "9999999.99"
     @ LIN,62 SAY TCOMM PICT "9999999.99"
ENDDO
SET PRINT OFF
CLOS DATA
RETU
```

PROGRAM 22

Write a procedure to create birth/death register using the following information:

Field Name	*Type*	*Width*	*Description*
P_Name	C	30	Person's name
F_Name	C	30	Father's name
M_name	C	30	Mother's name
P_Address	C	50	Address of the person
B_D_Code	C	01	Birth – B; Death – D
Date	Date	8	Date of birth/death
Place	C	20	Place of birth/death
Reg_no	N	07	Registration Number

```
* A PROCEDURE TO CREATE BIRTH/DEATH REGISTER
```

```
SET TALK OFF
SET STAT OFF
SET COUNF OFF
SET SAFE OFF
USE B_D_REG
INDE ON P_NAME TO B_D_REG
USE B_D_REG INDE B_D_REG
GO TOP
LIN=66
DO WHILE NOT EOF()
IF LIN>65
   @ 1,1 SAY 'BIRTH / DEATH REGISTER AS ON
   @ 1,40 SAY DATE()
   @ 2,1 SAY REPLICATE ('=',95)
   @ 3,1 SAY 'NAME OF THE PERSON'
   @ 3,25 SAY "FATERH'S NAME"
   @ 3,45 SAY "MOTEHR'S NAME"
   @ 3,65 SAY "ADDRESS"
   @ 3,71 SAY "BIRTH/DEATH"
   @ 3,81 SAY "DATE"
   @ 3,91 SAY 'PLACE'
   @ 3,110 SAY "REGN. NO."
   @ 4,1 SAY REPLICATE ('=',95)
   LIN=6
ENDIF
   @ LIN,1 SAY P_NAME
   @ LIN,25 SAY F_NAME
   @ LIN,45 SAY M_NAME
   @ LIN,65 SAY P_ADDRESS
   @ LIN,71 SAY B_D_CODE
   @ LIN,81 SAY DATE
   @ LIN,91 SAY PLACE
   @ LIN,110 SAY REG_NO
   LIN=LIN+1
   SKIP
   LOOP
ENDDO
CLOS DATA
RETU
```

PROGRAM 23

Write a program to generate control break report of the salesman, break on region is desirable. You can use the format of the sales files shown in earlier program. The following program would do the same for you.

```
* PROGRAM FOR PRINTING REGIONWISE SALES REPORT - INDIAN OFFICE
* AUTOMATION PRODUCTS
* THIS PROGRAM PRINTS A REPORT ON REGIONWISE/SALESMANWISE SALES
* AND ALSO TOTAL SALES OF ALL REGIONS.
SET TALK OFF
SET STAT OFF
SET CONS OFF
SET SAFE OFF
SET DATE BRIT
*** TRANSACTION FILE
USE SALES
INDE ON S_REGIONS+S_NAME+PRODUCT TO SALES
USE SALES INDE SALES
GO TOP
STOR 0 TO TSALES,GTSALES, PAGE
LIN=25
DO WHILE NOT EOF()
REG1=S_REGION
REG2=REG1
DO WHILE REG1=REG2 AND NOT EOF()

*** HEADING
   IF LIN>24
      PAGE=PAGE+1
      @ 1,25 SAY 'INDIAN OFFICE AUTOMATION PRODUCTS'
      @ 2,25 SAY '                NEW DELHI
      @ 3,1 SAY 'DATE : '
      @ 3,10 SAY DATE()
      @ 3,60 SAY 'PAGE NO: '
      @ 3,70 SAY 'PAGE PICT"999"
      @ 4,1 SAY REPLICATE('=',78)
      @ 5,25 SAY ' REGION WISE SALES REPORT'
      @ 6,1 SAY REPLICATE ('=',78)
      @ 7,1 SAY 'SALESMAN NAME'
      @ 7,28 SAY 'REGION OF SALES'
      @ 7,54 SAY 'PRODCUT'
```

```
        @ 7,70 SAY 'SALES'
        @ 8,1 SAY REPLICATE ('=',78)
        LIN=10
     ENDIF
*** PRINTING TILL THE REGION IS SAME
     IF LIN<24
        @ LIN,1 SAY S_NAME
        @ LIN,28 SAY S_REGION
        @ LIN,54 SAY PRODUCT
        @ LIN, 67 SAY SALES
        LIN=LIN+1
        TSALES = TSALES + SALES
        GTSALES = GTSALES + SALES

        SKIP
        REG2 = S_REGION
        LOOP
     ENDIF
ENDDO

**** REGION TOTAL SALES PRINTING
     @ LIN, 1 SAY 'SALES OF'
     @ LIN, 10 SYA REGI
     @ LIN, 67 SAY TSALES PICT "999999999"
     LIN=LIN+2
     STOR 0 TO TSALES

ENDDO
**** TOTAL SALES FOR ALL REGIONS PRINTING
     LIN=LIN+2
     @ LIN, 1 SAY 'TOTAL SALES'
     @ LIN, 67 SAY GTSALES PICT "999999999"
     LIN=LIN+2
     @ LIN,1 SAY REPLICATE ('=',80)

WAIT
CLOS DATA
RETU
```

PROGRAM 24

A table address contains name and address of employees working in a company. Write a program to accept the name of person in a variable and check if it exists in the table. If yes, displays the name and age from the table, otherwise display a message = "name not found".

You can use the following structure for the name file.

Name	*Type*	*Width*	*Decimal*
Name	character	25	
Age	numeric	2	0

The following program would do the same for you.

```
* PROGRAM FOR DISPLAY OF NAME AND AGE
* THIS PROGRAM ACCEPTS NAME OF AN EMPLOYEE AND DISPLAYS THE AGE
* AFTER LOCATING THE NAME
SET STAT OFF
SET CONS OFF
SET TALK OFF
SET SAFE OFF

**** MASTER FILE
SELE A
USE NAMEAGE
INDE ON NAME TO NAMEAGE
USE NAMEAGE INDE NAMEAGE
SELE A
GO TOP
SET DEVI TO SCREE
STOR SPAC(25) TO G_NAME
DO WHILE NOT EOF()
SELE A
GO TOP
   CLEA

***** INPUT OF EMPLOYEE NAME'
   @ 12,10 SAY "ENTER EMPLOYEE'S NAME :"
   @ 12,40 GET G_NAME PICT "! ! ! ! ! ! ! ! ! ! ! ! ! ! ! ! ! ! !
!"
   READ
   IF G_NAME=SPAC(25)
      EXIT
   ENDIF
   SELE A
```

```
    SEEK G_NAME
    IF EOF()
       WAIT WIND 'NAME NOT FOUND....'
       SELE A
       GO TOP
    ENDIF

 **** DISPLAY OF AGE AFTER LOCATING THE RECORD
    IF FOUND()
       @ 14,10 "EMPLOYEE'S AGE :"
       @ 14,40 SAY AGE
    ENDIF
    WAIT WIND
    STOR SPAC(25) TO G_NAME
 ENDDO
 CLOS DATA
 CLEA
 RETU
```

QUESTION PAPER JANUARY 2004

M1-R3: BUSINESS SYSTEMS

NOTE:

1. There are **TWO PARTS** in this Module/Paper. **PART ONE** contains **FOUR** questions and **PART TWO** contains **FOUR** questions.
2. **PART ONE** is to be answered in the **TEAR-OFF ANSWER SHEET** only, attached to the question paper, as per the instructions contained therein. **PART ONE** is **NOT** to be answered in the answer book.
3. Maximum time allotted for **PART ONE** is **ONE HOUR**. Answer book for **PART TWO** will be supplied at the table when the answer sheet for **PART ONE** is returned. However, candidates, who completes **PART ONE** earlier than one hour, can collect the answer book for **PART TWO** immediately after handling over the answer sheet for **PART ONE**.

TOTAL TIME: 3 HOURS **TOTAL MARKS: 100**

(PART ONE – 40; PART TWO – 60)

PART ONE

(Answer all the questions)

1. **Each question below gives a multiple choice of answers. Choose the most appropriate one and enter in the "tear off" answer sheet attached to the question paper, following instructions therein.** **(1 x 10)**

1.1 Using Visual FoxPro, the number of tables that we can use simultaneously is:

A) 225
B) 205
C) 255
D) 252

1.2 The Windows element in Visual FoxPro are:

A) Application Window
B) Project Manager Window
C) Command Window
D) All of the above

1.3 One of the following is not true for the Status Bar of a Visual FoxPro Window

A) the bar is placed at the bottom of the application window
B) It provides the details of the currently open window
C) an active window will make the colour of the status bar to change to dark
D) Information like OVR, NUM, Caps, etc., is displayed on the Status Bar.

1.4 Which one of the following is not true for the Memo data type in Visual FoxPro?

A) Memo fields act as variable-length character fields.
B) The limit to the length of the Memo field is 254 characters

C) Memo data type can hold scanned images and digitized sound

D) You can minpulate this data type by using any of the functions that manipulate Character fields

1.5 In an Accountant's system, collection of all money on temporary and permanent accounts is maintained in the

A) Cash journal

B) General ledger

C) Accounts payable component

D) Double entry balance system

1.6 Which of the following is a valid SQL command:

A) SELECT Emplist.lname, Emplist.fname, Wages.date, Wages.wage;
FROM Wages, Emplist;
WHERE Wages.empno = Emplist.empno

B) SELECT Emplist.lname, Emplist.fname, Wages.date, Wages.wage
FROM Wages, Emplist
WHERE Wages.empno = Emplist.empno

C) SELECT Emplist.lname, Emplist.fname, Wages.date, Wages.wage,
FROM Wages, Emplist,
WHERE Wages.empno = Emplist.empno

D) SELECT Emplist.lname, Emplist.fname, Wages.date, Wages.wage;
FROM Wages, Emplist;
WHERE Wages.empno = Emplist.empno

1.7 In a program, if you desire to exit unconditionally out of SCAN - ENDSCAN loop, you will use the following command:

A) RETURN

B) LOOP

C) SKIP

D) EXIT

1.8 The Visual FoxPro lets you use floating toolbars to work with Reports. They are:

A) Report Control toolbar

B) Layout toolbar

C) Color Palette

D) All of the above

1.9 Consider the following expressions:

A="11/08/03"

B=SUBSTR(A,7,2)

?B

What is the value of B?

A) 11/08

B) /08/03

C) 03

D) 08

1.10 Consider the following code:

Status = IIF(debit>=credit,"Amount due","Credit")

The above code is equivalent to:

A)
```
IF debit>=credit
        Status = "Amount due"
ELSE
        Status="Credit"
ENDIF
```

B)
```
IF debit>=credit
        Status="Credit"
ELSE
        Status="Amount due"
ENDIF
```

C) Both A) and B) above are correct

D) There is no equivalence of the code listed in the problem.

2. Each statement below is either TRUE or FALSE. Choose the most appropriate one and Enter in the "tear-off" sheet attached to the question paper, following instructions therein. (1 x 10)

2.1 While deciding on the media for Real Time Systems, you will ensure that it is a magnetic tape based system.

2.2 A suspense account is one, which are to be used for unforseen expenses during the financial year.

2.3 In ABC Analysis, we clasify items, which are small in numbers but contribute maximally into C category.

2.4 On the liability side of the balance sheet, you will normally keep the Reserves and the Surpluses.

2.5 In a double entry book keeping system, it is not necessary that debits equal credits.

2.6 ?? will display the contents of a field, memory variable or a result of a mathematical equation at the beginning of a new line.

2.7 UNIQUE command can be used to prevent the display or access of the duplicate records.

2.8 You can modify the structure of an existing table using the MODIFY TABLE command.

2.9 In Visual FoxPro, indexing can be done on the multiple fields of different types.

2.10 Balance Sheet shows the compnay's health at an instant while Profit and Losss Account shows the company's performance over a period of time.

3. **Match words and phrases in column X with the closest related meaning/word(s)/phrases in column Y. Enter your selection in the "tear-off" answer sheet attached to the question paper, following instructions therein.** **(1 x 10)**

X		Y	
3.1	Inventory valuation	A.	The SELECT command
3.2	Loan to employees is recorded in	B.	Uses data from an existing database file as the basis for changes to data records in the active database file.
3.3	Skills Inventory	C.	Working capital
3.4	Hash totals	D.	Subsidiary Ledger
3.5	Current assets	E.	Personnel Systems
3.6	Selects a work area	F.	It is used to remove the trailing blanks from a character string
3.7	SET RELATION	G.	Causes an active database file to appear to contain only the records meeting the specified condition
3.8	TRIM()	H.	Validation
3.9	UPDATE	I.	Links the active database file to another open database file according to key expression that is common to both files.
3.10	SET FILTER	J.	LIFO
		K.	Random access
		L.	Low Inventory Storage
		M.	Payroll Systems
		N.	SKIP

4. **Each statement below has a blank space to fit one of the words or phrases in the list below. Enter your choice in the "tear – off" answer sheet attached to the question paper, following instructions therein.** **(1 x 10)**

A.	**Record key**	**B.**	**Buffer stocks**	**C.**	**Trial Balance**
D.	**Subsidiary ledger**	**E.**	**Pseudocode**	**F.**	**Loop**
G.	**ABC Analysis**	**H.**	**Utility programs**	**I.**	**Top down**
J.	**Testing**	**K.**	**Dummy**	**L.**	**Transaction**
M.	**Books of accounts**	**N.**	**Balance sheet**		

4.1 In a ____________ approach, the main program is decomposed into progressively lower level modules.

4.2 At the end of every year the accountant carries the balance of Profit and Loss Account to ________.

4.3 A(n) ________ is a listing of the ledger of accounts, along with their net debit or credit balances.

4.4 The process of executing the developed programs with various data inputs in order to detect programming errors or an omission is called as ________.

4.5 An unique identifying value that is found in every record in a file is called as a ________.

4.6 Purchases from vendors form part of the ________.

4.7 Variations in demand of a product are taken care by carrying ________.

4.8 ________ is a programming term used to represent a set of instructions in a programme, which is to repeated.

4.9 The ________ shows classification of various stock items on the basis of their values.

4.10 A term that describes program segments written in ordinary language, rather than in a programming language is ________.

PART TWO

(Answer all questions)

5. Answer any **three** of the following in not more than 100 words:

a) Visual FoxPro permits four different types of indexes. Describe in brief about each one of the them.

b) Write the steps to change the structure of an existing table in Visual FoxPro.

c) Write the steps that you will take to create multiple key index using the Table Designer dialog box.

d) Explain with an example the use of a Macro (&) command. **(5 x 3)**

6. Answer any **three** of the following.

a) Visual FoxPro has some built in date functions by which you can do any date-oriented tasks. Describe any five of them in the following tabular format.

Date Function	Meaning of the Date Function	Format in whcih you will see

b) The subscribers' details of a magazine are maintained in a database. The fields are Subscriber number, Subscriber name, Address (three fields) and Expiry Date (Month and Year in the form MM/YY).

Write a command module to accept month and year through terminal and printout names and addresses of all subscribers whose subscriptions are expiring in the next month. The printing should be done in such a way that the name and address could be used as address sticker.

c) Consider the following library database

Field Name	*Description*	*Type*	*Width*
TITLE	Book Name	Character	50
AUTHOR	Name of author	Character	30
CLASS	Number of book	Character	10
DETAIL	Details of the book	Memo	10
STOCK	Quantity in stock	Numeric	3
ISSUED	Quantity issued	Numeric	3

Write procedures that will handle the following queries on such a database:

i) A query enquiring whether a particular book is available.

ii) A query enquiring about the books written by an author.

iii) A query enquiring about books of the same name but by different authors.

d) The names of persons are available in a database split into three fields: FIRSTNAME, MIDNAME and LASTNAME.

It is desired that names of the persons be printed in alphabetical order of LASTNAME. It is however found that some records have blanks in the field LASTNAME. In such cases the MIDNAME should be taken as LASTNAME. Write a program in Visual FoxPro to print it as directed. **(5 x 3)**

7. A credit card company maintains the records of its customers in a table named CUSTOMER.DBF. The structure of the table is given below.

Fieldname	*Type*	*Width*	*Dec*	*Remarks*
CUST_NO	Char	5		Customer Number
C_FNAME	Char	10		Customer's First Name
C_MNAME	Char	10		Customer's Middle Name
C_SNAME	Char	10		Customer's Surname
C_ADRS	Char	10		Customer's Address
C_PHONE	Num	10		Customer's Phone Number
AMT_DUE	Num	9	2	Amount Due
AMT_DEP	Num	7	2	Amount Deposited
AMT_WITH	Num	7	2	Amount Withdrawn
DATE	Date	8		Date of transaction
D_DATE	Date	8		Due Date
M_DATE	Date	8		Maturity Date

Witer a program in Visual FoxPro for the company to find the information about any existing customer by entering the customer with proper windowing facility. **(15)**

8. In a Payroll system, you are provided with Employee number, Employee name, Department, Designation, City which is either a Metro or a Non-Metro and Basic pay. Write a Visual FoxPro program to read this file, calculate allowances and total salary as follows:

a) Dearness allowance (DA)-

Up to Rs. 3500	110% of basic pay
Above Rs. 3500	90% of the basic pay subject to a minimum of Rs. 3850 and a maximum of Rs. 6300.

b) House Rent Allowance (HRA) is 15% of the basic pay subject to a miximum of Rs. 800.

c) If City is Metro, City Compensatory Allowance (CCA) = 800 else if it is Non-Metro, City Compensatory Allowance (CCA) = 600.

d) Provident fund (PF) is 12% of the basic pay.

c) Total salary = Basic Pay + Dearness Allowance + House Rent Allowance + CCA - PF. Each payslip printed should contain all information of input record, all allowances, deductions and total salary for each employee. **(15)**

Signature of Invigilator

SPECIAL ANSWER SHEET

Use Blue or Black Ball Point Pen to shade your answer.

LEVEL	PAPER/MODULE CODE	Enter your Roll number
O	M1-R3	

1. MULTIPLE CHOICE:
(Shade the box, corresponding to your answer)

	A	B	C	D
1.1	☐	☐	☐	☐
1.2	☐	☐	☐	☐
1.3	☐	☐	☐	☐
1.4	☐	☐	☐	☐
1.5	☐	☐	☐	☐
1.6	☐	☐	☐	☐
1.7	☐	☐	☐	☐
1.8	☐	☐	☐	☐
1.9	☐	☐	☐	☐
1.10	☐	☐	☐	☐

2. TRUE OR FALSE
(Shade the box, corresponding to your answer)

	TRUE	FALSE
2.1	☐	☐
2.2	☐	☐
2.3	☐	☐
2.4	☐	☐
2.5	☐	☐
2.6	☐	☐
2.7	☐	☐
2.8	☐	☐
2.9	☐	☐
2.10	☐	☐

3. MATCH THE FOLLOWING:
(Write the alphabet in capital letters corresponding to your answer, in the box)

3.1	☐
3.2	☐
3.3	☐
3.4	☐
3.5	☐
3.6	☐
3.7	☐
3.8	☐
3.9	☐
3.10	☐

3. FILL IN THE BLANKS:
(Write the alphabet in capital letters corresponding to your answer, in the box)

4.1	☐
4.2	☐
4.3	☐
4.4	☐
4.5	☐
4.6	☐
4.7	☐
4.8	☐
4.9	☐
4.10	☐

For the Use of Evaluator

Marks in Figures	Marks in Words	Signature of Examiner

ANSWERS TO QUESTION PAPER JANUARY 2004

M1-R3: BUSINESS SYSTEMS

PART ONE

1. MULTIPLE CHOICE QUESTIONS

1.1 A) 255

1.2 D) All of the above

1.3 C) An active will make the colour of the status bar to change to dark

1.4. B) The limit to the length of the Memo field is 254 characters

1.5 A) Cash journal

1.6 A)

1.7 D) EXIT

1.8 D) All of the above

1.9 C) 03

1.10 A)

```
IF debit>=credit
    Status = "Amount due"
ELSE
    Status = "Credit"
ENDIF
```

2. TRUE OR FALSE QUESTIONS

2.1 False

2.2 True

2.3 False

2.4 True

2.5 False

2.6 False

2.7 True

2.8 False

2.9 True

2.10 True

3. MATCHING QUESTIONS

3.1 J. LIFO

3.2 M. Payroll systems

3.3 L. Low Inventory Storage

3.4 H. Validation

3.5 C. Working capital

3.6 A. The SELECT command

3.7 I. Links the active database file to another open database file according to key expression that is common to both files

3.8 F. It is used to remove the trailing blanks from a character string

3.9 B. Uses data from an existing dtbase file as the basis for changes to data records in the active database file

3.10 G. Causes an active database file to appear to contain only the records meeting the specified condition

4. FILL IN THE BLANKS

4.1 I. Top down

4.2 N. Balance sheet

4.3 C. Trial balance

4.4 J. Testing

4.5 A. Record key

4.6 D. Subsidiary ledger

4.7 B. Buffer stocks

4.8 F. Loop

4.9 G. ABC Analysis

4.10 E. Pseudocode

Signature of Invigilator

[ ]

SPECIAL ANSWER SHEET

Use Blue or Black Ball Point Pen to shade your answer.

LEVEL	PAPER/MODULE CODE	Enter your Roll number
O	M1-R3	

1. MULTIPLE CHOICE:
(Shade the box, corresponding to your answer)

	A	B	C	D
1.1	■	□	□	□
1.2	□	□	□	■
1.3	□	□	■	□
1.4	□	■	□	□
1.5	■	□	□	□
1.6	■	□	□	□
1.7	□	□	□	■
1.8	□	□	□	■
1.9	□	□	■	□
1.10	■	□	□	□

2. TRUE OR FALSE
(Shade the box, corresponding to your answer)

	TRUE	FALSE
2.1	□	■
2.2	■	□
2.3	□	■
2.4	■	□
2.5	□	■
2.6	□	■
2.7	■	□
2.8	□	■
2.9	■	□
2.10	■	□

3. MATCH THE FOLLOWING:
(Write the alphabet in capital letters corresponding to your answer, in the box)

3.1	J.
3.2	M.
3.3	L.
3.4	H.
3.5	C.
3.6	A.
3.7	I.
3.8	F.
3.9	B.
3.10	G.

3. FILL IN THE BLANKS:
(Write the alphabet in capital letters corresponding to your answer, in the box)

4.1	I.
4.2	N.
4.3	C.
4.4	J.
4.5	A.
4.6	D.
4.7	B.
4.8	F.
4.9	G.
4.10	E.

For the Use of Evaluator

Marks in Figures	Marks in Words	Signature of Examiner

PART TWO

5. Answer any **three** of the following in not more than 100 words:

a) Visual FoxPro permits four different types of indexes. Describe in brief about each one of the them.

Ans. First among them is Index which creates an index file to display table/.DBF records in logical order

Syntax

```
INDEX ON <exp>TO<idx file> | TAG<tag name>[OF<cdx file>]
    [FOR<expL>]
    [COMPACT]
    [ASCENDING | DESCENDING]
    [UNIQUE]
    [ADDITIVE]
```

Records in a table/.DBF that has an index file are displayed and accessed in the order specified iby the index expression. The physical order of the records in the table/.DBF is n't changed by an index file. If TALK is SET ON, FoxPro reports how many records are indexed during the indexing process. The record interval displayed during indexing can be specified with SET ODOMETER.

FoxPro lest you create two types of index files.

Compound .CDX index files containing multiple index entries called tags

.IDX index files containing one index entry

You can also create a structural compound index file, which is automatically opened when the table/ .DBF is opened, they are the preferred index type.

Include COMPACT to create compact .IDX index files. Compound index files are always compact.

b) Write the steps to change the structure of an existing table in Visual FoxPro.

Ans. Steps to be taken for modification of a DBF file:

1. Open the DBF file using USE command or any other open command.
2. Type MODIFY STRUCTURE command in command window to open structure box.
3. The structure box will allow you to perform any kind of modification that you want to do.

c) Write the steps that you will take to create multiple key index using the Table Designer dialog box.

Ans. Steps to be taken for creating multiple key index using the Table Designer dialog box.

1. Either during table designing or by giving modify command, open the table structure dialog box.
2. Click on index tab for the field you want.
3. Click on another field index tab to make it index field.
4. To activate a particular index field give command SET ORDER TO file name in the command window.

d) Explain with an example the use of a Macro (&) command.

Ans. This command is used for macro substitution.

Syntax

&<memvar>[.<expC>]

Macro substitution treates the contents of a memory variable or array element as a chacter string literal. When an ampersand (&) precedes a chacter type memory variable or array element, the contents of the variable or element replace the macro reference. You can use macro substitution in any command or function that accepts a character string literal.

6. Answer any **three** of the following.

a) Visual FoxPro has some built in date functions by which you can do any date-oriented tasks. Describe any five of them in the following tabular format.

Date Function	Meaning of the Date Function	Format in whcih you will see

Ans. 1. CTOD() Converts a character expression to a date expression. CDOD(), the chacter to date function, returns a date type value from a character expression.

2. DTOC() Returns a character type date from a date expression. DTOC() returns a character string corresponding to the date expression <expD>. The date format is determined by SET CENTURY and SET DATE.

3. DTOC() Returns a character string date in the format YYYYMMDD from a specified date expression. This function is useful for indexing tables/.DBFs on a date field. It is equivalent to DTOC() when its optional 1 argument is included. The character string returned by DTOS() isn't afected by SET DATE or SET CENTURY.

4. CDOW() Returns the day of the week from a given date expression. CDOW() the character day of the week function, returns from a date expression the name of the day of the week. For example, Sunday or Monday.

5. CMONTH() Returns the name of the month from a given date expression. CMONTH() the character month function, returns the name of the month as a string in proper noun format

b) The subscribers' details of a magazine are maintained in a database. The fields are Subscriber number, Subscriber name, Address (three fields) and Expiry Date (Month and Year in the form MM/YY).

Write a command module to accept month and year through terminal and printout names and addresses of all subscribers whose subscriptions are expiring in the next month. The printing should be done in such a way that the name and address could be used as address sticker.

Ans. The following program would give the required result.

Clear

Close all

```
Use subscrib
M1=0
Y1=0
Flag=0
Input "enter the month" to M1
Input "enter the year" to Y1
Clear
Scan
    If year(exdate)=Y1
    If month(exdate)-M1<=1 and month(exdate)-M1>=0
        Flag=0
            ?"name" at 5,sname
            ?"address1" at 5,add1
            ?"address2" at 5,add2
            ?"address3" at 5,add3
            endif
endif
endscan
            if flag=0
            ?"there is no such list to print"
            endif
```

c) Consider the following library database

Field Name	*Description*	*Type*	*Width*
TITLE	Book Name	Character	50
AUTHOR	Name of author	Character	30
CLASS	Number of book	Character	10
DETAIL	Details of the book	Memo	10
STOCK	Quantity in stock	Numeric	3
ISSUED	Quantity issued	Numeric	3

Write procedures that will handle the following queries on such a database:

i) A query enquiring whether a particular book is available.

ii) A query enquiring about the books written by an author.

iii) A query enquiring about books of the same name but by different authors.

Ans. The following program would give the required result.

i)

```
Procedure bankdetails
Clear
Close all
Use book
Bn=space(60)
Accept "enter the book name" to bn
Flag=0
Scan
If alltrim(bn)=alltrim(title) and stock>0
    ?"title" at 5,title
        accept to title
    ?"author" at 5f
        accept to author
        flag=1
        endif
    endscan
        if flag=0
    ?"no book is avilable"
    endif
```

ii)

```
Proc library
Use book
Aut=space(30)
Accept "enter the author name" to aut
Flag=0
Scan if alltrim(aut)=alltrim(author)
Accept "enter the title" to title
Flag=1
Endif
Endscan
If Flag=0
?"no book is available in library"
endif
```

```
iii)
Proc inquiry
Use book
Accept "enter the book name" to bn
Scan
    If bname=title
        Accept "enter the auth" to aut
    Endif
Endscan
```

d) The names of persons are available in a database split into three fields: FIRSTNAME, MIDNAME and LASTNAME.

It is desired that names of the persons be printed in alphabetical order of LASTNAME. It is however found that some records have blanks in the field LASTNAME. In such cases the MIDNAME should be taken as LASTNAME. Write a program in Visual FoxPro to print it as directed.

Ans. The following program will do the job.

```
Use names
?"last" at 5,"firstname" at 50
scan
?"firstname" at 5,"first name"
    if lastname=null
        ?middle name
    endif
endscan
```

7. A credit card company maintains the records of its customers in a table named CUSTOMER.DBF. The structure of the table is given below.

Fieldname	*Type*	*Width*	*Dec*	*Remarks*
CUST_NO	Char	5		Customer Number
C_FNAME	Char	10		Customer's First Name
C_MNAME	Char	10		Customer's Middle Name
C_SNAME	Char	10		Customer's Surname
C_ADRS	Char	10		Customer's Address
C_PHONE	Num	10		Customer's Phone Number
AMT_DUE	Num	9	2	Amount Due

AMT_DEP	Num	7	2	Amount Deposited
AMT_WITH	Num	7	2	Amount Withdrawn
DATE	Date	8		Date of transaction
D_DATE	Date	8		Due Date
M_DATE	Date	8		Maturity Date

Witer a program in Visual FoxPro for the comapny to find the information about any existing customer by entering the customer with proper windowing facility.

Ans. The following program would the job.

```
Close all
Define window user title "customer window" from 1,1 to 30,100 float grow close;
mini zoom
acti wind user

defi menu my
defi pad a of my prompt "find"
defi popup find form 1,0
onselect pad a of may acti popup find
on select bar 1 of find do search

acti menu my

proc search
hide popup find
use customer
cmo=space(10)
accept "enter the cust_no" to cno
locate for cst_no=cno
if found()
display off
else
?"record not found"
endif
deac popup all
deac wind all
```

SAMPLE PAPER 1

M1-R3: Business Systems

NOTE:

1. There are **TWO PARTS** in this Module/Paper. **PART ONE** contains **FOUR** questions and **PART TWO** contains **FOUR** questions.
2. **PART ONE** is to be answered in the **TEAR-OFF ANSWER SHEET** only, attached to the question paper, as per the instructions contained therein. **PART ONE is NOT to be answered in the answer book.**
3. Maximum time allotted for **PART ONE** is **ONE HOUR**. Answer book for **PART TWO** will be supplied at the table when the answer sheet for **PART ONE** is returned. However, candidates, who completes **PART ONE** earlier than one hour, can collect the answer book for **PART TWO** immediately after handling over the answer sheet for **PART ONE**.

TOTAL TIME: 3 HOURS **TOTAL MARKS: 100**

(PART ONE – 40; PART TWO – 60)

PART ONE

(Answer all the questions)

1. **Each question below gives a multiple choice of answers. Choose the most appropriate one and enter in the "tear off" answer sheet attached to the question paper, following instructions therein.** **(1 x 10)**

1.1 In Stone age, business was done using :

(A) Computers

(B) Pebbles

(C) Money

1.2 MICR is mostly used in :

(A) Schools

(B) Banks

(C) Railways

1.3 Sequential file orgranization has records in :

(A) serial

(B) sequence

(C) random

1.4 In top down design, the main program is written:

(A) Fist

(B) Last

1.5 How many wizards are there in Visual FoxPro:

(A) 20

(B) 22

(C) 21

1.6 Logical field can take up value T or :

(A) S

(B) F

(C) U

1.7 Find command is under :

(A) File menu

(B) Edit menu

(C) Tool menu

1.8 A form is displayed on :

(A) Printer

(B) Screen

(C) Hard disk

1.9 You can add shapes to the report :

(A) Yes

(B) No

1.10 An indexed file can be activated using :

(A) Set order

(B) Set index

(C) Set sort

2. **Each statement below is either TRUE or FALSE. Choose the most appropriate one and Enter in the "tear-off" sheet attached to the question paper, following instructions therein. (1 x 10)**

2.1 Computers are very effectively used in running business.

2.2 Information is needed in virtually every field of human action.

2.3 Secondary record keys are not necessarily unique.

2.4 Softcopy output can be taken on terminals and voice output systems.

2.5 A tansaction file contains the records that are used to update the records of the master file.

2.6 A record is a collection of fields relating to a specific entity.

2.7 Alphanumeric code contains both numeric and alphabetic characters.

2.8 Flow chart is the representation of the programming steps.

2.9 Procedural programming is not based on certain procedures.

2.10 A database comprises of forms.

3. **Match words and phrases in column X with the closest related meaning/word(s)/phrases in column Y. Enter your selection in the "tear-off" answer sheet attached to the question paper, following instructions therein. (1 x 10)**

X		Y	
3.1	Keyboard	A.	Value of which changes in the program
3.2	Mouse	B.	Collection of all files relating to an application
3.3	Bar Code Reader	C.	Containing both alphabets and numerics
3.4	Bit	D.	Program following various procedures
3.5	Database	E.	A pointing device
3.6	Alphanumeric code	F.	To extract information from table
3.7	Variable	G.	Media to key in the data
3.8	Procedural programming	H.	Used for creating tables, etc.
3.9	Query	I.	Binary digit
3.10	Visual Designer	K.	Device to read bar codes

4. **Each statement below has a blank space to fit one of the words or phrases in the list below. Enter your choice in the "tear – off" answer sheet attached to the question paper, following instructions therein.** **(1 x 10)**

A.	**Keyboard**	**B.**	**Transaction**	**C.**	**Report**
D.	**Debugging**	**E.**	**Movement**	**F.**	**Command**
G.	**Memo**	**H.**	**Pointing**	**I.**	**Queries**
J.	**files**				

4.1 __________ is an input device.

4.2 Mouse is in fact a __________ device.

4.3 Data is stored in terms of __________.

4.4 __________ file contains data which is used to update the master file.

4.5 The process of correcting errors is called __________.

4.6 Processing is used in a flowchart to represent arithmetic and data __________ instructions.

4.7 A __________ is printed based on information from the tables.

4.8 Window that is used for typing commands is called the __________ Window.

4.9 When you have very long data to be filled in, you use the field called __________.

4.10 To get information from the table we use __________.

PART TWO

(Answer all questions)

5. Answer **any five** of the following:

a) What is a Master file?

b) How are Wizards used?

c) How is AND condition used in the query?

d) What is Mail Merge?

e) How is CANCEL command used?

f) What operations you can perform on the files? **(2 x 5)**

6. Answer **any three** from the following:

a) How would you handle large volume of data?

b) How do you create command files?

c) What is Project Manager?

d) How would you use the option of Grid? (5 x 3)

7. Answer **any three** of the following:

a) How would you save and print a report?

b) How would you create a new relational database using Visual FoxPro?

c) Which commands form the looping?

8. (5 x 3)

a) How does computer help in printing invoices?

b) Which are the basic tasks in Data Processing?

c) What sort of queries you can generate from the table?

d) How would you add records through program?

e) What are the advantages and disadvantages of flow chart? ([2+4]+[1.5x4]+[1+1+2]+2+2)

Signature of Invigilator

SPECIAL ANSWER SHEET

Use Blue or Black Ball Point Pen to shade your answer.

LEVEL	PAPER/MODULE CODE	Enter your Roll number
O	M1-R3	

1. MULTIPLE CHOICE:

(Shade the box, corresponding to your answer)

	A	B	C	D
1.1	☐	☐	☐	☐
1.2	☐	☐	☐	☐
1.3	☐	☐	☐	☐
1.4	☐	☐	☐	☐
1.5	☐	☐	☐	☐
1.6	☐	☐	☐	☐
1.7	☐	☐	☐	☐
1.8	☐	☐	☐	☐
1.9	☐	☐	☐	☐
1.10	☐	☐	☐	☐
1.11	☐	☐	☐	☐
1.12	☐	☐	☐	☐
1.13	☐	☐	☐	☐
1.14	☐	☐	☐	☐
1.15	☐	☐	☐	☐

2. TRUE OR FALSE

(Shade the box, corresponding to your answer)

	TRUE	FALSE
2.1	☐	☐
2.2	☐	☐
2.3	☐	☐
2.4	☐	☐
2.5	☐	☐
2.6	☐	☐
2.7	☐	☐
2.8	☐	☐
2.9	☐	☐
2.10	☐	☐
2.11	☐	☐
2.12	☐	☐

3. MATCH THE FOLLOWING:

(Write the alphabet in capital letters corresponding to your answer, in the box)

3.1	☐	3.6	☐
3.2	☐	3.7	☐
3.3	☐	3.8	☐
3.4	☐	3.9	☐
3.5	☐	3.10	☐

4. FILL IN THE BLANKS:

(Write the alphabet in capital letters corresponding to your answer, in the box)

4.1	☐	4.8	☐
4.2	☐	4.9	☐
4.3	☐	4.10	☐
4.4	☐	4.11	☐
4.5	☐	4.12	☐
4.6	☐	4.13	☐
4.7	☐		

For the Use of Evaluator

Marks in Figures	Marks in Words	Signature of Examiner

SAMPLE PAPER 2

M1-R3: Business Systems

NOTE:

1. There are **TWO PARTS** in this Module/Paper. **PART ONE** contains **FOUR** questions and **PART TWO** contains **FOUR** questions.
2. **PART ONE** is to be answered in the **TEAR-OFF ANSWER SHEET** only, attached to the question paper, as per the instructions contained therein. **PART ONE** is **NOT** to be answered in the answer book.
3. Maximum time allotted for **PART ONE** is **ONE HOUR**. Answer book for **PART TWO** will be supplied at the table when the answer sheet for **PART ONE** is returned. However, candidates, who completes **PART ONE** earlier than one hour, can collect the answer book for **PART TWO** immediately after handling over the answer sheet for **PART ONE**.

TOTAL TIME: 3 HOURS **TOTAL MARKS: 100**

(PART ONE – 40; PART TWO – 60)

PART ONE

(Answer all the questions)

1. **Each question below gives a multiple choice of answers. Choose the most appropriate one and enter in the "tear off" answer sheet attached to the question paper, following instructions therein.** **(1 x 10)**

1.1 Source data elements are Raw, Stored and :

(A) Developed

(B) Designed

(C) Derived

1.2 Printers can be used for outputting the results, which copy it is called:

(A) Soft

(B) Medium

(C) Hard

1.3 In batch processing, processing is done in terms of:

(A) batches

(B) groups

(C) items

1.4 A syntax error occurs when the system cannot understand a :

(A) command

(B) logic

(C) flow

1.5 You can extract information from table and work on it by using :

(A) Query

(B) Table

(C) Form

1.6 Can you use the same field name twice :

(A) Yes

(B) No

1.7 You can resize fields on the screen using the mouse and then :

(A) pushing

(B) dragging

(C) pulling

1.8 You can run a form using the :

(A) Form menu

(B) File menu

(C) Edit menu

1.9 Report file in Visual FoxPro is saved with extension:

(A) .scf

(B) .scx

(C) .frx

1.10 Macros have this character in the beginning :

(A) *

(B) &

(C) %

2. Each statement below is either TRUE or FALSE. Choose the most appropriate one and Enter in the "tear-off" sheet attached to the question paper, following instructions therein. (1 x 10)

2.1 Controlling includes the various aspects which can enhance production.

2.2 Scope covers the various aspects of the product as far as the market is concerned.

2.3 Data must be recorded or captured in some form or other before they can be processed.

2.4 Using Data communication you can transmit data from one place to another.

2.5 The files can also be stored on direct access storage.

2.6 Serial file has the records are stored without any consideration of their order or sequence.

2.7 A database consists of all the files of an organization, structured and integrated to facilitate updation of files and retrieval of information from them.

2.8 The process of modifying an old file with current information is known as file updation.

2.9 Flowchart helps in correcting errors in the programming logic too.

2.10 Top down design approach is performed in a special way, the main program is written first.

3. Match words and phrases in column X with the closest related meaning/word(s)/phrases in column Y. Enter your selection in the "tear-off" answer sheet attached to the question paper, following instructions therein. (1 x 10)

	X		Y
1.	Light Pen	A.	Basic unit of information
2.	Scanner	B.	Calculates the largest of all values
3.	Point of Sale Terminals	C.	Device like pen to put data into computer
4.	Byte	D.	In flow chart the connecting lines
5.	Record length	E.	Errors occuring due to error in logic
6.	Flow lines	F.	Printing information from table
7.	Logic errors	G.	Faster way of creating tables, etc.
8.	Report	H.	Collection of various related tables
9.	Wizard	I.	Used in department stores
10.	Database	J.	Fixed or variable

4. Each statement below has a blank space to fit one of the words or phrases in the list below. Enter your choice in the "tear – off" answer sheet attached to the question paper, following instructions therein. (1 x 10)

A.	Expression Builder	B.	General	C.	program
D.	Query	E.	Title bar	F.	Transactions
G.	Serial	H.	Middle	I.	Procedural
J.	programs				

1. _______ level managers are responsible for making the tactical decisions.
2. Most of the ________ give rise to the data.
3. Program files are used to store ______.
4. _______ file has the records are stored without any consideration of their order or sequence.
5. Functional testing is carried out independently of the code used in the ______.
6. _________ programming is based on certain procedures.
7. A ______ can be generated to get results based on the data in the tables.
8. _______ is at the top of the screen and displays the name of the program, i.e., Microsoft Visual FoxPro.
9. For storing graphics in tables, you use the type as ________.
10. ______________ allows you to build valid expressions.

PART TWO

(Answer all questions)

5. Answer **any five** of the following:

a) What is programming?

b) What is a Query?

c) What is a Transaction file?

d) How would you identify the relevant data?

e) How would you run the query?

f) What sort of report can you generate from the table? **(2 x 5)**

6. Answer **any three** from the following:

a) How would you use Nested if?

b) What are Application Wizard and Builder?

c) Which are the different methods of file updation?

d) What is the function of GoTo command? (5 x 3)

7. Answer **any three** of the following:

a) Describe the MailMerge process.

b) How would you use One-to-Many Report Wizard?

c) What do you understand by Object Linking and Embedding?

8. **(5 x 3)**

a) What does ZAP command do?

b) Describe the various reports printed in accounting system.

c) How would you create a table using Table Designer?

d) How do you run the programs?

e) Describe the various steps involved in Computerized Accounting.**([2+4]+[1.5x4]+[1+1+2]+2+2)**

Signature of Invigilator

SPECIAL ANSWER SHEET

Use Blue or Black Ball Point Pen to shade your answer.

LEVEL	PAPER/MODULE CODE	Enter your Roll number
O	M1-R3	

1. MULTIPLE CHOICE:

(Shade the box, corresponding to your answer)

	A	B	C	D
1.1	☐	☐	☐	☐
1.2	☐	☐	☐	☐
1.3	☐	☐	☐	☐
1.4	☐	☐	☐	☐
1.5	☐	☐	☐	☐
1.6	☐	☐	☐	☐
1.7	☐	☐	☐	☐
1.8	☐	☐	☐	☐
1.9	☐	☐	☐	☐
1.10	☐	☐	☐	☐
1.11	☐	☐	☐	☐
1.12	☐	☐	☐	☐
1.13	☐	☐	☐	☐
1.14	☐	☐	☐	☐
1.15	☐	☐	☐	☐

2. TRUE OR FALSE

(Shade the box, corresponding to your answer)

	TRUE	FALSE
2.1	☐	☐
2.2	☐	☐
2.3	☐	☐
2.4	☐	☐
2.5	☐	☐
2.6	☐	☐
2.7	☐	☐
2.8	☐	☐
2.9	☐	☐
2.10	☐	☐
2.11	☐	☐
2.12	☐	☐

3. MATCH THE FOLLOWING:

(Write the alphabet in capital letters corresponding to your answer, in the box)

3.1	☐	3.6	☐
3.2	☐	3.7	☐
3.3	☐	3.8	☐
3.4	☐	3.9	☐
3.5	☐	3.10	☐

4. FILL IN THE BLANKS:

(Write the alphabet in capital letters corresponding to your answer, in the box)

4.1	☐	4.8	☐
4.2	☐	4.9	☐
4.3	☐	4.10	☐
4.4	☐	4.11	☐
4.5	☐	4.12	☐
4.6	☐	4.13	☐
4.7	☐		

For the Use of Evaluator

Marks in Figures	Marks in Words	Signature of Examiner

SAMPLE PAPER 3

M1-R3: Business Systems

NOTE:

1. There are **TWO PARTS** in this Module/Paper. **PART ONE** contains **FOUR** questions and **PART TWO** contains **FOUR** questions.
2. **PART ONE** is to be answered in the **TEAR-OFF ANSWER SHEET** only, attached to the question paper, as per the instructions contained therein. **PART ONE** is **NOT** to be answered in the answer book.
3. Maximum time allotted for **PART ONE** is **ONE HOUR**. Answer book for **PART TWO** will be supplied at the table when the answer sheet for **PART ONE** is returned. However, candidates, who completes **PART ONE** earlier than one hour, can collect the answer book for **PART TWO** immediately after handling over the answer sheet for **PART ONE**.

TOTAL TIME: 3 HOURS **TOTAL MARKS: 100**

(PART ONE – 40; PART TWO – 60)

PART ONE

(Answer all the questions)

1. **Each question below gives a multiple choice of answers. Choose the most appropriate one and enter in the "tear off" answer sheet attached to the question paper, following instructions therein.** **(1 x 10)**

1.1 Merging is done on key:

(A) Field

(B) Lock

(C) Master

1.2 In computer data is stored in terms of :

(A) files

(B) records

(C) marbles

1.3 A bit can have two values 0 and .

(A) 3

(B) 1

(C) 4

1.4 Common field to various tables in the database is called :

(A) Key

(B) Common

(C) Same

1.5 Application Wizard is used for developing the :

(A) Project

(B) Application

(C) Table

1.6 A field can be renamed :

(A) Yes

(B) No

1.7 Query works on :

(A) Table

(B) Forms

(C) Reports

1.8 Form takes field from :

(A) Report

(B) Table

(C) Wizard

1.9 Append command adds the data to the :

(A) Beginning

(B) Last

(C) Middle

1.10 List command displays on :

(A) Printer

(B) Screen

(C) Plotter

2. **Each statement below is either TRUE or FALSE. Choose the most appropriate one and Enter in the "tear-off" sheet attached to the question paper, following instructions therein. (1 x 10)**

2.1 Directing means getting the job done by directing the management.

2.2 You need not know where your product is going to sell.

2.3 Keyboard is an important part for getting the data out of computer.

2.4 Data files are used to store data records.

2.5 An indexed file is one that has an index for looking up locations of records on a disk.

2.6 Record length can be either of Fixed length record or Variable length record format

2.7 Programming is one of the step in system development cycle.

2.8 Program flow charts may not use conventional symbols.

2.9 The process of correcting errors is called Debugging.

2.10 Queries are not used to get result from the database.

3. **Match words and phrases in column X with the closest related meaning/word(s)/phrases in column Y. Enter your selection in the "tear-off" answer sheet attached to the question paper, following instructions therein. (1 x 10)**

X		Y	
1.	Printer	A.	Data about attributes of an entities
2.	MICR	B.	Records of different length
3.	Smart Cards	C.	Pictorial representation of program
4.	Field	D.	Displaying on screen to fill in the data
5.	Variable length	E.	Codes written in English
6.	Flow chart	F.	Magnetic cards
7.	Pseuecode	G.	Collection of data
8.	Syntax error	H.	Magnetic Ink Character Reader
9.	Form	I.	Information on the screen by touch
10.	Table	J.	Error due to wrong command

4. Each statement below has a blank space to fit one of the words or phrases in the list below. Enter your choice in the "tear – off" answer sheet attached to the question paper, following instructions therein. **(1 x 10)**

A.	Indexed	B.	Table	C.	Top Down
D.	English	E.	Validation	F.	Go To
G.	.obj	H.	Cross Tab Wizard	I.	Status bar
J.	Manipulation				

1. Derived data are the result of processing or __________ of raw or stored data.
2. Data __________ can be done performing various checks.
3. Object code file has an extension of____.
4. An _______ file is one that has an index for looking up locations of records on a disk.
5. __________ design approach is performed in a special way, the main program is written first.
6. Pseudocode is written in plain ________ language..
7. ________ contains data in rows and columns.
8. ________ displays various kinds of information related to the window that is currently opened.
9. ________ command will take the curser to a particular record.
10. Wizard which allow you to change the positioning of the data is called ______________

PART TWO

(Answer all questions)

5. Answer **any five** of the following:

a) What is data handling?

b) Which are the data elements by functions?

c) What is a database?

d) Which kind of files are used in Visual FoxPro?

e) What are Pseudocodes?

f) How is Find command used? **(2 x 5)**

6. Answer **any three** from the following:

a) What are the forms used for?

b) Describe the various types of files.

c) What do you understand by top down design?

d) What is a Report? (5 x 3)

7. Answer **any three** of the following:

a) How would you modify the structure of the table?

b) What does the Cross Tab Wizard do?

c) How would you run the Query?

8. (5 x 3)

a) What are the methods of creating arrays?

b) What are Procedures?

c) What is command window used for?

d) How is the combination Do while and End do used?

e) What are the advantages of Relational Databases? ([2+4]+[1.5x4]+[1+1+2]+2+2)

Signature of Invigilator

[ ]

SPECIAL ANSWER SHEET

Use Blue or Black Ball Point Pen to shade your answer.

LEVEL	PAPER/MODULE CODE	Enter your Roll number
O	M1-R3	

1. MULTIPLE CHOICE:

(Shade the box, corresponding to your answer)

	A	B	C	D
1.1	☐	☐	☐	☐
1.2	☐	☐	☐	☐
1.3	☐	☐	☐	☐
1.4	☐	☐	☐	☐
1.5	☐	☐	☐	☐
1.6	☐	☐	☐	☐
1.7	☐	☐	☐	☐
1.8	☐	☐	☐	☐
1.9	☐	☐	☐	☐
1.10	☐	☐	☐	☐
1.11	☐	☐	☐	☐
1.12	☐	☐	☐	☐
1.13	☐	☐	☐	☐
1.14	☐	☐	☐	☐
1.15	☐	☐	☐	☐

2. . TRUE OR FALSE

(Shade the box, corresponding to your answer)

	TRUE	FALSE
2.1	☐	☐
2.2	☐	☐
2.3	☐	☐
2.4	☐	☐
2.5	☐	☐
2.6	☐	☐
2.7	☐	☐
2.8	☐	☐
2.9	☐	☐
2.10	☐	☐
2.11	☐	☐
2.12	☐	☐

3. MATCH THE FOLLOWING:

(Write the alphabet in capital letters corresponding to your answer, in the box)

3.1	☐	3.6	☐
3.2	☐	3.7	☐
3.3	☐	3.8	☐
3.4	☐	3.9	☐
3.5	☐	3.10	☐

4. FILL IN THE BLANKS:

(Write the alphabet in capital letters corresponding to your answer, in the box)

4.1	☐	4.8	☐
4.2	☐	4.9	☐
4.3	☐	4.10	☐
4.4	☐	4.11	☐
4.5	☐	4.12	☐
4.6	☐	4.13	☐
4.7	☐		

For the Use of Evaluator

Marks in Figures	Marks in Words	Signature of Examiner

SAMPLE PAPER 4

M1-R3: Business Systems

NOTE:

1. There are **TWO PARTS** in this Module/Paper. **PART ONE** contains **FOUR** questions and **PART TWO** contains **FOUR** questions.
2. **PART ONE** is to be answered in the **TEAR-OFF ANSWER SHEET** only, attached to the question paper, as per the instructions contained therein. **PART ONE** is **NOT** to be answered in the answer book.
3. Maximum time allotted for **PART ONE** is **ONE HOUR**. Answer book for **PART TWO** will be supplied at the table when the answer sheet for **PART ONE** is returned. However, candidates, who completes **PART ONE** earlier than one hour, can collect the answer book for **PART TWO** immediately after handling over the answer sheet for **PART ONE**.

TOTAL TIME: 3 HOURS **TOTAL MARKS: 100**

(PART ONE – 40; PART TWO – 60)

PART ONE

(Answer all the questions)

1. **Each question below gives a multiple choice of answers. Choose the most appropriate one and enter in the "tear off" answer sheet attached to the question paper, following instructions therein.** **(1 x 10)**

1.1 In Payroll system, most important print out is :

(A) Earnings

(B) Payslips

(C) Deductions

1.2 Object files have an extension of :

(A) .doc

(B) .exe

(C) .obj

1.3 A byte of information is stored using how many bits:

(A) 8

(B) 7

(C) 6

1.4 A database consists of various :

(A) Tables

(B) Chairs

(C) Stools

1.5 Table wizard is in :

(A) Tools menu

(B) File menu

(C) Edit menu

1.6 In Appending the records are added in :

(A) Between

(B) First

(C) Last

1.7 Query can have multiple conditions using Or and :

(A) OR

(B) TO

(C) AND

1.8 Bottom is one of the buttons on the control bar of the form.

(A) Yes

(B) No

1.9 ? command is used to display :

(A) table

(B) data items

(C) form

1.10 One To Many Form Wizard creates Form using :

(A) One Table

(B) Two Tables

(C) Two Forms

2. **Each statement below is either TRUE or FALSE. Choose the most appropriate one and Enter in the "tear-off" sheet attached to the question paper, following instructions therein. (1 x 10)**

2.1 Planning means to foresee the outlook of the company.

2.2 Top level management should know in advance when the resources are needed and when not.

2.3 Mouse is in fact a pointing device.

2.4 Object code files contain the machine codes and are created with an extension .EXE.

2.5 Batch processing is done in small patches.

2.6 Variable Length record format may contain the records of different lengths.

2.7 A person engaged in the activity of programming is referred to as operator.

2.8 System charts stress on what data is used and produced at various points in a sequence of operations.

2.9 A syntax error occurs when a program cannot understand the command that has been entered.

2.10 Reports are generated to print information from tables.

3. **Match words and phrases in column X with the closest related meaning/word(s)/phrases in column Y. Enter your selection in the "tear-off" answer sheet attached to the question paper, following instructions therein. (1 x 10)**

X	Y
1. Touch Screen	A. Collection of field relating to an entity
2. OCR	B. Writing instructions for computer
3. Data Validation	C. Changing file with corrections
4. Record	D. Information on screen by touch
5. Alphabetic code	E. Relational Database Management System
6. Programming	F. Used for extracting information from table
7. File updation	G. A collection of tables pertaining to a kind of data
8. Database	H. Optical Character Recognition
9. RDBMS	I. Containing only alphabets
10. Query	J. Performing checks on input data

4. Each statement below has a blank space to fit one of the words or phrases in the list below. Enter your choice in the "tear – off" answer sheet attached to the question paper, following instructions therein. (1 x 10)

A.	**Minimize**	**B.**	**Query Wizard**	**C.**	**Terminals**
D.	**Standard Toolbar**	**E.**	**Processing**	**F.**	**Forms**
G.	**System**	**H.**	**Arrow**	**I.**	**EXE**
J.	**DATA**				

1. To run any business you need to develop a ________ to run it.
2. Softcopy output can be taken on ________ and voice output systems.
3. Executable files have an extension of ________.
4. Program flow charts stress on how ________ is transformed.
5. Flow chart is the representation of the ________ steps.
6. ________ are displayed on screen to fill in the data.
7. To reduce Visual FoxPro to an icon, we use the ____________ button.
8. ________ contains buttons for performing the most common actions in Visual FoxPro.
9. For correcting mistakes, you use the ________ keys.
10. You can create query using ____________.

PART TWO

(Answer all questions)

5. Answer **any five** of the following:

a) What is information?

b) What is Relational Database Management System?

c) What all the steps in program life cycle?

d) What is Data Processing?

e) How program testing is done?

f) What is the difference between Pseudocode and flow chart? **(2 x 5)**

6. Answer **any three** from the following:

a) How would you classify the different data files?

b) What is AutoForms?

c) Which are the various tools used in Visual FoxPro?

d) Which are the data elements by source? (5 x 3)

7. Answer **any three** of the following:

a) How would you add, delete and rename the fields of the table?

b) What is the function of Replace command?

c) What is sorting and how it is done?

8. (5 x 3)

a) Describe Numeric functions.

b) What are the advantages of using RDBMS?

c) Describe the following SQL functions: Order By and Group By.

d) What do you understand by passing parameters?

e) How are relationships among tables developed? **([2+4]+[1.5x4]+[1+1+2]+2+2)**

Signature of Invigilator

SPECIAL ANSWER SHEET

Use Blue or Black Ball Point Pen to shade your answer.

LEVEL	PAPER/MODULE CODE	Enter your Roll number
O	M1-R3	

1. MULTIPLE CHOICE:

(Shade the box, corresponding to your answer)

	A	B	C	D
1.1	☐	☐	☐	☐
1.2	☐	☐	☐	☐
1.3	☐	☐	☐	☐
1.4	☐	☐	☐	☐
1.5	☐	☐	☐	☐
1.6	☐	☐	☐	☐
1.7	☐	☐	☐	☐
1.8	☐	☐	☐	☐
1.9	☐	☐	☐	☐
1.10	☐	☐	☐	☐
1.11	☐	☐	☐	☐
1.12	☐	☐	☐	☐
1.13	☐	☐	☐	☐
1.14	☐	☐	☐	☐
1.15	☐	☐	☐	☐

2. TRUE OR FALSE

(Shade the box, corresponding to your answer)

	TRUE	FALSE
2.1	☐	☐
2.2	☐	☐
2.3	☐	☐
2.4	☐	☐
2.5	☐	☐
2.6	☐	☐
2.7	☐	☐
2.8	☐	☐
2.9	☐	☐
2.10	☐	☐
2.11	☐	☐
2.12	☐	☐

3. MATCH THE FOLLOWING:

(Write the alphabet in capital letters corresponding to your answer, in the box)

3.1	☐	3.6	☐
3.2	☐	3.7	☐
3.3	☐	3.8	☐
3.4	☐	3.9	☐
3.5	☐	3.10	☐

4. FILL IN THE BLANKS:

(Write the alphabet in capital letters corresponding to your answer, in the box)

4.1	☐	4.8	☐
4.2	☐	4.9	☐
4.3	☐	4.10	☐
4.4	☐	4.11	☐
4.5	☐	4.12	☐
4.6	☐	4.13	☐
4.7	☐		

For the Use of Evaluator

Marks in Figures	Marks in Words	Signature of Examiner

G Glossary

Abort To exit a function or application midway and without saving any data that has been changed. It is also, in DOS commands, the option for cancelling a command that cannot be implemented (for example, trying a DIR of A: without a floppy in it). The key combination - Ctrl+Break or Esc also abort commands.

Accept This command is used to accept the character string from the screen.

Active window The open window in respect of Microsoft Windows programs which a program is being executed. In respect of Clipper debugger, window to which all key strokes (except those valid in the command window) apply.

Add button This button moves the highlighted field from the available fields list box to the selected fields list box.

Add all button This button moves the highlighted field from the available fields list box to be selected fields list box.

Address (1) Number of a particular memory or peripheral storage location. Each byte of memory and each disk sector have its own unique address. Programs are compiled into machine language, which references actual addresses in the computer. (2) As a verb, to mange or work with. For example, "The computer can address 2MB of memory."

Alphanumeric Use of alphabetic letters mixed with numbers and special characters as in name, address, city and state. The text you are reading is alphanumeric.

AND A conjunction. It gives the result as True if both the conditions are true, otherwise false.

Append To add data to the end of an existing structure. For example, the dBASE APPEND commands starts the data entry mode and allows users to add records to the end of the file. Also refers to adding a text block at the end of a file in word processing applications. In DOS, a text file can be attached (appended) to the end of another text file.

Argument In programming, a value that is passed between programs; subroutines or functions. Arguments are independent items or variables, that contain data or codes. When an argument is used to customize a program for a user, it is typically called a parameter.

Arithmetic operators Symbols for arithmetic functions: + for 'add', - for 'subtract', * for 'multiply', / for 'divide'.

AArray Ordered arrangement of data elements. A vector is a one dimensional array, a matrix is a two-dimensional array. Most programming languages have the ability to store and manipulate arrays in one or more dimensions. Multi-dimensional arrays are used extensively in scientific simulation and mathematical processing; however, an array can be as simple as a pricing table held in memory for instant access by an order entry program.

ASCII (American Standard Code for Information Interchange) Pronounced "ass-key." It is a binary code for data that is used in communications, mostly in minicomputers and all personal computers. ASCII is a 7-bit code providing 128 possible character combinations, the first 32 of which are used for printing and transmission control. Since the common storage unit is an 8-bit byte (256 combinations) and ASCII uses only 128, the extra bit is used to hold a parity bit or special symbols. For example, the PC uses the additional values for foreign language and graphics symbols. In the Macintosh, the additional values can be user-defined to enhance a font.

Attribute In many word processing and graphics programs a character emphasis, such as boldface and italic and other characteristics such as typeface and type size. In MS-DOS and Microsoft Windows 95, information about a file that indicates whether the file is a read-only file, a hidden file or a system file.

Auxiliary storage Same as secondary shortage.

Backup Additional resources or duplicate copies of data on different storage media for emergency purposes.

Backup files To make a duplicate copy of a file or disk for safe keeping. A spare copy of data used for when things go wrong and to avoid the disaster which can follow the damaging or corruption of disks or data. All users should have at least one duplicate copy or backup of their program or data though more would be advisable. The ancestral file method offers additional security for data. Back-up copies may or may not be working copies of the original file.

Band (1) Range of frequencies used for transmitting a signal. A band call can be identified by the difference between its lower and upper limits as well as by its actual lower and upper limits, for example, "a 10MHz band in the 100 to 110MHz range." (2) Contiguous group of tracks that are treated as a unit. (3) Printing element in a band printer.

Bar code A set of lines of varying widths which can be read by passing a light pen across them. On house hold goods there may be 30 lines giving a unique 13-digit code number to each product. When the cashier records this price from memory and is able to register that there is now one less of that item in stock. Library cards and library books sometimes have bar codes, though with more lines. The borrowing of books during the day is recorded on to tape by means of a light pen and the data is transferred to the computer at the end of the day.

Batch processing Processing a group of transactions at one time. Transactions are collected and processed against the master files (master files updated) at the end of the day or some other time period. Contrast with transaction processing.

Block A group of related items (records, characters, etc.) handled as a unit during input and output. A section of program coding treated as a unit.

Browse To View and possibly edit a file on screen like text in a word processing document. Browse commands let the user scroll through the data horizontally by the field and vertically by row or screen to view and edit the class hierarchy of the objects in an object-oriented programming language.

Bubble memory A form of static memory which uses impregnated garnet as the storage medium. It is a garnet chip enclosing one or more thin layers of magnetic film. A bubble represents the presence of a bit and the lack of a bubble represented the absence of a bit.

Buffer Reserved segment of memory used to hold data while it is being processed. In a program, buffers are created to hold some amount of data from each of the files that will be read or written. A buffer may also be a small memory bank used for special purposes.

Cache memory A high-speed temporary storage area in the CPU for storing parts of program or data during processing. This is used to hold another copy of data which has recently been accessed by the microprocessor in anticipation of its use again in the near future. When next needed the data can be accessed very quickly, though the least accessed data in cache memory is replaced by newly accessed data.

Call by value In programming, a call to a subroutine that passes the actual data of the parameters used in the subroutine.

Candidate It is like a primary key index, except that you can have more than one candidate index per table.

Case sensitive Distinguishing lower case from upper case. In a case sensitive language, 'a' is treated differently than 'A'.

Clause A class of commnds that have a specific goal. A clause may control the format of displayed or printed information, or the structure of a table.

Clipboard A temporary storage location used to transfer data between documents and between applications. Typically, you transfer data to the Clipboard by using an application's Copy or Cut command and you insert data from the Clipboard by using the application's Paste command. You use Clipboard Viewer to the view the contents of the Clipboard. Clipboards usually produce ASCII text files and can store graphics files.

Command A word or phrase usually found in a menu that you choose in order to carry out an action. You choose a command from a menu or type a command at the MS-DOS prompt. You can also type a command in the run dialog box in File Manager or program Manager. An instruction given to the CPU rather by a software application, for example: a database package initiating the creation of a new file, or directly by the computer via the operating system. For example, on a VAX machine the command DIR lists the currently available files. In either case the command (if it is valid) will be converted to machine code and acted upon by the CPU.

Command file A series of instructions, or commands, that you can use to perform a repetitive task.

Command scope A condition that specifies the general set of tables records to which a command applies.

comment A brief line of commentary embedded into a computer program. Comments aim to provide a "road-map" through a program, enabling programmers, including the original writer, to follow the overall logic of the program. Since comment occupy a line of code it is best to be brief, rather then verbose in commentary.

Compound index file An index file containing multiple index entriess, called tags.

Concatenated key In the Hierarhical model, a physical record is a hierarchicaal arrangement of segments, each segment having a sequence filed. To pick out a unique segemnt in the record, the sequence fields of aall segments above it in the hierarchy are concatenated to the segment's own sequence field. This forms the concatenated key for the segment.

Connector symbol A flowcharting symbol used to represent a junction in a line of flow. A small circle, possibly containing some identifier, connects broken paths in the line of flow on the same page. A pentagonal shape connects the flow on different ages of the same flowchart.

Constant In programming any data with fixed values within the program. Minimum and maximum amounts, dates, prices, headlines and error messages are examples of constants.

Context-senstive Able to perceive the situation in which an event occurs. For example, an application program might present help information specific to the particular task you are performing, rather than a general list of commands, such help would be content-sensitive.

Control break Change of category used to trigger a subtotal.

Control program Software that controls the operation of and has highest priority in a computer. Operating systems, network operating systems and network control programs are examples. Contrast with application program.

CRT Cathode Ray Tube - Vacuum tube used as a display screen in a video terminal or TV. The term often refers to the entire terminal.

Cycle time Time interval between the start of one cycle and the start of the next cycle.

DASD Direct Access Storage Device - Pronounced "dazdee." Peripheral device that is directly addressable, such as a disk or drum.

Data (1) Technically, raw facts and figures which are processed into information. However, in common usage, both data and information are used synonymously the amount of data kept in the computer versus the amount of information is a tradeoff. Data can be processed into different forms of information, but it takes time to sort and sum transactions. Data is "processed". Software is "run", (2) Any form of information whether on paper or in electronic form. In electronic form, data refers to data fields, records, files and databases, word processing documents, graphic images and digitally-encoded voice and video. (3) Data items in data files and databases in contrast with text, graphics, voice and video files.

Data level model A data model concerned only with stored data, and not with its interpretation or the physical structure of data.

Data communications system A system consisting of computers, terminals and communications links.

Data file A collection of data records stored on a disk.

Data flow chart A flow chart showing the path of the data step in a problem solution or though a system.

Data flow diagram A graphic diagramming tool which was a few simple symbols to illustrate the flow of data among external entities, processing activities and data storage elements.

Data grouping Categorizing data in groups in a report corresponding to a sepecified order. Headers and footers can be defined to print every time the value for a group changess.

Data hiding A property whereby the internal data structure of an object is hidden from the rest of the program. The data can be accessed only by the functions declared within the class of that object.

Data processing Capturing, storing, updating and retrieving data and information. It may refer to the entire computer industry, to only datacenter operations or to only data processing activities, in contrast with word processing and office functions.

Data processing system The network of data processing hardware, software, people and procedures capable for accepting information, processing it according to a plan and producing the desired results.

Data processor A digital device that processes data.

Data transfer rate The rate, in kilobytes or megabytes per second, at which data can be read/ written from/to CDROM, disk, tape etc.

Data type Category of data Typical data types are numeric, alphanumeric (character), dates and logical (true/false). Programming languages allow for the creation of different data types. When data is assigned a type, it cannot be treated like another type, For example, character data cannot be calculated and digits within numeric data cannot be isolated. Data types can only contain valid dates.

Database (1) Set of interrelated files that is created and managed by a DBMS. (2) Any electronically-stored collection of data. A collection of logically related records of files. A database consolidates many records previously stored in separate files so that a common pool of data records serves as a single central file or data bank for many data processing applications. About data and database, it holds the name, type, range of values, source and authorization for access for each data element in the organization's files and databases. It also indicates which application programs use that data so that when a change in a data structure is contemplated, a list of affected programs can be generated.

Database administrator Person responsible for the physical design and management of the database and for the evaluation, selection and implementation of the DBMS. In smaller organizations, the database administrators are one in the same; however, when the two responsibilities are managed separately, the database administrator's function is more technical.

DBMS DataBase Management System - Software that controls the organization, storage, retrieval, security and integrity of data in a database; 1t accepts requests from the application and instructs the operating system to transfer the appropriate data. DBMSs let information systems be changed more easily as the organization's requirements change. New categories of data can be added to the database without disruption to the existing system.

Database sever Computer in a LAN dedicated to database storage and retrieval. Contrast with the server which stores many kinds of files and programs for shared use.

Debug To correct a problem in hardware or software. Debugging software is finding the errors in the program logic. Debugging hardware is finding the errors in circuit design.

Delete Marks records for deletion.

Delimiter Character or combination of characters used to separate one item or set of data from another. For example: in comma delimited records, a comma is used to separate each field of data.

Dialog box A type of communications connection established using a modem and POTS (Plain Old Telephone Service) to connect another computer, network, or the Internet.

Dimension One axis in an array. In programming, a dimension statement defines that array and sets up the number of elements within the dimensions.

Direct access processing The same as direct processing and random processing. Contrast with sequential processing.

Disk A generic name for magnetic storage media, using flat, circular platters. It is a flat circular plate covered in magnetic material which is able to store data on concentric tracks. As the disk spins a read/ write head travels from edge to middle selecting only the required tracks. Each track is divided into sectors. A format program is used to lay down the tracks and sectors on a blank disk and this has to be done on every disk before it can be used. Disks allow fast direct access time compared to the much slower sequential access tapes.

Distributed data processing System of computers connected together by a communications network. The term is loosely used to refer to any computers with communications between them. However, in true distributed processing, each computer system is chosen to handle its local workload and the network has been designed to support the system as a whole. Contrast with centralized processing and decentralized processing.

Dock The act of minimizing a window and placing it in the lower right corner of the screen.

Document file Files created in a work processor such as MS Word which contain formatting information.

Document reader An optical input device that is used to read document printed in a special type font.

Documentation A collection of documents or information that describes a computer program, information system or required data processing operations. Written explanations of the development, design, coding and operation of a program or system is known as documentation.

Double-click drag To double click without releasing the mouse button, move the mouse and then release the mouse button.

Edit The task of changing and improving a program by adding or removing instructions or by modifying the data. This is sometimes done with the help of a special program called an editor. EDIT is also a text-editor that comes with MS-DOS 5.0 and above for creating and editing text files.

Embedded command Command inserted within text or other codes. In word processing, proprietary codes inserted into the text that commands the printer to change fonts, print underline, boldface, etc. They may be partially or totally invisible on screen, but usually can be revealed when necessary. When a document is printed, the text is copied to a temporary file and the embedded commands are converted into printer commands for specific printer. When printing is finished, the temporary file is erased.

Error message When an error occurs it may be possible for the program to indicate what has gone wrong by putting a message on the screen. Such word wording is known as an error message and helps the user find the fault quickly. For example, 'cannot divide by zero at line 230' is an error message which tells the operator that the value of the denominator is zero at instruction number 230 in the program.

Escape character Control character often used in conjunction with other codes. In ASCII, escape is decimal 27, hex 1B; in EBCDIC, it is hex 27.

Execution error An error detected during the execution of a program, e.g., division by zero or insufficient data values to be read into main memory.

execution time Time in which a single instruction is executed. It makes up the last half of the instruction cycle.

Expression builder It is a dialog box that contains menus, field names and variables from the active database(s), and an area where an expression appears as you are building it.

Extended memory In Intel 286s and up, standard memory above one megabyte used for RAM disks, disk caches and applications using DOS extenders. Windows also uses extended memory. Contrast with expanded memory (EMS) which is specialized memory above one megabyte. Memory boards can usually be set up as a mix of the two.

field Physical unit of data that is one or more bytes in size. A collection of fields make up a record. A field also defines a unit of data on a source document, screen or report. The field is the common denominator between the user and the computer. When you interactively query and update your database, you reference your data by field name. Technically, a field is the physical unit of storage, whereas a data. Element or data item refers to the data itself. For example, it is correct to say, "these data elements are stored in this field." the terms field, data element, data item and variable refer to the same unit of data and are often used interchangeably.

Field object It represents the data that will appear in the printed report. Field objects can be actual fields from a table or calculated fields resulting from calculations of the data.

File A collection of related records. Also, a document, table, program, or similar entity that has filename, a beginning, and an end. It consists of discrete records having a length of from one to 4,000 characters or bytes.

File management program A program that enables you to manage files, directories and disks by displaying a disk's directory structure and listing existing files. Commands available on the program's menus are used to move and copy files, create directories and perform other housekeeping tasks that help improve disk performance and protect your data. The Windows Explorer and XTree Gold are popular file management programs.

Floppy disk Removable storage medium. Also called a diskette, the medium is a single round disk of flexible, tape-like material housed in a square envelope or cartridge. The disk drive grabs II the disk at its center and spins it inside its envelope. Like tape, floppy disks can be recorded and erased over and over. Older floppies were recorded on only one side (single sided); however, most are recorded on both sides (double sided).

Flowchart A graphical representation in which symbols are used to represent operations, data flow, logic equipment and so on. A program flowchart illustrates the structure and sequence of operations of a program, while a system flowchart illustrates the components and flows of information systems. You can call a flowchart as a pictorial representation of program logic using a set of standard symbols. It is used to plan the logic of program as well as to document a completed program.

Footer The text that appears on all (or almost all) pages of a document or book at the bottom of the page. In the case of a document it may be the company name in books it may simply be the number.

Form feed A command built into the control panel of most printers. A Form Feed command advances the paper one page length for example from one perforation line to the text.

Format Physical structure of an items. A screen format is that layout of fields on the screen. A report format is that layout of the printed page including print columns, page headers and footers. A record format is the layout of fields within the record. A file or database format is the layout of fields and records within a data file, layout codes within a word processing document or display lists (vector) or bitmaps (raster) within a graphics file. It also includes the structure of header data or identification data that is typically affixed to the beginning of the file.

Function In programming, a routine that does a particular task. When the program passes control to a function, it performs the task and returns control to the instruction following the calling instruction. It may perform a stand-alone task, such as printing a message, or it may accept values (arguments) from the calling instruction process them and pass the results back. Programming languages generally provide a set of standard functions and allow programmers to define their own. C is built entirely around functions. Contrast with command which is a fundamental instruction within the language. Though in programming, the term is specific, outside of programming, it is used to describe any operation such as the data entry function."

Function keys Set of keyboard keys used to command the computer (labeled Fl, F2, etc.). The commands associated with these keys are defined by the program Function keys are also used with the control, alt and shift keys, allowing 40 functions to be per-formed with 10 keys. Software packages that make extensive use of these keys come with plastic templates that fit around them for visual identification. PC and AT keyboards have 10 function keys in a cluster on the left (Fl-Fl 0). On the Enhanced keyboard, all function keys were relocated across the top of the keyboard (Fl-F12).

Graphics objects These are lines and boxess that you draw to enhance a report. Graphic objects also include pictures.

Hard copy The printed output usually on paper which can be taken away and studied. A data medium or data record that has a degree of permanence and that can be read by people off the machine.

Hashing A file-organization technique based on the ide of calculating rather than searching for the Address of Records in a file.

Index (1) In data management, the most common method for keeping track of data on a disk. Indexes are directory listings maintained by the OS, DBMS or the application. An index of files contains an entry for each file name and the location of the file. (2) In programming, a method for keeping track of data in a table.

Input/Output Pettaining to the techniques, media, and devices used for man machine interaction.

Indexed file A file that includes an index directory to facilitate random access.

Indexed sequential access method A method whereby records are organized in a sequential order and can be referenced directly through an index based on some key or characters.

Indexing (1) Creating indexes based on key data fields or key words. (2) Creating timing signals based on detecting a mark, slot or hole in a moving medium.

Information Summarization of data. Technically, data are raw facts and figures that are processed into information, such as summaries and totals. But since information can also be raw data for the next job or person, the two terms cannot be precisely defined. Both terms are used synonymously and interchangeably. As office automation and data processing merge, it may be more helpful to view information the way data is defined and used, namely: data, text, spread-sheet, pictures, voice and video. Data are discretely defined fields. Text is a collection of words. Spreadsheets are data in matrix (row and column) form. Pictures are lists of vectors or frames of bits. Voice is a continuous stream of sound waves. Video is a sequence of frames. Future databases will routinely integrate all these forms of information.

Information hiding Keeping details of a routine private. Programmers only know what input is required and what outputs are expected.

Information technology IT – Hardware, software, telecommunications, database management and other information processing technologies used in computer-based information system.

Input The items of data needed by a computer program to perform its operations. Pertaining to a device, process or channel involved in the insertion of data into a data processing system.

Input device Any hardware, such as a keyboard, scanner, digitiser, barcode reader, light pen, mouse, ATM, remote sensing equipment etc, that generates computer compatible input.

Interface Connection and interaction between hardware, software and the user. Hardware interfaces are the plugs, sockets and wires that carry electrical signals in a prescribed order. Software interfaces are the languages. Codes and messages programs use to communicate with each other. User interfaces are the keyboards, mice, commands and menus used for communication between you and the computer. Hardware "communicates to" other hardware. All this is interfacing. The software "communicates to" the hardware and other software. Users "communicates to" the software. All this is interfacing.

Join In relational database management, to match one file against based on some condition creating a third file with data from the matching files. For example, a customer file can be joined with an order file creating a file of records for all customers who purchased a particular product.

K An abbreviation for the prefix "Kilo". It is used to indicate the capacity of computer storage, 1K=210=1024 characters. Example: 64K=65,536 characters of storage.

Key Keyboard button. Data item that identifies a record. As an identifier, each key value must be unique in each key record. Numeric code used by an algorithm to create a code for encrypting data for security purposes.

Key field A unique field in a record used to distinguish one record from another.

Key word Word used in a text search. Word in a text document that is used in an index to best describe the contents of the document. A Reversed word in a programming or command language.

Label In data management, a made-up name that is assigned to a file, field or other data structure. In spreadsheet descriptive text that is entered into a cell. In programming a made up name used to identify a variable or a subroutine. In computer operation, a self-sticking form attached to the outside of a disk or tape in order to identify it. In magnetic tape files a record used for identification at the beginning or end of the file.

Label object They are any text that you type on the report, such as titles, labesl, or column headings.

Label record A machine readable record that is used to identify a data file. It is the first record of the file.

LAN Local Area Network – Communications network that serves users within a confined geographical area. It is made up of servers, workstations, a network operating system and a communications link. Servers are high-speed machines that hold programs and data shared by all network users. A workstation is a user's machine which can also function as stand-alone personal computer. Diskless workstations or floppy only workstations retrieve all software and data from the server. A printer can be attached to the workstation or it can be attached to a server and be shared by network users.

Language processor Language translation

software. Programming languages, command languages, query languages, natural languages and foreign languages are all translated by software.

Layout window The work area is which you design and define the look and content of a report or label.

light pen Light - sensitive styles wired to a video terminal used to draw pictures or select menu options. The user brings the pen to the desired point on screen and presses the pen button to make contact. Screen pixels are constantly being refreshed. When the user presses the button, allowing the pen to sense light, the pixel being illuminated at that instant identifies the screen location.

literal In programming, an unchanging item written into the program, such as a message displayed on screen. It is translated into machine language without conversion.

Local variable A variable whose value is controlled by a program module, such as a subroutine. The variable may or may not be accessible to the main program and/or other modules, however only the module containing the "local variable" can alter its value. This is a useful programming technique as it allows compartmentalisation and therefore safeguarding, of different program variables.

Logical database A schmea that describes the database as seen by one user. Different users of Applications may have different views of the same database.

Logical error An error that occurs when the actual logic of a program is different from the desired logic.

Logical operator One of the Boolean logical operators (AND, OR and NOT).

Logical record Reference to a data record that is independent of its physical location. It may be physically stored in two or more locations.

Looping It allows user to execute one or more lines of code as many times as necessary.

Macro Series of menu selections keystrokes and/or commands that have been recorded and assigned a name or key combination. When the name is called or the key is pressed, the macro is executed from beginning to end. It is used to shorten long menu sequences into one keystroke as well as to create miniature programs within an application. Macro languages often included programming controls (IF THEN, GOTO, WHILE, etc.) that automatic sequences like any programming language. In assembly language a prewritten subroutine that is called for throughout the program. At assembly time, the macro calls are substitute with the actual subroutine or instructions that branch to it. The high level language equivalent is a function. In dBASE programming a variable which reference another variable that actually contains the data. At runtime, the macro variable is substitute with the data variable.

Macro instruction Instruction that defines a macro. In assembly language, MACRO and ENDM are examples that define the beginning and end of a macro.

Magnetic Ink Character Recognition (MICR) An input device that can read cards and paper documents printed with a special magnetic ink.

Magnetic tape Sequential storage medium used for data collection, backup and historical purpose. Like videotape, computer tape is made of flexible plastic with one side coated with a ferromagnetic material. Tapes come in reels, cartridges and cassettes of many sizes and shapes. As with any tape, locating a specific item requires reading everything before it. There is no way to fast forward. Data bits are usually recorded on parallel recording tracks that run the length of the tape. For example, 9-track tape holds one byte of data across the tape's width (8 bits plug parity). Data is recorded in blocks of contiguous bytes, separated by a space called an inter record or inter block gap. Tape is often used to exchange data between minis and mainframes, since ½" open-reel tape provides a common standard. Storage capacity is measured in bits per inch (bpi). Since tape is laid out in parallel tracks, bpi is equivalent to bytes per inch. Common ½" recording densities are 1650 and 6250 dpi; early densities were 200, 556 and 800 dpi. Tape drive speed is measured in inches per second (ips), thus transfer rate is computed as :ips X bpi.

Magneto-optical (MO) drive A data storage device that uses laser technology to heat an extremely small spot on a magneto-optical (MO) cartridge so that the magnetic medium used in the MO disk becomes capable of having its magnetic orientation changed by the read/write head. Though magneto-optical drives are slow (average seek time of 30 ms, compared to about 15 ms for hard drives) and expensive (the average internal drive costs about $750, including disk), they are highly suitable for backup storage and for storing large programs or data that's accessed infrequently.

Many to many relation A situation in which one or more records in on table are related to one or more records in another.

Many to one relation A situation in which one or more records in one table are related to just one record in another.

Mass storage Secondary storage device with extra large storage capacities such as magnetic or optical disks.

Master file Collection of records pertaining to one of the main subjects of an information system. Master files contain descriptive data as well as summary information.

Megabyte One million bytes. More accurately 2 to 20th power or 1,048,576 in decimal notation.

Memo field Data field that holds a variable amount of text. The text may be stored in a companion file but it is treated as if it were part of the data record.

Memory variable FoxPro allows you to store any data of your choice in the RAM (Random Access Memory) of the PC. In all, you can store up to 256 different data items. Almost anything, such as intermediate or final result of a calculation; current or the next bill number; a date; fixed number etc. can be stored in RAM. The data items stored in RAM are called memory variables. You need to assign a unique name called the memory variable name to each data item. This is required so that you can refer to a required variable by name and use it in calculations or for some other applications. For naming a memory variable, follow the same rules as used for naming a field. That is, a memory variable name can be letters, numerals or the underscore character (_). You can use spaces and punctuation marks in memory variable names. Although a memory variable name can begin with the underscore character, it is advisable to avoid it. In fact, FoxPro automatically crates a few variables that are called print system variables. The print system variables always begin with the underscore character. Memory variables play a very important role in FoxPro programming. (Programming is described later.) You can store the data entered by the user in memory variables, validate the data, process the data (e.g. calculate square root). Thus, you do not have to store the data directly in a database file. Finally, when the data has been validated and processed, you can store it in the database file.

Memory The computer's workspace physically a collection of RAM chips. It is an important resource, since it determines the size and number of programs that can be run at the same time, as well as the amount of data that can be processed instantly. The program's instructions are copied into memory from a disk or tape and are then extracted from memory for analysis, execution or processing (calculated, compared and copied). Then the results can be output from memory to a screen, printer, disk, tape or communications channel. As data is entered into memory, the previous contents of that memory space is lost.

Menu bars A horizontal strip that appears at the top of the screen and contains menu pads.

Menu pads A word, phrase or icon on the menu bar that designates one menu. Positioning the cursor on a menu titile highlights the title and displays its options below it.

Microprocessor CPU on a single chip. In order to function as a computer, it requires a power supply, clock and memory. First-generation microprocessors were Intel's 8080, Zilog's Z80, Motorola's 6800 and Rockwell's 6502. The first microprocessor was created by Intel.

Microsecond One millionth of a second.

Modify structure Database command that changes a file's structure. Field lengths and field names can be changed and fields can be added or deleted. It may convert the old data file into the new structure without data loss, unless fields have been truncated or deleted.

Mouse A small device that is electronically connected to a computer and is moved by hand on a flat surface in order to move the cursor on a video screen in the same directories. Button on the mouse allows users to issue commands and make responses or selections.

Multiprocessing Simultaneous processing with two or more processors in one computer or two or more computers processing together. When two or more computers are used, they are tied together with a high-speed channel and share the general workload between them. If one fails, the other takes over. It is also accomplished in special purpose computers, such as array processors which provide concurrent processing on sets of data. Although computers are built with various overlapping features, such as executing instructions while inputting and outputting data, multiprocessing refers specifically to concurrent instruction execution.

Multiprogramming Pertaining to the concurrent execution of two or more programs by a computer by interleaving their execution.

Network Arrangement of objects that are interconnected. In communications, the transmission channels and supporting hardware and software.

NOT Boolean logic operation that reverses the input. If a 0 is input, a 1 is output and vice versa.

Offline A device not directly connected to the CPU.

Online (1) Peripheral device (terminal, printer, etc). which is ready to operate. A printer can be attached and turned on, yet still not online, if the ONLINE button will usually turn it back online. (2) An online computer system refers to a system with terminals, but does not imply how the system is an online system that implies data entry and updating. A transaction processing system is an online system that updates the necessary files as the work comes in, such as in an order processing system. A realtime system is an online system that provides an immediate response to a question.

operating system Master control program that runs the computer. It is the first program loaded when the computer is turned on and its main part, called the kernel, reside in memory at all times. It is an important component of the computer system because its sets the standards for the application programs that runs in it. All programs must work through the operating system.

Optical character reader An input device which can read characters directly from an ordinary piece of paper by using a scanning mechanism. These characters are written in special type fonts.

Optimize To cause something to work as effectively as possible. For example, optimizing an application means to use code that causes the application to run as quickly as possible in a given environment.

OR A logical operation in which the bit patterns of two values are compared and in which all bits are turned on that are on in one or both of the two component values. Boolean logic operation that is true if any of the inputs is true. An exclusive OR is true if only one of the inputs is true, but not both.

Output Any computer-generated information displayed on screen, printed on paper or in machine readable form, such as disk and tape to transfer or transmit from the computer to a peripheral device or communications line.

Overflow The inability of computer (RAM) to handle a particular calculation, often caused by programming logic errors, for example, attempting to divide by zero.

Pack (1) To compress data in order to save space. Unpack refers to decompressing data. (2) Instruction that converts a decimal number into a packed decimal format. Unpack converts a packed decimal number into decimal. (3) In database programs, a command that removes records that have been marked for deletion.

Parameter list Communicates a list of constants, variables, and/or arrays between a calling program and a subprogram.

Pass by reference A mean of passing a variable to a function. The calling routine passes the address of the variable to the called routing which can then use that address to retrieve or modify the variable. When the function changes the value of the passed variable, the variable's original value in the calling program is also changed.

Peripheral device In a computer system, any unit of equipment distinct from the central processing unit which may provide the system with outside communication. Peripheral devices are so called as they are attached to the periphery of the central processing unit or system box.

Point A measure of the size of a printer font, with one point being approximately 1/72.27 inches, 0.351 millimeters. Some software applications refer to point sizes, other to pitch sizes. The majority of the text in this book is sent in an 8 point font. To convert pitch to point, divide the pitch into 120, for example, 15 pitch = 120/8 point = 15. The greater the point size the greater the size of the font, inversely for pitch which is a measure of how many characters can be printed per linear inch.

Primary index The index that controls the current processing order of a file.

Procedure Manual procedures are human tasks. Machine procedures are lists of routines or programs to be executed, such as described by the job control language (JCL) in a mini or mainframe or the batch processing language in a personal computer in programming, another term for a subroutine or function.

Processing Manipulating data within the computer. The term is used to define a variety of computer functions and methods.

Processing symbol A rectangular figure used in flow charts to indicate a processing operation.

Processor May refer to software. A hardware device or software system capable of performing operations upon data.

Program A collection of instructions that tell the computer what to do. A program is also called software; hence, program, software and instructions are synonymous. A program is written in a programming language and is converted into the computer's machine language by software called assemblers, compilers and interpreters.

Project A project is a special file that keeps track of all programs, reports, labels, queries, format files and other type of files that are needed to create an application.

Pseudocode An algorithm expressed in English to conceptualize the algorithm before coding it in a programming language.

Random access file processing Same as Direct Access File Processing.

Random-access memory RAM – The computer's primary working memory in which program instructions and data are stored so that they can be accessed directly by the central processing unit (CPU) via the processor's high-speed external data bus. RAM often is called read/write memory to distinguish it from read/only memory (ROM), the other component of a personal computer's primary storage. In RAM, the CPU can write and read data. Most programs set aside a portion of RAM as a temporary work space for your data, so you can modify (rewrite) as needed until the data is ready for printing or storage on secondary storage media, such as a hard or floppy disk. RAM doesn't retain its contents when the power to the computer is switched off, so save your work frequently.

Real time systems Pertains to on line computer processing systems which receive and process data quickly enough to produce output to control, direct, or affect the outcome of an ongoing activity or process.

Recall Restore the records marked for deletion.

Record Group or related fields that store data about a subject (master record) or activity (transaction record). A collection of records make up a file. Master records contain permanent data, such as account number and variable data, such as balance due. Transaction records contain only permanent data, such as quantity and product code. A record is an entry in a database. For example, a payroll database may hold information on 300 employees and is therefore a 300 record database.

Record length A measure of the size of a record, usually specified in units such as characters.

Record pointer In a database management program, an onscreen status messages that states the number of the data record now visible (or in which the cursor is positioned).

Regular index Regular determines the order in which records are displayed but allows duplicate data to be entered into a field.

Relational database management system RDBMS – A relational database management program, especially one that comes with all the necessary support programs, programming tools and documentation needed to create, install and maintain custom database applications.

relational operator A symbol that specifies a compari-son between two values.

Relational	*Operator*	*Symbol*
EQ	Equal to	=
GT	Greater than	>
GE	Greater than or equal to	>=
NE	Not equal to	<> or # or!
LE	less than or equal to	<=
LT	less than	<

Relationship A connection between entities that has meaning for an appliction.

Remove button The Remove button moves the highlighted field from the selected fields list box to the available fields lsit box.

Remove all button Remove All button moves all the fields from the selected fields list box to the available field list box.

Replace In word processing programs, a feature that searches for a string and replaces it with another string. Always save your work before performing a replace operation. With most programs, you can improve the accuracy of the replacement operation by specifying capitalization and whole-word options. If you tell the program to match the capitalization pattern in the search string, such as Tree if you want the change only when tree begins a sentence, the program replaces only those strings that match the characters and capitalization pattern (Tree is replaced, but not TREE or tree).

Report detail band The area between the page header and the page footer, consisting of detail lines based on the records from the selected database(s).

Reserved word In a programming language or operating system a word – also called a keyword – that has a fixed function and can't be used for any other purpose. In BASIC, for example, the word REM is reserved to indicate the beginning of a remark. You can use a reserved work only for its intended purpose; you can't use the word for naming files, variables or other user-named objects.

Restore The Restore command reads the saved memory variables from disk back to your computer's memory.

Run-time error This is an error that occurs during program execution. A run-time error may occur during the program development stage or in real-life usage due to hardware failure. In the program development stage, run-time error may occur if a data file has not been previously closed and an attempt is made to open it. In real-life usage a run-time error will occur, for example, if the software application tries to access a printer that is out of paper, turned off or disconnected. Thorough and professional programming techniques ensure that the trauma of run-time errors is minimized. Preferably data should not be lost and the program should be recoverable at or close to the error point.

Run-time The period of time during which a computer program is a actually running.

Rushmore technology A data access technique that permits sets of records to be accessed very efficiently, at speeds comparable to single record indexed access.

Scientific notation Display of numbers in floating point form. The number (mantissa) is always equal to or greater than one and less than 10 and the base is 10. For example, 2.345E6 is equivalent to 2,345,000. The number following E (exponent) represents the power to which the base should he raised (number of zeros following the decimal point).

Scope (1) CRT type of screen, such as used on an oscil-loscope or common display terminal. (2) In program-ming, the visibility of variables within a program. (3) In dBASE, a range of records, such as the "next 50" or "current record to end of file."

Security Protection of data against unauthorized access. Programs and data can be securred by issuing identifications numbers and passwords to authorized users of a computer individual, will ultimately have access to these codes. Data transmitted over communications networks can be secured by encryption to prevent eavesdropping.

Seek To move the access arm to the requested track on a disk. Assembly language instruction that activates a seek operation on disk. High-level programming language commmand used to select a record by key field.

Sequential access An information storage and retrieval technique in which the computer must move through a sequence of stored data items to reach the desired one. Sequential access media such as cassette tapes are much slower than random-access media, such as hard disk drives.

Sequential file A file that has been organized in ascending or descending record key sequence so that the records are written or retrieved one after another in sequence.

Serial access A storage device or medium where the access time is dependent upon the location of the data. Magnetic tape is a typical serial access device.

Sort To reorder data into a new sequence. Sorting capabilities are provided within the operating system and many application program, such as word processing and DBMSs.

Sorting Physical arrangement of records in a table. Sorting does not make any changes to the existing table rather it creates a new table that stores ordered data.

Source document A document that is the original formal record of a transaction, such as a purchase order or sales invoice.

Source program Program in its original form, as writ-ten by the programmer.

Special character Non-alpha or non-numeric character, such as @,#,$,%,&,* and +.

SQL Structured Query Language – pronounced "SQL" or "see qwill," a language used to interrogate and process data in a relational database. Originally developed by IBM for its mainframes, there have been many implementations created for mini and micro database applications. SQL commands can be used to interactively work with a database or can be embedded within a programming language to interface to a database.

Storage The retention of program instructions and data within the computer so that this information is available for processing purposes. See primary storage and secondary storage.

String (1) In programming, a contiguous set of alphanumeric characters that does not contain numbers used for calculations. Names, addresses, words and sentences are strings. (2) Any connected set of structures, such as a string of bits, fields or records.

String function String function are tools that let you control the way you can store or display strings. You can also use them to determine certain characteristics about them. There are string functions that let you convert numbers to characters, characters to numbers, decimal numbers to whole numbers (called integers), determine how many characters in a string, and so on.

String variable A unique variable such as NAME or DATE that you assign to a string value.

Structural compound index A structural compound index file is created when you include TAG<tag name> without including the optional OF <cd file> clause. Structural CDX files always have the same base name as the table. A structural compound index file is automatically opened every time the table is opened.

Structure chart A design and documentation technique to show the purpose and relationship of the various modules in a program.

Structure design A system design approach in which a difficult problem is broken into smaller problems that are small enough to manage but independent enough to sove separately.

Structured programming Variety of techniques that impose a logical structure on the writing of a program. Large routines are broken down into smaller, modular routines. The use of the GOTO statement in discouraged. For documentation, certain programming statements are indented, so that beginnings and endings of loops are easily identified. Structured languages, such as Pascal, Ada and dBASE, force the programmer to write a structured program.

Subroutine Group of instructions that perform a specific task. A large subroutine is usually called a module or procedure; a small one, a function or macro, but all terms are used interchangeably.

Syntax Rules that must be followed white coding program instructions, similar to grammatical rules for the English language.

Syntax error Error that occurs when a program cannot understand the command that has been entered.

System A group of integrated parts (people, methods, machines, and materials) that have the common purpose of achieving some objective(s).

System analysis Analyzing in detail the components and requirement of a system Analyzing in detail the information needs of an organization, the characteristics and components of presently utilized information systems and the requirements of proposed information system.

Systems analyst Persons responsible for the develop-ment of an information system. They design and modify systems by turning user requirements into a set of functional specifications which ate the blue-print of the system. They design the database or help design it if data administrators are available.

System flowchart A graphic diagramming tool used to show the flow of data media as they are processed by hardware devices and information processed procedures in an information system.

Table A dbf file created in a previous version of Visual FoxPro is a free table until it is added to a database.

Transaction Activity or request. Orders, purchases, changes, additions and deletions are examples of transactions that are recorded in a business informa-tion environment. Queries and other requests are also transactions to the computer, but are usually just acted upon and not recorded in the system. Transaction volume is a major factor in determining the size and speed of a computer system.

Transaction file Collection of records that record the activity of an organization. The data in transaction files is used to update the data in master files which contain the subjects of the organization. Transaction files also serve as audit trails and are usually transferred from active disk files to the data library after some period of time. As optical disks become more economical, transaction files will remain online in the computers so that an organization's history will be immediately available for adhoc queries.

Type head buffer A buffer that accepts and holds characters that are typed faster than the computer can process them.

Unique It selects and orders a subset of records based on the first occurrence of a value in the field you specify.

Updating The process of keeping master files accurate and up-to-date by processing them with the latest transactions contained in the transactionf file.

User Any individual who interacts with the computer at an application level. Programmers, operators and other technical personnel are not considered users when working in a professional capacity on the computer.

Validation In programming, providing that a program does its job. Many programmers prefer the term "validation" to "testing" or "debugging," since it has a more positive ring.

Variable In programming, a structure that holds data and is uniquely named by the programmer. It holds the data assigned to it until the program is finished. Variable are used to hold control values. In some languages, the type of data must be declared before it is assigned. A local variable is one that can be referenced only within the subprogram, function or procedure it was defined in. A global variable can be used by the entire program.

View window The window lets you set up a special view of your data. You can open multiple tables and define relationship among them.

Window (1) The area that displays information on the screen. You can open or close a windows, move it around on the disktop, and sometimes change its size, scroll through it, and edit its contents. (2) The portion of a collection of information such as a document, picture, or worksheet that is visible in a viewing area on the display screen.

Wizard The wizard prompts you with simple questions as you go through a brief series of steps, in which you specify the table and fields that you want to use to create control on your report.

Zap Command that typically deletes the data within a file but leaves the file structure intact so that new data can be entered.

Zoom A feature of many graphics and some spreadsheet packages which allows the user to get a magnified view of a particular part of the graphics object (spreadsheet). This is a word borrowed from photography (zoom lens).

Index

I

J

K

L

M

N

O